A HISTORY OF TWELFTH-CENTURY
WESTERN PHILOSOPHY

A History of
Twelfth-Century
Western Philosophy

EDITED BY
PETER DRONKE

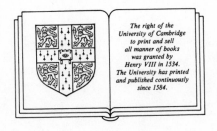

The right of the
University of Cambridge
to print and sell
all manner of books
was granted by
Henry VIII in 1534.
The University has printed
and published continuously
since 1584.

CAMBRIDGE UNIVERSITY PRESS

CAMBRIDGE

NEW YORK   NEW ROCHELLE

MELBOURNE   SYDNEY

B
721
.H58
1987

Published by the Press Syndicate of the University of Cambridge
The Pitt Building, Trumpington Street, Cambridge CB2 1RP
32 East 57th Street, New York, NY 10022, USA
10 Stamford Road, Oakleigh, Melbourne 3166, Australia

© Cambridge University Press 1988

First published 1988

Printed in Great Britain by Bath Press, Bath, Avon

British Library cataloguing in publication data

A history of twelfth-century western philosophy.
1. Philosophy, Medieval
I. Dronke, Peter
189   B721

Library of Congress cataloguing in publication data

A history of twelfth-century western philosophy.
Bibliography: p.
Includes index.
1. Philosophy, Medieval. I. Dronke, Peter.
B721.H58 1987   189   87-13847

ISBN 0 521 25896 0

CE

CONTENTS

v

PREFACE

It gives me deep pleasure to express my thanks to all the collaborators in this volume, not only for their generous written contributions but also for their helpful participation at every stage of its making. I am likewise grateful to the three translators – Jean Stewart, Jonathan Hunt and Rodney Livingstone – for the care with which they have rendered the often demanding French, Italian and German of their originals into English, and thus enabled us to produce a truly international volume.

Certain topics have been touched on in more than one chapter. It is hoped that the minor overlaps, which have been allowed to remain, bring with them the advantage of showing diverse facets of questions through diverse contexts of discussion.

I have greatly valued the steady encouragement of Jeremy Mynott, at Cambridge University Press, who first invited me to embark upon this volume, and the substantial help of Maureen Street in assembling the General Bibliography and of Jenny Swanson in compiling the Indices. A special word of thanks, finally, to Jane Hodgart, who, with her gentle and perceptive copyediting, has once again given of her expertise, making light of the complexities of adjustment in so many-sided a publication.

P.D.

CONTRIBUTORS

CHARLES BURNETT is Lecturer at the Warburg Institute in the University of London. He is the editor of Hermann of Carinthia's *De essentiis* (1982) and of *Pseudo-Bede, De mundi celestis terrestrisque constitutione* (1985).

PETER DRONKE, FBA is Reader in Medieval Latin Literature in the University of Cambridge. His books include *Fabula: Explorations into the Uses of Myth in Medieval Platonism* (1974), an edition of Bernardus Silvestris' *Cosmographia* (1978), and *Dante and Medieval Latin Traditions* (1986).

DOROTHY ELFORD is the author of *Developments in the Natural Philosophy of William of Conches* (PhD dissertation, Cambridge, 1983).

KAREN MARGARETA FREDBORG is the editor of Thierry of Chartres's *Commentary on Cicero's De inventione* (1987), and the author of several studies of medieval speculative grammar in the *Cahiers de l'Institut du Moyen-Age Grec et Latin*.

STEPHEN GERSH is Professor of Medieval Studies in the University of Notre Dame. He is the author of Κίνησις Ἀκίνητος (1973), *From Iamblichus to Eriugena* (1978), and *Middle Platonism and Neoplatonism: The Latin Tradition* (2 vols., 1986).

TULLIO GREGORY is Professor of the History of Philosophy in the University of Rome. His books include *Anima Mundi* (1955), *Platonismo medievale: Studi e ricerche* (1958), and *Giovanni Scoto Eriugena* (1963).

KLAUS JACOBI is Professor of Philosophy in the University of Freiburg. He is the author of *Die Modalbegriffe in den logischen Schriften des Wilhelm von Shyreswood* (1980), and editor of *Nikolaus von Kues: Einführung in sein philosophisches Denken* (1979).

DANIELLE JACQUART has a research appointment at the Centre National de Recherche Scientifique. She is the author (with Claude Thomasset) of *Sexualité et savoir médical au Moyen Age* (1985), and has published several studies of Latin and Arabic medical terminology.

JEAN JOLIVET is Professor at the Ecole Pratique des Hautes Etudes. His books include *Godescalc d'Orbais et la Trinité* (1958), *Arts du langage et théologie chez Abélard* (2nd ed., 1982), and *L'intellect selon Kindī* (1971).

MICHAEL LAPIDGE is Lecturer in the Department of Anglo-Saxon, Norse, and Celtic in the University of Cambridge. He is the author of several essays on the traditions of Stoic philosophy; his books include (with Richard Sharpe) *A Bibliography of Celtic–Latin Literature 400–1200* (1985) and (with James Rosier) *Aldhelm: The Poetic Works* (1985).

D. E. LUSCOMBE, FBA is Professor of Medieval History in the University of Sheffield. He is the author of *The School of Peter Abelard* (1969), the editor of Peter Abelard's *Ethics* (1971), and a contributor to *The Cambridge History of Later Medieval Philosophy*.

ENZO MACCAGNOLO († 1985) was Professor of the History of Philosophy in the University of Genoa. He is the author of *Rerum Universitas: Saggio sulla filosofia di Teodorico di Chartres* (1976) and of *Il divino e il megacosmo: Testi filosofici e scientifici della Scuola di Chartres* (1980).

JOHN MARENBON is a Fellow of Trinity College, Cambridge. He is the author of *From the Circle of Alcuin to the School of Auxerre* (1981), *Early Medieval Philosophy* (1983), and *Later Medieval Philosophy* (1987).

MARTIN TWEEDALE is Professor of Philosophy in the University of Auckland. He is the author of *Abailard on Universals* (1976), and a contributor to *The Cambridge History of Later Medieval Philosophy*.

WINTHROP WETHERBEE is Professor of English at Cornell University. His books include *Platonism and Poetry in the Twelfth Century* (1972), and a commented translation of *The Cosmographia of Bernardus Silvestris* (1973).

ABBREVIATIONS

AHDLMA	*Archives d'Histoire Doctrinale et Littéraire du Moyen Age*
BGPTM	Beiträge zur Geschichte der Philosophie und Theologie des Mittelalters ('Beiträge zur Geschichte der Philosophie des Mittelalters' in the case of fascicules before 1930)
CC	Corpus Christianorum
CC CM	Corpus Christianorum, Continuatio Mediaevalis
CHLMP	*The Cambridge History of Later Medieval Philosophy*, ed. N. Kretzmann, A. Kenny, J. Pinborg (Cambridge 1982)
CIMAGL	*Cahiers de l'Institut du Moyen-Age Grec et Latin*
CSEL	Corpus Scriptorum Ecclesiasticorum Latinorum
H	*The Commentaries on Boethius by Gilbert of Poitiers*, ed. N. M. Häring (Toronto 1966)
Harvard 1982	*Renaissance and Renewal in the Twelfth Century*, ed. R. L. Benson, G. Constable (Cambridge, Mass. 1982)
MARS	*Mediaeval and Renaissance Studies*
MGH	Monumenta Germaniae Historica
P.L.	Patrologia Latina
R	Boethius, *The Theological Tractates, The Consolation of Philosophy*, ed. and tr. E. K. Rand, H. F. Stewart, S. J. Tester (Cambridge, Mass.–London 1973)
RMAL	*Revue du Moyen Age Latin*
RSPT	*Revue des Sciences Philosophiques et Théologiques*
RTAM	*Recherches de Théologie Ancienne et Médiévale*
S	*S. Anselmi Opera Omnia*, ed. F. S. Schmitt (6 vols., Seckau–Rome–Edinburgh 1938–61, repr. Stuttgart–Bad Cannstatt 1968)
SVF	*Stoicorum Veterum Fragmenta*, ed. H. von Arnim (3 vols., Leipzig 1903–5; *Indices*, ed. M. Adler, Leipzig 1925)
TK	*A Catalogue of Incipits of Mediaeval Scientific Writings in Latin*, revised and augmented ed. by L. Thorndike, P. Kibre (London 1963)

INTRODUCTION

PETER DRONKE

It is an exciting moment to be looking at twelfth-century philosophy. The last thirty years have seen the discovery in manuscript of many major texts in this field, and the appearance of an imposing number of new editions and specialist studies. Many of those who have worked at first hand with the documents of twelfth-century thought have come to see the achievements in this century as among the most original and most brilliant in the whole of pre-Renaissance philosophy. Till now, however, the histories of philosophy have lagged behind. In Bernhard Geyer's medieval volume (1927) in the standard history begun by Ueberweg, the twelfth century was given some ninety pages – about one ninth of the space devoted to the Middle Ages as a whole. In the best histories available in English from the post-war period, however, the century that spans from St Anselm to Alan of Lille occupies only a twelfth of the space in Etienne Gilson's *History of Christian Philosophy in the Middle Ages*, and less than a fifteenth in the early medieval volume of Frederick Copleston's *History of Philosophy*, a volume that does not extend beyond the thirteenth century. In the recent *Cambridge History of Later Medieval Philosophy*, which treats the period 1100–1600, apart from a brief chapter on 'Abelard and the Culmination of the Old Logic', twelfth-century thought features only in incidental allusions.[1]

There is thus a need to chart, at least provisionally, the full range of the contributions that were made to philosophy in twelfth-century Europe, taking account of all the detailed research of recent decades and attempting to set the newly accessible works, as well as those of renowned figures such as Anselm and Abelard, in their cultural context.

Winthrop Wetherbee, in the first chapter, looks particularly at this wider

1 F. Ueberweg, *Grundriss der Geschichte der Philosophie II: Die Patristische und Scholastische Philosophie*, ed. B. Geyer (11th ed., Basel–Stuttgart 1927); E. Gilson, *A History of Christian Philosophy in the Middle Ages* (London 1955); F. Copleston, *A History of Philosophy: Augustine to Scotus* (London 1950); *The Cambridge History of Later Medieval Philosophy*, ed. N. Kretzmann, A. Kenny and J. Pinborg (Cambridge 1982) [= *CHLMP*]. The bio-bibliographical section of *CHLMP* (pp. 855–92) includes only nine of the authors who have entries below (pp. 443–57); even such major figures as Adelard of Bath, David of Dinant, Gilbert of Poitiers, Gundissalinus, Hermann of Carinthia and Thierry of Chartres are omitted.

intellectual context, which, since Haskins' classic study (1927), has been aptly designated *The Renaissance of the Twelfth Century*. Wetherbee adumbrates the role of philosophical enquiry in relation to the methods of teaching and learning current at the time, and the educational programmes, both traditional and more adventurous, that were then devised. He also shows how certain kinds of cosmological speculation, far from being confined to the schoolroom or the cloister, left their mark on major works of literature.

In the chapters that follow, the contributors have outlined as precisely as possible the range of texts that were or became available to twelfth-century philosophers, the texts that quickened their writing. A leading historian of medieval thought has even in a recent standard work affirmed as a 'fact that until the middle of the twelfth century the only ancient philosophy directly accessible to the Latin medievals was contained in two of Aristotle's works on logic'.[2] How far from fact this is emerges, among other things, from Chapters 2 and 3. First and foremost, the whole of the twelfth century stands under the sign of Plato's *Timaeus*. In the Latin *Timaeus* and its commentaries from Calcidius (in the fourth century) onwards, to cite Raymond Klibansky, 'the Middle Ages became acquainted with the classical formulation of the principle of causality ... The emphasis they laid on Plato's doctrine that "Whatever comes to be must be brought into being by the action of some cause" and on the necessity to "give reasons" (*reddere rationes*) taught the mediaeval scholar to search in every phenomenon, not excluding the creation of the world, for its "legitimate" cause and reason.'[3] Admittedly, this was the only Platonic dialogue that was widely diffused, and Calcidius' Latin version was not complete. The two dialogues that Henry Aristippus translated in the 1150s – the Latin *Phaedo* (which survives in two recensions, seven manuscripts in all) and *Meno* (five manuscripts) – appear to have had scant influence. Yet the many-sidedness of the Platonism of the ancient world that was handed down (through Calcidius' commentary, through Macrobius and various popularizers of the Roman world, as well as Greek and Latin Fathers), and how freshly this variegated Platonism was utilized in the twelfth century, becomes clear in Tullio Gregory's chapter (Ch. 2).

The nature and the extent of Stoic influences still pose more problems than the Platonic; yet Michael Lapidge (Ch. 3) is able to map the principal paths of transmission. While the *Peri hermeneias* ascribed to Apuleius will have given twelfth-century scholars only a partial conception of Stoic logic, the extent

2 N. Kretzmann, in *CHLMP*, p. 5.
3 *The Continuity of the Platonic Tradition during the Middle Ages, with a new preface and four supplementary chapters* ... (Munich 1981), pp. 74f.

to which key works of Cicero and Seneca were read in the twelfth century, that could convey precise notions of Stoic cosmology and ethics, emerges here, I believe, for the first time. It also becomes clear that a number of widely read authors who have commonly been held to transmit Platonic and Neoplatonic ideas – Calcidius, Martianus Capella, the 'Hermes' to whom *Asclepius* is ascribed – were likewise influential in the dissemination of Stoic thought.

But many of the most fecund new arrivals in the Latin twelfth century hail from the Arabic world. Whilst Averroes (1126–98) was not yet known in northern Europe – the first sure traces of his presence there are not seen till around 1230, in Paris – the second half of the twelfth century shows us the translation and diffusion of vital works by Averroes' greatest predecessors: al-Kindī († after 870), al-Fārābī († 950), Avicenna (980–1037), and Algazel (1058–1111). The plenitude of the Arabic contribution is evoked in Chapters 4 and 5, which are in some measure complementary. Where Jean Jolivet (Ch. 4) brings out especially the transformations of the language and conceptual framework of western philosophy in the later twelfth century, and the interplay, throughout the century, of translating and creative thought, in the work of such men as Adelard of Bath, Petrus Alfonsi, Hermann of Carinthia, and Gundissalinus, Charles Burnett (Ch. 5) concentrates especially on what the extraordinary range of scientific translations, both from Arabic and Greek, brought with them that leavened philosophical speculation. First came the medical works translated from the Arabic in late-eleventh-century Salerno, by 'the cursed monk, daun Constantyn' (as Chaucer's Merchant sardonically calls him, disappointed at having found him no help as a guide to sexual bliss), and by scholars in Constantine's circle. In northern Europe these Constantinian translations had already by about 1120 reached Chartres, where they were used creatively, with a keen sense of their philosophical implications, by William of Conches[4] (cf. Ch. 11). Only a little later, in the first half of the twelfth century, the stream of scientific translations becomes a flood. Burnett sketches the ways in which newly accessible works of astronomy and astrology (particularly the two

---

4 While our sources offer no outright statement that William, who had studied with Bernard of Chartres, was still there as a teacher at the time when he first cites the newly translated works (in his *Philosophia*, *ca.* 1125), the circumstantial evidence that William taught at Chartres is considerable: see most recently O. Weijers, 'The Chronology of John of Salisbury's Studies in France (*Metalogicon*, II 10)', in *The World of John of Salisbury*, ed. M. Wilks (Oxford 1984), pp. 109–16. For a contrary view see R. W. Southern, *Harvard 1982*, p. 129: 'The chief claimants for [William's] school have been Chartres and Paris, but on present evidence neither can be strongly supported.' On p. 133, by contrast, Southern writes (on account of a printing error?) that William taught John of Salisbury 'certainly in Paris'.

translations of Abū Ma'shar's *Introductorium*, that helped to make Aristotelian cosmology familiar), as well as of mathematics and physics,
provided stimuli to fresh philosophical endeavour.

In some ways it would have been desirable to include a further chapter,
'The Aristotelian inheritance', in the 'Background' section of the volume, so
that the importance of this inheritance, alongside the Platonic, Stoic, and
Arabic, should be made plain. This has not been done, however, since
Aristotelian influences take historically a very different shape from the rest:
the Aristotelianism in logic (discussed in Chapters 7 and 8) follows a path
that scarcely crosses the other path, of Aristotelian natural philosophy,
epistemology, and metaphysics, which becomes clearly visible only in the
later decades of the century, and to which the fourth section of the book is
dedicated.

Many new perspectives emerge from Chapters 6–8, which again in several
important aspects complement one another. The speculative grammar of the
thirteenth century has become well known in recent decades, through a fine
series of editions (Boethius of Dacia, Martin of Dacia, and others) and
studies, in which the late Jan Pinborg played a leading part.[5] The beginnings
of speculative grammar in the twelfth century, on the other hand, are still
largely an undiscovered country. It is significant that Margareta Fredborg,
who provides an orientation here (Ch. 6), has, more than any other
contributor to the volume (except perhaps Danielle Jacquart in Chapter 15),
had to cite unpublished sources from manuscripts. What emerges in particular is the significance of the new kinds of grammatical analysis, from
William of Champeaux to the 'Porretans' (the disciples of Gilbert of
Poitiers), for the semantic discussions of the logicians, and their famous
quarrel over the nature of 'universals'.

This problem of universals is central to Martin Tweedale's survey of the
developments in logic that culminate with Abelard (Ch. 7). He sketches a
tradition that reaches back to the eleventh century, to the comprehensive
Dialectica (probably towards 1040) of Garlandus and to the highly individual
contributions to logical theory in two early works by Anselm; he also evokes
the rich diversity of problems that Abelard as dialectician broached, and the
kinds of already existing controversy that he entered. While the later part of
the century, as Klaus Jacobi shows (Ch. 8), produced no single logical
innovator of Abelard's stature, the argumentation in this field – in such

5 The texts have been published particularly in the journal *CIMAGL* and the series Corpus
  Philosophorum Danicorum Medii Aevi; see also J. Pinborg, *Logik und Semantik im Mittelalter
  — Ein Überblick* (Stuttgart–Bad Cannstatt 1972).

matters as sophisms, and the semantics of terms and propositions – reached a degree of subtlety in the works of several Parisian schools that makes understandable (even if we do not concur) John of Salisbury's criticism in his *Metalogicon* (1159), that logic was being transformed from an aid to knowledge into a self-sufficient discipline, endlessly refined for its own sake.

In the chapters (9–14) that comprise the third section of the volume, the writings of six thinkers are outlined in greater detail, with special emphasis on the elements of philosophical originality embedded in them. I should like to suggest briefly some of the reasons why it was decided to focus more closely on these six, rather than others. The choice of Anselm and Abelard hardly needs explanation. The other four have not yet been favoured with detailed discussion as major figures in any history of philosophy. It has been difficult to do them justice till now, partly because their writings have only recently become available in scholarly editions: those of N. M. Häring for Gilbert (1966) and Thierry (1971), and of Charles Burnett for Hermann (1982). For William of Conches, the problem is only partially resolved: there are good modern editions of his *Philosophia* (by Gregor Maurach, 1980) and his *Glosae super Platonem* (by Edouard Jeauneau, 1965); but for William's masterpiece, the *Dragmaticon*, one must still turn to the *editio princeps* (1567), and for his other commentaries, except for occasional printed extracts, to the manuscripts.[6]

There is also another way in which this choice of authors distinguishes itself from those made in older histories of medieval philosophy. Both Geyer and Gilson, for instance, included chapters on the twelfth-century mystics. It might well be argued that, if one were to understand the expression 'medieval philosophy' in a wider sense, that includes medieval spirituality – a sense that is clearly also fruitful and valid in its own terms – then figures such as St Bernard, Richard of Saint-Victor, Hildegard of Bingen, and Joachim of Fiore would have to be among the protagonists chosen for extended consideration in any study of the twelfth century. Yet this would obviously lead to a book of a somewhat different kind. Similarly, most of the works in that fascinating borderland of medieval Platonism, where cosmology is nourished by imaginative fictions more than by analytic thought

---

6 *The Commentaries on Boethius by Gilbert of Poitiers* (Toronto 1966); *Commentaries on Boethius by Thierry of Chartres and his School* (Toronto 1971); Hermann of Carinthia, *De essentiis* (Leiden–Cologne 1982); Wilhelm von Conches, *Philosophia* (Pretoria 1980); Guillaume de Conches, *Glosae super Platonem* (Paris 1965). The edition of the *Dragmaticon* by G. Gratarolus – *Dialogus de substantiis physicis . . . a Vuilhelmo Aneponymo philosopho* (Strasbourg 1567) – exists in a facsimile edition (Frankfurt/Main 1967).

– to which Winthrop Wetherbee and I have both devoted books[7] – are not included here, or are discussed only incidentally, as Bernard Silvestris' *Cosmographia* is, for example, in Chapter I. Detailed treatment, however (not only in the section on individual authors but throughout the volume), has been limited to those writings in which reasoned argument, bearing on a traditional sphere of philosophical enquiry (such as logic, epistemology, or metaphysics), plays an important role.

Nonetheless, the question of the relations especially between philosophical and theological discussion in the authors and works treated in Part III is a complex, many-branched one. The contributors have broached this question in diverse ways, as best fitted their particular topics. Thus David Luscombe, for instance, has indicated certain philosophical impulses that underlie Abelard's more strictly theological work as much as they do his explorations in dialectic, metaphysics, and ethics. Dorothy Elford has aimed primarily to single out what is of intrinsic philosophical interest in the thought of William of Conches; John Marenbon, by contrast, argues that Gilbert of Poitiers, to be seen aright, must be considered as principally a theologian, and he proceeds to show how a new range of philosophical language and problems arises as it were within Gilbert's theological discourse itself.[8] Stephen Gersh writing on Anselm, and I on Thierry, are concerned particularly to delineate areas of philosophical argument in the works of two thinkers who saw no impropriety in using such argument in the same context as theological speculation.

The various ways in which philosophical and theological aims could converge did not, at least for the most gifted and original minds, imply any constriction of rational enquiry. Both Jolivet and Burnett allude to a celebrated passage in Adelard of Bath's *Quaestiones naturales* that bears on this, and that I should like to cite a little more fully here, in an attempt to set it in a certain intellectual and historical perspective. When Adelard's nephew

---

7 W. Wetherbee, *Platonism and Poetry in the Twelfth Century: The Literary Influence of the School of Chartres* (Princeton 1972); P. Dronke, *Fabula: Explorations into the Uses of Myth in Medieval Platonism* (Leiden–Cologne 1974).

8 A twelfth-century MS of Gilbert's Boethian commentaries, Valenciennes Bibl. municipale 197, fol. 4v, has a splendid picture of Gilbert, in episcopal regalia, teaching his most advanced students 'theological philosophy': the heading begins: 'Magister Gillebertus Pictaviensis episcopus altiora theologice philosophie secreta diligentibus auctius pulsantibus reserans discipulis quatuor . . . (Master Gilbert, Bishop of Poitiers, unlocking the higher secrets of theological philosophy for four diligent disciples who knock more forcibly)'. The page is reproduced, with elucidations by E. Jeauneau, in *Notre-Dame de Chartres* (11ème année, no. 44), Septembre 1980, p. 12. On the uses of the term *philosophia* up to 1200, see particularly E. R. Curtius, 'Zur Geschichte des Wortes Philosophie im Mittelalter', *Romanische Forschungen* LVII (1943) 290–309.

asks him to explain the nature of living beings, Adelard in his dialogue replies that it is difficult to discuss such matters with him:[9]

For I have acquired one type of learning, with reason as guide, from my Arabic teachers, while you, fettered by the appearance of authority, follow another, as a halter. For what else should authority be called but a halter? Indeed as brute beasts are led by a halter, not discerning in what direction or to what purpose they are led, following only the rope that holds them fast, so there are not a few among you whom written authority leads into danger, caught and bound as you are in bestial credulity ... For your listeners do not understand that reason has been given to each person to distinguish between true and false, reason being the prime judge. If reason were not to be that universal judge, she would have been given to each one in vain ... Moreover, those who are called authorities did not gain their first credence among lesser mortals except in that they followed reason ... I do not cut to the quick, saying authority should be despised. But I affirm that reason must be sought out first, and when she is found, authority, if she lies near, can then be made to follow ... For I am not one of those whom the painting of the skin (*pictura pellis*) can satisfy. Indeed every written statement is a wanton, exposed now to these[10] affections, now to those.

With his witty sexual innuendo – the 'painting of the skin' means both the writing on the parchment and the false lures of the seductress – Adelard seems to arrive at a radical scepticism, at least in questions of natural philosophy. What is more surprising is that towards the end of the century (1185–95) Alan of Lille, writing a theological work directed against heretics,[11] should likewise make such a witty contrast between reason and authority. To counter those who deny that the human soul is immortal, Alan adduces both biblical and pagan authorities – including (for the first time in northern Europe) the Neoplatonic *Liber de causis*, based on Proclus, as well as alluding to Plato's *Phaedo*. He continues:

But because authority has a waxen nose, that can be bent in different ways, she must be fortified by reasons.

Alan was here, I believe, recalling a phrase of Thierry of Chartres's:

Plato says that primordial matter is flexible like wax, for what exists in potentiality can be bent to this and to that.[12]

9 Adelard von Bath, *Quaestiones naturales*, ed. M. Müller (BGPTM xxxi 2), pp. 11f.
10 Reading *nunc ad hos nunc ad illos affectus* (*nunc ad hoc* Müller).
11 *De fide catholica*, also known as *Contra haereticos* (P.L. 210, 305ff); on the date of the work see M.-Th. d'Alverny, *Alain de Lille: Textes inédits* (Paris 1965), p. 156 n. 4 (citing the study by C. Vasoli). The quotation from the *Liber de causis* (here called *Aphorismi de essentia summae bonitatis*) and the passage cited below both occur at I 30 (331 C, 333 A).
12 Thierry 1971, pp. 76f; the 'Plato' allusion appears to be to Calcidius ch. 310 (ed. Waszink, *Plato Latinus IV: Timaeus a Calcidio translatus commentarioque instructus* (2nd ed., London–Leiden 1975), p. 311): see Häring's note *ad loc.*

Alan's wit lay not only in transferring the flexibility from *materia* to *auctoritas*, but in adding the dimension of illusion. A wax nose is a disguise, a false nose – it is potentially of any shape only because it is unreal.

Yet I also think that Alan (and perhaps Adelard too) was echoing a much earlier affirmation of the ideal of reason vis-à-vis authority, that he found in Scotus Eriugena's *Periphyseon* (composed 864–6).[13] The master (*Nutritor*) in Eriugena's dialogue has been arguing that all verbs that apply properly to mutable creatures can be used only metaphorically of God. The pupil (*Alumnus*) replies:

A. You strongly press me to admit that this is reasonable. But I should like you to bring in some supporting evidence from the authority of the Holy Fathers to confirm it.

N. You are not unaware, I think, that what is prior by nature is of greater excellence than what is prior in time.

A. That is known to almost everybody.

N. We have learnt that reason is prior by nature, authority in time. For although nature was created together with time, authority did not come into being at the beginning of nature and time, whereas reason arose with nature and time out of the Principle of things.

A. Even reason herself teaches this. For authority proceeds from true reason, but reason certainly does not proceed from authority. For every authority which is not upheld by true reason is seen to be weak, whereas true reason is kept firm and immutable by her own powers and does not require to be confirmed by the assent of any authority.[14]

Eriugena's influence in the twelfth century has been studied in a fine essay by Paolo Lucentini;[15] much further work still remains to be done. It is clear at least that Eriugena's independent, daring spirit found response more than once in the later period.

13 Alan names 'Johannes Scotus' and cites the *Periphyseon*, e.g. in his *Summa 'Quoniam homines'* (ed. P. Glorieux, *AHDLMA* xx (1953) 113–364), pp. 138, 140, 154, 263.
14 *Periphyseon* I, ed. and trans. I. P. Sheldon-Williams (Dublin 1968), pp. 196–9 (= P. L. 122, 513 A–B); I cite Sheldon-Williams' translation.
15 *Platonismo medievale: Contributi per la storia dell' eriugenismo* (2nd ed., Florence 1980); Lucentini's study 'Giovanni Scoto e l'eresia di Amalrico' is forthcoming in the *Colloquium zur Wirkungsgeschichte Eriugenas*, ed. W. Beierwaltes.
       An extensive knowledge of the *Periphyseon* is revealed in the recently edited *Comentum* of William of Lucca on the Dionysian *De divinis nominibus* (ed. F. Gastaldelli, Florence 1983); at the same time William, writing between 1169 and 1177, is influenced in his method by Gilbert of Poitiers (see below, p. 354). Another work that draws profoundly on Eriugena (as well as on the *Liber de causis* and Avicenna), and also has 'Porretan' features of argument, is the *Liber de causis primis et secundis*, composed in the late twelfth or early thirteenth century (see below, p. 354).
       Most recently C. Meier, 'Eriugena im Nonnenkloster?', *Frühmittelalterliche Studien* xix (1985) 466–97, has argued for the knowledge of Eriugena by Hildegard of Bingen – whose first major work, *Scivias* (1151), interestingly enough, is alluded to by William of Lucca,

Another area of major importance where further studies (and indeed in this case editions) are needed is the Aristotelianism of the later twelfth century. The uses of Aristotelian logical texts in this century, and the advent of new translations from Aristotle's *Organon*, have become well documented recently; the more pervasive use of Aristotle in the mid thirteenth, by men such as Albertus Magnus, Thomas Aquinas, and Siger of Brabant, has long been known. But no history of philosophy to my knowledge has yet charted the twelfth-century influence and creative uses of Aristotle's non-logical treatises. Despite the outstanding work of scholars such as Lorenzo Minio-Paluello in defining the achievements of the twelfth-century 'freelance' translators of Aristotle from the Greek,[16] the myth that most of his writings reached the West only in the thirteenth century, or that they made no impact earlier, retains exceptional tenacity.

The knowledge and use of some of Aristotle's works of natural philosophy among the medical writers in Salerno, in the third quarter of the twelfth century, was pointed out by Alexander Birkenmajer in a pioneer article half a century ago.[17] Nonetheless, as Danielle Jacquart observes (Ch. 15), though significant details have meanwhile been added to Birkenmajer's picture, the majority of the relevant Salernitan texts are still unpublished and must be cited from manuscripts. She thus makes accessible, and clarifies in the light of the latest researches, much evidence that histories of philosophy have not yet taken into account. Already soon after 1150, commenting on Johannitius' 'introduction to Galen's art' (*Ysagoge*), Bartholomew of Salerno and Petrus Musandinus cite Aristotle's *Physics* (which had been recently translated from the Greek by James of Venice), his *De generatione et corruptione* and *Nicomachean Ethics* (of which the earliest translations from the Greek remain anonymous). In the 1170s Urso of Calabria

who appears to have visited Hildegard in person (see *Comentum*, p. 221). Meier, who bases her argument principally on Hildegard's alleged use of Eriugena's *Expositiones* of pseudo-Dionysius, does not take the problems of transmission sufficiently into account. Of Eriugena's *Periphyseon* and its abridgement, Honorius' *Clavis Physicae* (ed. P. Lucentini, Rome 1974), there survive 24 MSS in all; of his *translation* of the Corpus Dionysiacum, more than 100 MSS; of his *Vox spiritalis aquilae* (ed. E. Jeauneau: Jean Scot, *Homélie sur le Prologue de Jean* (Paris 1969)) there are 54 MSS, though it is ascribed to Eriugena only in 5 (cf. *ibid.* p. 53). These are works of Eriugena's that Hildegard might plausibly have known (the last perhaps not under his name). His *Expositiones*, which survive only in one complete and four incomplete MSS, are much less likely to have been accessible to Hildegard.

16 L. Minio-Paluello, *Opuscula: The Latin Aristotle* (Amsterdam 1972), esp. the essays 'Iacobus Veneticus Grecus' (pp. 189–228) and 'Giacomo Veneto e l'Aristotelismo Latino' (pp. 565–86).

17 'Le rôle joué par les médecins et les naturalistes dans la réception d'Aristote aux xIIe et xIIIe siècles' (1930), repr. in his *Etudes d'histoire des sciences et de la philosophie du Moyen Age* (Wrocław–Warsaw–Cracow 1970), pp. 73–87.

shows his familiarity not only with these works but also with the *Meteorologica*, and uses his Aristotelian texts more profoundly and extensively than his predecessors, in order to give his medical discussions a coherent philosophical basis.

Still more far-reaching than the Aristotelianism in Salerno is the knowledge and understanding of Aristotle that David of Dinant brought to Paris, probably shortly before 1200. David, like the Salernitans, was a physician; but he had studied in Greece, where, he says, the *Problemata* ascribed to Aristotle 'came into my hands *(pervenit ad manus meas)'*.[18] Not only did David translate the *Problemata*, but he compiled a group of 'Notebooks *(Quaternuli)'* in which his own philosophical thoughts – set out in the succinct, discrete form he had learnt from the *Problemata* – alternate with passages from a wide range of genuine Aristotelian writings, which he cites in his own renderings, adding notes and comments. As well as quoting from the works known in Salerno, David gives long extracts from *De generatione animalium* and *De somno et vigilia*, and knows the *De anima* and the *Parva naturalia*.

When the Parisian Synod of 1210 ordered the destruction of all copies of David's *Quaternuli* (which had clearly been widely circulated) and forbade the reading and teaching of 'Aristotle's books on natural philosophy and their commentaries' – *nec libri Aristotelis de naturali philosophia nec commenta legantur*[19] – David was fortunately out of the Synod's reach, probably living in Rome as the chaplain of Pope Innocent III. The reasons for the Parisian ecclesiastics' hostility towards David's own thought, and towards the 'natural' Aristotle that he had brought with him, will have lain partly in David's attempts (basically similar to those of William of Conches and Thierry of Chartres earlier in the century) to use principles of natural explanation for the alleged miracles in the Bible – to account for the Flood, or the plagues of Egypt, or the star of the Magi, physically, without the need to postulate specific divine interventions – and even more in David's venture to think through the implications of the relationship between body and soul, matter and spirit, in a radically Aristotelian way, banishing every vestige of Platonic dualism in his attempt to see these not as two realms but as one. It is this initiative that has been called, imprecisely, David's 'pantheism'.

In Paris before 1204, quite possibly even before the arrival of David with his *Quaternuli*,[20] an Englishman, John Blund, who later taught in Oxford

---

18 *Davidis de Dinanto Quaternulorum Fragmenta*, ed. M. Kurdziałek, Studia Mediewistyczne III (Warsaw 1963), p. 3.
19 See below, pp. 429ff.
20 Thus D. A. Callus and R. W. Hunt, in their edition: Iohannes Blund, *Tractatus de anima* (London 1970), p. xi.

and was in 1232 elected Archbishop of Canterbury (though he did not take up the office), composed his *Tractatus de anima*, a work that has not yet featured in histories of philosophy. Though he is more deeply indebted to Avicenna's *De anima* than to Aristotle's, John shows intimate knowledge both of this Aristotelian text and of the *Parva naturalia*, as well as of four other physical treatises of Aristotle's and the *Metaphysics*. The twenty-six extant chapters of John's treatise, which survives in three manuscripts, are in the form of *quaestiones*, often quite elaborately articulated, so that in a series of arguments for and against a particular thesis, leading to a *solutio*, some may be extended by corollaries, or by objections that are answered in their turn. Crucial to John's problematic, as it had been to Avicenna's, is how to reconcile Aristotle's conception of the soul as 'the perfection of an organic body that has life potentially' with the conviction that the human soul is capable of existence separately from the body, and hence immortally. And he is adamant that this is a problem of metaphysics, not of theology: the theologian can speak of how the soul earns rewards or punishments, but to define the nature of the soul is beyond his ken.[21]

John's treatise, notwithstanding his mastery of much new learning, at times displays strange juxtapositions of new and old: thus, when he discusses the various meanings of 'mind (*intellectus*)' in Aristotle's *De anima*, and Avicenna's concept of a transcendent or angelic intelligence which is the 'giver of forms (*dator formarum*)' to human souls, he suddenly adds (from a very different, religious context): 'for a human being has two angels, a good one and a bad, each of which is a servant of the human soul'.[22] And when, on basically Aristotelian premises, John rejects Plato's notion of the world-soul – 'We say that the world has no soul' – he continues: 'For we believe there is no other world-soul than the Holy Spirit ruling and vivifying the universe.'[23] William of Conches and Thierry of Chartres, identifying Plato's world-soul with the Christian Holy Spirit, had seen this as a reason for accepting Plato's concept; for John it has become a reason for rejecting that concept as outworn.

For the present we have only two substantial texts – David's fragmentary Notebooks, expertly reconstructed by their editor Kurdziałek, and John's *De anima* – to testify to this first 'wave' of Aristotelian thought in Paris. Yet the decree of 1210 suggests that a tradition not only of reading and commenting but of lecturing publicly on Aristotle's natural philosophy had

---

21 *Ibid.* p. 7.
22 *Ibid.* p. 94. See also below, Ch. 4, pp. 146f.
23 *Ibid.* p. 98.

arisen and flourished – a tradition about which it is to be hoped that new investigations will bring more to light.

While the earliest of the thinkers considered in this volume, St Anselm († 1109), is truly an innovator, it would also be true to say that he scarcely influences the other major innovators in twelfth-century philosophy;[24] he crowns an earlier era of speculation rather than points to the fresh developments in the next. Anselm is also the only one among the innovators here discussed in detail whose principal formation was in a monastery – as Lanfranc's pupil, at Bec – and not in a city. As Jacques Le Goff has argued persuasively in his *Les intellectuels au moyen âge*, a new type of intellectual seems to emerge in the urban milieux from about 1100 onwards: it is the cities which have come to flourish by this time that see the rise of the 'modern intellectual', whose first striking embodiment is Abelard – the scholar–teacher who approaches his work as a professional, a technician or specialist. The new intellectuals are intent upon circulating their knowledge, rather than hoarding it as an heirloom, which had been the characteristic attitude of the earlier monastic schools.[25] Beryl Smalley, too, in her classic *The Study of the Bible in the Middle Ages*, in order to define the exceptional nature of the Abbey of Saint-Victor (founded by William of Champeaux and some other Augustinian canons on the left bank of the Seine in 1110), begins with a sharp contrast:

A gulf had opened between monks and scholars. Contemporaries constantly stress their difference in function: the scholar learns and teaches; the monk prays and 'mourns'. The canons regular courageously refused to admit the dilemma ... Until about 1140, at least, the Victorines seem to have kept an open school; they were unique at Paris in being both *scholares* and *claustrales*.[26]

The difference of orientation between the scholastic and monastic worlds, while it has often and with justice been stressed, should also admit of some qualification in other contexts than Saint-Victor. As Claudio Leonardi points out, for instance, in his perceptive recent introduction to the 'Golden Letter' of William of Saint-Thierry, William, who became a Cistercian and St Bernard's closest friend, who attacked the philosophical approach to God of Abelard and William of Conches, nonetheless shared with them, and Gilbert of Poitiers, as also with the biblical exegetes of the school of Laon, the conviction 'that one could no longer simply use the words of the faith, of the

24 Though, as the editors indicate, John Blund's discussion of free will (*Tractatus* xxv) owes much to Anselm's *De libertate arbitrii*.
25 J. Le Goff, *Les intellectuels au moyen âge* (Paris 1957), esp. pp. 9f, 40, 67f.
26 *The Study of the Bible in the Middle Ages* (2nd ed., Oxford 1952), pp. 83f.

Bible and of the Fathers, even if it be with the support of the liberal arts, in order to comprehend God, man and history; that one needed a different language, and one that was rigorously ordered'.[27] William's own approach was mystical, not philosophical: for him the problem of knowing God was that of experiencing God, in a loving theosis. Yet he had been trained, like Abelard and William of Conches, in an urban cathedral school, and even his mystical masterpiece, as Michael Lapidge indicates in Chapter 3, shows a notable debt to Stoic moral philosophy.

Conversely, some of the major teachers – Alan of Lille, and very probably Thierry of Chartres – end their days as Cistercian monks.[28] It might seem easy to interpret this simply as their renunciation of secular career and aspirations as death approached – and yet a striking number of the 'worldly' texts of twelfth-century philosophy have survived chiefly because they were copied and preserved in Cistercian abbeys. Again, there are a number of anonymous philosophical texts of which, in our present state of knowledge, we cannot even say with confidence that they originated in a secular or a monastic milieu – texts that cannot yet be ordered with any certainty into our total picture of twelfth-century philosophy. I should like to pause briefly at one of these.

In 1984 Paolo Lucentini published the *Liber Alcidi de immortalitate animae*, which survives in five manuscripts of Italian provenance.[29] His careful discussion of the texts the author knew leads him to suggest that the *Liber* was written in the second half of the twelfth century, possibly in Sicily. The work is at once a dialogue, a *consolatio*, and an allegorical vision. It is set in an imaginary Greece of the end of the first century AD. The protagonist, Alcidus, mourns the death in battle of his brother. There appears to him first a vain young Rhetor, symbolizing the 'outer man *(exterior homo)*',[30] whose speech, dwelling only on earthly values, affections, and griefs, leaves Alcidus in more desperate sorrow than before. Then a radiant ancient sage – the inner man – accompanied by three young nobles, who evoke three aspects of the human soul (intellect, passion, and will), inveighs against the

27 Guillaume de Saint-Thierry, *La lettera d'oro* (Florence 1983), p. 10.
28 On Alan's *moniage*, see d'Alverny 1965, pp. 22–6; on that of Thierry, see A. Vernet, 'Une épitaphe inédite de Thierry de Chartres', in *Recueil de travaux offert à Cl. Brunel* (2 vols., Paris 1955) II 660–70, at pp. 666–9, and lines 37ff of the epitaph (p. 670). It is unfortunate that M. Gibson, in editing R. W. Hunt's *The Schools and the Cloister: The Life and Writings of Alexander Nequam (1157–1217)* (Oxford 1985), cites Vernet's essay, as reprinted in his *Etudes médiévales* (Paris 1981), in support of the assertion '"Terricus" never became a monk' (p. 6 n. 26) – the precise contrary of what Vernet demonstrates.
29 *Liber Alcidi de immortalitate animae: Studio e edizione critica* (Naples 1984); on the MSS, pp. xix–xxxviii.
30 *Ibid.* p. 5.

Rhetor's limitations and puts him and his retinue to flight. He brings Alcidus true comfort, by affirming that the soul is immortal, and also (though he makes no overt Christian reference) that the body will rise again: Alcidus' brother is alive, in the only true life. He bids the first youth, Altividus ('high-seeing' intellectual vision), to argue for the soul's immortality, and the second, Iramalus ('irascible' passion), to teach Alcidus the virtues by which immortal beatitude is won. Their discourses fill most of the rest of the dialogue. Though much in the detail of the arguments can be traced to long-familiar texts – of Boethius and Augustine, Cicero, Macrobius, and Calcidius – the elegant *montage* of the whole, and the attempt to create a convincing fictive world of Hellenistic thought, make this a notable testimony to twelfth-century humanism. The dialogue is studded with allusions to invented historical personages, and to writers of Greek philosophy that the author cannot have known directly (once he even falls into anachronism, mentioning the reading of Plotinus in his first-century world). Yet the range of his real reading is equally surprising: as Lucentini skilfully shows, he is familiar with the trinitarian speculations of Abelard and the Victorines, on the one hand, and with a lost translation of Diogenes Laertius' *Lives of the Philosophers* (probably made by Henry Aristippus in 1156–60) on the other.[31] At present we simply do not know of a twelfth-century milieu in which both Richard of Saint-Victor and Diogenes Laertius were read. An analysis of the elaborate patterns of rhythmic *clausulae* in the work, which well deserves undertaking, may eventually enable us to locate it in a particular stylistic current, even if not at a particular centre.

Another text, which has not yet been published, raises some crucial questions about specific philosophical achievements in the early twelfth century. In a learned and interesting essay of 1984, Paul Edward Dutton has argued for the attribution of a substantial commentary on the *Timaeus*, which begins with the words 'Socrates de re publica' and survives anonymously in five manuscripts, to the legendary Bernard of Chartres,[32] whose philosophical thought we have hitherto known only indirectly, chiefly by way of citations and allusions in John of Salisbury.[33] Dutton's claim will have to be fully tested when the critical edition of this commentary, which he

---

31 *Ibid.* pp. xcix–ciii, cv–cvi.
32 'The uncovering of the *Glosae super Platonem* of Bernard of Chartres', *Mediaeval Studies* XLVI (1984) 192–221. In the discussion below, I refer to the *Glosae* in question by their incipit, 'Socrates de re publica', in order to distinguish them from the published *Glosae super Platonem* of William of Conches (see above, n. 6).
33 See especially E. Jeauneau, '*Nani gigantum humeris insidentes*', in his *Lectio philosophorum* (Amsterdam 1973), pp. 53–73.

has promised, appears. The observations that follow are based on the passages published in Dutton's essay, on those cited earlier (as anonymous) by Tullio Gregory, and on some substantial extracts that I transcribed in 1971 from two of the manuscripts.[34]

Certain indications that Dutton has given do seem to point to the presence of Bernard of Chartres in this commentary. Its author takes up the distinction that John of Salisbury saw as characteristic of Bernard, between the ideas (*ideae*) as eternal exemplars in the divine mind, and the images of those ideas, the 'forms as born (*nativae formae*)', which exist in the physical world.[35] Noteworthy too is a comment, some twenty lines long, on the components of the world-soul, which, as Dutton shows, is cited in a mid-twelfth-century Irish gloss on the *Timaeus*, with the added instruction 'read Bernard here and you will find still more (*Hic lege Bernardum et adhuc invenies*)'.[36] Since in the 'Socrates de re publica' commentary the gloss for this lemma does in fact have a remarkable allegorical continuation,[37] it would seem that this passage at least represents the work of 'Bernardus', and there is no doubt that in the early twelfth century the Bernard most celebrated for his Platonism was Bernard of Chartres.

Yet I still sense some possible difficulties about seeing the 'Socrates de re publica' commentary in its entirety as a work by the Chartrian. Dutton, indicating its relation with other *Timaeus* glosses of the period, mentions for instance that a London manuscript (B.L. Royal 12 B xxii) reveals 'a heavy, though not exclusive, dependence' on this work that he attributes to Bernard. Yet the London manuscript is one that a recent scholar has 'dated to "circa 1100"';[38] J. H. Waszink in his edition of Calcidius likewise sets it at

---

34 T. Gregory, *Platonismo medievale: Studi e ricerche* (Rome 1958), pp. 66–71, 76 n. 1, 103, 120f; in *Fabula* (cit. n. 7), I printed a passage (again as anonymous) from the MS Munich Clm 540 B (p. 89 n. 1); my other transcriptions are also from this MS, collated for some passages with the (incomplete) MS Vienna 2376, 2.

35 *Metalogicon* IV 35; cf. E. Garin, *Studi sul platonismo medievale* (Florence 1958), pp. 50–4.

36 Dutton 1984, pp. 208f.

37 As this point is not made explicitly, and the continuation is not printed, in Dutton's article, I give the text, for convenience, below, from Munich Clm 540 B, fols. 16v–17r (the promised critical edition may bring some modifications):
   Puritas etiam anime per VII habetur, quia septenarius a veteribus dictus est Minerva, quia sicut illa sine matre et prole est, ita septenarius infra X nec gignit nec gignitur; qui X perfectus dicitur, quia quod eum sequitur non est numeratio sed replicatio numeri. Item per VI intervalla VII limitum perfectio anime notatur, quia sextarius perfectus est. Item inter VII partes omnes musice consonantie notantur, per quod anime armonia naturaliter insita denotatur, et per hec omnia scientia quadruvii intelligitur, in quo est perfectio scientie: per numeros, arimethice; per hoc quod lineares, superficiales, cubici sunt numeri, geometrie; per consonantias proportionaliter notatas, musice et astronomie, in qua de musico concentu sperarum agitur.

38 Dutton 1984, p. 199.

the very beginning of the twelfth century.[39] If the influence indeed goes from 'Socrates de re publica' to the London glosses, then the earlier work must already have been in circulation at the latest by the 1090s. On the other hand, our most solid chronological evidence for Bernard of Chartres as a teacher (*magister scolae*) points to the years 1119–24,[40] and there is no record of his teaching before the second decade of the twelfth century. Is it not a little hazardous, then, to assume that long before this Bernard had already completed and published an influential work? Naturally such a supposition cannot be ruled out; but in our present state of knowledge it cannot be accepted as certain either.

It seems to me at least possible that the full edition may reveal that the 'Socrates de re publica' commentary has more than one layer, and that we may have to reckon with the presence in it of earlier eleventh-century speculations inspired by the *Timaeus* as well as of contributions ascribable to Bernard of Chartres. It should not be overlooked, for instance, as Garin pointed out in his penetrating pages on Bernard, that the Bernardian distinction between exemplary and 'born' forms is already to be found under the definition of *idea* in Papias' *Elementarium*[41] (which according to the most recent scholarship was completed probably in 1041).[42] Papias explains that the Greeks 'gave the name "ideas" to the exemplary forms which were in the divine mind when it created these born forms; for they said that the ideas in the divine mind, or archetypal world, are always in existence'. Papias here uses not *nativae formae* but the synonymous *nativae species* (cf. Calcidius, ed. Waszink, pp. 336.5–7, and 339.2–3). Yet it is evident from his definition that the distinction John of Salisbury associates with Bernard of Chartres was already a talking-point at a time when Bernard could not yet have been born. The first three chapters of Tullio Gregory's *Platonismo medievale* have shown clearly the level of discussion of Platonic problems of which the eleventh century was capable. This emerges especially through Manegold of Lautenbach's polemic against Wolfelmus of Cologne, the *Libellus contra Wolfelmum* (*ca.* 1085).[43] Where Manegold complains that Platonists such as Wolfelmus see 'matter also as intelligible (*materiam etiam intelligibilem*)', and thereby

---

39 Waszink (see n. 12), p. cxxiii: 'saec. XII in.'.
40 See especially R. W. Southern, *Medieval Humanism* (Oxford 1970), p. 68 n. 1; however, Otto of Freising's testimony (*Gesta* I 53), that Gilbert studied with 'Bernardus Carnotensis' *before* studying with Anselm of Laon († 1117), gives us an earlier *terminus ante quem* for the start of Bernard's teaching.
41 Garin 1958, p. 53 n. 1 (citing in full the Papias passage from which I translate below).
42 Cf. V. de Angelis (ed.), *Papiae Elementarium: Littera A* I (Milan 1977), ii–iii.
43 On the date: Manegold von Lautenbach, *Liber contra Wolfelmum*, ed. W. Hartmann (MGH, Weimar 1972), p. 13.

'detract from God's omnipotence, allowing nothing to be made *ex nihilo*',[44] he would seem to be referring to a question very like that discussed in 'Socrates de re publica', where all the *nativae formae* are said to have existed potentially (*potentialiter*) in matter, even 'before the establishing of the world (*ante constitutionem mundi*)', so that 'philosophers say that God did not make the world *ex nihilo* but only adorned it'.[45]

At least we must say that some of the principal questions that surface in 'Socrates de re publica' are rooted in earlier, eleventh-century discussions of Platonic problems. However, some distinguished contributions notwithstanding – such as Gregory's chapters, already mentioned, or de Rijk's edition of Garlandus[46] – our picture of eleventh-century philosophical speculation is still more fragmentary than that of the twelfth. Yet for the twelfth century too it is best to end on a note of caution. What we have at present is less a picture than a picture-puzzle, with many pieces not yet inserted in their place, some that we do not yet know where to insert, and some where we may never know, because too many vital linking pieces are lost. The present volume is a first attempt to evoke the picture, by a group of scholars each of whom has worked at particular parts of the puzzle, not only picking up pieces that already lie to hand (in printed sources), but also searching out pieces that are still hiding (in manuscripts). The picture as evoked is not yet at a stage where it will yield precise answers to the historians who, for example, want to ask: to what extent can we see these thinkers as the product of their society? to what extent did they change the outlook of their society? But I hope it will also be of help eventually towards the answering of such challenging questions. What we can offer, however (to return to Le Goff's contrast), is something for circulation, not for hoarding; not a fixed corpus of information that will somehow encapsulate twelfth-century philosophy, but above all an opening-up of problems, and an invitation to take them further.

I should like to conclude with two more personal reflections. The first is to commemorate Enzo Maccagnolo, who met with a tragically sudden death in the summer of 1985, while he was engaged on writing the concluding chapter of this volume. I had long known his deeply probing book on Thierry of Chartres and his anthology of translations of Chartrian philosophy;[47] in recent years I had also come to know him as a warm and

44 Manegold 1972, ch. 8 (pp. 60f).
45 Dutton 1984, p. 217 and n. 122.
46 Garlandus Compotista, *Dialectica*, ed. L. M. de Rijk (Assen 1959).
47 *Rerum universitas (Saggio sulla filosofia di Teodorico di Chartres)* (Florence 1976); *Il divino e il megacosmo: Testi filosofici e scientifici della scuola di Chartres* (Milan 1980).

generous friend. Since at our last meeting, in April 1983, he told me he was preparing an extended study of David of Dinant, I was particularly delighted by his agreeing to write Chapter 16. His widow very kindly sent me the chapter as it was left, much of it still unfinished, and with some passages in two or three alternative rough versions. Though he might not have wished his work on David to be published in this form, without the benefit of his own later thoughts, the importance of the subject makes it vital to include here at least a substantial portion of his draft. Moreover, Maccagnolo's central intuition about David's thought – that, far from simply reproducing Aristotelian notions, or extending them in heretical directions, David was attempting an individual *itinerarium mentis in deum*, in which knowledge is a continuum that begins with the study of physical phenomena and makes its way to God as final point – seems to me of exceptional interest and freshness. I have edited the draft as best I could, rounding the chapter off with a quotation from David's editor, Marian Kurdziałek, in place of a conclusion, and have added the notes that are in square brackets.

The second is to pay a brief but affectionate tribute to the scholar who is cited more than any other by the writers of this volume, who appears as an *auctoritas* in literally dozens of our notes: Marie-Thérèse d'Alverny. Ever since she gave me some of her precious time and help, nearly thirty years ago, when as a complete beginner I looked at manuscripts in the Bibliothè-que Nationale, I have learnt incalculably much from her counsels and her writings, especially in the field of twelfth-century thought. Her capacity to bring a wealth of new materials to light through the study of unpublished texts, her unfailing clarity of perception and exposition, and her ability to see intellectual links that eluded her predecessors, have played a large part in transforming the subject to which this book is devoted.

I
BACKGROUND

I

PHILOSOPHY, COSMOLOGY, AND THE TWELFTH-CENTURY RENAISSANCE

WINTHROP WETHERBEE

This chapter is an exercise more in literary history than in the history of philosophy. In it I will attempt to isolate one particularly influential strain in the thought of the early twelfth-century schools, define the emphases that distinguish it from other intellectual currents in the period, and trace its influence in several areas of twelfth-century intellectual culture. The group of thinkers with whom I will be chiefly concerned, and whom I have labelled for convenience the 'cosmologists', are united by their interest in the study of the natural universe as an avenue to philosophical and religious understanding. Because some of the most prominent among them were associated at different points in their careers with the cathedral school at Chartres, it has been traditional to assume that this school was the centre of such studies, and Chartres has been extolled as the nurse of humanist values and intellectual freedom in the early twelfth century.[1] While we are now learning to see the activity of the School of Chartres as part of a broader scholastic movement, it remains clear that there are important and widely influential common elements in the thought of those masters whose names have been most frequently associated with Chartres. It is largely the appropriation of the themes and methods of these 'cosmologists' by thinkers in other areas that accounts for the persistent tendency to associate the twelfth century with ideas of progress and renewal, and it is clear that the work of a John of Salisbury or Alan of Lille reflects the impact of a 'discovery of man and nature' that is a distinctive achievement of the period. It is also, however, necessary to recognize that the promulgation of the ideas of the cosmologists

---

1 Raymond Klibansky, 'The School of Chartres', in *Twelfth Century Europe and the Foundations of Modern Society*, ed. Marshall Clagett, Gaines Post, and Robert Reynolds (Madison, WI 1961), pp. 3–14. The importance of the school of Chartres is questioned in three essays by R. W. Southern: 'Humanism and the School of Chartres', in *Medieval Humanism and Other Studies* (Oxford 1970), pp. 61–85; 'The Schools of Paris and the School of Chartres', in *Harvard 1982*, pp. 113–37; *Platonism, Scholastic Method, and the School of Chartres* (Reading 1979). Responses to Southern are offered by Peter Dronke, 'New Approaches to the School of Chartres', *Anuario de Estudios Medievales* VI (1969) 117–40; Nikolaus Häring, 'Chartres and Paris Revisited', in *Essays in Honor of Anton Charles Pegis*, ed. J. R. O'Donnell (Toronto 1974), pp. 268–329.

by John, Alan and others is accompanied by a growing sense of the limits of philosophy, and the dangers associated with its too-enthusiastic pursuit, which sound very much like the traditionalist scepticism of Hugh of Saint-Victor and the other early opponents of the cosmologists themselves. And it will be necessary for us too to give some consideration to the limited resources with which the cosmologists were working, in assessing the character of their influence.

Perhaps we should begin by asking in more general terms how the achievement of twelfth-century philosophy is to be measured. Within philosophy itself, strictly defined, the most important original work in the period is probably Abelard's use of dialectic to explore the relations of language, thought, and reality. But despite his innovative brilliance, Abelard's influence was limited, and this is only partly due to the suspicions raised against his work on doctrinal grounds. Recent historians have tended to view his achievement in logic less as a new departure than as a culmination, the fullest development of a movement which begins in the early eleventh century, and which is cut off from later developments by limited access to the 'new logic' and other works of Aristotle.[2]

The broader effect of philosophy on the culture of the period is largely a matter of the intrusion of dialectic into the fields of grammar, theology, and law. Here too achievement is limited. It is clear that a new, speculative theology comes to coexist with the traditional programme, grounded in biblical exegesis: Hugh of Saint-Victor, Abelard, and especially Gilbert of Poitiers explore its relations with philosophy, and Chenu can speak of it as a new science, based on 'criteria stemming from the intelligible nature of its subject matter'.[3] But in the early twelfth century theology is confined for the most part to the reconciling of traditional authorities in new ways, like the closely related and widely influential movement toward the codification of canon law.[4] Insofar as it manifests a genuine desire to establish rational bases

---

2 Norman Kretzmann, 'The Culmination of the Old Logic in Peter Abelard', in *Harvard 1982*, pp. 488–511; Martin M. Tweedale, 'Abelard and the Culmination of the Old Logic', in *CHLMP* pp. 143–57. For qualifications of this view, Klaus Jacobi, 'Peter Abelard's Investigations into the Meaning and Functions of the Speech Sign "Est"', in *The Logic of Being*, ed. Simo Knuuttila and Jaakko Hintikka (Dordrecht 1986), pp. 170–1. Jean Jolivet, surveying Abelard's use of the arts of the Trivium, notes the difficulty of tracing his influence, and the vagueness of such testimony as that of John of Salisbury: *Arts du langage et théologie chez Abélard* (Paris 1969), pp. 338–40.

3 *La théologie au douzième siècle* (Paris 1957), p. 326; trans. Jerome Taylor and L. K. Little, *Nature, Man, and Society in the Twelfth Century* (Chicago 1968), p. 276; Lauge Olaf Nielsen, *Theology and Philosophy in the Twelfth Century* (Leiden 1982), pp. 136–42, 362–70.

4 Joseph de Ghellinck, *Le mouvement théologique du xiie siècle* (2nd ed., Bruges–Brussels–Paris 1948), pp. 7–9, 52–65. See also L. M. de Rijk, *Logica Modernorum* (Assen 1962–7) II. 1 126–30.

of enquiry, it points toward the swallowing-up of its own achievements in the more decisive reorganization of knowledge in the later twelfth and thirteenth centuries.

There is no avoiding the fact that to a great extent the original thinkers of the early twelfth century inhabit a sort of limbo, suspended between old and new, yet it is equally clear that an interest in new intellectual ventures is one of the distinctive characteristics of the period. 'Traditional terms and schemata spring into new life',[5] and there is much discussion of the scope and interrelation of the Liberal Arts. The widespread concern with the organization of knowledge is accompanied by a new sense of its applicability to man's condition in the world, including his politics, economics, and technology. The major figures in the new urban schools are *magistri*, teacher-scholars with a new sense of their professional role, and a new awareness of the practical importance of systematic thought. There can be no doubt that the status and influence of men of learning rose tremendously in our period, and that the practical value assigned to arithmetic, astrology, and even magic had a significant effect in encouraging the revival of scientific study, as well as enhancing the prestige of learning in general.[6]

We must not overemphasize the newness and significance of these interests: when Hugh of Saint-Victor devotes a chapter of his *Didascalicon* to justifying the place of *mechanica* among the types of knowledge which make up philosophy, or when his follower Richard discovers in agriculture and other practical arts 'the dignity of a divine gift', it is easy to feel that we have located the Promethean strain in twelfth-century thought, the 'humanisme intégral' that views all human skills as means to redemption.[7] But the thinking of the Victorines is in a tradition which goes back through Augustine to antiquity; what they value is not the practice of the mechanical arts but the *ratio* in the light of which they become sources of a knowledge that leads ultimately to God.

5 R. W. Hunt, 'The Introductions to the "Artes" in the Twelfth Century', in *Studia medievalia in Honorem . . . R. J. Martin* (Bruges 1948), pp. 85–6; repr. in his *Collected Papers on the History of Grammar in the Middle Ages*, ed. G. L. Bursill-Hall (Amsterdam 1980), pp. 117–18.

6 On the status of *magistri* see Philippe Delhaye, 'L'organisation scolaire au xiie siècle', *Traditio* v (1947) 211–68; Chenu 1957, pp. 323–50 (Taylor–Little 1968, pp. 270–309). On the general status of scientific learning, Alexander Murray, *Reason and Society in the Middle Ages* (Oxford 1978), pp. 110–24; Brian Stock, *The Implications of Literacy* (Princeton 1983), pp. 30–4, 86–7.

7 Hugh, *Didascalicon* ii 20, ed. C. H. Buttimer (Washington 1939), pp. 38–9; Richard, *Benjamin Major* ii 5 (P. L. 196, 83); Guy Beaujouan, 'Réflexions sur les rapports entre théorie et pratique au moyen âge', in *The Cultural Context of Medieval Learning*, ed. John E. Murdoch and Edith D. Sylla (Dordrecht–Boston 1975), pp. 437–9; Franco Alessio, 'La filosofia e le "artes mechanicae" nel secolo xii', *Studi Medievali*, ser. 3, vi (1965) 110–29; Maurice de Gandillac, 'Place et signification de la technique dans le monde médiéval', in *Tecnica e casistica* (Rome 1964), pp. 265–75.

Moreover, the emphasis on coherence and the sense of new goals is often misleading. The concern to expand the scope of systematic study is continually undermined by an inadequate appreciation of the properties of the individual Arts, and an inability to distinguish their proper domains. New knowledge is assimilated in random ways, and while it helps to generate a sense of the possibility of a more comprehensive approach to learning, the proliferation of new texts and methods exerts a distracting influence. It is one of the many paradoxes of the intellectual life of the period that the concern for synthesis coexists, even in the work of individual masters, with a tendency toward the pursuit of isolated specialities. There are, of course, instances of genuine co-operation among the Arts: for both Thierry of Chartres and Gilbert of Poitiers the ascent to theological understanding, in conformity with the classic definition in Boethius' *De trinitate*, requires a clear understanding of the complementary spheres of the subordinate disciplines of natural science and mathematics.[8] The problem of universals itself was approached through questions of signification and predication which are grammatical as well as philosophical, and the pursuit of these questions by Abelard and others looks forward to the later reconstitution of grammar on a philosophical basis in the work of the thirteenth-century speculative grammarians. But the project of the philosopher-theologians is hindered by the absence of a common standard for defining physical fact, or the status of number,[9] and the tentative synthesis of logic and grammar remains, even in the work of the grammarians themselves, wholly unconnected with such traditional pursuits of the *grammaticus* as the study of classical authors. In both areas, new methods and ambitions simply coexist with traditional practice rather than transforming it.

This opposition between the spirit and the substance of twelfth-century learning is nowhere more striking than in the area where the spirit of the 'twelfth-century Renaissance' has seemed to express itself most vividly in philosophical terms: the study of the universe and of man in his relation to the universal order. The cosmologists of the early twelfth century, Bernard and Thierry of Chartres, William of Conches, and a host of anonymous commentators, exhibit a Platonism which is not just the ingrained idealism of the Augustinian tradition, but reflects a new interest in Plato himself and in his late-antique followers Macrobius, Martianus Capella, Calcidius, and

8 G. R. Evans, *Old Arts and New Theology* (Oxford 1980), pp. 119–36.
9 Nielsen 1982, pp. 90–6, 153–4.

Boethius.[10] 'Plato' meant the cosmology of the *Timaeus*, and study of this central text as a way of explaining the relationship of God, the eternal ideas of things, and the material expression of these ideas was the chief project of these Platonists. That the visible universe is a coherent cosmos, informed by soul and modelled on an ideal exemplar, was fundamental, and to the extent that the world-soul and the archetype were seen as manifestations of God, expressions of his goodness and wisdom, they could render his activity accessible to reason through the visible universe. 'In the creation of things', says William of Conches, 'divine power, wisdom, and goodness are beheld', and these three attributes, under various names, seemed to thinkers of widely diverse orientation a manifest expression of the Trinity.[11]

Equally important are the anthropological implications of these ideas. As even the incomplete *Timaeus* accessible to the Middle Ages makes plain, man is himself a universe, composed of the elements and subject to the physical laws of the cosmos at large, and endowed with a soul which reflects the divine wisdom and is by nature subject to its providential influence. To know nature is to know man, and hence an appreciation of the organicity and inner coherence of the universe could lead to a view of nature and natural law as a standard for the regulation of human society. 'Natural justice', the theme of the *Timaeus*, is the foundation of the 'positive justice' of moral and political order, and in the philosophical poetry of the later twelfth century Natura becomes, like Boethius' Philosophia, a goddess, a manifestation of Wisdom.[12] The continuity of human and cosmic life was also emphasized in the Stoic physics with which the cosmologists augmented their Platonism, drawing from Cicero and Seneca the idea of an *ignis artifex*, a vital force which sustains and renews universal life at all levels, from mere vegetable existence to the level of cognition and intelligence.[13] Medicine, in the form of the Galenic view of the properties and behaviour of the elements in the human constitution, provided a further link.[14] And the Hermetic treatise

---

10 Edouard Jeauneau, 'Note sur l'École de Chartres', *Studi Medievali*, ser. 3, v (1964) 821–65, repr. in Jeauneau's *'Lectio Philosophorum': Recherches sur l'École de Chartres* (Amsterdam 1973), pp. 5–49; 'Macrobe, source du platonisme chartrain', *Studi Medievali*, ser. 3, I (1960) 3–24 ('*Lectio Philosophorum*', pp. 279–300).
11 William, *Glosae super Platonem*, ed. E. Jeauneau (Paris 1965), p. 60. Tullio Gregory, *Anima mundi. La filosofia di Guglielmo di Conches e la Scuola di Chartres* (Florence 1955), pp. 123–74; *Platonismo medievale: studi e ricerche* (Rome 1958), pp. 122–38.
12 Gregory 1958, pp. 138–50.
13 See *ibid.* pp. 135–42; B. Stock, *Myth and Science in the Twelfth Century* (Princeton 1972), pp. 138–62; Gerard Verbeke, *The Presence of Stoicism in Medieval Thought* (Washington 1983), pp. 35–44.
14 Richard McKeon, 'Medicine and Philosophy in the Eleventh and Twelfth Centuries: the Problem of the Elements', *The Thomist* XXIV (1961) 211–56, at pp. 231–43; Heinrich

Asclepius, widely influential in the period, dwells at length on the importance of contemplation of the cosmic order to the recovery of man's lost capacity for rational conduct and understanding of God.[15] The ideas are not new, but they appear in the context of a new sense of the possibility of 'progress through knowledge', as in this passage from the *De eodem et diverso* of Adelard of Bath:

The creator of things, supremely good, drawing all creatures into his own likeness, so far as their nature allows, has endowed the soul with that mental power which the Greeks call *Nous*. This power she freely enjoys while in her pure condition, untroubled by disturbance from without. She examines not only things in themselves but their causes as well, and the principles of their causes, and from things present has a knowledge of the distant future. She understands what she is in herself, what the mind is by which she knows, and what the power of reason by which she seeks to know. Once bound by the earthly and vile fetters of the body she loses no small portion of her understanding, but that elemental dross cannot wholly obliterate this splendour.[16]

Adelard's concern with *causae* and *principia* defines the programme of twelfth-century Platonic 'science', a programme which would seem to be putting secular knowledge to new and significant uses. It is in glosses on Plato's cosmology, and in such new departures as the cosmological treatises and philosophical poems which the study of the *Timaeus* inspired, that we can see the clearest evidence of the new ambitiousness of twelfth-century thought, and the effect of the incorporation into the curriculum of the schools of scientific concerns which had previously been pursued in random and often primitive ways. This is a new, 'literate' science, in which the principles governing natural phenomena appear in a fully intellectualized form, and the use of abstraction to 'control' the natural world has been hailed as the symptom of a dawning sense of man's capacity to reclaim his proper place in the scheme of things.[17]

Underlying this intellectual confidence is a new confidence in the learning of the past. The treatise on the work of the six days attributed to Thierry of

Schipperges, 'Einflüsse arabischer Medizin auf die Mikrokosmosliteratur des 12. Jahrhunderts', *Miscellanea Mediaevalia* I (1962) 129–53, at pp. 138–45; Dronke 1969, pp. 124–5.
15 *Asclepius* 12–14, ed. A. D. Nock and A.-J. Festugière (Paris 1960), pp. 311–14.
16 *De eodem et diverso*, ed. Hans Willner, BGPTM IV. 1, pp. 9–10:
  'Rerum conditor optimus omnia ad sui similitudinem trahens, quantum eorum natura patitur, animam mente, quam Graeci noyn vocant, exornavit. Hac ipsa, dum in sua puritate est, tumultu exteriore carens plane utitur. Nec modo res ipsas, verum etiam earum causas et causarum initia assequitur et ex praesentibus futura longo tractu cognoscit; quidque ipsa sit, quid mens, qua cognoscit, quid ratio, qua inquirit, deprehendit. Eadem testeo et lutulento corporis amicta carcere non parvam suae cognitionis amittit portionem. Sed nec faex illa elementaris ad plenum potest hoc decus abolere.'
17 Stock 1983, p. 243.

Chartres is remarkable in the virtual autonomy it assigns to the elements as operative *causae* in the generation of the universe, and Thierry's commentaries on Boethius' theological tractates employ arithmetical formulations with a new freedom to define the principles of the created order and its relation to the operations of the Trinity.[18] In their implicit conviction that such scientific studies can be reconciled with an ultimately religious conception of philosophy as a whole, they give expression to the ideals of the Platonist cosmologists. A similarly vivid sense of the autonomy and coherence of the natural order pervades the writings of William of Conches on the *philosophia mundi*. For him as for Thierry natural processes are the channels through which divine power informs the universe, and hence to study nature is to acknowledge God's grandeur, rather than to encroach upon it. Both authors are remarkable also in viewing their work as ancillary to the propagation of ancient wisdom. Though many of his contemporaries tended to reject the substance of the teaching of pagan authors while borrowing from their methodology, the noble preface to the *Heptateuchon*, Thierry's great compendium of material on the Liberal Arts, boasts of presenting, not Thierry's own thoughts, but the very texts of the *auctores* in each Art.[19] William could view his own treatises, as well as his glosses on ancient texts, primarily as aids to the study of 'the philosophers who are read nowadays in the schools'.[20]

In the remainder of this chapter I will be concerned very largely with the fortunes of the thought of these scientist-philosophers, whom I will call 'cosmologists' despite the fact that the term is inadequate to comprehend the work of a Gilbert of Poitiers and applies to only certain aspects of that of Thierry. Their impact on the development of medieval philosophy was short-lived, but their influence in other areas is clear and striking. It is their reading of the natural order that comes to inform moral, political, and legal thought in the later twelfth century, and provides the inspiration for important new ventures in the criticism and imitation of ancient authors. In general, it is through their work that the effects of the philosophical activity of the early twelfth century come to bear on the culture of the period. But the particular forms in which their influence appears are due in large measure to the same combination of lofty educational ideals with limited scientific resources that led to their neglect in the increasingly specialist atmosphere of

18 Jeauneau 1964, pp. 824–9; 1973, pp. 8–13; 'Mathématiques et Trinité chez Thierry de Chartres', *Miscellanea Mediaevalia* II (1963) 289–95; Jeauneau 1973, pp. 93–9; Evans 1980, pp. 119–36.
19 *Prologus in Eptateuchon*, ed. Jeauneau, *Mediaeval Studies* XVI (1954) 174.
20 *Dragmaticon*, ed. Guilielmus Gratarolus (Strasbourg 1567; repr. Frankfurt 1967), p. 83.

philosophical studies during the later twelfth century. Thus before attempting to trace their influence it will be necessary to look more closely at the
limitations of their work, in order to distinguish more clearly that in it which
was of enduring importance.

After a century during which the stature of Thierry, William, and their
fellow-Platonists as intellectual pioneers, humanists, and champions of
intellectual freedom had been generally acknowledged, it has recently been
argued with considerable force that too much has been made of their
orginality, and that their programme was in fact hopelessly old-fashioned.[21]
The *Timaeus*, it is argued, could stimulate scientific investigation, but it
could not provide material for new thought; most of the science it inspired
was pseudo-science, and it was already being 'elbowed aside' by newly
recovered texts at the time when its influence is most visible.[22] The
paradoxical result is that the most ardent Platonists of the twelfth century
were forced to abandon philosophical Platonism in favour of a cosmology
which vacillates between a crude form of natural science and wholly intuitive
exercises in myth and metaphor. William of Conches could present a
seemingly forward-looking claim to scientific objectivity with his assertion
of the right to explain *how* that was done which is said in Scripture to have
been done,[23] but he is very far from an empirical thinker, and incapable of
seriously investigating conflicts between Platonic idealism and the functional
concepts of medicine, or winnowing out the elements of magic and crude
astrology in his preferred sources. Like so much of the thought of his day,
William's project is essentially one of reconciliation, one more manifestation
of the preoccupation of the earlier Middle Ages with the harmonizing of
authorities, and brings into play little that is new in the way of knowledge or
methodology. Even Thierry's well-known attempt to explain the creation
secundum physicam, reading Genesis in the light of the *Timaeus*, is finally just a
manifestion of the same concern, an attempt to reconcile ancient *auctores* with
Patristic tradition. Even the authority assigned to the *Timaeus* by Thierry
and William does not serve to set them apart from those whose concern was
with theology in a stricter sense: 'they all used the same methods, they all
drew their ideas from ancient texts, and often from the same ancient texts,
which kept reappearing in all areas of study'.[24] Where scientific originality
does appear, it is not a matter of new ventures in syncretism, but of the

21 Southern 1970, pp. 78–83; 1979, pp. 8–15.
22 Margaret Gibson, 'The Study of the *Timaeus* in the Eleventh and Twelfth Centuries',
   Pensamiento XXV (1969) 183–94, at p. 190.
23 *Philosophia*, ed. G. Maurach (Pretoria 1980), I 44 (p. 39); = P. L. 172, 56.
24 Southern 1979, p. 29.

recovery of new sources, and the tentative exploration of new areas of study. Adelard of Bath, for all his Platonist eloquence, is a case in point. The passage quoted above echoes Boethius, Plato and the *Asclepius*, but its stress on the soul's power to read nature for evidence of things to come is astrological, and reflects a growing respect for Arabic thought. Adelard was to contribute actively to the undermining of the scientific authority of the *Timaeus* by his assiduous cultivation of the Quadrivium.

It could of course be answered that the authority of the *Timaeus* involves far more than its power to answer specific questions, and a case can certainly be made for the originality and significance of Thierry's deployment of mathematical concepts, or William's essays in defining the relation of the physical elements to ideal *principia*. But such questions are for later chapters to address, and here I would like to take issue only with the suggestion that there is nothing distinctive in the cosmologists' use of non-Christian texts. Here at least, I believe, we can make some useful distinctions, and ones which will have an important bearing on the lines of influence I am concerned to trace.

The 'scientific' Platonism of the early twelfth century coexists with a more or less mystical, hierarchical Neoplatonism which reflects the attempt to come to terms with Greek Patristic thought, and whose two great sources were Dionysius the Areopagite, in the Latin version of his writings made by Johannes Scotus Eriugena, and Eriugena's own *summa*, the *Periphyseon* or *De divisione naturae*. There were innumerable points of contact between these Platonisms,[25] and in themselves they were not irrevocably opposed. Both were concerned with the higher significance of *naturalia*, with the ascent of the mind to the vision of truth, *per creaturas ad creatorem*, and with the relation of created multiplicity to the uncreated One, the *Idem*, whether conceived as 'Father of lights (*Pater luminum*)' or as that 'form of forms (*forma formarum*)' whose nature and relation to the forms of creation were revealed, as Calcidius had tantalizingly declared, in Plato's still unrecovered *Parmenides*.[26] But the two kinds of Platonism differed significantly in their attitudes toward the actual works, as opposed to the methods, of the ancient *auctores*, and in their sense of the value of such wisdom as philosophy alone is capable of attaining.

25 Chenu 1957, pp. 108–41, Taylor–Little 1968, pp. 49–98; Roger Baron, *Science et sagesse chez Hugues de St. Victor* (Paris 1957), pp. 171–79.
26 Calcidius, *Commentarius in Timaeum Platonis*, ed. J. H. Waszink (2nd ed., London–Leiden 1975), 272, pp. 281–3, as reported in a gloss attributed to Thierry on Boethius *De trinitate* II 35, ed. Häring, *Commentaries on Boethius by Thierry of Chartres and His School* (Toronto 1971),

As an index to these differences we may note the various uses made of Boethius' *De institutione arithmetica*, and especially of the *Proemium* to the first book of that work, a preface which, like the treatise itself, combines the technicalities of its subject with a pervading awareness of their implications from a Pythagorean and Platonic point of view. The first book of the treatise itself builds from the definition of number to address 'that most profound discipline', as Boethius calls it, and that 'which bears the utmost relevance to all natural activity and to the integrity of creation', the perception of the final dependence of all inequality upon a higher equality, an exercise in 'pure understanding' which Boethius declares is morally as well as intellectually valuable. This breadth of treatment is paralleled by the scope of the *Proemium*, which sets a definition of arithmetic within the context of a characterization of the Quadrivium as a whole, and this in turn within a definition of the mission of philosophy, the pursuit of that wisdom which consists in 'the knowledge and full comprehension of those things that truly are'. The four sciences of the Quadrivium – Arithmetic, Music, Geometry, and Astronomy – through their respective emphases on the principles of identity, relationship, dimension, and motion, make it possible to talk in general terms about the multiplicity of life (which is in itself potentially infinite and therefore intractable in philosophy). Thus Boethius declares of the Quadrivium, in a passage which was to be much quoted in the twelfth century, that it affords a vehicle for those privileged thinkers

... whom a higher sense of purpose (*excellentior animus*) leads onward, away from those senses which are born with us, to more certain kinds of understanding. For there are certain definite stages and dimensions of advancement through which it is possible to rise and progress until the eye of the mind (that eye which, as Plato says, is far worthier of existence and preservation than all our organs of sensory perception, since only by its light may truth be sought or perceived) – until, I say, this eye, which has been submerged and blinded by our bodily senses, may be illuminated once again by these disciplines.[27]

The passage was adapted by twelfth-century thinkers to address a variety of epistemological questions. In the context of Boethius' known affinities with the Plato of the *Timaeus*, it could sanction that sense of the ideal

p. 276; R. Klibansky, 'Plato's Parmenides in the Middle Ages and Renaissance', *MARS* I (1941–3) 282–3.

27 *De institutione arithmetica*, ed. Gottfried Friedlein (Leipzig 1867), pp. 9–10:
'Hoc igitur illud quadruvium est, quo his viandum sit, quibus excellentior animus a nobiscum procreatis sensibus ad intelligentiae certiora perducitur. Sunt enim quidam gradus certaeque progressionum dimensiones, quibus ascendi progredique possit, ut animi illum oculum, qui, ut ait Plato, multis oculis corporalibus salvari constituique sit dignior, quod eo solo lumine vestigari vel inspici veritas queat, hunc inquam oculum demersum orbatumque corporeis sensibus hae disciplinae rursus inluminent.'

correspondence between the system of the Liberal Arts, the *cohaerentia artium*, and the order of the universe which fired the twelfth century's interest in natural science, medicine and astrology. At the same time the Neoplatonic associations of the 'eye of the mind (*oculus animi*)' invited spiritual interpretation. For the scientist and the spiritual thinker alike it could evoke a sense of the process by which music, geometry and astronomy, ordering our perceptions of harmony, form, and regular motion, render them reducible to number. The numerical basis of all such coherence is a basic principle of twelfth-century aesthetics,[28] and that unity underlay number was both a scientific principle and an article of belief.

Equally importantly, however, the *Proemium* and the passage just quoted could be regarded as a vindication of the employment of secular resources in the pursuit of truth. As such they reached the twelfth century already endorsed by Johannes Scotus Eriugena, who quotes the *Proemium* approvingly in his *Periphyseon*, and applauds 'the magnificent Boethius' for his insight into the dependence of material existence on the concurrence of those immaterial essences 'that truly exist (*quae vere sunt*)', an intuition in which Eriugena sensed an affinity with the thought of his beloved Cappadocian Fathers.[29] But the precise function that the Boethian insight might perform in the context of Eriugena's Neoplatonist system is harder to determine. Describing the descent of God from his own proper superessentiality, Eriugena speaks suggestively of how God becomes 'the principle of all essence, all life, all intelligence, and all those things which "gnostic theory" considers in their primordial causes'.[30] A case might be made for seeing in 'gnostic theory' either a mystical or a scientific conception of the speculative activity of the Quadrivium. Elsewhere Eriugena describes the initial impulse of inchoate matter to return to God as 'a yearning to be shaped by the various numbers of sensible creatures'. This conception anticipates Bernardus Silvestris' portrayal of the physics of chaos and may well seem to be solidly grounded in the tradition of the *Timaeus*,[31] though the yearning of the material in Eriugena's system is always charged with hints of transcendent aspiration.

The scientific status of Eriugena's use of Boethius remains equivocal, but we may distinguish clearly between two quite different appropriations of the *Proemium* in the two major pedagogical statements of the earlier twelfth

28 Edgar de Bruyne, *Études d'esthétique médiévale* (3 vols., Ghent 1946) I 9–26.
29 Johannes Scotus Eriugena, *Periphyseon* I 54–61, III 11 (P.L. 122, 498–503, 654–7).
30 *Ibid.* III 20 (P.L. 122, 683).
31 *Ibid.* II 16 (P.L. 122, 549); see Winthrop Wetherbee (trans.), *The Cosmographia of Bernardus Silvestris* (New York 1973), pp. 37–8, 52–5.

century, the *Didascalicon* of Hugh of Saint-Victor and Thierry's preface to the *Heptateuchon*. Hugh repeatedly quotes Boethius' definition of wisdom as 'the comprehension of those things which truly exist', and his opening chapter defines the mission of the Arts as the restoration, to minds which have been enticed by bodily sensation, of a recognition of ourselves, and so of the image of the divine Wisdom within ourselves. This process is defined a little further on as 'an illumination of the apprehending mind' by the divine Wisdom, in a passage quoted directly from Boethius' first dialogue on Porphyry's *Isagoge*. Such passages, together with a number of 'Pythagorean' speculations on the human soul's innate affinities with the rational order of things and the creative union of the principles of *Idem* and *Diversum*, reflect the application of the principles of knowledge defined in the *Proemium*.[32] Hugh, however, is not concerned to elaborate any but the spiritual implications of his ideal curriculum. He uses the notion of the soul's analogy with the universe, not to urge the study of philosophy, but as an image for the soul's more profound affinity with the divine Wisdom.[33]

But if Hugh considers only the final cause of philosophy, Thierry is concerned with what it can accomplish in its own sphere. His preface echoes the *Proemium* in its definitions of philosophy and wisdom, and Thierry's own commentaries, 'bathed in a Pythagorean atmosphere' and making frequent reference to Boethius' treatise,[34] provide perhaps the purest example we have of the scientific application of Boethius' definition of the roles of Arithmetic and the Quadrivium. And at the risk of seeming to have merely revived the old, misleading notion of Thierry and his fellow cosmologists as the proponents of a rationalism and humanism without precedent in medieval thought, I would argue that it is largely their willingness to engage an ancient source, directly and as nearly as possible on its own terms, that distinguishes the work of Thierry, Bernard of Chartres, and William of Conches from that of their contemporaries.

A second, closely related trait of this group of thinkers is their concentration on the mythic and metaphorical aspects of the texts with which they deal. Thierry's careful characterization of the operations of the elements in his hexaemeral treatise is set in a context in which the authority of Vergil is invoked together with that of Plato and Boethius, and all seem to be reconciled by a highly imaginative syncretism. This tendency is even more

---

32 *Didascalicon* I 1–2, II 1–2, pp. 4–7, 23–5. See also the commentary of J. Taylor (trans.), *The Didascalicon of Hugh of St. Victor* (New York 1961), pp. 175–82, 195–6.
33 Taylor 1961, pp. 11–19.
34 Jeauneau 1963.

marked in the work of William, and represents another area in which the work of these thinkers combines the old and the new. Bernard of Chartres, in many ways the father of the group, has been called the last of the Carolingian grammarians,[35] and in what we know of his teaching there is little that differs from the methods of glossing curriculum authors that had been used by Eriugena and Remigius of Auxerre. The scope and emphasis of William's glosses on Plato and Boethius are anticipated in Eriugena's pioneering commentary on Martianus Capella; both authors juxtapose discourse on psychological and cosmological topics with moralizing mythography and attempts to extract meaning from etymology and the minutiae of syntax. Indeed no author did more than William to justify and perpetuate this tradition of 'grammatical Platonism', which had served as a substitute for the resources of dialectic and mathematics during several centuries, and which survived the twelfth century as a basic resource of commentary on classical authors.[36]

Though reliance on myth is one of the grounds on which the cosmologists have been found wanting as philosophers in a strict sense, it has been answered that the fictive imagination is a fundamental and legitimate resource of Platonism in all periods, and that its use in the twelfth century was prompted by a conviction, as much philosophical as religious, that 'there are certain vital aspects of metaphysics where we can proceed only by images'.[37] R. W. Southern, while questioning the 'Platonic' character of this use of imagination, concedes a certain role to poetry and allegorical interpretation in 'propagating and fixing scholastic doctrines',[38] and it is essentially this propagation that I wish to follow forward from its source in the work of the cosmologists. If the effect of the new scientific literacy of the twelfth century was to make men view nature in the light of 'a *ratio* synonymous with the inner logic of texts',[39] the *Timaeus* is surely the example *par excellence* of the authoritative text. To study nature was in effect to decode the *Timaeus*, and as a result the literary character of that text had a tremendous influence on the thinking to which it gave rise.

The *Timaeus* indeed offers a powerful precedent for mythic thinking. Its cosmogony is avowedly a 'likely story'. Its treatment of physics and metaphysics is conditioned by a clear awareness that there can be no exactly

35 Southern 1970, p. 78.
36 Jean Jolivet, 'Quelques cas de "platonisme grammatical" du vııe au xııe siècle', in *Mélanges offerts à René Crozet* (2 vols., Poitiers 1966) I 93–9.
37 P. Dronke, *Fabula* (Leiden–Cologne 1974), p. 52.
38 Southern 1979, p. 40.
39 Stock 1983, p. 318.

truthful account of the natural order, and set in perspective by the essentially religious function of its narrative of creation, which aims to illustrate the purposive presence of a benevolent creator at the origin of cosmic life. Its choice of the image of artist and model to express the creative activity of the Demiurgos, its association of secondary causality with a hierarchy of 'gods', its use of numerical proportion to illustrate the harmony of the soul, are essentially exercises in metaphor. To read the *Timaeus* as philosophy or science requires that one should come to terms with its surface of literary myth.

The influence of this aspect of the *Timaeus* was reinforced by the great authority assigned to the texts which were recognized as the work of Plato's followers. These included, in addition to Boethius' *Consolation*, the Hermetic *Asclepius*, with its powerful and highly mythological view of a universe pervaded by the love of a bisexual cosmological deity; Macrobius' Commentary on the *Somnium Scipionis* of Cicero, which provides an explicit rationale for the use of myth in philosophical speculation; and the elaborate allegory *De nuptiis Mercurii et Philologiae* of Martianus Capella, in which education and spiritual experience are intricately worked together and set off by a Latinity charged with hints of the philosophical and religious implications of mythology. Each of these works in its way seems to offer the promise of a philosophical understanding accessible through largely literary means, and they renewed for the twelfth century the late-classical ideal, most strikingly illustrated in Macrobius' reverence for the *Aeneid*, of the great work of literature which is *ipso facto* an expression of the truths of philosophy.

There is evidence of such an approach in the teaching of Bernard of Chartres, as reported in John of Salisbury's *Metalogicon*. There the *senex Carnotensis*, whom John, perhaps with a certain scepticism, calls 'perfectissimus inter Platonicos seculi nostri',[40] is almost a mythic figure, whose aphorisms and philosophical ideas frequently appear, like those of the Presocratics, in fragments of gnomic verse. But the concrete importance of his philosophical thought is borne out by the recent identification of a set of glosses on the *Timaeus* which are very probably his, and which confirm John's account of his widely influential attempt to bring Plato's cosmogony into line with what was seen as the more rigorous procedure of Boethius' *De trinitate*. To reconcile Plato's division of the *principia rerum* into 'God, matter, and idea' with Boethius' declaration that ideas, or pure form, cannot be in direct contact with matter, Bernard posits the existence of *formae nativae*,

40 *Metalogicon* IV 35, ed. C. C. J. Webb (Oxford 1929), p. 205.

secondary forms which 'dispose' matter, and which he equates with the Aristotelian *endelichia* or *forma corporis* that draws the sheer potentiality of matter into particular things.[41] The doctrine of *formae nativae* proved remarkably stimulating for both theological speculation and poetry. Its Aristotelian tendency is developed in a commentary on Boethius' *De trinitate* attributed to Thierry, where form and matter become *actus* and *possibilitas* respectively, and appears in various ways in other commentaries associated with Thierry's name;[42] Bernard's concern with the relations of immanent and transcendent form appears again in the trinitarian speculations of Gilbert of Poitiers.[43] But the notion of intermediary, formative presences in the generation of cosmic life has mythic potentiality as well, and was to provide the inspiration for a renewal of the world of poetic allegory in Bernardus Silvestris' *Cosmographia*.

Bernard of Chartres's own work has a literary aspect which is of great importance in itself. Though the *Timaeus* glosses are concerned almost entirely with philosophical questions, they touch as well on the rhetorical aspect of Plato's text, and on his figurative use of language. To this extent they corroborate the vignette John provides of Bernard's method of expounding texts in the classroom, an account prefaced with a vivid picture of the text of the ideal *auctor*, an 'image of all the arts' in which grammar and poetry serve to set off the truths of mathematics, physics, and ethics.[44] John was not Bernard's student, and we must allow for a degree of idealizing nostalgia in his report of the work of an early champion of that Liberal Arts curriculum whose value is a central theme of the *Metalogicon*. But we may nonetheless take his picture of the *opus consummatum*, the authoritative text in which all the Arts collaborate to lead the student to virtue and an understanding of the *consilia naturae*, as embodying the larger objectives that the pedagogy of Bernard and his followers was intended to realize.

We have further evidence for this kind of teaching, and for the use of literary criticism in the *lectio philosophorum*, in the commentaries of William of Conches, who was almost certainly Bernard's student, and who, John of Salisbury tells us, carried forward Bernard's methods. In his glosses on the *auctores* William pursues an underlying wisdom largely by analysing the

---

41 Paul E. Dutton, 'The Uncovering of the *Glosae super Platonem* of Bernard of Chartres', *Mediaeval Studies* XLVI (1984) 212–19; cf. *Metalogicon* IV 35, pp. 205–6.
42 Häring 1971, pp. 82–7, 95–6, 275; Stephen Gersh, 'Platonism–Neoplatonism–Aristotelianism: A Twelfth-Century Metaphysical System and Its Sources', in *Harvard 1982*, pp. 512–32; John Marenbon, *Early Medieval Philosophy (480–1150). An Introduction* (London 1983), pp. 146–8.
43 Bruno Maioli, *Gilberto Porretano* (Rome 1979), pp. 261–8.
44 *Metalogicon* I 24, pp. 54–5.

figurative language, what he calls the *integumenta* in their texts. The *integumentum*, the verbal 'covering' which at once veils and expresses philosophical truth, is commonly an image or fabulous narrative derived from classical mythology, but particular words can also be treated as *integumenta* and 'broken open' by etymology to yield philosophical meaning, as in Isidore or Fulgentius, and in a technical discussion such as Plato's treatment of soul in the *Timaeus*, the term can be applied to mathematical formulae, or the use of such terms as *idem* and *diversum*.[45] Identifying *integumenta* in ancient texts could help the twelfth-century commentator to deal with passages outwardly at odds with Christian truth, but they were also seen as a fundamental resource of the philosophers themselves in conveying their deepest intuitions.

Though the technical use of the term integumentum seems likely to have originated, like so much else, in the work of Bernard,[46] William develops its practical and theoretical implications. Glossing Macrobius' commentary on the *Somnium Scipionis*, he questions Macrobius' strictures on the use of myth or *fabula* in philosophy. Where Macrobius had excluded myths which imputed violence or adultery to the gods, William argues that these, too, can harbour meaning that is *pulcrum et honestum*.[47] His approach is grounded in Plato's view of the world as the image of a divine archetype, and it is clear that thinking through myth and image plays a far more important cognitive role, and one more clearly integrated with William's sense of the task of the philosopher, than in Macrobius' view. For William indeed the language of philosophy is fundamentally 'integumental' in character, and his discussion makes explicit assumptions which are pervasive in the work of Bernard and Thierry. Boethius, who speaks in the *De trinitate* of the need to 'veil' his deepest philosophical insights in 'novorum verborum significationes', was understood to be alluding to the necessary 'translation' involved in applying philosophical language to theological speculation. The commentaries attributed to Thierry acknowledge that mathematical language is a recourse for dealing with the ineffable and incomprehensible, and make frequent reference to the necessarily 'imaginary' character of the perceptions of divine reality we can gain from the study of the *imagines* or *similitudines* of divine forms which are imposed on the *materia* of universal nature.[48] Thus the

45 E. Jeauneau, 'L'usage de la notion d'integumentum à travers les gloses de Guillaume de Conches', *AHDLMA* xxiv (1957) 66–84; Jeauneau 1973, pp. 158–76.
46 Dutton 1984, p. 218.
47 Dronke 1974, pp. 13–55.
48 Boethius, *De Trinitate*, Prologue, ed. H. F. Stewart and E. K. Rand (Cambridge, MA 1918), p. 4; Häring 1971, pp. 164–6, 268–71.

figurative aspect of philosophical language and the 'imagining' to which it invites us are an inseparable part of natural philosophy. And at certain moments the cosmic *imago* seems a translucent medium: both William and Thierry are capable of seeing in the operation of Plato's world-soul not only a link between the physical and ideal worlds but a direct expression of God's love, capable of identification with the *spiritus sanctus*.[49]

But the question of how far such insights could legitimately be pursued, where philosophy gives way to another order of imaginative thought, remains elusive. It has been observed that the authority of the Timaean cosmology gives to the natural phenomena which it treats as *integumenta* a significance which resembles that of the symbolic *res* of Scripture, and at least one twelfth-century commentator found it possible to contrast Plato with Aristotle on the grounds that the former had dealt with substantial reality while the latter was a philosopher of mere words.[50] William, too, must have sensed a continuity between the philosophical and the sacramental view of *naturalia*. He doubtless saw the value of images as enhanced by the Incarnation, a perfect manifestation of the divine in natural form, and there are resemblances between his discussion of philosophical imagery and the role assigned to symbols and *enigmata* in the thought of the pseudo-Dionysius.[51]

There can be no precise account of such resemblances, for no twelfth-century thinker seems to have been drawn to develop a sustained comparison between the philosophical approach to imagery and the hermeneutics associated with religious symbolism. But we may note that William does not pursue the mystical or symbolic implications of the texts he studies. In practice his approach to *integumenta* is conditioned by an awareness that Plato's cosmology is an image, a way of representing the workings of a cosmic order which is itself a remote and inferior expression of the wisdom that resides archetypally in the divine mind. It is illuminating in this regard to compare his thought with that of Abelard, to which it bears certain superficial resemblances. Abelard, too, emphasizes the rational coherence and the self-perpetuating power of the natural order, and dwells at length on the religious significance of the *integumenta* or *involucra* of the Platonic cosmology. He even claims for such intuitions the status of a divinely

49 Gregory 1958, pp. 122–50; Dronke, 'L'amor che move il sole e l'altre stelle', *Studi Medievali*, ser. 3, VI (1965) 389–422, at pp. 410–13, repr. in Dronke's *The Medieval Poet and His World* (Rome 1984), pp. 463–6; Dronke 1969, pp. 134–7.
50 De Bruyne 1946, II 328–34; Jeauneau 1960, pp. 12–16; M. de Gandillac, 'Le platonisme au xiie et au xiiie siècles', in *Association Guillaume Budé. Congrès de Tours et de Poitiers, 1953* (Paris 1954), p. 273.
51 Dronke 1974, pp. 32–47.

ordained vehicle of revelation, serving for pagan philosophers the function of the biblical *lex scripta* for the Jews.[52] Like William he expresses scorn for those whose ignorance makes them mistrustful of such philosophical evidence for religious truth.

But where William, like Thierry, is concerned to show how God's power is expressed through natural law and process, Abelard's view is grounded in the belief that the thought of the ancient philosophers was in the service of a divine purpose which enabled them to speak truer than they knew. We come to grasp this purpose not by science, but in the light of faith, which compels us to make sense out of images and ideas which would otherwise be absurd. Thus while William in certain commentaries identifies the world-soul with the Holy Spirit in terms of its cosmological function, Abelard emphasizes repeatedly that the association, while legitimate, is wholly allegorical. Rather than reflecting the conscious strategy of a philosopher confronted by the exigencies of rational thought, it shows Plato prompted by divine grace to express truths beyond his ken.[53] Though Abelard seems at times to give more credit to intention, and cites Macrobius on the philosophers' deliberate veiling of religious truth, he is consistent in his lack of interest in physical questions, and views nature only as a vehicle of revelation.[54]

The distinction between Abelard's position and William's is obscured in the polemic of theological conservatives against the work of both. William of Saint-Thierry underplayed the allegorical emphasis of Abelard's treatment of Plato, and claimed to see in William of Conches Abelard's intellectual heir, while Thomas of Morigny detected in Abelard's use of *involucra* traces of the suspect Platonism of Eriugena.[55] Their censures seem to have led Abelard to distance himself from even the allegorical reading of Plato in his later writings, but it is clear that William is much more directly implicated by their accusations, and in other polemic of the period it is clearly the cosmologists and their approach to creation and nature that are the focus of concern. At the simplest level attacks were directed at their presumption in analysing the work of creation, since in so doing they could

52 *Ibid.* pp. 55–67; W. Wetherbee, *Platonism and Poetry in the Twelfth Century* (Princeton 1972), pp. 38–43.
53 D. E. Luscombe, 'Nature in the Thought of Peter Abelard', in *La filosofia della natura nel Medioevo* (Milan 1966), pp. 314–19; Tullio Gregory, 'Abélard et Platon', in *Peter Abelard*, ed. E. M. Buytaert (Louvain 1974), pp. 39–63; 'Ratio et Natura chez Abélard', in *Pierre Abélard – Pierre le Vénérable* (Paris 1975), pp. 569–81.
54 On the limits of Abelard's knowledge of, and interest in, natural philosophy, see J. Jolivet, 'Éléments du concept de nature chez Abélard', in *La filosofia della natura nel Medioevo* (Milan 1966), pp. 297–304; Jolivet 1969, pp. 334–5.
55 D. E. Luscombe, *The School of Peter Abelard* (Cambridge 1970), pp. 125–6.

seem to imply the pre-existence of other *principia* than the sole omnipotent God.[56] Physical questions are what most concern William of Saint-Thierry in his *De erroribus Guillelmi de Conchis*,[57] and they are a recurring theme in what is certainly the most interesting and penetrating critique of the presumptions of natural philosophy, that of Hugh of Saint-Victor.

Hugh is in many ways closely allied with thinkers like Thierry and William, in his insistence on the importance of a complete Liberal Arts curriculum, and in his vivid sense of the coherent vision of reality for which the Arts prepare the way.[58] He was plainly well grounded in the Platonist tradition, and insists on the necessity of understanding natural justice, and the process by which 'each nature reproduces its essential form', as a stage in the ascent to truth. But for Hugh such knowledge is important only insofar as it enables one to realize and penetrate the letter of Scripture. He never recommends the texts of pagan authors in his *Didascalicon*, and he is eloquent on the limitations of secular literature, the vanity of cosmological specu-lation, and the futility of studying poetry, which 'touches in a scattered and confused fashion on topics lifted out of the Arts', but which can never be more than a by-product of true learning.[59] It is not hard to hear a condemnation of something very like William's treatment of the *integumenta* of Plato in Hugh's harsh remarks on those pseudo-philosophers 'who are always taking some small matter and dragging it out through long verbal detours, obscuring a simple meaning in confused discourses'.[60] For the wisdom concealed by *integumenta* is restricted by the inspiration of the human philosopher or poet, and unless one accepts Abelard's view of the *auctor* as prophet, his meaning can never transcend the natural world, the *opus conditionis*, literal and non-symbolic. The felt need to preserve the authority of Scripture led Hugh to stress the opposition between the natural and supernatural worlds with a new firmness, and the result was an equally firm denial of the transcendental implications of philosophy.

The limits implied for rational speculation by the criticisms of Hugh and William of Saint-Thierry seem to be representative of the traditionalist response to the work of the cosmologists. It is probably to some extent the force of these criticisms, as well as important shifts that were taking place in the activity of the schools, that account for the noticeable decline in the prominence of Platonist thought after the mid-century. Certain issues

---

56 Chenu 1957, pp. 21–7; Taylor–Little 1968, pp. 4–15; Dronke 1969, pp. 136–9.
57 P.L. 180, 333–40.
58 Taylor 1961, pp. 12–14.
59 *Didascalicon* III 4, p. 54; but see also III 14, pp. 64–6, and Baron 1957, pp. 93–6.
60 *Ibid.* III 4, p. 54.

introduced by the cosmologists were to remain alive in scholastic debate, and the *Timaeus* would continue to provide the basic model of the universe,[61] but already in the middle years of the century there was a growing awareness of a view of the natural order far more detailed and coherent than that developed by William and Thierry. Even a thinker like Hermann of Carinthia, whose *De essentiis* is modelled in many respects on the *Timaeus*, and who extols Thierry as Plato reborn, is nonetheless fundamentally removed from the world of the cosmologists by his deep interest in the Arab version of Aristotelian physics and the larger astrological context in which it was placed by thinkers like Abū Maʿshar.[62]

In the transitional period of compilation and codification which separates the scholastic milieu of Abelard, William, and Thierry from the new order introduced by the discovery of Aristotle, the influence of the cosmologists and of Plato himself becomes to a great extent the property of the schools of grammar and rhetoric. Commentaries on the poems of Vergil and Ovid appropriate the form and techniques of William's glosses, and the Platonic cosmology and its implications become a theme for new kinds of learned poetry. A harbinger of this shift is a Latin dream-poem, the *Metamorphosis Golye episcopi*, a curious combination of topical satire and visionary allegory which offers a suggestive insight into the academic world of the 1140s.[63]

In his dream the poet finds himself before a sumptuous palace surrounded by a richly detailed *locus amoenus*, the two together mirroring the harmony of the universe. Within the palace Jove and the gods are celebrating the marriage of Mercury and Philology, the union of eloquence and wisdom extolled in Martianus' famous allegory, and the poet enumerates the philosophers and poets in attendance. The list includes not only ancient authors, but modern ones, including Thierry of Chartres, Gilbert of Poitiers, and a host of students of Abelard. As the names of these *moderni* are reviewed, Philology laments that Abelard himself is not present. His pupils answer that the 'hooded primate' has caused him to be condemned to silence – presumably the condemnation of Abelard's writings instigated by Bernard

---

61 See, e.g., Godefroy de Saint-Victor, *Fons Philosophiae* 189–244, ed. Pierre Michaud-Quantin (Namur 1956), pp. 41–3; *Ordo artium* 1–80, ed. Ludwig Gompf, *Mittellateinisches Jahrbuch* III (1966) 107–10.

62 Hermann of Carinthia, *De essentiis*, ed. Charles Burnett (Leiden–Cologne 1982), pp. 20–5; Richard Lemay, *Abu Maʿshar and Latin Aristotelianism in the Twelfth Century* (Beirut 1962), pp. 193–257.

63 Ed. Thomas Wright, *Latin Poems commonly attributed to Walter Mapes* (London 1841), pp. 21–30; ed. R. B. C. Huygens, 'Mitteilungen aus Handschriften', *Studi Medievali*, ser. 3, III (1962) 764–72; Wetherbee 1972, pp. 127–34; John F. Benton, 'Philology's Search for Abelard in the *Metamorphosis Goliae*', *Speculum* L (1975) 199–217.

of Clairvaux in 1140. The poem ends with the gods' decree that the 'hooded mob' be banished from schools where the secrets of philosophy are explored.

It is easy to overinterpret a poem which seems to bring us so close to the centre of things. In broad terms the poet seems to identify himself with the intellectually adventurous, but sympathy with Abelard and other advanced thinkers is not enough to enable us to define his position more precisely. It is clear, however, that he is familiar with the work of the cosmologists. The palace, adorned with images which represent cosmic life 'all beneath a fabled covering (*totum sub involucro*)', is a poetic image of the Platonic cosmos:

> iste domus locus est universitatis,
> res et rerum continens formas cum formatis,
> quas creator optimus, qui praeest creatis
> fecit et disposuit, nutu bonitatis.

> This mansion is the realm of the universe itself,
> containing the forms of things together with things formed,
> which that best creator who oversees creation
> made and ordered as an expression of his goodness.

The poet dwells at length on the *figurae* which adorn the palace, and hints with what seems conscious daring at the transcendent significance of the cosmic powers embodied in the gods and goddesses who bestow their gifts on Philology.[64] Without reading his poem as a humanist manifesto, we may see in it clear evidence that for this anonymous writer the world view of the ancient *auctores* as renewed and developed by the cosmologists was the appropriate setting for serious intellectual activity. If the philosophical issues that engaged them were still very much *sub judice*, it is clear that the orientation and values of the cosmologists were contributing to the formation of a new literary culture.

It is clear as well that the *Metamorphosis Golye* is not an isolated example, for during the middle years of the century, the very time when their philosophical authority is declining, the influence of the cosmologists is plain and decisive in many areas of thought. Here again John of Salisbury offers invaluable evidence. The tradition underlying John's famous and elaborate comparison of the state to the human body in the *Policraticus* is complex, but the immediate stimulus was his familiarity with the development of similar ideas by William of Conches, whose glosses on Macrobius and Plato elaborate on Calcidius' tripartite analogy, derived from the *Republic*,

---

64 Wetherbee 1972, pp. 129–30.

between the city state and the human body.[65] While William is less interested
in the political implications of his analogy than in what it has to say about the
nature of man, John develops the metaphor in the direction of a more
sophisticated conception of political order itself, in which not the structure of
the body but the co-operation among its parts and faculties is the primary
focus. In the process he moves away from the Platonic–Calcidian model, but
it is clear that this model, and William's preoccupation with the human–
cosmological analogy, are a deep conditioning influence. John's thought
habitually moves back and forth between images of natural, rational, and
spiritual governance, stressing the analogous operation of ordering forces in
the soul, the state, and the cosmos, and he is clearly at one with William and
the cosmologists in seeing the state as grounded in 'universal truths
demonstrated by the cosmos and the human body'.[66] More broadly, his
sense that 'natural justice' is the proper basis of political order corresponds to
a new emphasis in the work of the canonists and legists, where the concept of
a divinely ordained *lex naturae*, understood with varying emphasis as a
natural instinct toward social co-operation and as a rational standard derived
from emulation of the order of the universe at large, is increasingly regarded
as the necessary condition for the attainment of justice.[67]

In relation to the twelfth century's well-known concern with history the
work of the cosmologists, as well as the widespread concern with other more
spiritually oriented Platonisms, poses a complex problem, for the effect of a
Platonist cosmology in which human life imitates the cyclical life of nature,
or is part of an all-embracing continuum of emanation and return, is to
'detemporalize and deexistentialize' the order of things, and to promote a
view in which human progress and decline can seem relatively independent
of the pivotal events of sacred history.[68] The problem appears in a striking
form in the work of Hugh of Saint-Victor. Staunch and consistent in his
devaluing of rational, scientific knowledge, Hugh was nonetheless deeply
engaged, through his interest in the pseudo-Dionysius and Neoplatonist
theology, with the notion of a coherent and symbolically meaningful natural

65 P. E. Dutton, '*Illustre ciuitatis et populi exemplum*: Plato's *Timaeus* and the Transmission from
   Calcidius to the End of the Twelfth Century of a Tripartite Scheme of Society', *Mediaeval
   Studies* XLV (1983) 79–119; Tilman Struve, *Die Entwicklung der organologischen Staatsauffassung
   im Mittelalter* (Stuttgart 1978), pp. 123–48; 'The importance of the organism in the political
   theory of John of Salisbury', in *The World of John of Salisbury*, ed. Michael Wilks (Oxford
   1984), pp. 303–17; Max Kerner, 'Natur und Gesellschaft bei Johannes von Salisbury',
   Miscellanea Mediaevalia XII (1979) 188–96.
66 Dutton 1983, p. 118.
67 Gaines Post, *Studies in Medieval Legal Thought* (Princeton 1964), pp. 494–561.
68 Chenu 1957, pp. 62–3; Taylor–Little 1968, pp. 162–3.

economy, which he could not fully reconcile with a linear view of history.[69] The same tension appears in a less obvious form, but one which more clearly reflects the influence of the cosmologists, in the *Chronica* of Otto of Freising, where an eschatological narrative of world history coexists with a philosophical perspective, in the light of which history becomes the realization of a collective human nature, capable through reason of progress and self-understanding.[70] In Otto's *Gesta Frederici* this conception of human progress is clearly associated with the advances of human thought in Otto's own day. The relation of this hard-won progress to the impending end of the world is never defined, but it is clear that Otto, with the cosmologists, accorded philosophy and the analysis of natural causation an important role in the discovery of truth.[71]

Finally one must attempt to assess the tremendous importance of Platonist cosmological thought in the study, and increasingly in the production, of imaginative literature. Here once again the most obvious influence is that of William of Conches, and it is clearest in the newly ambitious commentaries on classical poetry which begin to appear at about the time when William's career is drawing to a close, and which emulate in a more formulaic way the scope and orientation of his glosses on Boethius and the *Timaeus*. Already in the glosses tentatively assigned to Bernardus Silvestris, whose author was a younger contemporary and quite possibly a student of William, there is a difference of emphasis which reflects a new, less scientific orientation. Though his glosses on Martianus Capella contain some cosmological speculation, and make reference to his own earlier glosses on the *Timaeus*, their most striking feature is a new ease, and a greater reliance on sheer ingenuity, in the interpretation of Martianus' *integumenta*. The *accessus* to the commentary places *integumentum* and *allegoria* side by side, as distinct but closely comparable modes of figuration, one proper to scriptural history, the other to pagan fable, but both alike possessed of an inner *mysterium occultum*.[72] Elsewhere the commentator distinguishes between the 'open' and 'mystical' modes of philosophical discourse, illustrating the former by the terms *pater*, *nois*, *anima mundi* (Father, Mind, world-soul), the latter by

---

69 Chenu 1957, pp. 177–85; Taylor–Little 1968, pp. 127–8; Henri de Lubac, *Exégèse médiévale* (2 vols. in 4, Paris 1959–64), II. 1 418–35; Wetherbee 1972, pp. 56–9.

70 Karl Morrison, 'Otto of Freising's Quest for the Hermeneutic Circle', *Speculum* LV (1980) 207–36.

71 Joseph Koch, 'Die Grundlagen der Geschichtsphilosophie Ottos von Freising', *Münchener Theologische Zeitschrift* IV (1953) 79–94; repr. in *Geschichtsdenken und Geschichtsbild im Mittelalter*, ed. Walther Lammers, Wege der Forschung XXI (Darmstadt 1961), pp. 321–49.

72 Jeauneau 1964, p. 856; 1973, p. 40; Wetherbee 1972, pp. 113, 267; Dronke 1974, pp. 119–22.

'Jove', 'Pallas', and 'Juno', and correlating both 'trinities' with the Father, Son, and Spirit of *divina pagina*.[73] All of this is offered with the air of one summarizing standard doctrine for beginners, and there is none of the mingled assertiveness and defensiveness of William's earlier essays in the rationalization of myth. In the same writer's commentary on Vergil, and in those of Arnulf of Orleans on Ovid, the ancient authors appear as philosopher-poets, their common theme the intellectual and spiritual pilgrimage of a humanity which seeks always to transcend its condition by interpreting and passing beyond the distracting surface appearances of earthly life, the *integumenta* in which the order of things is veiled, and to ascend at last 'by way of creatures to the creator (*per creaturas ad creatorem*)'.[74] The common project is clearly defined in the *accessus* to the glosses on Martianus Capella, where the *De nuptiis* is said to be an 'imitation' of the *Aeneid*:

For just as in that work Aeneas is led through the underworld attended by the Sibyl to meet Anchises, so Mercury here traverses the universe attended by Virtue, to reach the court of Jove. So also in the book *De consolatione* Boethius ascends through false goods to the *summum bonum* guided by Philosophy. Thus these three *figurae* express virtually the same thing.[75]

That all three authors are imitating Plato goes without saying. The *Timaeus* is the paradigmatic literary text as well as a *summa* of philosophy, and to the extent that the poets had succeeded in emulating this great model, virtually the embodiment of the natural order itself, their own works attain a similar scope and coherence. The result of all this is a new sense of the importance of poetry and poetic form, which not only conditions the study and production of poetry in the schools, and the poetics implicit in the new *artes poeticae*, whose appearance is a further symptom of the new trend,[76] but will affect fundamentally the generation of the new poetic 'world' of vernacular romance, and the way in which this world gives shape to the ideology of *courtoisie*.[77]

73 Jeauneau 1964, p. 840; 1973, p. 24; Wetherbee 1972, pp. 123–4, 270–1.
74 Wetherbee 1972, pp. 11–13, 104–25; J. Jolivet, 'Les rochers de Cumes et l'antre de Cerbère. L'ordre de savoir selon le Commentaire de Bernard Silvestre sur l'Énéide', in *Pascua Medievalia. Studies voor Prof. Dr. J. M. de Smet* (Leuven 1983), pp. 263–76; P. Dronke, 'Integumenta Virgilii', in *Lectures médiévales de Virgile* (Rome 1985), pp. 313–29.
75 Jeauneau 1964, p. 857; 1973, p. 41; Wetherbee 1972, pp. 124–5, 267; Dronke 1985, p. 327.
76 Wetherbee 1972, pp. 145–51; P. Dronke, 'Medieval Rhetoric', in *Literature and Western Civilization*, ed. David Daiches and Anthony Thorlby (6 vols., London 1973) II 315–45, at pp. 329–41; repr. in Dronke 1984, pp. 21–32.
77 Jean Győry, 'Le cosmos, un songe', *Annales Universitatis Scientiarum Budapestensis: Sectio Philologica* IV (1963) 87–110; Leo Pollmann, *Chrétien von Troyes und der Conte del Graal* (Tübingen 1965), pp. 86–99; *Das Epos in den romanischen Literaturen* (Stuttgart 1966), pp. 78–88; Wetherbee 1972, pp. 220–41; Claude Luttrell, *The Creation of the First Arthurian*

The first and in many ways the definitive expression of this new sense of the function of imaginative literature is the *Cosmographia* of Bernardus Silvestris, which, produced in the late 1140s and dedicated to Thierry of Chartres, both crystallizes in a remarkably comprehensive form the aspirations and attainments of the cosmologists of the earlier period and prepares for the more free-ranging poetic use of Platonism in the later twelfth century. The *Cosmographia*'s two main divisions, *Megacosmus* and *Microcosmus*, deal with the creation of the universe and of man. The work opens with Nature's appeal to Noys or Providence on behalf of Silva or primal matter, which though still an unformed chaos, yearns to be 'reborn' to form and beauty.[78] Noys responds by creating the greater universe, then orders Nature herself to convoke Urania, celestial reason, and Physis, the principle of physical life, who will create the human soul and body which Nature will then join together. The work concludes with an account of the lesser universe, the human constitution.

The *Cosmographia* is a significant new departure, a serious attempt to use images, *integumenta*, as a vehicle for original thought, to produce a new imaginative cosmology in the tradition of the *Timaeus*. In one aspect it is an extremely powerful affirmation of the coherence and meaning of the natural order. The 'unfolding' of this order in the opening chapters has a mythic vividness comparable to that of the *Timaeus* itself. Written in the *prosimetrum* form deployed by Martianus and Boethius and already imitated in a perfunctory way in Adelard's *De eodem et diverso*, it uses a range of rhetorical devices to make its narration an aesthetic counterpart to the coherent ordering it describes.[79] At times Bernardus' responsiveness to the ways in which the divine Noys shapes and informs its creation seems to strain the resources of language:

Romance (Evanston, IL 1974), pp. 1–79; Tony Hunt, 'Redating Chrestien de Troyes', *Bulletin Bibliographique de la Société Internationale Arthurienne* XXX (1978) 209–37; 'Chrestien and Macrobius', *Classica et Mediaevalia* XXXIII (1981–2) 211–27; Karl Uitti, 'A propos de philologie', *Littérature* XLI (1981) 30–46.

78 For the view that Bernardus' cosmogony implies a cyclical pattern of destruction and renewal see Stock 1972, pp. 67–86. P. Dronke (ed.), *Cosmographia* (Leiden 1978), p. 31, sees the work as opening with the cosmos 'at the nadir of one if its many cycles', having undergone 'disintegration, decomposition'. But this idea seems inconsistent with the view of a perpetually self-sustaining cosmos affirmed elsewhere in the *Cosmographia* (e.g. I ii 10–11, pp. 101–2; II xiv 171–4, pp. 154–5). At the outset, moreover, Silva is not *disintegrated*, but still *unintegrated* (*informis adhuc*: I i 1, p. 97): Silva first appears, like Milton's Chaos, with 'visage incomposed' (*vultibus incompositis*: I ii 2, p. 99). Here as elsewhere in the *Cosmographia* Bernardus is perhaps intentionally ambiguous.

79 Wetherbee 1972, pp. 158–86; Dronke (ed.), *Cosmographia*, pp. 51–63.

Ex mundo intelligibili mundus sensibilis perfectus natus est ex perfecto. Plenus erat igitur qui genuit, plenumque constituit plenitudo. Sicut enim integrascit ex integro, pulcrescit ex pulcro, sic exemplari suo eternatur eterno.[80]

From the intellectual universe the sensible universe was born, perfect from perfect. The creative model exists in fullness, and this fullness imparted itself to the creation. For just as the sensible universe participates in the flawlessness of its flawless model, and waxes beautiful by its beauty, so by its eternal exemplar it is made to endure eternally.

The *Megacosmus* complements this emphasis on beauty and continuity by repeatedly asserting the dignity of man and the destiny it implies. As for Adelard of Bath, man's self-knowledge is inseparable from a knowledge of the heavens and the secrets of the natural world. Once possessed of that mastery over nature which is the hallmark of his original stature, 'He will ascend the heavens, no longer an unacknowledged guest, to assume the place assigned him among the stars.'[81] Informed by the rhetoric of the *Asclepius*, in which the understanding of nature is explicitly a religious vocation, Bernardus' treatment of man as potentially victorious through knowledge is in many ways a dramatization of the pedagogical ideal embodied in Thierry's *Heptateuchon* and the glosses of William.

Not surprisingly the *Cosmographia* is commonly cited as an expression of the spirit of the 'twelfth-century Renaissance', optimistic in its sense of the possibilities of collaboration between nature and human science and philosophy, and so implicitly affirmative of man's power to continue the work begun by divine creativity, controlling and 'reforming' his environment and thereby reaffirming his position as the crown and centre of creation.[82] Noys, inviting Nature to share with her in the task of creation, praises her *ingenium*, and as the *Cosmographia* develops its theme, human *ingenium* too seems to participate in the divine project.

But there is another side to Bernardus' view of the human condition. The universe of the *Cosmographia*, and the life of man within it, are charged with conflict, and presided over by forces which convey strong suggestions of necessity. The intractability of Silva, the primal chaos, powerfully dramatized in the opening scene of the poem, has its counterpart in the unruliness of human passion and appetite. Like the life of the universe at large, human

---

80 *Cosmographia* i iv 11, p. 119, trans. Wetherbee (New York 1973), p. 89.
81 *Ibid.* ii x 53–4, p. 142, trans. Wetherbee 1973, p. 114.
82 Stock 1972, pp. 161–2, 236–7; T. Gregory, 'La nouvelle idée de la nature et de savoir scientifique au xiie siècle', in *The Cultural Context of Medieval Learning*, ed. J. E. Murdoch and E. D. Sylla (Dordrecht–Boston 1975), pp. 193–212; but see also Gerhart B. Ladner, 'Terms and Ideas of Renewal', *Harvard 1982*, pp. 6–7.

experience is an interplay of rational and irrational forces, and the tension between them as man seeks to maintain right relations with the cosmic order becomes at times a heroic, almost tragic theme. It is made clear that the stability of nature at large is more often than not a standard by which the instability of man is to be measured, and indeed that man's relation to nature is fundamentally neurotic. Its stasis repels him and he seems condemned to a futile attempt to emulate its self-sufficiency. The closing lines of the *Cosmographia* point the contrast between them:

> Influit ipsa sibi mundi natura, superstes,
>   Permanet et fluxu pascitur usque suo:
> Scilicet ad summam rerum iactura recurrit,
>   Nec semel – ut possit saepe perire – perit.
>
> Longe disparibus causis mutandus in horas,
>   Effluit occiduo corpore totus homo.
> Sic sibi deficiens, peregrinis indiget escis,
>   Sudat in hoc vitam denichilatque dies.[83]

The nature of the universe outlives itself, for it flows back into itself, and so survives and is nourished by its very flowing. For whatever is lost only merges again with the sum of things, and that it may die perpetually, never dies wholly.

But man, ever liable to affliction by forces far less harmonious, passes wholly out of existence with the failure of his body. Unable to sustain himself, and wanting nourishment from without, he exhausts his life, and a day reduces him to nothing.

The pessimism in these reflections is nowhere more evident than in Bernardus' account of the creation of man. The goddesses who collaborate in this task are endowed by Noys with historical perspectives appropriate to their rules. Urania, uncorrupted wisdom, who is to create the human soul, is granted the Mirror of Providence, a vision of life in its cosmic and temporal totality. Nature, who will join this soul to its mortal body, receives the Tablet of Destiny, which reveals the course of the mutable world, 'the sequence of those things that come to pass by the decrees of fate'. Physis, fashioner of the body, is given the 'Book of Memory', where life appears as an array of images of the processes and principles that produce the diverse forms of natural life. In all three perspectives man is a tentative, almost shadowy presence, and the goddesses must search anxiously to determine his place in the scheme of things. Together the Mirror, Table and Book imply a deeply enigmatic questioning of the relations of physics, metaphysics, and human history.[84]

83 *Cosmographia* II xiv 171–8, pp. 154–5, trans. Wetherbee 1973, pp. 126–7. Dronke (ed.), *Cosmographia*, pp. 48–9, offers a more ambivalent interpretation of these lines.
84 *Cosmographia* II xi, pp. 142–4, trans. Wetherbee 1973, pp. 114–17; Dronke 1974, pp. 122–6.

There is considerable evidence in the *Cosmographia* that Bernardus' world view may finally be less pessimistic than this. His language and imagery are often reminiscent of the Christian Neoplatonism of the pseudo-Dionysius and Eriugena's *Periphyseon*, and there are strong hints that Bernardus' goddesses are not only cosmic forces but participants in the great process of emanation and return which for Eriugena defines the true relationship of created life to God.[85] But the note of doubt is equally plain, and there is clearly no question here of that hesitation in the face of ambiguously related Platonisms so typical of the earlier twelfth century. Rather, the murkiness of life as viewed from the existential vantage-point of Bernardus' Nature and Physis poses a clear challenge to philosophy. It raises the question of whether unaided human understanding is capable of attaining more than a tenuous and uncertain purchase on natural reality, and amounts to a searching critique of the philosophical project of the cosmologists.

A similarly critical attitude is evident in John of Salisbury's reflections on learning and truth in the *Policraticus*. Though John was a staunch champion of the pedagogy of the cosmologists, and saw them as having saved the Arts at a time when opportunist specialists were debasing and fragmenting the curriculum of the schools, he has much to say about the dangers to which rational thought is liable at higher levels of speculation, and specifically the danger that it will founder in merely fabulous or imaginary 'similitudes' of truth. While he recognizes the striking affinities between the *Timaeus* and the biblical account of creation, and commends Plato's remarkable intuitions of the nature of God, he also stresses the danger of presumption in such pursuits. Having 'cleared their eyes of dross' and learned to contemplate the Artisan of the universe, philosophers have sought to 'capture' God's truth, each in the light of his own imperfect reason, and the result was a fragmentation of knowledge, which John compares to the confusion of tongues at the building of the tower of Babel. He is sceptical of the synthesizing ambitions of the Platonists of his own time, and his distrust of the overextension of any line of rational enquiry is not different from his wariness in the face of magic and astrology.[86] Otto of Freising, too, for all his admiration of the achievements of rational thought in his time, adverts to the dangers of philosophy at several points. Like John he is keenly aware of how the pursuit of natural causes can cause one to value *rationes* and *argumenta* more than the truths of faith, or simply to succumb to the enticing beauty of

---

85 Wetherbee 1973, pp. 32–3, 52–5.
86 *Policraticus* VII 1–2, ed. C. C. J. Webb (2 vols., Oxford 1909) II 93–9; Hans Liebeschütz, *Medieval Humanism in the Life and Writings of John of Salisbury* (London 1951), pp. 74–8.

the world for itself. Nature harbours demonic presences, and these are capable of 'fascinating' and deceiving human reason with 'occult machinations and hidden seeds of nature'.[87] John had cited Bernard of Chartres in pointing to humility as the initial prerequisite or 'key' to philosophical understanding,[88] and for Otto, too, the truest lessons of philosophy, even natural philosophy, are moral ones, a point on which he dwells with a sombre force like that of the closing lines of Bernardus' *Cosmographia*:

> There is a maxim well known to physicists who study the deceptive character of complexion: 'To be moving toward the zenith is better than to have attained it.' For since man, born to labour, living for only a brief time (since his nature is composed of many things and tends toward dissolution), is incapable of remaining in a single state, when he has attained his zenith, he is bound to descend. This being so, let us take a moment to philosophize about it, for indeed 'Happy is he who has come to know the causes of things.'[89]

That three thinkers so sympathetic to the philosophical movement of the earlier twelfth century should be so nearly at one in their sense of the uncertainty of the attainments of philosophy, is probably symptomatic of a growing awareness of the transition that was taking place in the middle years of the century. Bernardus' *Cosmographia* is in many respects a record of the intellectual history of his time. Though he is a product of the Platonist programme of the cosmologists, he was responsive to new developments on several fronts. The strong Neoplatonist undercurrent in his cosmology is a harbinger of the course that theology was taking in the work of Alan of Lille and the Porretani, who were seeking to reconcile the negative theology of the pseudo-Dionysius with the more philosophical Neoplatonism of Boethius. But his detailed account of the physics of creation reflects a newly practical and technical emphasis in the study of nature. Science can no longer be reconciled so readily or so completely with an idealist or hierarchical conception of the relation of the universe to God. Theology and science, in short, have become as Urania and Physis, and the waning of the old Platonist vision is strongly suggested by Bernardus' treatment of both figures. Before discovering Urania, Nature must search long and anxiously

87 *Chronica* VIII 4, I 26, ed. Adolf Hofmeister (Hanover 1912), pp. 398, 60.
88 *Policraticus* VII 13, p. 145.
89 *Gesta Frederici* I 4, ed. Georg Waitz and Bernhard von Simson (Hanover–Leipzig 1912), p. 16:
'Optime enim a phisicis fallaciam complexionum considerantibus dictum cognoscitur: Melius est ad summum quam in summo. Cum enim homo natus ad laborem, brevi vivens tempore, natura tamquam ex multis composita ad dissolutionem tendente, numquam in eodem statu manere valeat, si in summo fuerit, mox eum declinare oportebit. Cuius rei causa paulisper philosophari liceat, etenim
Felix qui potuit rerum cognoscere causas.'

through the universe; she seems an alien presence in the celestial regions, and the atmosphere in which she moves is that which Hugh of Saint-Victor associates with the natural philosopher, for whom the universe is finally a barren and unmeaning place.[90] The practical and limited scope of the new science is evident in Physis' Book of Memory. Written not in letters but in 'signs and symbols', it is the record of human understanding applying itself to the study of generation and decay, a record 'based often upon fact, but more often upon probable conjecture.'[91]

The implications of Bernardus' treatment of Urania and Physis become explicit in the *De planctu Naturae* of Alan of Lille. Written like the *Cosmographia* in the *prosimetrum* form, and marked by a keen appreciation of the importance of Bernardus' poem, the work is a dialogue between the poet–narrator and a personified Nature, who lament together the alienation of man from the larger order of the universe. In one aspect Alan's Nature is God's deputy, combining in herself the traditional functions of the Platonic world-soul and all aspects of natural law and process, and in her dialogue with the poet she deploys a series of elaborate metaphors of political, moral, and sexual harmony, which give a new explicitness to her role as a source and standard of order in human life.[92] As such she represents the culmination of the cosmologists' realization of the potential significance of that order, a significance which is summed up in the resonant hymn with which the poet responds to her appearance: she is love and light, the 'regula mundi',

> Quae, tuis mundum moderans habenis,
> Cuncta concordi stabilita nodo
> Nectis, et pacis glutino maritas
>   Coelica terris.[93]

You whose reins guide the universe, who hold all things in stable order with ties of harmony, and with the bond of peace marry heaven and earth.

As Nature's role develops in the *De planctu*, the universe becomes virtually a church, in which divine creativity unites with Nature to generate the *materiale verbum* of created life.[94]

But the richness of Alan's development of the idea of Nature is largely a foil to his clear and uncompromising delineation of the limits of Nature's authority. Though her abiding presence as guide and standard is a constant

---

90 *In Ecclesiasten Homiliae* 5, 10 (P.L. 175, 156, 177); Taylor 1961, pp. 20–2.
91 *Cosmographia* II xi 10, p. 144, trans. Wetherbee 1973, p. 116.
92 Gregory 1958, pp. 122–50; George D. Economou, *The Goddess Natura in Medieval Literature* (Cambridge, MA 1972), pp. 53–96; Wetherbee 1973, pp. 6–19.
93 *De planctu Naturae* VII (metrum IV) 13–16, ed. Häring, *Studi Medievali*, ser. 3, XIX (1978) 831.
94 Wetherbee 1972, pp. 198–9.

rebuke to errant humanity, she has no power to control human error or effect genuine change. The knowledge of God she affords is largely negative, a matter of the contrast between her cloudy manifestation of his wisdom and the lucidity of revelation.[95] And in the end, the lesson of the *De planctu Naturae* is negative, an extended demonstration of the haplessness of humanity in the absence of some divine supplement to Nature's ordering role.

Alan's second major literary work, the *Anticlaudianus*, deals with the regeneration of human nature, in the process offering a survey of human knowledge and defining its relation to theology. Nature resolves to create a 'new man' who will exhibit none of the flaws of fallen human nature. In consultation with Ratio and Concordia she resolves to send Prudentia (the human capacity for wisdom) to petition God to create a soul for this *homo novus*. In a chariot made by the seven Liberal Arts, drawn by the five senses and steered by Reason, Prudentia ascends through the cosmos. At the outer limit of the physical universe she must abandon all of her equipage save the sense of hearing and then, guided by a *puella poli* who imparts theological understanding,[96] she ascends to the presence of God the Father, who accedes to her request. The new man is created, and after he and the Virtues defeat an army of Vices he becomes the ruler of a new Golden Age on earth.

The long account of the preparations for Prudentia's journey provides the occasion for an idealizing review of the resources of philosophy as the earlier twelfth century had practised it, and Prudentia's ascent, in a chariot whose wheels are the work of the mathematical sciences, is a deliberate allusion to Boethius' *Proemium*, which stresses the need for *prudentia* and nobility of mind in the ascent, 'by a kind of quadrivium (*quodam quasi quadruvio*)', to the 'summit of perfection (*cumulum perfectionis*)' in the pursuit of wisdom.[97] For Alan, too, the Arts are essential, a divinely ordained means of approach *ad limen theologie*.[98] But once this threshold is attained, the Arts must be 'left in peace', for the barrier which confronts human understanding as it seeks to approach God is absolute. Theology for Alan is a negative theology, grounded in the conviction that human language and the propositions of reason are fundamentally incapable of addressing the divine reality directly,

95 *De planctu Naturae* VI 128–58, pp. 829–30.
96 *Anticlaudianus* V 83–100, ed. Robert Bossuat (Paris 1955), pp. 125–6. The enigmatic status of this figure is emphasized by Dronke, who compares her role to that of Dante's Beatrice: *Dante and Medieval Latin Traditions* (Cambridge 1986), pp. 12–13.
97 *Anticlaudianus* I 325–IV 270, pp. 82–115.
98 *Sermo*, 'De clericis ad theologiam non accedentibus', ed. Marie–Thérèse d'Alverny, *Alain de Lille. Textes inédits* (Paris 1965), p. 275.

and it involves a transformation of the work of the sciences so radical as to divorce language from all natural reference, reducing the Platonic cosmos, at best a *phantasma* of its divine model, to no more than a negative image of the divine infinitude.[99] The mode of understanding by which Prudentia in the *Anticlaudianus* is enabled to apprehend and address this reality beyond understanding is dramatized by Alan as a recovery of the 'erectness' of man's original nature,[100] and this new integrity evidently informs the character of the *homo novus*, whose triumph is the ostensible climax of Alan's narrative. But in a sense the working out of the relation of the Arts to theology that culminates in Prudentia's vision of God is the major theme of the poem, and there is something gratuitous and anticlimactic about the ensuing *psychoma-chia* and the new earthly order to which it leads. The virtues associated with the New Man are largely secular, and his creation has been explained as Alan's envisioning of the political mission of the Capetian monarchy.[101] Whatever its significance, the idealism of this 'triumph of Nature', as Alan calls it, is difficult to reconcile with the radical subordination of earthly knowledge in the central books of the poem.

The same disjunction appears in Alan's position relative to the intellectual activity of the earlier twelfth century. In his time he was the Doctor Universalis, famous for his knowledge in the Liberal Arts; the *Anticlaudianus* was treated as a *summa* of secular wisdom as the earlier twelfth century had known it, and was glossed and expounded with the respect normally accorded a classical *auctor*.[102] But Alan's sense of the limited scope of philosophy and the Arts is strict and uncompromising. He himself attempted to bridge the gap in his *Regulae caelestis iuris*, by formulating laws and methods of demonstration that would make possible the appropriation of geometry and the other sciences to the work of theology,[103] and the very ambitiousness of the project recalls the optimism of the early twelfth century. But where the old vision of the *cohaerentia artium* is directly evoked in Alan's work, it appears in an almost elegiac perspective. Deeply engaged by the idea of world harmony, and with a poet's sense of the potentially numinous

99 *Anticlaudianus* I 488–503, V 114–27, pp. 71, 126–7. See also Jan Ziolkowski, *Alan of Lille's Grammar of Sex. The Meaning of Grammar to a Twelfth-Century Intellectual* (Cambridge, MA 1985), pp. 109–39.
100 *Anticlaudianus* VI 291–4, p. 149; Wetherbee 1972, pp. 217–18.
101 Linda E. Marshall, 'The Identity of the "New Man" in the *Anticlaudianus* of Alan of Lille', *Viator* x (1979) 77–94; Michael Wilks, 'Alan of Lille and the New Man', in *Renaissance and Renewal in Christian History*, ed. Derek Baker (Oxford 1977), pp. 137–57.
102 Radulphus de Longo Campo, *In Anticlaudianum Alani Commentum*, ed. Jan Sulowski (Warsaw 1972).
103 G. R. Evans, *Alan of Lille* (Cambridge 1983), pp. 64–80.

power of nature, he nonetheless accepts unfalteringly the message of his own *Rhythmus de incarnatione Domini*, in which each of the Liberal Arts in succession is confronted and confounded by the mystery of the virgin birth: *in hac Verbi copula, stupet omnis regula*.[104] The literary influence of his allegorization of the relations of man and nature was vast and profound, and appears plainly in the *Roman de la Rose*, Dante's *Commedia*, and the work of Chaucer.[105] But the discovery of a new accommodation between secular learning and theology was to require resources which the old curriculum of the Liberal Arts could not provide.

104 M.-T. d'Alverny, 'Alain de Lille et la *Theologia*', in *L'homme devant Dieu. Mélanges Henri de Lubac* (3 vols., Paris 1964), II 126–8.
105 Andrea Ciotti, 'Alano e Dante', *Convivium* XXVIII (1960) 257–88; Paul H. Piehler, *The Visionary Landscape* (London 1971), pp. 47–110; Wetherbee 1972, pp. 218–19, 242–66; Christel Meier, 'Zum Problem der allegorischen Interpretation mittelalterlicher Dichtung', *Beiträge zur Geschichte der deutschen Sprache und Literatur* XCIX (1977) 250–96; Daniel Poirion, 'Alain de Lille et Jean de Meun', in *Alain de Lille, Gautier de Châtillon, Jakemart Giélée et leur temps*, ed. H. Roussel and F. Suard (Lille 1980), pp. 135–51; Dronke 1986, pp. 8–13.

2

THE PLATONIC INHERITANCE*

TULLIO GREGORY

For a characterization of twelfth-century Platonism – apart from the constant presence of Platonic influences mediated by the Greek and Latin Fathers, especially Augustine, which can be considered a 'common property', part of the natural 'climate' of the Middle Ages[1] – it is necessary to consider the influence of a group of writings which, though already known in the early Middle Ages, only now took on a central importance in many debates, and were responsible for establishing new themes: in the first place the *Timaeus*, the great philosophical Genesis, where Plato evolved the cosmological framework within which his programme of moral and political reform was to be located, proposing a new relationship between the sensible and the intelligible through the myth of the Demiurgos and the mediation of the world-soul. The dialogue had already been a major point of reference in the Hellenistic period, not only for the various Platonic schools, but for the whole wider context of philosophical speculation in late antiquity. In the Middle Ages the *Timaeus*[2] – of which only the first part, devoted to the cosmological exposition (17A–53B), was known – was accompanied by the commentary of Calcidius, who oriented his interpretation of the dialogue according to the hermeneutic suggestions of Middle and Neo-Platonism, in particular those of Numenius and Porphyry: Calcidius not only laid emphasis on the meaning and value – religious and at the same time rational – of the contemplation of the cosmos, the sensible incarnation of the intelligible order, but resolved the cosmological myth of the *Timaeus* into a more organized system, which provided an interpretation and location for figures whose ontological state and reciprocal relations had been left ill-defined in the poetic fabric of the Platonic dialogue. To cite just one example, Calcidius

---

* Translated by Jonathan Hunt.
1 See M.-D. Chenu, *La théologie au XIIe siècle* (Paris 1957), pp. 116 and 141.
2 For the reception of the *Timaeus* and its various developments in the Hellenistic period, a work of notable importance is A.-J. Festugière, *La révélation d'Hermès Trismégiste* (4 vols., Paris 1949–54), esp. vol. II, 'Le Dieu cosmique' (2nd. ed., Paris 1949). The three classic commentaries on the *Timaeus* should be kept in view: A. E. Taylor, *A Commentary on Plato's Timaeus* (Oxford 1928); F. M. Cornford, *Plato's Cosmology. The Timaeus of Plato* (London 1952); L. Bresson, *Le même et l'autre dans la structure ontologique du Timée de Platon. Un commentaire systématique du Timée de Platon* (Paris 1974).

accepts the Middle-Platonic distinction between the 'supreme God' ('who is the supreme good beyond all substance and nature'), the 'mind of God' (the 'second God', the place of ideas and providence), and the world-soul ('second mind', 'fate'),[3] thus initiating an interpretation of Plato which was to remain fundamental in pagan and Christian Neoplatonism; moreover, the ample discussion devoted in the commentary to questions of a cosmological nature supplied substantial fragments of Greek science (drawn in particular from Adrastus) and threw into relief certain fundamental nuclei of problems, such as the mathematical nature of the cosmic order, the relationships between time and eternity, the elements and primordial matter, world-soul and souls, and providence and fate, collecting around each theme extremely ample doxographies which were to guarantee the Middle Ages a knowledge of some significant themes of Hellenistic thought.

Calcidius' commentary is one of the happy examples of that late classical speculation in which elements of various different traditions and schools had gradually blended together against a common Platonic background until they formed an original synthesis, which was to exercise a profound influence on medieval culture, also through other authors connected with the great rebirth of Greek letters which marks the fourth and fifth centuries of our era.[4] Of exceptional significance – for the field which interests us here – are, together with Augustine, two great exponents of Latin Platonism, Macrobius and Boethius, who were always read with constant reference to the *Timaeus*. In the commentary on the *Somnium Scipionis* the teachings of Plato – 'in accordance with the arcanum of truth itself' – are filtered through Plotinus and, in particular, Porphyry (who is frequently referred to and quoted), and merge with the whole ancient philosophical tradition from Homer and Pythagoras to Cicero and Vergil ('a stranger to no branch of knowledge'[5]) around a series of themes (the procession God, mind, soul; the mediating function of the world-soul between the intelligible and the sensible; 'Homer's golden chain', the arithmological speculations on the monad as the principle of multiplicity, and others) to which later philosophers always returned. An impetus in the same direction was given by the influence of Boethius, who was linked to the whole of Neoplatonic culture, especially Porphyry, Ammonius and, above all, Proclus, by way of whose commentary Boethius read the *Timaeus*: this was a Neoplatonism with

---

3 *Timaeus a Calcidio Translatus Commentarioque instructus*, ed. J. H. Waszink (*Plato Latinus*, vol. IV, London–Leiden 1962), pp. 204–5, 306, 324–5, 182, 206.
4 The fundamental work is P. Courcelle, *Les lettres grecques en Occident. De Macrobe à Cassiodore* (Paris 1948).
5 A. T. Macrobius, *Commentarii in Somnium Scipionis* I 6 23, 44; ed. J. Willis (Leipzig 1963), pp. 22, 26.

Aristotelian and especially Neopythagorean motifs, and the authority of its
influence progressively increased with the growth of Boethius' fame as a
martyr of the faith.

It is still the same substantially Platonic cultural tradition, permeated with
religious motifs, which was handed down not only by the great masters of
Christian thought – Origen and Gregory of Nyssa, Ambrose and Augustine,
Marius Victorinus and pseudo-Dionysius – but by other pagan texts whose
reception is constantly linked with the reading of the *Timaeus*, such as
Apuleius, Martianus Capella, and the mythical Hermes Trismegistus, with
the Latin *Asclepius* and the whole complex of pseudepigraphic texts attributed
to him and known in the Middle Ages through the mediation of the Arabs.

These texts give twelfth-century Platonism a particular complexion, in
which it would be misleading to attempt to distinguish between elements
deriving directly from the *Timaeus* and those originating from other authors
directly or indirectly linked to the variegated Platonic tradition which we
have outlined: in reality, through the texts of Latin Neoplatonism the twelfth
century absorbed in an original manner a complex philosophical experience
which had been brought to maturity in the Hellenistic period and in the early
centuries of the Christian era, during which the *Timaeus* had exercised a
central and polyvalent influence, by proposing a physical and religious
cosmology which had been gradually enriched with diverse elements –
Aristotelian, Stoic and the Neopythagorean, Middle– and Neo-Platonic,
Gnostic and Hermetic, Jewish and Christian – to form a unique cultural
koinê. It is significant therefore that in the Platonists of the twelfth century
Plato implies not only Calcidius but Cicero and Macrobius, Boethius and
Martianus Capella, Apuleius and the *Asclepius*, and the ancient poets and
mythographers, all ranged alongside the *auctoritates* of the Greek and Latin
Fathers, who had themselves referred back to this same tradition to
demonstrate the close affinity between the teachings of the 'Platonists' and
Christianity ('you would only have to change a few words and expressions
and they would become Christians', Augustine had written[6]), even to the
extent of affirming the divine and prophetic origin of pagan philosophy.

... in the books of Plato we find many things consonant with the words of the
prophets. In the *Timaeus*, for example, during his subtle investigation of the causes of
the world, he seems clearly to express the Trinity which is God, when he locates the
efficient cause in the power of God, the formal cause in his wisdom, and the final
cause in his goodness, which alone induced him to make all creatures sharers in his

6 Augustine, *De Vera Religione* IV 7 (P.L. 34, 126); *Ep.* 118, III 21 (P.L. 33, 442).

goodness, according as the nature of each one is capable of beatitude. At the same time he seemed to understand and teach that there was a single substance in these, when he asserted that the craftsman and shaper of the world was one God, whom, because of his extraordinary goodness and sweetness, he called the Father of all, and whom, because of the boundlessness of his majesty, power, wisdom, and goodness, it is as difficult for us to find as it would be impossible for us to proclaim, should we ever find him ... There are, moreover, many things in common between the Platonists and our own thinkers ...[7]

This passage of the *Policraticus* faithfully reflects the reading of the *Timaeus* propounded in the circles which John of Salisbury had frequented as a student: the school of Chartres, and in particular the instruction of William of Conches, his teacher, to whom we owe the most ample commentary on the dialogue written in the Middle Ages. With great clarity William pointed out in his introduction (*accessus*) both the 'encyclopaedic' character of the *Timaeus* – 'that we might have a perfect knowledge of philosophy' – and the theological and religious conclusions of the contemplation of the physical world:

... the utility of his discussion of this subject is that, seeing the divine power, wisdom, and goodness in the creation of things, we fear one so powerful, venerate one so wise, and love one so beneficent.[8]

This hermeneutic perspective, which takes up many themes from the Augustinian tradition and the Platonism of the Fathers and proceeds virtually to check their accuracy against the text of Plato, is prevalent in the Platonists of the twelfth century: it presupposes a reading of the *Timaeus* – according to a method suggested by William – which takes account of its particular literary genre, that of a cosmogonic discourse woven out of fables and myths ('Plato's way of talking about philosophy through integuments') which it is the commentator's task to interpret and dissolve, eliciting their hidden philosophical meaning ('the most profound philosophy covered with the integuments of words').[9]

The importance of this particular approach to the Platonic text, which allowed the freest and most complex interpretations of it, has often been stressed:[10] it corresponds to a hermeneutic canon systematically applied in the twelfth century to the reading of ancient poets and philosophers whose

7 John of Salisbury, *Policraticus* VII 5, ed. C. C. J. Webb (Oxford 1909) II 108–10; cf. Plato, *Timaeus* 27c ff.
8 Guillaume de Conches, *Glosae super Platonem*, ed. E. Jeauneau (Paris 1965), p. 60.
9 Guillaume 1965, p. 211.
10 Cf. E. Jeauneau, 'L'usage de la notion d'*integumentum* à travers les gloses de Guillaume de Conches', *AHDLMA* XXIV (1957) 35–100; P. Dronke, *Fabula. Explorations into the Uses of Myth in Medieval Platonism* (Leiden–Cologne 1974).

mythic, fabulous language is always felt to be a vehicle of hidden meanings, of truths of a philosophical and religious nature:

... how much philosophy has always scorned to have its secrets published in naked words, and has been accustomed to talk, particularly about the soul and the gods, through certain fabulous *involucra*, is thoroughly explained by Macrobius, the expounder of the great philosopher Cicero, and no mean philosopher himself.[11]

So wrote Abelard, indicating Macrobius as the source for a theory that in fact goes back to the Hellenistic age, which is used to justify a hermeneutics wholly geared towards unveiling the teachings concealed under the veil of the letter; and, in a direct encounter with Macrobius, William of Conches had found a way of developing the suggestions of the ancient commentator to give newer and wider meanings to the interpretation of mythic and symbolic language.[12] Nor should we forget, if we are to understand the exceptionally wide spectrum of uses that this hermeneutic perspective was to take on, the link which was immediately established with biblical exegesis, which had long ago fixed the various 'senses' according to which it was possible, and at times necessary, to grasp the multiple teachings behind the sacred letter. A significant parallelism was thus formed between the style of the ancient poets and philosophers, who had wrapped their exposition in the veil of 'fabulous narrative' and in the 'mysteries of figures',[13] and that of the books of the Bible with their metaphorical and figured expressions and their

11 Abelard, *Theologia Christiana* I 102, ed. E. M. Buytaert, Petri Abelardi *Opera Theologica* II (Turnhout 1965) 114; cf. *Theologia 'Scholarium'* I 19 (P.L. 178, 1021); *Theologia 'Summi Boni'* I 5, ed. H. Ostlender, *Beiträge zur Geschichte der Philosophie des Mittelalters* XXXV. 2–3 (1939) 13–14. Cf. T. Gregory, 'Abélard et Platon', in *Peter Abelard* (Leuven–The Hague 1974), pp. 38–64 (= *Studi Medievali*, ser. 3a, XIII (1972) 539–62).

12 Cf. Dronke 1974, pp. 13–67, and the texts from the unpublished glosses on Macrobius, *ibid.* pp. 68–78; E. Jeauneau, 'Macrobe, source du platonisme chartrain', *Studi Medievali*, ser. 3a, I (1960) 3–24.

13 Macrobius 1963, I 2 9–21, pp. 5–8.
    It is interesting to note that the term *allegoria*, characteristic of biblical exegesis and relating to the interpretation of 'historical' facts, and the terms *integumentum* or *involucrum*, characteristic of the poetic and mythological accounts ('est enim allegoria oratio sub historica narratione verum et ab esteriori diversum involvens intellectum, ut de lucta Jacob. Integumentum vero est oratio sub fabulosa narratione verum claudens intellectum, ut de Orpheo'; see E. Jeauneau, 'Note sur l'Ecole de Chartres', *Studi Medievali*, ser. 3a. v (1964) 856), also become interchangeable: Abelard uses *integumentum* for the Gospel parables, and in the commentary on Macrobius attributed to William of Conches *integumentum* is used for a passage in Genesis (see Dronke 1974, p. 51); *sacre pagine integumenta* appears again in an anonymous commentary on Martianus Capella (see Jeauneau 1964, p. 850 n. 166). Also significant is the insistence on the multiple senses, *innumeri intellectus*, of a single text – pagan or biblical – according to a precise exegetical canon laid down by Gregory the Great (*Regist. Ep.*, III, Ep. LXII, ed. P. Ewald, in M.G.H., *Epist.* I 1, p. 223) and recalled by Abelard (*Theol. Christ.* I 117, p. 121; *Theologia 'Scholarium'* I 20 (P.L. 178, 1028)). Note also a passage of William of Conches: 'de eadem re secundum diversam considerationem diverse inveniuntur expositiones' (Jeauneau 1957, p. 47).

use of parables and similes. In the interpretation of the Platonic texts this parallelism reaches perhaps its most extensive development in Abelard, who systematically uses the theme of the 'wrapping (*involucrum*)' or 'covering (*integumentum*)' to bring into line with the Christian faith the most difficult texts of Plato and Hermes Trismegistus, Vergil and Macrobius. Convinced that revelation operated not only through the prophets but also through men of pagan antiquity, Abelard proposes a reading of the *involucrum* which is laden with typological meanings: myth and metaphorical language become for him a prefiguration of truths which, though unknown to the ancient authors, were destined to be accomplished in the course of time, in the history of salvation; here the 'wrapping' is no longer simply a concealment of truths of an intelligible kind, outside time, but a 'type', a prophecy:

... it is a highly characteristic mode of speech in philosophers and prophets alike, when they come to discuss the arcana of prophecy, not to say anything in vulgar words, but rather to entice the reader by the comparisons inherent in similes. For things that previously seemed merely fantastic and remote from any practical usefulness according to the surface of the letter are more pleasing when they are afterwards discovered to be full of great hidden meanings and to contain within them great doctrinal edification.[14]

The further the 'surface of the letter' seems from the truth, the more it requires a non-literal translation ('the letter itself compels us towards mystical exposition');[15] the more, therefore, the texts of Plato and the Platonists seem to present a doctrine contrary to the Christian faith, the greater must be the effort to reconcile the 'words of the philosophers with our faith', for it is the Holy Spirit itself which has spoken through them without their knowing, as has happened with other prophecies which are an integral part of sacred history. In this perspective, which aligns the 'testimonies of the philosophers' with the 'testimonies of the prophets', Abelard recognizes in the *involucra* of Plato and Macrobius, as in those of other ancient authors, the revelation of the trinitarian mystery ('they clearly expressed a compendium of the whole Trinity after the prophets')[16]: the 'unbegotten God' of the *Timaeus* is the Father Creator, 'begetter of the universe, most virtuous, omnipotent', the 'mind' of Calcidius, Macrobius, and the *Asclepius* is the Son (all the terms which indicate subordination are brought into conformity with an orthodox theory of generation); the

14 Abelard, *Theologia Christiana* I 98 (Abelard 1965, p. 112); cf. Gregory 1974, pp. 542–4.
15 Abelard, *Theologia Christiana* I 117 (Abelard 1965, p. 122); *Theologia 'Scholarium'* I 20 (P.L. 178, 1028).
16 Abelard, *Theologia Christiana* I 68 (Abelard 1965, p. 100); *Theologia 'Scholarium'* I 17 (P.L. 178, 1012).

world-soul is the Holy Spirit – an interpretation which was highly controversial in the twelfth century but taken as certain by Abelard, who
identifies the world-soul in a 'beautiful figure of *involucrum*', as the type –
according to a pregnant term of Christian exegesis – of the third person of the
Trinity: applying to the difficult Platonic texts the subtlest of exegeses, he
recognizes in the metaphor of the world-soul the procession of the Spirit
from the Father and from the Son and its charismatic mission through the
sevenfold grace 'offered to all in common'. This is the only possible
interpretation of the Platonic texts because otherwise, if they were taken
literally, they would turn Plato, the supreme philosopher, into the greatest
of fools.[17]

Abelard's exegesis is applied to many other themes and passages of his
authors: even leaving aside the Christian interpretation of the Platonic ethics
– whose martyr in the name of truth was Socrates ('through his assertion of
the truth a kind of martyr')[18] – we must not forget the attempt to read not
only in the prophecy of the Sibyl and in Vergil's Fourth Eclogue but also in
the *Timaeus* a prefiguration of the Incarnation, through a symbolic interpretation of the famous passage about the letter *chi* (the structure of the
world-soul which must control the regular motions of the cosmos):

> . . . as if he were affirming in mystical terms that the salvation of all mankind, which
> we understand to be the true constitution of the world itself, was consummated in the
> very passion of the cross of our Lord.[19]

But Abelard's exegesis of the Platonic texts, situated in the context of a
theological discourse and presupposing a prophetic inspiration on the part of
the ancient philosophers, can be taken only as an extreme development of the
use of the *Timaeus* and the philosophical tradition connected with it.

There is closer adherence to the text of the *Timaeus* – which is, however,
still read by way of the notion of integument, that constitutes the true
structure of the dialogue – in the commentary of William of Conches. There
the cosmological interest is dominant, once the author has established – and

---

17 Abelard, *Theologia Christiana* I 106 (Abelard 1965, p. 116): 'Clarum est ea, quae a philosophis
de anima mundi dicuntur, per involucrum accipienda esse. Alioquin summum philosophorum Platonem, summum stultorum esse deprehenderemus'; cf. *Theologia 'Scholarium'* I 20
(P.L. 178, 1023); *Theologia 'Summi Boni'* I 5 (Abelard 1939, p. 15). The same exegesis is given
in the *Sententie Magistri Petri Abelardi (Sententie Hermanni)*, ed. S. Buzzetti (Florence 1983),
pp. 63, 82–4.

18 Abelard, *Theologia Christiana* II 74 (Abelard 1965, p. 164).

19 *Ibid.* 16 (Abelard 1965, p. 140); the theme can already be found in early Christian literature:
see Gregory 1974, p. 61. On Plato as a prophet of Christ, compare the remarkable text of
Humbertus de Balesma in the *Sermo* published by M.-T. d'Alverny, 'Humbertus de
Balesma', *AHDLMA* LI (1984) 127–91, at p. 161.

he frequently refers back to the fact – the dialogue's substantial conformity with Christian doctrine.[20] The more purely theological problems remain marginal and within traditional limits, with an accentuation of the operation *ad extra* of the divine persons: interpreting in a creationistic sense the discourse of the *Timaeus* on the 'adornment of the world', William has no difficulty in identifying the 'Craftsman (*opifex*)' with the Creator (replacing Calcidius' 'Founder (*conditor*)' with the 'creator out of nothing'), the archetypal world with the Word ('the divine wisdom which is called the archetypal world . . . immutable, eternal, pure, in which are contained intelligible living creatures'),[21] while the world-soul – whose possible interpretation as an 'integument' of the Holy Spirit is mentioned – is seen rather as a universal principle of harmony, movement and life.[22] The development of the cosmological themes, however, is extremely wide-ranging: creation, primal matter, and the elements (with an assiduous polemic against the hypothesis of an original chaos, and a personal doctrine of the 'elements (*elementa*)' – 'simple and minuscule particles which never vary' – distinguished from the 'elemented things (*elementata*)'); time and eternity (developing an interesting doctrine of time and the 'aeon (*aevum*)', which takes up some suggestions from Boethius and exonerates Plato from the charge that he maintained the theory of creation *ab aeterno*); the world-soul and souls; the heavens and their influences; and the structure of the human body. Nor is William unaware of the link between the great cosmogonic discourses of the *Timaeus* and the programme of ethical and political reform which lies behind it:

Since Plato was the disciple of this Socrates, perceiving that his master had expounded on positive justice but had omitted to discuss its origin – that is, natural justice – and desiring to make good the parts omitted by his master, he composed this work on this same subject, so that we might have a perfect treatise on all justice, both positive and natural; which can rightly be called the cause of this book. But since natural justice is most apparent in the creation of things and the government of creatures – for whatever is created by God is right and just and is not invented by man – he moves on to discuss this, in order to show the nature and extent of the justice observed by the creator. Therefore it may be said that Plato's subject in this work is natural justice or the creation of the world, or rather of the sensible world, which is the same thing.[23]

20 Cf. Guillaume 1965, pp. 210–11; *Dragmaticon*, ed. Gratarolus (Strasbourg 1567), p. 13: 'Si gentilis adducenda est opinio, malo Platonis quam alterius inducatur: plus namque cum nostra fide concordat.'
21 Guillaume 1965, pp. 113, 126; cf. p. 192: 'in divina sapientia *sunt animalia* secundum illud: "Quod factum est in ipso vita erat", quia vivit sapientia que omnia comprehendit', where the linking of the Timaean phrase with John 1: 3–4, should be noted.
22 Guillaume 1965, pp. 144ff.
23 Guillaume de Conches, *Glosae super Platonem*, according to the version in the MS Venice, Marciana 1870 (*fondo antico* 225), in Guillaume 1965, pp. 294–5; cf. T. Gregory, *Platonismo medievale – Studi e ricerche* (Rome 1958), pp. 59ff.

After the lead given by Calcidius and William the theme recurs regularly in the numerous glosses on the *Timaeus* in the twelfth century, with a stress on the relationship between microcosm and macrocosm, and that between political order and the constitution of the world, whose hierarchical structure is reflected in the three orders of the Platonic city (governors, soldiers, workers) and in the organization of medieval society:

Socrates ... therefore proposed a certain republic and ordered it according to a certain disposition which he had observed in the macrocosm and the microcosm. For he saw in the macrocosm, that is, in the larger world, some high beings, such as God and the planets, some intermediate beings, such as the active and ministering spirits, and some low beings, such as the other spirits who move in our air, for example, the evil demons. Similarly he saw in the microcosm, that is, in man, some high qualities, such as man's wisdom, the seat of which is in the uppermost part of him, that is, in his head ... He also saw in man some intermediate qualities such as courage, whose seat is in the heart, and concupiscence, whose seat is in the kidneys or the loins; and low things, such as feet, hands, etc. According to this disposition, then, he disposed the republic, instituting high officials, such as senators, intermediate ones, such as soldiers on active service, and low ones, such as the specialists in the mechanical arts – furriers, cobblers, apprentices, and, outside the city, farmers.[24]

The contemplation of the cosmos thus constitutes – as Plato indicated – the prerequisite for a new moral and political order; if the medievals did not know the famous final passage of the *Timaeus* (90CD), which exhorted men to bring the motions of the spirit into conformity with those of the heavens, William of Conches grasps the new sense assumed in the dialogue by the contemplation of the cosmos, not only by underlining the link between political order and 'divine disposition', but by pinpointing the sense of sight – whose primacy was celebrated in the *Timaeus* in relation to the new theory of contemplation – as the main route to discovering the divine wisdom which guides the cosmos, a prerequisite for a moral reform

---

24 Gloss from the MS Digby 23, fol. 5r, published by P. E. Dutton, '*Illustre civitatis et populi exemplum*: Plato's *Timaeus* and the Transmission from Calcidius to the End of the Twelfth Century of a Tripartite Scheme of Society', *Mediaeval Studies* XLV (1983) 79–119 (the text is quoted on p. 98 nn. 69–70); see also Gregory 1958, p. 61 n. 3. A theme present in all the glosses on the *Timaeus* is echoed in the anonymous *Tractatus de Philosophia* written in the second half of the twelfth century:

Respublica est aggregatio rerum, inter quas sunt quedam imperantes, quedam agentes, quedam obtemperantes. Dicitur autem fuisse inventa ad exemplar et imaginem sensilis mundi et microcosmi, id est minoris mundi, scilicet hominis, a Moyse primitus constituta, consequenter a Socrate, Platonis preceptore, adumbrata, ad ultimum ab ipso Platone confirmata. Attendamus igitur mundi utriusque dispositionem, ut quemadmodum sit disponenda nostra res publica intelligere valeamus' (ed. G. Dahan, *AHDLMA* XLIX (1983) 190; cf. Guillaume 1965, p. 75).

which subjects 'the erratic ways of the flesh ... to the rational motion of the spirit'.[25]

It is impossible to mention here the particular aspects of the various cosmologies of the twelfth century inspired by the *Timaeus* and by the texts of Latin Neoplatonism, from Thierry of Chartres's commentary 'according to physics' on Genesis to Bernardus Silvestris' *Cosmographia*, from Hermann of Carinthia's *De essentiis* to Gundissalinus' *De processione mundi* and the poetic compositions of Alan of Lille: but it must be emphasized that the Platonic dialogue, with Calcidius' commentary, which transmitted some significant passages of Hellenistic science, not only provided the materials for a cosmology – among other things, a doctrine of the elements and the movements of the heavens, a mathematical conception of cosmic harmony, and a physiology – but above all indicated as the tasks of philosophical enquiry the discovery of the 'legitimate cause and reason' (28A) of the intelligible order of the cosmos, understood as an organic whole ('intelligent living being', 'perfect one': 30C, 33A), the work of a divine craftsman who, being good by nature ('he was supremely good': 29E), follows an eternal model to bring about the best of worlds and guarantees its order by entrusting its preservation to the world-soul, which in its very structure (the same, the different, the mixed) ensures the link between intelligible and sensible.

These are the motifs which recur in various forms in the cosmologies of the twelfth century, where, together with the Timaean physics, Stoic and Hermetic influences blend together, arriving at the formation – the 'discovery', as it has been called[26] – of an idea of nature as a complex of causes endowed with an ontological coherence of its own, and therefore outside the symbolic mentality of the early Middle Ages, which tended to reduce phenomena to a direct manifestation of God's will, to a 'sacrament of salutary allegory'. In its guise of 'genitive force', 'series of causes', 'crafting fire', nature is represented as a helpmate of the Creator, who completes his work: not only in Bernard Silvestris' *Cosmographia* or in the poems of Alan of

25 Guillaume 1965, p. 252; cf. p. 254: 'Dedit ergo Deus oculos homini ut, cum perciperet homo duos esse motus in celestibus et similes in se, quemadmodum divina ratio facit erraticum motum sequi rationabilem motum firmamenti, ita erraticos motus carnis subderet rationabili motui spiritus.'

26 Cf. Chenu 1957, pp. 21ff (which is a reworking of earlier essays); T. Gregory, *Anima mundi. La filosofia di Guglielmo di Conches e la scuola di Chartres* (Florence 1955), pp. 175–246; 'L'idea di natura nella filosofia medievale prima dell'ingresso della fisica di Aristotele', *La filosofia della natura nel Medioevo (Atti del III Convegno Internazionale di filosofia medievale*, Passo della Mendola-Trento, 31 August–5 September 1964) (Milan 1966), esp. pp. 38ff; 'La nouvelle idée de nature et de savoir scientifique au XIIe siècle', in *The Cultural Context of Medieval Learning*, ed. J. E. Murdoch and E. D. Sylla (Dordrecht–Boston 1975), esp. pp. 193–212.

Lille is nature presented as the great mediator between God and the world –
'You', sings Noys, 'blessed fecundity of my womb'; 'Offspring of God and
mother of all things, / fetter of the world and everlasting bond ... Who,
gathering up the pure ideas of Noys, / coining the species with the particulars
of things / clothe things in forms ... / To whom all things, as to the mistress
of the world, render their tribute'[27] – but also more technically, in the
treatises on physics, she is divided up into a succession of intermediaries, a
series of descending and connected causes, while God's work is limited to a
single creative act: hence the distinction between a 'first' and a 'second
geniture' (Hermann of Carinthia, Gundissalinus), the articulation of successive levels of causes and reality (*De sex principiis*), and the function of the
world-soul or, in Stoic terminology, of the 'fiery vigour (*igneus vigor*)', as the
principle which rules the 'entirety of things (*universitas rerum*)'.

The *Timaeus* offered a primary and fundamental suggestion in the myth of
entrusting to the 'gods sons of gods' – the stars and the inferior divinities –
the task of completing the work of the Demiurgos by forming the various
living beings and the human body.[28] William of Conches has no hesitation in
seeing in God's discourse as it is presented by Plato the 'integument' of a truth
fundamental to the whole of physics: the distinction between that which is
created directly by God and is, in accordance with his will, incorruptible, and
that which, on the contrary – in order to be corruptible – is created by
intermediate agents, the stars and the spirits, in other words 'all celestial
things' which 'dominate the four elements'.[29] They are entrusted with the
completion of creation, including the formation of the body of man, which
they render capable of receiving the soul created directly by God. This
theory of mediated creation – into which were also to be inserted at a later

27 Bernardus Silvestris, *Cosmographia*, ed. P. Dronke (Leiden 1978), I, II pp. 98–9; Alan of
   Lille, *De planctu Naturae*, ed. N. M. Häring, *Studi Medievali*, ser 3a, XIX (1978) 831 (= P.L.
   210, 447).
28 Plato, *Timaeus* 41A ff.
29 Guillaume 1965, pp. 203–4:
   '*His igitur*. Finito tractatu de creatione celestis animalis tam visibilis quam invisibilis,
   transit ad creationem ceterorum animalium, more suo ad integumentum se transferens
   quod tale est quod, creatis stellis et spiritibus, convocavit eos Deus in uno conventu
   habitaque oratione iniunxit eis officium formandi corpora ceterorum animalium, et
   maxime hominis, coniungendique animam corpori et conservandi eam cum corpore,
   dandi cibi incrementa et dissolvendi. Huius rei est veritas quod stelle et spiritus a Deo
   vocantur cum ab ipso ad aliquid agendum aptantur; ad ipsos loquitur cum providet que
   per ipsos fiant, iniungit predicta officia quia per effectum stellarum et ministerium
   spirituum implentur. [...] *Dii deorum*. Hec est oratio patris ad filios, id est creatoris ad
   stellas et spiritus [...] *O dii deorum*. Stelle et spiritus dii deorum sunt quia dominantur
   quatuor elementis' [...]
   Cf. pp. 221–3, 233; Bernardus 1978, pp. 134–5; Alan of Lille, *Theologiae Regulae* VI (P.L.
   210, 626), ed. N. M. Häring, in *AHDLMA* XLVIII (1981) 130; *Distinctiones* (P.L. 210, 871).

stage, at the turn of the century, the more exact Neoplatonic teachings of the *Liber de causis* and Avicenna – had an extremely wide circulation and conditioned the exegesis of Genesis as well, and not only to defend – against the Augustinian tradition of creation in a single act – the successive moments, the historicity of the formation of the world as a physical process without direct intervention by the Creator. William of Conches reworked in his commentary on the *Timaeus* the passage from the *Philosophia* on the formation of the elemental world, the living beings, and the human body, through the action of the heat which comes down from the heavens, proposing an allegorical interpretation of the Genesis account of the creation of Adam and Eve, 'for it must not be believed literally (*non enim ad litteram credendum est*)';[30] similarly Thierry, writing his commentary 'according to physics' on Genesis, limits the creative act to the creation of primordial matter, while the 'distinction of forms' takes place in time under the dominion of the heavens, whose movement marks out the days of the creation ('a natural day is the space in which one entire turn of heaven is completed from the rising')[31]: the 'adornment' is produced by that movement, through the progressive action of heat ('fire is, as it were, the craftsman and the efficient cause') according to a 'natural order' which proceeds from the formation of the heavenly bodies right down to the 'animals of earth', 'in whose number man is made in the image and likeness of God'.[32] The reply to the polemics of the traditionalist theologians, who saw in this new cosmology a negation of the 'will of God' as the cause of creation, is always the same:

I take nothing away from God; all things that are in the world were made by God, except evil; but he made other things through the operation of nature, which is the instrument of divine operation.[33]

---

30 Guillaume 1965, p. 122; cf. *Philosophia* I, XIII 43, ed. G. Maurach (Pretoria 1980), p. 38 (P.L. 172, 56).
31 Thierry of Chartres, *De Sex Dierum Operibus* 4, in N. M. Häring, *Commentaries on Boethius by Thierry of Chartres and his School* (Toronto 1971), p. 557. On Thierry, see also chapter 13 below.
32 Thierry, *De Sex Dierum Operibus* 14–17 (Häring 1971, pp. 561–2); cf. Clarembald, *Tractatulus super Librum Genesim* 40–4, in N. M. Häring, *Life and Works of Clarembald of Arras* (Toronto 1965), pp. 243–7. Echoing a passage of Firmicus Maternus, the author of *De sex principiis* wrote: 'ad omnifariam mundi imitacionem hominem artifex natura composuit ut, quicquid substanciam mundi aut format aut solvit, hoc eciam hominem et reformet et dissolvat'; see T. Silverstein, 'Liber Hermetis Mercurii Triplicis de VI Rerum Principiis', *AHDLMA* XXII (1955) 289; cf. Firmicus Maternus, *Matheseos Libri VIII* II 1 16, ed. W. Kroll and F. Skutsch (Stuttgart 1968) I 96.
33 William of Conches, *In Boetium*, ed. J. M. Parent, *La Doctrine de la création dans l'École de Chartres* (Paris–Ottawa 1938), p. 126; cf. Guillaume 1965 p. 122: 'Iterum dicet hoc esse divine potentie derogare sic hominem esse factum dicere. Quibus respondemus e contrario

In this new cosmology derived from the *Timaeus*, the 'gods sons of gods', the stars, the celestial creatures, become not only the messengers of the divine will but 'ministers of the creator'; it is significant that the author of the preface to the *Experimentarius*, in order to defend his astrological and geometrical manual, was later able to say:

> We . . . do not believe that the stars or planets are gods, nor do we worship them, but we believe that their creator is God omnipotent, and we worship him. Nevertheless, we believe that the omnipotent One gave to the planets that power which the ancients believed to proceed from the stars themselves. We also believe that the same planets have the same power over things now, and apportion each man his fate by their disposition.[34]

The Timaean physics, enriched with Stoic elements – the 'fiery vigour', 'nature the craftsman', the heat which comes down from the sun as 'initiator of all geniture' – provides an interpretative scheme of becoming in which room was easily found for the suggestions of Arabic culture, from the doctrine of creation through a hierarchy of intermediate agents to the most precise astrological doctrines: it is therefore significant, as has been rightly observed, that the new translations from the Arabic of scientific texts originate from Platonic circles and meet their most favourable reception in those circles.[35] Thus Adelard of Bath, the defender of Arabic science 'which almost wholly exists in the Quadrivium' and a prolific translator, recognized Plato as his master ('since both on philosophical contemplation' – the interlocutor in the *Quaestiones naturales* says to him – 'and on the physical effects of causes, and also on ethical questions, I perceive that you are entirely in agreement with Plato'; 'your Plato'[36]). In the *De essentiis*, by Hermann of Carinthia – a disciple of Thierry, to whom he dedicated his translation of Ptolemy's *Planisphere* as one in whom the spirit of Plato was reincarnated[37] – the teachings of the *Timaeus* constitute the background to a cosmology thick with references to, and borrowings from, Arabic science: here not only does

id esse ei conferre quia ei attribuimus et talem rebus naturam dedisse et per naturam operantem corpus humanum sic creasse'; *Philosophia* I, XIII 44, p. 39 (P.L. 172, 56); Adelard of Bath, *Quaestiones naturales* 4, ed. M. Müller, *Beiträge zur Geschichte der Philosophie und Theologie des Mittelalters* XXXI. 2 (1934) 8.

34 Guillaume 1965, p. 223; *Experimentarius*, ed. M. Brini Savorelli, 'Un manuale di geomanzia presentato da Bernardo Silvestre da Tours (XII secolo): l'*Experimentarius*', *Rivista critica di storia della filosofia* XIV (1959) 313; for the composite structure and the attribution of the *Experimentarius*, see C. S. F. Burnett, 'What is the *Experimentarius* of Bernardus Silvestris? A Preliminary Survey of the Material', *AHDLMA* XLIV (1977) 79–125 (the quoted passage is on p. 116).

35 See C. Burnett's *Introduction* to Hermann of Carinthia, *De Essentiis, A Critical Edition with Translation and Commentary* (Leiden–Cologne 1982), p. 21.

36 Adelard of Bath, *Quaestiones naturales* 24, p. 31; cf. 27–9, pp. 33–4.

37 Cl. Ptolemaei *Opera Astronomica Minora*, ed. J. L. Heiberg (Leipzig 1907), p. clxxxv.

nature take on the structure of the Platonic world-soul, but in it 'identical nature (*natura identica*)' is specified as the active part of the cosmos, the heavens, whose 'leadership' is exercised over all the processes of generation and corruption and over the history of mankind.[38] Similarly, in Bernardus Silvestris' Platonism, permeated with Hermetic and astrological elements, 'elementing nature (*natura elementans*)' is identified with heaven and the constellations,[39] and in the pseudo-Hermetic *De sex principiis* nature is the very 'quality of the planets', the 'principle of order and of life', the 'crafting vigour', which realizes in the elemental world the design of the heavens.[40]

'The movement of the higher bodies cannot achieve anything in these lower ones without the aid of nature' wrote Gundissalinus in the *De processione mundi*,[41] which by its very title evokes a typical Neoplatonic theme mediated by the Arabic tradition; in the same perspective – which makes use of Platonic themes in more precise astrological contexts – Raymond of Marseilles, identifying the world-soul with the Holy Spirit, makes it the principle which governs – through the heavens – the course of time:

... for after David had said that the heavens had been fixed by the word of the Lord, he then added, in order to imply that they were moved by soul without the planets, and that they cannot do what they are able to do without spirit, 'And the breath of his mouth is all their power'; as if to say: the power which heaven and the planets have, when they presage future events and revolve with a wonderful motion, they have not

38 Hermann of Carinthia, *De Essentiis*, ed. C. Burnett (Leiden–Cologne 1982), p. 154: 'ipsa natura primum tripertita dividenda videtur – in idem, diversum et mixtum – quam, si volumus, eodem nomine notare possumus quo Plato significans mundi animam vocat'. For the astrological development in the physics of Hermann, who revives the Arab tradition and uses it also for his anti-Hebraic polemic in defence of Christianity, see *ibid.*, esp. pp. 80–2, 164ff, with Burnett's commentary; on the problem as a whole see Gregory 1964, pp. 51–61; Gregory 1975, pp. 202ff.

39 Bernardus 1978, I, IV, p. 118: 'Est igitur elementans Natura celum stelleque signifero pervagantes.'

40 Silverstein 1955, p. 282:
  'planetarum et signorum nature in naturalibus operantur. Status huius nature est effectus precedentis cause in celescium corporum qualitate consistens divina disposicione. Hec quidem qualitas a philosophis natura dicitur, que iuxta varias vires suas in universis et singulis sub lunari globo variatur [...] Hinc rerum temporalium qualitas appellatur natura, quia in universis vis innativa, in singulis operosa comprehenditur; in universis artifex, in singulis opifex comprobatur.'
  For the heavens' dominion over the history of mankind, see *ibid.* pp. 266–7, 290–1 (from Firmicus 1968, III 1 11–15, vol. 1 pp. 94–5). See also Bernardus 1968, pp. 104–5: 'Scribit enim celum stellis, totumque figurat / Quod de fatali lege venire potest / [...] Preiacet in stellis series quam longior etas / Explicat et spatiis temporis ordo suis...', with his use of the horoscope of Christ, which was to enjoy a wide diffusion in the twelfth century, drawing on a famous passage of Abū Ma'shar.

41 Gundissalinus, *De Processione Mundi*, ed. G. Bülow, *Beiträge zur Geschichte der Philosophie des Mittelalters* xxiv.3 (1925) 52.

from themselves but from the spirit ... When we read the philosophers' opinions about the world-soul, we find preferable and more sane the view of those who have said that the Holy Spirit is the soul both of heaven and of the seven planets.[42]

The debate about the world-soul, which in various forms pervades the whole century, in the effort to find it a place both in the theologico-Christian framework and in the new physics, took on a particular prominence even in authors who rejected the identification of it with the Holy Spirit, for there was an awareness of being faced with a structure fundamental to the Timaean world, a unifying principle of the whole of sensible and intelligible reality:

... the adornment of the world is whatever can be seen in the individual elements, such as the stars in heaven, the birds in the sky, the fish in the water, men on the earth, etc. But because some of them are always in motion, some grow, some discern, and some feel, and they have this property not from the nature of the body but from the nature of the soul. Thus Plato begins by discussing the soul, that is, the world-soul. And the world-soul is a kind of spirit inherent in things, conferring motion and life on them. This spirit is whole and entire in all things, but does not operate equally in all things.[43]

This universal soul – on another occasion identified by William of Conches with the Holy Spirit[44] – has the task of ensuring the movement, life, and harmony of the all, uniting 'undivided' and 'divided' nature – spirit and bodies – the same and the different, reality divided and at the same time united in the species and the *genera* or – according to another interpretation – capable of exercising different powers while remaining unique in itself. Thierry of Chartres – 'the foremost of philosophers in all Europe' – significantly develops an analogous exegesis when writing his commentary on Genesis and gathering around the phrase 'and the spirit of the Lord moved upon the waters' testimonies from the *Asclepius*, the *Timaeus*, and the *Aeneid*, according to a doxography which was frequently repeated.[45] But as a result of the prevalent cosmological use, consistent with the teachings of the *Timaeus*, the world-soul tended to leave the theological sphere – the condemnation by the Council of Sens of the thesis attributed to Abelard, 'that the Holy Spirit is the world-soul', and William of Saint-Thierry's

---

42 Published in R. Lemay, *Abu Ma'shar and Latin Aristotelianism in the Twelfth Century* (Beirut 1962), pp. 151 n. 2, 191 n. 1.
43 Guillaume 1965, pp. 144–5.
44 Gregory 1955, pp. 133ff.
45 Häring 1971, pp. 566–7; Theirry cites, together with the verse from Genesis (1: 2), a passage from the Psalms (32: 6) – the same one mentioned by Raymond of Marseilles – and one from Wisdom 1: 7. On the various interpretations of the biblical verse, see A. Tarabocchia Canavero, *Esegesi biblica e cosmologica. Note sull'interpretazione patristica e medioevale di Genesi 1, 2* (Milan 1981).

attacks on Abelard, and later on William of Conches, must have had their effect[46] – and become identified with nature, as the *De septem septenis* defines with extreme precision:

> The created spirit, that is, the universal and natural motion, fastens a form that in itself is invisible to matter of itself invisible, in such a way that what is composed of them is transformed into a kind of actual and visible substance. This spirit is a natural and universal motion, containing the four 'hylements (*ylementa*)', as it were the ligaments of its *hylê* or matter, and diffused in the firmament by the stars, in the sublunary world by fire, air, water, earth, and all other things which naturally move in the world. This motion is called by Hermes nature, by Plato the world-soul, by certain others fate, and by the theologians divine disposition.[47]

Thus around the world-soul, which has now become resolved into nature, there grows a cluster of philosophical and religious notions of varying origin, but all traceable to a single Platonic matrix; in Thierry the 'determinate necessity', the 'seriate connection of causes'

> ... some have termed natural law, others nature, others the world-soul, others natural justice. But others have called it fate, others the *Parcae*, others the intelligence of God.[48]

Similarly the anonymous author of the *Compendium philosophiae*, passing in review the various interpretations of the Platonic text ('There are some who say that the world-soul is the sun ... There are others who think that the world-soul is none other than the divine benignity or the Holy Spirit') is able to assert that

> ... there is an opinion held by others, who say that the world-soul is a certain vigour inherent in all things ... this opinion is praised by almost everyone,

adding immediately that 'better than all the others is a new opinion ... in which it is asserted that fate or order or divine disposition is the world-soul': an opinion which – as the commentator emphasizes – denies the world-soul a substantial existence of its own ('it is said to be excogitated and not created,

46 Cf. Gregory 1955, pp. 150–2.
47 *De septem septenis*, P.L. 199, 951–2 (MS British Library, Harley 3969, fol. 214v); the citation of 'Hermes' refers to the pseudo-Hermetic *De sex principiis*, published in Silverstein 1955, pp. 248–9.
48 Thierry of Chartres, *Glosa super Boethii librum de Trinitate* II 21 (Häring 1971, p. 273); note also the doxographies of Calcidius in his commentary on the *Timaeus*, especially for the identification of the *anima mundi* with *fatum*, Calcidius 1962, pp. 181ff; cf. also Clarembald 1965, II 19, p. 201.
   On the attribution to Thierry of the *Glosa* and also of the *Commentum super Boethium de Trinitate* and of the *Lectiones in Boethii librum de Trinitate*, see the introduction by Häring 1971; the attribution remains debatable (even Häring speaks of a 'moral certainty', and uses the phrase 'reasonable to conclude'), but the common Chartrian matrix of these works is universally accepted.

lest it should be understood as corporeal, or as some spiritual essence') and reduces it to the realization in time of the order which is present *ab aeterno* in the divine mind, with an interesting exegesis of the Timaean text suggested by Calcidius' commentary.[49]

If the influence of the *Timaeus* is prevalent in the cosmogonies of the twelfth century, far from insignificant – in fact particularly important for its originality with respect to the tradition – is the presence in theological reflection of more purely Neoplatonic themes: the vehicle for them, together with the writings of pseudo-Dionysius and Eriugena, was provided by the works of Boethius, where there was an equally strong influence from Neopythagorean motifs, which had been fused, in the Hellenistic period, in the same crucible of cultural experiences as those transmitted by Macrobius and Calcidius: one need only think, as far as the commentary on the *Somnium Scipionis* is concerned, of the arithmological articulation of the procession monad, mind, world-soul (whose structure, according to the generation of numbers 'from even and odd', always provided an opportunity for arithmological digressions) and the precise connection – which reflects a well-defined doxographical tradition – established by Calcidius between Pythagoras and Plato, concerning the doctrine of the relationship between God and matter resolved into that between unity and multiplicity.[50]

49 *Compendium Philosophiae*, ed. C. Ottaviano, *Un brano inedito della 'Philosophia' di Guglielmo di Conches* (Naples 1935); for the attribution cf. Gregory 1955, pp. 28–40; for the importance of the debate on the *anima mundi* in the twelfth century see in particular E. Garin, *Studi sul platonismo medievale* (Florence 1958), pp. 33ff (with an analysis of the composite *De mundi constitutione*, attributed to Bede in Migne but reallocated by Garin to the twelfth century; on this text, see now the edition by Charles Burnett: *Pseudo-Bede: De mundi celestis terrestrisque constitutione*, Warburg Institute Surveys and Texts x (London 1985).

50 Macrobius 1963, I 6, pp. 18–36; Calcidius 1962, XXVI–LIV, pp. 76, 103; cf. CCXCV, p. 297: 'Numenius [. . .] Pythagorae dogmate, cui concinere dicit dogma Platonicum, ait Pythagoram deum quidem singularitatis nomine nominasse, silvam vero duitatis.' Cf. Thierry, *Commentum* II 28 (Häring 1971, p. 77): 'sunt igitur secundum Platonem duo rerum principia: actus scilicet sine possibilitate i.e. Deus vel necessitas et – quasi ex adverso posita – materia i.e. possibilitas [. . .] nemo tamen existimet quod Plato materiam Deo coeternam esse voluerit, licet Deum et materiam rerum principia constituerit. Immo a Deo descendere voluit materiam. Ubique enim magistrum suum sequitur Pythagoram qui unitatem et binarium duo rerum principia constituit: unitatem Deum appellans per binarium materiam designans'; similarly Thierry's pupil, Clarembald of Arras, established a direct connection between Pythagoras' one and Plato's *necessitas absoluta*, between the *absoluta possibilitas* and the *binarium*: 'Pitagoras quoque diu admiratus quare numerus in denario terminaretur [. . .] tandem huius ammirationis hoc modo exitum invenit ut in unitate Deum i.e. necessitatem absolutam, in binario materiam i.e. absolutam possibilitatem ratione alteritatis constitueret'; Clarembald, *Tractatulus* (Häring 1965, p. 236). Note also Bernardus 1978, p. 146: 'Erant igitur duo rerum principia: unitas et diversum [. . .]. Unitas deus, diversum non aliud quam yle, eaque indigens forma' (the importance of the *silva* as a principle of evil is stressed by Garin 1958, pp. 58–9). Cf. the glosses of William of Conches: '[. . .] dividuam substantiam dicamus illam primordialem materiam, scilicet ilem, individuam archetipum mundum [. . .]' (Guillaume 1965, p. 153); and the discussion on the arithmetical structure of the *anima mundi*

Calcidius' suggestion, adopted together with the Pythagorizing speculations of Boethius, opened the way to a representation of creation as a procession or generation of the numbers starting from unity: 'the creation of numbers is the creation of things'.[51] In this perspective there re-emerged a theme which, after its introduction by Plato's *Parmenides*, had constituted – right down to its final developments in Plotinus and Proclus – an essential nucleus of Middle- and Neo-Platonism: the relationship between God and world is articulated according to the dialectic unity–multiplicity, where the first term – which properly speaking is not a number, is not being, and is not intelligible, since it is placed above all categorical distinctions – is the radical foundation which in itself 'implies' the multiple, the expression or 'explication' of the superabundance of the one.[52] In a Christian context, the creation – freed from any empirical and spatial representation – is interpreted according to a deeper ontological relationship, developing here, too, a Plotinian motif ('all things are beings through the one') transmitted by pseudo-Dionysius ('all beings exist by being one' was Eriugena's translation)[53], and by Boethius in a constantly repeated axiom: 'every thing that is, is because it is one'.[54] Now that the one is thus identified with

---

(ibid. pp. 153ff); at the beginning of the *Glosae*, on the words *Unus, duo, tres* in the *Timaeus* (17A) he noted: 'Plato igitur, ut pitagoricus, sciens maximam perfectionem in numeris esse, quippe cum nulla creatura sine numero possit existere [...]'; the theme recurs in the *Dragmaticon (Dragmaticon* 1567, pp. 52–3).

51 Thierry, *De sex dierum operibus* 36 (Häring 1971, p. 570).

52 Cf. *Lectiones in Boethii librum de Trinitate* II 4 (attributed to Thierry of Chartres), in Häring 1971, p. 155:

'Deus est enim unitas in se conplicans universitatem rerum in simplicitate. Sicut enim unitas conplicatio est omnis pluralitatis et non est tamen pluralitas sed unitas nisi vi, unitas enim vi et potestate pluralitas. Et pluralitas vero explicatio est unitatis et unitas est principium et origo pluralitatis.'

The trinitarian relationship is also divided up according to a 'mathematical' relationship – taking up a suggestion by Augustine (*De doctr. christiana* I (P.L. 34, 21)) – thus becoming fixed in a form which became extremely widespread in the twelfth century, from Thierry of Chartres (*Commentarium super Boethii librum de Trinitate* II 38 (Häring 1971), p. 80; *Lectiones in Boethii librum de Trinitate* IV 16 (*ibid.* p. 218)) to Alan of Lille, who makes it one of his 'theological rules': 'in Patre unitas, in Filio equalitas, in Spiritu Sancto unitatis equalitatisque connexio' (P.L. 210, 625; ed. N. M. Häring, *AHDLMA* XLVIII (1981) 128). The formula is attributed to Parmenides by the *De septem septenis* (P.L. 199, 961).

53 Plotinus, *Enn.* VI 9 1; pseudo–Dionysius, *De Divinis Nominibus* XIII 2 (P.G. 3, 977): τῷ εἶναι τὸ ἓν πάντα ἐστὶ τὰ ὄντα; Latin translation in P.L. 122, 1169.

54 Boethius, *In Porphyrium* (P.L. 64, 83); cf. *Liber de persona et duabus naturis* 4 (P.L. 64, 1346): 'Esse enim atque unum convertitur, et quodcumque est, unum est'; referring to Boethius, Alan of Lille later gave as the first 'theological rule': 'monas est qua quelibet res est una', where he is making a commentary on 'Unitas autem a nullo descendit. Omnis pluralitas ab unitate defluit' (P.L. 210, 623; Häring 1971, pp. 124–5). Cf. Gundissalinus 1925, p. 29: 'quia esse et unum inseparabilia sunt, quoniam, quicquid est, ideo est, quia unum est'; and the

being ('unity as if it were beingness (*unitas quasi onitas*)'[55]), and therefore with 'act' and the 'form of being', the relationship with the many is defined in terms of participation and immanence ('God is everywhere entire and is essentially'), going beyond the exemplarism prevalent in the Platonic–Augustinian tradition and the Timaean myth of the Craftsman who models the cosmos by contemplating an eternal model. The distinction between the two extreme terms seems to become blurred, the more the presence of the one in the multiple is accentuated, resolving all forms into the single form:

> . . . unity therefore is divinity itself. But divinity is the form of being for individual things. For just as a thing is bright because of light, and hot because of heat, so individual things derive their being from divinity. Whence God is truly said to be entire and essentially everywhere. Therefore unity is the form of being for individual things. Whence it is truly said, 'every thing that is, is because it is one'.[56]

And again:

> . . . for just as heat is the form of being hot, and whiteness is the form of being white, so God is the form of being (*forma essendi*). And just as whiteness is in a white thing, so the form of being is in every thing that is. But God is the form of being. Therefore God is everywhere entire and is essentially in all things. So it comes about that when we speak of being in relation to a creature we are predicating participation in being; but when we speak of it in relation to God we are designating being itself. For God is being itself.[57]

The dialectic of participation takes on an exceptional richness, the presence of God is affirmed with accents which recall the boldest expressions of John Scotus Eriugena: 'the unity of all things is the first and unique being', 'since divinity itself is unity itself, therefore the unity of all things is unique being',[58] while the forms, which are multiple in their inherence in matter, are resolved, when they are freed from it, into the one, from which they have

---

same author's *De unitate*, ed. Correns, *Beiträge zur Geschichte der Philosophie des Mittelalters* I. I (1891) 3.

55 Thierry, *Commentum* II 22 (Häring 1971, p. 75): 'actus [. . .] sine possibilitate necessitas est. Hec autem a Platone eternitas, ab aliis unitas quasi onitas ab on greco i.e. entitas, ab omnibus autem usitato vocabulo appellatur Deus.' Attention was drawn to the diffusion of the theme, even outside the philosophical circles of Chartres, by M.-D. Chenu, 'Platon à Cîteaux', *AHDLMA* XXI (1954) 99–106; note also an important passage in Arnaud de Bonneval, *Comm. in Ps. 132, hom.* I 5 (P.L. 189, 1572): 'Et nota quod haec ipsa unitas, de qua hic agitur, longe ab illa unitate quae pars est numeri separatur [. . .]. Trahit autem etymologiam de graeco, et dicitur *unitas* quasi *onitas*, idest *entitas* sive *essentialitas*; unde et apud Graecos ὄν, idest substantialis, videlicet in se et per se solum immutabiliter semper subsistens, Deus vocatur.'

56 Thierry, *De sex dierum operibus* 31 (Häring 1971, pp. 568–9); the final words are a quotation from Boethius (cf. n.54).

57 Thierry, *Commentum* II 17 (Häring 1971, pp. 73–4).

58 Thierry, *De sex dierum operibus* 41–2 (Häring 1971, pp. 572–3).

'emanated' ('from that simple divine form the forms of all things are said to emanate'; 'in one and the same form all things are resolved'; 'to speak truly, all forms of things will revert to one form').[59]

The use of a certain symbolism, too – bound up with the theme of emanation, flux, and the reflection of the one form in various mirrors like various planes of being in which the original unity multiplies itself as it grows weaker,[60] 'in the likeness', Gundissalinus was to add, echoing Avencebrol, 'of the emission of water flowing from its source, and its outpouring'[61] – evokes the whole complex range of Neoplatonic themes: the very concept of creation as an absolute beginning tends to be resolved into the dynamic flow of the multiple from the fontal origin, while the emphasized relationship of participation which joins the divine form (or the forms, that constitute a unity in the Word) to the manifold forms, leads to the rediscovery of the significance of the Parmenidean position according to Calcidius' account:

... this is the reason why Plato in the *Parmenides* says that all forms, inasmuch as they are form and without discretion, are the form of forms. Nor are they many forms but one form which, because it is not joined to mutability, cannot be embodied.[62]

Perhaps precisely to avoid the risks of a direct relationship of participation between the forms in the divine mind and the embodied forms, Bernard of Chartres – 'the most perfect among the Platonists of our century' – had not only asserted that the 'eternal reasons' were in their multiplicity inferior to the creator, taking up a theme from John Scotus Eriugena and, significantly, accepting Macrobius' doctrine that the *nous* is inferior to the one (if certain glosses on the *Timaeus* are indeed by Bernard[63]), but posited between them and concrete, material reality the 'embodied forms (*forme native*)', 'that is, the

---

59 Thierry, *Commentum* 41, 44 (Häring 1971, pp. 81–2); *De sex dierum operibus* 42 (Häring 1971, p. 573).

60 Cf. Thierry, *Commentum* 64, 48 (Häring 1971, pp. 88–93); Clarembald, *Tractatus* II 21, 60 (Häring 1965, pp. 115, 130); Gundissalinus 1925, pp. 40–1.

61 *Ibid.* p. 40.

62 Thierry, *Glosa* II 35 (Häring, p. 276); cf. *Lectiones* II 66 (Häring 1971, p. 176): 'Secundum quod Plato dicit in *Parmenide* Calcidio testante quod unum est exemplar omnium rerum et plura exemplaria in quo nulla diversitas, nulla ex diversitate contrarietas sicut in Platone dicitur' (cf. Calcidius 1962, pp. 276–7; Gregory 1958, pp. 117ff); *Commentum* II 66 (Häring 1971, p. 88): 'omnes rerum omnium forme in mente divina considerate una quadam forma sunt in forme divine simplicitatem inexplicabili quodam modo relapse'.

63 Cf. P.E. Dutton, 'The Uncovering of the *Glosae super Platonem* of Bernard of Chartres', *Mediaeval Studies* XLVI (1984) 192–221; for the passage to which I allude, see p. 215: 'Nota archetipum nec principium nec finem habere et tamen secundum philosophos diversum esse a deo et inferiorem; diversum quia colligit in se omnium rerum ideas [...]. Inferior est, cum Macrobius dicat ideas esse in mente dei, quae inferior est Deo'; for the reference to Macrobius, see Macrobius 1963, I 2 14, I 6 8, I 14 3, 6, pp. 6, 19–20, 55–6.

images of exemplars which are created with individual things'; a doctrine which not only drew on a reference to Boethius, but was derived directly from the *Timaeus* and Calcidius' commentary ('the second form (*species*) that is embodied borrows its substance from the principal form, which is without beginning'), as is also confirmed by certain glosses which have been attributed to Bernard on the basis of their use of a characteristic terminology ('embodied forms, which are images of ideas').[64]

If in this perspective – which was later taken up with more complex developments by Gilbert of Poitiers[65] – Platonic exemplarism was accepted, the more marked Neoplatonism of Thierry and his school was not unaware of the risk of a dialectic of participation and of the symbolism linked with it: significantly, if on the one hand they stress the presence of the one in the multiple, of the unique form in the forms, on the other they constantly emphasize the clear distinction between the one and the multiple, and between the divine form and the immaterial forms, which are properly speaking images, copies:

... but when we say that divinity is the form of being for individual things, we do not say that divinity is some form which has existence in matter ... for divinity cannot be embodied;[66]

they therefore strongly reject (as a 'sophistical inference', a 'ridiculous inference') the objection of those who try to deduce from those more radical

64 The evidence for the teaching of Bernard of Chartres is in John of Salisbury, *Metalogicon* II 17 (P.L. 199, 875–6; ed. Webb (Oxford 1929), pp. 94–5), who directly connects with Plato the thesis of the inferiority of the forms with respect to God and the teaching of Bernard on the *forme native*. Cf. *Metalogicon* IV 3 (P.L. 199, 938; Webb 1929, p. 205): 'Ideas tamen quas post Deum primas essentias ponit, negat in seipsis materie admisceri aut aliquem sortiri motum; sed ex his forme prodeunt native, scilicet imagines exemplarium quas natura rebus singulis concreavit'; for the cited passage of Calcidius, see Calcidius 1962, 344, p. 336, and cf. Gregory 1958, pp. 112–15. For the quotation from the *Glosae super Platonem* attributed to Bernard of Chartres, cf. Dutton 1984, pp. 216–17; the expression *forme native* also appears in the glosses on the *Timaeus* in the MS Vienna, Lat. 2376, 2; Munich, Clm. 540B (cf. Dronke 1974, p. 89 n. 1).
    That the embodied forms are properly speaking *imagines* and not *forme* is constantly repeated in the twelfth century in relation to a passage of Boethius' *De Trinitate* (2; P.L. 64, 1250) also quoted by John of Salisbury (*Metalogicon*, IV 3 (P.L. 199, 938; Webb 1929, p. 205)); cf. Thierry, *Glosa* II 49 (Häring 1971, p. 279): 'Inde est quod nec vere forma est quia inmateriata est. Sed ea et consimilibus *abutimur* vocando eas *formas* cum potius *sint imagines* formarum. Non enim sunt ydee sed ydos'; *Lectiones* II 19, II 41, II 47 ('imago enim a philosophis vocatur forma inmateriata'): Häring 1971, pp. 161, 168, 170. See also the scale of forms in the imaginary palace described by Alan of Lille in the *Sermo de sphaera intelligibili*, in Alan of Lille, *Textes inédits*, ed. M.-T. d'Alverny (Paris 1965), pp. 299–300 (and cf. *ibid.* pp. 167–9). Cf. also Garin 1958, pp. 50–3.
65 Cf. John of Salisbury, *Metalogicon* II 1 (P.L. 199, 875–6; Webb 1929, pp. 94–5): 'universalitatem formis nativis attribuit et in earum conformitate laborat. Est autem forma nativa' – John explains – 'originalis exemplum, et quae non in mente Dei consistit, sed rebus creatis inhaeret'.
66 Thierry, *De sex dierum operibus* 32 (Häring 1971, p. 569).

affirmations the identification of the one with the many, of the one form with the various forms ('if the divine form is all forms, then, some will say, it is humanity'; 'but let no one think that because God is in all things, he is therefore a stone or a piece of wood or such things').[67]

Nevertheless, a significant indication of the presence of Neoplatonic themes – together with some Eriugenian elements – is the emphasis on the great theme, 'God is all things', affirmed under the authority of John the Evangelist and Hermes Trismegistus, with a significant juxtaposition of authorities drawing on one and the same cultural background:[68] thus the Platonism of the twelfth century seems to repeat the complex conclusions of the Platonism of late antiquity, tending on the one hand to underline the immanence of the one in the multiple to the point of identifying the two terms – as was to happen in the radical developments attributed to Amalric of Bène near Chartres ('God is all things in all things ... God is stone in stone, Godinus in Godinus')[69] and attested in David of Dinant's *Quaternuli* ('mind and *hylê* are the same. Plato seems to agree with this when he says that the world is a sensible God ... Therefore it is manifest that there is only one substance ... and that this substance is none other than God himself')[70] – and

---

67 Thierry, *Commentum* IV 8 (Häring 1971, p. 97): 'Quod autem deus sit omnia testatur Iohannes Apostolus dicens *omnia* inquit *in ipso vita erant*, i.e. sapientia [...] Quod quidem in *Trismegistro* Mercurius asserit ubi omnia unum esse confirmat et astruit'. Cf. John 1: 4; *Asclepius* 1, ed. A. D. Nock and A.-J. Festugière, *Corpus Hermeticum* II (Paris 1945) 296.

68 On the presence of Eriugenian themes in the twelfth century and on the *Clavis physicae* by Honorius of Autun, which transmits – transcribing them in full – sizeable fragments of the *De divisione naturae*, cf. P. Lucentini, *Platonismo medievale. Contributi per la storia del eriugenismo* (Florence 1979), especially pp. 45ff, 57ff (and the bibliography given there), and also the edition of the *Clavis physicae* (Honorius Augustodunensis, *Clavis Physicae*, ed. P. Lucentini (Rome 1974)). Here we meet all the well-known Eriugenian formulas: 'Deus namque solus et vere omnium essentia, ut ait Dionisius Ariopagita' (p. 5); 'Patris Verbum est "forma omnium"' (p. 41); 'profecto dabitur omnia ubique Deum esse, et totum in toto, et factorem et factum [...]' (p. 126); 'Verbum Dei est natura omnium que in ipso et per ipsum facta sunt: essendo enim ipsum fiunt omnia, quoniam ipsum omnia est' (p. 133); for the inferiority of the *principales cause* 'non omnino coeterne' ('causa omnium precedit principales causas in se eternaliter constitutas') cf. pp. 64–5.

69 Cf. G. C. Capelle, *Autour du décret de 1210: III. – Amaury de Bène. Étude sur son panthéisme formel* (Paris 1932), p. 92: the reference to the text of John 1:4 is significant: 'Quicquid in Deo est, Deus est; sed in Deo sunt omnia, quia "quod factum est in ipso vita erat"; ergo Deus est omnia' (from the *Contra Amaurianos*); the condemnation of 1210 had already repeated: 'Omnia unum, quia quicquid est, est Deus' (*ibid.* p. 89); the connection with the Eriugenian tradition is clearly indicated by Henry of Suse (*Ostiensis*): 'dogma istud colligitur in libro magistri Johannis Scoti qui dicitur periphision, idest de natura, quem secutus est iste Amalricus' (*ibid.* p. 94), who also condemns the doctrine of the *primordiales cause que vocantur idee* inferior to God (*creant et creantur*), because it is against the 'Saints' ('cum tamen secundum sanctos, idem sint quod Deus in quantum sunt in Deo': p. 94); cf. also the testimony of Martin of Poland, *ibid.* p. 105.

70 *Davidis de Dinanto Quaternulorum fragmenta*, ed. M. Kurdziałek, *Studia Mediewistyczne* III (1963) 70–1; in the *Chronica* by the anonymous author of Laon we read: 'Erat enim idem

on the other to exalt the absolute transcendance of the ineffable one: 'unity had no beginning: simple, intact, solitary, permanent of itself in itself, illimitable and eternal. Unity is God.'[71] Thus, in the same texts where the greatest stress is laid on the immanence of the one, and the theme of God as form of being or form of forms dominates, his absolute transcendence and ineffability are exalted at the same time: that God who is the 'being of all things' manifests his radical alienness to the multiple, and becomes the ineffable principle which 'is not being'; in the *Lectiones* on Boethius' *De Trinitate* which are attributed to Thierry, God, 'the essence itself or entity of all things', the unity in which all forms are one form ('many exemplars of things which are all one exemplar in the divine mind'), is negatively defined as 'neither substance nor accident', 'not a being', because he is 'above all substance and above all accident'.[72] The theme – which recurs in all the writings of the school of Thierry – is Dionysian and Eriugenian, as is attested by its unequivocal terminology: but what is important here is to point out the constant effort to trace that theme back to a Platonic matrix, juxtaposing with the *auctoritas* of Dionysius and Augustine the *Timaeus* and the *Asclepius*, almost the extreme terms of a single identical tradition, points of reference and meeting-places between Platonism and Christianity. Thus the author of the *Glosa* on Boethius, in a text permeated with Dionysian elements, develops his whole exposition of divine ineffability by starting from a passage of Calcidius ('God ... is neither *genus* nor subject to any *genus*') – which recalls, via the Middle Platonist Albinus, a passage of the *Republic* which is of prime importance for the development of Neoplatonism, and particularly dear to Proclus[73] – and concludes it with a famous quotation from the *Asclepius* about the names of God, emblematically sketching the story of an idea from Plato to its last developments in Hellenistic Neoplatonism:

David subtilis ultra quam deceret, ex cujus quaternis, ut creditur, magister Almaricus et caeteri haeretici hujus temporis suum hauserunt errorem' (Capelle 1932, p. 98). On David see also Chapter 16 below.

71 Bernardus 1978, II 13, p. 146.

72 Thierry, *Lectiones* II 56, IV 27, II 66, IV 10, IV 27 (Häring 1971, pp. 173, 195, 176, 189, 195); cf. Clarembaldi *Expositio super librum Boethii 'De hebdomadibus'* II 19, pp. 200–1.

73 Calcidius 1962, 319, p. 315 (the reference to Albinus is in the apparatus); cf. Plato, *Respublica* VI, 509B (and cf. *Parmenides* 142A): this passage is mentioned by Proclus in conjunction with the *Timaeus* in his commentary on the *Parmenides*, which was to be translated in the thirteenth century by William of Moerbeke; cf. *Parmenides [. . .] nec non Procli Commentarium in Parmenidem*, ed. R. Klibansky and C. Labowsky (London 1953), pp. 21, 28. Note the words of Johannes Scotus, following pseudo-Dionysius, in a passage transcribed by Honorius of Autun, in Honorius 1974, p. 78: 'neque genus neque forma neque species neque numerus neque usia' (cf. P.L. 122, 589A).

... but God is neither a general nor a special nor an individual substance, nor a universal nor a particular accident ... and therefore can neither be predicated nor made a subject. Therefore he is neither a *genus* nor subordinated to a *genus*, nor is he a species nor subordinated to a species, nor is he an individual nor an accident ... And thus he cannot be signified by any name ... From this it is similarly clear that God is not comprehended by the intellect: for all understanding is possessed concerning a general or special or individual substance or concerning a universal or particular accident. But God is neither substance nor accident but is *yperiesiosis*, that is, above all substance and above all accident. Therefore no understanding can be possessed concerning God. Moreover, the fact that no name can signify God is attested by Mercury in the book entitled *Trismegister*, where he says that if God had a name it would signify all things which other words signify. For God is all things, that is, the entirety of things woven together into a kind of simplicity; which entirety no word can signify ... This is why Trismegister says that either God has no name or, if he has a name, it must be all names.[74]

The insistence with which twelfth-century Platonism returns to the *Timaeus* to find in it the matrix of all later theological speculation recalls an analogous development in Hellenistic religious speculation, which saw Plato as the divinely inspired master: apart from the continual comparisons of the Timaean Genesis with the Mosaic Genesis, even more significant seems the adoption of certain passages of the Platonic dialogue as points of reference for the discussion on the divine names, on the ineffability of the one, and on learned ignorance: even William of Conches, who does not get involved in the subtle speculations of the school of Thierry, cannot resist interpreting the Platonic theology as an apophatic theology, developing a hint from Macrobius ('Thus Plato, when he was of a mind to talk about the good, did not dare to say what it is, since the only thing he knew about it was that its nature cannot be known by man') and leading it back to the high road marked out by Augustine: 'whence it is said, "learned ignorance is not to know what God is" '[75]; while another well-known passage of the *Timaeus* ('understanding

74 Thierry, *Lectiones* IV 9–11 (Häring 1971, pp. 189–90); Calcidius' name is explicitly mentioned in Thierry, *Glosa* IV 14 (Häring 1971, p. 287), and also in the so-called *Fragmentum Londinense* (Häring 1971, p. 243), with the same reference to Trismegistus (*Asclepius* 1945, 20, p. 321). The same combination of *auctoritates* occurs in other texts from the school of Thierry, such as the *Abbreviatio Monacensis* 10–11 (Häring 1971, p. 367), and later in the *Summa 'Quoniam homines'* by Alan of Lille (ed. P. Glorieux, *AHDLMA* xx (1953) 139–40; cf. also pp. 123, 135). The *Asclepius* passage was later taken up by Nicolas Cusanus, *De docta ignorantia* I 24. The term *yperiesiosis* recurs also in Thierry, *Glosa* IV 16, Häring 1971, p. 288 ('Cum ergo dico *Deus* est *substantia* immo quid ipse non sit. Atque ex hoc relinquo subintelligendum quid ipse sit scilicet substantia supra substantiam quod grece *yperusyon* dicitur'). *Superessentialis* as an attribute of God also appears in Bernardus 1978, p. 127 (the editor points out the Eriugenian origin, p. 29).

75 The text is published by Dronke 1974, p. 73 (for Macrobius, see Macrobius 1963, I 2 15, p. 7); cf. also William's commentary on another important passage of the *Timaeus* (28c: 'igitur opificem genitorem universitatis tam invenire difficile quam inventum digne

is peculiar to God and to a very few chosen human beings') is adopted by the author of the *Glosa super Boethium de Trinitate* as a premise to the extreme development of unitive contemplation, as was indicated by Trismegistus ('and becomes God, according to Mercury'), indicating a historically verifiable link.[76]

Along with the *Timaeus*, the insistence on the name of Trismegistus is equally significant: in the *Asclepius* the Platonists of the twelfth century saw a compendium of Platonic speculation in complete harmony with the Christian tradition: concerning the theme of God as 'non-being' and that of ineffability, the author of the *Glosa* juxtaposes Augustine and Dionysius, Victorinus and Hilarius, Calcidius and Isidore of Seville, finding, finally, in Trismegistus the confirmation of Paul's speech on the Areopagus:

And all this is attested by Mercury in the book entitled *Trismegistrus* (*sic*). It is for this reason, too, that the pagan philosophers set up an altar to 'the Unknown God', in expectation of him whose identity cannot be known.[77]

It was to Trismegistus again that an anonymous text of the late twelfth century was attributed, the *Liber XXIV philosophorum*, where certain themes of medieval Neoplatonism are fixed in formulas which were to enjoy an extremely wide diffusion: the definition of God as a monad that is explicated in the trinitarian relationship ('God is a monad begetting a monad in itself reflecting its own ardour'), as 'infinite sphere whose centre is everywhere and whose circumference is nowhere', which creates 'through the overflowing of its goodness', which in itself is 'beyond being' because – as Eckhart was to repeat later – 'every . . . being declares the closing of some finitude'; hence he is unattainable except by the way of negation and ignorance, in darkness: 'God is he who is really known only through ignorance'; 'And this

profari'): 'Probato aliquem autorem mundi esse, subiungit quis sit scilicet ille qui nec digne potest inveniri nec digne demonstrari. Et hec est bona Creatoris diffinitio' (Guillaume 1965, p. 109); the *Timaeus* passage enjoyed a significant diffusion: see, for example, Hermann 1982, p. 80; John of Salisbury, *Policraticus* VII 5 (Webb 1909, p. 109); Peter of Celle, *Ep.* 166 (P.L. 202, 508); Alan of Lille 1953, p. 139. The author of the *Compendium philosophiae* also evokes Plato in a perspective of negative theology: 'maxima namque cognitio de ipso est scire quid non sit: unde Plato solummodo solem simillimum deo repperit' (*Compendium* 1935, p. 38).

76 Thierry, *Glosa* II 9–10 (Häring 1971, p. 270):
    'Ac deinde se extendens usque ad universarum rerum simplicem universitatem fit intelligibilitas que solius dei est et admodum paucorum hominum [. . .]. At vero cum ad simplicem universitatem unionum vix aspirat quantum tamen potest suspendit animum in intelligibilitatem erectum profecto se ipso supra se utitur fitque etiam iuxta Mercurium deus.'
    Cf. *Asclepius* 1945, p. 303.

77 Thierry, *Glosa* IV 11 (Häring 1971, p. 286); *Asclepius* 1945, 20, p. 321; *Acta Ap.* 17, 23.

is true ignorance, namely, knowing what is not, while not knowing what
is.'[78]

If in the twelfth century the theme of negative theology – with the whole
complex of Proclian elements handed down by pseudo-Dionysius – found
its most fertile terrain in the Platonism nourished on the reading of the
Timaeus and Boethius, together with influences from John Scotus Eriugena,
whose diffusion is attested by the *Clavis physicae*, it was to undergo more
complex developments after the translations – in the second half of the thirteenth century – of the writings of Proclus, preceded towards the end of the
twelfth by the *Liber de causis*. But with this very work, as with the translations of the Arab Platonists, in particular Avicenna, it is possible to
discern the establishment of a Christian Neoplatonism in which the Dionysian themes of the 'hierarchy' and the superessential God are absorbed into
a system of processions, according to a scale of intermediaries much more
complex than that of the Platonism of Chartres, Gundissalinus and the
pseudo-Hermetic texts. An emblematic case, at the beginning of the thirteenth century, is the *Liber de causis primis et secundis*: here, around themes
either Dionysian ('in the beginning of beginnings the glorious and exalted
God, whose entity is ineffable and whose unity is indivisible') or Eriugenian ('exemplars of things not entirely coeternal'), or Boethian (according
to the axiom 'what is, is because it is designated as one'), with a skilful
juxtaposition of texts often transcribed word for word from Augustine and
John Scotus Eriugena, Avicenna and the *Liber de causis*, a procession of the
multiple from the one is evolved according to a succession of levels, from
the first cause 'above all reason and intellect', to the first intelligence ('the
first of the creatures, therefore, is intellectual, and is intelligence') from
which the multiple proceeds according to successive intellectual acts
('therefore intelligence understands itself, so that there proceed from it
those things over which it holds its command'), through which are formed
the intelligences, the souls, the heavens, and finally the agent intellect
('until the agent intelligence is reached, which is active upon our souls').
This is the light of the human intellect, which is conjoined to it ('so that
according to the quantity of its light it may receive form from the agent
intelligence, in which there is a multitude of forms, and through its recep-

78 The text of the *Liber XXIV philosophorum* was edited by C. Baeumker and included in
   vol. xxv.1–2 of *Beiträge zur Geschichte der Philosophie des Mittelalters*, ed. M. Grabmann
   (1927) 194–214; for the quoted passages see pp. 208, 210–11, 213–14. For the history of the
   MSS, see M.-T. d'Alverny, 'Liber xxiv Philosophorum', in *Catalogus Translationum et
   Commentariorum* I: 'Hermetica Philosophica' (Washington, 1960) 151–4; see also Alan of
   Lille's *Sermo de sphaera intelligibili*, in Alan of Lille 1965, pp. 163–80, 297–306.

tion begin to be in effect, whereas previously it had only been in potentiality').[79]

The juxtaposition of new authorities with the ancient ones, and the prevalence of themes drawn from Arab Neoplatonism, in particular from Avicenna, indicate the new cultural horizon which was opening up for the Latin West; soon even the Platonic physics – the *Timaeus* was still read in the schools in the early decades of the thirteenth century – would be replaced by the more organic Aristotelian science.

79 The *Liber de causis primis et secundis* is in R. De Vaux, *Notes et textes sur l'avicennisme latin aux confins des XIIe–XIIIe siècles* (Paris 1934), pp. 88–140; for the passages quoted see pp. 88, 92, 88–9, 98, 100, 102, 130. Attention was drawn to the particular significance of the work by E. Gilson, 'Les sources gréco-arabes de l'augustinisme avicennisant', *AHDLMA* iv (1929) 5–149, esp. pp. 92–102, 142–9; M.-T. d'Alverny, 'Une rencontre symbolique de Jean Scot et Avicenne', in *The Mind of Eriugena*, ed. J. J. O'Meara and L. Bieler (Dublin 1973), pp. 170–9; H. Corbin, *Avicenna and the Visionary Recital*, trans. W. Trask (London 1960), pp. 101–22.

3

THE STOIC INHERITANCE

MICHAEL LAPIDGE

From the third century BC until approximately the third century AD, Stoicism was the principal philosophy of the Graeco-Roman world.[1] Within the Roman sphere its position was even more prestigious than in Greece, in the sense that it could number among its proponents some extremely eminent statesmen: the younger Seneca,[2] sometime adviser to the Emperor Nero, and the Emperor Marcus Aurelius himself.[3] Stoicism was a system of compelling originality and coherence,[4] marked by striking and characteristic doctrines: that, for the wise man, pleasure and pain (to say nothing of riches and reputation) were matters of indifference, as was death itself (hence, for the Stoic sage, suicide was in some cases a commendable option); that the wise man was to live in accord with nature, which was defined as an all-pervasive divine and fiery spirit that penetrated, animated, and unified the universe, and periodically consumed it. Thus nature, the universe itself, and the godhead were regarded as one and identical, and were conceived of as material. As this spirit penetrated the universe spatially, so it had temporal extension, which linked all events together in an inexorable chain of fate, which it was the wise man's obligation to contemplate and understand, but which he was powerless to alter or control.

These doctrines were first enunciated in outline by the founder of

---

1 The best general account of Stoicism is M. Pohlenz, *Die Stoa. Geschichte einer geistigen Bewegung* (4th ed., 2 vols., Göttingen 1970). There is no general treatment in English on the scale of Pohlenz's work, but see the concise and penetrating study by F. H. Sandbach, *The Stoics* (London 1975), as well as J. M. Rist, *Stoic Philosophy* (Cambridge 1969), which treats certain philosophical problems in depth rather than trying to give an overall account; individual themes and problems are also treated in two collaborative volumes: *Problems in Stoicism*, ed. A. A. Long (London 1971), and *The Stoics*, ed. J. M. Rist (Berkeley–Los Angeles–London 1978). A. A. Long and D. N. Sedley, *The Hellenistic Philosophers* (Cambridge 1987), contains excellent discussion of most aspects of Stoicism (with texts) and includes a comprehensive bibliography.
2 See M. T. Griffin, *Seneca: A Philosopher in Politics* (Oxford 1976).
3 There is no detailed, full-length study of the Stoicism of Marcus Aurelius; but see H. R. Neuenschwander, *Marc Aurels Beziehungen zu Seneca und Poseidonios* (Bern 1951).
4 See J. Christensen, *An Essay on the Unity of Stoic Philosophy* (Copenhagen 1962).

Stoicism, Zeno of Citium[5] (332–262 BC), and elaborated by his two successors, Cleanthes[6] (*ca.* 330–232 BC) and Chrysippus[7] (*ca.* 280–208/204 BC).
These three philosophers and their immediate followers are known col-
lectively as the 'Old Stoa'; it would seem that the most powerful and original
mind among them was that of Chrysippus, who established Stoic logic as an
effective working tool and who refashioned the theories of his predecessors –
still preserving their outlines – into a consistent and coherent whole, such
that when in antiquity a Stoic notion was attacked, it was invariably the
theories of Chrysippus that were cited. By the first century BC Stoicism had
begun to undergo modification and re-elaboration: many of the founders'
theories were rejected and new directions attempted. This period is referred
to as the 'Middle Stoa'; its principal proponents were Panaetius[8] and
Posidonius.[9] By then Roman government had established itself throughout
the Mediterranean. Stoicism moved to Rome, and the final (and least
creative) phase was Roman.[10] In this final phase, Stoicism experienced the
influence of the Romans' concern with practicality: theoretical pursuits such
as logic and cosmology were abandoned, and Stoic philosophers now
directed their entire attention to questions of how a wise man should live. As
moral preceptors the Roman Stoics – Epictetus,[11] Musonius Rufus,[12] Marcus
Aurelius – make engaging reading even today, but less for the originality
than for the utility of their utterances.

All these Stoics wrote in Greek. For the Latin Middle Ages, up to and
including most of the twelfth century, Greek was simply inaccessible.[13] It
was the possession of a tiny number of scholars (among them John Scotus

---

5 A. Graeser, *Zenon von Kition: Positionen und Probleme* (Berlin–New York 1975); but see also
   the assessment of this book by J. Mansfeld, 'Zeno of Citium. Critical Observations on a
   Recent Study', *Mnemosyne* XXXI (1978) 134–78.
6 G. Verbeke, *Kleanthes van Assos* (Brussels 1949).
7 J. B. Gould, *The Philosophy of Chrysippus* (Leiden 1971).
8 M. van Straaten, *Panétius, sa vie, ses écrits et sa doctrine* (Amsterdam–Paris 1946); B. N.
   Tatakis, *Panétius de Rhodes* (Paris 1951).
9 K. Reinhardt, *Poseidonios* (Munich 1921); *Kosmos und Sympathie. Neue Untersuchungen über
   Poseidonios* (Munich 1926); in Pauly–Wissowa, *Realencyclopädie* XXII. 1 (1953), 558–826, *s.v.*
   'Poseidonios'; L. Edelstein, 'The Philosophical System of Posidonius', *American Journal of
   Philology* LVII (1936) 286–325; and M. Laffranque, *Poseidonios d'Apamée: Essai de mise au point*
   (Paris 1964); see also below, n. 18.
10 For a general account see E. V. Arnold, *Roman Stoicism* (Cambridge 1911), though this is
   much dated; see now the valuable study by M. Colish, *The Stoic Tradition from Antiquity to
   the Early Middle Ages* (2 vols., Leiden 1985), esp. vol. 1 ('Stoicism in Classical Literature');
   also useful are V. d'Agostino, *Studi sul Neostoicismo* (2nd ed., Turin 1962) and A. Bodson, *La
   morale sociale des derniers stoïciens, Sénèque, Epictète et Marc-Aurèle* (Paris 1967).
11 A. Bonhöffer, *Epiktet und die Stoa* (Stuttgart 1890) and *Die Ethik des Stoikers Epiktet*
   (Stuttgart 1894). Both these books are still valuable.
12 A. C. van Geytenbeek, *Musonius Rufus and the Greek Diatribe* (Assen 1963).
13 See W. Berschin, *Griechisch-lateinisches Mittelalter* (Bern–Munich 1980), esp. pp. 113–243.

Eriugena); and in cases where it was known and studied, this study was directed to texts such as the Septuagint Psalter and the Christian writings of pseudo-Dionysius, not to Epictetus and Marcus Aurelius. Stoic philosophers, in other words, were not – and could not be – known at first hand. But this situation was compounded by another aspect of the transmission of Stoic texts. From the third to the sixth century AD, the prevalent philosophies and theologies were idealist and transcendental: Platonism, Neoplatonism, Christianity. Stoicism, with its unyielding insistence on the material and corporeal nature of the godhead, went awkwardly against the grain. The result was that Stoic texts – especially those of the Old and Middle Stoa – ceased to be read and copied. Thus the writings of the great early Stoics did not survive the fall of the Roman Empire, and they have not come down to us in their original form (with the exception of the occasional papyrus fragment). The scale of this loss is devastating. Chrysippus is known to have written over 700 books, yet not a single one of these books has survived. Accordingly, if we wish today to study the Old and Middle Stoa, we are obliged to piece together fragments of the Stoics' utterances which survive as quotations in their (frequently hostile) critics,[14] or to reconstruct as best we can the reasoning which may have underlain the bald résumés of Stoic doctrine preserved in the Greek doxographers.[15] The Old Stoa today is studied in a collection of fragments (seldom longer than two or three sentences),[16] and similar collections have been made for Panaetius[17] and Posidonius.[18] Given this situation, it is simply out of the question that a twelfth-century philosopher would have had the resources or the knowledge of Greek to make for himself a similar collection. This is tantamount to saying that no twelfth-century thinker had – or could have had – first-hand knowledge of Stoic doctrine.

This is not to say, however, that Stoic doctrines were unknown during the twelfth century. Certain Latin writers whose works were read in the twelfth century record various aspects of Stoic teaching, though they characteristically omit the reasoning which lay behind this teaching. Cicero, though not himself a Stoic, discusses Stoic doctrine on numerous occa-

---

14 Especially Plutarch, Alexander of Aphrodisias, and Sextus Empiricus.
15 H. Diels, *Doxographi Graeci* (Berlin 1879).
16 *Stoicorum Veterum Fragmenta*, ed. H. von Arnim (3 vols., Leipzig 1903–5), with a fourth volume of indices by M. Adler (Leipzig 1925) (hereafter *SVF*). Still useful for its commentary is A. C. Pearson, *The Fragments of Zeno and Cleanthes* (London 1891).
17 M. van Straaten, *Panaetii Rhodii Fragmenta* (2nd ed., Leiden 1962).
18 *Posidonius I: The Fragments*, ed. L. Edelstein and I. G. Kidd (Cambridge 1972); see also W. Theiler, *Poseidonios: Die Fragmente* (2 vols., Berlin–New York 1982).

sions.[19] Seneca, who considered himself a Stoic, occasionally reproduces Stoic ethical doctrine (he was quite uninterested in logic and physics).[20] Similarly, early Christian authors often transmit doctrines that are Stoic in origin.[21] It need hardly be stressed that the central tenet of Stoicism, that of a corporeal godhead penetrating the universe and identical with it, would have been utterly rebarbative to a Christian theologian; but the Stoic *logos* behaved in ways similar to the Christian *logos* or Word, and it is not surprising that Stoic terminology and metaphors pertaining to the Stoic *logos* were adopted by Christian theologians. And Christian moralists found much that was acceptable and commendable in Stoic ethics. When twelfth-century thinkers studied Patristic authors, therefore, they may often unwittingly have been imbibing Stoic doctrine. But to speak of Stoic *influence* on twelfth-century thought is to misrepresent the case; rightly and judiciously has a scholar recently chosen to speak of the 'presence' of Stoicism in medieval thought.[22] In the following pages I shall attempt to indicate where and how this 'presence' was felt, without implying at any point that it was a decisive presence.

The Stoics divided the field of their philosophical enquiry into three: logic, ethics, and physics.[23] It will be convenient to consider the presence of Stoic doctrine in twelfth-century thought under these three headings. In each case I shall outline briefly the Stoic doctrine as known from Greek sources; then the principal Latin texts which preserve this doctrine and their transmission in twelfth-century Europe; and finally the presence of the Stoic doctrine purveyed by these Latin texts in twelfth-century philosophy.

19 See in general the remarks of von Arnim, *SVF* I xix–xxx, as well as R. Hirzel, *Untersuchungen zu Ciceros philosophischen Schriften* (3 vols. in 4, Leipzig 1877–83), esp. I 191–244 (*De natura deorum*) and II (*De finibus* and *De officiis*); W. Süss, *Cicero: Eine Einführung in seine philosophischen Schriften (mit Ausschluss der staatsphilosophischen Werke)*, Akademie der Wissenschaften und der Literatur (Mainz): Abhandlungen der geistes- und sozialwissenschaftlichen Klasse 1965 (Wiesbaden 1966), no. 5; and W. Görler, *Untersuchungen zu Ciceros Philosophie* (Heidelberg 1974).

20 P. Grimal, *Sénèque, sa vie, son oeuvre, avec un exposé de sa philosophie* (3rd ed., Paris 1966). There is a convenient digest of Seneca's Stoic doctrine: H. B. Timothy, *The Tenets of Stoicism assembled and systematized from the Works of L. Annaeus Seneca* (Amsterdam 1973).

21 There is an excellent study of Stoicism in the earlier Patristic authors by M. Spanneut, *Le Stoïcisme des pères de l'église de Clément de Rome à Clément d'Alexandrie* (2nd ed., Paris 1969); for the later Patristic period see now Colish 1985, vol. II 'Stoicism in Christian Latin Thought through the Sixth Century'.

22 G. Verbeke, *The Presence of Stoicism in Medieval Thought* (Washington 1983); useful, too, is M. Spanneut, *Permanence du Stoïcisme de Zénon à Malraux* (Gembloux 1973), pp. 179–209. There is also a briefer sketch by G. Verbeke, 'L'influence du Stoïcisme sur la pensée médiévale en occident', in *Actas del V Congreso internacional de filosofia medieval* (2 vols., Madrid 1979) I 95–109.

23 *SVF* II 35–44.

Logic

Very little needs to be said concerning the presence of Stoic logic in the twelfth century, for it was virtually unknown at that time; indeed it is only during the past fifty years that the originality and coherence of Stoic logic has been realized.[24] From late antiquity onwards, and especially during the twelfth century, Aristotelian logic (as set out in the *Organon* and elucidated by various late Latin commentators, especially Boethius) held sway.[25] The principal concern of Aristotelian logic was with universal terms, and its characteristic expression was in the form of the categorical syllogism which linked these terms: 'if all A is B, and all B is C, then all A is C.'[26] Although the Stoics appear to have been familiar with term logic, they apparently thought that propositional logic was more fundamental.[27] Accordingly, the Stoics formulated 'propositions' (ἀξιώματα), which could be either true or false; an argument, in their view, was a system of propositions set out in various forms (σχήματα).[28] Stoic syllogisms are referred to as 'inference schemata', and characteristically take the following form (the Stoics used ordinal numbers in lieu of Aristotle's letters): 'if the first, then the second; the first; therefore the second'.

It will be clear that the variables here must be propositions, not universal terms. Consider the following argument: 'if it is day, then it is light; it is day; therefore it is light.' The Stoics (in fact Chrysippus) identified five types of inference schemata the validity of which is so obvious that they need not be demonstrated (hence these five schemata are called 'undemonstrated', ἀνα-πόδεικτα);[29] the example just given is a Type I undemonstrated argument. The variables in Stoic inference schemata, then, are propositions; the constants[30] include the 'conditional' (συνημμένον) – in the above example, the connective 'if'. In a conditional, the first clause is the antecedent (ἡγούμενον:

---

24 See especially the following: J. Mau, 'Stoische Logik', *Hermes* LXXXV (1957) 147–85; B. Mates, *Stoic Logic* (2nd ed., Berkeley–Los Angeles 1961); W. and M. Kneale, *The Development of Logic* (Oxford 1962), pp. 113–76; I. Mueller, 'Stoic and Peripatetic Logic', *Archiv für Geschichte der Philosophie* LI (1969) 173–87; 'An Introduction to Stoic Logic', in Rist (ed.) 1978, pp. 1–26; M. Frede, *Die stoische Logik* (Göttingen 1974), and *Les stoïciens et leur logique*, ed. J. Brunschwig (Paris 1978). Mates 1961, pp. 95–131, provides convenient translations of all the ancient testimonies to Stoic logic.
25 In general see A. Van de Vyver, 'Les étapes du développement philosophique du haut moyen âge', *Revue Belge de Philologie* VIII (1929) 425–52, and S. Ebbesen in *CHLMP*, pp. 101–27.
26 See, *inter alia*, J. Łukasiewicz, *Aristotle's Syllogistic* (2nd ed., Oxford 1957), esp. pp. 1–12.
27 See Mates 1961, pp. 11–19.
28 *SVF* II 193–206.
29 *Ibid.* p. 242; see Mates 1961, pp. 67–74.
30 See Mates 1961, pp. 42–57, and Mueller in Rist (ed.) 1978, pp. 8–10.

'if it is day'), the second the consequent (λῆγον: 'it is light'). Two further constants are the 'conjunction' (συμπεπλεγμένον: 'it is day *and* it is light') and the 'disjunction' (διεζευγμένον: 'either it is day or it is light'). A final constant is 'negation' (ἀποφατικόν): here the Stoics made the important and original observation that, to negate a statement properly, the negation sign must be prefixed to it (hence in order properly to negate the statement 'it is day and it is night', one must say, 'not both: it is day and it is night', rather than 'it is not day and it is not night').[31] It may be seen even from this brief summary that the Stoics had worked out a very detailed vocabulary for describing the variables and constants of their hypothetical syllogisms, and that their propositional logic has a thoroughness and coherency of its own: it is a carefully worked-out and workable system.

It is interesting but pointless to speculate on what impact Stoic propositional logic might have had, say, on the twelfth-century debate concerning universals, for the Stoics had developed a viable logic which apparently avoided universal terms ('all x is y . . .') altogether. But in fact Stoic logic was then unknown; its outlines have been reconstructed by modern scholars largely from the Greek writings of Sextus Empiricus and Alexander of Aphrodisias. To the Latin West all that was known of Stoic logic was some few snippets in various authors, not enough to form a coherent notion of the whole system. Cicero in his fragmentary *De fato* includes some discussion of Chrysippus' theory of 'propositions' (ἀξιώματα) and of future contingents (x 20–1). In his *Topica* he discusses seven types of 'undemonstrated' argument (§§54–7), but in so doing reveals his misunderstanding of the system. *De fato* and the *Topica* circulated in the twelfth century as part of the so-called 'Leiden corpus' of Cicero's *philosophica*, but had no apparent effect. Seneca at one point (*Epist. ad Lucilium* CXVII 13) gives a cursory explanation of the Stoic distinction between the sound and meaning of words and the thing signified, but no medieval reader of the brief passage could possibly have divined how the Stoics derived from this distinction their propositional logic.

Somewhat more information about Stoic logic could have been derived from the *Peri hermeneias* ascribed to Apuleius.[32] This brief work, probably the earliest surviving Latin work devoted exclusively to logic and covering some of the ground covered by Aristotle's treatise of the same name, is concerned with the logic of propositions. The first part (§§1–4) presents an analysis of the proposition; this is followed by discussion of opposition,

---

31 Mates 1961, p. 31.
32 *Apulei Platonici Madaurensis Opera III: De Philosophia Libri*, ed. P. Thomas (Leipzig 1908), pp. 176–94.

equivalence and conversion of propositions (§§5–6), and the remainder of the work treats categorical syllogisms. Throughout the work Apuleius is concerned to criticize Stoic logic, and it therefore contains (for example) some account of the Stoics' 'undemonstrated' arguments and of the negation of sentences.[33] Although there are few surviving manuscripts, Apuleius' *Peri hermeneias* was evidently studied during the twelfth century, for it is listed (alongside Aristotle and Boethius) as a textbook on logic in Thierry of Chartres's *Heptateuchon* and in John of Salisbury's *Metalogicon*;[34] and according to the testimony of Alexander Nequam it was still in use at the school of Petit-Pont in Paris in the last quarter of the twelfth century.[35] An attentive twelfth-century reader could possibly have formed some (albeit incomplete) notion of Stoic logic from Apuleius, and a similar notion could have been derived from Book IV of Martianus Capella, *De nuptiis Philologiae et Mercurii*.[36] Martianus' discussion is based principally on Aristotle's *Categories* and *Prior Analytics* as well as on Apuleius's *Peri hermeneias*. However, after discussing Aristotle's categorical syllogism at length, Martianus turns near the end of Book IV to a consideration of the hypothetical syllogism (§§414–20). The fact that in his examples he uses ordinal numbers rather than letters indicates that his source is a Stoic one as yet unidentified. There are other traces of Stoic logic in his discussion, for example the formation of the negative of a statement by prefixing the negative to the entire statement, not merely to the verb (§402). Although by the twelfth century the period of Martianus' greatest ascendancy as a curriculum-text had passed, the substantial number of twelfth-century manuscripts of the *De nuptiis* indicates that it was still being read.

From the foregoing discussion it is clear that no twelfth-century logician could have formed a complete, or even adequate, notion of Stoic logic; at the most he could have known of the Stoic inference schemata (but without understanding their rationale). It is not surprising, then, that there is virtually no trace of Stoic logic in the twelfth century; indeed it is noteworthy that in his *Metalogicon* John of Salisbury states that logic was invented in order to dissipate the obscure fallacies of the Stoics (such as the notion that

---

33 See M. W. Sullivan, *Apuleian Logic: The Nature, Sources and Influence of Apuleius's Peri Hermeneias* (Amsterdam 1967), pp. 157–65.

34 John of Salisbury, *Metalogicon* II 16 and III 6 (ed. C. C. J. Webb, *Ioannis Saresberiensis Episcopi Carnotensis Metalogicon* (Oxford 1929), pp. 90 and 144 respectively). Thierry's *Heptateuchon* is unprinted; but see Sullivan 1967, pp. 204–5.

35 C. H. Haskins, *Studies in the History of Mediaeval Science* (2nd ed., Cambridge MA 1927), p. 373.

36 See W. H. Stahl, R. Johnson, and E. L. Burge, *Martianus Capella and the Seven Liberal Arts* (2 vols., New York–London 1971–7) I 108–10.

matter is coeternal with God).[37] There are some general similarities between Abelard's theory of 'consequences' (*consequentiae*) and the consequence (λῆγον) of the Stoic proposition, but there is no evidence of any direct influence.[38] It is probably symptomatic that, when discussing hypothetical arguments, Abelard follows Boethius closely; but where Boethius briefly treats Cicero's account of the Stoic inference schemata (*Topica* §§54–7), Abelard passes over Boethius' treatment in silence.[39] At one point in his *Dialectica* Abelard explains the difference of sense which results from placing the negative particle before the whole proposition, rather than before the verb, as for example between 'non quidam homo est iustus' and 'quidam homo non est iustus';[40] a similar distinction was maintained by Stoic logicians in their treatment of negation (ἀποφατικόν), and Abelard could have derived it from Martianus Capella, but he could equally well have arrived at it independently.[41] The same appears to be true of other twelfth-century logicians. In his *Ars disserendi*, Adam ('Parvipontanus') of Balsham quotes *Stoici* when discussing his ten disjunctive forms of statement (§133).[42] But he is simply quoting a sentence from Cicero's *De natura deorum* as an example of a disjunctive statement, and there is no evidence here that Adam was familiar with the Stoic treatment of disjunction (διεζευγμένον). That Abelard and Adam both remained impervious to (or unaware of) the possibilities of Stoic propositional logic is the clearest indication that Stoic logic exerted no influence in the twelfth century.

Ethics

The Romans were very much interested in Stoic ethics (unlike logic and physics, for which they manifested little or no interest). The result is that there exist in Latin several extensive treatments of Stoic ethics, principally in the writings of Cicero and Seneca, and these writings were widely accessible to twelfth-century thinkers. Similarly, many Stoic ethical doctrines – for example that virtue is the highest good – could easily be assimilated to Christian theology, with the result that the Stoic writings of Cicero, and especially Seneca, were most welcome to twelfth-century theologians. But

37 *Metalogicon* II 2 (ed. Webb 1929, p. 62).
38 See Kneale and Kneale 1962, pp. 219–20, and E. Stump in *CHLMP*, p. 303 n. 9.
39 *Petrus Abaelardus: Dialectica*, ed. L. M. de Rijk (2nd ed., Assen 1970), p. 515; Neale and Neale 1962, p. 222.
40 *Petrus Abaelardus* 1970, p. 178.
41 Thus Kneale and Kneale 1962, p. 210.
42 L. Minio-Paluello, *Twelfth-century Logic. Texts and Studies I: Adam Balsamiensis Parvipontani Ars Disserendi (Dialectica Alexandri)* (Rome 1956), p. 85.

the adaptability of Stoic ethics to Christian theology brings problems in its train, for many Patristic authors from Tertullian onwards had thoroughly assimilated Stoic ethical teaching.[43] To take one obvious example: Ambrose in his *De officiis* reproduced closely the *De officiis* of Cicero.[44] The problem for historians of twelfth-century thought is that of disentangling Stoic doctrine received directly from Cicero and Seneca from that received indirectly by way of Patristic authors. In what follows I shall be principally concerned to sketch the direct influence, through Cicero and Seneca, of Stoic ethics on twelfth-century thought.

The Stoic system of ethics was one of remarkable cogency and even boldness.[45] The early Stoics, especially Chrysippus, did not shrink from pushing simple premises to logical (and sometimes unpalatable) conclusions, and enjoyed creating paradoxes which would display their ethical doctrines in a daring and compelling light. For the Stoic wise man – and the Stoics were only concerned with the wise man, or the man striving to become one – the principal activity was the pursuit of moral excellence or 'virtue' (ἀρετή). Virtue was absolute moral perfection and hence equivalent to 'the good' (ἀγαθόν).[46] And everything that was not good was, so to speak, 'bad' (κακόν); hence the Stoics' notorious paradox that all sins are equal.[47] To the wise man, however, all things not pertinent to moral perfection were 'indifferent' (ἀδιάφορα), and these 'indifferents' included all those things normally prized by the man in the street: fame, wealth, honour, long life, to say nothing of fine food and clothing.[48] Such things were not the concern of the wise man; and those who concerned themselves with such things were not wise and thus were, so to speak, fools: another Stoic paradox.

How was the wise man to pursue moral perfection? The central tenet of

43 Spanneut 1969, pp. 231–65; Spanneut 1973, pp. 161–76; Colish 1985, vol. II.
44 See T. Schmidt, *Ambrosius. Sein Werk De officiis libri tres und die Stoa* (Erlangen 1897).
45 There is a clear and valuable introductory account in Sandbach 1975, pp. 28–68; see also Pohlenz 1970, I 111–58, as well as the following individual studies: A. Dyroff, *Die Ethik der alten Stoa* (Berlin 1897); O. Rieth, *Grundbegriffe der stoischen Ethik* (Berlin 1933); L. Labowsky, *Die Ethik des Panaitios* (Leipzig 1934); G. Nebel, 'Zur Ethik des Poseidonios', *Hermes* LXXIV (1939) 34–57; B. L. Hijmans, 'Posidonius' Ethics', *Acta Classica* II (1959) 27–42; N. P. White, 'The Basis of Stoic Ethics', *Harvard Studies in Classical Philology* LXXXIII (1979) 143–78; and especially M. Forschner, *Die stoische Ethik. Über den Zusammenhang von Natur-, Sprach- und Moralphilosophie im altstoischen System* (Stuttgart 1981).
46 *SVF* I 190 and III 70, 76 and 587; see E. Grumach, *Physis und Agathon in der alten Stoa* (2nd ed., Berlin 1966), pp. 6–43; A. Graeser, 'Zur Funktion des Begriffes "gut" in der stoischen Ethik', *Zeitschrift für philosophische Forschung* XXVI (1972) 417–25; and Forschner 1981, pp. 171–82.
47 *SVF* III 524–43; see Rist 1969, pp. 81–96.
48 *SVF* I 191 and 195–6 (Zeno); 559–62 (Cleanthes); and III 117–23, 147–68 (Chrysippus); see also M. E. Reesor, 'The "Indifferents" in the Old and Middle Stoa', *Transactions of the American Philological Society* LXXXII (1951) 102–10.

Stoicism was that the end or object (τέλος) of life was 'to live harmoniously with nature (ὁμολογουμένως τῇ φύσει ζῆν)'.[49] This tenet was variously interpreted by the Stoics themselves, and there was always some debate as to whether the 'nature' or φύσις in question was a man's individual nature, or was the nature of the universe.[50] For most Stoics, φύσις was the principle of life and growth within the universe, hence equivalent to the all-pervading spirit (πνεῦμα) or mind (νοῦς) or reason (λόγος) or providence (πρόνοια): all these names describe the one immanent godhead.[51] The wise man, therefore, was to live harmoniously with the universal order. And since for the Stoics this universal order was equivalent to the inexorable fate of things, it was the wise man's duty to attune himself to fate; otherwise he would be dragged along by it willy-nilly.[52] Attunement to the universal nature was aided by the fact that every man has in his soul a preconception of what is just and good, and a natural affinity (οἰκείωσις) for natural order.[53] Nevertheless, pursuit of moral perfection involved the acquisition of knowledge[54] and the exercise of choice. The wise man was to pursue the virtues (the Stoics discourse frequently on the four cardinal virtues),[55] but, they argued, a wise man could not very well possess one virtue without possessing them all, and hence paradoxically all virtuous men were equally virtuous.

Pursuit of the virtues involved control of the passions.[56] The Stoics argued that all men and animals were subject to physical impulses (ὁρμαί), as, for example, when a dog sees a cat and chases it automatically, or when a man sees and lusts after a woman. But the wise man did not permit himself to give in to such impulses, for the mind of man is capable of giving or withholding 'assent' (συγκατάθεσις) to such impulses, and it is the duty of the wise man to

49 SVF I 179 (Zeno); 552 (Cleanthes) and III 4–9 (Chrysippus); see A. Bonhöffer, 'Die Telosformel des Stoikers Diogenes', *Philologus* LXVII (1908) 582–605; O. Rieth, 'Über das Telos der Stoiker', *Hermes* LXIX (1934) 13–45; W. Wiersma, *ΠΕΡΙ ΤΕΛΟΥΣ. Studie over de Leer van het volmakte Leven in de Ethiek van de Oude Stoa* (Groningen 1937); 'Τέλος und Καθῆκον in der alten Stoa', *Mnemosyne* ser. 3, V (1937) 219–28; A. A. Long, 'Carneades and the Stoic Telos', *Phronesis* XII (1967) 59–90; I. G. Kidd, 'Stoic Intermediates and the End for Man', in Long (ed.) 1971, pp. 150–72; J. M. Rist, 'Zeno and Stoic Consistency', *Phronesis* XXII (1977) 161–74; and Forschner 1981, pp. 212–26.
50 Grumach 1966, pp. 44–71; H. and M. Simon, *Die ältere Stoa und ihr Naturbegriff* (Berlin 1956), pp. 53–94.
51 On these various equivalences, see below, n. 184.
52 The formulation is that of Cleanthes, as reproduced by Seneca: 'ducunt volentem fata, nolentem trahunt' (*SVF* I 527); on the Stoic notion of fate, see below, n. 121.
53 *SVF* I 197, II 87, 724 and III 188; see C. O. Brink, 'οἰκείωσις and οἰκειότης: Theophrastus and Zeno on Nature in Moral Theory', *Phronesis* I (1956) 123–45; S. G. Pembroke, 'Oikeiosis', in Long (ed.) 1971, pp. 114–49; and Forschner 1981, pp. 146–59.
54 G. B. Kerferd, 'What does the Wise Man Know?', in Rist (ed.) 1978, pp. 125–36.
55 *SVF* III 252–61.
56 *Ibid.* 169–72.

withhold assent from lustful or evil ones.[57] In other words, the mind of the wise man should be in a state 'without passion' (ἀπάθεια).[58] The wise man who attained to such a state of ἀπάθεια was free; all other men were, so to speak, slaves, in that they were enslaved by their passions.[59] As the wise man must give or withhold assent to his impulses, so he should be able to exercise the correct choice among matters that are, strictly speaking, morally indifferent to him; but among these indifferents, some are to be preferred (προηγμένα), others to be rejected (ἀποπροηγμένα).[60] The exercise of correct choice in such matters is described as 'taking appropriate action', or as 'duty' (καθῆκον),[61] and hence most Stoic treatises devote a good deal of attention to the analysis of 'duties'. In certain circumstances, for example, such as the avoidance of committing an immoral act, the appropriate action or duty might well be suicide.[62] (This was a feature of Stoic ethics which the Roman Stoics, especially Epictetus and Seneca, vaunted excessively.) In any event, the duty of the wise man is to live in accord with nature, as a member or particle of the universal commonwealth, to follow its inborn or natural laws, for these are identical to the will or reason of god and the universe. From this tenet evolved the Stoic theory of natural law.[63]

Unlike the situation obtaining with respect to Stoic logic, it was possible for a twelfth-century philosopher to form an accurate and balanced view of Stoic ethics from reading the writings of Cicero and Seneca. Cicero was not himself a Stoic, but in many respects he was inclined to Stoic views, and he

57 Ibid. 144, 201 and 448; see G. B. Kerferd, 'The Problem of Synkatathesis and Katalepsis in Stoic Doctrine', in Brunschwig (ed.) 1978, pp. 251–72. There is a full treatment of the Stoic theory of 'impulses' in the recent book by B. Inwood, Ethics and Human Action in Early Stoicism (Oxford 1985), esp. pp. 42–66.

58 SVF III 144 and 201; see T. Ruether, Die sittliche Forderung der Apatheia (Freiburg-im-Breisgau 1949), pp. 12–16, and J. M. Rist, 'The Stoic Concept of Detachment', in Rist (ed.) 1978, pp. 259–72.

59 See Inwood 1985, pp. 127–81.

60 SVF III 127–39; see I. G. Kidd, 'Moral Actions and Rules in Stoic Ethics', in Rist (ed.) 1978, pp. 247–58.

61 SVF III 491–9; see G. Nebel, 'Der Begriff des καθῆκον in der alten Stoa', Hermes LXX (1935) 439–60; Wiersma 1937; and Forschner 1981, pp. 184–96.

62 On suicide in the ancient world in general, see R. Hirzel, 'Der Selbstmord', Archiv für Religionswissenschaft XI (1908) 75–104, 243–84 and 417–76; on Stoic suicide see E. Benz, Das Todesproblem in der stoischen Philosophie (Stuttgart 1929), esp. pp. 54–65; and Rist 1969, pp. 233–55.

63 See A. H. Chroust, 'Some Historical Observations on Natural Law and "According to Nature"', Emerita XXXI (1963) 285–98; G. Watson, 'The Natural Law and Stoicism', in Long (ed.) 1971, pp. 216–38; and H.-T. Johann, Gerechtigkeit und Nutzen. Studien zur ciceronischen und hellenistischen Naturrechts- und Staatslehre (Heidelberg 1981) esp. pp. 57–153.

frequently took care to reproduce Stoic arguments in detail, even when he disagreed with them.[64]

The following works of Cicero are most relevant to Stoic ethics. In his *De finibus*, Book III is devoted to an extensive exposition of Stoic ethics placed in the mouth of Marcus Cato (Cato's outline follows more or less the outline of my previous paragraph);[65] Book IV contains Cicero's rebuttal. *De officiis* is a lengthy account of the wise man's 'duties' (*officia* = καθήκοντα), but Cicero has his eye especially on the role of the wise man in society. He argues, following Panaetius (for whom he is in this case a unique witness), that nature endows all men with instincts or affinities for reason and society, and he shows in detail (especially in Book II) what was appropriate to nature in every sphere of life.[66] The incomplete *De legibus* contains *inter alia* a substantial treatment of the Stoic theory of natural law (I xii 33 – xvii 47, I xxi 56 and II iv 8 and 10).[67] Finally the *Paradoxa Stoicorum* are a discussion of seven Stoic ethical 'paradoxes', such as the view that 'virtue is the only good' (no. 1), that 'all sins are equal' (no. 3) or that 'only the wise man is free' (no. 5).

All these works of Cicero were widely read in the twelfth century, and are preserved in numerous manuscripts. *De finibus* is preserved in two distinct families of twelfth-century French manuscripts;[68] the lost ancestor of one family was almost certainly at Orléans in the twelfth century, and the progenitor of the other survives in Paris, BN lat. 6331, written somewhere in northern France, s. xii² (this interesting manuscript also includes copies of Seneca *De beneficiis* and *De clementia*: thus it is a sort of compendium of Stoic

64 On Cicero and the Stoics, see M. Schäfer, *Ein frühmittelstoisches System der Ethik bei Cicero* (Munich 1934); P. M. Valente, *L'éthique stoïcienne chez Cicéron* (Paris 1956); and G. B. Kerferd, 'Cicero and Stoic Ethics', in *Cicero and Vergil: Studies in Honor of Harold Hunt* (Amsterdam 1972), pp. 60–74.
65 E. Kilb, *Ethische Grundbegriffe der alten Stoa und ihre Übertragung durch Cicero im dritten Buch De Finibus Bonorum und Malorum* (Freiburg-im-Breisgau 1934); D. Pesce, *L'etica stoica nel terzo libro del De finibus*, Antichità classica e cristiana XV (Brescia 1977); and G. Patzig, 'Cicero als Philosoph, am Beispiel der Schrift *De finibus*', *Gymnasium* LXXXVI (1979) 304–22.
66 M. Pohlenz, *Antikes Führertum: Ciceros 'De officiis' und das Lebensideal des Panaitios* (Leipzig 1934); and H. A. Gärtner, *Cicero und Panaitios*, Sitzungsberichte der Heidelberger Akademie der Wissenschaften, phil.-hist. Klasse (Heidelberg 1974), no. 5.
67 See M. van de Bruwaene, 'La règle de nature dans Cicéron', in *Miscellanea J. Gessler* (2 vols., Louvain 1948) II 234–40; R. A. Horsley, 'The Law of Nature in Philo and Cicero', *Harvard Theological Review* LXXI (1978) 35–59; and especially K. Girardet, *Die Ordnung der Welt. Ein Beitrag zur philosophischen und politischen Interpretation von Ciceros Schrift 'De legibus'* (Wiesbaden 1983).
68 See R. H. and M. A. Rouse, 'The Medieval Circulation of Cicero's "Posterior Academics" and the *De finibus bonorum et malorum*', in *Medieval Scribes, Manuscripts and Libraries: Essays presented to N. R. Ker*, ed. M. B. Parkes and A. G. Watson (London 1978), pp. 333–67; and *Texts and Transmission: A Survey of the Latin Classics*, ed. L. D. Reynolds (Oxford 1983), pp. 112–14.

ethics). *De officiis* was read and copied throughout the Middle Ages and was especially influential during the twelfth century;[69] in the latter part of that century it was commented on and studied in the Paris schools,[70] and Alexander Nequam referred to it as 'a most useful work'.[71] *De legibus* and the *Paradoxa Stoicorum* were read in the period before the twelfth century as parts of a manuscript corpus of Cicero's *philosophica* (known as the 'Leiden corpus'),[72] but from the twelfth century onwards both works were copied very frequently, especially *De legibus* (the first separate 'edition' of that work was produced in northern France in the twelfth century).[73]

The writings of the younger Seneca are also a valuable source for Stoic ethics, although they contain far less concentrated exposition of Stoic doctrine than those of Cicero. Particularly relevant are Seneca's *De beneficiis* and *De clementia*, as well as the collection of *Epistulae ad Lucilium*; the collection of treatises known as 'Dialogues' also contain isolated discussions of Stoic ethics but, as will be seen, they are less relevant to the twelfth century than the others.[74]

De beneficiis is seemingly based in part on a lost work by the Stoic Hecaton, a student of Panaetius, but it is a rambling and diffuse diatribe containing only occasional detailed and specific treatment of Stoic ethical doctrines, such as man's inheritance from nature and his duty to live in harmony with nature. *De clementia* is preserved incomplete; it is an obsequious letter of exhortation addressed to the young Nero, and contains almost incidental discussion of Stoic views on duty and magnanimity. The *Epistulae ad Lucilium* are more pertinent to Stoic doctrine; they are a collection of 124 letters, usually brief, addressed to Seneca's friend Lucilius on a variety of topics, including Stoic themes. Some few preserve valuable accounts of Stoic doctrine and are apparently based on Seneca's familiarity with the writings of his Stoic predecessors (especially *Epp.* LVIII, LXV, LXXXV, LXXXVII, XCII, XCIV, XCV, CII and CXIII). Of the 'Dialogues', several contain incidental treatment of Stoic ethical doctrine. With the exception of the 'Dialogues', all these works of Seneca were widely copied and circulated during the twelfth

69 See N. E. Nelson, 'Cicero's *De officiis* in Christian Thought: 300–1300', *University of Michigan Publications: Language and Literature* X (1933) 59–160, at pp. 89–112.

70 P. Delhaye, 'L'enseignement de la philosophie morale au XIIe siècle', *Mediaeval Studies* XI (1949) 77–99, at p. 83.

71 Haskins 1927, p. 372.

72 Reynolds (ed.) 1983, pp. 124–8.

73 P. L. Schmidt, *Die Überlieferung von Ciceros Schrift 'De legibus' im Mittelalter und Renaissance* (Munich 1974), pp. 201–16.

74 The 'Dialogues' include: *De providentia, De constantia sapientis, De ira, Consolatio ad Marciam, De vita beata, De otio, De tranquillitate animi, De brevitate vitae, Consolatio ad Polybium* and *Consolatio ad Helviam*.

century.[75] *De beneficiis* and *De clementia* circulated together; all surviving copies derive from a Carolingian manuscript of Italian origin, a copy of which was taken north to somewhere in the Loire valley by *ca.* 1100, whence there was an explosion of copies emanating from the Loire monasteries during the twelfth century.[76] Before the twelfth century the *Epistulae ad Lucilium* were transmitted in two discrete sections (nos. I–LXXXVIII and LXXXIX–CXXIV); during the century interest in these epistles caused copies to multiply, and it was then that the two separate parts were first recombined.[77] By contrast, the 'Dialogues' were not generally available in northern Europe before the second half of the thirteenth century,[78] although excerpts – notably of *De ira* – are preserved in a twelfth-century manuscript of possible French origin (now London, BL Add. 11983, 40r–43r). Finally, before turning to the influence of these texts, one further transmitter of Stoic ethics should be mentioned. Martin of Braga († 579), in his *Formula vitae honestae*, includes a concise account of the four cardinal virtues, and it has been thought that his source was Seneca's lost *De officiis*; in any event Martin's treatise circulated widely under Seneca's name from the twelfth century onwards.[79]

One of the principal means by which Stoic ethics (as conveyed by Cicero, Seneca, and Martin of Braga) became known during the twelfth century was through the compilation and circulation of florilegia.[80] In particular a number of florilegia were assembled which were devoted to matters of ethics, and Cicero and Seneca inevitably figured largely in these. It may be convenient to list the principal florilegia containing these two authors, for they give some notion of the dissemination of Stoic ethics during the twelfth century. The *Florilegium Gallicum*, which survives in two manuscripts and is by far the richest of the florilegia of classical authors, was compiled in northern France, arguably at Orleans, in the second half of the twelfth

---

75 On Seneca's influence in the twelfth century, see K. D. Nothdurft, *Studien zum Einfluss Senecas auf die Philosophie und Theologie des zwölften Jahrhunderts* (Leiden–Cologne 1963); there is also a brief account by G. M. Ross, 'Seneca's Philosophical Influence', in *Seneca*, ed. C. D. N. Costa (London 1974), pp. 116–65, at pp. 131–40.

76 Reynolds (ed.) 1983, pp. 363–5.

77 L. D. Reynolds, *The Medieval Tradition of Seneca's Letters* (Oxford 1965), esp. pp. 104–24, and Reynolds (ed.) 1983, pp. 374–5.

78 L. D. Reynolds, 'The Medieval Tradition of Seneca's Dialogues', *Classical Quarterly* XVIII (1968) 355–72, and Reynolds (ed.) 1983, pp. 366–9.

79 *Martini Episcopi Bracarensis Opera Omnia*, ed C. W. Barlow (New Haven, Conn. 1950); for the edition of the *Formula vitae honestae*, see pp. 236–50, and pp. 204–34 for discussion of its manuscripts and transmission.

80 B. Munk Olsen, 'Les classiques latins dans les florilèges médiévaux antérieurs au XIIIe siècle', *Revue d'histoire des textes* IX (1979) 47–121, and X (1980) 123–72.

century;[81] it contains *inter alia* excerpts from Cicero, *De officiis* and *Paradoxa Stoicorum*, and Seneca, *De beneficiis*, *De clementia* and *Epistulae ad Lucilium*. The *Florilegium Duacense*, preserved in three manuscripts of French origin, was probably also compiled in northern France in the second half of the twelfth century;[82] it includes excerpts from the following writings of Seneca: *De beneficiis*, *De clementia*, *Epistulae ad Lucilium* and *Naturales quaestiones* (on which see below). Yet another florilegium of French origin, the *Florilegium Angelicum*, is preserved in three manuscripts, all copied in France during the second half of the twelfth century;[83] it was apparently intended as a book of maxims or aphorisms rather than as a coherent source-book on ethical doctrine, but it includes extracts from Seneca, *De beneficiis*, *Epistulae ad Lucilium* and Martin of Braga, *Formula vitae honestae*. Finally, the massive *Florilegium morale Oxoniense*, probably an English compilation dating from the twelfth century,[84] includes excerpts from Cicero, *De officiis* and *Paradoxa Stoicorum*, and Seneca, *De beneficiis*, *De clementia* and *Epistulae ad Lucilium*.

From the evidence of manuscripts and florilegia it is clear that a twelfth-century moralist was in a position to be reasonably well informed on the subject of Stoic ethics. However, the availability of Stoic doctrine need not imply that it exercised philosophical influence. In many cases the writings of Cicero and Seneca were simply quarried for arresting and concise aphorisms – this is particularly the case with authors of twelfth-century homilies and preaching-manuals (for example, Alan of Lille in his *Summa de arte praedicatoria*)[85] – but such quarrying tells us little about how twelfth-century thinkers reacted to Stoic doctrine. It is clear that some tenets of Stoic ethics would have been unacceptable to Christian theologians. Thus Walter of Saint-Victor in his *Contra quattuor labyrinthos Franciae* openly rejected Seneca's praise of suicide.[86] But in general Stoic ethics could easily be assimilated to Christian teaching.

One aspect of this assimilation is seen in the *Moralium dogma philosophorum*,

---

81 See R. H. Rouse, 'Florilegia and Latin Classical Authors in Twelfth- and Thirteenth-century Orléans', *Viator* x (1979) 131–60.

82 Munk Olsen 1979, pp. 84–9.

83 R. H. and M. A. Rouse, 'The *Florilegium Angelicum*: its Origin, Content and Influence', in *Medieval Learning and Literature: Essays presented to Richard William Hunt*, ed. J. J. G. Alexander and M. T. Gibson (Oxford 1976), pp. 66–114.

84 P. Delhaye and C. H. Talbot, *Florilegium Morale Oxoniense MS. Bodl. 633*, Analecta Medievalia Namurcensia v–vi (2 vols., Lille–Louvain 1956–61).

85 See Nothdurft 1963, pp. 156–60.

86 P. Glorieux, 'Le "Contra quatuor labyrinthos Franciae" de Gauthier de Saint-Victor', *AHDLMA* xix (1952) 187–335, at 270; see also his 'Mauvaise action et mauvais travail: Le "Contra quatuor labyrinthos Franciae"', *RTAM* xxi (1954) 179–93.

a text attributed with some plausibility to William of Conches.[87] In some respects William's work is little more than a florilegium, for some seven-eighths of it consists of quotation. The work laid most heavily under contribution is Cicero's *De officiis*, particularly Books I and III (165 quotations),[88] but William also drew on Seneca's *De beneficiis*, *Epistulae ad Lucilium* and (surprisingly, in view of the textual transmission of the 'Dialogues') *De ira*.[89] The work is structured around five topics: 'On moral excellence (*De honesto*)', 'On the acquisition of excellence (*De comparatione honestorum*)', 'On the useful (*De utili*)', 'On the acquisition of useful things (*De comparatione utilium*)' and 'On the conflict between the morally excellent and the useful (*De conflictu honesti et utilis*)'. A number of essential points of Stoic ethics are treated: the wise man must realize that only moral excellence is of value;[90] what is not pertinent to moral excellence is valueless; for fools, fame and honour are goals of pursuit, but for the wise man, the goals are calm of mind and equilibrium;[91] the reward of moral behaviour is not to be sought in external things, but in oneself; moral excellence is 'a state of mind in natural harmony with reason'.[92] The conclusion of William's treatise is an exhortation to 'subject one's life to the rule of reason'.[93] This is a sentiment which would have been thoroughly acceptable to any Stoic.

A different kind of application of Stoic ethics was made by a Cistercian theologian. The Stoics in general, and Seneca in particular, rail at length against physical excess, especially excessive food and excessive drink. The wise man who lives in accord with nature is able to live on very meagre resources. It is apparent that a reformed monastic order such as that of

---

87 P. L. 171, 1007–56; also J. Holmberg, *Das Moralium dogma philosophorum des Guillaume de Conches* (Uppsala 1929). Questions concerning the authorship of this work, long attributed to Hildebert of Lavardin, were first raised by J. R. Williams, 'The Authorship of the *Moralium dogma philosophorum*', *Speculum* VI (1931) 392–411; various opinions have since been expressed, in favour of Alan of Lille (P. Glorieux, 'Le *Moralium dogma philosophorum* et son auteur', *RTAM* XV (1948) 360–6) or of Walter of Chatillon (R. A. Gauthier, 'Pour l'attribution à Gauthier de Chatillon du *Moralium dogma philosophorum*', *Revue du Moyen Âge Latin* VII (1951) 19–64). More recently, however, a reasoned consensus in favour of William of Conches has emerged: see P. Delhaye, 'Une adaptation du *De officiis* au XIIe siècle: le *Moralium dogma philosophorum*', *RTAM* XVI (1949) 227–58 and XVII (1950) 5–28; and T. Gregory, *Anima mundi. La filosofia di Guglielmo di Conches e la scuola di Chartres* (Florence 1955), pp. 21–6.
88 Nelson 1933, pp. 90–9; Delhaye 1949 and 1950; Verbeke 1983, pp. 48–50.
89 Nothdurft 1963, pp. 100–7.
90 Holmberg 1929, p. 72.
91 *Ibid.* p. 31.
92 *Ibid.* p. 7: 'virtus vero est habitus animi in modum nature rationi consentaneus' (from Cicero, *De inventione* II lii 157–8).
93 *Ibid.* p. 72: 'hec prescripta servantem licet in tranquillo honestatis vivere et ad normam rationis vitam ducere'.

Citeaux would find much to commend in (say) Seneca's praise of abstinence and self-denial, in short, in his asceticism. And so we find William of Saint-Thierry – a man of mystic inclination and an opponent of the rationalism of Abelard and William of Conches – writing a letter of moral exhortation in 1145 to the Cistercian community of Mont-Dieu, urging the monks to live a life in accord with nature.[94] Basing himself on Seneca's *Ep. ad Lucilium* 1 8, he argues that virtue is natural and sin, unnatural;[95] and at another point he quotes with approval Seneca's undertaking (*Ep. ad Lucilium* v 4) 'to live according to nature; for what is against nature is the following: to torture one's body . . . and to feed off food which is not only vile but foul and filthy'.[96] As in the case of William of Conches in the *Moralium dogma philosophorum*, a life in accordance with nature is also in accordance with reason. Later in the century we find Peter the Chanter († 1197), a canon of Rheims and master in Paris – hence in no sense a monk, Cistercian or otherwise – arguing nevertheless in favour of a life of abstinence lived according to nature.[97] In his *Verbum abbreviatum*, a work very largely based on Seneca (especially *De beneficiis* and *Epistulae ad Lucilium*)[98] Peter sets out a doctrine of austere asceticism; and like William of Saint-Thierry, the cornerstone of his argument is Seneca's exhortation (*Ep. ad Lucilium* v 4) to live according to nature and to reject the excesses of food and drink (§68).[99]

The preceding examples represent more or less unsophisticated responses to Stoic ethics as transmitted to the twelfth century: William of Conches in the *Moralium dogma philosophorum* follows the structure of Cicero's *De officiis*, buttressing its argumentation with relevant citations from elsewhere in Cicero and from Seneca; William of Saint-Thierry and Peter the Chanter find support for their ascetic inclinations in the moral *sententiae* of Seneca.

The best concerted attempt to come to terms with the principles of Stoic ethics was made (characteristically) by Abelard. In his *Ethica* (or *Scito teipsum*)

94 M. M. Davy, *Un traité de la vie solitaire: Epistola ad fratres de Monte Dei de Guillaume de Saint-Thierry* (Paris 1940); *Lettre d'or aux frères du Mont-Dieu*, ed. J. M. Déchanet (Paris 1956); and see now Guillaume de Saint-Thierry, *La lettera d'oro*, ed. C. Leonardi, trans. C. Piacentini and R. Scarcia (Florence 1983).
95 J. M. Déchanet, '*Seneca noster*: des Lettres à Lucilius à la Lettre aux frères du Mont-Dieu', in *Mélanges J. de Ghellinck* (2 vols., Gembloux 1951) II 753–66; Nothdurft 1963, pp. 135–46.
96 See in particular J. M. Déchanet, 'Le "naturam sequi" chez Guillaume de Saint-Thierry', *Collectanea Ordinis Cisterciensium reformatorum* VII (1940) 141–8. Seneca, *Ep.* v 4: 'nempe propositum nostrum est secundum naturam vivere: hoc contra naturam est, torquere corpus suum . . . et cibis non tantum vilibus uti sed taetris et horridis'.
97 Petrus' *Verbum abbreviatum* is printed P.L. 205, 23–528; see E. M. Sanford, 'The *Verbum abbreviatum* of Petrus Cantor', *Transactions of the American Philological Association* LXXIV (1943) 33–48.
98 Nothdurft 1963, pp. 146–52.
99 P.L. 205, 204–5.

Abelard devotes considerable attention to the question of sin and intentiona-
lity. In some ways his argument is remote from Stoicism. Thus he is unable
to accept the Stoic view that all sins are equal: 'certain philosophers' – and
here his reference is unmistakably to the Stoics – 'thought that all sins were
equal.'[100] As Abelard goes on to remark, such a viewpoint is 'manifest
stupidity (*manifesta stulticia*)'; instead he stresses the difference between
'criminal' and 'venial' sins. But in other respects Abelard's views approach
closely to those of the Stoics, and he has clearly profited from meditation on
them. So he argues: 'suppose that someone sees a woman, and falls into lust,
and his mind is affected by delight of the flesh: he is inflamed for the filth of
sexual intercourse. I reply: what if this will is restrained by the virtue of
temperance?'[101] What Abelard means is that it is not the lust that is sinful, but
the mental/wilful complicity in consenting to lust: 'accordingly it is not a sin
to desire a woman, but rather to consent to the desire; the desire for
intercourse is not damnable, but rather the agreement with the desire'.[102]
Abelard's argument here is precisely the Stoic doctrine of 'natual impulse
(ὁρμή)' on the one hand, and 'assent to the impulse (συγκατάθεσις)' on the
other. Where Abelard found this Stoic theory is not immediately clear (it is
mentioned briefly by Seneca and treated more extensively by Cicero);[103] but
it is Abelard's original contribution to apply the notion of assent to that of sin
in a Christian context.

In his perhaps incomplete, slightly earlier *Collationes* (dialogues, that is,
between a Philosopher, a Christian, and a Jew), Abelard had considered
questions raised by Stoic ethical theory more extensively. The Philosopher
at various points expounds doctrines that are manifestly Stoic. Thus he
quotes Cicero's *De officiis* at length to the effect that the wise man who has
one virtue has them all (it is not possible for a man to be truly just who is not
also wise, and vice versa) and, quoting from the *Paradoxa Stoicorum*,
maintains that just as good men are equal in virtue, so bad men are equal in
sin, for all sins are equal.[104] The Christian points out that this deduction is a
rash one; and we have seen that Abelard in his *Ethica* rejected it. Elsewhere in
the *Collationes* the Philosopher maintains with the Stoics that virtue is the
greatest good but, apparently referring to Cicero's *De finibus*, he remarks
that the philosophers (= the Stoics) did not define what things were good

---

100 *Peter Abelard's Ethics*, ed. D. E. Luscombe (Oxford 1971), p. 74.
101 *Ibid.* pp. 10–12.
102 *Ibid.* pp. 12–14.
103 Cf. Seneca, *Ep. ad Lucilium* CXIII 18 (= *SVF* III 169) and Cicero, *Acad. Pr.* II (= *SVF* III 115).
104 P.L. 178, 1647; *Petrus Abaelardus: Dialogus inter philosophum, Iudaeum et Christianum*, ed.
   R. Thomas (Stuttgart–Bad Cannstatt 1970), p. 108, lines 1773–92.

and what bad and what indifferent, but merely gave illustrations.[105] However, the point at which Abelard's discussion is most deeply and importantly indebted to Stoic ethics is in his treatment of natural justice and natural law. Quoting Cicero, Abelard's Philosopher argues that natural law (*ius naturale*) is that reason which is naturally instilled in everyone, and therefore remains in everyone, such as the inclination to worship God, love parents, and punish evildoers; positive law (*ius positivum*), on the other hand, is that which is instituted by men.[106] He goes on to argue, rather boldly, that some (not all) Old and New Testament laws are 'natural' (for example, loving God or one's neighbours), and some are 'positive' (for example, circumcision for the Jews, baptism for Christians). He draws the striking conclusion that 'men can be saved by natural law alone (*homines salvari posse sola naturali lege*)'.[107] Here is the restatement and application of a moral concept, ultimately of Stoic origin, which from the twelfth century onwards was to figure significantly in canon law; indeed the *Decretum Gratiani*, compiled *ca.* 1140 at virtually the same time as Abelard was composing his *Collationes*, states unequivocally that 'mankind is ruled by two laws: natural law and custom', although inevitably Gratian puts a different construction on this definition from that of Abelard.[108] It remained for the commentators on Gratian and for Thomas Aquinas in subsequent centuries to refine the question of natural and positive law.

Physics

The Stoic system of physics is a coherent body of principles,[109] many of which are couched in language that has been thought to anticipate modern physics.[110] On the basis of these principles the Stoics worked out an elaborate

---

105 P.L. 178, 1675; *Petrus Abaelardus* 1970, pp. 159–60, lines 3132–5.
106 P.L. 178, 1656; *Petrus Abaelardus* 1970, pp. 124–5, lines 2218–40; the quotation of Cicero is from *De inventione* II liii 161. The distinction between *iustitia positiva* and *iustitia naturalis* is made in Calcidius, *Comm.* VI (ed. Waszink p. 59); cf. S. Gagnér, *Studien zur Ideengeschichte der Gesetzgebung* (Uppsala 1960), pp. 182–264.
107 P.L. 178, 1623; *Petrus Abaelardus* 1970, p. 62, lines 569–70.
108 See discussion by Watson in Long (ed.) 1971, p. 236, and D. E. Luscombe, *CHLMP*, p. 707. Gratian's distinction was based on Isidore, *Etymologiae* V iv–vi. Here, as frequently in the *Etymologiae*, Isidore was basing himself on Stoic doctrine: see J. Fontaine, *Isidore de Séville et la culture classique dans l'Espagne wisigothique* (2 vols., Paris 1959), II 654–6 *et pass.*
109 See L. Bloos, *Probleme der stoischen Physik*, Hamburger Studien zur Philosophie IV (Hamburg 1971); A. G. Longrigg, 'Elementary Physics in the Lyceum and Stoa', *Isis* LXVI (1975) 211–29; and R. B. Todd, *Alexander of Aphrodisias on Stoic Physics* (Leiden 1976), esp. pp. 21–88.
110 As in the epoch-making study by S. Sambursky, *Physics of the Stoics* (London 1959).

and compelling cosmology,[111] and since it was cosmology which particularly held the interest of twelfth-century theologians, I shall concentrate
on the cosmology rather than on the physical principles which lay behind it.
The Stoics were monists[112] and materialists:[113] they posited that everything –
the universe, nature, the godhead – was one material substance (οὐσία). This
one substance has two 'aspects' or 'principles' (ἀρχαί), one of which is god
(θεός), the other matter (ὕλη).[114]

These two principles do not have separate existence; rather, the matter is
qualified by god, which penetrates its every part; put differently, god is the
active (ποιοῦν), matter the passive (πάσχον) aspect of the one substance. The
Stoics worked out a theory of 'total mixture' or 'total interpenetration
(κρᾶσις δι' ὅλου)' to explain the permeation of matter by (a material) god:[115]
from this permeation resulted the four elements and the created universe in
all its shapes and forms; the presence of 'seminal particles of reason (σπερματικοὶ λόγοι)' or of the godhead in created things shaped and animated them.[116]
For the earliest Stoics (Zeno and Cleanthes) the godhead was regarded as
equivalent to the fiery aether (αἰθήρ), the creative fire which is the substance
of the sun and stars (in distinction to terrestrial fire, which is destructive); this
creative fire, because of its generative, vital force, was for Zeno and
Cleanthes the equivalent of nature (φύσις), which, because of the unity of
the universe, was in turn equivalent to universal mind (νοῦς) or reason
(λόγος) or providence (πρόνοια).[117] Chrysippus (followed by Posidonius)
refined this position by arguing, on the analogy of living creatures, that god
was a fiery breath or spirit (πνεῦμα) which permeated or 'breathed through'

111 See M. Lapidge, 'Stoic Cosmology', in Rist (ed.) 1978, pp. 161–85; on the Aristotelian
background to Stoic cosmology there is a valuable study by D. E. Hahm, *The Origins of
Stoic Cosmology* (Ohio 1977). An engaging exposition of Zeno's cosmology (with translations of the appropriate fragments in *SVF*) is given by H. A. K. Hunt, *A Physical
Interpretation of the Universe: The Doctrines of Zeno the Stoic* (Carlton, Australia 1976).

112 See R. B. Todd, 'Monism and Immanence: The Foundations of Stoic Physics', in Rist (ed.)
1978, pp. 137–60.

113 Still the best study of Stoic materialism and its origins is C. Baeumker, *Das Problem der
Materie in der griechischen Philosophie* (Münster 1890), pp. 326–70.

114 *SVF* I 85–8, and II 299–328; see M. Lapidge, 'ἀρχαί and στοιχεῖα: A Problem in Stoic
Cosmology', *Phronesis* XVIII (1973) 240–78.

115 *SVF* II 463–81; see Sambursky 1959, pp. 11–17 and Todd 1976, pp. 29–73.

116 *SVF* II 580 (= I 102), 1027 and 1074; cf. H. Meyer, *Geschichte der Lehre von den Keimkräften
von der Stoa bis zum Ausgang der Patristik* (Bonn 1914), pp. 7–26.

117 *SVF* I 115–20 and 499–504; see F. Solmsen, 'The Vital Heat, the Inborn Pneuma and the
Aether', *Journal of Hellenic Studies* LXXVII (1957) 119–23; 'Cleanthes or Posidonius? The
Basis of Stoic Physics', *Mededelingen der koninklijke Nederlandse Akademie van Wetenschappen*
XXIV (1961) 265–89; Lapidge 1973, pp. 254–9; Hahm 1977, pp. 140–53; and J. Mansfeld,
'The Cleanthes Fragment in Cicero, *De natura deorum* II. 24', in *Actus. Studies in Honour of
H. L. W. Nelson*, ed. J. den Boeft and A. H. M. Kessels (Utrecht 1982), pp. 203–10.

all parts of the universe, so animating it;[118] at the same time, this spirit or πνεῦμα created a cosmic tension (τόνος), a sort of force-field between all parts of the universe, so that one part of it moved in unison with the movement of another (as, for example, is the case with the moon and the tides); the mutual interaction of parts was called 'sympathy (συμπάθεια)', and the force with which all parts were held together by πνεῦμα was described metaphorically as a 'bond (δεσμός)'.[119] And as there was spatial interconnection between parts of the universe as a result of the cosmic tension, so necessarily was there temporal interconnection between events; whence the Stoic theory of fate (εἱμαρμένη) as a 'chain (εἱρμός)' or 'interweaving (συμπλοκή)' of causes.[120] Every creature and every event was a link in the interconnected chain of fate: in other words, the fate of every creature is predetermined and ineluctable.[121] Indeed the fate of the universe itself is predetermined, so that the universe periodically dissolves in fire (the process is called ἐκπύρωσις) and then water, and from these two agents a new universe is created.[122]

No Latin source preserves a complete account of Stoic cosmology and the physical principles on which it was based, but various texts contain accounts of some of the salient features. By far the most important Latin source was Book II of Cicero's *De natura deorum*.[123] Here one of Cicero's interlocutors, the Stoic Balbus, by way of arguing that the marvellous intricacies of nature prove divine order, gives a brief account of Stoic cosmological doctrines, such as the interconnectedness of all universal parts through the inspiration

118 *SVF* II 439–62; see G. Verbeke, *L'évolution de la doctrine du pneuma du stoïcisme à S. Augustin* (Paris–Louvain 1945), pp. 11–174; Lapidge 1973, pp. 273–8 and in Rist (ed.) 1978, pp. 168–76; Bloos 1973, pp. 52–64; Hahm 1977, pp. 158–66; and P. Hager, 'Chrysippus' Theory of Pneuma', *Prudentia* XIV (1982) 97–108.

119 On τόνος see *SVF* II 441, 447 and 546, together with Sambursky 1959, pp. 21–44, Bloos 1973, pp. 65–73, and Hahm 1977, pp. 169–73. On Stoic συμπάθεια, see Reinhardt 1926 and Bloos 1973, pp. 90–105. On the Stoic metaphor of the cosmic δεσμός, see M. Lapidge, 'A Stoic Metaphor in Late Latin Poetry: The Binding of the Cosmos', *Latomus* XXXIX (1980) 817–37, at pp. 818–19.

120 *SVF* II 912–38 and 945–51.

121 The Stoic conceptions of fate, necessity, and free will are of course far more complex than is implied here: see M. E. Reesor, 'Fate and Possibility in Early Stoic Philosophy', *Phoenix* XIX (1965) 285–97; 'Necessity and Fate in Stoic Philosophy', in Rist (ed.) 1978, pp. 187–202; Rist 1969, pp. 112–32; and R. W. Sharples, 'Necessity in the Stoic Doctrine of Fate', *Symbolae Osloenses* LVI (1981) 81–97.

122 *SVF* II 596–632; see Bloos 1973, pp. 121–30; Lapidge in Rist (ed.) 1978, pp. 182–4; and J. Mansfeld, 'Providence and the Destruction of the Universe in Early Stoic Thought, and Some Remarks on the Mysteries of Philosophy', in *Studies in Hellenistic Religions*, ed. M. J. Vermaseren (Leiden 1979), pp. 129–88.

123 See Hirzel 1877–83, I 191–244; P. Finger, 'Die drei kosmologischen Systeme im zweiten Buch von Ciceros Schrift über das Wesen der Götter', *Rheinisches Museum* LXXX (1931) 151–200 and 310–20; and Süss 1965, pp. 93–119.

of spirit (II vii 19), the cosmic force of divine fire and heat (II ix 23 – xii 32), Zeno's definition of nature as a creative fire (II xxii 57–8), and the characteristics of the aether (II xl 101 – xlvi 118). Other philosophical writings of Cicero contain occasional exposition of Stoic doctrine, even within a non-Stoic framework: thus *De divinatione* contains some discussion of fate or εἱμαρμένη (I lv 125–6). These treatises of Cicero are found frequently together in manuscript from the eleventh century onwards, as part of the so-called 'Leiden corpus'; they were readily available during the twelfth century.[124]

For cosmology, the writings of Seneca are less important, but not negligible: above all his *Naturales quaestiones*. The principal concern of this work is with natural phenomena such as earthquakes, thunder and lightning, winds and clouds. It is probable that some of Seneca's physical explanations of natural phenomena derive from earlier Stoic physicists, particularly Posidonius, but he also drew on other sources, notably Aristotle's *De caelo* and *Meteorologica*; in other words, it would be misleading to regard Seneca's *Naturales quaestiones* as a textbook of Stoic physics.[125] Nevertheless, it contains many incidental references to the central tenets of Stoic cosmology, as I have outlined them above: the question of primal matter in its two aspects, active and passive (II i 4 and II ii 1), the nature of aethereal fire (VII ii 1–2), the tensional force of *spiritus* or πνεῦμα (II vi 2–6, II viii 1, IIII xv 1–8 and VI xiv 1–4), the woven 'chain' of fate (I i 4 and II xxxv–xxxviii), the destruction of the universe by fire (ἐκπύρωσις) and flood (κατακλυσμός) (III xiii 1–2, III xxviii 3–7 and III xxx 6),[126] and the nature of the godhead (II xlv 1–3). Other writings of Seneca advert to cosmology, but never at length: thus two of the *Epistulae ad Lucilium* (nos. LVIII and LXV) discuss the two primal causes;[127] *De beneficiis* gives a full account of the names and nature of the godhead (IV vii), and at various points in the 'Dialogues' cosmology comes under discussion.

These writings (excepting again the 'Dialogues') were certainly well known and widely studied during the twelfth century. No manuscript of the *Naturales quaestiones* earlier than the twelfth century survives, but it is clear

124 See Reynolds (ed.) 1983, pp. 124–8.
125 See E. Bernert, 'Seneca und das Naturgefühl der Stoiker', *Gymnasium* LXVIII (1961) 113–24; G. Stahl, 'Die *Naturales quaestiones* Senecas. Ein Beitrag zum Spiritualisierungsprozess der römischen Stoa', *Hermes* XCII (1964) 425–54; and especially F. P. Waiblinger, *Senecas Naturales Quaestiones. Griechisches Wissen und römische Form*, Zetemata XXX (Munich 1977).
126 F. Levy, 'Der Weltuntergang in Senecas *Naturales quaestiones*', *Philologus* LXXXIII (1928) 459–66.
127 E. Bickel, 'Senecas Briefe 58. und 65. Das Antiochus–Posidonius Problem', *Rheinisches Museum* CIII (1960) 1–20.

from manuscript evidence that the work was rediscovered in northern France in the early twelfth century.[128] Adelard of Bath used it in his own *Quaestiones naturales* (written between 1111 and 1116), for his discussions of the corporeal nature of vision (§23), the cause of earthquakes being *spiritus* compressed in the earth (§50), and the causes of thunder (§64) and lightning (§65).[129] William of Conches in his *Dragmaticon* (*ca.* 1145) quotes extensively and often verbatim from the *Naturales quaestiones*.[130] The author of *De mundi constitutione* drew on it for his accounts of earthquakes being caused by the passage of *spiritus* through terrestrial caverns (1 54–6), lightning (1 142) and haloes (1 156).[131] Thierry of Chartres probably drew his exposition of the four causes of *mundana subsistentia* from Seneca (*Ep. ad Lucilium* LXV, where however Seneca's classification is Platonic, not Stoic).[132] This brief list of twelfth-century debts to Seneca's writings on physics and cosmology could be extended considerably.

Stoic cosmology was transmitted to the twelfth century, albeit indirectly, by other sources which deserve mention. The Latin *Asclepius*,[133] a translation of a Greek Hermetic text which was probably made some time during the fourth century AD (it is cited by Augustine in *De civitate Dei*), and which is sometimes ascribed to Apuleius, is indebted in many respects to Stoic cosmology: in its monism, whereby god and universe are one (§3), in its concise statement of the two Stoic principles, θεός and ὕλη (§14), in its account of the *spiritus* or πνεῦμα which penetrates all things, so animating them (§6), and in its extended treatment of εἱμαρμένη or fate (§§39–40). This work too was well known (under the name of Mercurius Trismegistus) in the twelfth century: it survives in six manuscripts, all of the twelfth century,[134] and was known to and cited by Thierry of Chartres,[135]

---

128 See H. M. Hine, 'The Manuscript Tradition of Seneca's Natural Questions', *Classical Quarterly* XXX (1980) 183–217; and in Reynolds (ed.) 1983, pp. 376–8.
129 Adelard of Bath, *Quaestiones naturales*, ed. M. Müller, Beiträge zur Geschichte der Philosophie des Mittelalters XXXI.2 (Münster 1934), pp. 30 (*NQ* I v 1), 50 (*NQ* VI xii–xviii), 57 (*NQ* II xxvii–xxix) and 58–9 (*NQ* II xvii 1) respectively; see also Nothdurft 1963, pp. 176–7.
130 See C. Picard-Parra, 'Une utilisation des *Quaestiones naturales* de Sénèque au milieu du XIIᵉ siècle', *Revue du Moyen Âge Latin* V (1949) 115–26; and Nothdurft 1963, pp. 162–75.
131 Pseudo-Bede, *De mundi celestis terrestrisque constitutione*, ed. C. Burnett (London 1985), pp. 22 (*NQ* VI xii–xviii), 30 (*NQ* II xvii 1) and 32 (*NQ* I ii 5) respectively.
132 See N. Häring, 'The Creation and Creator of the World according to Thierry of Chartres and Clarembald of Arras', *AHDLMA* XXII (1955) 137–216, at pp. 184–5, and Nothdurft 1963, pp. 186–7.
133 *Asclepius*, ed. A. D. Nock, trans. A.-J. Festugière, *Corpus Hermeticum* II (2nd ed., Paris 1960), pp. 259–401.
134 *Ibid.* pp. 259–60 and 267–8.
135 Häring 1955, p. 193.

Bernardus Silvestris,[136] John of Salisbury[137] and Alan of Lille.[138]

Another text which mediated Stoic cosmology was the (Greek) treatise *De natura hominis* by the fourth-century Greek Church Father, Nemesius of Emesa. It was formerly thought that the greater part of Nemesius' anthropology derived directly from Posidonius;[139] such a hypothesis would today be severely qualified. Nemesius' treatise was translated during the eleventh century by Archbishop Alfanus of Salerno († 1085) under the title *Premnon physicon*.[140] What interested the Salernitan doctor was Nemesius' discussion of the human organism, rather than his cosmology; accordingly Alfanus omitted the important chapters at the end of the Greek text concerning fate and providence. Even shorn of these chapters, however, the *Premnon physicon* includes much discussion of the Stoic theory of the fiery nature of the soul (§2), particularly as set out by Cleanthes and Chrysippus, as well as an account of the active and passive elements (§5). Alfanus' translation survives in five twelfth-century manuscripts, and was certainly known to William of Conches[141] and John of Salisbury.[142] Nemesius was translated into Latin a second time by Burgundio of Pisa (*ca.* 1165), and this time the important discussions of fortune, fate, and providence (which occupy §§34–42 of Burgundio's version) were not omitted;[143] since Nemesius based part of his argument on Alexander of Aphrodisias, *De fato*, which is in turn much indebted to Chrysippus,[144] we have here another channel by which Stoic doctrine on fate and providence may have reached the twelfth century.[145]

Another source of Stoic doctrine on fate and free will, as well as on matter (ὕλη), was the Latin commentary on Plato's *Timaeus* by Calcidius.[146]

---

136 See R. B. Woolsey, 'Bernard Silvester and the Hermetic *Asclepius*', *Traditio* VI (1948) 340–4; and *Bernardus Silvestris: Cosmographia*, ed. P. Dronke (Leiden 1978), pp. 17 and 72–4.

137 *Ioannis Saresberiensis Episcopi Carnotensis Policratici sive de nugis curialium et vestigiis philosophorum libri VIII*, ed. C. C. J. Webb (2 vols., Oxford 1909), I 163 (II 28).

138 *P.L.* 210, 332.

139 See W. W. Jaeger, *Nemesios von Emesa* (Berlin 1914), esp. pp. 70–96; Jaeger's argument was followed implicitly by Reinhardt 1921 and 1926.

140 *Nemesii episcopi Premnon Physicon . . . a N. Alfano archiepiscopo Salerni in Latinum translatus*, ed. K. Burkhard (Leipzig 1917).

141 See T. Silverstein, 'Guillaume de Conches and Nemesius of Emesa: On the Sources of the "New Science" of the Twelfth Century', in *Harry Austryn Wolfson Jubilee Volume* (3 vols., Jerusalem 1965) II 719–34.

142 *Metalogicon* IV 20 (ed. Webb 1929, p. 187).

143 *Némésius d'Émèse, De natura hominis: Traduction de Burgundio de Pise*, ed. G. Verbeke and J. R. Moncho (Leiden 1975).

144 G. Verbeke, 'Aristotelisme et Stoïcisme dans le *De fato* d'Alexandre d'Aphrodise', *Archiv für Geschichte der Philosophie* L (1968) 73–100; and especially R. W. Sharples, *Alexander of Aphrodisias on Fate* (London 1983), pp. 18–23.

145 See Verbeke 1983, pp. 76–80.

146 *Timaeus a Calcidio translatus commentarioque instructus*, ed. J. H. Waszink, Corpus Platonicum Medii Aevi: Plato Latinus IV (2nd ed., London–Leiden 1975).

Although the principal orientation of Calcidius is Platonic, his commentary contains substantial discussion of Stoic physics, more possibly than is usually realized. Of the Stoic cosmological theories in question, Calcidius provides extensive and accurate discussion of the Stoics' conception of the soul as corporeal (§§220–1) and of their definition of the two principles, θεός and ὕλη, particularly the latter (§§289–94 and 311–13),[147] as well as an extensive refutation of the Stoic theory of fate and determinism (§§160–75).[148] There is no need to demonstrate that Calcidius was widely read during the twelfth century. The same may be said of Boethius, whose *De consolatione Philosophiae* contains a lengthy treatment of fate, providence, and free will (especially IV, pr. vi and v, pr. iv and v), the terminology and cast of which is directly indebted to Stoic theory, although Boethius does not specify his source as such.[149] Finally, mention should be made of an important and influential passage in Vergil's *Aeneid*, where Anchises explains to Aeneas the order of the universe:

> Principio caelum ac terram camposque liquentis
> lucentemque globum lunae Titaniaque astra
> spiritus intus alit, totamque infusa per artus
> mens agitat molem et magno se corpore miscet.
> inde hominum pecudumque genus vitaeque volantum
> et quae marmoreo fert monstra sub aequore pontus.
> igneus est ollis vigor et caelestis origo
> seminibus . . .[150]

Vergil's description of cosmic order here is manifestly Stoic: the *spiritus* which nourishes all things from within, and which is infused in all things so that it is mixed throughout the vast mass of the universe, is the Stoic πνεῦμα, which imparts to living creatures a 'fiery vigour (*igneus vigor*)', the origin of which is in the aether. Vergil was read everywhere during the Middle Ages, and we should not be surprised to find that his striking picture of the world-soul commended itself to twelfth-century cosmogonists.[151]

147 See J. M. C. van Winden, *Calcidius on Matter. His Doctrine and his Sources* (Leiden 1962).
148 J. den Boeft, *Calcidius on Fate. His Doctrine and Sources* (Leiden 1970), pp. 47–84.
149 On Boethius' debt to Stoicism, see H. Chadwick, *Boethius* (Oxford 1981), pp. 228–33; on his influence in the twelfth century, see P. Courcelle, *La Consolation de Philosophie dans la tradition littéraire* (Paris 1967), pp. 301–15; and J. Beaumont, 'The Latin Tradition of the *De consolatione Philosophiae*', in *Boethius: His Life, Thought and Influence*, ed. M. Gibson (Oxford 1981), pp. 278–305, at pp. 295–300.
150 *Aeneid* VI 724–31:
    'To begin with, Spirit [= πνεῦμα] from within nourishes the sky and earth and watery tracts and the shining globe of the moon and the Titanian stars, and this Mind [= νοῦς], infused in all cosmic parts, animates the entire mass of the universe and is mixed throughout this vast body [= κρᾶσις δι' ὅλου]. From this all races of men and beasts and birds, and the monsters which the sea produces beneath its marbled surface, draw their life. There is a fiery force in them and a celestial origin [=αἰθήρ] for their seeds [= σπερματικοὶ λόγοι] . . .'
151 It is quoted, for example, by Thierry of Chartres (Häring 1955, p. 193).

We are now in a position to assess the impact of these Stoic cosmological theories on twelfth-century thought. We may begin with the two principles (ἀρχαί), namely θεός and ὕλη. It is clear that knowledge of Calcidius and the *Asclepius* will have provided an attentive reader with some notion of how these Stoic principles operated. Certainly there is no excuse for the error made by John of Salisbury, who remarks that the Stoics posited *three* principles, matter, form, and God.[152] Many twelfth-century philosophers speak of *informis materia*, but they invariably have in mind the Platonic 'receptacle' in the *Timaeus*, ready to receive the informing ideas, rather than the Stoic ὕλη, which is coeternal with – and indeed one aspect of – the material and corporeal godhead. Thierry of Chartres quotes the passage from the *Asclepius* explaining the two Stoic principles: 'there was god and matter, which in Greek we take to be the universe. And *spiritus* was associated with the world, or rather, *spiritus* subsisted in the world.'[153] But Thierry makes no comment on this quotation and makes no effort to see how the conception squares with his (basically Platonic) conception of *materia*. Bernardus Silvestris draws the character Hyle or Silva at some length, but his too is a Platonic *silva*, existing before the advent of form, tending towards evil without the moderating influence of mind.[154] Such a conception is very remote from the Stoics' immanent ὕλη. It is hardly surprising that Christian philosophers should have been unable to accept the implications of the Stoic concept of ὕλη, for to do so would be to make God matter. As far as I am aware, only one thinker took so bold a step, and that at the very end of the twelfth century. David of Dinant in his fragmentary *Quaternuli* argued that the '*hyle* of the world' was identical to God:[155]

From these arguments it can be gathered that mind and matter (*hyle*) are the same thing ... It is clear therefore that there is one primal substance, not only of all bodies but also of all minds, and that it is nothing other than God.[156]

David names Zeno among others as his authority for this view. Presumably his source for Zeno's theory of matter was Calcidius (§§289–94), but

152 *Metalogicon* II 20 (ed. Webb 1929, p. 107).
153 Häring 1955, p. 193: 'Fuit Deus et hyle, quem Graece credimus mundum. Et mundo comitabitur spiritus vel mundo inerat spiritus.' The relative *quem* printed by the editor, following the critical edition of *Asclepius* (*Corpus Hermeticum*, ed. Nock–Festugière II 313) must be construed with *mundum*; the sense must be: 'ὕλη, which we believe is in Greek the equivalent of *mundus*'.
154 Bernardus Silvestris 1978, pp. 99–100 (*Megacosmus* II 2–4).
155 The fragments of David's *Quaternuli* were first recovered by A. Birkenmajer, 'Découverte de fragments manuscrits de David de Dinant', *Revue néoscolastique de philosophie* XXXV (1933) 220–9; they are edited by M. Kurdziałek: *Davidis de Dinanto Quaternulorum Fragmenta*, Studia Mediewistyczne III (Warsaw 1963).
156 Kurdziałek 1963, pp. 70–1.

whether study of these chapters in Calcidius could in itself have led to so daring a formulation is unclear, and it is a pity that so little of David's writing has survived.[157] (The condemnation of the *Quaternuli* by a Parisian synod in 1210 may largely account for the loss.)[158]

Other Stoic cosmological theories were more satisfactorily adapted to Christian purposes. A case in point is the Stoic conception of nature (φύσις). Provided the Stoics' equation of god, nature, and universe could be jettisoned, and the operations of nature could be clearly subordinated to those of God, it was possible to accommodate some aspects of the Stoic φύσις. Twelfth-century thought was characterized by its exploration of the operations of nature in all its aspects,[159] and it is not surprising that Zeno's striking definition of nature as 'a creative fire proceeding methodically to generation'[160] should have attracted comment. Thus Hugh of Saint-Victor in his *Didascalicon*, noting (with Cicero)[161] that it is difficult to define 'nature', proposes several definitions of the term, the third of which is unmistakably Zeno's: 'Nature is a creative fire, proceeding from a certain force towards creating sensible matter.'[162] Hugh's source is undoubtedly Cicero, *De natura deorum*. It has not been realized how widely influential was Zeno's definition; certainly John of Salisbury could refer to 'that master artisan, fire', which, he notes, in the opinion of some was equivalent to nature.[163] The conception of

157 A different view of David's sources for his materialism is taken by M. Kurdziałek, 'David von Dinant und die Anfänge der aristotelischen Naturphilosophie', in *La filosofia della natura nel medioevo. Atti del terzo congresso internazionale di filosofia medioevale* (Milan 1966), pp. 407–16, who suggests (p. 410) that David's source was the Aristotelian conception of the αἰθήρ, as known to him from the *Meteorologica*, *De caelo* and *De mundo* (this last work, however, being a pseudo-Aristotelian treatise heavily indebted to Stoic doctrine). It is true that there is some ambiguity in Aristotle's treatment of the substance of the αἰθήρ, but it is misleading to imply that he conceived of it as material: see H. Happ, *Hyle. Studien zum aristotelischen Materie-Begriff* (Berlin 1971), pp. 486–9. Nothdurft 1963, pp. 196–7, suggests that David's source was Seneca (*NQ* II xlv 1–3), which is closer to the mark. But neither Aristotle nor Seneca is as close to David's conception as is Calcidius' treatment in §§289–94; furthermore, of these three sources, only Calcidius names Zeno, and Zeno is named by David as one of his sources.

158 See G. Théry, *Autour du décret de 1210: I David de Dinant. Étude sur son panthéisme matérialiste* (Kain 1925), pp. 38–45.

159 See T. Gregory, 'L'idea di natura nella filosofia medievale prima dell'ingresso della fisica di Aristotele – il secolo XII', in *La filosofia della natura* 1963, pp. 27–65.

160 *SVF* I 171 (Zeno said) τὴν μὲν φύσιν εἶναι πῦρ τεχνικὸν ὁδῷ βαδίζον εἰς γένεσιν. Cf. Cicero, *De natura deorum* II xxii 57: 'Zeno igitur naturam ita definit ut eam dicat ignem esse artificiosum ad gignendum progredientem via'.

161 *De inventione* I xxiv 34.

162 *Hugonis de Sancto Victore Didascalicon, De Studio Legendi: A Critical Text*, ed. C. H. Buttimer (Washington 1939), p. 18 (I x): 'tertia definitio talis est: Natura est ignis artifex ex quadam vi procedens in res sensibiles' (cf. p. 13 (I vi)). In the light of the Greek text and Cicero's translation of it (above, n. 160), the words *ex quadam vi* should probably be emended to *ex quadam via* (= ὁδῷ).

163 *Metalogicon* I 8 (ed. Webb 1929, pp. 23–4).

nature as creative fire both raised problems and encouraged imaginative application. One problem which it raised was one that the early Stoics, particularly Cleanthes, had faced long ago: namely the distinction between creative fire as a cosmic force, and terrestrial fire, which is plainly destructive.[164] For Cleanthes there were two sorts of fire, one cosmic and creative, the other destructive, and it is interesting to observe Adelard of Bath in his *Quaestiones naturales* (§74) wrestling with Cleanthes' distinction: 'Fire, as Cleanthes argued, was either destructive (*peremptorius*) like the fire around us, or gentle and harmless, like the interior heat of our bodies.'[165] The source once again is Cicero, *De natura deorum*.[166]

This identification of the creative fire of the aether with the creative heat of animate bodies was a Stoic concept (adapted from Aristotle),[167] and certain twelfth-century thinkers were able to apply it to their cosmology. Bernardus Silvestris speaks of the *aether* as a 'purer sort of fire (*purior ignis*)',[168] able to effect the generation of all things: 'Ethereal fire, then, a lover and husband spilling into the womb of earth, his bride, and there effecting the generation of all things, which he draws forth into life by his heat (*quam de calore suo producit ad vitam*), gives that generation over to the nurture of the baser elements.'[169] Bernardus was here drawing once again on the exposition of Cleanthes' views on generative fire, as reported in Cicero, *De natura deorum*.[170] A similar application of the ultimately Stoic conception of 'vital heat' was made by Thierry of Chartres in his account of creation in the *De sex dierum operibus*:

When the stars had been created and set in motion in the firmament, this heat, increased by astral motion and developing into vital heat (*vitalem calorem*), first brooded on the waters ... Through the medium of water that vital heat naturally reached terrestrial things, whence the living creatures of the earth were created.[171]

164 *SVF* I 504; cf. *SVF* I 120 and discussion by Lapidge 1973, pp. 267–73.
165 Adelard of Bath 1934, p. 66: 'Ignis autem illarum, ut Cleanthes arguit, aut peremptorius dicendus est, ut ignis exterior, aut mulcebris et innoxius, ut ignis corporis nostri interior.'
166 *De natura deorum* II xv 40–1; see T. Silverstein, 'Adelard, Aristotle and the *De natura deorum*', *Classical Philology* XLVII (1952) 82–6.
167 Hahm 1977, pp. 142–53.
168 Bernardus Silvestris 1978, p. 104 (*Megacosmus* III 5); the phrase is Stoic (cf. *De natura deorum* II xi 30).
169 Bernardus Silvestris 1978, p. 117 (*Megacosmus* IV 2).
170 *De natura deorum* II ix 23–4; cf. the remarks of B. Stock, *Myth and Science in the Twelfth Century: A Study of Bernard Silvester* (Princeton NJ 1972), pp. 138–41.
171 Häring 1955, p. 189: 'Stellis autem creatis et motum in firmamento facientibus, ex earum motu calor adauctus et ad vitalem usque calorem procedens aquis primo incubuit ... Mediante vero humore, vitalis ille calor naturaliter usque ad terrena pervenit et inde animalia terrae creata sunt'; cf. discussion by P. Dronke, 'New Approaches to the School of Chartres', *Anuario de estudios medievales* VI (1969) 117–40, at 133–4.

The source yet again is Cicero, *De natura deorum*, but the application this time is original.

Of the early Stoics, it was Cleanthes who fully articulated the similarity of aethereal fire to the vital heat which animates living bodies; it remained for Chrysippus to develop this conception into that of the vital, fiery πνεῦμα which penetrates all the universe, thus animating it, and which in minute portions or 'seminal particles of reason (σπερματικοὶ λόγοι)' qualifies and vivifies all created things. Twelfth-century cosmologists could not have accepted the material and corporeal nature of Chrysippus' πνεῦμα, but it is interesting to see how their discussions of the world-soul frequently incorporated aspects of Chrysippus' doctrine. The most remarkable adaptation was made by Hugh of Saint-Victor. We have seen how, in his *Didascalicon*, Hugh quoted Zeno's definition of nature as a creative fire proceeding to creation. In that work Hugh made no further attempt to assimilate the concept; but in his second Homily on Ecclesiastes he developed the concept and in so doing strikingly paralleled the development in the Old Stoa of the concept of creative fire into fiery πνεῦμα. Hugh's account is worth quoting in full:

Pergit spiritus . . . etc. According to our previous discussion, we may – not inappropriately – take this 'spirit' to be the fiery force which, proceeding from the sun itself, infuses itself in all things and, permeating them all invisibly, animates and moves them. Whence the ancients said that nature was a creative fire proceeding towards the generation of corporeal beings. For this vital motion and fiery force of perceptible growth in all nascent things is the source of increase, and, nourishing and feeding them with invisible nutriment, it produces at last an invisible substance. The poet [= Vergil] called this hidden force of nature, which moves all things and nourishes them, the spirit.[172]

Hugh then cites the verses from *Aeneid* VI given above (p. 105). In the passage which follows this discussion, Hugh raises doubts about the apparently corporeal nature of the *spiritus* described by Vergil. Like other theologians of his age, Hugh was clearly troubled by the corporeal nature of the Stoic πνεῦμα; but it is much to his credit that he realized that Vergil's *spiritus* is nothing more than a development of Zeno's creative fire. Here, for once, is a

172 *P.L.* 175, 136:
'*Pergit spiritus* . . . secundum praecedentem expositionem, spiritum nunc non inconvenienter accipere possumus igneam vim quae ab ipso sole procedens, per cuncta se diffundit, et universa invisibiliter penetrans vegetat et movet. Unde et veteres naturam esse dixerunt ignem artificem procedentem in res sensibiles procreandas. Vitalis enim motus, et vegetationis sensibilis in cunctis nascentibus ignea vis origo est: quae rebus omnibus incrementum subicit, et invisibili eas nutrimento alens ac fovens, ad invisibilem tandem producit substantiam. Hanc autem occultam naturae vim cuncta moventem et alentem poeta quoque spiritum nominavit'.

twelfth-century theologian wrestling with the principles of Stoic cosmology rather than merely quoting them.

Other twelfth-century texts contain similar, if less thorough, attempts to
assimilate the Stoic theory of πνεῦμα. The compiler of *De mundi constitutione*
quotes the Stoics (via Calcidius) as saying that the (human) soul is a 'certain
natural spirit'.[173] William of Conches, discussing the world-soul at length in
his *Glosae super Platonem*, gives a definition which *mutatis mutandis* would
satisfactorily describe the Stoic πνεῦμα:

The world-soul is a certain spirit (*spiritus*) located in all things, conferring on them
motion and vitality; this spirit exists in all things as all and one.[174]

William goes on to remark that the world soul does not 'operate equally in
all things (*sed non in omnibus equaliter operatur*)'; although the wording is not
precise, William's remarks adumbrate the Stoic theory of the mixture of
πνεῦμα in bodies being responsible for their shape and substance, one aspect
of which was expressed in the theory of seminal particles of reason (σπερματικοὶ λόγοι). Seneca at one point had referred to this theory in commenting
that 'reason is nothing other than a particle of the divine spirit infused in the
human body' (*Ep. ad Lucilium* LXVI 2), and this very definition is reiterated
by John of Salisbury, who goes on to qualify Seneca's statement by adding
that Seneca should be understood as saying that reason is a 'virtual' rather
than 'quantitative' part of the Divine Spirit.[175] It is true that the Stoic
'seminal particles' were corporeal; but if their corporeality could be overlooked, they could usefully be adapted to Christian theology.[176] Augustine
in his *De Genesi ad litteram*[177] had already made the adaptation and, given the
wider context of thought about the *anima mundi* during the twelfth century,
it is not surprising that the concept of 'seminal reasons' should have been
rehabilitated. Thierry of Chartres speaks of 'seminal causes (*seminales
causae*)' which 'God the Creator inserted in all the elements and adapted
proportionally',[178] so as to give them order and balance; and Thierry's
disciple Clarembald of Arras expounded at length his theory of *seminales
rationes*:

---

173 Pseudo-Bede 1985, p. 62 (II 66), from Calcidius §220.
174 *Guillaume de Conches Glosae super Platonem*, ed. E. Jeauneau (Paris 1965), pp. 144–5; cf.
     William's *Philosophia*, ed. G. Maurach (Pretoria 1980) pp. 22f, and discussion by
     T. Gregory 1955, pp. 123–74.
175 *Metalogicon* IV 16 (ed. Webb 1929, p. 182).
176 See Spanneut 1973, p. 151, and Verbeke 1983, pp. 29–32.
177 *De Genesi ad litteram* IX 1 and 17.
178 Häring 1955, p. 190: 'Deus Creator omnium elementis inseruit (*sc.* seminales causas) et
     proportionaliter aptavit.'

Ratio seminalis is, as I have said, a force contained in the elements, which is to be understood as follows. 'Force': that is, a natural inclination according to which like is produced from like, whence it happens that a bean is not born from a grain of wheat, nor wheat from a bean, nor a man from livestock, nor livestock from a man.[179]

Clarembald goes on to link these 'seminal reasons' with a theory of causality, and in so doing he elaborates – independently – the logical implications in the Stoic theory of σπερματικοὶ λόγοι. For if the πνεῦμα is extended continuously throughout the created universe, so that all its parts are linked and held together, it follows that movement in one part must cause reciprocal movement in another part. And given the spatial interconnection of all things, it follows that all events are interconnected temporally as well. For the Stoics, therefore, the theory of fate or necessity as an unbreakable and inexorable series of events was the logical outcome of their theory of cosmic πνεῦμα. Clarembald, too, clearly recognized the implications of his 'seminal reasons' for the question of causality; thus he writes, like Thierry, that 'from this absolute necessity arises a necessity of interweaving or concatenation (*necessitas complexionis sive concatenationis*) when those things, which are linked in this absolute necessity and descend eternally in a series of fate, like interconnected links of chain, are so arranged';[180] he then goes on to argue that the 'effect of seminal reasons is the entire sequence of temporal events', for in that the Word or Son of God is or exists, 'it (or he) conceived the forms of things from eternity and ordered there to be a unity through the seminal reasons and a temporal sequence of events'.[181] If the reference to (Platonic) forms and the Son of God were excised from this statement, and 'Word' understood as the Stoic λόγος,[182] we would have here in Clarembald a concise definition of the Stoic theory of fate or εἱμαρμένη, complete with the characteristic Stoic metaphors of 'interweaving' (*complexio* = συμπλοκή) and 'concatenation' (εἱρμός, 'a chain', was taken by the Stoics as the etymon of εἱμαρμένη). Clarembald's source for his (Stoic) conception of fate could have been either the *Asclepius* (§§39–40) or, less probably,

---

179 *Ibid.* pp. 208–9: 'Est itaque, ut diximus, ratio seminalis vis insita elementis ... Quod ita debet intelligi. *Vis*, scilicet aptitudo naturalis juxta quam similia ex similibus producuntur. Unde fit ut de grano tritici non nascatur faba, vel de faba triticum, vel de pecore homo, vel de homine pecus.'

180 *Ibid.* p. 207: 'ab hac autem necessitate absoluta descendit necessitas complexionis sive concatenationis, cum ea, quae in absoluta necessitate complicata sunt, ab aeterno ad fati seriem descendentia quasi gradibus concatenatis et sese complectentibus administrantur'.

181 *Ibid.* p. 210: 'perfecta autem sunt formae rerum, effectus seminalium rationum, integra successio temporum. Nam in eo quod Filius Dei Verbum est vel existit, formas rerum ab aeterno concepit et seminalibus rationibus integritatem adesse jussit et temporalem successionem.'

182 Cf. *SVF* II 913: εἱμαρμένη ἐστὶν ὁ τοῦ κόσμου λόγος.

Cicero (*De divinatione* I lv 125) or Calcidius (§§160–75). Although Clarembald seems to have worked out for himself the logical implications of his 'seminal reasons', it is most unlikely that he would independently have invented the Stoic terminology. In any event, it seems clear that the theory of fate or εἱμαρμένη was under discussion among his circle of philosophically minded friends. Thierry of Chartres wrote of fate in his *Glosa* on Boethius' *De trinitate* in words closely resembling those of Clarembald:

> This determined (series) is called necessity, or the necessity of interweaving, for the reason that, when we are involved in its substance, we cannot avoid the serial interconnection of subsequent events. Some have called this natural law, others Nature, others the World-Soul, others natural justice, and others Ymarmene (= εἱμαρμένη).[183]

Several of the appellations of the *necessitas* here show their Stoic ancestry.[184]

Bernardus Silvestris, too, described his Imarmene in terms of the Stoic metaphors of weaving: 'Imarmene, which is the sequence of time and is set out in order, arranges, weaves and reweaves (or: unravels) all the things it embraces.'[185] It is fair to say in general, however, that these twelfth-century thinkers treated the question of fate as a cosmological notion only; they did not go on to explore the role of man's free will in a universe so strictly ordered. That exploration was left to theologians of a later period: Albertus Magnus, Ulrich of Strasbourg, Duns Scotus and Thomas Aquinas.[186]

---

183 N. M. Häring, *Commentaries on Boethius by Thierry of Chartres and his School* (Toronto 1971), p. 284 (II 22): 'hec vero determinata dicitur necessitas, vel necessitas complexionis, eo quod, cum aliquam eius materiam incurrimus, causarum reliquarum seriatam conexionem vitare non possumus. Quam alii legem naturalem, alii Naturam, alii mundi Animam, alii iusticiam naturalem, alii Ymarmenem nuncupaverunt.'

184 *SVF* II 1024 (= Seneca, *De beneficiis* IV vii 1–2).

185 Bernardus Silvestris 1978, p. 120 (*Megacosmus* IV 14): 'Imarmene, que continuatio temporis est, et ad ordinem constituta, disponit, texit et retexit que complectitur universa.' Cf. *ibid.* p. 99 (*Megacosmus* II 1): 'rigida et inevincibili necessitate nodisque perplexioribus fuerat illigatum'. The metaphors of binding and weaving used throughout by Bernardus are of Stoic origin: see Lapidge 1980, pp. 818–19 and 836.

186 See Verbeke 1983, pp. 71–96.

4

THE ARABIC INHERITANCE*

JEAN JOLIVET

From the middle of the thirteenth century, Arab philosophers played an essential part in the development of Western Christian thought, philosophical and theological. The number known was relatively small, but two at least were inevitably familiar: Avicenna and Averroes; these had to be reckoned with, and indeed it soon became imperative to choose between them when framing one's philosophy. Now, the importance of Arabic writing[1] to Western thinkers was no sudden occurrence but the result of a long process that had begun nearly a century before the Latin translations of Averroes' principal commentaries were completed (in about 1230). The twelfth century, indeed, witnessed the appearance, in the field of speculation, of a number of philosophic texts translated from the Arabic, following on certain scientific writings of the same provenance. Furthermore, twelfth-century thinkers studied this rich, newly discovered literature with as much zeal as those of the thirteenth century were to do, although inevitably they made a somewhat different use of it. Thus Adelard of Bath, in his *Quaestiones naturales*, praises the learning and rational method of his Arab teachers;[2] shortly before 1150 Peter the Venerable writes that the 'Saracens', as he calls them, are 'clever and learned men' whose libraries are full of books dealing with the liberal arts and the study of nature, and that Christians have gone in quest of these.[3] Hermann of Carinthia, at about the same time, reminds

---

* Translated by Jean Stewart.
1 Historians of philosophy and science who study the world of Islam are faced with the difficulty of finding an adjective exactly appropriate to these disciplines and to those who practised them: the words 'Muslim', 'Islamic', which are essentially religious terms, cannot be used about such subjects as logic or mathematics, and in many cases their use is questionable when dealing with metaphysics and ethics; 'Arabic' is unsuitable if one thinks of the ethnic connotation of that word, since many of the authors we study belonged to other ethnic groups. We shall retain the term here, however, since it is convenient and frequently used in this connection; moreover, Arabic was the language from which texts were translated in the twelfth century, and the term was much used by Western Christians (we obviously rule out certain other terms also used by them, which are obsolete and have various connotations, such as 'Saracens', 'Ishmaelites', 'Hagarenes').
2 '... a magistris Arabicis ratione duce didici': *Quaestiones naturales*, ed. M. Müller, BGPTM XXXI (1934) 11.
3 '... peritis et doctis hominibus': *Liber contra sectam sive haeresim Saracenorum*, in J. Kritzeck, *Peter the Venerable and Islam* (Princeton 1964), p. 238; 'habet gens nostra plurimos in utraque

---

Robert of Ketton of 'the trappings and decorations which long vigils, and [their] most earnest labour, had acquired for [them] from the depths of the treasures of the Arabs';[4] later Dominicus Gundissalinus refers to Arab thinkers, Avicenna in particular, simply as 'the philosophers'.[5] We shall return to these examples, the most significant of which is undoubtedly that of Peter: the other three, being scholars and translators, were naturally interested in the works they studied; but the Abbot of Cluny himself, concerned by reason of his function with very different matters, shared their feeling. Let us simply note this sequence of eulogies, this respect for Arab scholars and philosophers, for their writings and their scientific institutions: although the twelfth century was indeed constantly involved in crusades, it set great store by the wealth of learning of the 'infidels'.[6] Not that all the philosophy and theology of the twelfth century was influenced by Arabic thought; in fact it was mainly in the second half of that century that Arabic philosophical texts were translated into Latin. But the effects of these translations varied in character and in depth, as we shall try to show insofar as they can be traced. We shall confine ourselves, needless to say, mainly to the translations of Arabic originals.

To begin with, there were these translations. We shall not attempt a detailed study of their history (or what is known of it; many points are still obscure); certain essential characteristics must however be brought out.[7]

In the first place, that scientific works were being translated well before philosophical ones: by the end of the eleventh century, certain medical texts had been translated by Constantine of Africa; whether well or ill done, they made available to the Western Christian world elements of 'theoretical medicine' hitherto mainly unknown, which were to play a part during the

lingua peritos, qui non tantum ea quae ad religionem vel ritum vestrum pertinent, ex vestris litteris sollicite eruerunt, sed etiam quantum ad liberalia vel physica studia spectat, armario-rum vestrorum intima penetrarunt': *ibid.* p. 250. Note also this untranslatable tribute, which combines a technical philosophical distinction with a rhetorical subtlety: 'o homines . . . non solum natura rationales, sed et ingenio et arte rationabiles' (*ibid.* p. 233).

4 '. . . cultus et ornatus . . . quos ex intimis Arabum thesauris diutine nobis vigilie laborque gravissimus acquisierat': *De essentiis*, ed. and trans. C. Burnett (Leiden–Cologne 1982), p. 70.
5 See below, pp. 142ff.
6 See J. Jolivet, 'L'Islam et la raison, d'après quelques auteurs latins des xie et xiie siècles', in *L'art des confins* (*Mélanges Maurice de Gandillac*) (Paris 1987), pp. 153–65.
7 All histories of medieval philosophy and science provide data on this subject. A word of warning, however: the historiography of Latin translations from the Arabic was slow to shed certain errors or misleading points of view, and the earliest studies should therefore be consulted with caution. See the recent article by M.-T. d'Alverny, 'Translations and Translators', in *Harvard 1982*, for the most recent picture of the scholarship and an abundant bibliography.

twelfth century in the development of a new philosophy of nature (William of Conches was to make use of Constantine's *Pantegni*[8]). The same is true of works of astronomy: in Spain at the same period treatises about the astrolabe were being translated. Later, in the twelfth century and at the same time as works of philosophy, other astronomical studies were translated from the Arabic: by Adelard of Bath, by John of Seville (d. 1157; his translations include works by Abū Maʿshar and Thābit b. Qurra) and by Hermann of Carinthia (Abū Maʿshar); there were mathematical treatises – al-Khwārizmī's algebra was translated in 1145 by Robert of Ketton.[9] By the twelfth century there were Latin versions of Arabic works on optics (Ibn al-Haytham), chemistry (Rāzī), alchemy and pharmacology . . .

Secondly, we must note that this interest in Arabic texts was not confined to scientific and philosophical circles; it was also apparent in the sphere of religion, thus attaining the importance of a fact of world history. Peter the Venerable, whom we have seen praising the richness of 'Saracen' libraries, himself promoted the translation of writing that might serve an apologetic purpose: the aim being to provide Christians with a knowledge of basic works on the Muslim religion, so that possible controversies could be upheld by a precise acquaintance with the opponent's beliefs. The result of this project was a collection of texts of unequal value, at any rate as to the works translated, but which included notably a translation of the Koran, the first in Europe, and one of an exchange of letters supposed to be between two Arabs, one a Muslim, the other a Christian; the Christian's letter, which is the longer, is attributed to a certain ʿAbd al-Masīḥ b. Isḥāq al-Kindī (not to be confused with the philosopher to be mentioned later), and is an apologia for the Christian religion. Among the translators engaged in this undertaking we must note two names, Robert of Ketton and Hermann of Carinthia, both already cited for their work in the fields of astronomy and mathematics.[10] Note, too, that there were other translations with an

---

8 D'Alverny 1982, pp. 422–6.
9 These are a few names among many; for more details see d'Alverny 1982, pp. 444ff; C. Sánchez-Albornoz, 'El Islam de España y el Occidente', in *L'Occidente e l'Islam nell'alto medioevo*, Settimane di Studio XII (Spoleto 1965), pp. 282–3; d'Alverny *ibid.*, pp. 118–20. Note that Latin versions of a number of learned Greek works (Euclid, Ptolemy) came through translations from the Arabic; most of the works of Aristotle, however, were translated directly from the Greek, and only exceptionally by way of an Arabic intermediary (L. Minio-Paluello, 'Aristotele dal mundo arabo a quello latino', in *L'Occidente e l'Islam*, pp. 610–13): translations from the Arabic must be given their full importance, but not more.
10 On these see Kritzeck 1964; C. S. F. Burnett, 'A Group of Arabic–Latin Translators working in Northern Spain in the mid-12th Century', *Journal of the Royal Asiatic Society* (1977) 62–108; 'Arabic into Latin in 12th Century Spain: the works of Hermann of Carinthia', *Mittellateinisches Jahrbuch* XIII (1978) 100–34.

apologetic purpose, and also that the Koran was, at any rate partially, accessible from other sources.[11]

These translations from the Arabic of scientific works and religious texts were the work of a first generation of translators. In the second half of the twelfth century, while the interest in science remained undiminished, translations of Arab philosophers began to appear. Most of them were undertaken at Toledo, from 1150 onwards: it may have been at this date that Avendauth (Ibn Dawūd) translated the Prologue to the *Šifā'* (*Healing*), Avicenna's great encyclopaedia. The outstanding name in this second wave is that of Dominicus Gundissalinus, Archdeacon of Toledo, whose apogee was about 1180, and who worked in collaboration with Avendauth, translating several sections of the *Šifā'*.[12] It is often impossible to identify precisely the translators of the various other works. But leaving aside this question and the problems of chronology, we can assert that by the end of the twelfth century there existed Latin versions of a number of important Arabic thinkers, although Averroes was not among them.

The principal element in this collection consisted of portions of the *Šifā'*, some of them of considerable importance. As well as sections of the Prologue and the *Isagoge*, and some books or passages of the *Physics*, there was the *Treatise on the Soul*, translated by Gundissalinus and Avendauth between 1151 and 1166, and the *Metaphysics*, translated by Gundissalinus with an unknown collaborator at some point in the second half of the twelfth century.[13] Add to these the *Intentions of the Philosophers* (*Maqāṣid al-falāsifa*) by al-Ghazālī (Algazel); this work, the translation of which is attributed to Gundissalinus, is actually a résumé of Avicenna's philosophy.[14] The *Enumeration of the Sciences* by al-Fārābī had been translated by Gerard of Cremona,[15] and his *Treatise on the Intellect* by an unknown translator.[16] Al-Kindī was represented by four short texts (one a pseudepigraphos), the chief of which is the *Epistle on the Intellect* (*Risāla fī l-'aql*) in two translations, one by Gerard of Cremona, the other an anonymous one which was to be made use of in the

11 G. Monnot, 'Les citations coraniques dans le "Dialogue" de Pierre Alfonse', in his *Islam et religions* (Paris 1986), pp. 261–77.

12 D'Alverny 1982, pp. 444–6; 'Notes sur les traductions médiévales des oeuvres arabes d'Avicenne', *AHDLMA* xix (1952) 337–58.

13 *Ibid.* pp. 349–58. Editions: S. van Riet, *Avicenna Latinus. Liber de Anima seu sextus De Naturalibus, I-II-III* (Louvain–Leiden 1972); *IV-V* (1968); *Avicenna Latinus. Liber de Philosophia Prima sive Scientia Divina* (3 vols., incl. an index volume, 1977; 1980; 1983).

14 *Algazel's Metaphysics, A Mediaeval Translation*, ed. J. T. Muckle (Toronto 1939).

15 *Domingo Gundisalvo, De scientiis*, ed. M. Alonso (Madrid–Granada 1954).

16 Ed. E. Gilson in 'Les sources gréco-arabes de l'augustinisme avicennisant', *AHDLMA* iv (1929–30) 115–26; the Arabic title is: 'On the meanings of (the word) intellect' (*Fī-ma'ānī l-'aql*).

next century by Albertus Magnus.[17] We must further mention the *Fons vitae* (Source of Life) by Ibn Gabirol (Avencebrol), in a version attributed to Gundissalinus; the Arabic original is lost; although this philosopher was a Jew his book is a metaphysical treatise in the purest tradition of Arabic philosophy.[18]

These titles suggest the contents of a library of homogeneous character: a metaphysic whose main themes were being, essence, the one, emanation; a doctrine of the soul and the intellect conceived as a hierarchized series of functions or entities ultimately dependent on a First or Agent Intelligence which is not God. Common to these two doctrinal schemata, the ontological and the noetic, was the principle of a downward flow of being, of unity, of intelligible light. These new books, finally, provided a theory of knowledge which far surpassed in breadth and power the traditional framework of the Liberal Arts. This latter point takes us to the frontiers, often difficult to trace exactly, which in fact join rather than divide the realms of science and philosophy. We note in this connection that the increase in learning due to the Arabs (which included with their own sciences those of ancient Greece, assimilated and transformed by them) modified in its very structure the concept and practice of the 'arts'; 'they have become the arts of the *physici*', of scholars who take an interest in nature;[19] this implies a relation to things very different from the speculative relation characteristic of the 'Liberal Arts'.[20] By analogy, the same is true of philosophy: the Arabic contribution must not be considered as a massive influx of new elements juxtaposed with the old; its chief result was perhaps the change it brought about in the general structure of the doctrinal field,[21] thus inaugurating alterations which were to develop further in subsequent centuries. This is how we must try to present things, while realizing that their extent and the still incomplete character of our knowledge render the task strictly speaking impossible; nor must we neglect

17 A. Nagy, 'Die philosophischen Abhandlungen des Ja'qūb ben Ishāq Al-Kindī', BGPTM II. 5 (1897); the texts are: *De intellectu, De somno et visione, De quinque essentiis, Liber introductorius in artem logicae demonstrationis*; the Arabic original of the third text is lost, and the last is apocryphal.
18 C. Baeumker, 'Avencebrolis Fons vitae ex Arabico in Latinum translatus ab Johanne Hispano et Dominico Gundissalino', BGPTM I.2–4 (1891–5).
19 On these two points see R. McKeon, 'The Organization of Sciences and the Relations of Cultures in the Twelfth and Thirteenth Century', in J. E. Murdoch and E. D. Sylla (eds.), *The Cultural Context of Medieval Learning* (Dordrecht–Boston 1975), pp. 151–92 (at p. 158).
20 Even Hugh of Saint-Victor, who is often credited with an innovatory appreciation of the importance of practical and technical knowledge, remains bookish in his sources: see *Les arts mécaniques au Moyen Age*, Cahiers d'études mediévales VII, ed. G. H. Allard and S. Lusignan (Montreal–Paris 1982), *passim*.
21 See McKeon 1975, p. 157.

certain details, the mere enumeration of which would not be enough, but without which our picture of the whole would remain aridly schematic.

Since Arab philosophers were obviously introduced into the West by way of translations, a study of their contribution must naturally begin with an examination of their vocabulary. The Latin terminology of philosophers and theologians had added to its indispensable classical basis certain special elements derived essentially from the two great authors to whom these thinkers were chiefly indebted, Augustine and Boethius; John Scotus Eriugena had provided an original contribution, which was, however, less widely used. The grammatical effervescence of the Carolingian period, so rich in new or unusual words, had subsided. St Augustine's vocabulary is sober, with the indispensable minimum of technical terms. This vocabulary thus served chiefly to convey the concepts of the Latin Fathers and of Greek philosophy as introduced by Boethius. The translators from Arabic were faced with texts the vocabulary of which was also derived from two principal sources: that of Greek philosophy as transposed by Arabic translators of the second and third centuries of the hegira (ninth and tenth centuries AD) and, to some extent, that of Muslim theology as adapted by Avicenna for the elaboration of a doctrine integrating ancient philosophy with ontological speculation about the relation of created beings to God. Obviously, there was no straightforward equivalence between the Arabic vocabulary of the original texts and the Latin vocabulary used by the translators. A few significant examples will show various effects of this disparity and the attempts made to reduce it or to compensate for it.

We note first, examining the index to S. van Riet's edition of Avicenna's *Metaphysics*,[22] the great disproportion in the two languages as regards words meaning 'being'. The poverty of Latin in this field led Gundissalinus to adopt two extreme measures, either the repetition of the same word with several different meanings, or the fragmentation of equivalences. In either case the content of the text is confused. It would of course be vain and indeed misleading to assume that every Arabic term always has a clearly specified meaning; many terms function as synonyms. But in some cases it is important to distinguish between them, and at any rate when the single word *esse* is used to 'translate' thirty-four different Arabic expressions, its inadequacy is patent. It usually corresponds to *kāna* and *wuǧida*, the two words most frequently used to express Being, the former in principle carrying the particular implication of being-in-process-of-becoming (less forceful than

22 See above, n. 13.

ṣāra, which we also find translated as *esse*). But it likewise renders the words *ḥadaṯa*, *ḥudūṯ*, which are more correctly translated at other times by *contingere*, *provenire*, since they imply the coming-into-being of something previously non-existent.[23] Reciprocally, *contingere* is used to translate, among other terms, *ʿaraḍa* (to occur), *waqaʿa* (to happen), and several times ... *kāna*! Such an inventory of the successive dislocations of vocabulary could be pursued at length; we may merely note, on the one hand, the relative inaptitude of Latin to express the concept of being in all its complexity; on the other hand the bewilderment of the translator, whose philosophical culture has not accustomed him to analyse the nuances of ontology, and who diversifies his renderings instead of observing some semantic regularity. We may observe, likewise, that Avicenna uses three different words which normally mean 'eternal' according to three different modalities: *abadī* implies infinite duration in the future, *azalī* infinite duration in the past, and *qadīm* absolute anteriority. But Gundissalinus translates all three by *aeternus*; and if he varies his rendering of *abadī* by using also *perpetuus*, *sempiternus* and *semper*, this does not increase the precision of his text – quite the contrary.

On the other hand, translators seeking greater accuracy sometimes used Latin words in an unfamiliar technical sense; some of their inventions have survived, others have not. Take for instance Avicenna's terms *taṣawwur/taṣdīq*; *taṣawwur*, 'representation', is according to Avicenna primary knowledge, acquired by definition or some such process: e.g. the way we 'represent' to ourselves the essence, the quiddity of man. *Taṣdīq*, 'acceptance', can only be acquired by means of a syllogism or something analogous; thus we 'accept' the statement that the world has a first cause. The former word was translated either by *imaginatio* or *formatio*, according to the different connotations of the Arabic word; the latter either by *credulitas* or by *fides*. The later fortune of these terms varied: the former was often expanded into *imaginatio intellectus*, 'intellectual representation'.[24]

In the few examples we have looked at, the translator was seeking in the Latin language a term corresponding to the Arabic word he wished to render. But it sometimes happened that he unwittingly did what translators from Greek into Arabic had themselves done, simply transposing the

---

23 Note incidentally that the formulae *novitas mundi*, *innovatio mundi* seem not to appear before the first part of the thirteenth century, in the work of William of Auvergne and the *Summa Halensis* (according to the card-index of the 'Glossaire du latin philosophique médiéval', (Paris, Centre National de la Recherche Scientifique/Université de Paris 1).

24 M.-D. Chenu, 'Imaginatio. Note de lexicographie philosophique médiévale', in *Miscellanea G. Mercati* (Vatican City 1946) II 593–602 (at pp. 599–601). *Formatio et credulitas* are also found in the *Fontes quaestionum* of al-Fārābī: see M. Cruz Hernandez, 'El "Fontes Quaestionum" ('Uyūn al-Masāʾil) de Abū Naṣr al-Fārābī', *AHDLMA* XVIII (1950–1) 303–23.

original word into the foreign language by creating a purely phonetic neologism: e.g. the Arabic *hayūlā* represents the Greek ὕλη. Thus Gundissalinus, translating Avicenna's *Metaphysics*, was faced with the word *anniyya* or *inniyya*, which is a way of expressing the existence of a thing or a being. He translates this twice by *esse*, once by *quia est*, but in four passages (and in eight instances) he simply transposes it into *anitas*. This word in fact won little favour,[25] which may seem surprising and even regrettable; it might have had the same success as *quidditas*, which Gundissalinus uses profusely in this same translation to convey *māhiyya*. Of course *quidditas* is philologically sounder than *anitas*: *quid* corresponds exactly to *mā*, and the relative suffix *-itas* to the Arabic suffix, whereas in *anitas an-* is, as we have said, merely a phonetic transposition. But it is most unlikely that those who read and used these Latin translations were aware of this; their lack of enthusiasm for *anitas* was probably due to a lesser concern with the details of ontology, an insensitivity to the special implication in the word *aniyya* or *inniyya* of the assertion of a real or ideal presence.

But the instances cited hitherto must not make us forget an important fact: twelfth-century translations from the Arabic also contributed to a major degree to the Latin vocabulary of philosophy. As Gilson pointed out long ago, there is a clear 'tradition' in medieval manuscripts whereby certain treatises which formed a 'doctrinal chain' were copied consecutively or collected together. Such were the treatises *On the Intellect* by Alexander of Aphrodisias, by al-Kindī, and by al-Fārābī, and the *De anima* of Avicenna.[26] The originals of the last three were written in Arabic, but that of Alexander was made known to the Western Christian world through the Latin version, attributed by Father Théry to Gerard of Cremona, of the Arabic translation by Isḥāq b. Ḥunayn.[27] We shall not attempt a detailed comparison of all these texts, but merely record their effect in the enrichment of the Latin vocabulary of philosophy and correlatively in the development of the medieval noetic. Like the translator of Alexander, the three Arab philosophers mentioned above all use the same word *'aql* to render the Greek νοῦς. Their own elaboration of this, based on the many Aristotelian commentaries translated into Arabic, distinguishes between several sorts or levels of

---

25 See the detailed article devoted to this question by M.-T. d'Alverny, 'Anniyya–Anitas', in *Mélanges Etienne Gilson* (Paris 1959), pp. 59–91 (especially pp. 90–1).

26 Gilson 1929–30, p. 5.

27 G. Théry, *Autour du décret de 1210: II – Alexandre d'Aphrodise. Aperçu sur l'influence de sa noétique* (Kain 1926); see especially pp. 68–83; the Latin text is on pp. 74–82. The Greek text has been edited by I. Bruns, *Commentaria in Aristotelem Graeca, Supplementum Aristotelicum* II.1 (Berlin 1887); the Arabic translation, by J. Finnegan, *Mélanges de l'Université Saint-Joseph* XXXIII (Beirut 1956).

intellect. Thus if we consider only the Latin formulae and leave aside for the moment the case of Alexander, we find in al-Kindī 'intellect always in act, potential intellect, intellect in transition from potentiality to actuality, demonstrative intellect (*intellectus semper in actu, int. in potentia, int. cum exit de potentia ad effectum, int. demonstrativus*)';[28] in al-Fārābī, considering only those expressions that are strictly noetic,[29] 'potential intellect, intellect in act, acquired (*adeptus*) intellect, agent intelligence (*intelligentia agens*)';[30] and in Avicenna, 'material intellect (*int. materialis*), intellect in act, intellect in disposition (*in habitu*), acquired intellect, holy (*sanctus*) intellect, agent intelligence'.[31] It would be pointless to summarize the history of medieval noetics, particularly since this would involve a consideration of the subsequent translations of Averroes and the use made of these; we have only to read these formulae to gauge their importance in later thought, to which for a long period they provided a basis of vocabulary and consequently of structure.[32] A few comments, reintroducing Alexander, will clarify certain points:

(1) The *intellectus demonstrativus*, ascribed to al-Kindī, was understandably never followed up; it is a misinterpretation.[33]

(2) The *intellectus adeptus* of al-Fārābī and Avicenna comes from an interpretative translation of Alexander's νοῦς θύραθεν, 'the intellect come from without'; the Arabic translator in fact emphasizes less the transcendence of the intellect than the fact that it is *acquired* by the soul: he thus calls it al-ʿaql al-mustafād (whence *intellectus adeptus*), simply completing his formula, where required, by Alexander's term; which produces al-ʿaql al-mustafād min ḫāriǧ, the intellect acquired from without (θύραθεν), *adeptus ab extrinsecis* (or *extrinsecus*).

(3) The word *intelligentia*, which appears in al-Fārābī's and Avicenna's lists meaning 'the agent intellect', can be related to an initiative of the Latin translator in connection with the Arabic translation of Alexander: to emphasize the transcendent nature of the νοῦς θύραθεν he gives it this name, whereas the Arabic, like the Greek, uses one single word to represent the three kinds of intellect: ʿaql or νοῦς. It sometimes happens that both words are used in the same sentence:

---

28 Edition: see n. 17. Arabic text in Abū Rīda, *Rasāʾil al-Kindī al-falsafiyya* I (Cairo 1369/1950), 353–8, and in J. Jolivet, *L'intellect selon Kindī* (Leiden 1971), pp. 158–60. One can see from Nagy's edition that Gerard of Cremona prefers *ratio* to *intellectus*; this particular sense of *ratio* has not survived.

29 See n. 16; this short work is like an entry in a dictionary, elaborate and searching; the author also enumerates other meanings of the word than those chosen by philosophers.

30 See n. 16.

31 See n. 13.

32 See L. Gardet, 'De la terminologie à la problématique (quelques exemples à propos de l'Avicenne latin)', in *Actas del V Congreso internacional de filosofia medieval* (Madrid 1979) I 155–62.

33 Jolivet 1971, pp. 11–13, 73–86.

'the acquired intellect is, by its nature, an intelligence (*intellectus adeptus . . . est, de natura sua, intelligentia*)'.[34] We notice the same thing in the translations of al-Kindī and al-Fārābī, and in the writings and translations of Gundissalinus. This distinction, introduced in the twelfth century, was to be maintained subsequently.[35] It implies a hierarchy among thinking beings, a basic difference between men and angels, which is absent from the Greek and Arabic terms.

We have dwelt in some detail on the theme of the variety of intellects in order to bring out, by a specific example, the importance of the work of twelfth-century translators in the history of medieval thought.

Another term whose fortunes ought to be followed is *intentio*. But the word was complex from the start. Gundissalinus uses it to render the Arabic *ma'nā*, which is a difficult word to translate. It signifies the meaning of a statement, a real though not perceptible quality of something, what one has in one's mind . . . Avicenna uses it in his *Treatise on the Soul* in different senses: he gives the name to the object of '*aestimativa*', that is to say, a quality present in a thing, perceived and grasped by a particular kind of intuition (thus the lamb immediately knows that the wolf is hostile to him); but he also speaks of *intentio intellecta*, of *intentio universalis*, and then the word means 'concept'.[36] In short, in Avicenna's writing as in common use, the word holds a meaning of which the core is clear but the fringe is hard to define. It is questionable whether the Latin *intentio* translates it satisfactorily; but the word was accepted and became an essential term in the vocabulary of philosophy by the thirteenth century, and it cannot be ignored, for all its difficulties and possible inappositeness.

Apart from the examples cited, however, these translations from the Arabic do not seem to have done much to enlarge the scope of philosophical Latin in the Middle Ages.[37] Yet their impact was profound, for we must consider the weight and the doctrinal context of this handful of terms: through them, in particular, the whole noetic theory of Aristotle, elaborated

---

34 Théry 1926, p. 80.
35 Some aspects of this story are traced in J. Jolivet, 'Intellect et intelligence. Note sur la tradition arabo-latine des 12e et 13e siècles', in *Mélanges Henry Corbin* (Tehran 1977), pp. 681–702.
36 *Liber de anima*, ed. cit. n. 13; see the Index.
37 See S. van Riet, 'Influence de l'arabe sur la terminologie philosophique latine médiévale', in *Actas del V Congreso internacional de filosofía medieval* I 137–44.

by Arab philosophers, entered the stream of thought of Western Christendom.[38]

We must now consider in what way, and to what extent, the concepts and terms imported through Latin translations of scientific and philosophical writings in Arabic spread through the philosophical field in the twelfth century. This is no easy task, for a number of reasons: we do not know all these translations, and those that are known have not all been examined in sufficient detail to enable us to recognize with any certainty their echo in specific Latin texts of the twelfth century; the same uncertainty prevails when we consider the latter. It is thus hard to compare two groups the components of which remain unknown either as separate elements or as a whole. Furthermore, where it is clear that a Latin author has borrowed something from one or several Arabic authors, we need to ascertain his intention in so doing. This is impossible, strictly speaking, and in fact it is not very important; but we ought surely to determine the significance of his borrowings, not in his own mind but in the way his concepts function; and this we shall presently try to do, in specific cases. Finally, we should avoid overestimating the importance of these Arabic influences, or – since we are looking for them and expecting to find them – seeing them where they do not exist. In the first place, for a variety of reasons, many writings remained unaffected by these influences, and this not only in the realm of theology and religious thought in general: a *Treatise on Philosophy and its Parts* (*Tractatus de philosophia et partibus eius*), recently published and ascribed by its editor to the second half of the twelfth century, owes nothing to the Arabic treatises on the classification of sciences which were in fact known at that time. Whether it had perhaps been written somewhat before they became accessible, or whether its author had deliberately ignored them, we cannot tell.[39] Secondly, there may have been doctrinal coincidences not necessarily implying influence: an interesting case is that of Gilbert of Poitiers, whose work shows some striking analogies with ideas expressed by Ibn Gabirol in his *Source of Life*; as far as we can tell, it was chronologically impossible for

38 Note the curious case of one of the Arabic titles for Aristotle's *Metaphysics*: Kitāb mā ba'd al-ṭabī'iyya ('*The book of that which comes after natural things*'): Gundissalinus does not translate the concept 'metaphysics' in his *De scientiis*; then Gerard of Cremona, who knows Greek, renders it as *de metaphysicis*, and Gundissalinus repeats this translation in his *De divisione philosophiae*: see I. P. Fernandez, 'Influjo del árabe en el nacimiento del término latino medieval "Metaphysica"', in *Actas del V Congreso internacional de filosofia medieval* II 1099–107.

39 G. Dahan, 'Une introduction à la philosophie au XIIe siècle. Le *Tractatus quidam de philosophia et partibus ejus*', *AHDLMA* XLIX (1982) 155–93.

him to have known the translation of this book; perhaps the two philosophies had a common root, which we should endeavour to trace.

Finally, there may be cases where an influence appears confined to a single point, so that it is impossible to determine exactly whether it is mediated or direct; thus in the *Cosmographia* of Bernard Silvestris we find the words *elementans, elementatum*, which it is chronologically possible for him to have borrowed from the *Introductorium magnum* of Abū Ma'shar;[40] but these words, the second in particular, occur already in the *Philosophia mundi* of William of Conches, written even earlier than the translations of Abū Ma'shar.[41] What, then, are we to conclude? Does this fact suggest an Arabic influence on Bernard Silvestris – it would surely be the only instance in this work – or the influence of William of Conches? And was the latter solely responsible for this remarkable expression, or had he been in contact with translators before their work appeared? Or again, which is not impossible, were these translators using a term which was already current among philosophers and scientific thinkers? These various examples illustrate the difficulty of determining exactly, and in every case, the impact of these Arabic–Latin texts on twelfth-century writers; certainty is only possible if the concepts, and still more the words, are numerous and recognizable enough to eliminate all doubt. This methodological difficulty is absent, of course, in cases where authors mention their sources or incorporate recognizable passages of these in their writings. We shall therefore first enumerate several examples of indirect influence of philosophical and scientific Arabic texts before turning to authors who illustrate the last-mentioned possibility. Finally we shall examine what was the total result of these influences in the history of medieval thought.

As we have seen, scientific writings were the first to be translated, and it is therefore their contribution that must be studied first. Despite the importance of works on mathematics, optics, and chemistry which were thus introduced into the Western Christian world, it was clearly the treatises on medicine and astronomy/astrology which had the deepest influence on speculative thought; bearing on the structure of the world and created things, on the macrocosm and the microcosm, they were inevitably of

40 See Peter Dronke's introduction to his edition (Leiden 1978), p. 18: the translations of the *Introductorium* date from 1133 (John of Seville) and 1140 (Hermann of Carinthia); the *Cosmographia* dates from 1147–8 (p. 2). But the sources traced by Dronke are not Arabic. When Bernard writes: 'Astra notat Persis, Egyptus parturit artes' (p. 105, v. 49), he is not referring to Arabic scholars; see the following line: 'Grecia docta legit, prelia Roma gerit'.
41 See P. Dronke, 'New Approaches to the School of Chartres', *Anuario de Estudios Medievales* VI (1969) 129ff; William's *Philosophia* cannot be later than 1130 (p. 130).

interest to philosophers. In a parallel fashion, a book like Hermann of Carinthia's *De essentiis* belongs as much to the field of philosophy as to that of science. Moreover these writings promoted and modified the recasting of the classification of sciences, illustrating to some extent the specialized treatises of al-Fārābī and Avicenna on the subject. We must briefly consider this movement, which went on during the whole century and which also, though on the didactic plane, belongs on the borderline between philosophy and science.

At the beginning of the twelfth century the *De eodem et diverso* of Adelard of Bath[42] offers a classification of the sciences which in the main reproduces the classical schema of the Seven Liberal Arts: the Trivium, comprising Grammar, Rhetoric, and Dialectic,[43] and the Quadrivium, which comprises Arithmetic, Music, Geometry, and Astronomy.[44] But right at the end of this little work there appear two brief references to sciences outside this framework: first to medicine, more precisely to the three principal organs (the brain, the heart and their divisions, the liver and the four humours); then to physics (the nature of the magnet and a problem of statics). The reference to medicine is preceded by an exhortation to abandon 'the schools of Gaul' (*Gallica studia*) and follow those of Greece; that to physics cites 'a certain Greek philosopher, who had made a special study of the art of medicine and the nature of things' and whom Adelard had met when travelling 'from Salerno to Magna Graecia': a clear allusion to the work of translation and the enrichment of learning which had been going on there for a long time already when Adelard wrote *De eodem*, and to which we have already alluded. Clearly such innovations could not be integrated into the framework of the seven traditional Arts.

A sort of corroboration of this fact is provided by Hugh of Saint-Victor († 1141), whose *Didascalicon* proposes, in Book I, a division of philosophy rather than of science, philosophy being divided into four sections: theoretical, practical, mechanical, and logical, with the Quadrivium included under the head of theoretical philosophy as one of its three parts, the others being theology and physics, according to the Aristotelian schema handed down through Boethius, but here in the inverse order. The Trivium, expanded to

---

42 Ed. H. Willner, BGPTM IV.I (1903).

43 The order of precedence of the two latter arts determines two different cultural patterns; Adelard follows the same order as Abelard and William of Conches, not that of Martianus Capella and of Bernard Silvestris in his *Commentary on the Aeneid* (if it is indeed his). On the system of the Seven Arts, see I. Hadot, *Arts libéraux et philosophie dans la pensée antique* (Paris 1984).

44 This is the order handed down by Boethius in his *Institutio arithmetica*; here again Adelard diverges from Martianus.

include the study of sophisms, is identified with logic. The two intermediary parts include no science strictly speaking, medicine being included under mechanics. In short, Hugh ignores the contribution of Arabic science, despite his concern with 'mechanics': the fact that the double system of the Liberal Arts is scarcely modified, and that only as regards the Trivium, implies total adherence to tradition.[45] This point needed noting here and now, for we shall meet Hugh again on the same ground.

On the other hand the classification proposed by Gundissalinus is an undeniable shattering of the old framework. His *Division of the Sciences*[46] opens with the familiar three theoretical sciences; then come the Seven Arts, with medicine inserted between the Trivium and the Quadrivium; as regards the latter he follows the arrangement of Adelard of Bath, but includes between Geometry and Astronomy several sciences which had been founded or developed in the Arab world.[47] We shall see that these profound changes were suggested not by a practical knowlege of science but by the translations of philosophers; but this is unimportant. What is noteworthy is that the expanded Quadrivium included sciences particularly cultivated by the Arabs, and that it opened and concluded with the two sciences mentioned by Adelard as flourishing in southern Italy and Sicily: medicine[48] and statics.

The later writer's echo of his predecessor is enriched by the new knowledge and thought acquired over several decades. For the work of philosophers had, as we have said, benefited by that of translators. By the end of the first third of the twelfth century we find William of Conches, in his *Philosophia*, adding to the traditional authorities (Plato, Macrobius, and poets such as Vergil and Ovid) the name of Constantine, a *physicus* whose theory of the elements, he argues, does not conflict with the view of the *philosophi*.[49] Later (1143) the *De essentiis* of Hermann of Carinthia offers a

---

45 A similar criticism could be made of the *Tractatus de philosophia* (cit. n. 39). In none of the four types of division the author proposes do the sciences stand out at all distinctly; in one of them, which the editor considers original (p. 165), medicine, *physica*, is identified with the physics of Boethius' schema, and the Seven Liberal Arts are set against the Seven Mechanical Arts which are, with one exception, the same as in Hugh of Saint-Victor.

46 The precise details are discussed below.

47 See also G. Beaujouan, 'The Transformation of the Quadrivium', in *Harvard 1982*, pp. 463–87.

48 The persistent association of medicine with the Seven Liberal Arts is found not only in written documents, but, for example, in the rose window of the north transept of Laon cathedral, which is divided into eight parts showing the Seven Liberal Arts plus medicine.

49 See the chapter on the elements in William's *Philosophia*, ed. G. Maurach (Pretoria 1980), pp. 26ff, esp. pp. 26 and 30. For the influence of medicine on William in particular, see H. Schipperges, 'Die Schulen von Chartres unter dem Einfluss des Arabismus', *Sudhoffs Archiv für Geschichte der Medizin und der Naturwissenschaften* XL (1956) 193–210. As regards

significant illustration of the influence of translations from the Arabic, and particularly translations of works of science, on the most enquiring minds of the twelfth century. We know that Hermann had been involved in the project of translation for the purpose of apologetics, inaugurated by Peter the Venerable; and that, moreover, he had translated works of mathematics, astronomy, astrology, and meteorology.[50] The *De essentiis* is a personal work[51] dealing with cosmogony and cosmology, and is thus on the borderline between physics and natural philosophy. If we examine its sources, which have been diligently inventoried by its editor, we find them to be the most advanced representatives of characteristic trends in the scientific and philosophical culture of the twelfth century: beside the solid traditional basis provided by the *Timaeus* with Calcidius' commentary, by Boethius (*De institutione arithmetica*) and Macrobius, we find a Greek contribution transmitted via the Arabs (the *Almagest* of Ptolemy, the *Elements* of Euclid), and Arabic writers on astronomy (al-Battānī, Abū Ma'shar) and on medicine (Qusṭā b. Lūqā).[52] The basic concepts – the 'essences', which are cause, movement, place, time and the *habitudo* or way of life proper to each 'species' – thus function in all these areas, whether known of old or newly discovered. Hermann moreover is careful to assert his orthodoxy, not only his belief in one God but also in Jesus Christ, whose birth was foretold by astrologers, as Abū Ma'shar tells.[53] In the same way the *Philosophia mundi* of William of Conches opens with an exposé of two characteristic Christian dogmas, the Trinity and the Incarnation. At first glance, at any rate, no conflict can be assumed in the twelfth century between Greek and Arabic science and philosophy on the one hand and the Christian religion on the other.

Nevertheless a change was taking place. The ancient system of the Quadrivium symbolised and maintained a philosophy in which nature had no place; Arithmetic was an abstraction, and the other three mathematical arts provided no concrete ballast: Music was merely a consequence of Mathematics, Astronomy an application of spherical Geometry: Geometry

astronomy, there is some disagreement among historians as to the influence on William of Abū Ma'shar's *Introductorium* (Dronke 1969, p. 124 n. 21).

50 A list with commentary is given in Burnett 1978.

51 Hermann of Carinthia, *De essentiis*, A Critical Edition with Translation and Commentary by C. Burnett (Leiden–Köln 1982); the introduction and commentary are exceptionally rich in information.

52 These are only the most important sources of Hermann of Carinthia. On the intermingling of Greek and Arabic contributions and their influence in the twelfth century, see the controversial but stimulating book of R. Lemay, *Abū Ma'shar and Latin Aristotelianism in the Twelfth Century* (Beirut 1962).

53 *De essentiis*, pp. 80–3, 243, 245–6.

itself juxtaposed speculation about abstract space with the most modest technical applications; it is curious to find Adelard of Bath, the future translator of Euclid from the Arabic, offering in his *De eodem et diverso* merely a few hints for land-surveyors. The practical knowledge and control of nature was limited by the uncertain efficacy of techniques; the view of nature available to thinkers was a distorted one, seen through such media as Isidore's *Origins of things* (with the significant alternative title of *Etymologies*: it is less an encyclopaedia of things than a dictionary of words), ancient encyclopaedias in need of revision, or works in which nature is considered solely with a view to edification, a typical example being Book XXI of the *City of God* (according to the *De doctrina christiana* the interest of the scientific study of things lies in the mystical meaning to be discovered in them). Tullio Gregory has repeatedly stressed the emergence in the twelfth century of a secular conception of nature, representing order in the world and fertile energy, as it might be conceived by philosophers meditating on astronomy/astrology and on medicine.[54] Now, we know the part played by books translated from the Arabic in the development of these branches of learning in the West at this period. Each of these sciences is concerned with specific facts: influences passing from the heavens to the earth, interaction between internal activities in living beings who are also subject to external happenings; each thus contributes to shaping and enriching the concepts of causality. Not only do they lend one another support on the general plane of ideas: on another level the rivalry and possible conflict between them may stimulate enquiry. Of great interest from this point of view is the controversy between *medici* and *astrologi* to which William of Conches and Hermann of Carinthia bear witness: the *astrologi* seeking to explain physical facts with reference to the whole cosmos, the *medici* confining themselves to qualitative and perceptible events.[55] Thus, by direct or dialectic means, these sciences brought into twelfth-century thought ideas hitherto unknown, and the philosophers who accepted and developed them weakened thereby those conceptions which sacramentalized and offered a mystical interpretation of the cosmos: inevitably, and whether consciously or not (or indeed perhaps with deliberate unconsciousness) they carried on and amplified a movement of thought tending to substitute a new image of the world for the old: a secular image for a religious one. But already, as was to happen during the

---

54 Among Gregory's writings on this topic, see especially *Anima mundi* (Florence 1955); 'L'idea di natura nella filosofia medievale prima dell'ingresso della fisica di Aristotele. Il secolo XII', in *La filosofia della natura nel medioevo* (Milan 1966), pp. 27–65; 'La nouvelle idée de nature et de savoir scientifique au XIIe siècle', in Murdoch–Sylla 1975, pp. 193–218.

55 Summarized in Burnett 1982, pp. 22–5.

era of scholasticism, these different views were seen sometimes as complementary, sometimes as conflicting with one another. We find William of Saint-Thierry borrowing largely from Constantine of Africa in the first book of his treatise *Of the nature of body and soul*, while Hugh of Saint-Victor rejects the medical doctrine according to which the animal spirit, material but subtilized as it reaches the brain, is held to give rise to *intellectus* and *ratio*: he writes, in opposition to this, a pamphlet *On the union of body and soul* which locates the rational substance outside and above the imagination, in the general scheme of a hierarchized universe.[56]

The contribution of philosophical writings was obviously more direct. Yet it was not immediate, in that it did not fill a vacuum: concepts acquired from Arabic sources had to be accommodated with those already established; the same is true of the way they were formulated. The area of philosophy in which Western Christian thinkers learnt most from Arabic writings was perhaps that of noetics, the science of the intellect; until they translated al-Kindī, al-Fārābī, and Avicenna, they had at their disposal only the traditional views inherited from Augustine and Dionysius concerning ideas and illumination, which were doubtless inspiring and spiritually rich but which either gave little scope for conceptual analysis, for which they were not intended, or else had not been developed in that direction; and there was not much to be gained from a few remarks by Boethius about the process of abstraction. But certain elements of vocabulary existed, which were so to speak ready and waiting for a fresh content: in particular the pair *intellectus/intelligentia*. These two terms referred to the highest form of knowledge attainable by the human soul. Philosophers and spiritual thinkers distinguished several such modes, or different powers of the soul, associating them respectively with the divisions of philosophy and the steps by which the soul ascends to wisdom. At the highest level, the vision of the intelligible, or of things divine, was therefore called either *intellectus* or *intelligentia*. Sometimes the two words were used together. Then, either one or the other – according to the author – represented the highest level.[57] We have already noticed the interesting case of the translators of al-Fārābī, of Avicenna, and of the Arabic version of Alexander of Aphrodisias, who use both *intelligentia* and *intellectus* to render the 'aql of their texts; its theoretical importance justifies a second reference to it, in connection with the way data

56 V. Liccaro, 'Ugo di San Vittore di fronte alla novità delle traduzioni delle opere scientifiche greche e arabe', in *Actas del V Congreso internacional de filosofía medieval*, II 919–26.
57 For detailed discussion, see M.-T. d'Alverny, *Alain de Lille: Textes inédits* (Paris 1965) pp. 170–80.

new to the twelfth century were reconciled with the traditional basis. In this particular case the vocabulary of the translators was richer than that of the original authors, and the differentiation which it allowed them to make clearly altered the tenor of the text: the Arab reader of the word *'aql*, like the Greek reader of the word νοῦς, retained a certain freedom to interpret as he chose the similarity or dissimilarity between the faculty by which man thinks and the power from above which makes him think, which indeed governs the movement of the spheres. The reader of the Latin text was in fact bound to make a marked distinction between the transcendent *intelligentia* and the human *intellectus*. This decision, philological in form but philosophical in substance and primarily theological, since it is certainly based on the angelology of Dionysius, is one of the last episodes in a long story: that of the interpretation of the Aristotelian noetic and of the relation between the *Treatise on the Soul* III 5 and the *Metaphysics* XII 7–9. Latin writers inherited this unwittingly, and the translations they produced revived the problem in terms of their own philosophy and theology: in particular, whether to consider the *intelligentia agens* as external to man, and in that case whether as God or an angel; or whether to revert to the single term *intellectus*, and consider the intellect-as-agent as belonging to the human soul. The problem arose fairly soon, but was probably not clearly thought out at first. For the moment we may conclude that, while inheriting from the Arabs a whole new chapter of philosophy, Western thinkers also inherited the problems, sometimes seemingly insoluble ones, connected with its concepts, and that they revived these in their own fashion.

The concepts of noetics, although new, thus secured a firm footing in Western philosophy, somewhat adapted and transformed. Inversely, another important notion, which plays a key role in Avicenna's philosophy, did not at first have the success it deserved: namely the notion of essence, indeterminate in itself in relation to existence and its various modalities. Not until the thirteenth century did this theme enter the philosophy and theology of the Western Christian world, in particular with the use made of it by St Thomas in his *De ente et essentia*. The twelfth century seems scarcely to have been aware of it. We have already observed the inadequacy of terms denoting existence in the Latin translation of Avicenna's *Metaphysics*. Now the heterogeneity of vocabularies is naturally paralleled by a difference in the nature of problems. The situation here was just the opposite of that which we found regarding noetics: for Western thinkers in the twelfth century, the field of metaphysics was already occupied by a body of doctrine which, though original, was built on traditional foundations. It was, if not a system, at any rate a group of concepts and schemata elaborated by Gilbert of

Poitiers, author of commentaries on the short theological treatises of Boethius, who moreover partially reflected the philosophy of Bernard of Chartres. His influence was to last until the middle of the thirteenth century. Now the major theme of Gilbert's ontology was the complementary character of the *quo est* and the *quod est*, of subsistence and that which subsists, already formulated by Boethius, and linked with a conception of idea and image derived from Platonism. It was thus both close enough to and different enough from the conceptions of Avicenna to conflict with these, at least in a strictly ontological sense.

On the other hand the orientation towards unity in Avicenna's doctrine would strike a familiar note to Western readers: the theme of unity was essential to Christian theology in connection with the Trinity of Divine Persons, and moreover had been given philosophical emphasis by Boethius.[58] We may note also the theme of ontological hierarchy, illustrated by Avicenna as the successive emanation of Intelligences, souls and bodies from the heavenly spheres, which echoes the schema of Dionysius and thus that of Proclus (the *Liber de causis* was also translated in the twelfth century), and again the theme of illumination, which brings together that of hierarchy and that of noetics. We shall examine presently how these doctrinal elements are combined in particular writings. But here we must repeat an earlier warning: when one finds in a twelfth-century writer an idea or a formula that recall, for instance, Avicenna, one must not immediately assume that he has been influenced by Avicenna. One should first consider whether this is not a case of a special tradition. To take an obvious example, when Alan of Lille writes that 'unity of itself begets unity (*unitas de se gignit unitatem*)', it would be a mistake to see in this formula an echo of Avicenna's axiom that 'from the One only one proceeds', for Alan continues, a line further on: 'God begets another self, that is, the Son, and brings forth from himself an equal to himself, that is, the Holy Spirit (*Deus gignit alterum se, i.e. Filium, de se profert equalem sibi, i.e. Spiritum sanctum*)'. This conceptualization of the dogma of the Trinity in arithmetical form had already been proposed by Thierry of Chartres.[59] One final comment: we referred earlier to the *Liber de causis*. Arabic philosophy was closely, although not totally, dependent on that of Greece, particularly

58 The pioneer article of M. H. Vicaire ('Les Porrétains et l'avicennisme avant 1215', *RSPT* XXVI (1937) 449–82) is doubtless more intuitive than really demonstrative, despite – or perhaps because of – the profusion of data it offers. But it serves the useful purpose of drawing attention to the undoubted kinship, for all their diversity, between the two doctrines mentioned in his title, and also between those of Avicenna and Dionysius, whose Platonism Avicenna supports in the twelfth century against that of Augustine (p. 469).
59 N. M. Häring, 'Alanus de Insulis. Regulae caelestis iuris', *AHDLMA* XLVIII (1981) 125. The relationship is signalled by Häring himself, but in connection with the phrase immediately

Neoplatonism. It is natural, therefore, that the influence it exerted should be
reinforced by texts issuing from the doctrinal complex from which it originated: but that complex remains visible in the writings of Arabic philosophers. In our present study, therefore, we shall take account, as a rule, only
of the latter, even where Greek writings which were available at the same
time provided supportive influence. (The fact that the *Liber de causis* was
known only in Arabic does not prevent it from being essentially Greek; it
does not therefore call for special analysis in a study devoted to a particular
stage of medieval Latin philosophy in its relation to Arabic philosophy.)

We must now consider several Latin works of the twelfth century in search
of traces – whatever their degree of depth, extent, and clarity – of the influence of Arabic writings on individual texts. We shall begin with a small book
entitled *Disciplina clericalis*, written during the first part of the century, by a
contemporary and perhaps a collaborator of Adelard of Bath: a Spanish Jew
named Moses, who on his conversion received the Christian name of Petrus
Alfonsi,[60] under which he is commonly known. He helped to introduce
Arabic astronomy to the West; he became physician to Henry I of England.
Apart from his scientific work he is known for having written a *Dialogue
between Petrus and Moses the Jew*, an apologia for Christianity which incidentally provides many precise details about Islam.[61] The *Disciplina clericalis*
is quite different: it is a textbook of practical morality, 'a compilation', the
author tells us, 'consisting partly of philosophers' aphorisms and castigations,
partly of Arabic aphorisms and castigations, fables and verses, and partly of
comparisons with animals and birds'.[62] The combination of these three
sources is interesting, as is the fact that the author has troubled to enumerate
them: the traditional use of bestiaries as edifying literature is modified here
by some elements borrowed from classical antiquity, and by others from
Arabic literature, these being of a genre amply represented in educational
works (*adab*) and in collections of sayings and stories with a moralistic aim.[63]

preceding – 'omnis pluralitas ab unitate defluit' – where he refers to Thierry, *De trinitate* I
        14.
60 *Die Disciplina Clericalis des Petrus Alfonsi*, ed. A. Hilka and W. Söderhjelm (Heidelberg 1911).
61 P.L. 157, 535–706.
62 '. . . libellum compegi, partim ex proverbiis philosophorum et suis castigationibus, partim
        ex proverbiis et castigationibus arabicis et fabulis et versibus, partim ex animalium et
        volucrum similitudinibus': p. 2.
63 The aphorisms are most probably the equivalent of *ḥikam*; the castigations of *mawā'iẓ*; the
        fables, of *amṭāl*; as for poetic citations, these are customary among Arabic authors. On the
        Arabic books used by Petrus, see E. Hermes, *The Disciplina Clericalis of Petrus Alfonsi*
        (Berkeley–Los Angeles 1977), p. 7.

Without attempting a study of comparisons and sources, we may note that the *Disciplina* mentions the prophet Enoch, under both his names, the biblical and the koranic;[64] that it refers in several passages to Alexander and Aristotle, who figure frequently in Arabic philosophical literature;[65] and that it quotes Luqmān, the legendary sage who is also mentioned in the Koran (he is identified here with Balaam), to whom it ascribes five aphorisms.[66]

Adelard of Bath is another witness to Arabic influence at the beginning of the twelfth century; or more precisely, to the fame of the Arabs at that period. His is a curious case, very different from that of Petrus Alfonsi. The latter sought to introduce into the Christian world he had chosen to enter part of the Arabic culture which he had always known. Adelard, an Englishman whose writings testify to his presence at Tours and at Laon, had acquired knowledge of a philology and science that had been quite unfamiliar to him. We have already noted the contrast between the high level of the mathematical works he translated and the elementary treatment of geometry in his *De eodem et diverso*. His relation to the Arabic language and to Arabic science has its own story, the initial stages of which we can trace in the *De eodem* and the *Quaestiones naturales* (a work of uncertain date, but undoubtedly composed after the *De eodem* and before Adelard's translations). In the earlier book, as we have seen, he praised the sciences known to Magna Graecia, of which the 'Gallica studia' are ignorant. The later work speaks more precisely in praise of the Arabs. It takes the form of a dialogue between Adelard and his nephew – the same figure, presumably, as that to whom the *De eodem* was addressed. Its opening pages describe Adelard's return to England after a journey studying in the East, and a friendly encounter during which the nephew asks him to 'tell him about the Arabic schools, to say something new about them'.[67] Adelard consents, while reflecting that this will scarcely please his readers who, he says, reject all modern discoveries. He reminds his nephew that they two have followed different paths, one devoted to the teachings and doctrines of the 'Gallic schools', the other to those of the Arabs. From an opening dialogue, the contrast is marked: on the one hand the young man, an exclusive adherent of Western learning, who dismisses as 'futile' the teaching of the 'Saracens' and objects to his uncle's praise of them; on the other Adelard, pouring scorn on such submission to authority (you follow it, he tells his nephew, like an

---

64 'Enoch philosophus qui lingua arabica cognominatur Edric': p. 2 (Edric=Idris).
65 Pp. 10, 37, 48.
66 The gnomic genre is well represented in Arabic literature.
67 '... aliquid Arabicorum studiorum novum': *Quaestiones naturales*, ed. M. Müller, BGPTM
   XXXI.2 (1934) 1.

animal being led by its halter) and contrasting 'the lessons he has learnt from his Arab teachers, under the guidance of reason'.[68] Thus he is not merely setting certain theories against others, one cultural zone against another; his argument is epistemological. Reason is to be preferred to authority. This point is of particular interest: reason, at any rate in scientific matters, is according to Adelard not to be found in the Western world but among the Arabs.[69] Yet it is noteworthy that at the time of saying this, Adelard has not yet really assimilated Arabic learning. Historians disagree as to exactly how much of that learning the *Quaestiones* in fact transmit, but their estimate varies from very little to nothing at all.[70] Adelard's declarations are purely programmatic; but at the same time they imply a clear recognition of the differences between the scientific concepts of Western Christendom and those of the Arabic world: differences of content, of level, of method. The *Quaestiones* may indeed reveal nothing really new, but none the less they point to a new landscape which their author seeks to approach: Adelard here speaks for his century.

In the second half of that century Dominicus Gundissalinus[71] (who was still living in 1190) produced, beside his translations, a personal work which deserves examination. The word 'personal' is used here in a special sense: Gundissalinus works chiefly with scissors and paste; he has not yet reached the stage of integrating the new philosophical contribution into compositions with an organization of their own. But there is a historical interest in his method of juxtaposition, and the way it is applied raises questions and justifies hypotheses as to the role first played by Arabic philosophy in medieval Christian thought. Since the chronological sequence of these treatises is uncertain we shall consider them in the order that seems clearest.

The *De unitate*[72] provides a particularly clear example of the way the philosophical concepts present in works translated from the Arabic became associated with similar concepts already developed in the Western Christian

68 *Ibid.* pp. 4–5, 11.
69 This was not an isolated position in the twelfth century: see Jolivet 1987. It was shared in fact by all those who translated Arabic works.
70 According to B. Lawn (*The Salernitan Questions. An Introduction to the History of Medieval and Renaissance Problem Literature* (Oxford 1963), pp. 20–30), everything set forth in this work was already known in the West; M.-T. d'Alverny considers that Arabic influence on the *Quaestiones naturales* 'is not obvious' (1982, p. 441 n. 81); M. Clagett, 'Adelard of Bath', in *Dictionary of Scientific Biography* I (New York 1970) 61–4, quotes a passage which in his opinion displays such influence: the description of a vessel pierced with several holes at the bottom, a single one at the top, and filled with water: the water does not run out so long as the topmost hole remains blocked.
71 See C. Kren, 'Gundissalinus, Dominicus', in *Dictionary of Scientific Biography* v (New York 1972) 591–3.
72 Ed. P. Correns, BGPTM I.1 (1891).

tradition. Gundissalinus sets forth the primary character of unity, its omnipresence in all created beings, though subject to a hierarchy in which it becomes increasingly diluted as it moves downward towards multiplicity. Thus he enumerates twelve ways of being one, from the one in essence, *unum essentia*, which is God, to the moral one, *unum in more*, based on an association of wills, good or evil, and including between those, notably, what is one through conjunction of matter and form (the angel, the soul), and what is one through continuity (the tree, the stone) . . .[73] The two last kinds of oneness correspond to six sorts of form, each of which informs a material substance: the forms of intelligence, of the soul (rational, sensitive, animal), of nature, of the body.[74] P. Correns, in the notes and the study with which he accompanies his edition, points out the two currents that meet in this work: one derived from Boethius and Augustine, the other from the *Fons vitae* of Ibn Gabirol. Now Ibn Gabirol, in this dialogue written in Arabic but of which we know only the Latin translation[75] (made precisely by Gundissalinus, together with John of Spain), recapitulates, in an original fashion, a whole corpus of Neoplatonic doctrines developed in texts which derive in one way or another from Arabic philosophical literature: Greek works known only in their Arabic translations, such as the *Theology of Aristotle*, works written directly in Arabic, such as the epistles of the Brethren of Purity (Iḥwān al-Ṣafā'), or the treatises of the Jewish philosopher Isaac Israeli (a disciple of al-Kindī).[76] Of course as they passed from these sources to the *Fons vitae*, from the *Fons vitae* to the *De unitate*, these doctrines underwent at each stage a process of refraction and filtering: Gundissalinus does not retain Ibn Gabirol's special theme of the presence of matter at every level of being; he speaks of creation rather than of emanation. Yet it is undeniable that in the final analysis his treatise is largely, even if indirectly, dependent on the Arabic philosophical tradition.

Gundissalinus' other writings derive more directly from this source. Gerard of Cremona had translated al-Fārābī's *Enumeration of Sciences* (*Iḥṣa' l-'ulūm*); Gundissalinus takes up the same text again and adapts it in his *De scientiis*,[77] as 'translator and compiler' according to his editor; he does not follow the text through to the end, but introduces, on his own initiative,

73 *Ibid.* pp. 9–10.
74 *Ibid.* p. 8.
75 Ed. C. Baeumker, BGPTM I.2–4 (1892–5).
76 On Ibn Gabirol's probable sources, notably the Arabic ones, see J. Schlanger, *La philosophie de Salomon Ibn Gabirol. Etude d'un néoplatonisme* (Leiden 1968), ch. 4; the author speaks of a 'littérature néoplatonicienne judéo-musulmane' (p. 56).
77 Ed. M. Alonso Alonso (Madrid–Granada 1954); Gerard of Cremona's translation is edited by A. González Palencia, *Al-Fārābī, Catálogo de las ciencias* (2nd ed., Madrid–Granada 1953).

quotations from Arabic works and authors not included in his Arabic original: Aristotle's *Meteorologica* and *Parva naturalia*, Nicomachus of Gerasa and Hugh of Saint-Victor (here again the Latin tradition links up with the Greek and Arabic traditions). The Prologue contains a passage where Gundissalinus sketches the general curve of the history of learning, as he sees it: once there were philosophers and among them, at a higher level, sages; now, in this ageing world (*mundo senescente*), neither of these are to be found; all we can do now is to 'skim the surface' of the sciences, or at least of some of them.[78] This text is curious because, by recalling the pessimistic theme of the ageing world, so frequently expressed in the medieval view of history, it contrasts well with the prevailing spirit in which translations were undertaken and which implied, on the contrary, an opening on to unknown regions, and therefore an advancement of learning. This theme appears in other works by Gundissalinus himself.

In fact his *De scientiis* plays its part in that reorganization of the system of arts and sciences of which mention has already been made; so does his *De divisione philosophiae*,[79] but in a far more developed and complex fashion. Here the influence of al-Fārābī persists, but that of Avicenna is much more prominent: Gundissalinus introduces into his work a whole chapter of the *Šifā'*, which discusses the hierarchy of the sciences. He borrows moreover other elements from the same author: concepts, principles of classification which cannot here be discussed in detail; he combines them with other sources, some of them Latin (Isidore, Boethius, Bede).[80] The general plan, pruned of the complications due to the plurality of points of view assumed by the author, is as follows: after a Prologue devoted to 'philosophy' and the ways of dividing it, Gundissalinus first suggests a tripartite distribution of the sciences, in which he echoes Avicenna, Algazel and Boethius, and which in the last instance can be traced to the Aristotelian list of sciences: physics, mathematics, theology (*scientia naturalis, mathematica, divina*); then come grammar, poetics, rhetoric, logic, and medicine, which is thus inserted

78 'Cum plures essent olim philosophi, inter omnes tamen ille solus simpliciter sapiens dicebatur, qui omnium rerum scientiam certa cognitione comprehendere credebatur. Nunc autem, mundo senescente, non dico sapiens, sed, quod minus est, philosophus nemo dici meretur; quia, qui sapientiae studere velit, iam vix invenitur aliquis. Quapropter, parvitati nostrae satisfieri credimus, si postquam non omnia possumus, saltem de singulis aliqua, vel de aliquibus aliquid, degustemus.'

(De scientiis, pp. 55–6)

79 Ed. L. Baur, BGPTM IV.2–3 (1903).
80 The complex organization of the *De divisione philosophiae*, and the questions it raises, have been best analysed by H. Hugonnard-Roche, 'La classification des sciences de Gundissalinus et l'influence d'Avicenne', in *Etudes sur Avicenne*, ed. J. Jolivet and R. Rashed (Paris 1984), pp. 41–75.

between the former content of the Trivium and that of a considerably enlarged Quadrivium, as proposed by al-Fārābī: arithmetic, music, geometry, perspective (*de aspectibus*), astrology, astronomy, the science of weights, the science of technical processes (*de ingeniis*; *ingenia* corresponds to the Arabic *ḥiyal*); this review of the theoretical sciences is concluded by the translation of the chapter on logic from the *Šifā'* already mentioned; finally we come to practical philosophy. The novelty of this work is twofold: for one thing, it introduces into the customary system of knowledge branches which were unknown to tradition, but which would in any case have had to be included because of the contribution of scientific translations; for another thing, it provides a new view of the status and structure of the sciences through a number of suggestions: the distribution of sciences according to their method and according to their object, division into parts and into species, integration of logic into philosophy as one of its parts, and so forth.[81] In a highly complex and problematic, not to say confused, form, a whole new epistemology is here introduced into Western Christian thought under the influence of Arabic philosophers. To the names, already mentioned, of Gundissalinus' chief sources (Avicenna, al-Fārābī, Algazel) must be added that of al-Kindī: an entire paragraph of his *De quinque essentiis* (known only in its Latin version) appears in the *De divisione philosophiae*,[82] as does a passage from the (inauthentic) *Liber introductorius in artem logicae demonstrationis*, according to which geometry and logic are the two species of the *ars demonstrativa*.[83] Furthermore, of the six definitions of philosophy enumerated in the Prologue, four are borrowed (as L. Baur points out) from Isaac Israeli's *Book of Definitions*, translated by Gerard of Cremona, and the other two from Isidore. Isaac was a disciple of al-Kindī, so here again Arabic philosophy is introduced through its intermediary (and so, indirectly, is Greek philosophy, from which these definitions are borrowed). Their reading of all these authors led Gundissalinus and his contemporaries to envisage in a new way the relations between religious knowledge and secular learning, with the latter appearing to some extent a rival to the former: 'the ultimate aim of the first philosophy', writes Gundissalinus, echoing Avicenna, 'is to know the way in which the Most High God rules the world, to know the orders of spiritual angels, to know the laws according to which

---

81 On these three points, see Hugonnard-Roche 1984, *passim*.
82 'Nam quia philosophia non est nisi ordo animae, idcirco convenit, ut philosophia dividatur in duas partes, quae sunt scientia et operatio, sicut anima dividitur in duas partes, quae sunt sensus et ratio, videlicet ut per scientiam cognoscatur pars rationalis et per operationem pars sensibilis': ed. Nagy 1897, p. 28.
83 Baur 1903, pp. 33–4; Nagy 1897, p. 57.

the heavenly spheres are ordered; this knowledge can only be attained if one knows astronomy, and none can acquire the science of astronomy without a knowledge of arithmetic and geometry'.[84] If, as this text implies, and as other sources confirm, the angels are also the Intelligences that move the spheres, angelology is naturally connected with astronomy; in which case, a Christian reader might think, the writings of Dionysius (a new translation of whose work by Johannes Saracenus was completed in 1167) were not the only means of access to knowledge of the heavenly hierarchy; the writings of astronomers and of philosophers could now be ranked beside those of the saints. This was certainly an unfamiliar situation, created by the translation of Arabic authors.

The opening of the *De processione mundi*[85] (the title means, roughly, 'cosmogony') is steeped in the Bible and in traditional theology: the famous verse from Romans 1: 20 exhorts one to pass from visible created things to the invisible things of God; the greatness, beauty and usefulness of created beings (see Wisdom 13: 5 and 6: 17, also quoted here a little later) indicate the Power, the Wisdom, and the Goodness of God, and thus a creative Trinity; and after the 'first moving cause' there comes a second, then another of third rank (*tertiae dignitatis*), and so on. A second section, concerned with methodology, leads from an analysis of things to the faculties of the soul, then to the metaphysical categories of created things: we recognize here a composite structure, an order (*dispositio*), and hence a moving cause (*causa movens*), by means respectively of our reason, of demonstration and of intelligence (*intelligentia*); with these three faculties are associated the three methods which, according to Boethius, characterize the three theoretical sciences (*rationaliter, disciplinaliter, intellectualiter*) and three ways of apprehending things, according to possibility, necessity, or supra-discursive intuition (*simplex et mera conceptio*). Then the demonstrations are set forth, according to familiar schemata and concepts: being composite, the world has a principle, a first cause, which is the Being who is necessary (*necesse esse*) and One; created beings, considered in themselves, are possible and may be necessary by reason of that necessary Being who is God; as efficient cause and creator, God is the origin of a twofold movement, creation and composition; the movement produced by the second cause also consists of

84 '... intentio ultima in hac scientia est cognitio gubernationis Dei altissimi et cognitio angelorum spiritualium et ordinum suorum et cognitio ordinationis in compositione circulorum. Ad quam scientiam impossible est perveniri nisi per cognitionem astrologiae; ad scientiam vero astrologiae nemo potest pervenire nisi per scientiam arismeticae et geometriae': Baur 1903, p. 39; van Riet 1977, p. 21.
85 Ed. G. Bülow, BGPTM xxiv.3 (1925).

two parts: composition and generation. Creation produces to begin with the two first principles of things: the material principle and the formal; matter and form are the two 'simples' created by the simple One, and their conjunction is the first compounding. As to the creation of things, it consists in 'the issuing (*exitus*) of form out of the wisdom and will of the Creator and the impression of his image on matter, as water issues and flows from its source'.[86] In the final analysis, 'the entire universe proceeded from non-being to the potentiality of being, from that potentiality to being in act, from being in act to corporeal and incorporeal being: and all this immediately, outside time': 'reason required it to be so.'[87]

This very cursory summary indicates the principal points of reference of Gundissalinus, already visible in the *De unitate*. There is the Christian authority, of course; to the quotations and concepts at the opening of the book may be added the appearance, almost at its conclusion, of the trinitarian schema: Gundissalinus, here following a Chartrian tradition, relates the creation of matter to the Power of God, that of form to his Wisdom, that of their conjunction to 'the connection of One with the Other (*utriusque connexio*)'. But throughout this treatise the influence of the philosophers plays a major role. In a disquisition on the creation Gundissalinus alludes to authors whom he does not name but who are recognizable as Avicenna and Algazel: 'The philosophers say that through the ministry of angels new souls are created every day from matter and form, and that through them the heavens are moved.' But more generally, he exploits to the full two rich mines of speculative writing: Avicenna's *Metaphysics* and the *Fons vitae* of Ibn Gabirol. In the first fifteen pages of a fifty-page work, the dialectical discussion of the necessary and the possible, the twofold nature of created things (possible in themselves, necessary through another), come straight out of Avicenna. However, a little further on Gundissalinus asserts that a created being has to be twofold, and towards the end, that it cannot be eternal: two points that formally contradict Avicenna's doctrine of creation. The first leads us to the other source on which the rest of the treatise largely depends: for according to Ibn Gabirol matter and form are twin principles connected in their origin. If we note that Gundissalinus also makes use, though much

---

86 'Creatio namque rerum a creatore non est nisi exitus formae ab eius sapientia et voluntate et imperio eius in imaginem in materiam ad similitudinem aquae exitus emanantis a sua origine et effluxio eius': *De processione mundi*, p. 40; Bülow refers to Ibn Gabirol, *Fons vitae*, in Bülow 1925, p. 330.
87 'Sic igitur processit totius mundi constitutio de nihil esse ad possibiliter esse, de possibiliter esse ad actu esse et de actu esse ad corporeum et incorporeum esse; et hoc totum simul, non in tempore': *ibid*. p. 54.

less frequently, of Boethius, Augustine, and Apuleius, we recognize the Neoplatonic syncretism, with a predominant Arabic trend, that we already observed in the *De unitate*. For all that he is a Christian and even an archdeacon, Gundissalinus here constructs a metaphysical model borrowed wholesale from the infidel, an analysis of the genesis of things which no doubt owes a few of its initial data to biblical revelation, but all its detail to reason.

Two remarks in conclusion. First, in several places in the *De processione mundi* what Gundissalinus writes differs from the corresponding passages in his translation of Avicenna. Thus in the formula *intellectus essendi* the word *intellectus* is used instead of *intentio*, which in the translation renders the Arabic word *ma'nā* (a difficult word to translate, as we noted above); elsewhere the word *quidditas*, as a translation of *haqīqa*, is simply omitted.[88] Apparently Gundissalinus as author has deliberately chosen a less unfamiliar vocabulary than that which he used as translator. A second point: one page of this treatise enumerates the different Latin words that can describe matter, according to its situation and its function. It is called matter (*materia*), says Gundissalinus, when it is considered in relation to form; substance (*substantia*) when it is considered in itself; hylê (*yle*) when it is potentially fitted to receive a form; subject (*subjectum*) when it actually bears a form; mass or matter (*massa vel materia*) insofar as it is common to all forms; element (*elementum*) when other things can be reduced (*resolvantur*) to it; origin (*origo*) when it initiates the composite structure; element, again, when one returns to it. Now of these eight meanings five – from the third to the seventh – are taken from one page in the *Physics* of the *Šifā'*; the definitions are translated literally, and there is a close correspondence between the Arabic and the Latin vocabularies used in this text to discuss matter: we find *yle/hayūlā*; *subjectum/mawḍū'*; *massa/mādda*; *materia/ṭīna*; *elementum/usṭuqus*; *origo/'unṣur*.[89] This proves that when Gundissalinus was writing his *De processione mundi*, Book I of the *Physics*, at any rate its opening, had already been translated, and very likely by Gundissalinus himself. We note moreover the effort made by the translator to retain in Latin the variety of the Arabic terms.

---

88 Compare Gundissalinus, p. 6, lines 16–17, and Avicenna, p. 45, lines 57–8; Gundissalinus, p. 16, lines 16–18: 'quod sic est, omnino non est simplex', and Avicenna, p. 55, lines 50–1: 'id cui semper accidit, eius quidditas non est simplex'. A more complex case occurs with Gundissalinus, pp. 8–10 in relation to Avicenna, pp. 46–8: among the MSS of the translation, some give *coaequalia*, others *comitantia*, to translate *mutakāfi'āni*; the *De processione mundi* has, according to the MSS, *comitantia* or *concomitantia*.

89 *De processione mundi*, p. 31; *Al-Šifā'*, *Al-Ṭabī'iyyāt*, *Al-samā' al-ṭabī'ī* (Tehran n.d.), p. 6.

The *De anima*,[90] both in substance and in spirit, is akin to the preceding works. It consists for the most part of a collection of texts drawn from Arabic philosophers; its editor cites Avicenna's *Treatise on the Soul* (the sixth book of the *Physics* in the *Šifā'*, which, as we have seen, was translated by Avendauth and Gundissalinus), the *Source of Life* of Ibn Gabirol and the *Difference between the Soul and the Spirit* (*De differentia animae et spiritus*) of the ninth-century Christian Arab Qusṭā b. Lūqa,[91] both translated by the same writers; and the treatise *De motu cordis* by Alfred the Englishman (Alfredus Anglicus, Alfred of Sareshel).[92] But it also draws inspiration, in its final chapter, from Christian authors. This treatise follows an elaborate plan: it examines successively whether the soul exists, how it moves the body, what it is, whether it is created or uncreated, whether it has been created one or manifold, whether souls have been created from the beginning of the world, whether the soul was created from nothing or from something, whether it is mortal or immortal; finally it discusses the powers (*vires*) of the soul, the sensitive soul as such, the internal powers of animals (*animalia*) and the powers of the rational soul. There are ten chapters in all, of which the first eight are concerned with metaphysics and theology, the ninth with things 'physical', and the last with things noetic and mystical: this contains, in particular, the description of the hierarchy of intellects which we have referred to earlier.

The Prologue to the *De anima*, like that to *De scientiis*, deserves examination, both in itself and in comparison with that to the translation of the *De anima* of Avicenna. In the latter, Avendauth, its co-translator, writes that, thanks to the munificence of the dedicatee, Archbishop John of Toledo,[93] and to his own work,

Latin readers will know with certainty something hitherto unknown, namely whether the soul exists, what are its nature and its qualities according to its essence and its activity, and this will be proved by true reasons ... Here, then, is a book translated from the Arabic, whose author, you must know, has collected everything that Aristotle said in his book about the soul, sense-perception and the sensible, the intellect and the intelligible.[94]

90 Ed. J. T. Muckle, *Mediaeval Studies* II (1940) 23–103. See also E. B. Abeloos, 'Un cinquième manuscrit du "Tractatus de anima" de Dominique Gundissalinus', *Bulletin de Philosophie Médiévale* XIV (1972) 72–85.
91 Ed. C. S. Barach (Innsbruck 1878). M.-T. d'Alverny is preparing a new edition (cf. *Bulletin de Philosophie Médiévale* XXI (1981) 36).
92 Ed. C. Baeumker, BGPTM XXIII. 1–2 (1923).
93 See d'Alverny 1982, p. 445 and n. 101.
94 '... ut vestro munere et meo labore, Latinis fieret certum, quod hactenus exsistit incognitum, scilicet an sit anima, et quid et qualis sit secundum essentiam et effectum, rationibus verissimis comprobatum ... Habetis ergo librum ... ex arabico translatum: in

The Archbishop may well have been surprised to be informed that hitherto, in the Latin, Christian world people did not know whether the soul existed and what was its nature, or at any rate had no authentic proofs of it. In his *De anima* Gundissalinus replaces this passage by another, less provocative, but interesting from a historical point of view:

> I have carefully collected all the rational propositions about the soul that I have found in the works of the philosophers. Thus, at any rate, a work hitherto unknown to Latin readers, since it was hidden in Greek and Arabic libraries, has now, by the grace of God and at the cost of immense labour, been made available to the Latin world so that the faithful, who toil assiduously for the good of their souls, may know what to think about it, no longer through faith alone but also through reason.[95]

Avendauth seemed to say that Avicenna had merely made a compilation from Aristotle: now Gundissalinus speaks of philosophers in the plural, and mentions Greek and Arabic books; he thus expresses a truer view of the relations between these authors and of the accumulation of philosophical learning. Moreover, he considers that this learning adds a rational dimension to what Christians hitherto knew only by faith. From the outset of his book he stresses the advantage for religion of this philosophical study of the soul, which makes it possible to refute those who believe that only things perceptible by the senses exist and that there is no God – like those referred to in the Book of Job and in the Psalms; that is why, he says, 'I have thought it necessary to put forward the arguments which have convinced philosophers that the soul exists.'[96] In short, the philosophers guarantee the truth set forth in the Bible, and so we return to the Prologue: 'no longer by faith alone, but also through reason'. In chapter 8, where the question of the soul's mortality is raised, the philosophers prove that it does not die with the body, in opposition to those who think that it is merely a breath (*pneuma, spiritus*).

---

quo quicquid Aristoteles dixit in libro suo de anima, et de sensu et sensato, et de intellectu et intellecto, ab auctore libri sciatis collectum.'   (Van Riet 1972, pp. 3–4)
In the passage not translated, Avendauth explains the method that was followed:

'I first translated each word into the vernacular, and my lord archdeacon translated them one by one into Latin.'

95   'Quapropter quicquid de anima apud philosophos rationabiliter dictum inveni, simul in unum colligere curavi. Opus siquidem latinis hactenus incognitum utpote in archivis graecae et arabicae tantum linguae reconditum, sed jam per Dei gratiam quamvis non sine multo labore ad notitiam latinorum est deductum (deditum) ut fideles, qui pro anima tam studiose laborant, quid de ipsa sentire debeant, non iam fide tantum, sed etiam ratione comprehendant.'   (Muckle 1940, p. 31.)
For the variant *deductum/deditum*, see Abeloos 1972 *in fine*.
96   Muckle 1940, p. 32; Job 21: 15; Psalms 13: 1.

The editor points out that this chapter is made up of two long passages from Avicenna.[97] This raises again the question we have already encountered when dealing with the *De divisione scientiarum* and the *De processione mundi*: what role does Gundissalinus allot, in relation to faith, to those philosophers whose works he copies? what does he expect to gain from them? The *De anima* provides a fresh opportunity to tackle this problem,[98] particularly since it has been studied by Etienne Gilson in his preface to the edition by J. T. Muckle.

Here Gilson sets forth and criticizes the various interpretations made since 1890 of Gundissalinus' *De anima*,[99] dealing specifically, in conclusion, with the thesis of Father R. de Vaux. According to de Vaux, the *De anima* and the *Book of First and Second Causes*, to which we shall return, give evidence of a 'Latin Avicennism' corresponding to the 'Latin Averroism' of the thirteenth century.[100] In Gilson's view, on the contrary, this period witnessed the growth of 'un augustinisme avicennisant',[101] an Augustinian trend influenced by Avicenna. He therefore denies the existence of any philosophical current reproducing Avicenna's doctrines in their entirety: no known author, he says, has maintained that our knowledge depends on a separate substance, which is the agent Intellect, common to the whole human species – a thesis characteristic of Avicenna's noetic theory. He demonstrates that Gundissalinus – to confine ourselves to that author – clearly altered a statement of Avicenna's in this connection: where Avicenna described one of the aspects of the soul as turned 'towards the highest principles', Gundissalinus writes that 'the soul looks upward, to contemplate that which is above her: God'.[102] Similarly, he substitutes an angel for Avicenna's 'Giver of forms',[103] and declares that God is seen 'through intelligence alone, with no

---

97 *Ibid.* pp. 61ff.
98 We shall not discuss the *De immortalitate animae*, ed. G. Bülow, BGPTM II.3 (1897); this work was most probably not by Gundissalinus at all but by William of Auvergne: B. C. Allard, 'Note sur le "De immortalitate animae" de Guillaume d'Auvergne', *Bulletin de Philosophie Médiévale* XVIII (1976) 68–72. The question of its possible Arabic sources is still unresolved.
99 Gilson 1929–30, pp. 23–7.
100 R. de Vaux, *Notes et textes sur l'avicennisme latin aux confins des XII-XIIIe siècles* (Paris 1934). This volume includes an edition of the *Liber de causis primis et secundis* and the last part of Gundissalinus' *De anima*. It is not impossible that Gundissalinus is also the author of the *Liber*, but by no means certain: see E. Gilson, 'Avicenne en Occident au Moyen Age', *AHDLMA* XXXVI (1969) 99–100; if he is, it must be admitted that he takes up a more radical position there than in the rest of his work. (See *below*.)
101 Gilson, 1929–30.
102 Avicenne: 'versus principia altissima' (p. 94 van Riet); Gundissalinus: 'ad contemplandum suum superius quod est Deus' (p. 151 de Vaux; p. 86 Muckle).
103 That is, the *intelligentia agens*: the expression *dator formarum* does not occur in Avicenna's *De anima*; but this does not essentially affect the argument.

intermediary'[104] – which, according to Gilson, means the denial of the 'agent Intellect'. Add to this what Gilson had noted at the outset of his refutation, that Gundissalinus makes a number of quotations from St Augustine, Boethius, St Bernard, St James, and especially St Paul; one can therefore no speak of 'Latin Avicennism' in connection with this book, or indeed any other.

In actual fact things are not so simple, as is apparent when one looks closely at Gilson's first textual argument. Gundissalinus, he says, sets a phrase of Avicenna's beside one from Augustine to emphasize that illumination comes from God alone and not from the agent Intellect: 'just as sight does not occur without external light, so without the light of the agent Intelligence entering within us we have no understanding of the truth of a thing; reason is, in fact, to the mind what sight is to the eye'. Father de Vaux himself compares this last phrase with Augustine's *Soliloquies* I 6, 12: 'it is God himself who brings illumination: I am reason in men's minds, as sight is in the eye'. And Gilson concludes that by quoting the final words of this sentence at this precise place, Gundissalinus is reminding us that illumination comes from God. In fact the thing to be noted is that he omits the opening words, which refer expressly to God, and thus deprives the Augustinian formula of its theological aspect, keeping only its philosophical side: the analogy between reason and sight. It is not a case, here, of annexing Avicenna's text to Christian theology, but of bringing a fragment of Augustine's text to illustrate a point of Arabic philosophy. Yet Gilson's other arguments remain sound. It seems then that Gundissalinus has here performed, no doubt deliberately, a series of alterations which counterbalance one another: suppressing the mention of God in a sentence from St Augustine and adding it to a sentence of Avicenna's; referring to the angel where the philosopher does not, although he does so elsewhere. The direct sight of God is, to be sure, not a factor in Avicenna's doctrine, but why does not Gundissalinus add to his gloss (for that is what his *quod est Deus* is) the slightest mention of a Christian 'authority'? In fact it would seem as though he sought to replace the theology of the saints by a theology according to the philosophers, from which he is free to dissociate himself if need be, but which in its totality provides the broad conceptual framework in which can be inserted documents provided by the Scriptures, the saints and the mystics. Under the apparent unity of his text we can trace a marked movement away from traditional wisdom. Gundissalinus has two aspects, and that explains

104 'Ideo sola intelligentia Deus gustari dicitur quia ex omnibus viribus animae ea sola in praesenti et futuro nullo mediante quasi tangitur': de Vaux, p. 172; Muckle, p. 100.

how scholars like Father de Vaux and Etienne Gilson have been able to maintain contradictory theses about him. For all the Christian references with which he illustrates his texts (whether sincerely or not is not our concern here), their real drift is philosophical, and the analysis of the *De anima* is enlightening in this respect. The corpus of Gundissalinus' treatises transmitted to the Western Christian world a practically complete metaphysical system which does not conflict with the teachings of Augustine, Dionysius, and Boethius, which on the contrary forms a coherent whole with them – but which, in its bulk and above all by reason of the structures it offers, integrates them, like precious building-materials, into a secular edifice.

The Book of First and Second Causes, edited by Father de Vaux,[105] is close to the writings of Gundissalinus in this respect. Its editor puts its date after 1180, probably in the last years of the twelfth century or the first quarter of the thirteenth. In any case, this book also borrows from many sources, both philosophical and Christian. The first include Avicenna, of course, and a little of al-Fārābī, but also the *Liber de causis* (of Greek origin, but known in its Arabic version); the second include Augustine, Dionysius, and often John Scotus Eriugena (disguised, because suspect). The book sets forth a common Neoplatonist metaphysic in which the above-mentioned doctrines can be reconciled, though they do not entirely coincide; broadly speaking, there is one God, from which flow a hierarchy of Intelligences and celestial souls, and below these the material beings; the theory of knowledge is on the whole that of Avicenna. The treatise concludes with a statement of the impossibility of knowing the First Cause.

There is undoubted evidence here of Arabic influence in the twelfth century or the beginning of the thirteenth; but this is linked, to a marked degree, with that of Greek Christian writers: Dionysius and John Scotus Eriugena, the latter it is true writing in Latin. We shall confine ourselves to repeating the question we asked about Gundissalinus: is this a philosophical or a Christian work? Father de Vaux opts resolutely for the former hypothesis: referring in connection with it, as we have seen, to 'Latin Avicennism'. He emphasizes that 'the author eliminates from his material anything specifically Christian, or more precisely anything that might appear as an intrusion of theology into the realm of reason, to which he intends to confine it'.[106] He notes in particular two passages where long quotations

---

105 De Vaux 1934. One of the MSS bears the title: 'Liber Avicennae de primis et secundis substantiis et de fluxu earum'; the book is not by Avicenna, but the second part of the title gives a good indication of the contents.
106 De Vaux 1934, p. 72; see also pp. 72–9.

from Augustine's *Soliloquies* are cut or modified: in the first, several lines are omitted about the three theological virtues and about the vision of God; in the second, while the concept that 'God is intelligible' is retained, the words *quod intelligitur* ('that which is understood') are replaced by *quod intelligit* ('that which understands'),[107] which implies that God can be understood by himself alone, since the rest of the treatise is devoted to proving that he is unknowable to us. To these sound arguments we can add another, which would have persuaded Father de Vaux, if he had noticed it, not to assert categorically that this work is an 'explicit witness' to the current of Eriugenist thought; for the metaphysical schema it describes postulates a descent with no upward return, an *exitus* without a *reditus*. This theme, a basic one in Eriugena's philosophy, was of course not taken over unaltered by the whole Christian tradition: but to follow John Scotus, as in this instance, by describing the way down and saying nothing as to the way back, and moreover to deny all possibility of knowing God, marks an unmistakable allegiance to a non-Christian Neoplatonism. Indeed, on the first of these two points, the author parts company with Avicenna, and this precludes one from speaking unreservedly of 'Latin Avicennism' in connection with this work. The Avicennist trend is still not easy to make out, but if Gundissalinus is to the right of it, the *Book of First and Second Causes* is to the left.

This brings us to the end of our period. But of course doctrinal history cannot, any more than any other history, be split up into decimal sections: the *Treatise on the Soul* by John Blund,[108] who died in 1248, can be considered as a twelfth-century work. With respect to the point at issue the editors of this work have noted in it quotations from all the Arabic philosophers hitherto translated: al-Kindī, al-Fārābī, Algazel, Qusṭā b. Lūqā, above all Avicenna, who is quoted twenty times (the others only occasionally), and also Constantine of Africa and Gundissalinus. There is no mention of Averroes (the term *commentator*, used on two occasions, refers to Avicenna): this omission serves to distinguish two stages in the history of medieval thought. We find theses which are specifically those of Avicenna: the role of the Intelligences, separate substances which produce and move the heavens,[109] the infusion of souls into bodies by 'the First Giver of forms', following a 'natural preparation'.[110] True, the First Giver is here God, the

---

107 *Ibid.* pp. 132 and 133.
108 Iohannes Blund, *Tractatus de anima*, ed. D. A. Callus and R. W. Hunt (London 1970). This author is probably the first master in Paris or Oxford to make extensive use of Avicenna's *De anima* (d'Alverny 1982, p. 451).
109 *Tractatus de anima*, pp. 5, 9, 86.
110 *Ibid.* pp. 98–9.

First Cause, and it is God, too, who 'imprints the formal intellect in the soul'. Nevertheless, John Blund adds, many writers 'seem to imply' that this imprint is the work of an Intelligence under the authority of the First Giver of forms; others say that the Intelligence is an angel in the service of the human soul (*minister animae hominis*),[111] 'for man has two angels, a good and an evil, who are both at the service of the human soul'. Then again, 'the rational soul is that in which man communicates (*convenit*) with the angels and other Intelligences'; this soul and these Intelligences have a 'simple Being (*simplex esse*)'.[112] On these points John Blund parts company with the Arab–Latin tradition, at any rate in the broad lines we have sketched. It should also be remembered that William of Auvergne, an exact contemporary of John Blund's, who is familiar with the same authors, discusses several of Avicenna's theses from a theological point of view, and that his work (according to Father de Vaux) contains elements of a polemic against a certain 'Latin Avicennism'[113] – perhaps the same trend followed, about 1230–40, by some theologians who, influenced by Avicenna, denied the possibility of seeing God 'as he is'; their case has been studied by Father de Contenson.[114] But at this point we become involved with the beginnings of classic scholasticism.

Is it possible to estimate exactly the significance and historical importance of this irruption of Arabic philosophy into the Christian West? Etienne Gilson, who has emphasized – and doubtless overemphasized – the 'Christianization' imposed on these doctrines by such authors as Gundissalinus, has written that Gundissalinus' *De anima* 'integrates . . . with a Graeco-Arabic synthesis the results obtained in other fields by St Augustine and St Bernard of Clairvaux'.[115] The ambiguity of this sentence reflects that of the doctrinal situation described: was this integration to the advantage of the Graeco-Arabic synthesis or of the Christian ideas which had been integrated into it? It is not possible to give a purely factual answer to this question: judgements differ according to one's view of classic scholasticism, on the model of which Gilson bases his opinion of Gundissalinus' work. But to judge by the way the saints' writings are treated in *De anima*, and particularly in the *Book of First and Second Causes*, it is clear that the integration benefited philosophy: the

111 *Ibid.* p. 94.
112 *Ibid.* pp. 84, 90.
113 De Vaux 1934, pp. 17–43; see also pp. 53–4 ('Un témoignage de Guillaume d'Auvergne').
114 P. M. de Contenson, 'Avicennisme latin et vision de Dieu au début du 13e siècle', *AHDLMA* XXVII (1959) 29–97.
115 Gilson 1929–30, p. 91.

compatibility between the Christian religion and Arabic Neoplatonism made the process easier, but it confuses the historian's perception of it, since it makes it hard to say at first glance which of the two elements prevailed. I myself see the author of the *Book of First and Second Causes* as the final link in a chain which goes back in time to Bernard Silvestris and Adelard of Bath: thinkers who developed a purely secular philosophy. As for Gundissalinus, it may be that his conscious attitude to his work was that of a schoolman; but it was basically motivated by the same concept as that of Bernard and Adelard: the secularization of Christian wisdom. Of this process, initiated in the Western Christian world through the science of the Arabs,[116] then accelerated by means of their philosophy, we gained a first glimpse in the declarations of Adelard, who thus appears as emblematic to this whole story.

116 H. Schipperges, 'Einflüsse arabischer Medizin auf die Mikrokosmosliteratur des 12. Jahrhunderts', in *Antike und Orient im Mittelalter* (Berlin 1962), p. 138: Adelard's rationalism as the first result of the influence of the Arabic *Arztphilosophen*; J. Jolivet, 'Les *Quaestiones naturales* d'Adélard de Bath, ou la nature sans le Livre', in *Mélanges E. R. Labande* (Poitiers 1974), pp. 437–46.

II

NEW PERSPECTIVES

5

SCIENTIFIC SPECULATIONS

CHARLES BURNETT

In his *Dialogi* (an apologia for Christianity, couched in the form of a series of dialogues between the Christian Petrus and the Jew Moses) Petrus Alfonsi undertakes to prove God's existence 'philosophically':

Petrus: Those who make their faith correspond to the Scriptures do not deny that God exists, and therefore it was not necessary to prove this to those who believed in the Scriptures, but only to those who believed in no written word.
Moses: Since you refuse to prove through the Scriptures that God exists and he is able to be comprehended by no corporeal sense, I very much want to hear by what philosophical *ratio* this can be proved.[1]

In the *Tractatus de sex dierum operibus* Thierry of Chartres writes:

There are four kinds of *rationes* which lead man to the recognition of his creator – i.e. the proofs of arithmetic and music, geometry and astronomy.[2]

At another point in the *Dialogi* Petrus has Moses ask:

I would like you to explain this to me, if you know it: Wherefore and how, according to the laws of physics (*secundum physicam*), did Adam, because of disobeying the command, lose that equality in the composition of his body, which he had prior to the Fall?[3]

Again in his *Tractatus* Thierry undertakes to explain the first part of Genesis *secundum physicam*.[4]

Both Petrus Alfonsi and Thierry claim to be using proofs or ways of reasoning independent of scriptural authority for investigating divine things. In this chapter I should like to investigate what they might mean by *philosophica ratio* and the proofs of the mathematical and physical sciences.

---

1 P. L. 157, 555A.
2 N. M. Häring, *Commentaries on Boethius by Thierry of Chartres and his School* (Toronto 1971), p. 568.
3 P. L. 157, 642A. The phrase *secundum physicam* occurs again at 652C, with respect to a physical explanation of Elijah's ascent to heaven.
4 Häring 1971, p. 555.

Science, after all, was what was applied to human affairs; knowledge of God should only be able to be acquired by the intuitive intellect.[5]

Scientific arguments may be based either on authority or on reason. But reason itself can be inductive – the experience of particular individual objects can lead one to conclusions about a greater range of objects, that is, about the species and forms of those particular objects; or it can be deductive – the knowledge of the forms can lead one to the knowledge of the individuals. Adelard of Bath makes these divisions clear. In the *Quaestiones naturales* he writes, addressing his nephew:

> I have learnt one thing from my Arabic teachers with reason as a guide, but you are led by another thing – a halter, captivated by the allure of authority. For what should authority be called other than a halter?[6]

In the *De eodem et diverso* Adelard describes the deductive and inductive methods as leading to the same truth, and attributes them to Plato and Aristotle respectively:

> One [of the philosophers], borne aloft by the sublimity of his mind, and by those wings which he strenuously attempted to don, approached the comprehension of things from their very beginnings and described what they were before they entered into bodies, defining the archetypal forms of things. The other, gifted in constructing systems (*artificialiter callens*), so that he might instruct his subtle readers, started from sensible and composite things. And provided that they meet each other on the way, they cannot be called 'contrary'. For composition loves division and division loves composition, provided that each corroborates the other. Hence if any product arises from multiplication (whether one is calculating on one's fingers or using the abacus), the correctness of the calculation can be proved by the division of the same product.[7]

The inductive method is specific to speculation which arises from experiencing individual objects with the senses. Aristotle defined this 'experimental' method in his *Posterior Analytics*. Scientific premisses, he says, are known by a certain intuition which is based on experience, which in turn is formed by the memory of a repetition of sense-perceptions.[8] John of Salisbury, drawing on his knowledge of the *Posterior Analytics*, confirms that science cannot exist without sense-perception.[9] Petrus Alfonsi claims that astronomy cannot be

5 Wisdom (*Sapientia*), as John of Salisbury says (*Metalogicon* IV 13, ed. C. C. J. Webb, pp. 178–9), is what is applied to divine things; knowledge (*scientia*) is what is applied to human things. For Peter of Poitiers *scientia* depends on the authority of reason, *sapientia* on the love of truth (*Sententiae* 4 (ed. N. M. Häring, *Die Zwettler Summe* (Münster 1977), p. 25)).

6 Ed. M. Müller, BGPTM XXXI. 2 (1934), p. 11.

7 Ed. H. Willner, BGPTM IV.1 (1903) 11. The identification of Plato and Aristotle is made in the hand of the scribe in the margin of the unique manuscript of this work.

8 *Posterior Analytics* II 19, 100Aff.

9 *Metalogicon* IV 9, ed. C. C. J. Webb, p. 174: 'Philosophus quoque qui rationalem exercet, qui etiam tam phisici quam mathematici cliens est, ab his incipit que sensuum testimonio convalescunt et proficiunt ad intelligibilium incorporaliumque notitiam.'

known except through *experimentum* – i.e. through observation.[10] Ptolemy, at the beginning of his astronomical handbook, the *Almagest*, asserts that he uses as starting-points 'the obvious phenomena'.[11] Abū Ma'shar, in his influential *Greater Introduction to Astrology* (translated by John of Seville in 1133 and again by Hermann of Carinthia in 1140), defines the science concerning the effects of the movements of the heavenly bodies – i.e. astrology – as relying partly on certain experiences of the senses. He then gives examples of experiences common to all men – such as that of the effect of the sun's yearly course on the change of seasons – which corroborate astrology.[12] In medicine Galen had differentiated between the *via experimenti* of the Empirical School and the *via rationis* of the Dogmatic School, and his arguments were known through the translation of his *Megatechni* made by Constantine of Africa in the late eleventh century. Several works of astrology and medicine contain the word *experimentum* or a cognate word in their titles. These are works of a practical nature, which prescribe procedures that the author would have us believe have been proved effective by the frequent experimentation of the astrologer or doctor.[13] The word therefore spreads to other practical works, such as geomantic manuals and collections of alchemical recipes.[14]

Of course, once the scientific premises have been established by the experience or experimentation of a reputable authority there is no need to repeat the experiments. In general this is what we find in the twelfth century. Scientific authorities who previously had been glimpsed only dimly, through pale epitomes or at several removes from the original – Euclid in geometry, Ptolemy in astronomy, Artistotle in physics, and Galen in medicine – were rediscovered and were revered to such an extent that their

10 *Letter to the Peripatetics of France*, ed. J. M. Millás Vallicrosa in 'La aportación astronómica de Pedro Alfonso', *Sefarad* III (1943) 105.
11 *Almagest* I 2. The importance of the *Almagest* will be discussed below.
12 *Introductorium maius* I 1, ed. Melchior Sessa (Venice 1506), a3r, and variants from Manchester, John Rylands and University Library, MS lat. 67 (Hermann's translation): (The second species of the celestial science) 'stellarium corporum naturas ... partim crebris quibusdam sensibilibus experimentis, partim naturali speculatione quadam insequitur.' Cf. *ibid.* a3v: 'Nonnulli etiam numerosis obtinent experimentis ex diversis lune mansionibus diversa tempora variis qualitatibus affici.'
13 For astrology one may mention Abū Ma'shar, *De experimentis seu de revolutionibus annorum*, TK 51, and Bernardus Silvestris, *Experimentarius*, TK 1574. For medicine the best-known example is Rhases, *Experimenta*, TK 152.
14 See the numerous works with the title *experimenta* in the index of TK; a work of fortune-telling in Cambridge, Magdalene College, MS Pepys 911, fol. 44v is called *Documentum experimenti retrogradi*; in Paris, BN MS lat. 7486, fol. 56v we read: 'Ars ... geomantica libet experimentis seu experimentiis'; the author of the *Speculum astronomiae*, attributed to Albertus Magnus, 17 (ed. P. Zambelli *et al.* (Pisa 1977), p. 48) describes all works of divination by the elements as *libri experimentales*.

experimental results were not questioned. In spite of Adelard's statement, the real contrast in the twelfth century was not so much between authority and reason, as between revelation and reason. The newly discovered classical works of science provided models for rational modes of argument. These were set up against revealed knowledge, as much that of sacred books[15] as that of the pseudo-science of Hermes Trismegistus, which was not subject to rational analysis. The twelfth century was an age of reason, rather than of experimentation.

Contemporary authors, well versed in the logic of Aristotle, liked to distinguish between two kinds of reasoning, which were differentiated according to the nature of the premisses. In the first kind the premisses are not deduced from sensory experiences, but are intuited as self-evident axioms, and the arguments from these premisses are 'necessary' and lead to 'demonstration'. This is the kind of reasoning used in mathematics, and, to a certain extent, in metaphysics. In the second kind, the premisses are deduced from the experience of the senses. They are not axiomatic but based on opinion. The resultant arguments are *probabilis* – a word which has the sense of 'able to be approved of by reliable opinion' or 'plausible' rather than 'probable' or 'provable'. Their validity must be judged on the basis of their rationality.[16]

William of Conches differentiates between these two kinds of reasoning when he turns from the discussion of what (truly) is but cannot be seen (or does not seem to be) – i.e. metaphysics – to that which both exists and is seen to exist:

Up to now our discussion has been about what is, but is not seen. Now we turn our pen to those things which are and are seen. But before we start we beg that if, when speaking about visible things, we should say something plausible but not necessary, or something necessary but not plausible, we should not be blamed in consequence. For as philosophers we propose what is necessary, although not plausible, but as physicists we add what is plausible although it is not necessary. But if anyone among the moderns has dealt with the subject in a more plausible way, his arguments should be adopted.[17]

15 The main thrust of Petrus Alfonsi's *Dialogi* is to point out the irrationality of the revealed knowledge of the religion of the Jews. At the end of the century Maimonides in his *Guide for the Perplexed* tried to explain these same Jewish beliefs in terms which would satisfy philosophers.

16 For the logical context of 'necessary' and 'plausible' arguments see John of Salisbury, *Metalogicon* II 14, and Hugh of Saint-Victor, *Didascalicon* II 30, ed. C. H. Buttimer (Washington 1939), p. 46. These forms of argumentation are referred to by Adelard of Bath (*Quaestiones naturales*, ed. Müller, p. 46.13), Robert of Ketton, and Hermann of Carinthia (see below).

17 *Philosophia* 19, ed. G. Maurach (Pretoria 1980), p. 26.

The demonstrative method is particularly characteristic of the mathematical sciences of geometry and astronomy, which were rediscovered as scientific disciplines in the course of the twelfth century. The rational method based on plausible arguments is characteristic of physics and theoretical medicine, which developed notably during the same period. Each of these two methods and the texts which exemplify them will be discussed in turn.

Mathematical speculation and the via demonstrationis

The *locus classicus* for the enunciation of the demonstrative method is in Aristotle's *Posterior Analytics*. Scientific knowledge proceeds by the way of demonstration. Demonstration begins from 'premisses which must be true, primary, immediate and better known than, and prior to, the conclusion, which is further related to them as effect to cause'.[18] The conclusions necessarily follow from the premisses, but whereas whatever follows from the premisses is thereby demonstrated, the premisses themselves cannot be demonstrated. The premisses of demonstration are peculiar to the science in question: the premisses of one science cannot be used for drawing conclusions in another. The science to which Aristotle refers most frequently as that which exemplifies the demonstrative method, is geometry.

Although Boethius appears to have made a translation of the *Posterior Analytics*, no trace of this version has survived.[19] The earliest medieval translation is that made by James of Venice at some time in the second quarter of the twelfth century. This became the Vulgate. It was followed by a translation which was probably made by a 'Johannes'. Both these translations were made from Greek and before 1159, when John of Salisbury refers to them. Some time before 1187 Gerard of Cremona translated the work from Arabic.

John of Salisbury, in his *Metalogicon*, is the first European scholar to show a first-hand knowledge of the *Posterior Analytics*. For him it is a difficult book, whose obscurities have been compounded by the scribes and translators. John recognizes its subject-matter as the 'art of demonstration', and draws together many of the arguments of Aristotle. He writes:

18 *Posterior Analytics* I 2, 71B20–21. The translation is that of G. R. G. Mure in W. D. Ross, *The Works of Aristotle* I (Oxford 1928).
19 See the preface to L. Minio-Paluello's edition of the *Analytica Posteriora* in *Aristoteles Latinus* IV 1–4 (Bruges–Paris 1968). Minio-Paluello considers the possibility that some variant readings found in a manuscript margin could come from Boethius' version (*ibid.* p. xv).

[In demonstration] it is first of all necessary to know the principles of the various scientific disciplines, and thence, by weaving together rational arguments (*rationes*), to trace the sequence of conclusions which are necessarily true, and to do this, if I may say so, by 'digging in one's heels' and insisting that no hole in the argument should appear, arising as it were from a gap in the necessary sequence, which would prejudice that demonstrative science.[20]

John of Salisbury claims that demonstration is used by hardly anyone in his day except mathematicians, and amongst them almost exclusively by the geometers. It is true that the *Posterior Analytics* does not appear to have become well-known, either in the time of John of Salisbury († 1180) or later in the twelfth century.[21] However, both the *Posterior Analytics* and the demonstrative method which it describes were known indirectly through Arabic and Latin texts.

Aristotle's work existed in at least two different versions in Arabic, and was known to the Arabs specifically as *The Book of Demonstration* (*Kitāb al-Burhān*); Gerard of Cremona's translation retains the title *De demonstratione*. Citations from the work became known in the West through translations of Arabic works into Latin. One such citation occurs in the *Greater Introduction to Astrology* of Abū Maʿshar. In the third chapter of the first book the opening of Aristotle's second book is quoted.[22] Al-Fārābī in his *Catalogue of Sciences* lists the *Posterior Analytics* as the work dealing with the fourth of the eight parts of logic, which he considers the most important of all. Demonstrative statements produce certain knowledge concerning a question that is posed, and the rules in the *Posterior Analytics* are those on which philosophy is based.[23] Al-Fārābī's work was translated in the third quarter of the twelfth century by Dominicus Gundissalinus, who used it as one source for his own *De divisione philosophiae*. Another source he uses is a letter on demonstrative logic from the collection of the Ikhwān al-Ṣafāʾ (the Brethren of Purity), which brings out very clearly the use of demonstration in both logic and geometry.[24]

20 *Metalogicon* IV 8, ed. C. C. J. Webb, p. 172.
21 Only one manuscript which could have been written within the twelfth century is still extant: Vat. lat. 2982. The oldest manuscript, Chartres 92 (s. XII), was destroyed through bombing in 1943 (cf. L. Minio-Paluello, *Opuscula: The Latin Aristotle* (Amsterdam 1972), p. 194).
22 Arabic, Leiden, University Library, Or. 97, fol. 15v. The two Latin translations are discussed by R. Lemay in *Abū Maʿshar and Latin Aristotelianism in the Twelfth Century* (Beirut 1962), pp. 56–8.
23 Al-Fārābī, *Catálogo de las ciencias*, ed. A. González Palencia (2nd edn., Madrid 1953), p. 23 and pp. 28–9 (Arabic); pp. 137 and 142 (Gerard of Cremona's trans.).
24 *Liber introductorius in artem logicae demonstrationis, collectus a Mahometh discipulo Alquindi philosophi*, ed. A. Nagy, BGPTM II.5 (1897) 41–64.

The most readily available Latin source for Aristotle's work was the introduction to the first textbook in the corpus of classical texts on logic (the *logica vetus*) – i.e. Boethius' second commentary on the *Isagoge* of Porphyry. Here Boethius, referring to the *Postremi resolutorii* (i.e. the *Posterior Analytics*), describes the method of demonstration as:

... a trustworthy way of bringing reason to bear on a matter which is sought, working from [principles] which are already known in a natural way, which are appropriate, prior, the cause, are necessary, and inhere in themselves.[25]

Boethius, following Aristotle, explores the logical consequences of this statement. However, the passage on the *Posterior Analytics* in John of Salisbury's *Metalogicon* points us to another Boethian source which was to prove influential in the twelfth century. John calls the principles on which demonstration is based *communes conceptiones animi* ('common notions of the mind'). This term occurs nowhere in the twelfth-century translations of the *Posterior Analytics* where the words *dignitates, maximae propositiones* or *a(n)xiomata* are used instead. John takes his term from Boethius' *De hebdomadibus*, in which *communis animi conceptio* is defined as 'a statement which anyone accepts as soon as he hears it'.[26] Boethius goes on to say that there are two ways in which 'common notions' are used. One applies when the notion cannot be denied by anyone who hears it. He gives as an example an axiom from Euclid's *Elements*:

If you take two equal quantities away from two equal quantities, the remaining quantities are equal.

The other is a notion accepted only by a learned man, such as:

Those things which are incorporeal do not have fixed positions.

In other words, we have a mathematical and a metaphysical example of a premiss. Both kinds of premisses will be shown to have an important place in twelfth-century thought.

A twelfth-century preface to a Latin version of Euclid's *Elements* firmly establishes the method in the work as that of demonstration, and indicates that the theory in the *Posterior Analytics* is put into practice in this work:

The mode of procedure [in the *Elements*] is to demonstrate. Demonstration is a form of argumentation in which one argues from primary and true statements to their conclusions. For the art under discussion is arranged in such a way that the

25 *Commenta in Isagogen Porphyrii editio secunda* I.1, ed. G. Schepss and S. Brandt, Corpus Scriptorum Ecclesiasticorum Latinorum XLVIII (Vienna 1906), p. 157.
26 *De hebdomadibus (Quomodo substantiae in eo quod sint bonae sint . . .)*, ed. and trans. H. F. Stewart, E. K. Rand, and S. J. Tester in *Boethius, The Theological Tractates, The Consolation of Philosophy* (Cambridge MA 1973), p. 40.

consequences necessarily result from the premises or from the principles. For a
demonstrative science is either one that both teaches how to demonstrate and demonstrates, such as the *Posterior Analytics*, or one that demonstrates but does not teach
how to demonstrate, such as geometry.[27]

If the influence of the *Posterior Analytics* was patchy and indirect in the twelfth
century, the influence of works which put the demonstrative method into
practice was important. Aristotle and John of Salisbury suggest that the
demonstrative method is proper to all the mathematical sciences. It is most
conspicuously present, however, in geometry and astronomy and in those
subjects related to them, such as trigonometry and optics. The most
important text exemplifying the method was the *Elements* of Euclid.

We must remind ourselves of the form of this work.[28] The text begins
with definitions of terms, common notions (or axioms), and postulates. All
these establish the premises which the consequent material presupposes,
and are equivalent to the 'pre-existent knowledge' that, in the words of
Aristotle, is either the comprehension of the meaning of the term used (by
definition) or the admission of the fact that must be assumed (i.e. the
admission of the common notion or the postulate).[29] The definitions are
straightforward: 'A point is that which has no part', 'A line is that which has
length but not breadth, whose extremities are two points', and so on.
Examples of the common notions are: 'Whatever quantities are equal to the
same quantity, are equal to each other', 'If equal quantities are added to equal
quantities, the combined quantities will also be equal', and the common
notion cited by Boethius in *De hebdomadibus*: 'If equal quantities are taken
from equal quantities, those that remain are also equal'. The postulates give
constructions which are assumed to be possible (or impossible) – such as that
one should be able to draw a straight line from any point to any point, but
that two straight lines cannot contain an area. Following these three
categories come the theorems themselves. These consist each of a proposition, expressed either in the infinitive (such as the first proposition: 'On a
given straight line to construct an equilateral triangle'), or as a real condition
(such as the sixth proposition: 'If in a triangle two angles be equal to one
another, the sides which subtend the equal angles will also be equal to one

27 The preface is edited by M. Clagett in 'King Alfred and the Elements of Euclid', *Isis* XLV
    (1954) 269–77, at p. 275.
28 The most thorough analysis of the *Elements* remains that of T. L. Heath, *The Thirteen Books
    of Euclid's Elements*, Dover Reprint (3 vols., London 1956). See also I. Bulmer-Thomas,
    article 'Euclid' in C. C. Gillispie (ed.), *Dictionary of Scientific Biography* IV (New York 1971)
    415–28.
29 *Posterior Analytics* I 1, 71B11–15.

another'), or a statement in the present indicative tense (such as the seventeenth proposition: 'In any triangle two angles taken together in any manner are less than two right angles'). The propositions are followed by the proofs, which make use of geometrical diagrams with points marked by letters of the alphabet, and which demonstrate the truth of the proposition step by step, without leaving any intermediate stages in the argument unexplained. The proofs end with a restatement of the contents of the proposition and an affidavit that 'this is what it was necessary to demon-strate' (which every schoolboy knows as *quod erat demonstrandum*). Within each book the propositions become progressively more complex. The books discuss in turn triangles and other rectilinear figures, circles, proportions of lines and solid figures. It is important to realize that much that could be expressed in arithmetical or algebraic terms, using numbers and unknown quantities, is expressed in terms of geometry. For example, the well-known Pythagorean theorem (*Elements* I, Prop. 47) is expressed geometrically in the words 'In right-angled triangles the square on the side subtending the right angle is equal to the squares on the sides containing the right angle.' Expressed algebraically the same theorem would read (for a triangle with sides of lengths, a, b, and c): $a^2+b^2=c^2$, and values could be substituted for the triangle's sides. Books VII, VIII, and IX of the *Elements* are generally referred to as the 'arithmetical books', in that they are concerned with the relationship of numbers to one another, but the numbers are not given as digits, but are represented by lines of the required ratios. Books XIV and XV, concerning solid figures, though not originally part of Euclid's *Elements*, were regularly present in medieval versions of the text. At certain points in the course of the work further definitions are given, and from some theorems an immediate consequence is drawn; this is called the 'corollary'.

All works on mathematical astronomy and the subaltern sciences men-tioned above presupposed a knowledge of the *Elements*. Euclid's work was, as it were, the premiss for all these other mathematical works. As such it is difficult to overemphasize the importance of the translations of the complete work into Latin which were made in the first half of the twelfth century. In the early Middle Ages the torso of a translation probably made by Boethius survived, embedded in works on land-measuring (those of the *agrimensores*) and associated with the abacus. This torso consisted only of definitions, postulates, common notions, and propositions from the first four books of the *Elements*.[30] Above all, this version lacked proofs for all save the first three

30 The extent of this torso is discussed in M. Folkerts, *'Boethius' Geometrie II* (Wiesbaden 1970), pp. 70–82.

propositions. Thus the whole reasoning of the demonstrative method was absent. The propositions were set forth as self-evident truths – to all appearances of the same status as the common notions – and there was no attempt to show how one theorem derives from previous theorems.

Amongst the meagre amount of material we have on discussions concerning geometry in the period before the twelfth century there is a letter from Gerbert d'Aurillac to a correspondent who has failed to keep to Aristotle's dictum that the premisses of one science cannot be used in another science. For he has attempted to work out the area of an equilateral triangle by using the 'triangular' number of the requisite side (a numerological concept), instead of using Euclid's *Elements*.[31]

What happens in the first half of the twelfth century is that there is a sudden burst of interest in Euclid's text. By the third quarter of the century there was not one new translation of the complete work, but at least six.[32] Whereas the text of the Boethian excerpts had remained relatively stable over many centuries, the texts of the new versions of Euclid are exceedingly fluid, especially in the earliest manuscripts. One scribe might copy two versions into one manuscript. Another might write out two versions of the proofs to the propositions one after the other. A third might draw on several versions to put together his text of the work. Concern over the accuracy of the text is shown by extensive marginalia, giving Arabic and sometimes Greek equivalents of the terms used or comparing Euclid's definitions of arithmetical terms (at the beginning of the seventh book) with those in Boethius' *De institutione arithmetica*. All this witnesses to a lively interest in the text.

Early readers of the new Latin Euclid were aware of the demonstrative method which was being used. Hermann of Carinthia, probably translating a phrase in the Arabic text he was using, explained that the common notions are so called because

... they contain maxims of this kind – which we call *almukadimas* in Arabic, but *theoremata* in Greek – on which the whole reasoning (*ratio*) of the art seems to depend completely.[33]

---

31 The 'triangular' numbers are numbers which can be represented spatially by units arranged in the form of a triangle – such as three ∴ , six ∴∴ , and ten ∴∴∴ . They are described in Boethius, *De institutione arithmetica* II 7–8. For a discussion of this letter and its cultural context see M. S. Mahoney, 'Mathematics', in D. C. Lindberg (ed.), *Science in the Middle Ages* (Chicago 1978), pp. 145–78, at pp. 149–50.
32 See the article by John Murdoch on 'Euclid: Transmission of the Elements', in Gillispie 1971, pp. 437–59.
33 Ed. H. L. L. Busard (Leiden 1968), p. 11: 'quod maximas huiusmodi proposiciones quas arabice *almukadimas*, grece *theoremata* nuncupamus contineat, quibus artis racio omnino innixa videtur'.

In two early manuscripts of the Latin version of the *Elements* known as 'Adelard I' there are marginalia indicating how one proposition can be proved from an earlier theorem or theorems: e.g. against the proof of the third theorem in Book I is the gloss: 'The third follows from the second', and against the seventh theorem is the statement that 'it follows from the fifth'.[34] The most widely copied twelfth-century version of the *Elements* omits Euclid's proofs altogether and replaces them by instructions showing the reader which earlier theorems to use in order to obtain the proof. The framework of the argument is given, but the reader is left to fill in the details himself. In the case of the fourteenth proposition of the first book, for example, he is told to 'prove the proposition from the second part of the first postulate and from the preceding theorem, by means of an indirect process of reasoning'. The fullest twelfth-century version of the *Elements* (known as 'Adelard III') includes a long preface which contains the description of the demonstrative method quoted above (pp. 157–8). Relics of ancient philosophical exegesis of the *Elements* survive in (*a*) a short Arabic preface concerning what is required in a theorem, which derives from Proclus' commentary and was translated both by Hermann and by Gerard of Cremona,[35] and (*b*) the Arabic commentary on the *Elements* by al-Nairīzī, which quotes substantial portions from Simplicius and other Greek philosophers, and which was translated by Gerard.[36]

The kind of demonstrative method that we find in the *Elements* – which we may call the 'axiomatic method' – is also that of several mathematical works which first became known in the West in the twelfth century, such as the *Spherics* of Theodosius, Euclid's *Optics*, and Archimedes' *On the Quadrature of the Circle*. It is constantly used in the passages on calculation in Ptolemy's *Almagest*, in which Euclid is frequently cited. In his *Tetrabiblos* Ptolemy refers to the *Almagest* as expounding astronomy 'by the method of demonstration',[37] and several chapters – e.g. those in which the parameters of the planetary orbits are calculated[38] – are headed 'demonstration of . . . (*apodeixis* . . .)'. The earliest work on trigonometry in the Latin West – the *Liber Embadorum* which Plato of Tivoli translated from the Hebrew of Abraham bar Ḥiyya Savasorda in Barcelona in 1145 – uses Euclid's *Elements* as its

---

34 A full list of these glosses is given in H. L. L. Busard (ed.), *The First Latin Translation of Euclid's Elements commonly ascribed to Adelard of Bath* (Toronto 1983), p. 22, n. 10.
35 Heath 1956, pp. 129–30; Hermann, ed. Busard, p. 9; Gerard of Cremona, ed. Busard (Leiden 1983), p. 1.
36 Ed. M. Curtze, *Euclides Supplementum. Anaritii Commentarii* (Leipzig 1899).
37 Ed. F. E. Robbins (Cambridge MA 1971), p. 2.
38 *Almagest* XII 2–6.

starting-point. The work begins with the definitions, postulates and common notions from *Elements*, Book I, and the definitions from Book VII, describing them as *universalia proposita* belonging to geometry and arithmetic respectively, and then sets forth theorems on the calculation of areas, replacing Euclid's proportional lines with examples using numerical values.

One of the earliest works in which a Latin author tries his hand at using the demonstrative method of the *Elements* is that of Stephen of Antioch – if he can be identified with the Stephen who wrote the 'Liber Maimonis', which has survived in one twelfth-century manuscript. This author boasts that he is using geometrical proofs 'unknown to the Latin world', and he includes several geometrical theorems, complete with labelled diagrams, to illustrate the courses of the planets.[39] In 1143 Hermann of Carinthia was using Euclid's *Elements* along with constructions in the *Almagest* to 'demonstrate' the distances between the planets and the proportion of the earth's surface which was inhabitable. Thierry of Chartres, who had a reputation as a mathematician,[40] shows some understanding of the *Elements* in that he distinguishes between the geometrical books and the arithmetical books when he includes Adelard's translation of the work in the *Heptateuchon*.[41]

The wider philosophical implications of the *Elements* were already apparent to its earliest readers. Hermann of Carinthia compares the definitions, postulates, and common notions to *elementa* – a term which at that time was the property of physicists[42] – and to the *communes loci* of the rhetoricians,

39 C. H. Haskins, *Studies in the History of Mediaeval Science* (2nd ed., New York 1927), pp. 101–2. Recent research being carried out by Reuven Avi-Yonah in Harvard would tend to confirm Stephen of Antioch's authorship.

40 According to an anecdote in the Munich MS Clm 14160, he gave some secret lessons in mathematics to Peter Abelard (see D. E. Luscombe, *The School of Peter Abelard* (Cambridge 1970), p. 58).

41 Books VII–IX have been placed in the arithmetical section of the *Heptateuchon* (Chartres, Bibliothèque municipale, MS 498, fols. 122r–124v) alongside Boethius' *De institutione arithmetica* and the book of Martianus Capella's *Marriage of Mercury and Philology* devoted to arithmetic (Book VII). The very end of the *Elements* is found on fols. 141r–v of the same manuscript. Since 104 folios are missing immediately before fol. 141, it is difficult to know how much more of Euclid's work the *Heptateuchon* originally included. It is possible that Thierry did not have Books I–IV of Adelard's version copied into the *Heptateuchon*, in that most of the propositions of these books were included in Boethius' *Geometria II*, which is also in Thierry's collection; see my 'The Contents and Affiliation of the Scientific Manuscripts Written at, or Brought to Chartres, in the Time of John of Salisbury' in *The World of John of Salisbury*, ed. M. Wilks (Oxford 1984), pp. 142–3. The encyclopaedic rather than didactic purpose of the *Heptateuchon* is indicated by the fact that the proofs to the propositions have been omitted.

42 The twelfth-century translations of Euclid's work, following the example of the 'Boethian' version, offer titles such as *Ars (institutionis) geometriae* or simply *Ars geometrica*. The definitions are called *elementa* in Aristotle's *Categories* 14B1 (cf. Boethius' commentary on this passage, P.L. 64, 285A–B), but the earliest reference I have found to the work as a whole as *Liber elementorum* is in the translations of al-Fārābī's *Classification of the Sciences*, ed. A.

while referring to the common notions themselves as *maximae* ('maxims') – a term used by dialecticians. A gloss in the 'Adelard I' version of the *Elements* comments on the equivalents in physics and arithmetic to the definition: 'The point is that which has no part':

An element has no part; unity also has no part.[43]

That a minimal part exists would seem to be contradicted by *Elements* I.10 ('To divide a given line into two equal portions'), which implies that any line – no matter how short – can be further divided. This contradiction was realized by the 'editor' of the version known as 'Adelard III'.[44]

The mathematical and philosophical debates which the *Elements* engendered in the thirteenth and fourteenth centuries have been well described by John Murdoch.[45] However, the implications of the axiomatic method of the *Elements* for metaphysics and theology were already understood in the later part of the twelfth century.

John of Salisbury, in his *Policraticus*, compares the postulates and the common notions of geometry to those matters of faith which must not be questioned. In each case the structure of the art rests on the stable foundations of its premisses.[46] John might have had Boethius' *De hebdomadibus* in mind. In this work Boethius poses a theological problem and appeals to the example of mathematics in laying down definitions and rules by which one might deduce the answer to the problem. First comes the definition of 'common notion' which we have cited above. Then follow eight rules. These rules are applied to the question: 'How are substances good in virtue of their existence without being substantial goods?' Boethius' work was a popular text in the twelfth century. It received expositions by Thierry of Chartres, Clarembald of Arras and Gilbert of Poitiers, who comment on the axiomatic method Boethius uses, and point out which of the rules are used for solving the question Boethius poses. Before 1150 Peter of Poitiers, in his *Sententiae*, had put forward a similar set of 'natural' rules concerning such concepts as cause, identity, property, or diversity – rules that conform to 'human reasons' (*humanae rationes*). Like Boethius, he attempts to see how these rules can be applied to investigating the nature of the Trinity. For example, in addressing the statement that 'the cause of the saying that the

González Palencia, p. 148 (Gerard's translation); ed. M. Alonso Alonso, (Madrid–Granada 1954), p. 93 (Gundissalinus' version).
43 Bruges, Stadsbibliotheek, MS 529, fol. 1r: 'elementi nulla pars est, unitatis quoque nulla'.
44 See J. E. Murdoch, 'The Medieval Euclid', *Revue de Synthèse* LXXXIX (Paris 1968) 91.
45 *Ibid.*
46 *Policraticus* VII 7, ed. C. C. J. Webb, pp. 114–16. John cites *Elements*, postulate 1: 'A straight line can be drawn from any point to any point.'

Father or Son or Holy Spirit are called God is divinity', rules 1 and 5 are found to apply, but rule 2 does not apply.[47]

The example of Euclid's *Elements* was used directly for theological speculation towards the end of the twelfth century by Nicolas of Amiens in his *De arte catholicae fidei*.[48] In his Prologue Nicolas claims that arguments from authority have proved ineffective in convincing Jews and Gentiles of the truth:

> Therefore I have all the more studiously drawn up those bases (*rationes*) of our faith which can be approved, and which a keen intelligence can hardly refute, so that those who do not deign to agree with prophecy and the gospel may at least be led by human arguments.[49]

The 'human' arguments – as we have seen from John of Salisbury and Peter of Poitiers – are those of *scientia* rather than of *sapientia*. Nicolas calls his work the 'art (*ars*)' of Catholic faith:

> For, being composed in the manner of an art, it contains definitions, distinctions and propositions, proving what is proposed by a sequence of arguments which conform to rules.[50]

The *ars* that he has in mind is the *ars geometrica* – the usual name for Euclid's *Elements* in the twelfth century. He follows the example of Euclid by drawing up definitions (calling them *descriptiones*),[51] postulates (*petitiones*) and common notions (*communes conceptiones*). He states the reason for each of these:

> The descriptions are put forward for this reason: that it might be clear in what sense the words appropriate to this art should be used ... [The postulates] are so called because, though they are not able to be proved through other statements – being like

---

47 Ed. N. M. Häring, *Die Zwettler Summe* (Münster 1977), pp. 30–4. The rules in question are: 'Every statement (*dictum*) derives from a cause, to such an extent that if the cause did not exist, the statement would be empty' (1); 'The statement and the cause of the stating (*causa dicendi*) are different: e.g. when this body is called white, whiteness [not 'white'] is the cause of the stating' (2); 'The cause of the stating is partly intrinsic, partly extrinsic' (5).

48 This work was written between 1187 and 1191; see G. R. Evans, *Alan of Lille* (Cambridge 1983), for a discussion of the work.

49 P.L. 210, 596–7.

50 *Ibid.* 597A–B. Note that the problematic word *artificiosus*, which I have interpreted as 'conforming to rules', is also used in respect to Euclid's work by Alexander Nequam in *Sacerdos ad altare* (Haskins 1927), p. 374: 'Deinde ad theoremata geometrie que ordine artificiosissimo disponit Euclides in suo libro.' For Adelard, Aristotle is *artificialiter callens*; see above, p. 152. The association of mathematics with the adjective *artificiosus* goes back to Classical times: cf. Cicero, *De finibus* II 15: 'nec de re obscura, ut physici, aut artificiosa, ut mathematici ... loquitur'.

51 That he has changed the term *definitiones* to *descriptiones* in order to conform to the terminology of logicians is suggested by G. R. Evans, *Alan of Lille* (Cambridge 1983), pp. 184–5.

maxims, even if not as obvious as they – I nevertheless 'postulate' (*peto*) that they should be accepted in order that what follows should be approved . . . [The common notions] are so called because they are so obvious that the mind having once heard them immediately understands them to be true.[52]

Amongst the definitions are those of substance, matter, and form. Amongst the postulates are, that each composition should have a cause composing it, and that no causal order regresses to infinity. Amongst the common notions are the fact that every cause is prior to and more worthy than its effect, and that nothing is prior to, or more worthy or more sublime than, itself.

These are followed by the theorems, consisting of propositions and proofs, and often ending with a statement to the effect that the proposition has been proved.[53] Nicolas divides his work into five books and includes further definitions at the beginning of the second and fourth books. He continues to flavour his work with Euclidean spice by adding corollaries here and there. But the *De arte catholicae fidei* is more than a formal *tour de force*, superficially resembling the *Elements*. Nicolas *does* maintain the deductive approach, showing carefully how one proposition is proved by means of preceding theorems and the common notions.

When Petrus Alfonsi undertook to 'prove God's existence philosophically', he was not thinking so much of using the axioms of the *Elements* as of metaphysical premisses. Charles Lohr has pointed to a set of texts in which a non-Euclidean demonstrative method – which he calls a deductive method – is used.[54] In this no distinction is made between the axioms, which must be taken as presupposed and are not demonstrable, and the propositions, which are proved by necessary arguments from these axioms. Rather, the whole system evolves by necessary arguments from a first proposition which is so patently true that it is beyond hypothesis. This is the system avowedly embraced by Proclus in his *Elements of Theology* – a system that became known in the West through the twelfth-century translation from the Arabic of a cento from Proclus' work, the *Liber de causis*. Proclus' system is very similar to that adopted by Alan of Lille in his *Regulae caelestis iuris*, also known as *Regulae theologicae*. Alan claims Boethius' *De hebdomadibus* as his model, but, in fact, does not follow Boethius in making a distinction between the rules and the conclusions drawn from the rules. In Alan's work

52 P.L. 210, 597B–C. Hermann, too, compares common notions to maxims (see pp. 162f).
53 E.g. I 1, 4, 10, 17 and 20: 'et sic patet propositum'; I 12: 'et sic habebis propositum'.
54 C. H. Lohr, 'The Pseudo-Aristotelian *Liber de causis* and Latin Theories of Science in the Twelfth and Thirteenth Centuries', in *Pseudo-Aristotle in the Middle Ages*, ed. J. Kraye, W. F. Ryan, and C. B. Schmitt (London 1986), pp. 53–62.

there are only rules. There are 134 of them, and they unfold inexorably from the first rule: 'That the monad is that by virtue of which each thing is one'.[55]

Physical speculation

What would Thierry of Chartres and Petrus Alfonsi have understood by *secundum physicam*?

Before the assimilation of Aristotle's works on natural science, which did not start until the later twelfth century, there was no clear example, comparable to that of Euclid's *Elements*, of how physical speculation was put into practice. However, there are similarities between the demonstrative method and the kind of physical speculation which characterizes the early part of the twelfth century. For both witness to a concern with principles. The principles in mathematical demonstration are axioms; in the natural world the principles can either be regarded as the primary constituents of things, or as the ultimate causes. Both these – the elements and the causes – become prominent in twelfth-century physical discourse.[56] The concern for causes and reasons is characteristic of the new departures in other disciplines in the first half of the twelfth century. For example Hugh of Saint-Victor in his introduction to learning, the *Didascalicon* (composed in the late 1120s[57]), modifies Boethius' definition of physical speculation by describing the science as being primarily concerned with causes and effects, investigating both by analysis and synthesis:

Physics speculates by investigating the causes of things in their effects, and [deriving] the effects from the causes.

The examples Hugh gives are all of natural questions: the cause of earthquakes, tides, the virtues of herbs, the passions of wild animals, the origins of every kind of bush, stone, and reptile.[58]

---

55 This is demonstrated by J. Jolivet in 'Remarques sur les *Regulae theologicae* d'Alain de Lille', in *Alain de Lille, Gautier de Châtillon, Jakemart Giélée et leur temps*, ed. H. Roussel and F. Luard (Lille 1980), pp. 83–94.
56 The relationship between principles, causes, and elements in Aristotle and twelfth-century discussions of the elements has been magisterially discussed by R. McKeon, in 'Medicine and Philosophy in the Eleventh and Twelfth Centuries: the Problem of Elements', *The Thomist* XXIV (1961) 211–56.
57 This date is suggested by J. Taylor in *The Didascalicon of Hugh of St Victor* (New York 1961), p. 3.
58 *Didascalicon* II 16, ed. C. H. Buttimer, p. 35:
Unde tremor terris, qua vi maria alta tumescant,
Vires herbarum, animos irasque ferarum,
Omne genus fruticum, lapidum quoque reptiliumque.
It has been assumed that these three lines of verse are all given by Vergil. The first line is

The identification of physics with the study of causes is repeated in an anonymous twelfth-century *summa* of Boethius' *De arithmetica*:

Physics deals with the invisible causes of visible things.[59]

The author of the *summa* further points out that physics is the means by which the know-how of medicine is acquired:

Medicine is the science of making certain confections and of giving potions and putting into practice the knowledge attained through physics. For physics is one thing, the knowledge of practising according to physics is another. Physics is the recognition of the natures and hidden causes placed by God in things, which, although they are not known by anyone, nevertheless it is possible to have the knowledge of practising according to them.[60]

Most works on physical science which the twelfth century had inherited were not directed towards revealing principles or establishing systems. They include encyclopaedic works which classify phenomena without attempting to gauge the more universal causes that underlie them. Such works are Pliny's *Natural History*, Seneca's *Natural Questions*, Macrobius' *Commentaries on the Dream of Scipio* and *Saturnalia*, Aulus Gellius' *Noctes Atticae*, Isidore of Seville's *Etymologies*, and works which use these texts as sources: e.g. Bede's *De natura rerum*, pseudo-Isidore's *De ordine creaturarum*, and pseudo-Bede's *De mundi celestis terrestrisque constitutione*. The last work gives a good impression of the physical discussion of the latter half of the eleventh century. It gives several, often mutually incompatible, reasons for physical phenomena. For example, for the cause of earthquakes the author (or rather compiler) retails various theories: (*a*) the violent rushing of winds through cavities in the earth, (*b*) the collapse of huge masses of rock within a hollow earth, (*c*) the movement of the earth over the abyss, (*d*) the attempt of Leviathan (the dragon encircling the earth) to seize the sun.[61]

The compiler at one stage introduces a hypothetical objector who insists that 'when there is an efficient cause of something there should be an

---

Georgics II 479. However, the second and third lines are not Vergil's. Did Hugh make them up, or did he take them from another source? Müller's suggestion that the lines may be a reference to the contents of Adelard of Bath's *Quaestiones naturales* merits consideration (Adelard 1934, p. 89).

59 Bern, Bürgerbibliothek lat. 633, fol. 28r: 'Phisica vero de <in>visibilibus causis rerum visibilium.' I am grateful to Margareta Fredborg, Alison Peden, and Gillian Evans for transcribing passages of this text, and for identifying its nature. The *summa* is found on fols. 27r a – 30v a (incipit: 'Quoniam in unaquaque re legenda obscurior est tractatus . . .'), and includes a division of science which, in its general outline, follows that of Hugh of Saint-Victor. Hugh, however, does not give this definition, or associate medicine with physics.

60 *Ibid.* fol. 27v b.

61 Ed C. S. F. Burnett (London 1985), pp. 22–3.

effect',[62] but in general he does not seem to be at all concerned about the laws of causality.

In these encyclopaedic works and their derivatives there are echoes of Aristotelian, Neoplatonic, or Stoic physics, but no attempt is made to build a systematic picture of the universe. The tradition is continued into the twelfth century and beyond in works such as Honorius Augustodunensis' *Imago mundi*, Helinand of Froidmont's *Chronica*, Bartholomaeus Anglicus' *De proprietatibus rerum* and Vincent of Beauvais's *Speculum naturale*.

Of all the sciences, medicine is best represented in pre-twelfth-century Western Europe. However, most of the early medieval medical works were of a strictly practical nature. It was only when Constantine of Africa, in the latter half of the eleventh century, translated several important medical works from Arabic, that a fresh impetus was given to theoretical medicine.[63] Significantly, it was after the introduction of these works that the term *physicus* began to be applied to doctors, who previously had been called *medici*.[64] This shift is reflected in the definition of medicine – as being the science requiring the knowledge of physics – in the anonymous *summa* of Boethius' *De arithmetica*, quoted above (p. 167). Much pre-twelfth-century medical literature was couched in the form of questions, some of which ranged beyond medicine into other fields of natural science and metaphysics.[65]

Two works stand apart from this general picture. The first is Scotus Eriugena's *Periphyseon*, which was an exceptional work when it was written in the ninth century, and which hardly began to be read and understood until the twelfth. In the twelfth century it became influential, largely through the epitome from it made by Honorius Augustodunensis, called the *Clavis physicae*.[66] This is not the place to discuss the effect of this work on the thought of the twelfth century. A more central position, from the point of view of twelfth-century science, was occupied by the *Timaeus* of Plato, the first half of which had been translated in the fourth century by Calcidius, who had also provided an extensive commentary to the work. In Plato's text the hypothesis of a harmonious order at the physical level is set up to match

---

62 *Ibid.* p. 28: 'Ubi est efficiens causa alicuius rei, debet esse effectus.'
63 Brian Lawn, in his *Salernitan Questions* (Oxford 1963), p. 30, detects an increasingly theoretical tendency in the studies at Salerno in the first half of the twelfth century.
64 The term *physicus* for 'doctor' does not occur in Cassiodorus' *Institutiones* or Isidore's book on medicine (*Etymologiae* VI), and is still absent in Hugh of Saint-Victor's *Didascalicon*.
65 See Lawn 1963, pp. 19–20.
66 See P. Lucentini, *Platonismo medievale* (Florence 1979), pp. 5–75, and Lucentini's edition of the *Clavis* (Rome 1974); also M.-T. d'Alverny, 'Le cosmos symbolique du xiie siècle', *AHDLMA* xx (1953) 31–81.

the harmonious order of the perfect state. The world of pure forms (the world of being) is distinct from the created world (the world of becoming). The world of becoming is subject to certain principles. In particular, Plato states that everything which comes into being necessarily arises from a certain cause.[67] The phrase which immediately follows this injunction – 'for nothing comes into being, whose birth is not preceded by a lawful cause and reason'[68] – is Calcidius' elaboration of Plato's simpler assertion that 'nothing can come to be without a cause'. Calcidius adds that reason discovers the cause.

One of the earliest works in the twelfth century that shows a first-hand reading of Plato's *Timaeus* with Calcidius' commentary is the *Quaestiones naturales* of Adelard of Bath.[69] On the surface this appears to be just another work in the old tradition of question literature – an impression encouraged by the fact that several well-worn questions from this genre are taken up again by Adelard, such as 'Why is joy the cause of weeping?' 'Why are human offspring unable to walk when they are born, whereas those of brute animals can?' and 'Why does a live body, if it falls into a river, sink to the bottom, while the same body, when dead, after a few days floats on the surface?'[70] But the *Quaestiones naturales* is far more than a collection of natural questions and their answers. The title itself appears not to be original. Internal and cross references suggest that Adelard intended the work to be called *De rerum causis*, or even *Sic faciunt causae rerum*.[71] Adelard's insistence on causal necessity is apparent throughout the work. Beside the term *causalis necessitas* we find *causarum intentio* and *causae rerum*.[72] Adelard invites his readers always to look for causal connections.[73] Enquiry into the reasons for things must precede appeal to authority.[74] The cause must always be

67 Ed. Waszink, p. 20: 'Omne autem quod gignitur ex causa aliqua necessario gignitur.'
68 *Ibid.* 28A: 'Nihil enim fit, cuius ortum non legitima causa et ratio praecedat.'
69 I would favour the early date (1107) proposed by Haskins for this work (Haskins 1927, p. 27).
70 Lawn 1963, p. 24.
71 I owe this information to Michael Evans, who has been studying the early manuscripts of the work. There may be an echo of Vergil, *Georgics* II 490: 'Felix, qui potuit rerum cognoscere causas.'
72 Cf. Müller 1934, p. 49 (in reference to earthquakes disturbing the law that weights come to rest at the midpoint of the earth): 'Quid est quod ea ab hac causali necessitate mutare facit, instabilitatem inducit?' The other phrases are found on pp. 49.4 and 37.14.
73 Cf. phrases such as 'Hoc enim ad superiora sequitur' (p. 10.7–8); 'ex praedictis ea . . . procedunt' (p. 24.18). The language is reminiscent of Euclid's *Elements*, especially the version known as 'Adelard II', which Adelard may have been working on at about the same time.
74 Müller 1934, p. 12.5–6: 'Id autem assero, quod prius ratio inquirenda sit, ea inventa, auctoritas, si adiacet, demum subdenda.'

searched for. Appeal to God can be made when a rational explanation is
completely beyond one's grasp. Adelard expresses this thought in his usual
urbane way. The nephew in the dialogue tries to undermine Adelard's
rational argument by saying: 'If air is not able to add its own nourishment to
plants which need it in some way, your whole reasoning (*ratio*) is unstable
and the effects of all things should be referred rather to God.' Adelard replies:

> I do not undervalue God. For whatever exists comes from him and through him. But
> everything also exists in a confused way and is not without that division which – as
> far as human knowledge goes – should be attended to. In a case in which [human
> knowledge] fails wholly, the matter must be referred to God. But since we do not yet
> blanch with ignorance, let us return to [using] reason.[75]

As starting-points for chains of reasoning Adelard appeals to certain
general principles and unquestionable suppositions. All sublunar beings are
made from the four elements; matter is never destroyed completely, but is
forever being formed into new combinations;[76] similars attract similars;[77]
whatever is moved, moves something else.[78]

Adelard realizes that, in investigating sensible matter, one must resort to
opinion. But the rational opinion of philosophers is very different from the
opinions of the common people.[79] The philosopher should enquire into the
origins of things. 'Whoever does not know the beginning, cannot speak well
about the final result.'[80] The *Quaestiones naturales* go some way towards
seeking out the causes of specific phenomena, as they exist in a composite
state, but, as Adelard points out at the end of his treatise, a more lofty and
difficult enterprise remains: that of searching out the uncombined principles
which underlie the composites. This is the study of God, intelligence (*nous*),
prime matter (*hylê*), the simple forms and the pure elements. These Adelard
describes as the *initia*.[81]

While Adelard himself may have baulked at such an enterprise, other
investigators of physical science stepped in boldly. Hermann of Carinthia
considered that there were five principles which (following Boethius in the

75 Müller 1934, p. 8.
76 In support of his notion of the preservation of matter Adelard quotes Plato ('the philosopher') in the translation of Calcidius (Müller 1934, p. 9).
77 Müller 1934, p. 7.32: 'unumquodque suo simili nutriri'; *ibid.* p. 6.3: 'unde ista inferiora
   perpetua dissolutione ad sua similia recedunt'; p. 8.12: 'quae calida est, calidum [nutrimen-
   tum trahit], quae frigida est, frigidum . . .'
78 Müller 1934, p. 56.18: 'quidquid movetur, movet aliud.'
79 The opinions of the *vulgus* are frequently criticized; see Müller 1934, p. 15.29 and p. 49.12.
80 Müller 1934, p. 52.21: 'Quicumque principium ignorat, male de fine loquitur.'
81 Müller 1934, p. 69.13–20. In the fictitious context of the *Quaestiones naturales* Adelard
   suggests to his nephew that they discuss these subjects on the following day. There is no
   evidence that Adelard wrote a sequel to the *Quaestiones*.

De arithmetica) he called 'essences'. These are cause, movement, place, time, and 'habitude'. The cause itself is divided into two: the first cause is God, the secondary cause could be described as nature. Movement is the coming-together of matter and form.

Six principles are favoured by the anonymous author of another work, apparently written in England in the twelfth century: the *Liber Hermetis Mercurii Triplicis de VI rerum principiis*.[82] The principles are not the ultimate causes of things so much as basic aspects of the created universe – the principal law of the stars (their disposition), the secondary law of the stars (their movements), the world, the 'world-mechanism (*machina mundi*)', nature in natural things and time in temporal things.[83] Nevertheless, the *De VI rerum principiis* is concerned with fundamentals, and describes them at the beginning of the work as three in number:

There are three things which form, put together and establish the intellect of man more perfectly: cause, reason and nature. Cause precedes what it causes; reason constitutes the analysing and synthesising intellect; nature establishes for each thing not only its being, but also the mode of its being. Reason derives from cause, and nature comes from both.[84]

The author goes on to identify reason with the twofold law of the stars, and nature as that which, having derived from the heavens, and having been divided into four parts (i.e. the four elements), pours out the different qualities of things.

The impetus for specifying the essential principles of things may have been fuelled by translations of Arabic works. Al-Kindī's work *De quinque essentiis* describes in turn matter, form, movement, place, and time, but was probably only known through a translation made by Gerard of Cremona in the later twelfth century.[85] But already in the early years of the century Petrus Alfonsi was making known a set of five essences which had been espoused by Rāzī (Rhases): God, soul, matter, time, and place.[86] Pseudo-Apollonius, in a text translated by Hugo of Santalla some time before 1151,

---

82 Edited and discussed by T. Silverstein in *AHDLMA* XXII (1955) 217–302. Another English manuscript of the work is described by V. Flint in 'The "Liber Hermetis Mercurii Triplicis de VI Rerum Principiis" and the "Imago Mundi" of Honorius Augustodunensis', *Scriptorium* XXXV (1981) 284–7.

83 Silverstein 1955, section 7.

84 *Ibid.* sections 10–12.

85 Ed. A. Nagy, BGPTM II.5 (1897) 28–40.

86 *Dialogi*, P.L. 157, 560: 'Legi siquidem in libris philosophorum plerisque, quinque ante mundi constitutionem fuisse, Deum scilicet qui omnium rerum originem tenet; post eum vero animam et materiam, tempus et locum.'

speaks of two causes and five properties of all creatures, the properties being creation, alteration, time, matter, and connection.[87]

The question of matter and the elements was especially pressing for the physicist. In the first half of the twelfth century the debate becomes particularly lively. Ancient texts on this topic were being read with new interest.[88] The most detailed of these was the chapter concerning matter (*silva*) in Calcidius' commentary on Plato's *Timaeus*. Calcidius points out that it is necessary to use analysis to reach knowledge of the first things (*initia*) in the universe.[89] New translations also influenced speculation concerning the elements.[90] The most important of these was the translation of the *Kunnāsh al-Malikī* made by Constantine of Africa and known in Latin as the *Pantegni*. The discussion of the elements at the beginning of this work was the starting-point for William of Conches's account of the elements in his *Philosophia*, and William of Saint-Thierry's in *De natura corporis et anime*, and it was in reaction to Constantine's account – as that of the *medici* – that Hermann of Carinthia proposed his own theory. There are, moreover, several texts of this period with titles such as *De elementis*. The twelfth-century manuscript from Bury St Edmund's, Cotton Galba E.IV, contains two such works: an anonymous *De elementis*, which is one of the earliest texts to cite Aristotle's *Physics*, and the *De elementis* of 'Marius', whose author was probably Petrus Alfonsi; this contains references to a work *De elementis* attributed to Aristotle.[91] Another pseudo-Aristotelian work which contributed to the debate later in the twelfth century was the *De causis proprietatum et elementorum* translated by Gerard of Cremona,[92] as did Urso of Salerno's *De commixtionibus elementorum libellus*.[93]

---

87 *De secretis naturae*, Paris BN MS lat. 13951, fol. 2r (the two causes): 'prior per quid, posterior ad quid'; fol. 3r (the five properties): 'renovatio, alteratio, tempus, materia, coniunctio (vel connexio)'. The term *renovatio* raises problems. The Arabic is *al-ḥadath*, which normally means 'a new, unprecedented thing, an innovation', but in the context the nominal form of the verb *aḥdath* ('to bring forth, produce, create, establish'). Therefore both the idea of novelty and that of creation are present.

88 The texts available in the twelfth century include: Pseudo-Clement, *Recognitiones*; Isidore, *Etymologiae* XIII; Lactantius, *De ira dei* 10 (Lucretius was not much known).

89 *Commentarius* 302: 'Nos ergo, quia de initiis sermo est, quibus antiquius nihil est, utemur probationis remediis ex resolutione manantibus.'

90 E.g. Nemesius, *Premnon physicon* 5 De Elementis; Abū Ma'shar, *Maius introductorium in astronomiam* I 3, II 4 and IV 5; al-Kindī, *De quinque essentiis*, ed. Nagy, p. 31; al-Ghazzālī, *Metaphysics*, ed. Muckle, pp. 10–19.

91 See R. C. Dales, 'Anonymi *De elementis*: From a Twelfth-Century Collection of Scientific Works in British Museum MS Cotton Galba E.IV', *Isis* LVI (1956) 174–89, and M.-T. d'Alverny, 'Pseudo-Aristotle *De elementis*', in *Pseudo-Aristotle in the Middle Ages*, ed. J. Kraye, W. F. Ryan, and C. B. Schmitt (London 1986), pp. 63–83.

92 Ed. S. Vodraska, in a Ph.D dissertation (unpublished) (London University 1969).

93 Ed. W. Stürner (Stuttgart 1976).

Whereas the elements provided the material cause for existent bodies, the heavens provided the efficient cause. Even more prominent than works on the elements in the early twelfth century are works on astrology. Treatises necessary for the practice of astrology were the first to be translated from Arabic into Latin,[94] and by the mid twelfth century two to three times as many works had been translated in this field as in any other subject. Translations of works on geometry and astronomy were made for the sake of astrologers. The translations were diffused rapidly. A short introduction to astrology by Abū Maʿshar, translated by Adelard of Bath, appears in a twelfth-century manuscript from the Abbey of Mont Saint-Michel,[95] and a manuscript in Chartres – sadly now lost – once included several astrological works and astrological notes for the years 1135 and 1137–41. Thierry's *Heptateuchon* includes Adelard's translations of Euclid's *Elements* and the tables of al-Khwārizmī, both works which were useful for an astrologer, but not a single text of the new Aristotle.[96]

Most astrological literature cannot be regarded as having any philosophical value. It gives the data necessary for drawing up horoscopes. 'Judgements' are made from the positions of the planets and the nodal points of the moon in the twelve astrological 'places' into which the ecliptic is divided. Thus, on the one hand, one has the mathematical works and tables which enable the astrologer to calculate these positions; on the other hand, one has the books of 'nativities', 'revolutions of nativities', 'interrogations' and 'elections' which describe how to interpret the horoscope in the case of the newborn child, or the client wanting a yearly updating of his horoscope, asking for information, or seeking advice on when to initiate an activity. The most one can say about the second kind of astrological work is that it may exemplify a rational order of subject-matter. Already in the first half of the twelfth century one sees examples of the codification of astrological judgements, which may be compared with the codification of canon law and the *quaestiones disputatae* in theology.

One astrological work, however, did attempt to give the rationale of astrology. This is the *Greater Introduction to Astrology* of Abū Maʿshar. Abū Maʿshar defines astrology as the science that studies the natures and properties of the planets (including the sun and moon), and their 'leader-

94 A. Van de Vyver, 'Les plus anciennes traductions latines médiévales (x-xi siècles) de traités d'astronomie et d'astrologie', *Osiris* 1 (1936) 658–91.
95 Avranches 235; only the last folio of the work has survived in this MS.
96 See Burnett 1984 (n. 41), pp. 127–60.

ship'[97] over the happenings in the sublunary world. The fact that the changes of the elements in composite things follow the movements of the planets regularly and by a definite law seems to Abū Ma'shar a necessary proof that there must be some natural causal relationship between the planets and the sublunary elements. The planets cannot act directly on the material world, for they are not in physical contact with it. The movements in matter must follow the leading movements of the planets because of some natural relationship between the lower and upper world, just as the movements of the limbs and the soul of an auditor follow the song of a skilful singer. Abū Ma'shar sees the particular role of the planets as being that of an efficient cause. The elements cannot put themselves together, nor can form come together with matter on its own. Rather, an outside cause is needed to bring about the combinations. This outside cause is the celestial power, which distinguishes genus from genus, species from species, individual from individual, and determines sex, physical characteristics, and the length of a thing's existence. Aristotle had argued that the motion along the ecliptic (which is the sun's course) is the immediate cause of coming-to-be and passing-away.[98] Abū Ma'shar extrapolates from Aristotle's argument.

Richard Lemay has shown how Abū Ma'shar's theory is based to a large extent on Aristotelian physics, and how the *Greater Introduction to Astrology* was a vehicle by which aspects of this physics were introduced to Western scientists.[99] The profound interest in elements and causes amongst these scientists in the earlier part of the twelfth century prepared the way for the reception of Aristotle's own natural philosophy.

The full range of Aristotelian physics became known through the translations of al-Fārābī's *Classification of the Sciences* made in the third quarter of the twelfth century. In the fourth chapter of this work al-Fārābī defines physics, using phrases from Aristotle's treatise:

Physics speculates on natural bodies and on the accidents which arise in these bodies ... and it teaches that, for each physical body, there is matter, form, a maker and an aim for which that body exists.[100]

The reader is specifically referred to the Arabic canon of Aristotle's physical works – *Physica, De caelo et mundo, De generatione et corruptione, Meteorologica,*

---

97 *Greater Introduction* I.I. The double sense of the Arabic term *dalāla* – 'showing' and 'leadership' – is reflected in the choice of wording in the translations of John of Seville (*significatio*) and Hermann of Carinthia (*ducatus*).
98 *De generatione et corruptione* II 10, 336A32–4.
99 Lemay 1962, *passim*.
100 Ed. González Palencia, pp. 76 and 83 (Arabic), 106 and 108 (Latin).

Liber mineralium (i.e. an excerpt from Avicenna's *Shifā'* appended to the *Meteorologica*), *Liber plantarum* (i.e. Nicolas of Damascus' *De plantis*), *Liber animalium*, and *De anima*. Al-Fārābī describes the subject-matter of each of these books. Translations of all these works were completed at some time or other during the twelfth century.[101] However, knowledge of these translations was slow in spreading. Birkenmajer, in an old article, showed how many of the earliest citations of Aristotle's physical works in original Latin writings were made by doctors who were interested in the wider theoretical aspects of their profession – such as Urso and Maurus in Salerno – and scholars who were close to the centre of the translating activity – such as Daniel of Morley and Gerard of Cremona.[102]

Petrus Alfonsi received his early education in Spain in an Arabic milieu. In all likelihood he would have known Aristotle's works on natural philosophy in Arabic. When he speaks *secundum physicam*, however, it is in reference to the doctrines of medicine. Moses asks Petrus how 'according to physics' Adam lost that equality in his composition that he had before he sinned, in the context of a discussion of Adam's elemental constitution. Adam, in common with all created beings, had been made from the four elements, but in his case only were the subtler parts of the elements used and combined together in completely equal proportions. Thus he had the opportunity not to die. When he sinned, the equality of this mixture was disturbed, and he lost the potential for immortality. To underline the medical sense of this account, Petrus adduces the analogy of a man with a completely equable temperament who allows himself to be moved to anger by a rumour that he hears. The anger produces an excess of choler in his temperament and irrevocably upsets the equilibrium of the humours.[103]

Thierry of Chartres's concept of physics in his *De sex dierum operibus* is broader. It is the study of the causes in the cosmos. Thierry describes these causes before beginning the verse-by-verse exposition of the opening of Genesis.[104] The originality of Thierry's *De sex dierum operibus* lies in its use of physics for biblical exposition. That he could dare to do this indicates that by

---

101 For a convenient list of these translations, see *CHLMP*, pp. 74–9.
102 A. Birkenmajer, 'Le rôle joué par les médecins et les naturalistes dans la réception d'Aristote au xiie et xiiie siècles' (first published in 1930), in A. Birkenmajer, *Etudes d'histoire des sciences et de la philosophie du moyen âge*, Studia Copernicana I (Wrocław 1970), pp. 73–101.
103 P.L. 157, 641–2.
104 This section is chs. 2–17 in Häring's edition. The unity of the section is indicated by its opening and closing words: 'Causas ex quibus habeat mundus existere et temporum ordinem in quibus idem mundus conditus et ornatus est rationabiliter ostendit . . . De causis et de ordine temporum satis dictum est. Nunc ad expositionem littere veniamus.'

the time he was writing the work physics had acquired the status of a philosophical discipline. I hope I have shown that it owed this status to the fact that, like mathematics and metaphysics, it was concerned with the ultimate causes of things.

6

SPECULATIVE GRAMMAR

KAREN MARGARETA FREDBORG

The title of this chapter, 'speculative grammar', might need elucidation on two points. Firstly, from a historical point of view, the Latin equivalent of 'speculative grammar', *grammatica speculativa*, was used exclusively by and for modistic grammar of the late thirteenth and fourteenth centuries. Grammarians of the twelfth century speak instead of a grammar for the more mature students, the *provecti*.[1] Secondly, 'speculative' grammar is here chosen because it implies a focus on a purely theoretical framework of linguistic description, disregarding the concomitant practical training and pedagogical short-cuts as well as literary analysis of the Latin language and Latin literature. Sometimes, the German term *Sprachlogik* or, better, *Sprachtheorie* has been used to designate this theoretical approach, which grew more vigorous in the following centuries. For the twelfth century, the speculative parts of Latin grammatical description occasionally encroach upon logic, but generally they are concerned with questions such as universal grammar and definitions of a word or a part of speech, and with the question of meaning versus reference (to extralinguistic or extramental entities).

The sources

One of the main difficulties in the study of speculative grammar of the twelfth century is the state of the sources – most of the material is still unedited or only partially edited. Since grammatical manuscripts are particularly prone to extraneous additions (interpolations) and to rearrangements of material, even very early in the tradition of a certain text, we cannot always be confident that we have what the author actually meant to say.

A notorious example of this is the *Glosule*, an anonymous commentary on Priscian's *Institutiones grammaticae* I-XVI (s. VI[1]), that is, on the portions of the

---

1 J. Pinborg, *Die Entwicklung der Sprachtheorie im Mittelalter* (Münster–Copenhagen 1967).
C. H. Kneepkens, 'Robert Blund and the Theory of Evocation', in *English Logic and Semantics* (Nijmegen 1981), p. 61.

work which deal with the *littera*, the syllable, and the parts of speech. The earliest version of the *Glosule* goes back to the second half of the eleventh century, and several versions existed at quite an early date;[2] an early twelfth-century grammarian, Master G <?>, even comments upon interpolations made to the corresponding glosses to Priscian's books on syntax, *Institutiones* XVII–XVIII, which originally followed the *Glosule* in one manuscript. These glosses are now ascribed to Master Guido.[3] One of the versions of the *Glosule* was printed as a marginal gloss in a popular Renaissance edition of Priscian under the name of an otherwise unknown Johannes de Aingre.[4] Around the *Glosule*, quite a number of other anonymous commentaries are clustered, of which one has been assigned to Master Guido,[5] or Master G <?>, while another version of this could on equally plausible grounds be ascribed to a Master Guillielmus.[6] The opinions of Master G <?>, Master Guido and Master Guillielmus display many similarities, and at least one modern scholar has been tempted to identify the anonymous author of the *Glosule* with Abelard's rival and master, William of Champeaux.[7] This identification is not improbable, since the views ascribed to William by Abelard can indeed also be found in some versions of the *Glosule*, and would plausibly link the *Glosule* with William of Champeaux's school at Saint-Victor in Paris. Yet we badly need a modern critical edition of the *Glosule* before we can safely attribute one of the versions to Abelard's famous master.

Another difficulty is the stubborn anonymity of these authors; for this reason the grammatical commentaries and treatises are usually cited by a conventional name, most often derived from their opening words. Unfortunately, the general tendency is that the more polished the commentaries, the more reticent the grammarians are about the names of their contemporaries, while masters' names or at least initials abound in the more loosely structured notes and glosses.[8]

---

2 M. F. Gibson, 'The Early Scholastic *Glosule* to Priscian, *Institutiones grammaticae*: the Text and its Influences', *Studi Medievali* ser. 3, XX.1 (1979) 235–54.
3 C. H. Kneepkens, 'Master Guido and his View on Government: on 12th c. Linguistic Thought', *Vivarium* XVI.2 (1978) 119.
4 M. F. Gibson, 'The Collected Works of Priscian: the Printed Editions 1470–1859', *Studi Medievali* ser. 3, XVIII.1 (1977) 249–60.
5 Kneepkens 1978, p. 118.
6 MS Paris, Arsenal 910 fols. 133r a – 140v b (Priscian XVII 1–32), fol. 135r a: 'When I hear "William!" (*Willelme*), I understand from the vocative "come here!, listen!"' The long extract in Kneepkens 1978, pp. 119–20 n. 35, is also found in the Arsenal MS fol. 137r a–b.
7 L. Reilly, *Petrus Helias' Summa super Priscianum I–III: an Edition and Study* (D.Phil. Diss., Ann Arbor, Michigan 1978), pp. 575–83.
8 *Note Dunelmenses*, MS Durham, Cath. Lib. C.IV.29; *Promisimus*, MS Oxford, Bodl. Lib. Laud. Lat. 67 fols. 20r–88v: cf. R. W. Hunt, 'Studies on Priscian in the Eleventh and Twelfth

Irritating and bewildering as both the anonymity and interpolations can be, it is still possible to outline with some degree of certainty some identifiable schools of thought in which we can see the development of grammatical doctrine and terminology. In the first decade of the twelfth century one school is represented by the *Glosule* in its various versions, where the views of a Master Anselm and Master William are often juxtaposed.

A different school is centred on William of Conches, who wrote a commentary to Priscian I–XVI in the 1120s and revised it in the 1140s. The revised version also includes a commentary on Priscian XVII–XVIII. William clearly criticized and improved upon the *Glosule* tradition, and in turn influenced Peter Helias; Peter's very popular *Summa super Priscianum* added perhaps little new grammatical doctrine, but is a convenient and much used popularization of the doctrines of William and his predecessors.[9] This *Summa* probably dates from the 1140s.

In the second half of the century, the school of Ralph of Beauvais developed an interest in syntax and had, for its time, an unusually keen eye for substantiating grammatical rules by original, illustrative examples from classical authors. Such observations were generally much neglected by writers at this level. Rather, higher instruction in grammatical theories presupposed some grounding in dialectical reasoning and terminology. The late Richard Hunt, who was the first to take us into a serious study of twelfth-century grammar,[10] has rightly drawn attention to the fact that, in the first half of the twelfth century, grammar contributed directly to the development of logical doctrine, while the reverse was true in the second half of the century.[11] In this later period, dialectic intruded into grammar and the writings of several schools of dialectic, particularly those of Mont Sainte-Geneviève and the Petit Pont in Paris, are quoted in grammatical texts. These are cited by name, for instance, in the gloss known as *Promisimus*, which has links with the school of Ralph of Beauvais.

Another school, that of one of the most respected theologians and dialecticians of the twelfth century, Gilbert of Poitiers († 1154), left its

Centuries I', *MARS* I.2 (1941–3) 194–231; 'Studies on Priscian in the Twelfth Century II', *MARS* II (1950) 1–56.

9 Hunt 1950, p. 21; E. Jeauneau, 'Deux rédactions des gloses de Guillaume de Conches sur Priscien', *RTAM* XXVII (1960) 212–47. K. M. Fredborg, 'The dependence of Petrus Helias' *Summa super Priscianum* on William of Conches' '*Glose super Priscianum*', *CIMAGL* XI (1973) 1–57.

10 Hunt 1941–3, 1950.

11 R. W. Hunt, '*Absoluta*'. The Summa of Petrus Hispanus on Priscianus Minor', *Historiographia linguistica* II.1 (1975) 1–23. Cf. n. 79 below.

impact on grammar: recently not only a logical compendium, but also a fragmentary Priscian commentary, have been found from that school.[12]

So far only commentaries on Priscian have been mentioned as sources for speculative grammar – the grammarian Donatus was reserved for the more elementary level. While Priscian commentaries continued to be written throughout the Middle Ages, the second half of the twelfth century also saw the appearance of independent treatises on syntax, e.g. by Robert of Paris in the 1160s, by his student Huguccio, and by the Englishman Robert Blund writing towards the end of the century.[13]

The sifting through the work of many anonymous grammarians is still going on. To the above list I shall add only one new commentary, the *Anonymus Leidensis*,[14] since it is conversant with the views of the Porretans. The work of the grammarian Petrus Hispanus, on the other hand, exists in too many versions to be adequately considered here.[15]

The schools of linguistic thought represented by the *Glosule* and William of Champeaux, and those of William of Conches, Ralph of Beauvais, Robert of Paris, Robert Blund, and the Porretans, might ultimately not be the only schools worth studying. In the present state of research, however, these are of the greatest intrinsic interest and, significantly, coincide with some of the major philosophical schools of the century. I here take schools of thought in a wide sense, allowing for some internal dissent. The schools of Peter Abelard and Thierry of Chartres are not represented, though we may assume that both authors wrote on grammar.[16]

Phonology

Phonology appears to be a subject with little or no theoretical development in twelfth-century grammar, though correct pronunciation was taken to be one of the main goals of instruction. Still, the correct pronunciation of Latin was eagerly discussed – indeed, many commentators spent so much energy on the first two books of Priscian that they failed to continue beyond – but the theoretical framework remained that of Priscian and bore the mark of his

12 'Compendium Logicae Porretanum', ed. S. Ebbesen, K. M. Fredborg and L. O. Nielsen, *CIMAGL* XLVI (1983). K. M. Fredborg, 'A Porretan Grammar', forthcoming (MS Oxford, Bodl. Lib. Can. Misc. 281 fols. 73r–83v).
13 Kneepkens 1981, pp. 69, 62, 60. Cf. n. 79 below.
14 MS Leiden, U.B. BPL 154 fols. 41r a – 123v a.
15 Cf. Hunt 1975.
16 Thierry, cf. K. M. Fredborg, 'Tractatus Glosarum Prisciani in MS Vat. Lat. 1486', *CIMAGL* XXI (1977) 43; for Abelard, cf. D. Van den Eynde, 'Les écrits perdus d'Abélard', *Antonianum* XXXVII (1962) 467–80.

shortcomings.[17] Observations on local and unusual pronunciation surface occasionally in most grammars, but rarely with such precision that one could draw up something like a map of dialects. Practice and observation, not theory, was the rule in cases of dispute, if the dispute could not be settled on the authority of Priscian and the practical manuals, the *Artes lectoriae*.[18]

Semantics

Grammar deals with words and utterances insofar as they convey meaning. The *Glosule* point out that it is not the listener but the speaker who lends meaning to the word and articulates his intent (*voluntas*, later *intellectus*), with the utterance. It makes no difference whether the listener understands immediately or whether the person uttering a sound uses words or another code, as do thieves signalling by whistling to each other in the woods.[19] Thus, the *Glosule* continue, the strict tradition based on Priscian concentrates much of the discussion on the speaker's intent and on name-giving (*impositio vocis ad significandum*). This is in contradistinction to Boethius, who looks at meaningful utterances from the listener's standpoint.[20]

Simplifying matters just a little, one may say that the grammarians of the first half of the century preferred to discuss the nature of the individual parts of speech from the viewpoint of signification rather than from that of syntactic function. 'Words should not be judged according to the actual manner of construction, but according to the special nature of their origin' say the *Glosule*,[21] and Abelard notes that signification is prior to construction.[22] The 'nature of origin (*natura inventionis*)' reflects a well-known twelfth-century grammatical concept, the *causa inventionis*, which can perhaps best be translated by the French *raison d'être*, or paraphrased as the reason why words express both a primary meaning and secondary semantic–syntactic features.

William of Conches, who upheld the notion of a universal grammar for all

17 R. H. Robins, *A Short History of Linguistics* (London 1967), p. 24.
18 Magister Siguinus, *Ars Lectoria*, ed. J. Engels (Leiden 1979).
19 *Glosule* (*Prisciani Opera*, Venice 1500), fol. 4v; *Note Dunelmenses* fol. 19r a–b.
20 Cf. L. M. De Rijk, *Logica modernorum* II.1 (Assen 1967) 139–42 (from the school of Saint-Victor); 'The Commentary on Priscianus Maior Ascribed to Robert Kilwardby', ed. K. M. Fredborg, N. J. Green-Pedersen, L. Nielsen, and J. Pinborg, *CIMAGL* xv (1975) 56–65.
21 *Glosule* in De Rijk 1967, pp. 110, 114–15.
22 Abelard, *Dialectica*, ed. L. M. de Rijk (2nd ed., Assen 1970), p. 125. For a late representative, Radulphus Brito, see J. Pinborg, 'Some Syntactical Concepts in Medieval Grammar', *Classica et Mediaevalia Dissertationes* IX (1973) 501 n.17.

languages,[23] attached much importance to assigning a *causa inventionis* at every level of grammatical description. The *causa inventionis* of the utterance, letter, and syllable is the expression of the speaker's intent;[24] the *raison d'être* of the individual parts of speech is their particular signification. To take the two most important: nouns signify substance (a *what*) and quality (an *of what kind*), verbs signify action or (in the passive) suffering. All the accidental features of word-classes – the *species* of nouns, case, gender, person or mood – are accounted for by their special semantic–syntactic *causa inventionis*.

In a much-quoted passage from the end of William's lecture-course on natural philosophy, *Philosophia mundi*,[25] William severely criticized both his immediate predecessors and Priscian for not assigning the range of *causae inventionis* systematically, and this approach became popular with Peter Helias and the school of Ralph of Beauvais.[26] William's criticism is, in fact, justified only as regards the accidental features, since the *Glosule*, though not Priscian, assigned the *causa inventionis* for nearly all the parts of speech.[27]

William's predecessors preferred to discuss the accidental features in semantic terms of what was *not* the principal meaning of a word. For instance, says Master G <?>, reading is found both in the verb *to read* and in the noun *reader*. The principal meaning of *to read*, by the definition of the verb, is to signify an action as inherent in somebody. The noun *reader* signifies, in its principal meaning as a noun, a substance and a quality. For a *reader* signifies the very person in whom reading takes place, as its substance, and it signifies the act of reading as its quality. But, by its adjectival force (viz. a reader is a <u>reading</u> person), *reader* also signifies the reading as inherent, which is not its own principal meaning, whereas this is the principal meaning of the verb.[28]

23 K. M. Fredborg, 'Universal Grammar According to Some 12th c. Grammarians', *Historiographia Linguistica* VII (1980) 71.
24 Fredborg 1973, p. 13; cf. William, MS Florence, Bibl. Laur., San Marco 310 fol. 21v b:
   'Causa autem inventionis syllabae hic per se non est quaerenda; cum per se enim nil significet, propriam non habet causam inventionis, sed ea<n>dem cum littera, ut supra ostendimus, quae inventae sunt ad dictionem componendam, ut homo habe<re>t per quod alii voluntatem suam manifestare posset.'
   ('Here one looks in vain for a separate cause for the syllable; for, since by itself it does not signify anything, it does not have its own cause of origin, but the same cause as that of the letter, mentioned above; letter and syllable were invented for the composition of words in order that man might have a medium for showing his intent to other men.')
25 Jeauneau 1960, p. 218. Philosophy and grammar are also joined in the treatise on grammar by Hugh of Saint-Victor: cf. J. Leclercq, 'Le "De Grammatica" de Hugues de St. Victor', *AHDLMA* XIV (1943–5) 266.
26 Hunt 1941–3; Hunt 1950, pp. 7–10; de Rijk 1967, pp. 111–12.
27 *Glosule*, fols. 24v, 26r, 96v, 151r, 159r, 185v, 195r; Hunt 1941–3, pp. 212–13; de Rijk 1967, p. 110.
28 Text in Fredborg 1977, p. 36, n. 85; cf. Hunt 1941–3, p. 218 n. 1.

Kind or subclass, as with the verbal noun *reader* here, as well as number, gender, mood, and person, can be taken as secondary significations.[29] What belongs to the principal signification of one part of speech might be a secondary signification of another.[30]

William of Conches, and with him Peter Helias, eventually adopted a classification of the accidental features into either secondary signification or purely formal properties, such as the property 'conjugation' of verbs. What is new in the approach of these two is that the formal properties are generalized and called general properties, which again, I believe, is linked with William's and Peter's notion of a universal grammar for all languages.[31]

One great advance in the early discussions of word-classes that are related to the same meaning, such as the 'read-' group mentioned above, was the coinage of a term, *nominatum*, for the object named by a noun or adjective, as distinguished from the principal meaning, the *significatum*. The referent (*nominatum*) of a word is the object to which a name is given in the process of name-giving. The name-giving, which covers all word-classes except interjections, relates primarily to the citation-form, the *caput*. This citation-form (the nominative singular of nouns and adjectives, the first person singular present indicative of the verb) is naturally and cognitively prior to the other forms,[32] which are derived from it.[33] Only nouns and adjectives, not verbs, have a *nominatum* to which they refer.

As will be seen from the table below, the meaning of a word is not coextensive with the *nominatum*; furthermore, a heated debate took place over how the qualities, if at all, were part of the *nominatum*.

Glosule:

significata:		*nominata:*	
man signifies	the substance of individual men, by determining their quality	refers to	the substance (*res*) of individual men
white signifies	whiteness, which *white* represents as its principal cause	refers to	a body

---

29 *Glosule*, fols. 27r, 64r, 96r, 104r, 113r, 114v, 115v, 121r, 123v, 125v.
30 Texts in Hunt 1941–3, pp. 218–19; Kneepkens 1978, p. 119 n. 35 = MS Paris, Arsenal 910 fol. 137r a–b (Priscian XVII 17).
31 Fredborg 1973, pp. 32–43; Fredborg 1980, pp. 71–4; de Rijk 1967, pp. 110–11.
32 *I read* conveys direct action, the singular, present, first conceived by personal experience (*Glosule* fol. 113r–v, on Priscian VIII 64).
33 William of Conches: late version, MS Paris B.N. lat. 15130, fols. 75v b; 106r b; cf. the Vatican *Glosule* version, Fredborg 1977, p. 31.

Tractatus glosarum Prisciani:

significata:		*nominata:*	
man signifies	as substance, the special nature of man, being a mortal animal, able to laugh, + humanity, as its quality	refers to	the special nature of men by assigning its special form, humanity
white signifies	as substance, everything partaking in whiteness + whiteness, as its quality	refers to	everything partaking in whiteness, by assigning the quality whiteness
or:			
man signifies	(as before)	refers to	a special thing (*res*)

The view that the *significatum* and the *nominatum* could be one is often mentioned, but considered absurd, in the early texts.[34]

With William of Conches, the signification of the nouns and adjectives becomes as diversified as their referents, which may further change according to the context of the sentence, without any change of meaning of the word:[35]

William:

significata:		*nominata:*	
man signifies	a substance, by determining a general quality	refers to	individuals only
		or refers to	the form in 'man is a species'
		or refers to	itself in 'man is a noun'
Socrates signifies	an individual substance and an individual quality	refers to	the substance itself, in 'Socrates runs'
		or refers to	itself in 'Socrates is a name'
whiteness signifies	only a quality	refers to	the individual whitenesses
white signifies	a quality, secondarily hinting at a substance	refers to	a substance or a thing in which there is whiteness.

---

34 Text in Fredborg 1977, pp. 28–31; de Rijk 1967, p. 228 n. 1.
35 Text in K. M. Fredborg, 'Some notes on the grammar of William of Conches', *CIMAGL* XXXVII (1981) 27–39.

| *all*, or *none* signifies | neither substance nor quality, but modes of speaking (*modos loquendi*) | has no referent |
| *who* signifies | an indefinite substance | has no referent |

The last words in the list (classified as *nomina* rather than *pronomina* by Priscian), which have no referents, cannot be used as predicates in a sentence[36] – a rule which underlines that the particular usefulness of the distinction between meaning and reference was directed towards their use in the context of a sentence; the ultimate goal of the distinction was to (allow the logician to) establish whether a sentence was true or not.

The *nominatum*, or *appellatum*, as it was called by St Anselm (1033–1109)[37] and by authors of the second half of the twelfth century, covers both existing as well as non-existing entities to which nouns and adjectives refer. The early texts discuss reference not only within the framework of the meaning of the noun,[38] with all the logical implications which Abelard comments on,[39] but also from a semantic–syntactic point of view. When an adjective or adjectival word is used in the predicate position, as in

'Socrates is further outside than Plato, who is outside'
(*Socrates est ulterior Platone qui est ultra*)

the *further outside* refers to Socrates and, upon an extreme view, the sentence must be reformulated so that

'Socrates is a person-being-outside' about whom being-further-outside is predicated,

which lays the subscriber to this view open to the criticism of infinite regress (viz. 'Socrates is an outside-person-being-outside . . .'). The author of the *Glosule*, who outlines these positions, here prefers to say that the adjective *outside*, or rather the adverb used as an adjective here, does not refer directly to anything.[40] Still, in most cases, the predicate is endowed with a referent in the *Glosule*; thus, because of the nature of the *nominatum*, a string of adjectives used in predicate position must be linked with conjunctions (*and, but*), as for instance in

---

36 Fredborg 1981, p. 28; Robert of Paris, MS London, B. L. Harl. 2515 fol. 9v a.
37 D. P. Henry, *Commentary on De grammatico: the Historical–Logical Dimensions of a Dialogue of St. Anselm's* (Dordrecht–Boston 1974).
38 Text in Fredborg 1977, pp. 27–31; also *Note Dunelmenses*, fols. 64v b – 65r a.
39 *Dialectica*, ed. de Rijk, pp. 112–14.
40 *Glosule* fol. 36v a (Priscian III 1).

'Aeneas is pious and just and so forth',

since *pious* and *just* predicate different properties of Aeneas by referring to (*nominando*) these.[41]

In the first half of the twelfth century, grammatically well-formed sentences, in the context of disentangling signification from reference, are those which would satisfy logicians of a 'realist' tendency as regards the doctrine of Universals. Such concerns are not so dominant in the later period. Since the grammarians of the latter half of the century concentrated their efforts on encompassing syntax in semantics, their contributions are better discussed from the point of view of syntax.

Syntax

Certain grammatical notions which we today consider self-evident, like parsing a sentence into 'slots' or main components or, indeed, analysing a period into main and dependent clauses, were either foreign to medieval grammarians or tackled on a rather different basis. The grammarians analysed and systematized the explicit and implicit semantic relations of the Latin language, rather than furthering, as such, a more abstract operational syntactic analysis.

True, such things as construe marks did exist, that is to say a syntactic notation indicating, by pairs of dots, which words belong together. It was mostly used in the analysis of verse, where, for metrical or stylistic reasons, pairs of nouns and adjectives, or the subject and verb, might be placed far apart. This notation by dots could be expanded to a fuller syntactic analysis, where a series of numbers or letters would show how to rearrange the sentence into normal word order.[42] The normal word order would then indicate syntactic functions, first the subject, then the verb, then the accusative object and other oblique cases, and adverbial phrases.[43]

Although the theoretical treatises, to my knowledge, never discuss this

---

41 *Ibid.* fol. 152r; additions to *Glosule* in MS Metz, Bibl. Mun. 1224, fol. 110v b.

42 M. Draak, 'Construe Marks in Hiberno-Latin Manuscripts', in *Mededelingen der Koninklijke Nederlandse Akademie van Wetenschappen, Nieuwe Reeks deel 20.10, Afdeling Letterkunde* (1957) pp. 261–82; F. C. Robinson, 'Syntactical Glosses in Latin Manuscripts of Anglo-Saxon Provenance', *Speculum* XLVIII (1973) 443–75; G. R. Wieland, *The Latin Glosses on Arator and Prudentius in Cambridge University Library MS Gg. 5. 35* (Toronto 1983), pp. 98–107.

43 William of Conches, late version, fol. 86r a = *Licet multi in arte*, MS Oxford, Bodl. Lib. Can. Misc. 281, fol. 3r a; cf. Priscian XVII 105; C. Thurot, *Extrait de divers manuscrits latins pour servir à l'histoire des doctrines grammaticales au Moyen-Age* (Paris 1869; repr. Frankfurt a. Main 1964), pp. 87–9.

elementary and practical notational device, the concept of a normal word order in a minimal sentence is a key notion in syntactic analysis; it was also common to focus narrowly on two-part constructions of which one part governed the other.[44]

A minimal sentence, consisting of a noun and a verb, was, on the basis of Priscian (II 18), analysed according to the particular meaning of the two: the noun signifying substance and quality (a *what* and an *of which kind*), the verb signifying action or (if passive) suffering. The function of the noun was seen (following Aristotle) to be the subject of which something is said, while the verb was seen as the predicate indicating what is said of the subject. The dialectical terminology, subject and predicate, is widely used in grammar throughout the century, alternating in the second half of the century with new grammatical terms for this pair, *suppositum/appositum*, which were to have a long history in grammatical theory.[45]

Before going into the various shades of meaning of the terms *suppositum/ appositum*, it might be worthwhile to look at the phrase which brought this syntactic pair to the fore, namely 'the function of subjecting/predicating (*officium supponendi/apponendi*)'. Grammatical function was by Priscian called 'force (*vis*)', or, more rarely, 'function (*officium*)'. In our period, *function* fluctuates between being seen as a word's special meaning or as a syntactic property, that it has on account of its special meaning. Interestingly, the notion of function is brought in, as it were, by the back door, in the discussion of when a pronoun or the interrogatives *who*, *what* take the role of a noun, or of the uses of the verb *to be*, which syntactically behaves differently from other verbs.

The pronoun, says William of Conches, summarizing the early tradition, has a different meaning from the noun, which signifies either a common property – humanity in the common noun *man* – or a private property, as in the case of proper nouns. The pronoun, by contrast, lacks common or proper *qualitas*. But it has the same function as the proper noun, and may stand for a proper noun, since the pronoun by its signification directly singles out the locutionary object of a sentence.[46] Though it is not one of the two principal parts of speech, the pronoun may assume the function of one of these principal parts of speech because of its similarity to the proper noun in meaning, namely in making direct reference.

---

44 Pinborg 1973.
45 R. Pfister, 'Zur Geschichte der Begriffe von Subjekt und Praedikat', *Münchener Studien zur Sprachwissenschaft* XXXV (1976) 108–9. Cf. Thurot 1964, pp. 176–80, 216–18.
46 Text in Fredborg 1973, pp. 22–7.

In a similarly semantically oriented manner, the early *Glosule* and affiliated texts discuss the verb *to be*, which acts differently from other verbs when it functions as a predicate with a noun or adjective, acting as a *copula*. Hence, its meaning has two aspects: one in being a verb (*vis verbi*): *to be*; another in being a *copula* (*vis substantivi*): for instance, *to be good*.

A further function of *to be* is introduced in the *Glosule* tradition by the distinction between the copulative function, *vis substantivi*, and the predicative function, *vis praedicationis*. In the analysis of the sentence *Socrates is white*, whiteness is predicated of Socrates according to the *vis praedicationis*, while, according to the copulative force of *to be*, the sentence should be reformulated into *Socrates is a* (or *this*) *white thing*.[47] This distinction between the predicative and the copulative force of *to be* corresponds to the double (grammatical/dialectical) sense of propositions advocated by William of Champeaux and ridiculed by Abelard.[48] The matter in dispute was a question of divergent ontology, since William's stance in the grammatical issue of substituting *Socrates is the white thing* for *Socrates is white* lands him with those philosophers who take abstract qualities as properties inherent in the extralinguistic objects of the world. The origin of the quarrel is that, to William, a predicative sentence like *Socrates is white*, is grammatically intransitive; in other words, there is no transitivity or change of person between *Socrates* and *white*. The intransitivity of person is overtly indicated by the Latin masculine nominative singular ending in *-us* in *Socrates est albus*, where the grammatical gender corresponds to the real Socrates' sex; hence, to William, the grammatical and realist interpretation makes good sense.

In the early texts, the semantic bias of grammatical function is rather strong, but later, after William of Conches and Peter Helias, *officium* becomes more of a syntactic function. The debt to dialectic is acknowledged, as can be seen from the following passages:

Anonymus Leidensis (on Priscian II 15):
The dialectician concerns himself only with two functions, the function of standing as subject (*officium supponendi*) and the function of attributing something to the subject (*officium apponendi*). For these two suffice for rendering a sentence perfect. The subject

47 *Glosule*, Hunt 1941–3, pp. 226–7 (Priscian VIII 1), and ed. Venice 1500 fol. 103r–v (= fol. 177r–v, MS Cologne, Dombibl. 210 fol. 63r a); *Tractatus Glosarum*, MS Vat. lat. 1486, fol. 78v a; additions to the *Glosule*, MS Metz, Bibl. Mun. 1224 fol. 110v a–b; *Note Dunelmenses*, Hunt 1941–3, p. 215 n. 1.
48 William of Champeaux: cf. de Rijk 1967, pp. 183–6; N. J. Green-Pedersen, 'William of Champeaux on Boethius' *Topics* according to Orléans Bibl. Mun. 266', *CIMAGL* XIII (1974) 21–2; Abelard, *Scritti di logica*, ed. M. Dal Pra (2nd ed., Florence 1969), pp. 271.38–275.29.

is the thing about which something is said, the thing attributed is a thing which is said of something.[49]

Porretan grammar (on Priscian XVII 76):

Every verb, as we have frequently said, was invented in order to apposit or attribute its essence to its person. There are three kinds of being which are attributed. Since only properties can be attributed, some of these are the essences (*substantiae*) of the subjects, such as genera, species and specific differences of being. Others are their proper qualities, that is individual qualities. Others again are accidental features.

Because of these three kinds of attributes, three kinds of verbs were invented which apposit the attributes. The verb *I am, you are, he is*, was invented in order to apposit the essences of subjects. Hence, from the function of appositing these essences (*substantiae*), this verb is called the substantive verb . . .

Vocative verbs were invented in order to apposit individual properties, viz. *I am called, I am named*, and similar verbs. Such verbs are called vocative because of their function of appositing proper nouns, by which names are given. And these verbs were invented in order to signify equivocally the qualities of all proper nouns. Hence proper nouns are joined to these verbs so that the nature of the proper quality can be determined in the individual case . . .

The remaining verbs were invented in order to attribute accidental features. From their function of providing an accidental attribute, these verbs are called accidental or adjectival verbs, e.g. *he reads, he runs*, and suchlike.

There are, however, many accidents for which no corresponding adjectival verbs are invented, like length, curliness etc. Accordingly, the substantive verb is used, in a wider sense, to apposit these attributes; for, just as one may properly say *Socrates is a man*, in the same manner – but figuratively – we say *Socrates is tall* or *has curly hair*. And so the substantive verb is used in a wider sense to apposit all kinds of attributes and, so used, though transgressing its real function, it still keeps the name which it has from its true function, so that throughout it is called a substantive verb; it is construed substantively, with the noun or adjective following it in a sentence.[50]

49 MS Leiden, U.B. BPL 154, fols. 58v b – 59r a: 'Considerat ergo dialecticus tantum duo officia, scilicet officium supponendi et officium apponendi, quia haec duo sufficiunt in locutionem perfectam. Et est suppositum res de <qua> aliquid dicitur et appositum res quae de aliquo dicitur.'

50 MS Oxford, Bodl. Lib. Canon. Misc. 281, fol. 83r:

'Omne igitur verbum, ut saepe diximus, repertum est propter apponendam suam substantiam suae personae. Sunt autem tria genera eorum quae apponuntur. Cum enim proprietates tantum possint apponi, earum aliae sunt substantiae subiectorum, ut genera, species, differentiae. Aliae sunt propriae qualitates eorum, scilicet individua. Aliae sunt accidentia. Unde, propter triplex genus appositorum (ergo apposita MS) inventa sunt tria genera apponentium verborum. Est enim inventum hoc verbum *sum, es* (eis MS), *est* propter apponendas substantias subiectorum (substantivorum MS). Unde ex officio apponendi eas dictum est substantivum . . .

Propter apponendum vero proprias qualitates inventa sunt verba vocativa, scilicet *vocor* et *nominor* et similia, quae ex officio apponendi propria nomina, quibus fit vocatio, dicta sunt verba vocativa; et sunt ita reperta, ut significent (-ant MS) qualitates omnium propriorum nominum aequivoce. Et inde (unde MS) propria nomina eis adiunguntur, ut per hoc determinetur cuiusmodi propriam qualitatem hic praetendunt (praecedunt MS) vel ibi . . .

Propter apponendum utcumque accidentia inventa sunt cetera verba, quae ex officio

This tripartite division of verbs appositing essential, individual or accidental properties is found in all late twelfth-century Porretan discussions[51] of the verb and in other grammarians too.[52] Whether the Porretan school (but not Gilbert himself) in fact coined the terminology of *suppositum–appositum* is not known; but they worked out the implications to an extent which their contemporaries found original.

In the Porretan grammar we meet the distinction between the noun being the subject of the sentence (*substat appositioni*) and the noun being the referent, the person that the sentence is about.[53] Furthermore, if the noun is placed before the substantive verb in normal word order, noun–verb–noun (NVN), it signifies substance. But placed after the verb, as in *Socrates is a man*, the noun *man* only signifies quality. Accordingly, the noun used in the predicate position does not signify a person, but only a property.[54] Here we note the disappearance of the concept of intransitivity, which made William of Champeaux maintain that the same person must be expressed intransitively both by *Socrates* and *white* in *Socrates is white*.[55] Correspondingly, the Porretans distinguish between personal and substantive constructions of the verb. The verbs are construed personally with the subject, but substantively with a noun or adjective in the predicate position, irrespective of the kinds of verbs. E.g.

> apponendi accidentia dicuntur accidentalia verba vel adiectiva, ut *legit*, *currit* et similia. Quia tamen sunt multa accidentia ad <quae> significanda non sunt reperta verba adiectiva, sicut longitudo, crispitudo et similia, transsumptum est verbum substantivum ad hoc apponendum, ut, sicut proprie dicitur 'Socrates est homo', ita – licet praeter proprietatem – 'Socrates est longus vel crispus'. Et inde etiam propter similitudinem transsumptum est ad apponendum qua<e>libet alia, in quo usu, licet sit praeter officium, tamen retinuit nomen quod habet ex officio, ut ubique dicatur substantivum et substantive construi ad nomen sequens.'

51 'A Porretan Compendium on Logic', pp. 10–11; N. M. Häring, 'A Latin Dialogue on the Doctrine of Gilbert of Poitiers', *Mediaeval Studies* xv (1953) 253.
52 *Anonymus Leidensis*, fol. 60v a; Robert of Paris, fols. iv a, 12r b; Huguccio, MS Munich, Bayer. Staatsbibl. Clm 18908, fol. 7v a. The distinction is very common in the thirteenth and fourteenth centuries: cf. Thurot 1964, pp. 185, 239.
53 MS Oxford, Bodl. Lib. Canon. Misc. 281, fol. 76r: 'Substantia nominis substat appositioni, quae in logica praedicatio appellatur. Idem vocatur etiam persona, eo quod substat toti locutioni.' Cf. *Dialogus*, ed. Häring 1953, p. 254.
54 *Ibid.* fol. 80r: 'Positum ergo nomen post verbum non retinet vim [non] significandi personam, sed tantum apponendi qualitatem subiecto. Unde nec positum post verbum dicendum est alicuius personae.' Cf. 'A Porretan Compendium on Logic', p. 16; *Dialogus* (ed. Häring 1953), p. 269; J. Pinborg, *Logik und Semantik im Mittelalter, ein Überblick* (Stuttgart–Bad Cannstadt 1972), p. 49. This view was criticized in *Promisimus*: cf. Hunt 1950, pp. 51–2. We still need a detailed study of the notion of *persona* in the earlier grammatical texts, which appear to have been influenced by contemporary discussions of the persons in the Trinity.
55 See above, p. 188.

'I am called Vergil (*vocor Vergilius*)'[56]
N___V___N
personally substantively

'you will come as a welcome guest from Tiryns (*venies Tirynthius*)'
N___V___ N
personally substantively

'See, as a virgin she shall give birth' (*ecce, virgo concipiet*)'
substantively

According to Priscian's analysis (XVII 77) of the second example (from Juvenal, *Sat.* XI 61), *as a welcome guest from Tiryns* is taken as part of the subject, and the sentence is considered abnormal, *you* being second person singular, the Tirynthian guest third person.[57] In the third sentence, if *virgin* is taken as part of the subject, the prophetic and miraculous force of Isaiah's words (Isaiah 7: 14) would be gone – any number of virgins today, says the Porretan *Dialogus*,[58] will also give birth at some time in the future!

So far function, and particularly the predicate function, has been discussed – *officium* and *appositum*. The *suppositum* has a longer and more intricate history. In the early texts it refers mainly to the extralinguistic substratum of which we talk,[59] or to the bearer of a name or form[60] represented by the subject of a sentence. The real theoretical advance appears to have come about when *suppositum* was first freed from the narrow context of interrogatives and was used to refer to the general characteristic of a noun's meaning, by Thierry of Chartres († ca. 1157) and by the Priscian gloss *Promisimus*.[61] A further advance came when grammarians distinguished the grammatical subject of the sentence, *suppositum appositioni* or *praedicationi*, from the extralinguistic person, *persona*, which the sentence is about.[62] The distinction between the grammatical–logical subject and the extralinguistic referent is

56 MS Oxford, Bodl. Lib. Canon. Misc. 281, fol. 73v.
57 *Ibid.* fol. 79v–8or; cf. fol. 73v: 'Priscian does not recognize substantive constructions.' Other authors use the term 'non-personal' to refer to substantive constructions: cf. Alexander de Villa-Dei, *Doctrinale*, ed. D. Reichling (New York 1974), lines 1081–2.
58 *Dialogus*, ed. Häring 1953, pp. 253–4.
59 Petrus Helias, *Summa in Priscianum Minorem*, ed. E. Tolson, *CIMAGL* XXVII–XXVIII (1978) 89; Fredborg 1973, pp. 17–8.
60 S. Ebbesen, 'Early Supposition Theory (12th–13th Cent.)', *Histoire, Epistémologie, Langage* III.1 (1981) 37–8.
61 De Rijk 1967, p. 259 (*Promisimus, ca.* 1170); Thierry, in Fredborg 1977, p. 43.
62 As in the Porretan grammar: see above, p. 190.

fully brought out by Robert of Paris[63] and by *Anonymus Leidensis*, who was writing, it seems, at the end of the century. To be the subject of the verb, says the Leiden commentator, is to be of the same person as the verb; to be the subject of the sentence is to be the referent of which the sentence is true.[64]

The two kinds of *supposita* do not always overlap in surface grammar, e.g. *you and I read* (*ego et tu legimus*), where *read* (*legimus*) is first person plural, which *you* and *I*, taken separately, are not. More importantly, the author[65] recognizes complex sentence subjects, such as

> 'a-white-man runs'   and   'I-who-run read'
> | | | |
>   N   V   N   V

as distinct from complex sentence subjects with logical quantifiers, like *all* or *some*, where the quantifiers are not part of the supporting expressions. This last distinction reminds us of a difference in the dividing line between logic and grammar then and now. What now would be a grammatically permissible complex subject was not deemed so by twelfth-century grammarians, who, both in semantic concern for well-formedness[66] and in syntactical description, were keen to fasten upon and uphold semantic properties, which in their turn could be handled without contradiction by logicians.

Another grammatical advance lay in the development of the notion of governing. From a fine study by C. H. Kneepkens,[67] it appears that the early texts take governing to be a semantic determination of one word by another. For instance, in

> 'I   seem   to be good (*ego videor esse bonus*)'
> | | ‾‾‾‾‾‾‾‾‾‾‾‾‾
> subj. pred. determination of the predicate

the infinitive *to be* governs the complement *good*.[68]

---

63 C. H. Kneepkens, '"Legere est Agere": the First *Quaestio* of the First *Quaestiones*-Collection in MS Oxford C.C.C. 250', *Historiographia linguistica* VII (1980) 126 n. 4; '"Suppositio" and "Supponere" in Twelfth Century Grammar', *Acts of the 7th European Symposion on Medieval Logic and Semantics, Poitiers 1985* (forthcoming).
64 MS Leiden, U.B. BPL 154, fol. 66r a: 'Aliud est supponere verbo, aliud locutioni. Supponere verbo est esse eiusdem personae cum verbo; supponere locutioni est significare suppositum pro quo vera est locutio.'
65 *Ibid.* fol. 66v a.
66 Cf. Pinborg 1972, pp. 61–3. S. Ebbesen, 'The Present King of France wears Hypothetical Shoes with Categorical Laces. Twelfth Century Writers on Well-Formedness', *Medioevo* VII (1981) 91–113.
67 Kneepkens 1978.
68 *Note Dunelmenses* fol. 6r a (Priscian VIII 63).

As with the above-mentioned construe-marks, we are concerned with dyadic relations:

verbs govern *intransitively* the nominative	'I run' ←
verbs govern *intransitively* the vocative	'Peter, come!' ←
transitive verbs govern *transitively* the oblique cases	'I accuse you' →
transitive participles govern *transitively* the oblique cases	'accusing you' →
nouns govern *transitively* the oblique cases	'Peter's hat' →
adjectives govern *transitively* the oblique cases	'like him' →
adverbs from such adjectives govern *transitively* the oblique cases	'in the same manner as he' →
prepositions govern *transitively* the oblique cases	'by him'[69] →

Hugh of Saint-Victor, William of Conches and Ralph of Beauvais[70] stand slightly apart from the rest of the grammarians by holding that neither the verb nor the subject is governed by another word, because both are principal constituents of a sentence and, as such, are 'above' being governed.

Later, in the 1140s, governing became freed of semantic connotations and was taken to be a syntactic device, defined by Peter Helias as a means to the perfection of the construction.[71] Peter's definition of governing was short-lived, since the one given by Ralph of Beauvais prevailed,[72] but his efforts to distinguish clearly between syntactic governing and semantic determination bore fruit. The Englishman Robert Blund distinguishes thus:[73]

semantic determination by the verb:

↓   ← ←⌐   ← ←

'Socrates is a man'   'I see Plato'

syntactic governing: ← →   ← →

69 Guido: see Kneepkens 1978, p. 124.
70 Hugh: cf. Leclercq 1943–5, p. 290; William and Ralph, cf. Kneepkens 1978, pp. 131, 138; Ralph of Beauvais, *Glose super Donatum*, ed. C. H. Kneepkens (Nijmegen 1982), p. 11.
71 Petrus Helias, ed. Tolson 1978, p. 154.
72 Ralph of Beauvais, ed. Kneepkens 1982, p. 11; Robert Blund, MS London, B.L. Royal 2 D xxx, fol. 79r b; cf. Thurot 1964, p. 246.
73 Robert Blund fol. 79r b; cf. C. H. Kneepkens, 'The Quaestiones Grammaticales of MS Oxford, Corpus Christi College 250: an Edition of the First Collection', *Vivarium* XXI.1 (1983) 4–5, 21; Robert of Paris fol. 8r b.

According to Robert Blund, no word enters a sentence without being there either because of governing or because of determination. Certain cases of adjectival determination, however, involve no governing:

determination only:

$\longrightarrow$

'a white man runs'[74] $\longleftarrow$

                                                              'I see well'[75]

Though the explanatory powers of such a dyadic model were rather weak, sets of syntactic rules, and reflections on the grammatically or logically underlying structures, were accumulated, which remedied some of the model's weaknesses. To give just a few such rules:[76]

The verb governs its subject because of the identity of person, e.g. 'I read'.

The transitive verb governs the oblique cases because of transitivity, e.g. 'I read the book'.

The verb governs a specific case because of the mood (such as accusative + infinitive), e.g. 'you see me read'.

The verb governs certain oblique cases because of its accidental signification, e.g. 'I teach you grammar'.

The verb governs the accusative case by reference to the part instead of the whole, e.g. 'I feel pain in my foot'.

The verb governs the accusative (viz. of duration) by a tacitly understood preposition, e.g. 'the man lived (through) a hundred years'.

The verb governs (viz. figuratively) a case by the tacit reformulation to another verb with a similar meaning, e.g. 'he burns for (= loves) Alexis'.

The verb does not govern certain oblique cases which in reality are construed adverbially, e.g. 'he lives like an ass'.

The notion of governing was never extended to account for dependent clauses – indeed to construe clauses with clauses is explicitly said by Robert Blund to be beyond imagination.[77]

The concepts of governing and of the grammatical sentence constituents, *suppositum–appositum*, were the most far-reaching innovations in twelfth-century syntax. These concepts in turn helped to clarify semantic problems of words used in a context where the range of the meaning of individual words had to be determined. Such semantic problems were the domain of logicians and grammarians alike, and in seeking to resolve them, a fertile, but at times confusingly intricate, interplay between the two arts took place.

---

74 Robert Blund fol. 79r b, echoing Petrus Helias (ed. Tolson 1978), p. 156.
75 Robert Blund fol. 79r b, echoing Petrus Helias (ed. Tolson 1978), pp. 44, 72, 101, 150.
76 Robert of Paris, fol. 27v a.
77 Robert Blund, fol. 80r a: '"Socrates is a man and Plato is an animal" is not a construction, unless somebody would feign (*fingere*) that propositions are construed with propositions.'

Still, the role of grammar was never to discuss truth conditions as such, but ideally to frame the rules for grammatically well-formed sentences, so that the task of the logician was not obviated by obscure rules. In the process of discovering deep structures, a certain negligence in describing surface grammar became more discernible towards the end of our period. The use of standard examples rather than fresh observations occasionally gives the later grammars a certain sterile complexion compared with the liveliness and hurly-burly inventiveness of the beginning of the century.

Peter Helias had declared in the middle of the century that it would be possible to write a grammar of French.[78] However, in the face of the growing sophistication of rules, which were checked against abnormal expressions (a process that later contributed to the genre of grammatical sophismata), attention appears to have become directed elsewhere, away from collecting fresh data of surface grammar, not only from Latin but also such data as a vernacular would have supplied.[79]

78 Fredborg 1980, p. 72.
79 Since the completion of this chapter, the texts of Robert of Paris's and Robert Blund's grammars have been critically edited (with a working edition of Peter of Spain's *Summa*) in C. H. Kneepkens, *Het Iudicium Constructionis. Het Leerstuk van de Constructio in de 2de Helft van de 12de Eeuw* (4 vols., Nijmegen 1987).

7

LOGIC (i): FROM THE LATE ELEVENTH
CENTURY TO THE TIME OF ABELARD

MARTIN M. TWEEDALE

I The Ancient Scholastic Heritage

Around the beginning of the twelfth century the study of dialectic or logic achieved in Western Europe a pre-eminence within the fields of secular learning that it had never achieved before in the West and that it would never achieve again. Just what were the reasons for this intense interest in subjects which men in not a few other periods have thought were the driest dust of academic learning is not entirely clear. But in part it was no doubt due to the fact that of all the branches of ancient secular learning logic, and its cognate linguistic disciplines of grammar and rhetoric, managed in Western Europe best of all to preserve a continuity of tradition through the 'dark ages' of the seventh and eighth centuries. In fact, in the Latin West very little else did survive in any systematic form, and once the full panoply of Peripatetic science was restored in the thirteenth century, logic was forced to share equal honours with several other areas of study.

The tradition that was preserved was definitely Aristotelian, stemming from the *Organon*, passing through the great Greek commentators – Alexander, Ammonius, Porphyry, Themistius, Simplicius and others – acquiring in the process *supplementa* of Stoic origin, and making its way to the Western Middle Ages mainly via one remarkable figure: Boethius (*ca.* 480–524).[1] Thanks to him our period possessed or came to possess careful Latin translations of Aristotle's *Categories*,[2] *De interpretatione*, *Topics*, and *Sophistici elenchi*. Boethius' version of the *Prior Analytics*, however, was not introduced until around the middle of the twelfth century, and his translation of the *Posterior Analytics* did not survive at all. (James of Venice's version began circulating towards 1150.) In addition Boethius translated the *Isagoge* of the third-century Neoplatonist Porphyry, which had achieved an

---

1 Boethius' prominence as a logical authority dates only from the tenth century. The Carolingians relied on distinctly inferior works. See O. Lewry, O.P., 'Boethian Logic in the Medieval West', in *Boethius, His Life, Thought and Influence*, ed. M. Gibson (Oxford 1981), pp. 90–134. Also see *CHLMP*, pp. 105–9.
2 The version circulating is perhaps not entirely due to Boethius. See L. Minio-Paluello's preface to *Aristoteles Latinus* I 1–5 (Leiden 1961), pp. xii–xxii.

important place in the Greek scholastic logical canon as an introduction to the *Categories*.

Boethius also wrote commentaries on the canonical treatises. Available from the eleventh century on were those on the *Isagoge*, *Categories*, and *De interpretatione*, as well as one on Cicero's *Topica*. His second commentary on the *De interpretatione*, probably the most sophisticated of all Boethius' logical endeavours, does not seem, however, to have been widely used before Abelard. In addition to all this, Boethius transmitted the theory of syllogisms in two treatises called *De syllogismis categoricis* and *De hypotheticis syllogismis*. The latter treated conditional propositions and syllogisms built up from them, a topic not discussed by Aristotle but originally developed by the Stoics. He also wrote his own treatise on logical *topica* or *loci*, the *De topicis differentiis*, which has quite a different orientation to the subject than does Aristotle's work. Since the Boethian translations of Aristotle's *Topics* and *Sophistici elenchi* only surfaced again about 1130, Boethius' own treatment was the standard one for most of our period.[3]

Although this body of material formed by far the greater part of the logical canon around 1100, it does not quite account for all of Boethius' influence on the subject, for he had written as well five short theological treatises, which deployed technical logical notions to defend orthodox views of the Trinity and other dogmas. These works favourably impressed a number of theologians in the eleventh and twelfth centuries with the role that logic could play in dogmatic theology. As we shall see, the spirit in which these thinkers approached logic was quite different from and often more speculative than that of the pure logicians. Indeed, Boethius' own deployment of logic in the theological tracts shows a speculative Platonic bent that he largely excises from his purely logical works.[4]

Besides the logical tradition dominated by Boethius, logicians of our period were also very familiar with and influenced by the grammatical tradition stemming from Priscian's *Institutiones*.[5] In the area of semantics the

---

3 For a complete list of the Boethian logical corpus see J. Barnes, 'Boethius and the Study of Logic', in Gibson 1981, pp. 73–89.

4 Boethius' logical works are all contained in P.L. 64, but this edition is not entirely trustworthy. The second commentary on the *Perihermenias* (*De interpretatione*) has been edited by C. Meiser (Leipzig 1880). The two commentaries on Porphyry's *Isagoge* have been editied by G. Schepss and S. Brandt in CSEL XLVIII I. The *De topicis differentiis* has been translated into English by E. Stump in her *Boethius's De topicis differentiis* (Ithaca 1978). This volume also contains valuable interpretative essays by Stump. The theological tracts have been edited and translated into English by H. F. Stewart, E. K. Rand, and S. J. Tester (Loeb Classical Library, Cambridge MA 1973).

5 Priscian worked in Constantinople in the sixth century. His *Institutiones* have been edited by M. Hertz in *Grammatici Latini*, ed. H. Keil, II and III (Leipzig 1855 and 1858).

work of grammarians had an impact on logic perhaps equal to that of Boethius himself. Priscian's treatise does not itself probe very deeply into the semantic side of grammar, but it does attempt to distinguish the various parts of speech in a partly semantic fashion. For example, nouns are said to signify both substance and quality,[6] while verbs signify actions and receptions (*passiones*).[7] The problems with such distinctions led to interesting interactions between grammar and logic in our period. Priscian also is an important source for discussions of the verb 'to be', called by him a 'substantive' verb, since on his account it signifies the essence of its subject, not any accident.[8] No doubt future histories will devote much more attention to the grammatical background of logic in our period. But at this point only the groundwork has been laid for piecing together the story of how medieval grammar developed from fairly crude beginnings to the sophistication it had achieved by the end of the eleventh century.[9]

II Late Eleventh-Century 'Nominalists'

The *Dialectica* of Garland the Computist (*ca.* 1015–1084/1102), written before 1076, has been edited by L. M. de Rijk[10] and gives us a remarkable view of how logic was conceived at that time. The work is an attempt at a complete summary of the whole art; though it is divided by sections, each obviously related to some important treatise of the old logic (i.e. in the main the translations and works by Boethius already mentioned, save for the *Topics*, *Sophistici elenchi* and *Analytics*, which had not yet come into circulation), and though it relies openly on some earlier compendium, it is not a gloss but an independent treatise with a considerable amount of original material.

Garland retains the traditional view of the purpose of dialectic:

... the final cause and purpose of dialectic is to separate the false from the true.[11]

and goes on to assign the syllogism the key role in this endeavour. But he defines 'syllogism' fairly broadly as

---

6 *Inst.* II 18 (Keil II (1855) 55. 6); also II 22 (*ibid.* 56.29–57.7)
7 *Inst.* II 18 (*ibid.* 55.8); also VIII I (*ibid.* 369.2–5)
8 *Inst.* VIII 51 (*ibid.* 414.14–15)
9 See R. W. Hunt, 'Studies on Priscian in the Eleventh and Twelfth Centuries', *MARS* I (1943) and II (1950); L. M. de Rijk, ch. 2 of *Logica Modernorum* II.1 (Assen 1967); K. M. Fredborg, '*Tractatus Glosarum Prisciani* in ms. Vat. Lat. 1486', *CIMAGL* XXI (1977) 21–44; C. H. Kneepkens, 'Master Guido and his View on Government: on Twelfth-Century Linguistic Thought', *Vivarium* XVI.2 (1978) 108–41; K. M. Fredborg, 'Some Notes on the Grammar of William of Conches', *CIMAGL* XXXVII (1981) 21–41.
10 Garlandus Compotista, *Dialectica*, ed. L. M. de Rijk (Assen 1959).
11 Garlandus 1959, p. 2.3–5.

... a string of words (*oratio*) in which, once some items have been posited and conceded, some item other than those conceded necessarily comes about through what was conceded.[12]

This distinguishes syllogistic reasoning from induction – i.e. argument from particular cases to a general principle or to another analogous particular case – which lacks the necessity of the syllogism.[13] But it allows for syllogisms which do not fall under the traditional figures, for example, for those with singular terms. Sometimes the validity of these depends on the 'force of the syllogism', as here:

Marcus is Tullius.
Cicero is Marcus.
Therefore: Cicero is Tullius.[14]

where the arrangement of terms and quality of the propositions (in this case all affirmative) would produce a valid syllogism from universal propositions. But in the following this is not so:

Marcus is Tullius.
Socrates is not Marcus.
Therefore: Socrates is not Tullius.[15]

Here Garland says the validity depends on the 'nature of the terms', i.e. their singularity. (Note that he does not mark off a special sense of 'is' meaning identity for these propositions.)

Syllogisms are ultimately built up out of terms, and the study of terms leads to the doctrine of categories. It is here that Garland's 'nominalism' emerges quite clearly, for the category is simply the category-word, e.g. 'substance', and all the words that fall under it as its species or individuals, e.g. 'animal', 'man', 'Socrates'.[16] Both universals (items predicable of more than one thing) and individuals (items predicable of only one thing) are considered to be words. This 'nominalism' amounts simply to the refusal to think of logic as being about anything but words, and of itself has no ontological implications. But it does deny to a realist-oriented philospher an easy way through logic to the real universals and logical relationships he desires.

'Nominalism' has a number of strange consequences which Garland elaborates with relish. For example, every category word, i.e. every most

12 *Ibid.* p. 95.4–6
13 *Ibid.* p. 99.12–15
14 *Ibid.* p. 125.31–3
15 *Ibid.* p. 125.20–2
16 *Ibid.* p. 5.29–31

general genus, signifies itself. 'Substance' significes 'substance' because 'body' does, for any word, being a puff of air, is a body (as the medievals understood the term *corpus*). Since 'body' is a species of 'substance', 'substance' signifies whatever 'body' does.[17] It will be evident from this reasoning that by 'signifies' (*significat*) Garland means what we (following J. S. Mill) might call 'denotes': i.e. 'is predicable of, in a true sentence'. For Garland, then, the items a term signifies lie in what we would call its extension. The intensional aspect of meaning is called by Garland a 'mode of signifying (*modus significandi*)'[18] rather than something signified. Thus he can claim that all the most general genera signify the same items, but in different ways, for in fact each of them signifies everything. 'Substance' signifies each thing in virtue of the pure being of the thing (*purum esse rei*); 'quantity' signifies each thing in virtue of its amount; 'quality', in virtue of its being 'such'; and similarly with the other categories.[19]

As we just saw, Garland includes among the things so signified the words themselves that are in the categories. This means, of course, that for a word to 'fall under (*supponi*)' a generic term, such as a most general genus, is quite different from being signified by that term, and Garland makes this point explicit.[20] 'Man' is signified by both 'substance' and 'quality' (and by every other most general genus), but it falls under 'substance', not 'quality', and thus is in the category of 'substance', not that of 'quality'. Words are grouped into categories, then, not by differences in what they signify, but by differences in their modes of signifying.[21] This relegation of intensional aspects of meaning to modes removes yet another way in which the realist-inclined philosopher might try to gain easy access to real univerals through logic, i.e. in this case through a theory of signification.

Not all simple terms, however, fall into one or other of the categories, according to Garland, who here breaks with tradition. He proposes, for example, that 'house' (and presumably all species of artifacts) is in no category, since it is not a species of 'substance' (no artifact is), while everyone admits it is not in any other category.[22] But Garland fails to note here that those who felt it obvious that it was not in the categories of 'quality' or 'relation' were considering the concrete object it signified, not its mode of

17 *Ibid.* p. 21.9–18
18 For example, *ibid.* p. 15.5–19 and p. 78.17–24.
19 *Ibid.* pp. 22.32–23.17
20 *Ibid.* p. 23.19–27
21 *Ibid.* p. 15.11–15
22 *Ibid.* pp. 16.1–17.6

signifying. Garland's own approach would make it quite plausible that 'house' is in one or other of those categories.

Propositions about words, or what today we would refer to as sentences in the meta-language, Garland feels impelled to treat as a special class of categorical proposition.[23] He says they are made between a signifier (*significans*) and what it signifies (*significatum*). For example, in the sentence 'Animal is a genus', the word 'genus' is the signifier and the word 'animal' the item signified, whereas in a proposition like 'A man is an animal' the word 'man' is not what 'animal' signifies. Garland, in fact, holds that in the former proposition 'animal' has no signification at all by virtue of what the speaker intends, and in that respect the sentence is like those that have nonsense-syllables instead of meaningful expressions in them. Nevertheless, we can form a proposition, in the sense of a true or false sentence, using an expression that is without *significatum*. Note that Garland does not say that in such sentences a word is used to signify itself; rather it is not used to signify at all.

This concern with propositions about language – of which logic, in Garland's view, is composed – emerges clearly in what he says about the truth of categorical affirmative propositions. Most of his formula is given over to kinds of sentences of the meta-language:

It is to be noted that, in every true affirmative categorical proposition, either (1) the predicate and the subject co-signify, as in 'Every man is an animal'; or (2) the significate of the subject co-signifies with the significate of the predicate, as in 'A species is a genus', i.e. 'A man is an animal'; or (3) the significate of the subject co-signifies with the predicate, as in 'A species is an animal', i.e. 'A man is an animal'; or (4) the significate of the predicate co-signifies with the subject, as in 'A man is a genus', i.e. 'animal'; or (5) the one signifies the other, i.e. either the predicate the subject, as in 'Animal is a genus', or the subject the predicate, as in 'A genus is animal'.[24]

By 'co-signify' Garland means 'have some significate in common', i.e., in Mill's usage, there is something they both denote. In the case of the meta-language sentences, Garland's discussion manages to cover a number of unusual cases as well as the type constructed 'between signifier and signified'. In this way he deals with what was later referred to as taking the 'signified act (*actus significatus*)' for the 'exercised act (*actus exercitus*)' and giving terms 'material supposition'. All this evidences an unprecedented

23 *Ibid.* pp. 43.23–45.16
24 *Ibid.* p. 115.19–23

effort to take seriously the 'nominalistic' thesis that logic is about language, not about the world.

Garland also has something to say about the copula 'is' and the verb 'to be', a topic that was to be a lively issue in the early twelfth century. The copula, according to Garland, is not really a part of the proposition, although it is required there to link subject and predicate, and without it there would be no predication and thus no predicate.[25] This view would certainly seem to entail a sharp difference semantically between 'is' functioning as copula and 'is' used without a predicate. And indeed we find that Garland does make such a distinction, at least where the predicate is an accident. In 'Homer is', he says, the verb 'is' directs us to a thought of Homer's essence, while in 'Homer is a poet', it directs us to his *status* of poem-making.[26] Homer's essence is just the thing that is Homer, his substance, and thus the view is not far removed from Priscian's idea that 'to be' is a 'substantive' verb, in contrast to other verbs that indicate accidents.

One of Garland's main interests is hypothetical propositions (which include both consequences, i.e. conditionals in the modern sense and disjunctions) and the syllogisms formed from them. Like Boethius he does not view hypotheticals as truth-functional. In fact, he even allows that both parts of a consequence can altogether lack truth-value and the consequence still be true, as in 'If it were a man, it would be an animal', where no definite subject is intended for either antecedent or consequent and as a result neither is true or false.[27] A disjunction, however, must have at least one true disjunct in order to be true.

Particularly noteworthy is Garland's claim that certain equivalences hold between consequences, disjunctions and universal categorical propositions. The following equivalences, he says, hold (but remember, neither conditionals nor disjunctions are truth-functional):

(1) If A then B $\leftrightarrow$ Either not-A or B
(2) If not-A then not-B $\leftrightarrow$ Either A or not-B
(3) If A then not-B $\leftrightarrow$ Either not-A or not-B
(4) If not-A then B $\leftrightarrow$ Either A or B.

In these, following Boethius' practice, Garland lets 'A' and 'B' stand for predicates rather than propositions. Likewise:

(5) If A then B $\leftrightarrow$ Every A is a B
(6) If not-A then not-B $\rightarrow$ Every not-A is a not-B
(7) If A then not-B $\leftrightarrow$ No A is B.

25 *Ibid.* p. 47.12–26
26 *Ibid.* p. 79.29–33
27 *Ibid.* p. 137.1–3

(6) is perhaps intended as an equivalence as well.[28]

Garland, however, slips up at one point. He claims:

(8) If not-A then B → If A then not-B

and then goes on to assert the acceptable:

(9) If not-A then B → Every not-A is B

and proceeds to show:

(10) If not-A then B → No A is B

using (7) and (8) and the transitivity of '→'.[29] (10) is so clearly wrong that one wonders why Garland did not perceive the error. It seems he takes the disjunction 'Either A or B' to be true just in the case where 'A' and 'B' are immediate contraries: i.e. one must be true and one must be false; then by (4) 'If not-A then B' holds only if 'A' and 'B' are immediate contraries, and thus we get the problematic (8) and eventually (10).

Garland's preoccupation with consequences and hypothetical syllogisms manifests itself as well in a style of sophism that he deploys frequently and that seems distinctive of his work. A sophism is an apparently valid argument from accepted premises to an obviously false conclusion. The task of the logician is to locate the error in the argument. Garland's sophisms frequently use a contradiction as the conclusion, and this contradiction is typically totally unrelated to the subject-matter of the argument. For example, when constructing a sophism dealing with his thesis that the copula is not part of the proposition, he gives as conclusion: 'What is not a man is a man.' These sophisms always operate solely with hypothetical syllogisms, and have this form, where C is the absurd conclusion:

If P then C.
Is P the case?
If Q then P.
But is Q the case?
If R then Q.
But is R the case?

and so on until we reach a consequence whose antecedent is provable. All the consequences in the series are granted, so we can then proceed by iterated applications of *modus ponens* (i.e. arguing that since both the consequence and its antecedent are true, its consequent is as well) to the conclusion. Garland takes great care to state these arguments in a formally valid way. Even more

28 *Ibid.* pp. 131.1–133.30
29 *Ibid.* p. 134.9–16

remarkable is that the initial consequence often has an antecedent and a consequent that are unrelated, e.g. 'If what is not a proposition is a proposition, then what is not a man is a man.'[30] Evidently Garland thought any contradiction entailed any other contradiction.

Garland's discussion of *topica* or *loci*, which depends very much on Boethius' popular *De topicis differentiis*, is also oriented toward hypothetical syllogisms. In his treatise Boethius had examined arguments whose validity does not depend simply on the formal principles of the categorical syllogism, and he attempted to systematize the discovery of good arguments for desired conclusions. He gives many principles, called *maximae propositiones*, stating the grounds either for the validity of a certain class of arguments or the truth of one of their premisses. Depending on the sort of *maxima* involved, we get a *locus*, i.e. a sort of strategy for finding arguments for conclusions. Boethius listed twenty-eight of these. An example will give the general idea: Boethius said that if we set out to show that being praised is not a property of virtue we may argue that it is not because being reviled is not a property of vice. Here the *maxima propositio* is: Contraries are suited to contraries; and the *locus* is: from opposites.[31]

Garland holds that sometimes a *maxima* figures as a premiss in the argument which is based on it. Here he seems to treat axioms of sciences as *maximae propositiones*.[32] But on other occasions he sees the *maxima* as just stating why the conclusion follows from the premisses, and here he is willing to assign *maximae* to even formally valid categorical syllogisms.[33] Garland explicitly distinguishes these two sorts of *maximae* and is in effect progressing toward a sharper distinction between rules of inference and axioms.[34]

Garland does not seem to have had much impact on later figures; at least we find no mention of him by later logicians. But another figure with views obviously akin to Garland's 'nominalism' is frequently mentioned. This is the famous Roscelin (*ca.* 1050 – after 1120), whose works, save for one letter to Abelard, are now unfortunately lost. What gave Roscelin his notoriety were his forays into theology, where his logic, when confronted with the mystery of the divine Trinity, led him to a form of tritheism. In 1092 he was compelled to renounce these views under threat of excommunication.

All our knowledge of Roscelin's logical teachings comes either from his

---

30 *Ibid.* p. 46.16–30
31 Boethius, *De topicis differentiis* II, P.L. 64, 1191C; also in Stump 1978, p. 56.8–12.
32 Garlandus 1959, pp. 87–8.
33 *Ibid.* p. 92.25–33
34 See E. Stump, 'Dialectic in the Eleventh and Twelfth Centuries: Garlandus Compotista' in *History and Philosophy of Logic* I (1980) 1–18. Also see N. J. Green-Pedersen, *The Tradition of the Topics in the Middle Ages* (Vienna 1984), pp. 154–9.

irate opponent Anselm of Canterbury or from his student-turned-critic Peter Abelard. In Anselm's *De incarnatione Verbi* we learn that Roscelin denied that a universal is a real thing in the world and said it was merely the puff of air of an utterance (*flatus vocis*).[35] We have already seen that Garland held this view as regards both universals and individual terms. Secondly, Roscelin denied that the qualities of things are entities distinct from the subjects that possess them.[36] Colour is not something different from the body that is coloured, for example. This view too is implicit in Garland's thesis that 'substance' signifies everything that is and 'quality' signifies those same things but in a different way. It is also clear that Roscelin's denial of real universals was meant to rule out any real common thing that many particulars can be.[37] This was, no doubt, the source of his tritheism, for once it is admitted that the divine Persons are distinct particulars, Roscelin's logic forbade treating them as the same as any single real thing. Thus he was led to say that we speak of three persons but one substance by a manner of speaking.[38] Roscelin seems to have found even the division of a whole into parts in conflict with his principles.[39] The problem is, I think, that the whole is its parts, e.g. a house is its wall and its roof etc., but so is the wall the wall, and yet the wall and the house must be distinct if one is part of the other. Thus again we have distinct things being some one thing. (Abelard called this position insane.[40])

Roscelin may well have been an important conduit to the twelfth century for Garland's logic, but, unlike Garland, he was willing to bring his logical teachings to bear on other disciplines, and once he trespassed into theology he brought down on himself the enmity of the Church authorities and professional theologians. In this conflict Roscelin was not alone, and the resulting tension is an ever-present factor in the period. Nevertheless, a number of theologians continued to have a high regard for the dialectical art while despising some of its self-proclaimed practitioners.

III Theologians and Dialectic: Anselm of Canterbury

One such theologian was Anselm (1033–1109), the saint who studied under Lanfranc at the Benedictine Abbey of Bec, who later became Abbot of Bec and eventually Archbishop of Canterbury. He remains even today a well-

35 Anselm, S, II 9.21ff, 285.4ff.
36 *Ibid.* pp. 9.22 and 10.7
37 *Ibid.* p. 10.7–10
38 Epist. xv, P.L. 178, 365A.15–365B.3
39 See Abelard, *Dialectica*, ed. L. M. de Rijk (2nd ed., Assen 1970), pp. 554.37–555.2.
40 See E.-H. W. Kluge, 'Roscelin and the Medieval Problem of Universals', *Journal of the History of Philosophy* XIV.4 (October 1976) 405–14.

known figure in philosophy, mostly because of continued interest in his famous 'ontological argument' for the existence of God. Anselm was not a professional teacher of dialectic and wrote no commentaries on the classical works, nor even any general treatises on logic. We do possess, however, one complete short logical dialogue entitled *De grammatico*[41] and another incomplete one, usually called the 'Lambeth Fragments' or 'Philosophical Fragments'.[42] But evidence of Anselm's acute reflections on logical topics is scattered throughout his theological writings.

For Anselm mastery of dialectic provided the skills for correctly interpreting Church dogmas and diagnosing the fallacies in arguments that make these dogmas appear incoherent. For example, there is the ancient problem of how men can at the same time have free will and be so infected with sin that they cannot do what they ought.[43] Anselm's own view of freedom of will is that it is a power to keep one's will to the right path, so it seems it is straightforwardly contradicted by the effects of sin. Anselm solves this difficulty by speaking of a direct and an indirect sense of 'can'. The direct sense just means that the subject has in itself the requisite ability; the indirect sense that means there is nothing preventing the subject from doing something. Sinful man cannot will the right in this second sense of 'can', but he can in the first.

That Anselm thought a great deal about modal words like 'can' is evident from his 'Lambeth Fragments', which contain a remarkable attempt to systematize the ambiguities that befall such words. To begin with, Anselm asks us to view all verbs as analysable into the one verb *facere*, meaning 'bring about' or 'do', plus a phrase indicating what it is that is brought about. Then he distinguishes for *facere*, as for many other words, a proper sense and senses which it receives from its 'use in speaking (*usus loquendi*)'. For example, what is in the proper sense a not-bringing-about may in an improper way be treated as a bringing-about, as when we say a man does (*facit*) wrong when he does not love virtue.[44] We also say someone does (*facit*) something when what in the proper sense of *facit* happens is that he does not bring about (*non facit*) that something not be the case: thus when someone refuses to resuscitate (make not dead) a person, they can be said to have killed that

---

41 In Anselm, S, 1 145–68. Also with trans. in D. P. Henry, *The De grammatico of St. Anselm*, Univ. of Notre Dame Publications in Medieval Studies XVIII (1964); and in D. P. Henry, *Commentary on De grammatico*, Synthèse Historical Library VIII (Dordrecht 1974).
42 Ed. by F. S. Schmitt in 'Ein neues unvollendetes Werk des Hl. Anselm von Canterbury', BGPTM XXXIII (1936) 23–45.
43 *De libertate arbitrii* 3, 4 and 12, in Anselm, S 1.
44 Schmitt 1936, p. 27.

person, i.e. to have brought about his death. Also there are cases, called indirect modes, where we say the person does x, but in the proper sense he has only brought about something else which in turn brought about x. Anselm gives altogether five improper senses of *facere* and another five of *facere non*.[45] The way the analysis deploys multiple negations probably derives from Aristotle's *De interpretatione* 13, but the application of this formal schema to *facere*, and thus implicitly to all verbs, as well as the emphasis on proper and improper senses, is original and fairly successful.

Anselm says that similar analyses can be given for *debere* ('ought') and *posse* ('can') and proceeds to show how *debet* in its proper sense means 'owes' or 'is obligated to', but has a variety of senses established by the *usus loquendi* as well.[46] Thus we frequently say someone ought to do something when the situation in fact is that they are not obligated not to do something, e.g. we say 'x ought to marry', when he is not obligated not to marry. Also one can say in Latin x *non debet peccare* when in fact we mean not merely that x is under no obligation to sin but that he is under an obligation not to sin. There are indirect modes too, as when we say the poor ought to receive alms from the rich and mean not that the poor are under an obligation but that the rich are under an obligation to them.

We do not possess the analogous treatment of *posse* ('can'), but it is not too difficult to see how it would run and how Anselm's solution to the apparent incompatibility of free will and sin would fit in. When we say that the sin-corrupted man cannot choose what is right we mean not that he lacks this ability but that something else, namely sin, has the ability to keep him from choosing the right.

An analysis of 'can' naturally has implications for the classical modalities: necessity, possibility and impossibility. Necessity, Anselm says, is in its proper sense a matter of constraint,[47] since it amounts to *non posse non*, i.e. a lack of ability not to do or be something. And yet we say that God necessarily tells the truth, where we cannot possibly mean that God is constrained or lacks some ability. Rather we have here an indirect necessity, for the constraint really falls on things other than God; they lack the ability to prevent God from telling the truth.

Anselm always treats the modalities in their proper senses as properties of things: abilities and lacks of abilities. There is no notion equivalent to our logical necessity or possibility as propositional operators. The closest

---

45 *Ibid.* pp. 29–31.
46 *Ibid.* pp. 35–6.
47 *Cur Deus homo* II 17, in Anselm, S II 123–4.

Anselm comes to this is when he says that, although we say you are necessarily speaking when you are speaking, we do not imply that you are constrained to speak; rather we mean that nothing can bring it about that you do not speak when you are speaking.[48] It turns out that even the necessity of this tautology is in Anselm's view reducible to an inability to make something not be the case.

This postulation of improper senses exemplifies Anselm's insistence that we distinguish between what a sentence means in virtue of its verbal form (*secundum formam vocis* or *loquendi*) and what it implies about how things really are (*secundum rem* or *rerum naturam*). In its verbal form the sentence 'God of necessity tells the truth' appears heretically to set a constraint on God's actions, but when we see that 'of necessity' is being used in an improper and indirect sense there, we find that in reality the constraint falls on creatures, not on the divinity. This discovery that grammatical form might be positively misleading as to what a sentence really asserts, although generally admitted by Anselm's successors, was not really exploited to the full again until Ockham in the fourteenth century.[49]

This same theme appears in *De grammatico* as well. The starting-point of this dialogue is Aristotle's use of γϱαμματικός, in Latin *grammaticus* (literate), as an example of a non-substance and quality,[50] while Priscian treated it as a term signifying a substance as well as a quality.[51] The problem is engendered by the fact that, like all adjectives in Latin and Greek, *grammaticus* can be used as a substantive, much as the English word 'illiterate' performs the roles of both adjective and noun. Consequently, we can say *grammaticus est homo*, i.e. 'a literate is a man', and if a man, then certainly a substance. Nevertheless, to say *homo est grammaticus* ('the man is literate') is to ascribe a quality to a certain man. Anselm's solution, in brief, is to say that *grammaticus* has two significations, its *per se* or proper signification and its *per aliud* or indirect signification. *Per se* and properly it signifies the quality literacy; *per aliud* and indirectly it signifies the substance man.[52] The *per aliud* signification is linked by Anselm to the *usus loquendi*, whereas the *per se* signification, as we would expect, is something belonging to the term itself prior to its use.

In this way Anselm tries to make out the logical source of the distinction of 'denominative' terms, i.e. those that are not abstract but have an abstract

48 *Ibid.* pp. 124–5. See D. P. Henry, *The Logic of St. Anselm* (Oxford 1967), pp. 172–80.
49 Anselm's discussion of 'nothing' is another good example. See Henry 1967, pp. 207–19.
50 See Boethius' translation of the *Categories* 3A5 and 10A30, in *Aristoteles Latinus* I 1–5, pp. 9 and 27.
51 *Institutiones* II 25, in Keil II, 1855, 58.19–24.
52 Henry 1964, p. 37 (4.232).

form, e.g. 'literate'–'literacy', 'brave'–'bravery', from those that have no abstract form, e.g. 'man', 'animal'. The denominative terms signify a quality or other non-substance *per se* and substance *per aliud*, whereas the other non-abstract nouns, like 'man', signify substance, and the defining properties of a class, *per se*. If this were not the case, Anselm argues, *grammaticus* would be a species whose genus is *homo*.[53] One can see that Anselm is here exploring the basis of the quasi-grammatical distinction between the nouns that refer to genera and species and the nouns and adjectives that merely ascribe properties to things without sorting them. The question goes to the root of Peripatetic logic and ontology, but rarely received as full a treatment as Anselm gives it in *De grammatico*.

Anselm recognizes that his own solution has the odd consequence that there should be no problem about asserting *grammaticus est qualitas* ('literate is a quality'), for the subject term and the predicate term signify the same thing, literacy.[54] The student in the dialogue complains that this sort of remark is common among the dialecticians, even though they would never say it in ordinary conversation.[55] But Anselm's point is that *usus loquendi* leads us astray here, and that the logician is returning to the proper meaning of the term when he goes along with Aristotle and places *grammaticus* in the category of quality. In general, claims Anselm, when Aristotle says that A is in some category he means that the *per se* significate of 'A' is. This explains the prevalence of denominative terms rather than their abstracts when Aristotle lists items in the non-substantial categories.[56] To say that *grammaticus* is in the category of quality is the same as saying *grammatica* (literacy) is.

Anselm also says that *grammaticus* is 'appellative' of man even though it does not signify man properly speaking. The term 'appellative noun' is used frequently by Priscian to denote any common noun, but Anselm uses as well the verb *appellare* (to call, name), and makes it clear that a term 'names (*appellat*)' something when the term is predicable of that thing in a sentence acceptable to *usus loquendi*.[57] Thus *grammaticus* 'names (*appellat*)' man, but does not 'name' literacy, because accepted usage allows *homo est grammaticus*, but not *grammatica est grammaticus*.

Anselm's point is not, however, to limit the appellation of a term to the *particulars* that it is predicable of. When he says that 'man' both signifies *per se*

53 *Ibid.* pp. 37–9 (4.240–4.2415).
54 *Ibid.* pp. 41–3 (4.5).
55 *Ibid.* p. 36 (4.210).
56 *Ibid.* p. 42 (4.5142).
57 *Ibid.* p. 37 (4.2341).

and *appellat* substance[58] he does not mean particular substances but rather some single underlying substratum for all properties. Likewise when he says 'literate' signifies and *appellat* substance only *per aliud*, he refers to this same substratum, although no doubt he would allow that 'literate' *appellat* some particular substances as well.

Anselm's semantics, then, remains firmly intensional in contrast to what we found in Garland. We have already seen that he would place the *per se* significates of terms, not the terms themselves, in the Aristotelian categories, and, in general, he does not try to do away with *de re* questions in favour of *de voce* ones.[59] Furthermore, he takes it that the significates of words are *res* (things); there is no suggestion that they are ideas or concepts, as in Aristotle's *De interpretatione*.[60] There is in all this a kind of realism about intensions that goes beyond Boethius' logic and contrasts sharply with Garland's reduction of intensions to modes of signifying. No doubt this explains the hostility Anselm shows toward some of Roscelin's logical views.

An easy acceptance of the intensional realities signified by words is a mark of most of the theologians who favoured the use of logic in their discipline, and reveals the influence of Boethius' theological tracts. Odo of Tournai († 1113), for example, explains original sin as an imperfection that infects the substance that is common to all human beings, i.e. their specific human nature.[61] Odo takes very seriously the idea, found already in Boethius, that individuals within the same species differ only by accident, and draws from this the conclusion that their substance is a single common item corresponding to the species they all belong to. Anselm, though not so blatant, exhibits the same frame of mind.[62]

But Anselm's realism is naive. There is no awareness of the oddness of these intensional but objective realities, and no attempt to deal with the difficulties people might find in the idea of a thing common to many different things. Consequently, it can hardly be said that Anselm has a *theory* of universals; his realism is a largely unquestioned assumption rather than a carefully worked out and defended thesis.

58 *Ibid.* p. 36 (4.231).
59 Henry 1974, pp. 295–6.
60 Henry 1964, p. 43 (4.5143).
61 P.L. 160 1081D. See Tullio Gregory, *Platonismo medievale* (Rome 1958), ch. 3, and Peter King, *Peter Abailard and the Problem of Universals* (doctoral thesis for Princeton University 1982, publ. University Microfilms, Ann Arbor, Michigan), pp. 124–8.
62 There is dispute on this point. See Jasper Hopkins, 'The Anselmian Theory of Universals', ch. 3 in J. Hopkins and H. Richardson, *Anselm of Canterbury* IV (Toronto and N.Y. 1976). But King 1982, pp. 124–36, argues for Anselm's realism, successfully in my view.

IV Grammar and Dialectic

At the same time as dialectic became a force to be reckoned with in theology, it was also having a notable impact on grammar, and treatises on Priscian now became involved with important questions in semantics. The grammarians framed their semantics within the myth of an original 'imposition' of words on things at the time when words were invented.[63] We find much talk of the causes of the invention of this and that word, and a contrast is made between the meaning a term has because of these 'causes' and the meanings it receives as it gets used in various contexts. There is a clear similarity here to Anselm's distinction between *per se* signification and signification in virtue of *usus loquendi*.

An example of this technique occurs in a late eleventh-century gloss on Priscian (generally referred to as the *Glosulae*),[64] where the glossator considers what Priscian meant by saying that it is a property of nouns to signify substance and quality. He suggests that a common (appellative) noun like 'man' signifies many substances which all have a common property, that Priscian calls a quality, and indeed the 'cause of the inventing' of the noun in the first place was to signify that property, not the substances themselves. The glossator immediately goes on to explain that he is not saying that it signifies the quality by naming it; it only names or is 'imposed on' the substance. It signifies the quality by 'representing' it or 'determining' it with regard to a substance. And then he concludes:

Consequently every noun has two significations: one by way of imposition on a substance, the other by representation of a quality of that substance; for example 'man' by imposition signifies the reality (*rem*) of Socrates and of other men, i.e. by naming, while determining rationality and mortality as belonging to it, i.e. by representing.[65]

The glossator has clearly grasped the distinction between a noun's reference to things or realities that are subjects of properties and the noun's indicating the properties which belong to those things. In this he claims to be opposed by those who say that substance and quality compose a single item which is signified by the noun. For example, 'Socrates' signifies the combination of the thing or reality subject to Socrates' distinctive accidents,

---

63 See Hunt 1943, pp. 211–12.
64 Interesting portions of this are given in Hunt 1943, pp. 225–8, and in King 1982, ch. 4.4 Appendix, pp. 2–3.
65 King 1982, p. 2.34–8 of Appendix to ch. 4.4. In the last line I have altered *in hoc* to *id est* to make sense of the passage.

and those accidents – a view our glossator argues against at length.[66] His opponents seem to have shared the view of signification we saw Anselm maintained with respect to non-denominative nouns: they signify everything in their definition, i.e. substance plus all the differentiating features attached it. The glossator is clearly worried about the ontology which lies implicit in this conception.

Priscian's discussion of the verb led to equal controversy. He had distinguished verbs by saying they signify actions and receptions (*passiones*, i.e. what happens to a passive subject), but clearly nouns can signify actions and receptions too, so something more is needed to differentiate verbs from nouns. From dialectic comes the notion of an 'inhering', and our glossator claims that verbs signify actions and receptions in virtue of their inhering in something, namely the subject,[67] whereas nouns when they signify actions and receptions signify them simply for what they are. But then how can verbs be distingushed from what were called 'assumed names (*nomina sumpta*)', i.e. adjectives and denominative nouns, like white, for these too indicate an inhering of the quality they signify? Our glossator says that in fact the signification of verbs and *nomina sumpta* is not necessarily different, but verbs always carry along an indication of time and mood that *nomina sumpta* do not.[68]

A similar approach was apparently taken by a Master Guido or Wido in the first decade of the new century.[69] He clearly rejects the idea that a verb signifies that an action or reception inheres, for then on its own it would be a full proposition.[70] Instead it signifies the action in virtue of the inherence, and in this respect differs not at all from *nomina sumpta*.

What Priscian himself called the 'substantive verb', i.e. the verb 'to be', poses another problem for his view of verbs. What action or reception does it signify? The situation is complicated by the fact that 'to be' can be used without any complement, as in 'Socrates is', and with one (called *tertium adiacens*) as in 'Socrates is a man'. Here again we find the *Glosulae* and Master Guido holding like views. The verb 'to be' has a twofold nature, one by

66 *Ibid.* pp. 2.44–3.61.
67 *Ibid.* p. 3.24–5.
68 *Ibid.* p. 3.27–8.
69 A comparison of Fredborg 1977 and Kneepkens 1978 reveals that the views taken by Guido in his own gloss on Priscian are those ascribed to Master W in the work Fredborg refers to as *Sententiae* 1. It seems to me fairly certain that 'W' stands for 'Wido', not 'William' (of Champeaux) as Fredborg suggested. Guido is at least highly dependent on the *Glosulae*, if not their actual author. Kneepkens suggests that Guido was Master Guy d'Étampes, a famous teacher who became Bishop of Le Mans in 1125.
70 Fredborg 1977, p. 35.1–10.

being a verb, the other by being a substantive.[71] As a verb it designates an inhering action or reception; as a substantive it designates everything in essence. The *Glosulae* interpret the substantival sense as meaning that 'to be' applies to everything in virtue of existence.[72] Guido says it signifies all essences disjunctively, 'so that when we say "Socrates is", we mean he is a man or an ass or even whiteness'.[73] Both authors admit that the more frequent usage is as a substantive, and that in either case 'to be' is equivocal. As a verb, there is no one very general action or reception which it signifies; rather it signifies disjunctively all the actions signified by other verbs. Nor as a substantive is it univocal. This equivocality is directly implied by Guido's view, but the glossator too denies that existence is some one real property in all things.[74]

When 'to be' is used with a complement (*tertium adiacens*), both authors agree that it loses entirely the signification of an action or reception and retains from its verbal aspect only the function of linking (*copulat*).[75] In these cases its force as a substantive produces a sentence which amounts to saying 'this is that'.[76] The *Glosulae* put the matter thus:

For so far as the force of this sentence 'man is an animal' is concerned, 'is' signifies, not just by itself but in association with other words, that that thing which is man is that thing which is animal. But this holds not from its verbal force, but rather from its substantive force.[77]

But can we say this even when the predicate term is an adjective or a *nomen sumptum*? Both authors now distinguish what is a result of the predication from what is a result of the substantive verb. The former makes us read the sentence 'Socrates is white' as meaning that whiteness inheres in Socrates, while the latter causes us to read it as saying that the thing which is Socrates is a white body according to the *Glosulae*, a white thing according to Guido.[78]

We know from Abelard's gloss on Boethius' *De topicis differentiis* that his one-time teacher and persecutor, William of Champeaux (*ca.* 1070 – *ca.* 1120), carried a doctrine of this sort to the extreme of claiming that propositions of the kind 'Socrates is white' have two different senses, one

71 Hunt 1943, p. 226.12–14; Kneepkens 1978, p. 120.
72 Hunt 1943, p. 226.16.
73 Kneepkens 1978, p. 120.
74 Hunt 1943, p. 227.36–40.
75 Kneepkens 1978, p. 120; Hunt 1943, p. 227.5.
76 Kneepkens 1978, p. 121.
77 Hunt 1943, p. 227.10–14.
78 Hunt 1943, p. 228.25–9; Kneepkens 1978, p. 120.

their grammatical sense, and the other their dialectical sense.[79] The grammarians note the substantive verb, claiming it is an 'intransitive' construction
that means e.g. 'Socrates is a white thing.' The dialecticians, on the other
hand, note the predication and judge that it means 'whiteness inheres in
Socrates'. In fact, the dialecticians claim that really 'Socrates is white' and
'Socrates is whiteness' have this same meaning. William said the dialectical
sense was 'higher' and 'more general', but propositions are not true or false
in this sense; rather truth and falsity apply to them in their grammatical
interpretations.[80]

William was in his day a famous teacher of rhetoric, grammar, dialectic,
and theology, but he seems to have had a proclivity for extreme positions.
While listening to his lectures on rhetoric, Abelard tangled with him on the
nature of universals, and says that by arguments he compelled his teacher to
abandon the view that 'one and the same thing existed wholly at the same
time in each of its individuals.'[81] Very little of William's own writing has
been found, but some rhetorical commentaries on Cicero's *De inventione* and
the pseudo-Ciceronian *Rhetorica ad Herennium* have recently been brought to
light, and in the epilogue to the latter he says that 'true genera pre-exist in an
unformed state like matter, but they are informed so as to give species when
forms are added'.[82] This makes it virtually certain that it is William's position
that Abelard describes and devastates in two places,[83] for the heart of that
view is the thesis that genera relate to species and species to individuals much
as matter without some form does to matter informed.[84] Animal, for
example, when combined with certain forms, viz. those that differentiate
man from other animals, becomes man; when combined with certain other
forms, viz. those that differentiate some other animal species, it becomes that
species. And likewise man, when combined with Socrates' peculiar features,
becomes Socrates. In other words, Boethius' suggestion that individuals are
differentiated by accidents has been applied to species as well. This thesis
may well arise out of attempts to explain the signification of nouns in terms

79 Abelard, *Super topica glossae*, in Pietro Abelardo, *Scritti Filosofici*, ed. M. Dal Pra (Rome–
    Milan 1954), pp. 271.38–273.10.
80 See de Rijk 1967, ii. 1 183–5.
81 Abelard, *Historia calamitatum*, ed. J. Monfrin (Paris 1962), p. 65.85–9.
82 K. M. Fredborg, 'The Commentaries on Cicero's *De Inventione* and *Rhetorica ad Heren-
    nium* by William of Champeaux', *CIMAGL* xvii (1976) 1–39. See p. 35.31–2.
83 Abelard, *Logica 'Ingredientibus'* and *Logica 'Nostrorum petitioni sociorum'*, both ed. by B. Geyer
    in *Peter Abaelards philosophische Schriften*, in BGPTM xxi (1919–33), see pp. 10.17–34 and
    515.14–25. Also see M. Tweedale, *Abailard on Universals* (Amsterdam 1976), pp. 95–8; King
    1982, pp. 137–71.
84 This thesis finds some support in Boethius. See his *Liber de divisione*, P.L. 64, 879C.

of substance and quality, as authorized by Priscian.[85] In the case of nouns standing for genera and species, it is important to have a substance or subject be part of the signification of the term, otherwise it will be difficult to separate them from *nomina sumpta* and adjectives. Recall here Anselm's problem of distinguishing 'man' from denominative terms that 'name (*appellant*)' man, and his claiming that 'man' signifies a substance *per se*, where Anselm means some general substratum. (See above pp. 208–10.)

William's thesis follows more closely than Anselm's the grammar of defining species in terms of a genus-noun plus an adjective. He takes the genus-noun to name the substrate, and the adjective the quality. Thus the substrate differs for species of different genera, although, given that those genera themselves result from their own substrata and qualities, we will eventually be forced back to the highest genera as the only ultimate substrate, a startling consequence that Abelard was not slow to point out.[86]

William's realist tendencies emerge also in what we know of his doctrine of *topica* or *loci*. He considers the *loci* themselves to be things which prove conclusions from certain premisses.[87] What he seems to mean here is that, for example, when we argue 'Socrates is a man, therefore he is an animal', the *locus* is the thing man, although when we indicate the strategy of the argument we say 'species', not 'man', and ultimately refer to the *maxima propositio* that what the species is predicated of, the genus is too.'Species' refers to man, but under the relationship of specificity; because of this relationship the argument is valid. Clearly William, in contrast to the early 'nominalists' like Garland, saw the terminology of logic as referring to reified intensional entities, not to linguistic expressions.

Consonant with this is his treatment of *maximae* as multiply ambiguous.[88] The various senses of a *maxima* are just those consequences (i.e. conditionals) which we would say exemplify the principle the *maxima* states. Thus one of the senses of the *maxima* 'What the species is predicated of, the genus is too' is 'If Socrates is a man, Socrates is an animal', and another is 'If a horse is an animal, a horse is a substance', and so on indefinitely. Abelard's discussion of this doctrine cites two reasons for holding it: (1) *Maximae* often contain pronouns the reference of which varies with the reference of the antecedent.

85 We find it in a gloss on Priscian from this period. See Fredborg 1977, pp. 27–31.
86 Abelard 1919–33, p. 12.27–32.
87 See pp. 16–19 of N. J. Green-Pedersen, 'William of Champeaux on Boethius' Topics according to Orleans Bibl. Mun. 266', *CIMAGL* XIII (1974) 13–30. The Master W referred to appears to be William. Also see Green–Pedersen 1984, pp. 165f.
88 *Ibid.* pp. 21–3, fragments 8, 10, 12; and p. 28. My account here relies entirely on Green-Pedersen's summary.

In this they are like 'Everyone loves himself', for there 'himself' cannot be said to refer to just one person. (This shows the beginning of an awareness of the logical problems involved in pronouns associated with quantifiers, a topic that was to loom large in fourteenth-century logic but which was perhaps never fully resolved until Frege.) (2) The *maxima* would never be able to 'prove' any consequences if it were not about the things those consequences are about. It is no good having it be about either words or things of its own. Hence it must just amount to an indefinite list of all the consequences it proves.[89]

William had retreated from some of his more extreme realist doctrines by the time he wrote his theological works,[90] but his earlier views remain a witness to the considerable confusion that existed on semantic questions early in the twelfth century. No doubt this is due largely to the various contradictory influences operating: the Boethian logical semantics were at odds with the grammatical tradition resting on Priscian, and the 'nominalist' tendencies of many logicians were in conflict with the naive realist approach of theologians familiar with the realism of Boethius' theological tracts. A very clear and penetrating mind was needed to sort out the fundamentals of the subject. Fortunately, one with such talents was available, Peter Abelard.

V Abelard and his Contemporaries

Abelard (1079–1142), it seems, was the first philosopher in the Latin West since ancient times to make full use of Aristotle's *De interpretatione* and Boethius' commentaries on it.[91] The main effect of this appears to have been a greatly increased role for psychological considerations in semantic theory. Abelard promotes ideas (*intellectus*) to a key position in his analysis of how words signify. Having a simple idea is a mental act of attending to some

89 For more on *maximae* and *loci* in this period see N. J. Green-Pedersen, 'The Doctrine of "maxima propositio" and "locus differentia" in Commentaries from the 12th Century on Boethius' "Topics"', *Studia Mediewistyczne* XVIII (1977), 125–63, and Green-Pedersen 1984.
90 See G. Lefèvre, *Les variations de Guillaume de Champeaux et la question des universaux* (Lille 1898), p. 25.
91 Abelard composed two major logical treatises: one is the *Logica 'Ingredientibus'*, consisting of glosses on the *Isagoge*, *Categories*, and *De interpretatione*. Most of this is edited in Geyer 1919–33, and the remainder in L. Minio-Paluello, *Twelfth Century Logic* II (Rome 1958). The other is his *Dialectica*, edited in de Rijk 1970. There is another gloss on the *Isagoge* usually called *Logica 'Nostrorum petitioni sociorum'*, also in Geyer 1919–33, pp. 505–80. Finally there are five shorter glosses on the *Isagoge*, *Categories*, *De interpretatione*, Boethius' *De divisionibus*, and Boethius' *De topicis differentiis*, edited in Dal Pra 1954. A work that closely adheres to Abelard's point of view is the *Tractatus de intellectibus*, edited in L.U. Ulivi, *La psicologia di Abelardo e il 'Tractatus de intellectibus'* (Rome 1976), pp. 101–27. But this is probably not by Abelard himself.

nature of a thing; it differs from acts of sensing (*sensus*) in that it does not require an actually existent object or 'subject thing', whereas sensing does. Imagining too does not require the actual existence of what is imagined, but unlike having an idea it does not distinguish out any particular nature.[92] There are, as well, complex ideas corresponding to whole propositions, whereas simple ideas correspond to nouns and verbs. To construct a complex idea out of simple ones requires a joining activity of the mind.[93] Some words we use function merely as joiners or disjoiners without signifying any idea; such are the copula and various conjunctions like 'if' and 'or'. Other words modify ideas without themselves signifying an idea; the modal operators and quantifiers are examples of this class. Such is Abelard's attempt to differentiate psychologically 'definite' and 'indefinite' terms, i.e. what later were to be called 'categorematic' and 'syncategorematic' terms.[94]

Where we do have ideas, there must be in addition either some act of sensing or some image thrown up by the imagination. Abelard is very careful to distinguish mental images both from the physical things they are images of and from real psychological entities such as ideas. They are no sort of thing (*res*) at all.[95] Neither are they what an idea is an idea of, i.e. the 'subject thing' for the idea. Rather the mind uses the image to think of something else, namely a nature or property.[96]

Nouns and verbs, Abelard allows, can be said to signify the ideas they generate in the listener, but more frequently he claims they signify what those ideas are of – the 'subject things'. In the case of proper nouns the subject thing is just the single item that is named, but in the case of common nouns (*appellativa*) naming and signification come apart, so that what the noun names (*appellat*) is the particulars which it can be predicated of, while it signifies a nature or *status* which those particulars exhibit. The extensional and intensional realms are here clearly distinguished, with signification limited to the intensional.[97]

Abelard gives special attention to the distinctive character of verbs, and it

92 Abelard 1919–33, pp. 317.9–15 and 20.20–8. See also the *Tractatus de intellectibus*, Ulivi 1976, pp. 103–4. For more on Abelard's psychology see Tweedale 1976, pp. 169–79; J. Jolivet, *Arts du langage et théologie chez Abélard* (2nd ed., Paris 1982), pp. 368–9; and K. Jacobi, 'Die Semantik sprachlicher Ausdrücke, Ausdrucksfolgen und Aussagen in Abailards Kommentar zu *Peri Hermenias*', *Medioevo* VII (1981) 41–89, at pp. 47–9.
93 Abelard 1919–33, p. 339.20–30.
94 Abelard 1919–33, pp. 337–40, and Minio-Paluello II 1958, 20–1. A different view is found in Abelard's *Dialectica* in de Rijk 1970, pp. 118–20. See I. Dambuska, 'La sémiotique des "Dictiones Indefinitae" dans la Dialectique d'Abélard', *CIMAGL* XXI (1977) 10–20.
95 Abelard 1919–33, pp. 20–1, 314–15.
96 Abelard 1919–33, p. 329.
97 See Tweedale 1976, pp. 162–5; Abelard 1970, pp. 111–14.

is here that his semantics begins to diverge widely from those of his predecessors. The verb is responsible for the completeness of propositions, as against the incompleteness of mere noun-phrases, no matter how complex. Verbs achieve this by providing a 'saying or 'proposing' force with respect to the inherence of one item in another.[98] Abelard completely dismisses Priscian's idea that the distinctiveness of verbs lies in their signifying actions and receptions; it lies not in what they signify but in how they signify, i.e. the function they are performing.[99] Every verb implicitly involves a copula or 'substantive' verb, whose function is to propose an inherence, to link items signified by subject and predicate. But this does not mean that the copula or any verb (other than 'inheres' itself) signifies a relation of inherence in the way 'marries' signifies a relation of marriage, for if it did so signify it would not be able to link what it actually signifies but could link only that inherence.[100]

Abelard is very concerned to get straight the much-debated 'substantive' verb. (See above pp. 212–14.) He rejects the idea that as a copula it signifies existence, for there are true affirmative predications where the subject is non-existent. Eventually he reaches the view that the copula on its own is not a semantic unit in the sentence, and neither is the predicate noun accompanying it. Rather it is the complex of copula and noun which is a significant unit, functioning like a verb in the sentence. The copula is a kind of verb-maker.[101] The predicate noun turns out not to be a noun in the strict sense, since in this context it has no *appellatio* on its own. It serves only to bring in an idea of some objective content. When the predicate noun is used as a genuine noun, Abelard believes, the copula is implicit in it, for the *appellatio* it has is limited temporally in a way that demands an implicit verb.[102] The upshot of this is that verbs are semantically prior to nouns, and the 'saying' force they bring to a proposition is involved in nouns as well, although nouns do not give that force to the whole sentence of which they are a part.

Complete sentences, whether propositions, questions, commands, pleas, or wishes, signify by saying something. They generate complex ideas in the mind of the listener, but is there any 'subject thing' such an idea is an idea of? Abelard says that there is: it is the *dictum*, what the sentence says, and it is this

98 Abelard 1970, pp. 123–4, 148–50.
99 *Ibid.* pp. 130–4.
100 *Ibid.* p. 159. See Tweedale 1976, pp. 237–44.
101 Abelard 1970, pp. 130–40; Abelard 1919–33, pp. 361–2, 348–50. See Tweedale 1976, pp. 285–304; Jacobi 1981, pp. 73–8, and K. Jacobi, 'Diskussionen über Prädikationstheorie in den logischen Schriften des Petrus Abailardus', in R. Thomas (ed.), *Petrus Abaelardus (1079–1142); Person, Werk und Wirkung* (Trier 1980), pp. 165–79.
102 Abelard 1970, pp. 122.22–123.5

that is primarily to be called true or false. But then he turns right around and cautions us not to believe that *dicta* are things, since, if they were, the necessary truth of some consequences (i.e. entailments) would turn out to be dependent on the existence of certain things, namely the *dicta* of the antecedent and consequent, and thus would not be necessary at all.[103] (Abelard never considers a realm of eternal abstract things; he is no Platonist.[104]) We could defend the view that *dicta* are things only if we thought of sentences as names of something, but this would be to confuse saying with naming.[105]

Abelard is working out here, sometimes in virtually self-contradictory assertions, the view that language only refers to real things by virtue of the presence in it of names. Expressions which signify, but not by naming, do not commit us to assuming there are things which these expressions signify. In this way Abelard tries to remove the ontological sting of his intensional notion of signification.

Verbs are not names, nor do common nouns name what they signify, since they are disguised verbs, as we saw. Common nouns 'name (*appellant*)' things, but it is not things that they signify. Yet surely if we can say, '"man" signifies man', there is something named by the second occurrence of 'man' in this sentence, and it is what 'man' signifies. Abelard replies that we misunderstand the use of 'man' there as the direct object of 'signifies' if we think it names (*appellat*) anything. A hearer of the word 'man' thinks of man, but again the object expression here does not name. We might say it is not a direct object at all, logically speaking. Rather it qualifies or determines the sense of the verb. In other words, the search for intensional things rests on a too-easy acceptance of grammatical structure as directly representing semantic structure.[106]

It is against this background that we should understand Abelard's attack on realism as regards universals, i.e. on the doctrine that universals are things (*res*), not words. Abelard's first teacher was Roscelin, from whom he learnt the sort of 'nominalism' that was current in the late eleventh century, a legacy he never really renounced. It is true that in one treatise he rejects the idea that universals are *voces* (utterances) in favour of saying they are *sermones*

---

103 Abelard 1919–33, pp. 365.31–366.26. See Tweedale 1976, pp. 234–7; Jolivet 1982, pp. 82–3; and W. L. Gombocz, 'Abaelards Bedeutungslehre als Schlüssel zum Universalienproblem', in Thomas 1980, pp. 153–64, at p. 157.
104 But see Jolivet 1982, pp. 353–4.
105 Abelard 1970, p. 160.14–36. See Tweedale 1976, pp. 237–54.
106 Abelard 1919–33, pp. 530.38–533.9. See Tweedale 1976, pp. 180–4; also L. M. de Rijk, 'Peter Abälard (1079–1142): Meister und Opfer des Scharfsinns' in Thomas (1980), pp. 125–38, at pp. 135f.

(meaningful expressions). But this is because he came to see the need sometimes to distinguish entities which are nevertheless 'essentially' the same. A *vox* is the sound speech produces, a physical entity properly studied by natural science. The *sermo* is the word or expression which, although it is always the same thing as some *vox*, is a linguistic entity dependent for its existence on the conventions of language.[107] Abelard believed that the essential sameness of two items did not guarantee that what was correctly predicable of one would always be correctly predicable of the other as well. For example, Socrates is essentially the same as the matter that makes him up, but although this matter is the matter of Socrates, Socrates is not the matter of Socrates. Socrates and his matter, like a statue and the bronze composing it, and like a *sermo* and its *vox*, differ not essentially but 'in definition'. The *status* of the two are different, i.e. to be Socrates is different from being his particular matter, and that difference is sometimes sufficient to establish different subjects of predication. In his theology Abelard deploys this clever logical manoeuvre, which to some extent anticipates the real–versus–formal distinction of later scholastics, to rescue the doctrine of the Trinity from the attacks of impudent pseudo-practitioners of dialectic.[108]

But all this is rather a way of making 'nominalism' more sophisticated than any sort of rejection of it. Abelard proceeds to reduce the sort of naive realism taught by William of Champeaux (see above pp. 214f) to ruins by showing how it involves claiming that some one thing, viz. a genus, possesses simultaneously and wholly two or more incompatible attributes, viz. the differences of its various species. Naive realism seems never to have recovered from the blow.[109]

Abelard's own ontology allows for two types of things (*res*), both individual: substances and forms. In this he differs from Garland, and probably from Roscelin, who reduced everything to substances. (See above, p. 205.) But Abelard helps himself generously to a host of non-things as well: *status*, *dicta*, natures, properties, states, and events, among others. Is this not blatantly at odds with his claim that language commits us to holding that whatever we name is a thing (*res*)? Here we have, no doubt, one of the most troublesome features of Abelard's theory. Evidently he feels that, once he has shown that the primary way of signifying these items is not by

---

107 Abelard 1919–33, pp. 522.10–524.24. See Tweedale 1976, pp. 142–62.
108 Abelard, *Theologia Christiana*, ed. E. M. Buytaert in CC CM XII (Turnhout 1969), III 136–71, IV 34–40, 57–9, 86–91, 102–6. Abelard is concerned not so much to propose a rational explanation of the Trinity as to show that the arguments of some arrogant logicians are too simple-minded to refute the dogma.
109 Abelard 1919–33, pp. 11.25–12.14. See Tweedale 1976, pp. 98–107; King 1982, pp. 151f.

naming them, he is free to construct nouns like *status, proprietas,* and *natura* that appear to name them, with no new worries about their being genuine things (*res*) after all.[110] Abelard's theology is deeply committed to this way of having your ontological cake while throwing it out at the same time. The doctrine of the Trinity requires that we agree there are three distinct relational properties in God, but if we claim these are genuine *res,* forms of some sort, we have something in God not essentially the same as God, and God's simplicity is lost. On the other hand, if we take the denial that they are *res* to mean that they simply do not exist in the objective world, then the distinction of the three Persons disappears.[111] Abelard's solution is that the properties are not *res* but nevertheless have objective existence. In this way Abelard attempts to reconcile theology, hitherto firmly in the grips of naive realism, to a 'nominalist' logic.

Although support for naive realism seems to have collapsed under Abelard's attack, a marvellous variety of sophisticated realisms were invented in Abelard's own lifetime as alternatives to his nominalism. One approach was simply to disregard Abelard's warnings that *status, dicta* and the rest are not *res* and to treat them Platonically,[112] i.e. as denizens of an eternal, non-physical but intelligible realm. Then, just as Garland treated both singulars and universals as words, both can be treated as being among the eternal entities. This approach was worked out in great detail and subtlety by the school of Melun, a place where Abelard taught on at least two occasions. The Melidunenses also carry Abelard's separation of naming and signification to its logical completion, by applying it to proper names as well as common. Thus 'Socrates' signifies intensionally a property in the realm of intelligibles while naming a physical inhabitant of ancient Athens.[113]

Another response was that of Walter of Mortagne (who became Bishop of Laon in 1155 and died in 1174), whose view is cited by John of Salisbury[114] as one no longer held in his day (1159). Walter explains and defends his position in the *Tractatus 'Quoniam de generali'.*[115] The basic thesis, paradoxically

110 See Gombocz 1980.
111 Abelard 1969, IV 156–7.
112 Or perhaps Stoically. The obvious affinities with Stoic semantics and ontology encourage scholars to continue the so-far-unrewarded search for a route whereby such Stoic ideas might have made their way to twelfth-century France. [But on this see above, ch. 3, pp. 85–8.]
113 Important sections of the *Ars Meliduna* are found in de Rijk 1967, II.1 264–390. See especially Pt I ch. 8, Pt II ch. A, 4–6, ch. E, 1.
114 *Metalogicon* II 17, p. 93.9 in the edition by C. C. J. Webb (Oxford 1929).
115 Ed. B. Hauréau in his *Notices et extraits de quelques manuscrits latins de la Bibliothèque Nationale* V (Paris 1892) 298–320. King 1982, pp. 128*–142*, contains an English translation.

enough, is that any individual is also a species and a genus, but he is an individual inasmuch as he has, for example, the *status* of Socrates, a species inasmuch as he has the *status* of man, and a genus inasmuch as he has the *status* of animal. The term 'man' refers to individual men, but it does so in virtue of their common *status*. Walter has obviously adopted quite a bit of Abelard's theory but has tried to contrive a way of avoiding 'nominalism' by saying the terms such as 'universal', 'species', and 'genus' denote the individual things which would normally be said to fall under the universal, while admitting that what makes an individual an individual is not what makes it a species, genus or universal. Abelard himself criticized such a view in two places,[116] and in general the solution envisaged for the many absurdities that seem attendant on the view is far from clear.

A notable feature of Walter's realism is that it grants that all things are individual, none are common to many. It is realist only in that it claims that universals, species, and genera are *res*, not words. Another proposal that is realist only in this attenuated sense was made by Joscelin of Soissons (Bishop of Soissons, 1122–51).[117] He attempts to retain the naive realist tenet that species and genera are the matter for what falls under them, but denies that any one thing is common to many. Rather the species man, for example, is just a collection of particulars, one of which serves as the matter for Socrates, another for Plato, and so on. It is important to note that here the species is not just the collection of all men, but a collection of items each of which serves as the substratum for the individuating forms which give us a particular man. Similarly the genus is a collection of items each of which serves as the substratum for the differences of some species.[118]

Joscelin evidently developed this view with considerable ingenuity. A follower of his explains, for example, that we can say humanity is found in Socrates even though only one part of it is, in just the same way as we say a person is touching a wall even though only the tip of his finger is in contact with the wall. Also, when it is objected that on the birth of new men the species man must be a new collection, and so is really different things at different times, he replies that in a sense the new species is the same as the old, just as Socrates as a man consists of more atoms than he did as a boy, and yet is the same.

116 Abelard 1919–33, pp. 14–15, 518–20.
117 A follower of his has left us a detailed defence of this view in the tract entitled *De generibus et speciebus*, incompletely edited by V. Cousin in *Ouvrages inédits d'Abélard* (Paris 1836), pp. 507–50, and now completely edited in King 1982, pp. 144*–185*.
118 Abelard criticizes a 'collection' theory in his *Logica 'Ingredientibus'* (Abelard 1919–33, pp. 14–15), but that view says the universal is just the collection of the particulars falling under it; e.g. the species man is the collection of all men.

Perhaps the most thoroughgoing attempt of all to avoid 'nominalism' while giving up naive realism was the remarkable theory devised by Gilbert of Poitiers (1085–1154). This and other aspects of Gilbert's thought are discussed later in Chapter 12 of this volume.

Another area in which Abelard's work was very influential was the doctrine of *topica* or *loci*. Abelard may have seen the recently recovered Boethian translation of Aristotle's *Topics*, but it seems not to have influenced his work. He is one of the last scholastics to rely mainly on Boethius' own *De topicis differentiis*, with its emphasis on *maximae propositiones* and their *differentiae*. Abelard's most original contribution here is to distinguish those *maximae* which express the reason certain premisses constitute a good *argument* for a given conclusion from those which guarantee the truth of a *consequence*, i.e. of a conditional sentence expressing an entailment.[119] Abelard does not view arguments and consequences as equivalent. That is, we cannot say that an argument 'P, Q, therefore R' is good just because the consequence 'If P and Q, then R' is true. First of all, in proposing an argument disputants commit themselves to the truth of the premisses, but in asserting a consequence they do not commit themselves to the truth of the antecedent. But it is more important to notice that an argument can be good even though the conclusion does not follow with necessity from the premisses, as in arguments from authorities.[120] Abelard seems to take the view that an argument need only convince opponents of the truth of the conclusion, whereas a consequence requires that the antecedent cannot be true unless its consequent is. Some *maximae* are no more than rules for producing convincing arguments, and they should be distinguished from ones which can genuinely be used to guarantee the truth of consequences.

Accompanying this distinction are two incompatible ways in which Abelard describes *maximae*. In his *Dialectica*,[121] where he is giving a theory of consequences, he comes up with a view not unlike that which William of Champeaux evidently held. (See above pp. 215f.) Here the *maximae* are conditional propositions 'containing the senses of many consequences', i.e.

---

119 In this section I rely heavily on the excellent work done by Christopher Martin in his soon-to-be submitted doctoral dissertation for Princeton University, in which he studies doctrines of the conditional through the whole medieval period. The major findings as regards early twelfth-century logic will be found in his 'Embarrassing Arguments and Surprising Conclusions in the Development of Theories of the Conditional in the Twelfth Century', forthcoming in the *Proceedings of the VIIth European Symposium on Medieval Semantics* (Poitiers, 17–21 June 1985).

120 Abelard 1970, pp. 438.23–439.5.

121 *Ibid.* pp. 253–454, 469–98.

they are something like schemas for valid consequences.[122] The *maximae* can be considered to be about the same things as are the consequences that instance them. But in his gloss on Boethius' *De topicis differentiis*,[123] where he is concerned with a theory of arguments, Abelard rejects the view that *maximae* have multiple senses and takes instead the 'nominalist' line that the terms of the *maxima* are words that stand for words. Then the *maxima* need not be a conditional proposition; in fact categorical propositions are preferable. Just how much these conflicting theories represent a genuine change in Abelard's views and how much they simply result from the fact that the theory of consequences is different from the theory of arguments is yet to be determined by Abelard scholars.

For Abelard, a consequence asserts a connection between the *dicta* of its antecedent and its consequent; Abelard is very clear that the connection cannot be considered either as between objective things or as between the complex ideas generated by the antecedent and consequent.[124] But his view is not the one common today, that a consequence asserts merely that two *dicta* are so connected that the antecedent one cannot be true unless the consequent one is true as well. Certain arguments evidently convinced Abelard that this criterion for the truth of a consequence was too weak.[125] He discovered that two commonly accepted *loci*, the *locus ab oppositis* and the *locus ab immediatis*, generate consequences which can be used to prove false conditionals.[126] An example is the following:

(1) If Socrates is a man and a stone, Socrates is a man. (Consequent included in the antecedent.)

(2) If Socrates is a man, Socrates is not a stone. (*Locus ab oppositis*, i.e. from opposed items.)

(3) Therefore: If Socrates is a man and a stone, Socrates is not a stone. (By transitivity from (1) and (2).)

(4) But if Socrates is not a stone, it is not the case that Socrates is a man and a stone.

(5) Therefore: If Socrates is a man and a stone, it is not the case that Socrates is a man and a stone. (By transitivity from (3) and (4).)

Now this conclusion (5) has the form 'If P then not P', and Abelard

---

122 See Green-Pedersen 1977, pp. 132–7. Green-Pedersen fails to note, though, that the *Dialectica* passages concern the treatment of consequences and not arguments, while the passage in the *Glossae* concerns only arguments.

123 Abelard 1954, pp. 205–330, especially pp. 231–40.

124 Abelard 1919–33, pp. 366.2–367.9.

125 The proper interpretation of Abelard on this matter, and of the arguments of Alberic against him, is due to the work of Christopher Martin mentioned in n. 119.

126 These arguments are credited to Abelard by the author of the *Introductiones Montane minores*, in L. M. de Rijk, *Logica Modernorum* II.2 (Assen 1967) 7–71. See especially pp. 63, 64, 67. Similar arguments can be found in Abelard 1970, pp. 276, 395.

accepted that no statement could entail its own negation, the converse of a principle found in Aristotle and Boethius and at least as evident as theirs.

Abelard's solution to this problem was to claim that (2) is false, i.e. that the *locus ab oppositis* did not always generate true consequences. And yet certainly the antecedent of that consequence cannot be true unless the consequent is; so why is it false? Abelard then draws up a more stringent requirement for the truth of a consequence: the antecedent *by its own meaning alone* must require the truth of the consequent.[127] Abelard means, in effect, that the meaning of the consequent is contained in the meaning of the antecedent as the meaning of 'animal' is contained in the meaning of 'man'. The *locus ab oppositis* fails to generate true consequences because, given two opposing terms, A and B, the negation of B is not included in A, and conversely. In this way Abelard defends a view of consequences as 'laws of nature', i.e. principles expressing relationships of containment between natures or *status*, and thus gives them an ontological as well as semantic dimension.

Abelard's reasoning on this point was rightly shown to be fallacious by his successor at the school on Mont Sainte-Geneviève near Paris, one Alberic, who began teaching there in 1137.[128] Alberic discovered that, even granting Abelard's stricter criterion for consequences, arguments could be devised against this similar to the ones Abelard had used against the *locus ab oppositis*. For example:
(1) If Socrates is a man and is not an animal, Socrates is not an animal.
(2) If Socrates is not an animal, Socrates is not a man.
(3) If Socrates is not a man, it is not the case that Socrates is a man and not an animal.
(4) Therefore: If Socrates is a man and not an animal, it is not the case that Socrates is a man and not an animal. (By transitivity from the premisses.)
Again the conclusion has the form 'If P then not P'. But here the premisses are all true even on Abelard's criterion for the truth of consequences.

Abelard and Alberic had, in effect, discovered a grave defect in the theory of conditionals as handed down from Aristotle through Boethius, and logicians now had to turn their attention to revising the theory. We hear no more from Abelard on the subject, but Alberic and his school, the Montani, decided that transitivity should be abandoned, i.e. that it was not always valid to argue 'If P then Q, and if Q then R, therefore if P then R', since

127 Abelard 1970, pp. 283.37–284.17.
128 John of Salisbury studied under both Abelard and Alberic at that time. See John 1929, II 10.
     This Alberic is not to be confused with Alberic of Reims, Abelard's accuser at the Council of Soissons, who became Bishop of Bourges in 1137.

consequences did not always express a causal relationship between antecedent and consequent.[129]

Another school, already mentioned, the Melidunenses, noted that the arguments that caused the trouble always involved as a premiss a conditional with an impossible antecedent (for example, Abelard's or Alberic's (1) above), and claimed that nothing follows from what is false. Thus they could deny (1).[130] The Porretani (followers of Gilbert of Poitiers) denied that a consequence was always valid if the consequent was a conjunct in the antecedent. Thus they too could deny (1) in Alberic's argument.[131]

Finally, there was another school, the Parvipontani, who took as their master Adam of Balsham (fl. 1132). We have no record of Adam himself tackling this problem, but his followers came up with the solution that came to be standard in later scholastic logic: we stick with the idea that a consequence is true if and only if it is impossible for the antecedent to be true while the consequent is false, and allow that impossible propositions entail anything, even their own negations, and that necessary propositions are entailed by anything, even their own negations. This position makes a clean break with the Aristotelian–Boethian tradition.

---

129 De Rijk 1967, II.2 65.1–3. C. J. Martin 'The Compendium Logicae Porretanum', CIMAGL XLVI (1983) xviii–xlvi, at pp. xxxv–xxxvi, contains a brief summary of the various responses to the problem.
130 De Rijk 1967, II.1 386–90.
131 Compendium Logicae Porretanum, ed. S. Ebbesen, K. M. Fredborg, and L. O. Nielsen, CIMAGL XLVI (1983) 1–93, at pp. 22f.

8

LOGIC (ii): THE LATER TWELFTH CENTURY*

KLAUS JACOBI

John of Salisbury as witness: was there a degeneration of logic in the second half of the twelfth century?

John of Salisbury's *Metalogicon*,[1] which was written in 1159,[2] is commonly held to be an important narrative source for the history of logic in the first half of the twelfth century. Between 1136 and 1147 John studied logic, grammar, and theology at various schools in Paris and, in all probability, also in Chartres.[3] His work 'On Logic' is rich in vivid descriptions of his teachers, their idiosyncrasies, and their teaching methods.

We propose to use this work as a starting-point for an account of the characteristic features of the history of logic in the *second* half of the century. At the time when he wrote the *Metalogicon* John had been employed for ten years (from 1147) as secretary to Theobald, the Archbishop of Canterbury. In this capacity he devoted himself to legal affairs and he was also frequently entrusted with diplomatic missions. He had not concerned himself with logic since his student days,[4] and even now he had no leisure for such matters: his duties left him scarcely any free time.[5] Even though he took

---

* This chapter was translated by R. S. Livingstone, who wishes to acknowledge the help of Lubor Velecky (Department of Philosophy, University of Southampton) on a number of technical points.

1 *Metalogicon*, ed. C. C. J. Webb (Oxford 1929); *The Metalogicon of John of Salisbury*, trans. D. McGarry (Berkeley and Los Angeles 1955). Unless otherwise stated, I refer in what follows to Webb's Latin edition. A good introduction to the present state of research can be found in the proceedings of the conference that took place in Salisbury in 1980 to mark the eighth centenary of John's death: M. Wilks (ed.), *The World of John of Salisbury*, Studies in Church History III (Oxford 1984).

2 Cf. McGarry's introduction to his translation, p. xix n. 26.

3 That John studied in Chartres as well as Paris used to be generally accepted until doubt was cast on this assumption by R. W. Southern, 'Humanism and the School of Chartres', in *Medieval Humanism and other Studies* (Oxford 1970), pp. 61–85. Nowadays the earlier view has reasserted itself; cf. P. Dronke, 'New Approaches to the School of Chartres', *Anuario de Estudios Medievales* VI (1969) 117–140, esp. pp. 121–3; C. Brooke, 'John of Salisbury and his World', in Wilks (ed.) 1984, pp. 1–20, esp. p. 6; D. Luscombe, 'John of Salisbury in Recent Scholarship', in Wilks (ed.) 1984, pp. 21–37, esp. p. 24; O. Weijers, 'The Chronology of John of Salisbury's Studies in France (*Metalogicon*, II.10)', in Wilks, pp. 109–16.

4 *Met.* III [*Prologus*], p. 117.2–19.

5 *Ibid. Prologus*, p. 3.1–10.

pleasure in recalling his life as a student,[6] writing a book on logic was, on the whole, a chore which he undertook only because he felt compelled to do so.[7] Around him at the archiepiscopal court[8] there were people who held the arts of the Trivium in general and logic in particular in low esteem. Having studied abroad for almost twelve years, John now found himself attacked and belittled by envious ill-wishers. He felt impelled to defend himself[9] by taking up the cudgels on behalf of logic and its usefulness.[10]

John does not call his opponents at court by name. He uses the name 'Cornificius',[11] an allusion to a personage of antiquity known for his contempt for culture. Cornificius and his supporters maintained that the ability to speak and argue well is a natural gift to be developed by practice. Theoretical study and a knowledge of rules did not lead to eloquence.[12] Of course, taken on their own such assertions are not difficult to refute. The counter-claim that knowledge of the rules and practice can effectively reinforce each other is – just as in the case of the development of other skills – more plausible than a one-sided insistence on natural gifts and practice.[13] If such contempt for the Liberal Arts could become widespread there must be deeper reasons for it. John saw the underlying cause in the way logic was taught in the schools.[14] His book was directed in the first instance against people who had learnt nothing but who belittled those who had made a

---

6 *Ibid.* III [*Prologus*], p. 119.27; IV [*Prologus*], p. 165.9–12.
7 *Ibid. Prologus*, pp. 1.11–3.18; III [*Prologus*], p. 118.11–19.
8 *Ibid. Prologus*, p. 1.13: 'concuriales'.
9 *Loc cit.*, p. 3.1.
10 That John defends logic and the study of logic for its utility is something he stresses from the outset in the Prologue (p. 4.5–10) and in many other places.
11 Cf. Webb 1929, p. 8 n. 1; McGarry 1955, p. 11 n. 13. Following a suggestion made by P. Mandonnet (*Siger de Brabant et l'Averroïsme latin au 13ᵉ siècle*, Pt I 'Etude critique', Les Philosophes Belges VI (2nd ed., Louvain 1911), pp. 122–3 n. 5), L. M. de Rijk has argued ('Some New Evidence on Twelfth Century Logic: Alberic and the School of Mont Ste. Geneviève (Montani)', in *Vivarium* IV (1966) 1–57) that the model for Cornificius was a certain Magister Gualo, who was active during the twenties in Paris, where he came into conflict with the Chancellor of the Cathedral (*ibid.* pp. 4–8). Since there is no doubt that John's polemic was directed at his contemporaries, such a claim would mean that the memory of this Gualo must have undergone a revival at the very time that John was in Paris. I do not believe that all the features John gives his 'Cornificius' can be explained by this identification. However, I do not wish to go into the question further here. Even if de Rijk's suggestion proves correct, I do not regard it as an obstacle to my attempt to learn from John about the development of logic in the second half of the twelfth century. On the controversies in the first half of the twelfth century, there is abundant information in J. O. Ward, 'The Date of the Commentary on Cicero's "De inventione" by Thierry of Chartres (ca. 1095–1160?) and the Cornifician Attack on the Liberal Arts', *Viator* III (1972) 219–73.
12 *Met.* I 1, pp. 6.27–7.1; cf. I 6–7, I 9–11.
13 Cf. *ibid.* I 10–12.
14 *Ibid.* I 3.

thorough study of the subject.[15] But, as he progressed, the thrust of his argument changed direction. In opposition to the new teachers, who in his view teach nothing of value,[16] John, who recalled his own teachers with feelings of respect,[17] developed his view of the educational value of the study of logic.[18]

Not without satirical exaggeration,[19] but obviously well informed, he gives an account of current school practice both as it had shown signs of becoming in his student days[20] and, above all, as it had developed in subsequent years.

Ex arte at de arte agere idem erat

Speech in which the words 'consistent' and 'inconsistent' (*'conveniens' et 'inconveniens'*), 'argument' and 'reason' (*'ratio'*), did not resound, with negative particles multiplied and transposed through assertions of existence and non-existence (*multiplicatis particulis negativis et traiectis per esse et non esse*), was entirely unacceptable (*inconveniens*). So true was this that one had to bring along a counter whenever he went to a disputation, if he was to keep apprised of the force of affirmation or negation.[21]
They spoke only of 'consistence' (*'convenientiam'*) or 'reason' (*'rationem'*) . . . Not even an argument was admitted unless it was prefaced by its name. To act with reference to an art and according to the art were (for them) the same (*Ex arte et de arte agere idem erat*).[22]
Even though one might try to get to the root of a question (*si intellectui rerum que videbantur in questione versari operam dabat*), noisy verbosity (*verbosus clamor*) would suffice to win the victory, regardless of the kinds of arguments advanced (*et qui undecumque aliquid inferebat, ad propositi perveniebat metam*).[23]

Novae sectae

If anyone applied himself to studying the ancients, he became a marked man and the laughing stock of all . . . Everyone enshrined his own and his master's inventions. Yet even this situation could not abide. Students were soon swept along in the current, and, like their fellows in error, came to spurn what they had learned from their teachers, and to form and found new sects (*novas sectas*) of their own . . . Behold, all

---

15 *Ibid.* I 5, p. 17.11–20.
16 Cf. *ibid.* I 3, I 25, II 6–9, II 15–19.
17 *Ibid.* I 5, p. 20.8–10.
18 In Books III and IV of the *Metalogicon* John goes through the logical writings of Porphyry and Aristotle. In each case he indicates what he perceives to be the educational value of the work. Cf. Luscombe 1984, p. 26; P. Riché, 'Jean de Salisbury et le monde scolaire du XIIe siècle', in Wilks (ed.) 1984, pp. 39–61, esp. p. 26.
19 Cf. esp. *Met.* II 6.
20 *Ibid.* I 5, p. 17.4–7; II 10, p. 79.17–20.
21 *Ibid.* I 3, 10.23–11.1 / McGarry's trans., pp. 14–15.
22 *Ibid.* I 3, p. 12.6–14 / p. 16.
23 *Ibid.* I 3, p. 11.8–11 / p. 15.

things were 'renovated' (*Ecce nova fiebant omnia* [cf. Apoc. 21: 5]). Grammar was [completely] made over (*innovabatur gramatica*); rhetoric was despised (*contemnebatur rhetorica*).[24]

The presupposition of the critique: logic as organon

Ex arte et de arte agere idem erat – this formula contains the essence of John's objections.[25] He understands logic as a discipline by means of which one learns to reason.[26] He commends it as a discipline, in the conviction that without such schooling in articulateness neither practical wisdom[27] nor theoretical knowledge of any given realm[28] can be acquired. Precisely for this reason, however, and while emphasizing its educational value, he consciously and categorically classifies logic as a mere means, as an organon.[29] To be able to act 'with reference to art' – that is the proper aim. The newer teachers of logic, in contrast, spend their entire lives in the pursuit of a subject which is useful only as a propaedeutic.[30] They know nothing but logic and are at a loss when they are asked to find applications for the rules.[31]

24 *Ibid.* I 3, pp. 11.12–19, 12.2–4 / pp. 15–16.
25 Cf. the recurrence of the phrase, *ibid.* II 9, p. 77.14–16. On the distinction between *ex arte* and *de arte agere*, cf. R. W. Hunt, 'The Introduction to the "Artes" in the Twelfth Century', in *Studia Mediaevalia in honorem . . . Raymundi Josephi Martin* (Bruges 1948), pp. 85–112, and J. O. Ward 1972. Hunt (p. 99) draws attention to the following passage in Hugh of Saint-Victor's *Didascalicon* (III 5, ed. Buttimer, p. 56):
'Duo sunt, agere de arte et agere per artem; verbi gratia, agere de arte, ut est agere de gramatica, agere per artem, ut est agere gramatice. Distingue hec duo, agere de gramatica et agere gramatice. De gramatica agit qui regulas de vocibus datas et precepta ad hanc artem pertinentia tractat. Gramatice agit omnis qui regulariter loquitur vel scribit.'
This distinction, Hunt adds (p. 100), becomes 'with a change of preposition, *ex arte* for *per artem*, which makes it clearer', a normal constituent of introductions to commentaries (cf. also pp. 101–4). Ward notes (p. 249) that the distinction derives from Cicero's *De inventione* I 6, 8. Thierry of Chartres took it over; it is likelier that John of Salisbury adopted it from Thierry than that he found it in Hugh of Saint-Victor. Ward (p. 251) adduces a passage in one of John's letters that is probably contemporary with the *Metalogicon* (*Ep.* 179, P.L. 199, 175BC), which significantly confirms the emphasis John lays on *ex arte agere*.
26 *Ibid.* I 10, p. 27.8–12; cf. II 1, II 3.
27 *Ibid.* II 1; cf. I 1, p. 7.2–7, on the interdependence of *eloquentia* and *sapientia*.
28 *Ibid.* II 2–3.
29 Cf. e.g. *ibid.* II 11, IV 29–30.
30 *Ibid.* II 7, p. 72.15–23 / McGarry's trans. p. 88:
'It has not been my purpose in the foregoing to belittle logic which is both a fortunate (*iocunda*) and useful science. I have rather wanted to show that those who are haranguing at the crossroads, and teaching in public places (*in triviis* [cf. Jerome, *Ep.* 11; P.L. 22, 512]), and who have worn away, not merely ten or twenty years, but their whole life with logic as their own concern, do not really possess what they are pretending to teach. Even as old age descends upon them, enfeebling their bodies, dulling their perceptions, and subduing their passions, logic alone still remains their exclusive topic of conversation, monopolizes their thought, and usurps the place of every other branch of knowledge. As these Academicians age and grey, they remain preoccupied with the concerns of boyhood.'
31 *Met.* II 6, pp. 70.29–72.8; cf. II 15.

In John's judgement, logic as studied lately deals with nothing but itself. But studied in this fashion, it appears harmful rather than useful in his eyes.[32]

They meticulously sift every syllable, yea, every letter, of what has been said and written, doubting everything, 'forever studying, but never acquiring knowledge' [cf. 2 Tim. 3: 7]. At length 'they turn to babbling other nonsense' [cf. 1 Tim. 1: 6–7], and, at a loss as to what to say, or out of lack of a thesis, relieve their embarrassment by proposing new errors ... They make compilations of what everybody has ever thought on the subject ... They cannot omit anything because they lack the knowledge to discriminate as to what is better. So towering does this mixed-up heap of opinions and counter-opinions become that even the compiler himself can hardly keep track of all it contains ... Their commentaries are not only filled, but even stuffed with encumbrances which have been spun by logicians, and which [counter-propositions] are rightly called 'oppositions', for they detain one from going to better studies, and constitute impediments to progress.[33]

These logicians appeal to the authority of Aristotle, but they could learn from him to be as subtle as the object under investigation permits and requires, instead of seeking out subtlety at the expense of usefulness and seriousness.[34] They could learn from him that there is no need of proof where a matter is not in doubt, and that they ought not 'to argue about every matter with equal intensity'.[35]

Chief themes of the debates de arte

From John's discussions one can gather which were the main points that caused controversies *de arte* to flare up – controversies that John considered empty and sterile, but in which each school championed its own doctrines.

Semantics

The question of universals was a key issue in his student days. Under the heading 'In what a pernicious manner logic is sometimes taught; and the ideas of moderns about [the nature of] genera and species',[36] John reports on the linguistic, conceptualist, and realist interpretations of universals. He himself regards all these debates, which were sparked off by Porphyry's *Isagoge*, as misguided. Instead of delving into this work for mysterious revelations of supreme wisdom,[37] scholars should read it as its title suggests, namely as an introductory treatise.[38]

32 *Ibid.* II 9. Cf. Ward 1972, p. 229.
33 *Met.* II 7, pp. 72.23–73.14 / McGarry, pp. 88–9; cf. II 17, p. 91.9–25.
34 *Met.* II 8; cf. M. Wilks, 'John of Salisbury and the Tyranny of Nonsense' in Wilks (ed.) 1984, pp. 263–86, esp. p. 267.
35 *Met.* II 8, pp. 75.25–76.9; cf. II 15.
36 *Ibid.* II 17, p. 91.9–10 / McGarry, p. 111.
37 *Ibid.* II 17.
38 *Ibid.* II 16, pp. 90.27–91.8; cf. II 20.

Theory of consequences

A second focal point of scholastic debate can be deduced from John's narrative. John makes mention of one of his students, William of Soissons, whom he taught privately for a time and then sent on to his fellow-countryman, Adam of Balsham, the teacher of logic on the 'Petit Pont' (over the Seine), from which he derived his name 'Parvipontanus'. 'William later, according to his followers, invented a device (*machinam*, an artificial method of argumentation and reasoning, called a "machine" because it was devised to construct and to demolish . . .) to revolutionize the old logic by constructing unacceptable conclusions (*consequentiae inopinabiles*) and demolishing the authoritative opinions of the ancients.'[39] John conjectures that William must have learnt from Adam 'that the same conclusion may be inferred from either of two contradictories (*idem esse ex contradictione*)',[40] whereas Aristotle had taught that nothing follows from a contradiction and that it is impossible for a contradiction to be inferred from anything.[41] John rejects the thesis of his former pupil with indignation.[42] He makes no effort to understand it. But from the information he gives we may infer that the argument was based on a purely formal, truth-functional interpretation of conditionals.[43] According to this, a conditional is false if and only if the antecedent is true and the consequent false. If this interpretation of conditionals is assumed, then the so-called paradoxes of implication – which formally have nothing paradoxical about them – follow: *ex falso* or *ex impossibili quodlibet* and *verum* or *necessarium ex quolibet*. The aforementioned theses could be inferred from both paradoxes, firstly as the claim that one and the same consequent Q can be implied by both the antecedent P and also its contradictory; and, secondly, as the proposition that the contradiction P and not-P implies whatever you like, and hence also Q.

39 *Ibid.* II 10, p. 81.11–14 / McGarry's trans. and note, p. 98.
40 *Ibid.* II 10, p. 81.16 / p. 99.
41 *Ibid.* II 10, pp. 81.16–82.1.
42 *Ibid.* II 10, p. 82.2–3: 'nec amici machina impellente urgeri potui ut credam ex uno impossibili omnia impossibilia provenire'.
43 This supposition is by no means anachronistic, despite my formulation of it in modern terminology here. Cf. my studies of the distinction between *consequentia naturalis* and *consequentia non naturalis*: 'Drei Theorien über die Funktion aussagenverknüpfender Zeichen. Die Diskussion des Junktors "si" bei Wilhelm von Shyreswood', in *Sprache und Erkenntnis im Mittelalter* (= *Miscellanea Mediaevalia* XIII. 1 (1981)), pp. 385–97. C. J. Martin is at present preparing a study of the theory of entailment, particularly in the twelfth century, 'Theories of Entailment in the Middle Ages from Boethius to the Twelfth Century Schools' (Princeton University, D.Phil. Diss.). At the 7th European Symposium on Medieval Logic and Semantics, which took place in Poitiers, 17–22 June 1985, he read a paper on 'Embarrassing Arguments and Surprising Conclusions in the Development of the Conditional in the

Fallacies

A third pointer has been decoded by de Rijk.[44] John began his studies with Abelard on the Mont Sainte-Geneviève in Paris, and, on Abelard's departure, he studied for another two years with Alberic and an Englishman, Robert of Melun.[45] John depicts Alberic as a meticulous questioner who was able to discover problems in everything.[46] At a time when John had already turned to other teachers, Alberic went to Bologna, according to John's account. There he 'unlearned (*dedidicit*)' what he had formerly taught; and subsequently, on his return to Mont Sainte-Geneviève, he 'untaught' it (*dedocuit*).[47] The words *dedidicit* and *dedocuit* are not neutral in John's use of them, but have a negative connotation.[48] Hence he adds, not without malice, *An melius, iudicent qui eum ante et postea audierunt*[49] ('Whether he was better, let them judge who heard his lectures both before his departure and after his return'). The man from whom Alberic revised or unlearned his previous knowledge was probably James of Venice. It was he who discovered Aristotle's *Sophistici elenchi* and translated it with a commentary.[50] Alberic's journey was no more of a chance event than the discovery of Aristotle's text – the treatise was searched for and found.[51] Alberic must have undertaken the journey in order to study it at first hand. Now this work was not unknown to John of Salisbury. He recommended it as a practical manual, so that the student would be in a position to discover his own errors and to reject simulated knowledge.[52] What must have incurred John's displeasure was the use Alberic made of the treatise after his return.

Twelfth Century'. I am most grateful to Mr Martin for giving me a copy of his paper and allowing me to make use of it for the present essay.

44 L. M. de Rijk, *Logica Modernorum. A Contribution to the History of Early Terminist Logic* (henceforth cited as *Log. Mod.*) I: 'On the Twelfth Century Theories of Fallacy' (Assen 1962) 85–8.

45 *Met* II 10, p. 78.6–13.

46 *Ibid.* II 10, pp. 78.10–79.17.

47 *Ibid.* II 10, p. 79.17–19.

48 Cf. Wilks 1984, p. 273.

49 *Met.* II 10, p. 79.19–20.

50 De Rijk, *Log. Mod.* I 85–8.

51 C. H. Lohr, 'The Mediaeval Interpretation of Aristotle', in *CHLMP*, p. 83: 'The full range of the Aristotelian logic which became known in the latter half of the twelfth century was not used because the treatises were translated, but the treatises were translated because this new generation wanted to use them.'

52 *Met.* IV 22. It does not become clear from John's discussions just how well he knew the *Sophistici elenchi*. It is altogether possible that he knew the contents only by hearsay or from Boethius' references.

Logic in the second half of the century reconsidered: the research mentality

In the last twenty-five years or so numerous treatises on logic dating back to the second half of the twelfth century have been edited and been more or less tentatively ascribed to different schools: to the Parvipontani, the Montani, the Porretani, and the Melidunenses.[53] All these names point to the period in which John was writing; for the treatises which have been edited up to now, dates have been proposed which put them all later than the time when he was writing. Nevertheless, they all fit remarkably well with his descriptions. This may mean that some of these texts should be given an earlier date. Alternatively, and I think this the more plausible explanation, the tendency that John describes with such venom may simply have gained acceptance. At any rate, we now possess so much textual knowledge that we can confirm that the *Metalogicon* is of enormous value for our understanding of the logic of the second half of the century, as well as of the earlier period.

Whether we should share John's value-judgements is another question. His assessment is based on the assumption that logic has the function of an organon, but that it has no intrinsic interest of its own.[54] Writers who spent their entire lives dealing with logic *de arte*, to use John's expression, are unlikely to have accepted this assumption. If logic is regarded as a foundation science, this will lead to quite a different assessment. In that case logic simply cannot be studied 'with too much subtlety'. Plausibility does not suffice; every thesis must be scrutinized to the point where its most precise formulation has been established.

In order that we may understand the mentality of the logicians against whom John of Salisbury's polemics are directed, we have no choice but to

---

53 In his *Logica Modernorum* L. M. de Rijk has completely edited no fewer than twenty treatises, in additon to a number of fragments and two further treatises which are reproduced in lengthy excerpts. Through his work he has stimulated further studies and editions. Instead of cataloguing them here in detail, I refer in general to the periodical *Vivarium*, to the *Cahiers de L'Institut du Moyen-Age Grec et Latin* (*CIMAGL*), and to the series *Artistarium* (with its supplementary volumes). A fruitful source of information about the state of research are the volumes of the Acts of the European Symposia on Medieval Logic and Semantics. The history of logic in the twelfth century was touched on in 1979 at the Symposium at Leiden and Nijmegen (*English Logic and Semantics. From the End of the Twelfth Century to the Time of Ockham and Burleigh. Acts of the 4th European Symposium . . .*, ed. H. A. G. Braakhuis, C. H. Kneepkens, and L. M. de Rijk, *Artistarium* Supplementa I (Nijmegen 1981)) and in 1983 at the Symposium in Oxford (*The Rise of British Logic. Acts of the 6th European Symposium . . .*, ed. P. O. Lewry, OP, Papers in Mediaeval Studies VII (Toronto)); it was the subject of all the papers at the 7th Symposium in Poitiers in 1985. These are to be published by A. de Libera. Copious information can also be gleaned from the *Cambridge History of Later Medieval Philosophy*.

54 Cf. Wilks 1984, pp. 273–4.

study their commentaries, treatises and *Summae* and to immerse ourselves in their way of thinking. There are no programmatic writings in which a spokesman for the new logic defends his conception of logic or sets it out independently of John's attacks. It appears that they were so preoccupied with their researches that it would have been superfluous to make a special point of drawing up a specific programme of research. The controversies of the second half of the twelfth century were not concerned with asking questions about the tasks facing logic or what its precise educational value might be, but with individual semantic and syntactic issues. It was, to use Thomas Kuhn's phrase, a period of 'normal science'.[55] Scholars were preoccupied with 'puzzle-solving'. The first half of the century had been notable as an age of great individuals, each of whom was powerful enough to create a style of his own. It is significant that the logical treatises of the second half of the century have all come down to us anonymously. To be sure, within the 'scientific community' schools were differentiated. They were highly suspicious and intolerant of one another and anxious to emphasize their own particular teachings. But Parvipontani, Montani, Porretani, and Melidunenses are not as easily distinguished by their method of posing questions as had been the case with Adam of Balsham, Alberic, Gilbert, and Robert of Melun, from whom the schools took their names and to whom they owed their origins. In their approach to problems they had come to resemble one another; the differences lie in their responses to specific individual questions. The *Ars Meliduna*,[56] for example, and the *Compendium logicae Porretanum*[57] differ greatly in terms of content. But they are both divided into four books which deal respectively with terms, with what is signified by terms, with propositions, and with what is signified[58] or asserted by propositions[59] (i.e. by the propositional content).[60] And within the individual books the individual topics succeed one another in more or less the same order.[61]

---

55 T. S. Kuhn, 'The Structure of Scientific Revolutions', in *International Encyclopedia of Unified Science* II.2 (1962).

56 L. M. de Rijk, *Logica Modernorum* II.1: 'The Origin and Early Development of the Theory of Supposition' (Assen 1967). De Rijk gave this *Ars* its name and published extensive extracts from it (*Log. Mod.* II.1, chs. 6–10, pp. 264–390). A complete critical edition is in course of preparation by Y. Iwakuma. Mr Iwakuma was kind enough to give me a copy of Book I in manuscript and I should like to express my thanks to him here.

57 *Compendium logicae Porretanum*, ed. S. Ebbesen, K. M. Fredborg, and L. O. Nielsen, *CIMAGL* XLVI (1983).

58 *Comp. Log. Porr.*, p. 1.

59 *Ars. Melid.*, Prooemium, ed. Iwakuma, line 9 / ed. de Rijk, *Log. Mod.* II.1 264.

60 In the *Compendium logicae Porretanum* the book on terms is followed first by the book dealing with propositions and only after that do we find the book on what is signified by terms.

61 On 'Affinities to *Secta Meliduna*', cf. the editors of the *Compendium logicae Porretanum*, Introduction, pp. viii–ix. They have found similarities in both style and subject-matter:

In what follows the attempt will be made to throw light on the mentality of the logicians of the second half of the century by taking a closer look at the very issues which John of Salisbury found so disconcerting. I propose to adopt this route because these issues are the ones which are liable to discredit the logic of this epoch, if it is only considered from outside, instead of the effort being made to look at it from within.

Logica Nova – *Concentration on the question of fallacies*

In the Age of Scholasticism teaching and research were, as is well known, governed for the most part by texts that were held to be authoritative. In logic Aristotle was the undisputed authority. But by no means all of his writings on logic were known to the early Scholastics.[62] In the first half of the century they were familiar with the *Categories* and with *De interpretatione*, as well as with Porphyry's *Isagoge*. These works were studied in the translations by Boethius, together with the commentaries which he provided. Boethius had also translated Aristotle's other writings on logic. However, instead of supplying commentaries on these, he wrote treatises of his own which, on the one hand, enriched the material on syllogisms and the theory of argumentation ('Topics') with elements of Stoic teaching, and, on the other, were designed to tighten up the subject-matter and present it in a more easily assimilable form. Together with some smaller works by other authors, Boethius' *De syllogismis categoricis*, *De syllogismis hypotheticis*, *De divisione* and *De differentiis topicis* were among the basic textbooks taught at the cathedral and monastic schools and at the civic schools which were newly established in the first half of the twelfth century. This was the canon of the *logica vetus*.

The intensive study of this canon was bound to lead to the discovery that it contained gaps: Boethius mentions works by Aristotle that were not to be found in any library. From 1120 scholars looked for and found Boethius' translations of the *Prior Analytics*, the *Topics* and the *Sophistici elenchi*; the *Posterior Analytics* were newly translated from the Greek by James of Venice. How and where these writings were discovered is unknown. The city of Venice, with its excellent connections with Byzantium, may well have acted

'Though the theses are generally different from those of our Compendium, the range of subjects covered is much the same.'

62 On what follows cf. the accounts of B. G. Dod, 'Aristoteles Latinus'; C. H. Lohr, 'The Medieval Interpretation of Aristotle'; S. Ebbesen, 'Ancient Scholastic Logic as the Source ...', all in *CHLMP*. A good overview is given by J. Pinborg, *Logik und Semantik im Mittelalter. Ein Überblick*, Problemata x (Stuttgart–Bad Cannstatt 1972), pp. 16–18. Cf. also A. Maierù, *Terminologia logica della tarda scolastica*, Lessico Intellettuale Europeo VIII (Rome 1972), pp. 9–17.

as the gateway. This newly discovered logic (*logica nova*) was by no means fully integrated into the teaching-programme. A commentary on the *Posterior Analytics* was not forthcoming until much later in the thirteenth century. In the twelfth century their theoretical discussion was apparently held to be too stringent. John of Salisbury, for example, suggests that Aristotle's art of demonstration was really only suitable for geometry.[63] As far as the *Prior Analytics* are concerned, crucial passages were increasingly cited in the treatises of the second half of the twelfth century. Yet this text did not by any means receive special attention. John would have liked to see the *Topics* introduced into the schools as a textbook – alongside the treatises of the *logica vetus*. He discusses the individual books of the *Topics* in detail, draws attention to their variety and recommends them strongly as a source of arguments on contentious issues.[64] Nevertheless, he seems to have been alone in his partiality for the work. He reports that the students of Robert of Melun found the book more or less worthless.[65] In general we can say that the logicians of the second half of the century made use of the book, but that serious debates and commentaries did not begin until the thirteenth century.[66]

Of the newly discovered writings of Aristotle only the treatise on fallacies, the *Sophistici elenchi*, attracted detailed attention.[67] It was soon glossed, provided with commentaries and adapted for use in the schools.

The study of fallacies in theory and for practical ends

What attracted the logicians of the time so powerfully to this work? Because research and teaching were intimately connected with each other in the Scholastic period, it is advisable to reformulate the question. What did the teachers wish to show their students by assigning an important place in the curriculum to the study of fallacious arguments? Various objectives can be

---

63 *Met.* IV 6.
64 *Ibid.* III 5–10.
65 *Ibid.* IV 24, p. 191.9–10.
66 Cf. N. J. Green-Pedersen, *The Tradition of the Topics in the Middle Ages. The Commentaries on Aristotle's and Boethius' Topics* (Munich and Vienna 1984), p. 87; cf. his remarks on the twelfth-century commentaries on Boethius' *De differentiis topicis*, pp. 123–6 and Appendix B, pp. 418–31.
67 Cf. on the following L. M. de Rijk, *Log. Mod.* I, *passim*; *Log. Mod.* II.1 491–512. After de Rijk, S. Ebbesen is the scholar who has done most to investigate the reception of the *Sophistici elenchi* and to edit further texts of the twelfth century; see his publications in *CIMAGL* VIII (1972) 3–32; IX (1973) 79; X (1973) 1–20; XVI (1976) 1–128; XXI (1977) 1–9, in conjunction with XXXIV (1979) xlii; XXXIV (1979) i–xlviii; further, his monograph *Commentaries and commentaries on Aristotle's Sophistichi elenchi. A study of post-Aristotelian ancient and medieval writings on fallacies*, Corpus Latinum Commentariorum in Aristotelem Graecorum VII (3 vols., Leiden 1981).

distinguished. These objectives are mutually compatible and can subsist simultaneously. However, the sequence in which they are considered here corresponds to the periods in which they were most prominent.

In the *Ars disserendi* of Adam of Balsham 'Parvipontanus',[68] which was completed in 1132,[69] the author's aim in discussing the fallacies was practical. Obscurities and ambiguities in speech are to be avoided, or exposed when they are encountered. Anyone who desires to become a master of the 'art of reasoning', must familiarize himself with the traps inherent in language into which the unwary can fall or which can be consciously set by an opponent.[70] Adam gives rules and advice about how to detect equivocations and other defects of speech. He says, for example, 'Test if the same word in different contexts proves to be equivocal';[71] 'Test if the same word has two different meanings deriving respectively from the original imposition (. . .) of the word and from its metaphorical usage';[72] 'Test if equivocity of a word may appear in another word closely connected with it because of their relation of *derivativum, paronymum, denominativum* or any kind of declension or conjugation';[73] 'Test if equivocity of a word becomes evident if one tries to assign the contrary to the meaning of a word.'[74]

From the canon of the *logica vetus* scholars had arrived at a classification of fallacies into six types. When Aristotle's *Sophistici elenchi* became known, it was discovered that it contained further types and that Aristotle's method of classification differed from that of Boethius in his reports.[75] Now all

68 L. Minio-Paluello, *Twelfth Century Logic. Texts and Studies* I: 'Adam Balsamiensis Parvipontani Ars Disserendi (Dialectica Alexandri)' (Rome 1956).
69 *Ibid.* Introduction, p. xxi. On the second recension (by Alexander Nequam?), cf. *ibid.* pp. xviii–xxiii. Cf. also L. Minio-Paluello, 'The "Ars Disserendi" of Adam of Balsham "Parvipontanus"', *MARS* III (1954) 116–69.
70 For the following, compare the survey provided by Minio-Paluello 1956, pp. xxiv–xxxiv, and the analysis in de Rijk, *Log. Mod.* I 64–74.
71 Here and in what follows I am quoting from the analyses of de Rijk, adding the references for the *Ars disserendi*; here: DRA I (2) = Detection rule for equivocation in the first class (A), second rule, *Log. Mod.* I 68 / *Ars Diss.* p. 36.6–10.
72 DRA I (3), *Log. Mod. ibid.* / *Ars Diss.* p. 36.10–12.
73 DRA I (7), *Log. Mod.* I 69 / *Ars Diss.* pp. 37.16–38.15. A 'paronym', according to Aristotle's definition in his *Categories* (1A12–15), is 'a thing that takes its name from some other, in such a way that it is given a new verbal form, as for instance "grammarian" from "grammar", "hero" from "heroism"'. *Denominativum* is the Latinized form of the Greek term. On the theory of *denominatio*, cf. esp. D. P. Henry, *The De grammatico of St Anselm* (Notre Dame 1964) and *The Logic of St Anselm* (Oxford 1967). *Derivativum* is a technical term in medieval grammar. Entities take their names from one another, words are derived from one another. As Aristotle's examples show, grammatical and semantic analysis do not always run parallel: the hero takes his name from 'heroism', while 'heroism' itself is a derivative of the word 'heroic'.
74 DRA I (12), *Log. Mod.* I 70 / *Ars Diss.* pp. 39.17–40.4.
75 Cf. the survey provided by Pinborg 1972 pp. 66–9. Pinborg bases his findings on De Rijk's detailed investigations, *Log. Mod.* I 24–48, 94–8, 134–52.

Scholastic thinkers were agreed that classifications were a source of knowledge. The more accurate they were, the more completely they opened up a field of study to investigation and the more precisely they enabled the observer to pinpoint a particular object within that field. It can easily be imagined, therefore, that teachers of logic would have been deeply disturbed by the discovery that the authorities operated with divergent systems of classification, and that such a discovery would inevitably have been of the greatest interest to them. It may well have been this feeling of disquiet which led Alberic to go to Bologna and, subsequently, to his 'unlearning' what he had previously known.

In the debates about how to classify fallacies correctly there must also have been a change in the motives for investigating them at all. Behind the desire to provide a complete classification of every type of fallacy imaginable there no longer stood the practical wish to avoid false reasoning. Instead there was now a theoretical interest. By finding out how arguments go awry – even if certain kinds of error occur only rarely in practice – you could discover the conditions that are necessary for an argument to succeed – even if the majority of these conditions are satisfied in most cases as a matter of course. What motivated logicians was not so much how to avoid dysfunctions, or how to diagnose them when they appear, but rather the question of how language functions.

Sophisms

When teachers of logic went through the various types and subtypes of fallacy in their classes or in the treatises intended as teaching-manuals, they explained each type with the aid of examples. Many of the examples given originated in the received Aristotelian texts and hence routinely reappeared in all the schools. But the teachers also found or invented new examples. It would be a valuable labour to sift through the edited treatises enquiring whether the examples in any of them exhibit specific common features, or at least 'family resemblances'. I shall confine myself here to repeating and amplifying an observation I have already made elsewhere.[76] In the *Dialectica Monacensis*, which was probably written towards the end of the twelfth century, or perhaps 'shortly after 1200',[77] we encounter artificially constructed examples. These examples occur neither in everyday speech nor in

---

76 K. Jacobi, 'Wilhelm von Shyreswood und die Dialectica Monacensis', *Artistarium*, Supplementa I, pp. 99–122, esp. pp. 100–1.

77 So S. Ebbesen surmises, 'Anonyma Aurelianensis I, Commentarium in Sophisticos Elenchos', *CIMAGL* XXXIV (1979) xvii.

scientific discourse. They were *sophismata*, specially designed for classroom use. At the same time they are not as perverse as they may at first appear. They were not just invented so as to compel students to practise on artificially abstruse examples, or to enable the teacher to display his virtuosity in mastering such difficult examples. The sophisms constructed in this way are all concerned with ordinary parts of speech – prepositions, quantifiers, relative pronouns, excluding and modal expressions – i.e. with 'syncategorematic' words in general.[78] The examples show that precisely such operators are frequently not unambiguous, but multifunctional. It is necessary in every case to determine the scope to which they apply. That this is essential is made clear by experimenting with language. An expression which is normally understood correctly in context is subjected to procedures which test its limits. The purpose of these tests is primarily theoretical and scientific (and only indirectly practical). The aim is to determine the function of logical signs with precision. A little later, or even simultaneously, such exercises were developed into independent treatises 'On Syncategorematic Expressions'. In the thirteenth century such examples were collected under such titles as *Abstractiones*[79] or *Sophismata*. We are less concerned here with the way in which subsequent developments in logic were made possible by the achievements of the second half of the twelfth century, or with how the logic of this period looks when seen in retrospect from the standpoint of terministic logic.[80] Our aim is to analyse the style of the logical treatises of the second half of the twelfth century for clues as to the mentality of their authors and the schools for which they were written. The striking features here include a mode of argumentation which takes subtlety to the point of splitting hairs and a predilection for artificially constructed examples of ambiguity as opposed to 'natural' examples. Such features, which are

---

78 The term 'syncategorematic' – which medieval logicians had found in Priscian – was used for all expressions that cannot occur alone as subject or predicate of a sentence; those that can do so were called 'categorematic'. For the logician *syncategoremata* are of the greatest interest, because through them – the quantifiers, negators, modal operators, conjunctives – the logical form of a simple or complex proposition is expressed. The existence of a treatise 'On Syncategorematic Expressions' is already indicated by the author of the *Dialectica Monacensis*, ed. De Rijk, *Log. Mod.* II.2 610.33. On the subsequent development see H. A. G. Braakhuis, *De 13de Eeuwse Tractaten over Syncategorematische Termen* (2 vols., Nijmegen 1980).

79 Cf. A. de Libera, 'La littérature des *abstractiones* et la tradition logique d'Oxford', in Lewry (ed.) 1985, pp. 63–114.

80 That this is the starting-point of de Rijk's *Logica Modernorum* 1962 and 1967 can be seen from the subtitle of the whole work, *A Contribution to the History of Early Terminist Logic*, as well as the title of vol. II. 1: 'The Origin and Early Development of the Theory of Supposition'. Cf. also L. M. de Rijk, 'The Origins of the Theory of the Properties of Terms', in *CHLMP*, pp. 161–73.

characteristic of the treatise on fallacies in the *Dialectica Monacensis*, can also be discovered in other treatises.

Implicitae propositiones

A treatise roughly contemporary with the *Dialectica Monacensis*, but probably originating in another school,[81] is the *Tractatus implicitarum* edited by F. Giusberti.[82] The author defines his theme in the very first sentence:

Logicians describe as 'implicit' those propositions in each of which two propositions are implied or contained. Implicit propositions are brought about by the use of such terms as 'that which', 'those which', 'alone', 'only', 'besides', 'begins', 'ends', 'now for the first time', 'now for the last time' (*id quod, ea quae, solum, tantum, praeter, incipit, desinit, nunc primo, nunc ultimo*).[83]

The author gives general and specific rules about how implicit sentences can be made explicit, and he illustrates the procedure by analysing a number of examples. Here, too, the primary goal is evidently not a pedagogic exercise for teaching students scientific reasoning. The aim is rather the precise investigation of the laws of logic. An example can be used by way of illustration. In the sentence *Si falsum est Socratem esse id quod est asinus, verum est Socratem non esse id quod est asinus*, the inference is held to be invalid. For the propositions 'Socrates is what an ass is' and 'Socrates is not what an ass is', can both be false. If the inference is admitted, it can be contested by a chain of inferences. 'It is false that Socrates is what an ass is→ It is true that Socrates is not what an ass is→ Socrates is not what an ass is→ Something is an ass, and Socrates is not that something→ Something is an ass.' Now the initial sentence is necessary while the last sentence is contingent. This means that the chain is faulty. The author avoids the first step which inaugurated the chain.[84]

---

81 Attempts to assign the *Dialectica Monacensis* to one of the schools have not been successful to date. The treatise may have originated in England. On the *Tractatus implicitarum* cf. the introduction to the edition, Giusberti 1982 (see n. 82, below), p. 22, where other treatises from the same Codex are ascribed to the 'Gilbertine School'.

82 F. Giusberti, *Materials for a Study on Twelfth Century Scholasticism*, History of Logic II (Naples 1982), sect. I: 'A Treatise on Implicit Propositions from around the Turn of the Twelfth Century: an Edition with some Introductory Notes', pp. 21–85. First published in *CIMAGL* XXI (1977) 45–115. Cf. also L. M. de Rijk, 'Some Notes on the Mediaeval Tract *De insolubilibus*, with the Edition of a Tract Dating from the End of the Twelfth Century', *Vivarium* IV (1966) 83–115; here de Rijk also edits a short treatise *De inplicationibus*, pp. 100–3, which was written in the same hand in the codex and which follows directly after *De insolubilibus*.

83 Giusberti 1982, p. 43.

84 *Ibid. Tractatus implicitarum* 4.1–4.1 a 4 dictum, p. 52.

The method of instantiae

There are also treatises from an earlier period in which the same intellectual stance is evident. Y. Iwakuma has edited a *Tractatus de locis argumentationum*, which he assigns to the last third of the twelfth century and tentatively ascribes to the School of the Montani.[85] Iwakuma came across this treatise in the course of his work on a complete edition of the *Ars Meliduna*,[86] which must have been written earlier, between 1154 and 1180.[87] Giusberti, too, had regarded the *Ars Meliduna* as a preliminary stage of the *Tractatus implicitarum*, which he had edited, and he included parts of it in an appendix.[88] As Iwakuma points out,[89] what these and other works have in common is a certain method of proceeding in logic. This method consists in the use of objections to theses or rules which have been proposed. In some texts counter-instances to each thesis are piled up, regardless of whether they are valid and so force a revision of the proposed thesis or rule, or whether the counter-arguments are fallacious and the proposed thesis or rule is valid.[90] Such treatises serve as exercises. Students are trained to scrutinize the formulation of rules very closely, to discover counter-arguments, and to attack and defend theses. In other texts, theses which are regarded by a particular school as its own property are defended against every conceivable objection and counter-example. In such a case the *instantiae* have to be refuted. The more ingenious and – at first glance – plausible the objections are, the more brilliantly the thesis of the school will be vindicated, when, finally, all objections have been overcome. The Melidunenses in particular – the school in Paris named after Robert of Melun – appear to have favoured this method of presenting their own theses.[91]

The literature of *instantiae* is extremely inaccessible. We recall John of

85 Y. Iwakuma, 'Instantiae. A Study of Twelfth Century Technique of Argumentation with an Edition of MS Paris BN lat. 6674 f. 1–5', *CIMAGL* xxxviii (1981) 1–91; on the problems of date and place of origin see pp. 7–8.
86 Cf. n. 56, above.
87 De Rijk, *Log. Mod.* ii.1 280–1. Cf. Iwakuma 1981, p. 7 n. 23.
88 Giusberti 1982, pp. 77–85.
89 The list given in Iwakuma 1981, pp. 2–3 has been augmented since: Y. Iwakuma, 'Instantiae Revisited', *CIMAGL* xliv (1983), 61–80, esp. p. 61.
90 Iwakuma 1981, pp. 3–4, and 1983, p. 62. Iwakuma also includes the *Tractatus de locis argumentationum*, which he has likewise edited, in this category.
91 Iwakuma 1983, p. 62. From the excerpts published by de Rijk in *Log. Mod.* ii.1 292–390, this stylistic feature, so characteristic of the *Ars Meliduna*, cannot be detected. On the theses specific to particular schools cf. the notice by S. Ebbesen and Y. Iwakuma, 'Instantiae and 12th century "schools"', *CIMAGL* xliv (1983) 81–5. In his contribution to the 7th Symposium on Medieval Logic and Semantics (Poitiers 1985; cf. n. 53), 'Logique et théologie dans la Summa "Quoniam homines" d'Alain de Lille', A. de Libera has drawn attention to this author's employment of a similar method in theology.

Salisbury's polemical attacks on the logicians 'who doubt everything, constantly study and never attain knowledge', and are tempted to agree with him in this instance at least. 'Many *instantiae* seem incomprehensible at first sight', complains the editor of the *Tractatus de locis argumentationum*; and a little further on he reaffirms, 'I cannot pretend to have understood all the *instantiae*.'[92] Nevertheless, we should not cast doubt on the philosophical value of this kind of literature simply because we have difficulty in understanding it. Iwakuma has correctly diagnosed the source of our difficulties. That the literature of *instantiae* is so hard for us to comprehend 'is due to the many semantical, logical and social presuppositions which were familiar to men of the time, but not to us.'[93] The philosophical point of this method may be described as follows: logical propositions must be universally valid. The rules of logic tolerate no exceptions. The objections, counter-examples and attempts at falsification ought, if they have any cogency, to lead to the precise formulation of theses and rules. If the *instantiae* prove to be lacking in cogency or relevance, their refutation helps us to understand better what state of affairs is described by the thesis or encompassed by the rule.

Let us describe some of the arguments in order to clarify what is at stake here.

In the first example[94] the problem is how to make inferences from the part to the whole. More accurately, the discussions concern the relation of the *totum universale* to its *partes subjectivae*, which the author does not distinguish explicitly from other kinds of relation of part to whole. Here, an affirmative argument is valid: 'Socrates is a man; therefore, Socrates is an animal.' A negative inference, on the other hand, is not valid: the sentence 'Socrates is not an ass; therefore, he is not an animal', for example, 'has no necessity'. Examples are then adduced as *instantiae* which correspond to the rule in question, but which contain obviously fallacious inferences. 'Socrates alone (*solus*) is a man; therefore, Socrates alone is an animal.' 'This man begins to see a man; therefore, he begins to see an animal.' 'This man ceases to see a man; therefore, he ceases to see an animal.' 'This man now sees a man for the first time; therefore, he sees an animal for the first time.' 'This man now sees a man for the last time; therefore, he now sees an animal for the last time.' 'Adam was the first man; therefore, he was the first animal.' 'Every man is

92 Iwakuma 1981, p. 6.
93 *Ibid.*
94 *Tractatus de locis argumentationum, loc cit.*, 7.1, pp. 27–8.

inside here; therefore, every animal is inside here.' In a brief sentence the author explains the fallaciousness of these *instantiae*: all the counter-examples contain a term 'that implies a negation'. Thus they do not contain affirmative arguments, but a mixture of affirmative and negative ones. The 'concealed negation' prevents the validity of the argument from the *pars subjectiva* to the *totum universale*. Let us attempt to uncover the veiled negations, something the author evidently regards as superfluous: 'Socrates alone' = no one who is not Socrates; 'this man begins' = in the moment before this one, he didn't . . .; and likewise the following examples; 'Adam was the first man' = before him there was no one. But how are we to understand the last example? Is it not that the deduction here fails because of the position of the term – it stands in the position of subject and not, as in the previous examples, as the predicate or part of the predicate? In that case shouldn't the rule be made more precise? – Practice is needed if we are to grasp the author's point. 'Every' is equivalent to 'not anyone who isn't'. But it is invalid to infer from 'there is not any man who isn't . . .' that 'there is not any animal that isn't'.

At a later point the author tests whether propositions with a relative pronoun can be split up into the conjunction of two sentences, the second of which is governed by the same subject as the first and is signalled by the use of a demonstrative pronoun.[95] The inference 'a man who runs, disputes; therefore, a man runs and he disputes' seems valid. Nevertheless, objections are advanced. 'Only a single animal, which is a phoenix, runs; therefore, only a single animal runs, and this is a phoenix.' 'I love every person whom I see; therefore, I see every person, and I love that person (i.e. every person whom I see).' The author's treatment of these counter-examples is as unsatisfactory as it could possibly be. He maintains that they are correct and declares that such inferences are only probable, not necessary. A precise syntactical analysis of such examples would have been desirable; it would then have become apparent that the scope of functors like 'only' and 'every person' is different in the consequent from what it was in the antecedent.

The style of reasoning of the *Ars Meliduna* cannot be adequately illustrated here. The treatise is simply packed with detail. The opinions of the different schools on every conceivable issue are reproduced at length; objections are canvassed, attempts at proof are scrutinized and alternative theses are tested. In de Rijk's excerpts several folio pages are sometimes represented in a few

---

95 *Ibid.* 21.1, p. 50.

lines.[96] When the edition is ultimately available in full it will provide material for a host of studies. It will then be possible to establish the focal points of the debates between the different schools. The analyses in the *Ars Meliduna* are conducted with extraordinary care throughout. The level of debate among the various logicians is astonishingly high and the confident and judicious manner in which the author threads his way through the jungle of theses and antitheses is highly impressive. The *Ars* is the climactic achievement of logic in the second half of the twelfth century, just as the writings of Peter Abelard had been in the first.[97]

The theory of categories in the Compendium logicae Porretanum

To praise a compendium emanating from the school named after Robert of Melun implies no disparagement of treatises from other schools.[98] Every school developed its own answers to controversial questions of the day, and concentrated on certain focal themes of its own. The Melidunenses established strikingly close links between logical and grammatical problems. The Porretani, on the other hand, in the compendium already mentioned, which in structure resembles that of the *Ars Meliduna*,[99] tended to intermingle logical and semantic questions with ontological ones.

The individual books of the *Compendium logicae Porretanum* begin with lists of theses. The way these are formulated makes them sound strangely alien; they are by no means immediately self-evident. The author presents them as

96 For example, what de Rijk designates as 'cap 5' of Pt I begins on fol. 211 v b, and 'cap 6' on fol. 213r a. In the typescript this 'cap 5' fills ten sides; in de Rijk, *Log. Mod.* II.1 293–4, it takes up only fifteen lines.

97 At the 7th Symposium on Medieval Logic and Semantics (Poitiers 1985; cf. n. 53) Joel Biard and H. A. G. Braakhuis both read papers on the *Ars Meliduna*, although both relied entirely on the excerpts published in de Rijk's *Logica Modernorum*. Despite this, both contributions are strongly recommended: J. Biard 'La signification des termes dans l'*Ars Meliduna*'; H. A. G. Braakhuis, 'Problèmes Sémantiques dans l' *Ars Meliduna*'. Cf. also the Princeton dissertation by P. O. King, which regrettably has not yet been published, 'Peter Abailard and the Problem of Universals' (2 vols., 1982), ch. 10.1, 'The *Ars Meliduna* and the Influence of Grammar', pp. 235–40.

98 Following in the footsteps of de Rijk F. Bottin and E. P. Bos have recently made notable contributions to our knowledge of the treatises originating on the Mont Sainte-Geneviève, whose principal author was Alberic. Bottin is preparing an edition of the commentary on the *Categories* discovered by de Rijk in the MS Padua, Bibl. Univ. 2084. E. P. Bos is doing likewise with the treatise from the Paris MS B. N. lat. 15141, to which de Rijk has given the name of *Introductiones Montanae Maiores*. Cf. L. M. de Rijk, 'Some New Evidence on Twelfth Century Logic: Alberic and the School of Mont Ste. Geneviève (Montani)', *Vivarium* IV (1966) 1–57; L. M. de Rijk, *Log. Mod.* II.1 146–50, 213–15. The contributions of F. Bottin, 'Quelques discussions sur la transitivité de la prédication dans l'école d'Albéric du Mont', and of E. P. Bos, 'Quelques remarques sur les vues sémantiques des *Introductiones Montanae Maiores* et *Minores*', are due to appear in the Acts of the 7th Symposium on Medieval Logic and Semantics (cf. n. 53).

99 Cf. n. 57, above.

the intellectual property of the group or the school to which he feels he belongs. Every thesis is supported by argument. This is done without any polemics and without taking issue with conflicting theses, unless they stem from 'renegade' Porretani. The *Compendium* does not defend the theses of the school against outsiders, but instead expounds the meaning of these theses for the members of the school itself.[100]

One of the areas in which the *Compendium* expounds original and noteworthy theories of its own is in its teaching concerning the categories.[101] The author reverts to this question on numerous occasions. Thus in Book I we find Thesis 6: 'Only a term which belongs to the knowledge of nature (*ad naturalem facultatem*) is a means of predicating (*predicamentum*).'[102] In Book II the thesis is defended that 'not every predicative statement predicates something (*non omni predicativa aliquid predicari*).'[103] In Book III, Thesis 19 touches on the theme of the categories: 'Not everything predicable is something substantial or accidental (*Non omne predicabile est substantiale vel accidentale*).'[104] Lastly, the whole work concludes with an appendix entitled 'The three kinds of predicable contents and means of predication'.[105]

The arguments in support of all these theses obviously cannot be reported here in detail. But some of the main points can be summarized briefly, so as to convey an impression at least of the independence and rigour of the theory of categories in this treatise. In order to answer the question posed by Aristotle in his *Categories*, the author starts with the term used by Boethius to translate the word 'category'. A *praedicamentum* signifies a means of predicating something, just as *vestimentum* signifies a means of clothing something

---

100 According to M.-T. d'Alverny, *Alain de Lille, Textes inédits* (Paris 1965), pp. 19–20, Alan of Lille and Simon of Tournai, who were both students of Gilbert of Poitiers, 'lived and taught in Paris in the second half of the twelfth century, doubtless on the Mont Ste Geneviève.' If we assume that the *Porretani* had their school on the Mont Sainte-Geneviève, this leads to the question of where the *Secta Meliduna* was based. It can scarcely be imagined that the two schools shared the same site. G. R. Evans, *Alan of Lille. The Frontiers of Theology in the late Twelfth Century* (Cambridge 1983), suggests that Simon of Tournai taught at the Cathedral School of Notre Dame (p. 8). If this were true of the *Porretani* as a whole, the Melidunenses might have had their school on the Mont Sainte-Geneviève. This hypothesis would still leave unresolved whether the *Melidunenses* and the *Montani*, like their founders Robert and Alberic, can be imagined teaching peaceably side by side.

101 Cf. the Editors' introduction, pp. xii–xv.

102 *Comp. Log. Porr.*, p. 1.19–20. The explanation of this thesis contains a more precise statement: 'Every term that belongs to the knowledge of nature, and only such a term, is a category (*predicamentum*)' (p. 4.(1)08–9).

103 *Ibid.* II 3, p. 14.97. The preceding thesis lists the types of statement in which nothing is predicated. They include statements in which the predicate-position is taken by a noun which in terms of content belongs to logic (*nomen rationale*) or ethics (*nomen morale*) (p. 12.7–10).

104 *Ibid.* p. 30.27; p. 43.(4)31–2. Cf. also Theses 29–39 in Book III and the surrounding discussions.

105 *Ibid.* pp. 73–93; the title comes from the editors.

and *ornamentum* a means of adorning something. The categories, therefore, are words. But not every word is a category in the strict sense. In order to understand this, it is essential to attend to what is being predicated (*praedicatum*). Strictly speaking, one would have to say that it is the subject which is asserted – the subject in a double sense: logically and grammatically, as the subject of a sentence, and ontologically, as the bearer of properties. Despite this, we have become accustomed to saying that a property (*proprietas*) is being predicated of a particular subject. The subject is expressed (*declaratur*) by the assertion of this property. But not everything that can be said of a thing is a property which expresses what that thing is or what sort of thing it is that is being spoken about. For example, to say of a pearl that it is costly says nothing about the nature of the pearl, but only about the value men have given it in the course of trade. The only lexical items which merit the title of 'categories' are those which enable us to describe natural objects as things given in nature and to say what sort of things they are. It is this vocabulary alone that was classified by Aristotle. The author proceeds to identify two other vocabularies, apart from the vocabulary of natural knowledge: the language of ethics and that of logic. These have still to be classified, although the manner in which Aristotle set about classifying the predicable objects of natural knowledge could serve as a model and a guide. The language of ethics includes, apart from the vocabulary of morality proper, the words for professions and offices, for social classes and for aspects of the human condition, such as 'rich' and 'poor', and, finally, for artifacts of every kind. The language of logic includes all the words by means of which man is able to reflect on the processes of making distinctions, understanding, naming, predicating, and reasoning.

The principal contentious issues

The semantics of terms

The principal debates between the Schools – which were also frequently attempts to establish their own philosophical profile – were of course fought out on terrain which was of interest to all the logicians of the day. Up to now the attention of recent scholars has been drawn largely to the semantic discussions, above all to the debates surrounding the semantics of terms, in the course of which the theory of supposition was developed.[106] There is

---

106 Twelfth-century logicians, starting from the analysis of fallacious conclusions and from grammatical analyses, discovered that the way a subject term is to be understood depends on the predicate term as well as on the logical functors of a proposition. For instance *homo* is understood differently in each of the following: *homo est nomen*, *homo est species*, *homo currit*, and *homo est animal*. The question 'What does the term stand for (*supponit*) in this

some fruitful cross-fertilization here between logical and grammatical approaches.[107] Because of the complexity of the issues involved it is not possible here to give an account of even the most important tenets. All we can do is to refer to the main subjects of debate. One issue concerned the relationship between the signifying and naming functions of categorematic expressions. The signified is a general meaning, a form. The abstract form of nouns is often used to identify such meanings: as in the case of whiteness, colour, or corporeality. The thing or things named are extramental. Only concrete nouns, such as 'a white thing', 'a coloured thing' or 'a body', name things, each from a specific point of view. Controversy focused on the issue of whether the signifying or the naming function was primary, or whether this question produced one answer for substances and another for properties. It emerges with increasing clarity that such questions can only be answered profitably if a 'contextual approach' (de Rijk) is used in the analysis of words. As in Abelard at an earlier stage, the path has to be traversed from the question of the meaning and function of nouns and verbs to the question of the meaning and function of subject-phrases and predicate-phrases, i.e. the terms in a sentence.

The semantics of propositions

Research into the controversies of the second half of the twelfth century *de significatis propositionum* has not advanced with the same degree of differentiation as research into the debates *de significatis terminorum*.[108] The debate here focuses on the relationship between the content of a sentence – i.e. what is said, the *dictum* of a statement, or that which can be said, *enuntiabile* – and truth or falsity. The problem cannot be expounded more precisely here, since that would mean tracing it back to Abelard. But should an edition of the *Ars Meliduna* ever be completed, a comparison with the *Com-*

proposition?' is a search for the interpretation that enables the given proposition to be true. The distinction between types of 'supposition' is a distinction between typical modes of usage. On the theory of supposition, apart from vol. II of L. M. de Rijk's *Logica Modernorum*, which opened the gates to all subsequent research, cf. Pinborg 1972, pp. 43–79; N. Kretzmann, 'Semantics, History of', in P. Edwards (ed.), *The Encyclopedia of Philosophy* VII–VIII (New York–London 1967) 358–406, esp. pp. 370–3; L. M. de Rijk, 'The Origins of the Theory of the Properties of Terms', in *CHLMP*, pp. 161–73.

107 On the grammatical aspect cf. C. H. Kneepkens, '"Suppositio" and "supponere" in 12th Century Grammatical Theory', which is due to appear in the Acts of the 7th Symposium on Medieval Logic and Semantics (see n. 53).

108 Cf. G. Nuchelmans, *Theories of the Proposition. Ancient and Medieval Conceptions of the Bearers of Truth and Falsity* (Amsterdam–London 1973); 'The Semantics of Propositions', in *CHLMP*, pp. 197–210.

pendium logicae Porretanum will make new research into twelfth-century truth theory and modal theory both necessary and possible.[109]

Logical syntax: Consequentiae

John of Salisbury is not alone in finding it difficult to discover any meaning in the debates on logical syntax which took place in the twelfth century. The same may be said of modern historians of philosophy. A familiarity with modern research into such matters of formal logic as material, formal and strict implication, inference, entailment and relevance logic is perhaps essential if we are to follow medieval logicians in their theories about the structure of propositions (*propositio hypothetica*) and about *consequentiae*.[110] But anyone who is conversant with modern research into logical syntax may find medieval formulations excessively cumbersome. In modern logic, symbols are used which make clear distinctions between the signs for variables (e.g. for propositions where the content is arbitrary) and the signs for logical constants (such as for the connectives 'if . . . then'), and the scope of each logical operator is made unambiguous by the use of brackets. Medieval logic, on the other hand, is constantly forced to redefine its definitions by analysing new examples. Or, at best, it formulates metalinguistic rules about forms of argument and deduction in which the metalanguage is only distinguished from the target language by a special vocabulary (*termini secundae intentionis*).

Nevertheless, to study questions to which philosophers of quite different ages have devoted their efforts, even where there is no evidence that the later thinkers have been influenced by the earlier ones, and to compare the treatment of similar questions within very different theoretical frameworks, is a task not without its own interest and importance.[111] So we must warmly welcome the recent emergence of studies which set out to make a systematic comparison with the twelfth-century theory of consequences.[112]

What is at stake in the twelfth-century debates – as also in modern theories – can be summed up in a single sentence. The aim is to discover the validity conditions for conditionals, each of which must be necessary and which all

109 Cf. in the meantime K. Jacobi, *Die Modalbegriffe in den logischen Schriften des Wilhelm von Shyreswood und in anderen Kompendien des 12. und 13. Jahrhunderts. Funktionsbestimmung und Gebrauch in der logischen Analyse*, Studien und Texte zur Geistesgeschichte des Mittelalters XIII (Leiden–Cologne 1980).
110 Cf. I. Boh, 'Consequences', in *CHLMP*, pp. 300–14.
111 Cf. my essay 'Abelard and Frege: The Semantics of Words and Propositions', in *Atti del Convegno Internazionale di Storia della Logica, San Gimignano, 4–8 December 1982* (Bologna 1983), pp. 81–96.
112 Cf. n. 43 above.

together coalesce into a coherent, sufficiently determined theory. Every attempt to formulate rules is exposed to objections: whatever examples are adduced, a conditional framed in accordance with the rules must never give rise to inferences that run counter to intuition. It is not possible here to illustrate the subtlety and ingenuity of the arguments used by twelfth-century logicians to test the solutions they propose. But I hope that I have succeeded in making it seem a little more plausible that it was precisely in this area that the individual schools of logic should have rigorously competed for the most satisfying theory, so that a clearly defined position on this issue – as well as on the problems of semantics – could become the distinguishing mark of a school.

Logic as a part of philosophy (scientia)

John of Salisbury's powerful plea was uttered on behalf of a logic which conceived itself as an art (ars). He advocated the study of logic as a schooling in the arts of thinking, reasoning, and speaking. In the second half of the twelfth century logic was studied without regard to its practical applicability. Thus logic became a science (scientia).[113] Whoever studied logic, studied theory. Theory has its sense and purpose in itself. It stands in no need of justification in terms of any benefit it may yield. Logic, which had been the indispensable tool of the philosopher, was imperceptibly transformed into a fundamental constituent part of philosophy.

. . . and its applications in theology

Theory often produces results which have practical relevance even when, or precisely because, it is pursued without an eye to practical applicability. This was also the case in the second half of the twelfth century. In recent studies of Alan of Lille[114] and Peter the Chanter[115] attention has been drawn to the fact that the works of these writers were powerfully influenced by the procedures characteristic of logic in the second half of the twelfth century. Of the two Alan of Lille was undoubtedly the more original, more important and more rigorous thinker. Works like that of Peter the Chanter 'constitute the point of arrival of many decades of theological [and, I would add, of logical: K.J.]

---

113 I leave open the question whether Abelard too did not think of logic as *scientia* rather than *ars*.
114 Evans 1983; cf. esp. pp. 5–10, 25–41; A. de Libera (forthcoming, cf. n. 91).
115 F. Giusberti, 'A Twelfth Century Theological Grammar. The *Tractatus de tropis loquendi* by Peter the Chanter', in Giusberti 1982, pp. 87–109. G. R. Evans, 'A work of "Terminist Theology"? Peter the Chanter's *De Tropis Loquendi* and some *Fallacie*', *Vivarium* xx (1982) 40–58.

teaching in Paris and of many *reportationes*, texts, glosses and fragments, which were gathered in different forms at different times; and which at the same time represent the point of departure for other *summae*, compilations and glosses.'[116]

116 Giusberti, *loc cit.* p. 99. Cf. Evans 1983, pp. 49–50:
'Peter uses, without definition or explanation, a number of technical terms which now require some explanation if they are to be intelligible. It is to be supposed that the structure of his treatise was clear to his students, or at any rate that they understood what was implied by the headings he gave them. Certainly, there is an orderliness about his approach, an internal logic in his arrangement of his topics, which strongly suggests that this was no exploratory exercise, but rather a mature work, resting upon tried foundations, and dealing with matters which were relatively familiar to the student of theology.'

III

INNOVATORS

9

ANSELM OF CANTERBURY*

STEPHEN GERSH

The details of Anselm's life and career are fairly well known to us on account of the *De vita et conversatione Anselmi Archiepiscopi Cantuariensis* and the *Historia novorum* written by his English secretary and disciple Eadmer.[1] We know that Anselm was born near Aosta in 1033, left Italy at the age of twenty-three, and eventually settled at the Benedictine abbey of Bec in Normandy in 1059. To Bec he had been attracted by the reputation of Lanfranc, the prior of the abbey and master of its school, and in 1060 he formally entered the novitiate. Thereafter Anselm's rise to ecclesiastical distinction was rapid: he became Prior of Bec on Lanfranc's departure to Caen in 1063, and Abbot after the death of Herluin in 1078. Finally he moved to England in order to succeed Lanfranc in the archbishopric of Canterbury, a position which he occupied until his death in 1109.

Among the external circumstances of Anselm's life, it is perhaps his association with Lanfranc which had the greatest influence upon the formation of his philosophical mentality. However, despite the praise bestowed upon Lanfranc for his intellectual abilities in Eadmer's *Vita*[2] and the obvious fact that he must have exercised considerable personal magnetism as a teacher to have convinced the young Anselm that he should settle at Bec, the extent of Lanfranc's influence over his younger contemporary has only been

---

* For the text of Anselm's writings see *S. Anselmi Opera Omnia*, ed. F. S. Schmitt (6 vols., Seckau–Rome–Edinburgh 1938–61; repr. Stuttgart–Bad Cannstatt 1968) [S]. All citations in the present chapter will be according to volume, page, and lines of this edition. For an English translation see *Anselm of Canterbury* I–IV, ed. and transl. J. Hopkins and H. Richardson (London–Toronto–New York 1974–6). Recent general studies of Anselm's thought include P. Mazzarella, *Il pensiero speculativo di S. Anselmo d'Aosta* (Padua 1962); J. Vuillemin, *Le Dieu d'Anselme et les apparences de la raison* (Paris 1971); J. Hopkins, *A Companion to the Study of St. Anselm* (Minneapolis 1972); H. Kohlenberger, *Similitudo und Ratio. Überlegungen zur Methode bei Anselm von Canterbury* (Bonn 1972); G. Cenacchi, *Il pensiero filosofico di Anselmo d'Aosta* (Padua 1974); G. R. Evans, *Anselm and Talking About God* (Oxford 1978); and K. Kienzler, *Glauben und Denken bei Anselm von Canterbury* (Freiburg–Basle–Vienna 1981).

1 See *The Life of St. Anselm, Archbishop of Canterbury, by Eadmer*, ed. and transl. R. W. Southern (London 1962). Anselm's intellectual milieu is discussed by R. W. Southern, *St. Anselm and his Biographer. A Study of Monastic Life and Thought 1059 – c.1130* (Cambridge 1963) and G. R. Evans, *Anselm and a New Generation* (Oxford 1980).

2 Eadmer, *Vita* I 4.

revealed by the most modern scholarship. Thus, whereas scholars like J. Hopkins writing as late as 1972 can still classify Lanfranc as a 'lesser influence' on Anselm,[3] the more recent studies of M. Gibson[4] and M. Colish[5] have demonstrated the extent to which Lanfranc's expertise in grammar and dialectic and his application of these arts to theological problems suggested a definite programme to Anselm. That Lanfranc was a specialist in dialectic is indicated by contemporary and later reports,[6] by references in medieval library catalogues to works now lost entitled 'Questiones Lanfranci' and 'Lantfrancus de dialectica',[7] and by evidence in his extant writings of interest in specific dialectical questions. This last category includes references to the Aristotelian–Boethian distinction of first and second substances in the *Liber de corpore et sanguine domini*, in which Lanfranc attacked Berengarius' theory of the Eucharist,[8] his apparent recourse to the doctrine of substance (οὐσία) presented by the pseudo-Augustinian *De decem categoriis* in a gloss on Jerome (?) in MS London B. L. Sloane 1580, fol. 16r,[9] and by his advocacy of the 'equipollence of propositions' as a technique of argument in the *Liber de corpore et sanguine domini*.[10] That Lanfranc was also an expert in grammar is suggested by medieval testimony that he was active in teaching all the arts,[11] by the numerous grammatical observations contained in his notes on Gregory the Great's *Moralia in Iob*,[12] and by his contributions to the glosses on Priscian which were in the process of assembly during the eleventh century.[13] A particularly interesting example of such a gloss was contained in

3 Hopkins 1972, p. 32.
4 M. Gibson, *Lanfranc of Bec* (Oxford 1978), pp. 34–5, 39f.
5 M. Colish, *The Mirror of Language. A Study in the Medieval Theory of Knowledge* (2nd ed., Lincoln, Nebraska 1983), pp. 71f.
6 By William of Malmesbury, Sigebert of Gembloux etc. The *testimonia* are listed in R. W. Southern 'Lanfranc of Bec and Berengar of Tours', in *Studies in Medieval History presented to F. M. Powicke*, ed. R. W. Hunt, W. A. Pantin, and R. W. Southern (Oxford 1948), pp. 30, 36–7.
7 See Southern 1948, p. 30.
8 See *ibid.* pp. 40–1; Gibson 1978, p. 90.
9 See Gibson 1978, pp. 41–2.
10 See Southern 1948, pp. 41–2, Gibson 1978, pp. 87–8, and Colish 1983, pp. 73–4. The phrase 'equipollences of propositions (*aequipollentiae propositionum*)' is apparently inspired by the pseudo-Apuleian *Perihermeneias* – a work which was coming back into vogue during the eleventh century. As used by Lanfranc, the phrase seems to indicate an argument constructed in the form: A = B = C = D, therefore A = D, in contrast to a syllogism taking the form: all A is D, B is A, therefore all B is D.
11 This is stated, for example, by Ordericus Vitalis: the *testimonia* are discussed in Colish 1983, pp. 71–3.
12 See M. Gibson, 'Lanfranc's Notes on Patristic Texts', *Journal of Theological Studies* XXII (1971) 435–50, and Gibson 1978, pp. 43f.
13 See R. W. Hunt, 'Studies on Priscian in the Eleventh and Twelfth Centuries', *MARS* I (1941–3) 206–7, and Gibson 1978, pp. 47–8.

MS Chartres B. Mun. 209, fol. 86v, where the verb 'to be' was explained simultaneously in relation to active and passive and substance and accident.[14] The importance of this evidence regarding Lanfranc's intellectual activity cannot be underestimated as soon as we realize that many of these discussions are echoed in the writings of his former pupil. For example, Anselm also has recourse to dialectical methods in distinguishing first and second substances[15] and in employing the equipollency of propositions,[16] or to grammatical methods in reflecting on the verb 'to be'.[17]

To the information which we possess regarding Anselm's life and career we are fortunate in being able to add many details concerning the chronology of his writings. This topic has been conclusively investigated by F. S. Schmitt, who assembled three kinds of data: cross-references within the treatises themselves, certain statements in the Anselmian *Epistolae*, and references to literary activity in Eadmer's biography.[18] There are slight discrepancies between the order of the earliest treatises indicated by the cross-references and that suggested by Eadmer's report, which can perhaps be explained by saying that Eadmer's information was incomplete for the period prior to his own personal contact with Anselm. Allowing for this, we can therefore conclude that at Bec were completed the *Monologion* in 1076, the *Proslogion* about 1077–8, *De grammatico, De veritate*, and *De libertate arbitrii* between 1080 and 1085, *De casu diaboli*, and the first recension of *De incarnatione verbi* in 1092; at Canterbury the second recension of *De incarnatione verbi* in 1094, *Cur deus homo* between 1094 and 1098, *De conceptu virginali et de originali peccato* between 1099 and 1100, *De processione spiritus sancti* in 1102, *De sacrificio azimi et fermentati* and *De sacramentis ecclesiae* about 1106–7, and *De concordia* about 1107–8. The establishment of this chronology allows us to draw one major conclusion regarding the evolution of

---

14 See Hunt 1943, pp. 224–5, and Gibson 1978, pp. 47–8.
15 *Monol.* 27 (S 1 45.4–12). On Anselm as dialectician see G. R. Evans, 'The "Secure Technician". Varieties of Paradox in the Writings of St. Anselm', *Vivarium* XIII (1975) 1–21 and Evans 1980, pp. 111f.
16 Examples are given in M. Colish, 'Eleventh-Century Grammar in the Thought of St. Anselm', in *Arts libéraux et philosophie au moyen âge (Actes du IVᵉ Congrès International de Philosophie Médiévale, Montréal 27 août – 2 septembre 1967)* (Montreal–Paris 1969), pp. 794–5, and Colish 1983, p. 92. The parallelism between Lanfranc's and Anselm's methodologies here was first noted by Southern 1948, pp. 41–2.
17 *Monol.* 6 (S I 20.11–19). On Anselm as grammarian see G. R. Evans, 'St. Anselm's Technical Terms of Grammar', *Latomus* XXXVIII (1979) 413–21, and M. Colish, 'St. Anselm's Philosophy of Language Reconsidered', *Anselm Studies* I (1983) 113–23.
18 F. S. Schmitt, 'Zur Chronologie der Werke des hl. Anselm von Canterbury', *Revue Bénédictine* XLIV (1932) 322–50. Schmitt's conclusions here and in other writings have been generally accepted by scholars. They are conveniently summarized by Mazzarella 1962, pp. 65–99, and Hopkins 1972, pp. 9–16.

Anselm's style: that, despite the general agreement in doctrine which all the treatises present, there is a marked development of method between Bec and Canterbury. Thus, the earlier works mostly pursue non-scriptural arguments in order to reinforce the tenets of faith, these arguments being either in the form of a meditation or in that of a philosophical dialogue. In the later writings, these non-scriptural arguments are interwoven with much actual exegesis of biblical texts in a more directly expository format.

In the treatises of Anselm of Canterbury, and especially in the earlier treatises, one overwhelming philosophical question forces itself upon the reader's attention: what is the precise relation between reason and faith? The writer himself comments that in the *Monologion* his aim had been to investigate what he literally terms the 'reason of faith (*ratio fidei*)',[19] and on turning to the preface of this work we can learn that what was envisaged there was a method of discovering certain things regarding the divine being in which there was 'absolutely no appeal to scriptural authority (*auctoritate scripturae penitus nihil in ea persuaderetur*)', and where whatever conclusions might emerge would do so through 'the necessity of reason (*rationis necessitas*)'.[20] Unfortunately, despite Anselm's obvious attempt to define his aims precisely, considerable uncertainty has arisen in the minds of modern interpreters about the precise nature of this reason which can bring us to the comprehension of truths about God. Does Anselm postulate a reason which can function in this way without starting from scriptural presuppositions, or is any such reason ultimately dependent upon premisses whose truth is only known through revelation?

There is abundant evidence in the treatises of their author's belief that, on some occasions at least, truths regarding the divine nature can be deduced by using reason in complete independence of credal assumptions. In *Cur deus homo* Anselm explicitly states that the arguments by which it is proved that mankind can be redeemed only through Christ's sacrifice, and which are based on reason alone, have a power of persuading not only believers but also unbelievers.[21] In other words, they are expressed in a form which both the Christian and the atheist can appreciate, rather than in one which only an adherent of the faith could be led to accept. Similarly, in *Contra Gaunilonem* he underlines his own conviction that the argument which proves the necessity of postulating God's existence, and which is an attempt to understand the content of faith, compels the assent even of those who reject

19 *Prosl.* pr. (S I 94.6–7).
20 *Monol.* pr. (S I 7.5–11). Cf. *ibid.* I (S I 13.5–11).
21 *Cur deus homo* I 3 (S II 50.18–20), II 22 (S II 133.5–11).

the sacred authority.[22] In the light of such texts, it is initially difficult to see why scholars like E. Bréhier,[23] E. Gilson,[24] and R. Roques[25] have continued to argue that the reason which is postulated as leading to knowledge of God cannot operate without some dependence upon the assumptions of faith.

The solution to this puzzle lies in the manner in which the premisses and the deductive processes inherent in this notion of reason are conceived. Such interpreters work with the implicit assumption that a genuine reason, first, must start from premisses whose truth is accepted independently of revelation (e.g. by being self-evident); and, secondly, must consist of deductions which are valid according to the principles of formal logic (i.e. Aristotelian or syllogistic logic). Such a reason, when employed to discover truths about the divine nature, would actually render the content of faith redundant. Yet Anselm clearly states in various passages that revelation has a function which can never be supplanted by reason.[26] So he must rather have believed that this reason, although consisting of deductions valid according to the rules of formal logic, actually begins from premisses whose truth is guaranteed by revelation alone.

This process of thought underlies the account in Gilson's *History of Christian Philosophy in the Middle Ages.*[27] It stems from the implicit assumption that this Anselmian notion of reason could not have been a valid complement to faith unless its proponent viewed it as deviating from the purely scientific notion of reason in abandoning the first of the two criteria mentioned above. However, the evidence explicitly presented by the treatises and the character of eleventh-century logic in general indicate a different conclusion:[28] namely, that the notion of reason involved here was held to be a valid complement to revelation because it deviated from the purely scientific form of reason in avoiding the second criterion instead. But this situation will perhaps emerge more clearly after a brief survey of relevant passages.[29]

22 *Contra Gaunil.* 8 (S 1 137.27–30).
23 E. Bréhier, *Histoire de la philosophie* 1 (Paris 1943) 557–8.
24 E. Gilson, *History of Christian Philosophy in the Middle Ages* (London 1955), pp. 128–30.
25 *Anselme de Cantorbéry, Pourquoi Dieu s'est fait homme*, ed. R. Roques (Paris 1963), pp. 96–8.
26 *Cur deus homo* 1 1 (S 11 48.16–24), 1 2 (S 11 50.7–13), 1 25 (S 11 96.6f), *De concord.* 111 6 (S 11 271.28f)
27 See Gilson 1955, pp. 129–30, where it is explicitly asserted that (i) In the eleventh century philosophy consisted essentially of Aristotelian dialectic; (ii) Anselm's aim was not to render the mysteries of faith intelligible in themselves, 'which would have been to suppress them'; and (iii) the order of procedure was strictly first to believe in the faith and secondly to strive for understanding.
28 Anselm's frequent use of equipollent rather than syllogistic arguments, in which he follows Lanfranc's practice, has already suggested that this is so.
29 Collection of these passages is much facilitated by Schmitt's excellent index.

As used in Anselm's writings, the Latin technical term *ratio* does not simply indicate the content of Aristotelian–Boethian logic. It has a much wider range of philosophical connotations, of which the following are perhaps the most important:[30]

Ontological senses of ratio

(1) The structure of reality. Reason can signify the manner in which something exists,[31] and in several passages specifically the manner of spatio-temporal existence.[32]

(2) 'Ontological' necessity. A situation which compels things to be or act in a certain way: for example, those circumstances which made it necessary for God to become man.[33] The 'necessity' implied here provides the basis in objectivity for the logical necessity mentioned below.[34]

The theological ratio

An aspect of the divine nature. This usage, which is arrived at by analogy from the microcosm to the macrocosm, is especially frequent in the *Monologion*.[35]

Ratio in epistemology

(1) Many passages speak of reason as a state of mind contrasted with 'faith (*fides*)'.[36] Sometimes the precise relation is specified by characterizing reason negatively as something posterior to faith in the order of being[37] or in the order of time;[38] or positively as that which stabilizes the faith[39] or adds delight to its contemplation.[40] But at all events the exercise of reason is enjoined by Scripture.[41]

30 I shall translate the Latin term *ratio* as 'reason' whenever possible. However, on certain occasions we must substitute 'manner', 'argument', or 'necessity' to convey the correct sense.
31 *Monol.* 6 (S I 18.23–6).
32 *Ibid.* 21 (S I 36.18) and 22 (S I 40.16–18).
33 *Cur deus homo* I 1 (S II 47.11–48.5) and I 4 (S II 52.7–11)
34 See n. 51.
35 *Monol.* 9 (S I 24.12–20), 10 (S I 25.23–7), 16 (S I 31.4), and 34 (S I 53.17–18).
36 *Ibid.* 1 (S I 13.5–11), 64 (S I 75.1–6); *Prosl.* pr. (S I 94.6–7), *De incarn. verbi* 1 (S II 6.10f), 6 (S II 20.16–19), *Cur deus homo* I 1 (S II 47.5–7), I 3 (S II 50.16–18), etc. In many other texts 'intellect (*intellectus*)' is substituted for reason in the same context.
37 *Cur deus homo* I 1 (S II 48.19–24); *De concord.* III 6 (S II 271.28f)
38 *Cur deus homo* I 1 (S II 48.16–18).
39 *Ibid.* [*Comm. operis ad Urban.*] (S II 40.1–2).
40 *Ibid.* [*Comm. operis ad Urban.*] (S II 39.4–6); *ibid.* I 1 (S II 47.8–11), and *ibid.* II 15 (S II 116.8–12).
41 *Ibid.* [*Comm. operis ad Urban.*] (S II 40.7–10), *De incarn. verbi* I 4 (S I 284.20–2), and *De incarn. verbi* I (S II 8.19–9.1).

(2) Other passages speak of reason as a state of mind without reference to faith. Such a reason is described in *De incarnatione verbi* and *Cur deus homo* as the characteristic of dialecticians, Jews or pagans, and faithless Christians.[42]

The psychological ratio
A faculty of the human soul. Sometimes reason is described simply as an aspect of the soul,[43] but more often it is viewed specifically as the highest part,[44] that which is synonymous with 'mind (*mens*)',[45] and the part which operates independently of imagination and sense.[46]

Logical senses of ratio
(1) The context of discourse. In some passages reason signifies a specific argument by which something is proved,[47] in others the activity of debating philosophical questions in general.[48]

(2) 'Logical' necessity. An argument which compels our admission of certain facts: for example, the demonstrations that God should have a certain nature,[49] or that the term 'grammarian' should signify either a substance or a quality.[50] The 'necessity' invoked here is a subjective and objective correlate of the ontological necessity previously distinguished.[51]

That the term *ratio* has such a variety of meanings must always be taken into account when reading Anselm's writings. This fact in itself shows that the simple equation with the content of Aristotelian–Boethian dialectic is totally unsatisfactory as a basis of interpretation.[52]

42 *De incarn. verbi* I 4 (S I 285.3f) and *De incarn. verbi* I (S II 9.20–10.4): dialecticians; *Cur deus homo*, pr. (S II 42.9–11), I I (S II 47.11–48.5), and II 22 (S II 133.5–11): Jews and pagans; *Cur deus homo* I 2 (S II 50.16–18): faithless Christians.
43 *Monol.* I (S I 13.15–14.1); *De conc. virg.* 10 (S II 152.5–6), and *De concord.* I 6 (S II 257.17–18).
44 *De incarn. verbi* I 4 (S I 285.7–9); *De conc. virg.* 13 (S II 155.15–16); and *De concord.* III 11 (S II 279.4f)
45 *Monol.* 10 (S I 24.27); and *De concord.* III 13 (S II 286.11).
46 *Monol.* 10 (S I 25.4–9), 33 (S I 52.15–18); and *De verit.* 11 (S I 191.11–18).
47 *Cur deus homo* I 24 (S II 94.13–18).
48 *Ibid.* I 1 (S II 48.6–9), II 13 (S II 113.17–48); *De concord.* III 6 (S II 270.26), and III 6 (S II 271.28).
49 *Monol.* pr. (S I 7.1–11), 18 (S I 33.6–7), 64 (S I 75.7–10), and 79 (S I 86.12–14).
50 *De gramm.* I (S I 145.4–9).
51 The contrast between objective (ontological) and objective/subjective (logical) necessity emerges in those passages where Anselm speaks of reasons which exist yet are incomprehensible to *our* reason. See *Cur deus homo* I 2 (S II 50.7–13), II 15 (S II 115.24–116.7), II 16 (S II 117.18–22), and II 19 (S II 131.13–15). Because the second necessity is not arbitrary but grounded in the first, we should speak of it as objective/subjective rather than as subjective alone.
52 When Anselm uses *ratio* in the senses of 'argument' and 'logical necessity', he follows varying practices in relation to both his choice of premisses and his mode of deduction. (i) Premisses: these can be (a) self-evident conclusions, (b) derived from Patristic writers, (c) derived from Scripture, (d) conclusions in other Anselmian texts. On the variety of

Further, a solution to our main problem has emerged: that it is because the Anselmian notion of reason deviates from the purely scientific form of reason in avoiding not the first but the second of the two criteria discussed earlier[53] that it was held to be a valid complement to revelation. Thus, the interpretative strategy which seemed absolutely inescapable to Gilson and others has turned out to be quite unnecessary. But how does this notion of a reason which begins from non-credal premisses but need not consist of valid formal–logical deductions operate in practice? To answer this question we must embark on the detailed analysis of Anselm's two most important philosophical texts.

Ratio *in the* Monologion

In the preface to the *Monologion*, the author defends himself against possible criticism that he is proposing novel or false doctrines by underlining the agreement of his own book's teachings with those of Augustine's works and especially of the *De trinitate*.[54] This explicit reference to a literary source, which is a relatively unusual one for Anselm, is most interesting in revealing the extent of his dependence upon the Fathers and upon Augustine in particular.[55] We know from a few other citations that Anselm had followed his teacher Lanfranc in immersing himself in authors like Ambrose, Jerome, Cassian, Gregory the Great, and Bede.[56] From the *Monologion* we now learn that for him it is the Bishop of Hippo who occupies the primary rank among authorities of the ecclesiastical tradition.[57]

If Augustine is the principal influence upon this book, whose central theme is an investigation of the nature of God by means of reason, is he also

premisses see J. McIntyre, 'Premises and Conclusions in the System of St. Anselm's Theology', *Spicilegium Beccense* I (1959) 95–101. (ii) Deductions: these can be (a) syllogistic (explicitly or implicitly), (b) non-syllogistic (equipollent, analogical etc). On the forms of deduction see G. R. Evans, 'St. Anselm's Analogies', *Vivarium* XIV (1976) 81–93; 'St. Anselm's Technical Terms of Rhetoric', *Latomus* XXXVI (1977) 171–9; and Colish 1983, pp. 71f.

53 See p. 259.

54 *Monol*. pr. (S I 8.8–20)

55 Augustine's *De trinitate* is also cited at *De incarn. verbi* 16 (S II 35.10–13), in *Epist.* 77 (S III 199.24–6) and *Epist* 204 (S IV 97.45–7).

56 For Ambrose see *Epist.* 23 (S III 130.10–13); for Jerome *Epist.* 23 (S III 130.10–13), for Cassian *Epist.* 425 (S V 371.13–15); for Gregory the Great *Epist.* 23 (S III 130.8–10), 25 (S III 133.23–31), 26 (S III 134.3–11), 65 (S III 183.60–184.66), 161 (S IV 32.27–33.34); and for Bede *Epist.* 42 (S III 154.32–6). Lanfranc had written glosses or commentary on Ambrose, Jerome, Cassian, and Gregory the Great. The importance of Gregory the Great in forming the philosophical and religious mentality of Anselm has been emphasized by A. Stolz, 'Das Proslogion des hl. Anselm', *Revue Bénédictine* XLVIII (1935) 331–47.

57 Lanfranc had written extensive notes on Augustine's *De civitate dei*. For Lanfranc's study of the Fathers see Gibson 1978, pp. 39f.

the source for the notion of reason contained there? To this question the answer is clearly affirmative, for as we peruse the text we quickly discover that the senses of reason which have been categorized as theological and psychological are paramount here, and these senses are undeniably the most prominent although not the exclusive ones in *De trinitate* and other works of Augustine. If this is the case, then we can learn much about the structure and purpose of the eleventh-century treatise by comparing it with its predecessor on specific points.[58]

In the preface, Anselm describes the subject-matter of his work as an account, expressed in the form of a meditation, of various questions discussed with the brothers 'concerning meditation on the divine being (*de meditanda divinitatis essentia*)'.[59] He characterizes its methodology as one involving no appeal to the authority of Scripture and leading to conclusions emerging from the 'necessity of reason (*rationis necessitas*)'.[60] This clearly defined programme is carried out in the main body of the text, which comprises, first, a series of arguments yielding certain conclusions regarding the nature of the supreme principle abstractly conceived and, secondly, a further series producing conclusions about the nature of the trinitarian God of Christianity;[61] yet towards the end of his discussion Anselm makes some further remarks about method.

In chapter 64 Anselm raises an important question: if the supreme nature is actually ineffable, how can we accept the various arguments which have preceded as a 'true reason (*vera ratio*)'?[62] To this he replies that the kind of language implied there does not tell us anything directly about that being, although it does reveal certain things 'through something else (*per aliud*)', just as we sometimes do not look directly upon the face of a person but only

---

58 Anselm's debt to Augustine in general has been studied by A. Cicchetti, *L'Agostinismo nel pensiero di Anselmo d'Aosta* (Rome 1951). More specific influences are treated by F. J. Thonnard, 'Caractères augustiniens de la méthode philosophique de saint Anselme', *Spicilegium Beccense* I (Paris 1959) 171–83; M. Schmaus, 'Die theologie-geschichtliche Tragweite der Trinitätslehre des Anselm von Canterbury', *Analecta Anselmiana* IV.1 (1975) 29–45.

59 *Monol.* pr. (S I 7.2–5).

60 See p. 258 and n. 20.

61 On the structural division see p. 265.

62 *Monol.* 65 (S I 75.19–23). Anselm's emphasis upon the ineffability of the supreme nature is discussed by P. Evdokimov, 'L'aspect apophatique de l'argument de saint Anselme', *Spicilegium Beccense* I (Paris 1959) 233–58; H. de Lubac, 'Sur le chapitre XIVᵉ du Proslogion', *Spicilegium Beccense* I (Paris 1959) 295–312; F. Ulrich, 'Cur non video praesentem? Zur Implikation der "griechischen" und "lateinischen" Denkform bei Anselm und Scotus Eriugena', *Freiburger Zeitschrift für Philosophie und Theologie* XXII (1975) 70–170; and H. de Lubac, '"Seigneur, je cherche ton visage". Sur le chapitre XIVᵉ du Proslogion de saint Anselme', *Archives de Philosophie* XXXIX (1976) 201–25 and 407–25.

upon its 'likeness or image (*similitudo aut imago*)' reflected in a mirror.[63] When we consider the meaning of terminology employed in speaking of the supreme nature as being or wisdom, we succeed in conceiving only something 'among created things (*in rebus factis*)'. But our perceptions are not totally false if we are able to apprehend certain aspects of the divinity through something else, especially when the latter is of a nature which most closely approaches it: the 'rational mind (*mens rationalis*)'.[64] So the language employed in our arguments actually tells us something directly about the created image, but through this image also provides certain intimations of the supreme being; it utilizes that which is 'a mirror to itself (*sibimet velut speculum*)' as a means of access to what cannot be seen 'face to face (*facie ad faciem*)'.[65]

This section is crucial to the understanding of Anselm's methodological application of reason and reveals how much he is building upon Augustinian foundations.[66] In *De trinitate* Augustine had also emphasized that the divine nature is incomprehensible[67] yet can be perceived 'through an image (*per imaginem*)',[68] this image being either created things in general[69] or specifically the human mind.[70] Such an assumption, which derived from the exegesis of three scriptural texts – (i) Romans 1: 20, on seeing the invisibles of God through things that are created;[71] (ii) Genesis 1: 27, where God creates man in his own image;[72] and (iii) 1 Corinthians 13: 12, on seeing God through a mirror in an enigma[73] – structurally underlay the entire work. Thus, Augustine had summarized his own argument saying that by Book viii the ineffability of the divine nature was apparent, and so in Books ix to xiv he turned aside to contemplate God through his 'creature (*creatura*)', Book xv being where a further attempt to speak of the divinity became possible.[74]

---

63 *Monol.* 65 (S 1 76.10–24).
64 *Ibid.* 65–6 (S 1 76.24) – 66 (S 1 77.24).
65 *Ibid.* 67 (S 1 77.27–78.1).
66 The importance of this section for understanding Anselm's method has generally been overlooked by modern scholars. However, a notable exception is P. Vignaux, 'Structure et sens du Monologion', *RSPT* XXXI (1947) 192–212; and 'Note sur le chapitre LXX du Monologion', *Revue du Moyen Âge Latin* III (1947) 321–34.
67 Augustine, *De trin.* xv 2 2 (CC 50A, 461).
68 *Ibid.* xv 23 44 (CC 50A, 522).
69 *Ibid.* vi 10 11–12 (CC 50, 241–2). Cf. *ibid.* ii 15 25 (CC 50, 113–14).
70 *Ibid.* xiv 2 4 (CC 50A, 425), xiv 19 25 (CC 50A, 456–7), xv 3 5 (CC 50A, 465–6), xv 8 14f (CC 50A, 479f), xv 20 39 (CC 50A, 516–17), and xv 23 43–4 (CC 50A, 520–2).
71 See *Ibid.* ii 15 25 (CC 50, 114), vi 10 11–12 (CC 50, 241–3), xv 2 3 (CC 50A, 462), and xv 6 10 (CC 50A, 472–3).
72 See *Ibid.* xiv 3 4 (CC 50A, 426), xiv 19 25 (CC 50A, 456), and xv 6 10 (CC 50A, 472–3).
73 See *Ibid.* xv 8 14f (CC 50A, 479f) and xv 23 44 (CC 50A, 522).
74 *Ibid.* xv 6 10 (CC 50A, 472–4). For another summary see *ibid.* xv 3 4–5 (CC 50A, 462–7). The texts of Romans and Genesis are juxtaposed at *ibid.* xv 6 10 (CC 50A, 472–3).

That Anselm had this Augustinian argument in mind can hardly be doubted, even if modern scholars have curiously tended to ignore the fact.

If we take this philosophical methodology into account, we can see that the obvious main division of the *Monologion* text – into a series of arguments yielding conclusions about the nature of the supreme principle abstractly conceived, and another series producing conclusions regarding the nature of the trinitarian God of Christianity – is justified in terms of logic. Clearly the two parts correspond to an approach to the divine being through analysis of created things in general and of the human mind respectively, it being natural in the Augustinian context to expect the former to produce a primarily abstract notion of divinity and the latter an essentially trinitarian one.[75]

The precise aim of the first set of arguments: to prove by reason alone that there exists 'a single nature, supreme among all things which exist, alone self-sufficient in its eternal blessedness, giving and causing all other things to be something or to be well in some respect through its omnipotent goodness', is stated at the beginning of chapter 1.[76] Anselm carried out this undertaking very carefully in the course of the first twenty-seven chapters, although he does not treat all the questions in the same detail or in the exact order stated at the beginning, no doubt being forced to observe certain logical connections among the ideas themselves.[77]

Chapters 1–4 of the *Monologion* can be considered as a unit in which Anselm appeals to a single form of argument to demonstrate that the first principle is a unity, and that as supreme and self-sufficient in the categories of goodness, greatness, and being, it is the cause of all other things. This single form of argument is the traditional Platonic one,[78] which proves from the

75 In *De vera religione* Augustine arrived at a trinitarian notion of God by reflecting on the created world. However, Anselm does not seem to have been influenced by this text.
76 *Monol.* 1 (S I 13.5–8): 'unam naturam, summam omnium quae sunt, solam sibi in aeterna sua beatitudine sufficientem, omnibusque rebus aliis hoc ipsum quod aliquid sunt aut quod aliquomodo bene sunt, per omnipotentem bonitatem suam dantem et facientem.' Cf. *ibid.* 4 (S I 17.32–18.3).
77 The basic scheme for this section is:
     unity (chs. 1–4)
     supremacy (chs. 1–4)
     self-sufficiency (chs. 1–4, 5–7)
     eternity (chs. 18–24)
     omnipotence (chs. 15, 18)
     goodness (ch. 1)
     cause of being (chs. 1–12)
     cause of well-being (ch. 13)
78 The Platonic character of this argument (and of the *Monologion* as a whole) has been unjustifiably questioned by F. S. Schmitt, 'Anselm und der (Neu–) Platonismus', *Analecta Anselmiana* I(1969) 39–71. For conclusive defence see K. Flasch, 'Der philosophische Ansatz des Anselm von Canterbury im Monologion und sein Verhältnis zum augustinischen

existence of a number of things having the characteristic x that there is a single x-*in-itself* from which the plurality derive this characteristic. Anselm applies the argument first to goodness,[79] then to greatness,[80] and then to being,[81] his only additions to the traditional schema being the corollaries that the x-*in-itself* in each of the categories must be identical,[82] that an x-*in-itself* must always be greater than something merely exhibiting the characteristic x,[83] and that the x-*in-itself* must be the first in a finite hierarchy of reality.[84] It is Augustine who provides the inspiration for the proof of the supreme principle's goodness, in Book VIII of his treatise on the Trinity,[85] while the notions that this principle is also greatness and substance,[86] and that its attributes are identical, can be derived from other parts of the same work.[87] Anselm's chapters 5–8 take up the question how it is that the first principle is cause of all other things, and conclude that it produces (i) as an efficient cause[88] and (ii) from nothing.[89] Here, the argument is formulated by contrasting the supreme nature, which cannot be a material or instrumental cause,[90] cannot be produced by an efficient, material, or instrumental cause,[91] and cannot arise from nothing,[92] with created things, which can be all of the above. This account of the varieties of cause is derived from Boethius' commentary on Cicero's *Topics*,[93] the reflections upon the concept of nothingness perhaps from certain Augustinian passages.[94]

Chapters 9–12 continue with the question how the first principle is cause

Neuplatonismus', *Analecta Anselmiana* II (1970) 1–43; and M. Adams, 'Was Anselm a Realist? The Monologium', *Franciscan Studies* XXXII (1972) 5–14.

79 *Monol.* 1 (S I 14.5–15.12).
80 *Ibid.* 2 (S I 15.15–23).
81 *Ibid.* 3 (S I 15.27–16.28).
82 *Ibid.* 1 (S I 15.10–12), 2 (S I 15.20–3), and 3 (S I 16.23–6)
83 *Ibid.* 1 (S I 15.7–10).
84 *Ibid.* 4 (S I 16.31–17.32).
85 Augustine, *De trin.* VIII 3 4–5 (CC 50, 271–4).
86 *Ibid.* V 10 11 (CC 50, 217–18), VIII 2 3 (CC 50, 270–1): greatness; *ibid.* V 2 3 (CC 50, 207–8): substance.
87 *Ibid.* VI 7 8 (CC 50, 237) and XV 5 7f (CC 50A, 468f)
88 *Monol.* 7 (S I 20.22–22.1).
89 *Ibid.* 7 (S I 21.32–22.10).
90 *Ibid.* 7 (S I 20.22f)
91 *Ibid.* 6 (S I 18.21f)
92 *Ibid.* 6 (S I 19.10–20.19).
93 Boethius, *In Topic.* V (P.L.64, 1145cf). Schmitt 1969, pp. 43–4, argues that Anselm only knew the Ciceronian text itself. However, *De grammatico* clearly uses material from Boethius' commentary. See D. P. Henry, *The Logic of Saint Anselm* (Oxford 1967), p. 9; and L. Steiger, 'Contexe syllogismos. Über die Kunst und Bedeutung der Topik bei Anselm', *Analecta Anselmiana* I (1969) 119. On Anselm's knowledge of Boethius in general see Hopkins 1972, pp. 28–30.
94 See Augustine: *De mag.* 2 3 (CC 29, 160–1) and *Contra Iulian. Opus imperf.* V 44 (P.L.45, 1480f) for some parallels.

of all other things, and now attribute to it a further mode of causality: the formal.[95] This discussion evolves by contrasting the human being's 'speaking' of external things – either through (i) the articulation of phonetic sounds, (ii) the contemplation of such sounds, (iii) the contemplation of the objects' visible shapes, or (iv) the contemplation of the objects' logical definitions[96] – with the supreme nature's employment only of the two latter modes.[97] The identification of the divine formal causality with inner 'speaking' is clearly derived from Augustine's *De trinitate*,[98] although some minor definitions are added from the Aristotelian–Boethian logical tradition.[99] Finally, chapters 13–27 can be considered as a group of related arguments, in which reflections upon the omnipresence of the atemporal and non-spatial first principle in the temporally and spatially defined objects of the created world[100] are interspersed with observations regarding the applicability to the supreme being of various kinds of terminology: such as relatives versus non-relatives,[101] the unity of attributes,[102] and substance or accident.[103] This section seems to have a logical connection with the previous material in that, whereas chapters 1–4 prove the existence of a first principle, which is identified as efficient cause of created things in chapters 5–8 and as formal cause of created things in chapters 9–12, the chapters from 13 onwards explain precisely how the relationship between this principle and creation is to be visualized. The emphasis upon the theme of omnipresence again reflects the Augustinian antecedents,[104] although here the influence of Gregory the Great's *Moralia in Iob*[105] may have almost equal significance.

The earlier part of the *Monologion* delineates the supreme principle in a

95 *Monol.* 9 (S I 24.10–20) and 12 (S I 26.26–33). The 'speaking' (*locutio*) introduced below is explicitly identified with formal causality at *ibid.* 10 (S I 24.24–27).
96 *Ibid.* 10 (S I 24.29–25.25).
97 *Ibid.* 10 (S I 24.27–9). Anselm also contrasts the supreme nature's causality with that of a human artisan at *ibid.* 11 (S I 26.3–23). The latter can only (a) imagine an object (i.e. contemplation mode iii) if he has already seen one physically realized, and (b) create an object if his notion of it (i.e. contemplation modes iii and iv) is accompanied by physical action. Such limitations do not apply to the higher creativity.
98 Augustine, *De trin.* XV 10 17–11 20 (CC 50A, 483–9) elaborates this thesis using a number of New Testament texts.
99 For example, Boethius, *In Isag. ed. pr.* I 20 (CSEL 48, 60.6) provides the Aristotelian definition of 'man'.
100 *Monol.* 14 (S I 27.19–26) and 18 (S I 32.7) – 24 (S I 42.29).
101 *Ibid.* 15 (S I 28.3–29.33).
102 *Ibid.* 16 (S I 30.32) – 17 (S I 32.4).
103 *Ibid.* 16 (S I 30.5–31), 25 (S I 43.3) – 27 (S I 45.22).
104 The Augustinian texts are too numerous to list here. However, the material has been studied in detail by S. Grabowski, *The All-Present God. A Study in St. Augustine* (St. Louis, Missouri 1954).
105 On this theme see M. Frickel, *Deus totus ubique simul. Untersuchungen zur allgemeinen Gottgegenwart im Rahmen der Gotteslehre Gregors des Grossen* (Freiburg i. Br. 1956).

relatively abstract manner, and its philosophical method may perhaps be summarized as follows. In the first place, the argument seeks to understand this principle through things subsequent to it in general, not in the weaker sense that knowledge of the higher will be achieved only *after* reflection upon the lower, but in the stronger sense, that understanding of the higher can be accomplished only *through* examination of the lower. This recognition that our perceptions of the first principle must always be indirect follows from Anselm's insistence upon the method of the image in chapters 64–6, and especially from his argument that even terms like 'being' properly represent created things alone.[106] Secondly, the earlier section of this work attempts to understand the supreme principle using a sequence of dialectical arguments, yet it terminates by achieving a perception not of that principle itself but of its ordering of subsequent things. In other words, the application of what has previously been termed the 'logical *ratio*' leads on – given the limitations of the epistemology of the image – to a knowledge of the 'ontological *ratio*' as defined earlier.[107]

The purpose of the second set of arguments also seems to be stated at the beginning of chapter 1, where, after listing the things which can be proved by reason alone, the words 'and many other things concerning God and his creation' are added.[108] Since it is in chapter 28 that Anselm first considers aspects of the supreme principle that are not actually mentioned in chapter 1, the arguments being thereafter more explicitly trinitarian in character, it is reasonable to consider the section beginning in chapter 28 as constituting a new development. This will correspond to the part of the programme outlined in chapter 1 with the words 'and many other things . . .'[109]

Chapters 28–38 of the *Monologion* can be considered as a unit in which Anselm employs a central epistemological analogy to demonstrate how a supreme spirit is identifiable with the 'speaking' mentioned earlier in the text. Here, he starts from the genuine philosophical problem: if this spirit is equivalent to the speaking,[110] then it must embrace the formal causes of all created things;[111] but if the spirit contains the formal causes of all created

106 *Monol.* 65 (S 1 76.24–77.3).
107 See pp. 260f.
108 *Monol.* 1 (S 1 13.8–9): 'aliaque perplura . . . de deo sive de eius creatura'. Cf. n. 76.
109 Anselm achieves the transition between the earlier and later sets of arguments by focusing on the notion of spirit, since this term, although having a trinitarian connotation, is also well-established in the philosophical tradition.
110 *Monol.* 29 (S 1 47.4–48.5).
111 *Ibid.* 30f (S 1 48.8f) Throughout this discussion, the formal causes are termed 'words (*verba*)', the unity of those formal causes 'the word (*verbum*)' or 'the speaking (*locutio*)'.

things, then it must be multiple and not unitary;[112] but the spirit has already been demonstrated to be unitary.[113] To this difficulty Anselm proposes two solutions: (i) although created things are similar to the first principle, since this relation cannot be reversed, their differentiation among themselves does not necessitate a corresponding situation in the higher sphere;[114] and (ii) the causes of various created things do not really belong to such things themselves but to the first principle, and so their status is commensurate not with the differentiation of the former but with the unity of the latter.[115]

The exposition of both the problem and its solutions is accompanied by the drawing of various analogies from the human mind to the supreme spirit,[116] and these analogies are brought into the centre of the discussions in the next two main sections of the text. Thus, in chapters 39–48 the relation between the supreme spirit and its speaking is indicated to be causal by invoking the analogy of a father's begetting of a son,[117] but to be non-subordinative by introducing that of the human memory's understanding of its own contents.[118] This means that terms like power, truth, justice, and wisdom can be more correctly applied to the son than to the father,[119] although terms in the form x-*in-itself* are affirmed with equal validity of father and son.[120] In chapters 49–61 the relation between the supreme spirit and its speaking is shown to be reciprocal by using the analogy of a lover's relation to his beloved,[121] this relation itself being as great as the things related and therefore identifiable with them.[122] Furthermore, the relation between the supreme spirit, its speaking, and their love can be revealed as causal by appealing to the analogy of a father and son breathing their mutual

112 *Ibid.* 32 (S I 50.16f), 33 (S I 51.21–52.7) etc.
113 *Ibid.* 29 (S I 47.4–48.5).
114 *Ibid.* 31 (S I 49.1) – 32 (S I 50.18).
115 *Ibid.* 33 (S I 51.21–52.1), 33 (S I 52.29–53.12), 34 (S I 53.15–54.3), and 35 (S I 54.6–13). On Anselm's understanding of divine formal causality see P. Mazzarella, 'L'esemplarismo in Anselmo d'Aosta e in Bonaventura da Bagnoregio', *Analecta Anselmiana* II (1969) 145–64; and E. M. Porcelloni, 'Le problème de la dérivation du monde à partir de Dieu chez Scot Erigène et chez saint Anselme', *Analecta Anselmiana* II (1970) 195–208.
116 These analogies are (i) From the human mind's knowledge of the supreme, the supreme spirit's eternal knowledge at *Monol.* 32 (S I 51.7–12); (ii) From the human mind's self-knowledge, the supreme spirit's consubstantiality with its word at *ibid.* 33 (S I 51.21) – 35 (S I 54.13) and 37 (S I 55.14–25); and (iii) From the human mind's levels of knowledge, the supreme spirit's creative knowledge at *ibid.* 36 (S I 54.16–55.10).
117 *Ibid.* 39 (S I 57.3) – 42 (S I 59.12).
118 *Ibid.* 47 (S I 63.4–7).
119 *Ibid.* 45 (S I 61.28) – 46 (S I 62.26).
120 *Ibid.* 44 (S I 60.14–61.24).
121 *Ibid.* 49f (S I 64.16f)
122 *Ibid.* 52 (S I 65.21) – 53 (S I 66.13).

love,[123] but as non-subordinative by introducing that of the human memory's understanding and love of its own contents.[124] Throughout these arguments there is continuous recourse to Augustinian models, the general progression from discussing the relation of father and son to considering that of father, son, and love following the argument of *De trinitate* xv,[125] the analogies drawn from psychological analysis parallelling those contained in Books xv and viii-x of the same work,[126] and the exemplarist theory of creation reflecting numerous statements of Augustine's there and elsewhere.

The later part of the *Monologion* elaborates an explicitly trinitarian account of the supreme principle, and its philosophical method may be contrasted with that of the previous section. In the first place, the argument strives to understand that principle not through things subsequent to it in general but through the most excellent part of the created world: the human mind. Although the characterization of the first principle not only as spirit, father, and son but also as truth, wisdom, and self-sufficiency involves the transfer of attributes from the created world as a whole, the more philosophical accounts of that principle as word, memory, understanding, and love are analogies of entirely psychological origin.[127] Secondly, the later section of the work endeavours to understand the supreme principle using a series of dialectical arguments in relation to an object which has the special character of being itself the subject of dialectical activity. In short, it is through an investigation of what has earlier been termed the 'psychological *ratio*' that we come to possess – to the extent that this is possible – some intimation of the 'theological' *ratio*' defined above.[128]

Ratio *in the* Proslogion

In the preface to the *Proslogion*, Anselm defines the subject-matter of his work by comparing it with that of the previous treatise. Whereas the earlier

123 *Ibid.* 54 (S I 66.17) – 57 (S I 69.13). There is an etymological connection between 'spirit (*spiritus*)' and 'to breathe (*spirare*)'.

124 *Ibid.* 51 (S I 65.13–18) and 59 (S I 70.3–17). On Anselm's trinitarian theories see R. Perino, *La dottrina trinitaria di S. Anselmo nel quadro del suo metodo teologico e del suo concetto di Dio* (Rome 1952); M. Schmaus, 'Die metaphysisch-psychologische Lehre über den Heiligen Geist im Monologion Anselms von Canterbury', in *Sola ratione. Anselm-Studien für F. S. Schmitt zum 75. Geburtstag*, ed. H. Kohlenberger (Stuttgart 1970), pp. 189–219; H. Kohlenberger, 'Konsequenzen und Inkonsequenzen der Trinitätslehre in Anselms Monologion', *Analecta Anselmiana* v (1973) 149–78; and G. R. Evans, 'St. Anselm's Images of Trinity', *Journal of Theological Studies* xxvii (1976) 46–57.

125 Augustine: *De trin.* xv 10 17f (CC 50A, 483f) deals with father and son; *ibid.* xv 17 27f (CC 50A, 501f) with love.

126 See especially Augustine: *De trin.* viii 8 12 f (CC 50, 286f)

127 See nn. 116, 118, and 124.

128 See pp. 260f.

was a meditation on the reason of faith consisting of an 'arrangement of many interlinked arguments (*multorum concatenatione contextum argumentorum*)',[129] the later treatise comprises 'a single argument which alone, requiring no other than itself to prove itself, is enough to demonstrate (*unum argumentum, quod nullo alio ad se probandum quam se solo indigeret, et solum ad astruendum ... sufficeret*)' various things about the nature of God.[130] However, both works have the same general aim: to bring the human mind also to understand what it believes about the divinity.

Precisely what is proved regarding God's nature by the single argument is carefully stated in the preface: with its aid we can demonstrate 'that God truly exists, that he is the supreme good which needs no other but which all other things need in order to be and to be well, and that he is whatever we believe regarding the divine substance'.[131] The different results are indeed achieved in this order within the main body of Anselm's text, although not all these topics receive an equally detailed treatment at his hands.[132] Thus, in chapters 2–4 it is demonstrated that God truly exists, in the fifth chapter that he is self-sufficient creator of all things from nothing, and in the remaining chapters that he possesses certain other attributes.

The relationship between the *Monologion* and the *Proslogion* is perhaps the crucial factor in understanding the purpose and method of the later work, a relationship which consists of important similarities between the two combined with equally revealing differences. A point of similarity is that both treatises underline the fact that God's nature is ultimately unknowable to man and that, just as the earlier work emphasizes the necessity of achieving knowledge of the supreme principle either through created things in general or through the human mind in particular,[133] so does the later reiterate the inaccessibility of God and the indirectness of any perception of his nature. This feature of the *Proslogion* is revealed in Anselm's statements that God is something greater than can be thought[134] and, using the traditional analogy between God and the mind and the sun and the eye, that one cannot look upon the sun itself but only upon other things reflecting its

129 On the reason of faith in the *Monologion* see p. 258.

130 *Prosl.* pr. (S I 93.2–10). It is interesting that the term 'God (*deus*)' is applied to the first principle from the beginning of the *Proslogion*. The first principle was described more abstractly throughout the argument of the *Monologion*, the term 'God' appearing only in the introductory and concluding remarks.

131 *Ibid.* pr. (S I 93.7–9): 'quia deus vere est, et quia est summum bonum nullo alio indigens, et quo omnia indigent ut sint et ut bene sint, et quaecumque de divina credimus substantia'.

132 Cf. p. 274.

133 Cf. pp. 263f.

134 *Prosl.* 15 (S I 112.14–17).

light.[135] If the two works agree in these epistemological assumptions, then both their extended discussions of the divine attributes must be interpreted in the same way: as attempts to grasp the highest nature as it manifests itself in things subsequent to it.[136]

Among points of difference is the relationship to sources, for, although the earlier treatise appeals explicitly to Augustine as an authority on the matters under discussion,[137] the later one adopts what was to become the standard Anselmian approach in avoiding all direct reference to literary forerunners. It seems clear that this silence is a deliberate strategy designed to show that the central argument of the *Proslogion* is totally independent of Scripture, in that (i) it has appeared in secular writers not normally meriting citation in a devotional text,[138] and (ii) it has certain claims to being self-evident rather than justified by any authority.[139] This independence represents the reason of faith in its boldest form.

Another point of difference is the multiplicity or unity of argument, since, whereas the earlier work relies on a number of interconnected arguments to prove the theses under discussion,[140] the later one attempts to discover a single argument capable of achieving the same results. Unfortunately, Anselm does not make absolutely clear what this single argument is and, although most modern scholars have interpreted this as the definition of God as that than which a greater cannot be thought,[141] it is obvious that this is only used in proving the first of the theses whose discussion is promised in the preface to the *Proslogion* and not the whole set. So perhaps some more fundamental element in the text remains to be identified.

These similarities and differences in their turn illuminate the notion of reason contained in the later treatise. For example, it is easy to see that the first part of the *Monologion* and the second part of the *Proslogion*, which are concerned with the problem of divine attributes, both lead the reader from

135 *Ibid.* 16 (S I 112.20–7).
136 *Ibid.* 17 (S I 113.8–15) illustrates our perception of the divine attributes by saying that the soul listens but does not hear the divine harmony, smells but does not perceive the divine fragrance, etc., and that God has these attributes in an 'ineffable (*ineffabilis*)' manner but has given them to created things in a 'sensible (*sensibilis*)' one. Anselm's thesis is that God's nature can only be described in terms of our intellectual or (as here) sensible perception of created things. The doctrine of spiritual senses stems ultimately from Origen and was known to Anselm through Augustine, *Conf.* x 6 (CSEL 33, 231.14f), and numerous passages in Gregory the Great's *Moralia*.
137 Cf. p. 262.
138 The 'secular' character of this argument will be discussed on pp. 273f.
139 The self-evident character of the argument is explicitly noted in Anselm's preface. See the text cited on p. 271.
140 Cf. pp. 263f.
141 *Prosl.* 2 (S I 101–5).

the sense of reason which has been categorized as logical to that which was termed ontological.[142] On the other hand, the second part of the *Monologion* alone deals with those senses of reason which have been classified as psychological and theological respectively, while the first part of the *Proslogion* alone treats that which was called epistemological. In fact, from these two texts taken together we can obtain illustrations of every interpretation of reason that appears in Anselm's writings.

That the *Proslogion* avoids all reference to sources is consistent with its method of arguing without appeal to Scripture. If the sources of its premisses are not given, it is because these are found in all kinds of authors both sacred and secular; and if the sources of its premisses are equally sacred and secular, it is because they are known independently of revelation. This non-scriptural character is especially apparent in the case of the earlier part of the text, for here both the famous premiss that God is 'something than which nothing greater can be thought *(aliquid quo nihil maius cogitari possit)*'[143] and the suggestion that this premiss is self-evident[144] have their roots equally in Christian and pagan philosophical literature. The premiss occurs expressed in varying phraseology in Augustine's *De moribus ecclesiae catholicae et de moribus Manichaeorum,*[145] *De libero arbitrio,*[146] *De diversis quaestionibus LXXXIII,*[147] *De vera religione,*[148] *Confessiones,*[149] and *De doctrina christiana,*[150] and Boethius' *De consolatione Philosophiae*[151] within Christian literature; and in Cicero's *De natura deorum,*[152] and Seneca's *Naturales quaestiones*[153] within the

142 For the division of the two texts see p. 265 n. 77, p. 268 n. 109, and p. 277.
143 *Prosl.* 2 (S I 101.5).
144 See the passage cited on p. 271.
145 Augustine, *De mor. eccl. cath. et Manich.* II 11 24 (P.L. 32, 1355) 'than which nothing better is able to be or be thought *(quo esse aut cogitari melius nihil possit)*'. Cf. *ibid.* I 3 5 (P.L. 32, 1312), I 16 29 (P.L. 32, 1323–4), and II 1 1 (P.L. 32, 1345).
146 Augustine, *De lib arb.* II 6 14 (CC 29, 246–7).
147 Augustine, *De div. quaest. LXXXIII* 18 (CC 44A, 23) and 28 (CC 44A, 35).
148 Augustine, *De vera relig.* 39 72 (CC 32, 234).
149 Augustine, *Conf.* VII 4 (CSEL 33, 145.11–15).
150 Augustine, *De doctr. chr.* I 7 7 (CC 32, 10).
151 Boethius, *De consol. philos.* III, pr. 10 57–8.
152 Cicero, *De nat. deor.* II 77.
153 Seneca, *Nat. quaest.* I, pr. 13: 'than which nothing greater can be thought *(qua nihil maius cogitari potest)*'. It is impossible to say which of these Christian and pagan texts influenced Anselm's own formulation. The precise wording of the premiss at *Prosl.* 2 (S I 101.5) is closest to Seneca: *Nat. quaest.* I, pr. 13. However, the substitution of 'better *(melius)*' for 'greater *(maius)*' at *Prosl.* 3 (S I 103.5) and the contrast of 'non-being *(non esse)*' and 'conceived as non-being *(cogitari non esse)*' at *ibid.* 2 (S I 101.3f) and 3 (S I 102.6f) recalls Augustine, *De mor. eccl. cath. et Manich.* II 11 24 (P.L. 32, 1355). For discussion of the literary sources of Anselm's premiss see J. Vergnes, 'Les sources de l'argument de Saint Anselme', *Revue des Sciences Religieuses* IV (1924) 576–9; T. A. Audet, 'Une source augustinienne de l'argument de saint Anselme', in *Etienne Gilson, philosophe de la Chrétienté,* ed. J. Maritain *et al.* (Paris 1949), pp. 105–42; P. Faggiotto, 'La fonte platonica dell' argumento ontologico

pagan tradition. The notion that certain kinds of premiss are self-evident is similarly found among Christian writers in Boethius' *De hebdomadibus*,[154] where the example given is 'if equals are taken from equals the remainders are equal'; and among pagan authors in Cicero's *Tusculanae disputationes*,[155] where one of the examples is 'that fortitude is a disposition of the soul enduring vicissitudes in obedience to the highest law'. The view that the premiss defining the nature of God can be placed in the self-evident category is possibly an element which Anselm believed to be his own innovation,[156] although even this has an antecedent in Cicero's *De natura deorum*, where the notion that God surpasses all things is interpreted as a 'preconception' in the Stoic technical sense.[157] At all events, the fact that the premiss that God is 'something than which nothing greater can be thought', as well as its interpretation as self-evident, spring from the combination of Christian and non-Christian philosophical traditions, is enough to guarantee that conclusions drawn from it represent confirmations of the faith quite independent of the faith.

The earlier part of the *Proslogion* sets out to demonstrate that God exists even to the satisfaction of the Fool mentioned in Psalm 13, who denied this proposition.[158] Reduced to its barest essentials, this part consists of three arguments: (i) In chapter 2 the self-evident premiss that God is 'something than which nothing greater can be thought' is combined with a second premiss, that it is greater to exist (a) in both reality and thought than (b) simply in thought,[159] to yield the conclusion that God must exist (a) in both reality and thought.[160] (ii) In chapter 3 the self-evident premiss that God is

---

di Anselmo d'Aosta', *Rivista di Filosofia Neoscolastica* XLVI (1954) 493–5; and K. D. Nothdurft, *Studien zum Einfluss Senecas auf die Philosophie und Theologie des zwölften Jahrhunderts* (Leiden–Cologne 1963), pp. 192–7.

154 Boethius, *De hebd.* 18–27: 'A common notion of the mind (*communis animi conceptio*)'. These are classified into (i) those intelligible to all men and (ii) those intelligible to the educated.

155 Cicero, *Tusc. disp.* IV 53 'common notions (*communes notiones*)'. Cicero views all such notions as innate in the human mind. Cf. Cicero, *Topic.* 31.

156 See *Prosl.* pr. (S 193.2f), where the discovery of the single argument is described as a kind of illumination.

157 Cicero, *De nat. deor.* II 45 describes our idea that 'there is nothing more outstanding than God (*nihil eo sit praestantius*)' as 'our preconception and notion (*praesensio notioque nostra*)'.

158 The reference to the Fool underlines the fact that Anselm's argument is not designed simply to strengthen the believer's faith but to furnish rational proof independent of revelation. See p. 258.

159 *Prosl.* 2 (S I 101.16–17) 'exist in thought alone . . . exist also in reality, which is greater (*in solo intellectu esse . . . esse et in re, quod maius est*)'. Anselm seems to hold this premiss also as self-evident, since he demonstrates it neither here nor elsewhere.

160 *Prosl.* 2 (S I 102.2–3). On the background to the notion that God is defined by superiority see A. Koyré, *L'idée de Dieu dans la philosophie de saint Anselme* (Paris 1923), pp. 195f; and G. Mainberger, *Die Seinsstufung als Methode und Metaphysik. Untersuchungen über 'Mehr und*

'something than which nothing greater can be thought' is combined with a further premiss that (a) that which exists and cannot be thought not to exist is greater than (b) that which exists and can be thought not to exist,[161] to yield the conclusion that God is (a) that which exists and cannot be thought not to exist.[162] (iii) Chapter 4 raises the question how it is possible that the Fool could deny the existence of God, given the conclusion of chapter 3. The answer is that he can deny the proposition if he thinks of 'God' simply as a word, but not if he thinks of the object to which the word refers.[163]

It is clearly impossible to take account of the numerous scholarly controversies surrounding the interpretation of these three chapters,[164] although a few observations are perhaps useful at this point regarding Anselm's philosophical aims and method. First, it is obvious that the arguments are concerned with the being of God (that he exists) rather than his determinate being (his manner of existence), and therefore have a purpose which diverges from that of the later part of the *Proslogion* and of the *Monologion* as a whole. This distinction between questions regarding something's being and something's determinate being had been traditional since the time of Aristotle,[165] and the medieval writer reveals his awareness of its applicability to the divine nature in at least one passage.[166] In the second place, it follows that the first part of the *Proslogion* is concerned with understanding God in himself and not through his creature, and therefore again has a purpose contrasting with that of the other Anselmian discussions. The fact that the opening chapters have

Weniger' als Grundlage zu einem möglichen Gottesbeweis bei Platon und Aristoteles (Fribourg 1959).

161 *Prosl.* 3 (S I 102.6–8): 'For something can be thought to exist which cannot be thought not to exist. This is greater than that which can be thought not to exist (*nam potest cogitari esse aliquid, quod non possit cogitari non esse; quod maius est quam quod non esse cogitari potest*).' Anselm seems to hold this as yet another self-evident premiss.

162 *Ibid.* 3 (S I 102.8–103.2).

163 *Ibid.* 4 (S I 103.18–20): 'the term which signifies it . . . that which is the thing itself (*vox eam significans . . . id ipsum quod res est*)'.

164 Much of this literature approaches Anselm in such an anachronistic way that it is of little value to the serious student of eleventh- and twelfth-century thought. However, in recent years renewed attention has been given to the question of examining the text of the *Proslogion* itself in its genuine historical setting. For summary and evaluation of the various modern interpretations see A. C. McGill, 'Recent Discussions of Anselm's Argument', in *The Many-Faced Argument*, ed. J. Hick and A. C. McGill (New York 1967), pp. 33–110; W. L. Gombocz, 'Zu neueren Beiträgen zur Interpretation von Anselms Proslogion', *Salzburger Jahrbuch für Philosophie* xx (1975) 131–5; and Colish 1983, pp. 55–63.

165 See Aristotle, *Anal. post.* I 1 71A11–17. Anselm probably learned to make this distinction from texts like Augustine, *De trin.* VII 5 10 (CC 50, 260–1), where God's 'being (*essentia*)' is contrasted with his 'substance (*substantia*)'.

166 *Prosl.* 2 (S I 101.3–4) distinguishes between understanding of God 'that he is, as we believe (*esse sicut credimus*)' and 'that he is what we believe him to be (*hoc esse quod credimus*)'. This distinction corresponds to an important structural division in the text itself.

such a character makes them unique not only in their argumentative structure but also in their revelatory potential.[167] Finally, it is worth reiterating that the arguments are fashioned entirely from non-scriptural (and self-evident) premisses: in other words they are delineated in terms of the 'epistemological *ratio*' defined earlier.[168]

That the *Proslogion* is described as an elaboration of a single argument seems a little puzzling in view of the obvious multiplicity of arguments even in the early chapters. The most common interpretation of Anselm's statement is to maintain that the premiss defining God as 'something than which nothing greater can be thought' constitutes this single argument, yet the premiss on its own cannot adequately explain the structure of the opening chapters, still less that of the treatise as a whole.[169] As a means of unifying the earlier and later parts of the text, I would therefore suggest that underlying its discussions is a further unstated premiss: 'when two terms are compared as greater and lesser, then God corresponds to the greater'. In the earlier part of the work this premiss has appeared with the two terms understood as two predicates which are *different* from one another (x and y): for example, 'existing in both reality and thought' (x) and 'existing simply in thought' (y), or 'existing in such a way that its non-existence is unthinkable' (x) and 'existing in such a way that its non-existence is thinkable' (y).[170] In the later part of the text the same unstated premiss will appear this time with the two terms understood as two predicates which are *contradictory* to one another (x and non-x): for example, 'omnipotent' (x) and 'not omnipotent' (non-x), or 'transcending spatio-temporal limitation' (x) and 'not transcending spatio-temporal limitation' (non-x).[171] Of course, since the actual character of these pairs of terms varies considerably according to context, my classification of

---

167 It is debatable whether the *Monologion* also contains arguments of this kind. Certainly its opening discussion leads to the conclusion that there is a transcendent source of the being, goodness, and greatness in created things. See pp. 265f. Yet Anselm later concludes that even speaking of God as 'being' is really to conceive only things subsequent to his nature. See p. 268. It therefore seems that the finely-tuned distinction between the being and the determinate being of the first principle is peculiar to the *Proslogion*.

168 See pp. 260f.

169 Evans 1978, pp. 46–8, has rightly drawn attention to this fact. She suggests for the underlying premiss: 'God is in some sense "more than" whatever we can conceive as a good.' This is perhaps not totally adequate as a formulation, although it definitely points in the right direction.

170 At *Prosl.* 15 (S I 112.14–17) a similar pair of terms is utilized: 'something greater than can be thought' (x) and 'something than which a greater cannot be thought' (y). Cf. *ibid.* 9 (S I 107.6–11) and 11 (S I 109.10–14).

171 At *ibid.* 18 (S I 114.17–24) a similar pair of terms is implied: 'indivisible into parts' (x) and 'divisible into parts' (y). Cf. *ibid.* 6f (S I 104.20f) and 11 (S I 110.1–3).

the two basic forms in which the underlying premiss appears is only a rough one.[172] However, the unstated premiss itself is perhaps the only conceptual device by which the statement that the whole work elaborates a single argument – proving that God exists *and* that he possesses definite attributes – can be given a literal meaning.

The later part of the *Proslogion* is therefore linked with the earlier through the recurrence of the underlying premiss in various guises. However, the later section also takes a new direction in turning, in accordance with the programme outlined in the preface,[173] from the question of God's existence to that of his attributes. Thus, chapters 5–13 prove that he is self-sufficient, perceptive, omnipotent, merciful, just, impassible, and not spatio-temporal, using the premiss that he is 'whatever it is better to be than not to be'.[174] At chapter 14 a digression of a more epistemological character begins by emphasizing that all the attributes so far deduced cannot describe the supreme principle in itself, which remains inaccessible.[175] However, a greater comprehension can be achieved by reinterpreting the attributes in a transcendent manner[176] – that God is something greater than can be thought instead of something than which a greater cannot be thought;[177] that he is beauty, harmony, fragrance, life, wisdom, truth, goodness, blessedness, and eternity ineffably[178] – and in a manner consistent with his indivisibility.[179] Chapters 19–21 return to the notion that God is not spatio-temporal, with a detailed examination of the omnipresence in created things which this concept implies.[180] Finally, chapter 22 shows that this principle which is

---

172 Basically, the difference between the two versions of the premiss lies in the degree of complexity in its terms. In one case, they represent simple contradictories, but in the other, they exhibit more varied relations.

173 See p. 271.

174 The basic scheme for this section is:
        self-sufficiency (ch. 5)
        perceptiveness (= sensibility) (chs. 6, 11)
        omnipotence (chs. 6–7, 11)
        mercy (chs. 6, 8–9, 11)
        justice (chs. 9–11)
        impassibility (chs. 6, 11)
        non-spatiality/atemporality (ch. 13)
    An additional set of attributes – life, wisdom, and goodness – occurs in ch. 12 and is presumably justified by appealing to the same premiss.

175 *Prosl.* 14 (S I 111.8f)

176 *Ibid.* 17 (S I 113.13). Cf. *ibid.* 16 (S I 112.20–113.4).

177 *Ibid.* 15 (S I 112.14–17).

178 *Ibid.* 17 (S I 113.8) – 18 (S I 115.4).

179 *Ibid.* 18 (S I 114.22–4).

180 *Ibid.* 19f (S I 115.7f)

completely indivisible in relation to space and time is what exists in the proper and absolute sense.[181]

It is striking how the meagreness of scholarship devoted to these later chapters contrasts with the enormous activity expended on the beginning of the text, and so even such brief comments regarding their philosophical importance as have been ventured may be considered as redressing a balance. In conclusion, we should perhaps stress that the arguments contained in this part of the text are concerned primarily with God's determinate being (his manner of existence), and as such discharge a function similar to that of the first part of the *Monologion*; indeed they systematize some of the doctrine of the earlier work.[182] The arguments are therefore directed towards understanding God through the created world in general and, as in the case of Anselm's earlier treatise, towards the disclosure of the 'ontological *ratio*' through the exercise of its 'logical' correlate.[183]

181 The discussion of the range, transcendence, and unity of divine attributes represents a more systematic development of material in the *Monologion*. See especially *Monol.* 15 (S 1 28.3) – 17 (S 1 32.4). The ultimate literary sources of these ideas – which are of course held to be deducible from self-evident premisses – have already been discussed. See pp. 265–8.
182 Cf. pp. 265–7.
183 Cf. pp. 261f.

10

PETER ABELARD

D. E. LUSCOMBE

Peter Abelard received his early education in arts from Roscelin of Compiègne in the schools of Loches or Tours around the mid or late 1090s. He probably also studied at Angers, and he was taught by a *magister V.*, who may be Ulger or Vasletus.[1] He finally arrived at the most important centre for the study of dialectic, which was Paris;[2] here he sat at the feet of William of Champeaux. The sharpness of his attacks on William's realism is partly to be explained by his earlier nominalist training under Roscelin. From Abelard's autobiography, his *Historia calamitatum*, we know of his struggles to establish himself as a teacher at Corbeil (1102), at Melun (*ca.* 1104), and at Paris. We learn as well of his espousal of the study of theology, for the sake of which he went to the school of Anselm in Laon after 1113. How much of Abelard's logical writing was done before and how much after this turn to theology is far from certain. He presumably developed his commentaries on logic while teaching at the cathedral school of Paris from *ca.* 1116, at least until his affair with Heloise disrupted his life. His theological writings, on the other hand, were all prepared after his visit to Laon. They are important to an understanding of Abelard as a philosopher. It was on account of his application of dialectic to the study of theology that Abelard was condemned by a Church council held at Soissons in 1121. For the next few years Abelard, who was now a monk, attempted to live the life of a philosopher-hermit. His autobiography does not extend beyond the years when he was Abbot of St Gildas de Rhuys in Brittany (*ca.* 1127 – *ca.* 1131), but we know from John of Salisbury, who heard Abelard teaching dialectic on the Mont Sainte-Geneviève in 1136, that he

---

1 Petrus Abaelardus, *Dialectica*, ed. L. M. de Rijk (2nd ed., Assen 1970), Introduction, pp. xx–xxi (Ulger); M. T. Beonio-Brocchieri Fumagalli, *The Logic of Peter Abelard* (Dordrecht 1969), pp. 38–9 (Vasletus).
2 '... diversas disputando perambulans provincias, ubicunque huius artis vigere studium audieram, peripateticorum emulator factus sum ... Perveni tandem Parisius, ubi jam maxime disciplina hec florere consueverat, ad Guillhelmum scilicet Campellensem preceptorem meum in hoc tunc magisterio re et fama precipuum': Abelard, *Historia calamitatum*, ed. J. Monfrin (2nd ed., Paris 1962), lines 28–34.

was still active as a logician.[3] He taught in Paris again in 1140. Until then he remained busy writing works of theology, among them works to guide the nuns of the convent of the Paraclete of which Heloise was now abbess. The culmination of decades of controversy over Abelard's teaching of theology occurred in 1140, when he was again condemned for heresy and was excommunicated by Pope Innocent II.

Abelard as a logician

Abelard's logical writings are concerned with seven basic texts: the *Isagoge* of Porphyry; the *Categories* and *De interpretatione* of Aristotle; and the *De syllogismo categorico*, *De syllogismo hypothetico*, *De differentiis topicis* and *De divisione* of Boethius. Only to a limited degree did Abelard use the *Prior Analytics* and *Sophistici elenchi* of Aristotle. Not without reason was he called the Peripatetic from Le Pallet, his birthplace (*Peripateticus Palatinus*).

M. Dal Pra has linked to Abelard's early teaching career a series of brief glosses which Abelard may have written between 1102/5 and 1112/14 and which may be identical with those Abelard called *Introductiones parvulorum*, or introductions for beginners in the study of logic.[4] They are found in a Paris manuscript, Bibliothèque Nationale lat. 13368, fols. 128r–167v, and include glosses on the *Isagoge* (although the final quarter of the work is lost), on the *Categories* (but only a fifth of the text has survived), on the *De interpretatione* (almost complete), and on the *De divisione*. Probably there were once also glosses on the *De syllogismo categorico* and *De syllogismo hypothetico*, but these do not survive. Since Abelard's purpose in these glosses is to help beginners to become acquainted with the textbooks of logic, he rarely betrays elements of his own teaching, but from such of the prefaces as survive it would appear that when Abelard expresses himself on the nature of the subject he hovers between regarding logic as a study of language and regarding language as being related to the things which it serves to express.

In another series of commentaries Abelard provides much more developed glosses on the ancient textbooks of logic. Their principal editor, B. Geyer, dated their composition to the years before 1120 and viewed them as parts of a single work, the *Logica 'Ingredientibus'* – *Ingredientibus* being the opening

3 '... cum primum adolescens admodum studiorum causa migrassem in Gallias, anno altero postquam illustris rex Anglorum Henricus, Leo iustitie, rebus excessit humanis, contuli me ad Peripateticum Palatinum, qui tunc in monte sancte Genovefe claris doctor et admirabilis omnibus presidebat': John of Salisbury, *Metalogicon* II 10, ed. C. C. J. Webb (Oxford 1929), pp. 77.31–78.4; see also p. 78.6–7.
4 Pietro Abelardo, *Scritti filosofici*, ed. M. Dal Pra (Rome–Milan 1954).

word.[5] These glosses concern the *Isagoge*, the *Categories* and the *De interpretatione*. Originally perhaps they also included glosses on hypothetical propositions, but these have not survived. The glosses are sometimes known as the 'Milan glosses', since they are mostly found in a Milan manuscript, Biblioteca Ambrosiana M 63 sup., but this description is a little misleading, since Dal Pra has shown that the glosses on the *De differentiis topicis* which are found in Paris, Bibliothèque Nationale lat. 7493 also belong to the '*Ingredientibus*' series.[6] Furthermore, the complete text of the commentary on the *De interpretatione* is preserved only in Berlin, Preussischer Kulturbesitz Lat. Fol. 624, fols. 97r–146r; the last section of the Milan copy of this text (fols. 71r b–72r b) contains a spurious commentary which is not by Abelard.[7] The '*Ingredientibus*' glosses are roughly three times as long as the *Introductiones parvulorum*; in addition to providing fuller literal glosses, Abelard often goes beyond his source to pursue problems which have occurred to him or which were currently under debate by contemporary logicians. At one point, for example, Abelard refers to the teaching of William of Champeaux: *praeceptor* (or *praecessor*) *noster Willelmus eiusque sequaces*.[8] The Milan glosses on Porphyry underwent revision, and of this revision – which Geyer dates before 1125, and which he saw as the first part of a new *Logica 'Nostrorum petitioni sociorum'* – there survive only the glosses on the *Isagoge*, which are contained in a single manuscript at Lunel, Bibliothèque municipale 6.[9]

Abelard also wrote a major, independent, and unified treatise of logic which was free of the gloss form, although it nonetheless uses fully the seven ancient textbooks of Aristotle, Porphyry, and Boethius. The only known

5 Peter Abaelard, *Philosophische Schriften* I, ed. B. Geyer, BGPTM XXI.1–3 (Münster i.W. 1919–27).
6 Dal Pra 1954, pp. xxvi–xxxvii. Dal Pra has edited these glosses 1954, pp. 205–330.
7 See L. Minio-Paluello, *Twelfth-Century Logic. Texts and Studies II. Abaelardiana Inedita. 1. Super Periermenias XII-XIV. 2. Sententie secundum M. Petrum* (Rome 1958). The spurious section in the Milan MS was edited by Geyer 1919–27, pp. 497.20–503.28. Minio-Paluello corrects and completes Geyer's edition.
8 Dal Pra 1954, p. 271.38–9. Evidence for William's teaching in logic is discussed by N. J. Green-Pedersen, 'William of Champeaux on Boethius' Topics according to Orleans Bibl. Mun. 266', *CIMAGL* XIII (1974) 13–30. See also two tracts edited by L. M. de Rijk, *Logica Modernorum* (2 vols., Assen 1962, 1967) II.1 130–9 (*Introductiones secundum Wilgelmum*) and pp. 139–45. Some *sententiae* of theology written by William have been edited by O. Lottin, *Psychologie et morale aux XIIe et XIIIe siècles* V (Gembloux 1959) 189–227. On some aspects of Abelard's handling of William's teaching and on his own changes of viewpoint see N. J. Green-Pedersen 'The Doctrine of "Maxima Propositio" and "Locus Differentia" in Commentaries from the 12th Century on Boethius' "Topics"', *Studia Mediewistyczne* XVIII (1977) 125–63.
9 Peter Abaelard, *Philosophische Schriften* II, ed. B. Geyer, BGPTM XXI.4 (Münster i. W. 1933, 2nd ed. 1973). Geyer's *Untersuchungen* into the texts he edited are to be found here on pp. 589–633, with *Ergänzungen* (1973) on pp. vi–viii.

manuscript of this work, the *Dialectica*, is in Paris, Bibliothèque Nationale lat. 14614, but it lacks both the beginning and the end of the text. The editor, L. M. de Rijk, dates the composition of the final revision of the *Dialectica* to Abelard's last years.[10]

Abelard may have written a work called *Rhetorica* and one called *Grammatica*, but neither has been identified in any manuscript.[11] *Sentences* containing an analysis of a paralogism and of the use of *totum* have been tentatively ascribed to him and printed under his name.[12] Claims have been put forward for Abelard as author of other works of logic which betray many similarities with his known writings and teachings. These include a short treatise *De intellectibus*[13] and another gloss on the *Isagoge* known as *Secundum vocales*.[14]

The use of logic

In his writings and commentaries on logic Abelard presents himself as an expositor of ancient logic. He nonetheless provides interpretations and emphases that are his own. He explores with formidable energy and perceptiveness the tensions he found in the traditional texts. In much of his writing he advances chains of argument and of counter-argument, and it is not always possible to perceive his solution to problems so much as his discovery of further difficulties and opportunities that arise from past and contemporary theories.

Like Cicero and Boethius, Abelard defines the art of logic or dialectic (he

---

10 De Rijk 1970, pp. xxi–xxiii. The dating of the supposed versions of the *Dialectica* is much debated. See further E. M. Buytaert in his general introduction to Abelard's *Opera theologica* I, CC, CM XI (Turnhout 1969), p. xxv n. 45. C. Mews now suggests *ca.* 1117: 'On Dating the Works of Peter Abelard', *AHDLMA* LII (1985) 73–134, at pp. 95–104.

11 Buytaert 1969, p. xxi; Mews 1985, pp. 92–3.

12 *Secundum Magistrum Petrum Sententie*, ed. Minio-Paluello 1958. These *Sentences* may have been a part of a lost work on fallacies to which Abelard refers in his *Dialectica*, ed. de Rijk 1970, p. 448.3–4 (*primus Fantasiarum nostrarum liber*). See L. M. de Rijk, *Logica Modernorum* I (Assen 1962), 109–12.

13 Ed. L. U. Ulivi, *La psicologia di Abelardo e il 'Tractatus de Intellectibus'* (Rome 1976); also *Petri Abaelardi Opera*, ed. V. Cousin, II (Paris 1859) 733–53. Both these editors favour the attribution of the treatise to Abelard; Ulivi examines the possibility very thoroughly.

14 *Glossae super librum Porphyrii secundum vocales*, ed. C. Ottaviano, *Un opuscolo di Abelardo*, Testi medioevali inediti, Fontes Ambrosiani III (Florence 1933), pp. 106–207. Extracts were edited by Geyer 1973, pp. 581–8. Geyer (pp. 610–12) notes the close similarities between these Glosses and those found in Abelard's *Logica*, but concludes that they are a compilation by a follower of Abelard. C. J. Mews presents new arguments in favour of Abelard's authorship in 'A Neglected Gloss on the "Isagoge" by Peter Abelard', *Freiburger Zeitschrift für Philosophie und Theologie* XXXI (1984) 35–55. The gloss 'Secundum vocales' is found in the same Milan MS which contains the '*Ingredientibus*' glosses (on fols. 72v–81v).

uses both terms indifferently) as the art of judging and distinguishing valid arguments from invalid ones in any branch of knowledge, and also of explaining why they are valid or not.[15] A conclusive argument may take the form of a consequence (*consecutio* or *consequentia*) or of a syllogism. Abelard examines in detail different types of these. The presence or absence of conclusive force in an argument (*vis inferentiae, vis argumenti, vis sermonis*) sometimes rests on the form of the reasoning (*complexio* or *dispositio terminorum*), sometimes on the evidence brought to bear in the argument (its *locus*: the *natura* or *eventus rerum* or the *proprietas sermonis*). In the former case the argument is complexional, in the latter it is topical.[16] But in either case the evaluation of the argument entails a judgement about the structure of the proposition or propositions used. The matter (*res*) being considered is of secondary concern to a logician.[17] Enquiry into the nature of things belongs to the study of physics. But the one art is necessary to the other, for to understand words we must first investigate things. In logic the nature of things needs to be known, not on its own account, but for the sake of finding the meaning of words before combining words into meaningful propositions.[18] In his *Dialectica* Abelard first treats of the parts of speech (*partes orationis, dictiones*) and then of propositions and syllogisms. The parts of speech include the study of Porphyry's five predicables (genus, species, difference, property, and accident), Aristotle's categories (substance and nine accidents), and signification. Propositions and syllogisms are studied in

15 'Est autem logica Tulli auctoritate diligens ratio disserendi, idest discretio argumentorum, per quae disseritur, id est disputatur. Non enim est logica scientia utendi argumentis sive componendi ea, sed discernendi et diiudicandi veraciter, de eis, quare scilicet haec valeant, illa infirma sint': *Logica 'Nostrorum petitioni sociorum'* ed. Geyer 1973, p. 506.24–8.

16 *Logica 'Nostrorum petitioni sociorum'*, ed. Geyer 1973, p. 508.10–15.

17 'Magis enim eos qui logice deservire student, de rebus ipsis propter nomina quam de nominibus propter res agere decet': *Dialectica* 1970, p. 73.3–5. Fundamental to an understanding of Abelard as a student of language is the brilliant book of J. Jolivet, *Arts du langage et théologie chez Abélard*, Etudes de philosophie médiévale LVII (2nd ed., Paris 1982).

18 'Hoc autem logice discipline proprium relinquitur, ut scilicet vocum impositiones pensando quantum unaquaque proponatur oratione sive dictione discutiat. Phisice vero proprium est inquirere utrum rei natura consentiat enuntiationi, utrum ita sese, ut dicitur, rerum proprietas habeat vel non. Est autem alterius consideratio alteri necessaria. Ut enim logice discipulis appareat quid in singulis intelligendum sit vocabulis, prius rerum proprietas est investiganda. Sed cum ab his rerum natura non pro se sed pro vocum impositione requiritur, tota eorum intentio referenda est ad logicam. Cum autem rerum natura percontata fuerit, vocum significatio secundum rerum proprietates distinguenda est, prius quidem in singulis dictionibus, deinde in orationibus, que ex dictionibus iunguntur et ex ipsis suos sensus sortiuntur. Neque enim absque partium discretione composita perfectio cognosci potest.'
Dialectica 1970, pp. 286.31–287.5.

their different forms, categorical and hypothetical, and then Abelard studies divisions and definitions.[19]

Vox

The basic element in speech is the word. With words we signify ideas and things but words are themselves physical things. When we say 'Socrates is reading' our voice strikes the air and the listener through his ear interprets the sound. Not every noiseful utterance is meaningful: voiced sounds have to be intentionally organized if meaning is to be communicated. Words therefore have a psychological as well as a physical aspect; language is indivisibly physical and intellectual. The Latin word *vox* is therefore ambiguous, for it denotes both sound uttered at a certain time (*materia vocis*) and what this sound signifies (*sensus*). The latter is communicated to the intellect of the hearer and enters his memory. The ambiguity of the term *vox* led Abelard in his *Logica 'Nostrorum'* to complement it by another term, *sermo*. *Sermo* represents the second meaning of *vox*, its *sensus*.

Signification

The *sensus* or significance of words is twofold: words generate a concept (*intellectus*) and also refer to something (*res*).[20] To signify with words is to generate an idea (*generare intellectum*), and the idea corresponds to something that can be grasped by understanding. Of this thing (*res*) there must first be an idea or concept before it can be named or expressed in a word. Between reality and language lies understanding.[21] For language to be able to express

19 I have followed here the clear analysis of L. M. de Rijk in his introduction to *Dialectica* 1970, pp. xxiii–xxv.
20 'Nomina enim et verba duplicem significationem habent, unam quidem de rebus, alteram de intellectibus. Res enim significant constituendo intellectum ad eas pertinentem, hoc est naturam aliquam earum vel proprietatem attendentem. Intellectum quoque designare dicuntur, sive is sit intellectus proferentis vocem sive audientis eam. Nam intellectum proferentis in eo significare vox dicitur, quod ipsum auditori manifestat, dum consimilem in auditore generat.'
                     Logica 'Ingredientibus', ed. Geyer 1919–27, pp. 307.26–308.1.
21 'Cum enim voces duplicem habeant significationem, de rebus scilicet et de intellectibus, res intellectibus naturaliter priores sunt; prius enim in rerum natura oportet constare, quod possit intellectus concipere, et qui vocabulum invenit, prius rei naturam consideravit, ad quam demonstrandam nomen imposuit. Intellectus itaque, qui rei naturam sequi debent, naturaliter posteriores sunt, res vero priores. Quantum tamen ad causam impositionis nominis prima et principalis significatio intellectus dicitur, quia scilicet ideo tantum vocabulum rei datum est, ut intellectum constituat. Sed cum sit in causa impositionis nominum significatio intellectus prior, ipse tamen intellectus in natura suae substantiae re naturaliter posterior est. Unde bene quantum etiam ad significationem rerum, quae

such understanding certain rules are required. They are partly grammatical, partly dialectical. Grammatical because sentences have to be formed, dialectical because such sentences have to make sense. The two disciplines – grammar and dialectic – predominate in Abelard's analyses of language, yet he was also an incomparable rhetorician or literary stylist.

Propositions

Abelard discusses extensively the question of what is signified by a proposition.[22] Like words, propositions have a twofold significance: they deal with things (res) and generate ideas (intellectus).[23] Propositions, as distinct from single words, generate more complex concepts and purport to express something true or false – true or false, that is, according to what the proposition has to say about it. A true proposition expresses how something is in reality: it does not state the thing itself. What a proposition states – the dictum propositionis – is not a thing but the mode in which a thing (or things) relates to another; i.e. it states the necessity or otherwise of their connection.[24] And beyond these things, beyond also the understanding of them that is generated by the proposition, lies the realm of meaning, which subsists even when we do not have it mind and even when the things that are contained in a proposition cease to exist. The significance of a proposition is only a quasi res. It is not a thing nor is it an act of thought, though it is the content of such an act. What the proposition says, id quod propositio dicit, the dictum, is not something external to the mind nor is it the mental act as such, but the objective content of such a mental act, a res in anima as distinct from a res extra animam, something held in the mind and not beyond it.[25] A

naturaliter priores sunt intellectibus, primae quoque voces hic dicuntur.'
  Logica 'Ingredientibus', ed. Geyer 1919–27, pp. 112.31–113.3.
22 Ibid. pp. 365.13–370.22; Dialectica, ed. de Rijk 1970, pp. 157.13–160.36.
23 'Sicut ergo nomina et verba duplicem significationem habent, rerum scilicet vel intellectuum, ita etiam concedimus duplicem esse propositionum, secundum intellectus scilicet compositos ex intellectibus partium et dicta eorum, quae sunt quasi res propositionum, cum tamen nullae penitus essentiae sint': Logica 'Ingredientibus' ed. Geyer 1919–27, p. 367.9–13. Cf. Dialectica 1970, p. 154.20–3.
24 'Et est profecto ita in re, sicut dicit vera propositio, sed non est res aliqua quod dicit. Unde quasi quidam rerum modus habendi se per propositiones exprimitur, non res alique designantur': Dialectica 1970, p. 160.33–6. 'Socratem sedere et non sedere, quae sunt dicta propositionum, licet non sint aliquae essentiae': Logica 'Ingredientibus', ed. Geyer 1919–27, p. 257.5–6.
25 Cf. L. M. de Rijk, 'La signification de la proposition (Dictum Propositionis) chez Abélard', in Pierre Abélard. Pierre le Vénérable. Colloques Internationaux du Centre National de la Recherche Scientifique DXLVI (Paris 1975), pp. 547–55; G. Nuchelmans, Theories of the Proposition, North Holland Linguistic Series VIII (Amsterdam 1973), pp. 150f. On the use of the word res by Abelard see J. Jolivet 'Notes de lexicographie abélardienne', in Pierre Abélard.

categorical proposition (e.g. 'man is an animal') loses its value if the things
which it combines in a relationship cease to exist. On the other hand, a
hypothetical proposition (e.g. 'if man is, he is an animal') is independent of
the condition of existence. Such a hypothetical proposition does not refer
simply to things (man, animal) or their relationship, but to their meaning, to
an understanding of them (intellectus de rebus). The relationship of consequences which is proposed (the habitus consecutionis) is not a thing (non est
aliquid) but it is a logical fact. Even if all men were destroyed, the
consequence would still necessarily hold that 'if man is, he is an animal'.
Actual relations between things (expressed by a categorical proposition) are
insufficient to produce a necessary consequence. To establish dialectical
necessity Abelard goes beyond the level of things and of concepts, for logical
truth lies not in existent being but in necessary and eternal consequences.[26]

Predication

Abelard's examination of the nature of propositions is inseparable from his
analysis of predication as it is found in the De interpretatione. In a proposition
(e.g. 'Socrates is white') something is said about something else and a
relationship is proposed. The nature of this relationship, which is called
predication, is a matter for debate. Abelard focuses upon the meaning and
function of the verb 'to be' in a proposition: it functions as a copula or link
which serves as a phrase-maker and provides completeness of sense in a
sentence; it also signifies as a verb with existential and temporal import.
Without the verb the proposition does not exist; without the act of

Pierre le Vénérable 1975, pp. 531–45, at pp. 534–8. Abelard sometimes means by res (a
physical) thing and sometimes what is signified (in language) by a proposition or word. It
proved difficult for him to separate reality completely from the understanding of it as
conveyed in language. See A. de Libera, 'Abélard et le dictisme', in Abélard. Actes du Colloque
de Neuchâtel, 16–17 novembre 1979. Cahiers de la Revue de Théologie et de Philosophie VI
(1981) 59–97.

26 'Omnibus enim rebus destructis incommutabilem consecutionem tenet huiusmodi consequentia: "si est homo, est animal", et quecumque vere sunt consequentie, vere sunt ab
eterno ac necessarie': Dialectica, ed. de Rijk 1970, p. 160.17–21; 'cum omnes vere consequentie ab eterno sint vere, antequam etiam res earum create essent': ibid. pp. 264.38–
265.1; cf. also pp. 278.9–16, 279.13–26, 282.25–9. Abelard devotes considerable attention to
the study of topics. He defines a topic or locus as vis inferentie, from which a hypothetical
proposition gets its validity. See Dialectica, ed. de Rijk 1970, pp. 253–466; and Super topica
glossae, ed. Dal Pra 1954, pp. 205–330. On the importance and originality of Abelard's
search for logically necessary rules see the articles by O. Bird, 'The Logical Interest of the
Topics as Seen in Abelard', Modern Schoolman XXXVII (1959) 53–7; 'The Formalizing of the
Topics in Mediaeval Logic', Notre Dame Journal of Formal Logic I (1960) 138–49; 'The
Tradition of the Logical Topics: Aristotle to Ockham', Journal of the History of Ideas XXIII
(1962) 307–23.

predication significance is not created. Abelard oscillates between regarding the verb 'to be' purely as a link between the subject and the predicate and regarding it as stating the existence of the subject and the predicate. In a proposition concerning non-existent or no-longer-existent entities, e.g. 'a chimera is thinkable' or 'Homer is a poet', it is clear that the copula does not signify the existence of the subject and is purely a link. A further difficulty concerning predication is the question whether in a proposition such as 'Socrates is a man' the copula affirms an identity of essence (the identity theory), or affirms that a universal nature designated by the predicate – man – inheres in an individual designated by the subject – Socrates – (the inherence theory). Abelard saw points for and against each approach.[27]

Universals

Abelard's arguments concerning universals are an aspect of his general study of propositions. In his discussion in the *Logica 'Ingredientibus'* of the question whether universal nouns are only words or whether they also refer to universal things, Abelard begins with Aristotle's definition of the universal as 'that which is by its nature predicable of many things (*quod de pluribus natum est aptum praedicari*).'[28] A universal noun is one which has been instituted expressly for the sake of serving as a predicate for several terms taken one by one. So in the propositions 'Socrates is a man', 'Plato is a man', 'Aristotle is a man', the predicate – man – stands for the species, which includes any number of individual men. But what does the predicate signify that enables me to link 'man' with individual men such as Socrates, Plato, and Aristotle by means of the verb 'to be'? The predicate we give to a group of subjects results from our perception that there is in things both similarity and dissimilarity, agreement and diversity. A number of similar individuals grouped together in a species or a genus share a common nature even though

27 Important on this are the studies of N. Kretzmann, 'The Culmination of the Old Logic in Peter Abelard', *Harvard 1982*, pp. 488–511; K. Jacobi, 'Peter Abelard's Investigations into the Meaning and Functions of the Speech Sign "Est"', in *The Logic of Being*, ed. S. Knuuttila and J. Hintikka (Dordrecht 1985), pp. 145–80. Also K. Jacobi, 'Diskussionen über Prädikationstheorie in den logischen Schriften des Petrus Abailardus, Versuch einer Übersicht', in *Petrus Abaelardus (1079–1142)*, ed. R. Thomas, Trierer Theologische Studien xxxviii (Trier 1980), pp. 165–79; 'Die Semantik sprachlicher Ausdrücke, Ausdrucksfolgen und Aussagen in Abailards Kommentar zu Peri hermeneias', *Medioevo* vii (1981) 41–89; 'Abelard and Frege: the Semantics of Words and Propositions', in *Atti del Convegno Internazionale di Storia della Logica. San Gimignano, 4–8 dicembre 1982* (Bologna 1983), pp. 81–96; 'Diskussionen über unpersönliche Aussage in Peter Abaelards Kommentar zu Peri Hermeneias', in *Medieval Semantics and Metaphysics. Studies dedicated to L. M. de Rijk, Ph.D. on the occasion of his 60th birthday*, Artistarium Supplementa ii (Nijmegen 1985), pp. 1–63.
28 *Logica 'Ingredientibus'* ed. Geyer 1919–27, p. 9.19.

as individuals they exhibit particular differences. They agree in their nature (*conveniunt ex creatione naturae*), for a nature, as Boethius said, is an original similarity between things (*similitudo nascentium*). Socrates, Plato, and Aristotle share an undeniable resemblance (*convenientia*) as men. What they have in common, however, is not a thing called 'man' but a state or a nature which is that of being man (*esse hominem, status hominis*).[29] 'We call this "being man" the *status hominis*, which is not a thing.'[30] This state of likeness is abstracted by the human mind from the evidence present to the human senses. Universal nouns perform a certain function within propositions and exist in language. They are not things. But they may not be arbitrarily attributed to any subjects, for they have a basis in or a correspondence to things. According to Abelard a thing is always individual and separate; it cannot be found (*convenire*) in any other thing that a universal noun can designate. There is no universal thing. Moreover, a universal name, being by definition a common name, cannot be attributed to individual things on their own. There is no thing underlying this name. As Boethius wrote, the noun 'man' creates difficulty: it causes us to think neither of Socrates nor of any other man nor of all men together. It produces a concept of no thing because it designates no thing. So a universal name, like a proposition, states no thing, and yet both mean something. This something which is signified by a universal name Abelard calls a 'common and confused image of a large number of beings'.[31]

Abelard's criticism of realism

In his autobiography Abelard attributes his rise to fame in no small measure to his success in combating the views of William of Champeaux on essences. Abelard's objections to William's views arise from his analysis of the

29 'Singuli homines discreti ab invicem cum in propriis differant tam essentiis quam formis . . . in eo tamen conveniunt, quod homines sunt. Non dico in homine, cum res nulla sit homo nisi discreta, sed in esse hominem. Esse autem hominem non est homo nec res aliqua . . . in re . . . nulla possit esse convenientia': *Logica 'Ingredientibus'* ed. Geyer 1919–27, p. 19.21–30.

30 'Statum autem hominis ipsum esse hominem, quod non est res, vocamus, quod etiam diximus communem causam impositionis nominis ad singulos, secundum quod ipsi ad invicem conveniunt': *Logica 'Ingredientibus'*, ed. Geyer 1919–27, p. 20.7–9. For a comparison of Abelard's understanding of *status* with his understanding of the *dicta* of propositions, see M. M. Tweedale, *Abailard on Universals* (Amsterdam 1976), ch. 5.

31 *Logica 'Ingredientibus'*, ed. Geyer 1919–27, pp. 21.27–22.6. Cf. also *Logica 'Nostrorum'* 1973, pp. 524.35–527.7. The somewhat ambivalent position of Abelard was noted by B. Geyer in a study of abiding value, 'Die Stellung Abaelards in der Universalienfrage nach neuen handschriftlichen Texten', BGPTM Supplementband I (1913), pp. 101–27. Of value among more recent studies is C. Wenin, 'La signification des universaux chez Abélard', *Revue Philosophique de Louvain* LXXX (1982) 414–48.

function of words and propositions and of their relationship to non-verbal reality. His detailed arguments are found not in the *Historia calamitatum* but in his *Logica 'Ingredientibus'*. Here he writes that some have maintained that individual things are distinguished from one another by their forms (*per formas*), but that where things share likenesses as members of a species they have in common a substance which is the same in its being (*essentialiter*) in each individual in the species. Take away the forms and all differences would disappear between the individual things, because their matter is essentially the same.[32] Thus the substance of the species 'man' is the same in all men, even though they are numerically distinct. Just as a piece of wax can be modelled into a figure of a man and then into a figure of a cow, so too the universal is at one and the same time wholly in all beings of which it is the substance. It is universal in itself, singular through the forms which are added to it. Without these it subsists in its nature, but cannot exist in actuality.[33]

To this view Abelard presents the difficulty that it is contradicted by physics (*physica . . . repugnat*).[34] If a single essential reality exists in separate species within a genus, it follows that a rational animal is an irrational animal and that contraries coexist at the same time in Socrates and in an ass. Individuality disappears.[35] A single essence cannot wholly and simultaneously subsist in diverse subjects.[36] To avoid these difficulties others have proposed a second doctrine which is closer to the truth: individual beings are distinct in their being and not only in their forms. No thing shares its essential matter or its essential forms with anything else. But to account for resemblances (i.e. to safeguard realism) they say that individual beings share some non-differences in their nature, e.g. men share in being men – that is, they share the nature of humanity.[37] To sustain this non-difference thesis it is necessary first to remove what is called the doctrine of collection, that is, the doctrine that

32 *Logica 'Ingredientibus'*, ed. Geyer 1919–27, p. 10.17–25. We are reminded of Abelard's account of the first position adopted by William of Champeaux in his dispute with Abelard, as narrated in the *Historia calamitatum*, ed. Monfrin 1962, lines 85–9: 'Erat autem in ea sententia de communitate universalium, ut eamdem essentialiter rem totam simul singulis suis inesse astrueret individuis, quorum quidem nulla esset in essentia diversitas sed sola multitudine accidentium varietas.'
33 *Logica 'Ingredientibus'* ed. Geyer 1919–27, pp. 10.23–11.9.
34 *Ibid.* p. 11.11.
35 *Ibid.* pp. 11.10–13.17.
36 '. . . manifestum est eam penitus sententiam ratione carere qua dicitur eandem penitus essentiam in diversis simul consistere': *ibid.* p. 13.15–17.
37 *Ibid.* pp. 13.18–14.6. This reminds us of Abelard's report of the revised teaching of William of Champeaux, *Historia calamitatum*, ed. Monfrin 1962, lines 89–91: 'Sic autem istam tunc suam correxit sententiam, ut deinceps rem eamdem non essentialiter sed indifferenter diceret.'

all men together or all animals together, not one by one, can be predicated of many and are respectively the species 'man' and the genus 'animal'.[38] Secondly, there has to be repudiated the doctrine that every individual man is himself a species and a universal, i.e. that universality and individuality can characterize one and the same thing and indicate both similarity and dissimilarity.[39]

So it is that in his *Logica 'Ingredientibus'* Abelard lists the different ways in which the universal may be defined and by a series of reasonings reduces to absurdity the doctrine that the universal is *res*. As a result the only doctrine that survives is that the universal is *vox*.[40] In his *Logica 'Nostrorum'* Abelard offers a renewed criticism of realism, which is very different from that found in *'Ingredientibus'*, even though the difference lies largely on the level of presentation. Here he lists three theses: (1) that universals are things; (2) that they are concepts; (3) that they are words.[41] (1) and (3) find support in the writings of Aristotle, Porphyry, and Boethius. (2) is supported in the *Timaeus* of Plato, in Boethius, and in Priscian's famous text on the forms of things which are in the mind of God (*Institutiones grammaticae* XVII 44).

Abelard's criticism of the first thesis, the *sententia de rebus*, overlaps at points with his criticism in the *'Ingredientibus'* of the doctrine of essences. He once more rejects the doctrine that there are universal *res* which are essentially present in a plurality of subjects that are diverse in forms.[42] He rejects, too, the doctrine that the universal is a thing which is present in its subjects not essentially but indifferently, i.e. that the same *res* is present in Socrates as in Plato, the similarity between them being their non-difference. Such a doctrine would mean that a *res* is both a universal and a particular according to the viewpoint from which it is considered (*diversis tamen respectibus*).[43]

Abelard's own view is (3): universals are words. Whereas in the *'Ingredientibus'* Abelard called the universal *vox*, now in the *'Nostrorum'* he eliminates the ambiguity by which *vox* can mean both the word spoken here and now, an articulated physical sound with but a fleeting existence, and the word as the carrier of signification.[44] He does so by preferring the term *sermo* to that

38 *Logica 'Ingredientibus'* ed. Geyer 1919–27, p. 14.7–17, pp. 14.32–15.22.
39 *Ibid.* p. 14.18–31, pp. 15.23–16.18; Tweedale 1976, pp. 113–27, calls these two doctrines the collection theory and the identity theory.
40 'Nunc autem ostensis rationibus quibus neque res singillatim neque collectim acceptae universales dici possunt in eo quod de pluribus praedicantur, restat ut huiusmodi universalitatem solis vocibus adscribamus': *Logica 'Ingredientibus'* ed. Geyer 1919–27, p. 16.19–22.
41 *Logica 'Nostrorum'* ed. Geyer 1973, pp. 512.19 f.
42 *Ibid.* pp. 515.14–518.8.
43 *Ibid.* pp. 518.9–522.9.
44 *Ibid.* pp. 522.10–524.10.

of *vox, sermo* meaning *vox* in its second sense as a significant word. *Vox* – the uttered noise – is a natural thing, whereas to show or to signify is the function of *sermones*. 'We say that universals are *sermones* because they can be predicated of several subjects and have been made for that purpose, that is, instituted by men. But neither *voces* nor *res* can in any way be universals, even though all *sermones* are *voces*.'[45] Universal names designate common forms; to conceive these by means of names (*nomina*) is to signify. Common forms are not things nor are they intellections. The idea of signification assumes an important place in Abelard's criticism of realism; it stands between reality and understanding: *praeter rem et intellectum tertia exiit nominum significatio.*[46]

The second thesis, that universals are concepts (*intellectus*), is therefore rejected, because concepts are what the universal generates. What kind of concepts?[47] Abelard is closer to realism here than one might expect. Although he concludes that the universal noun is a *vox* or *sermo*, it signifies something. In the *'Ingredientibus'* Abelard writes that a *nomen* appears to signify a *forma*, and the *forma* is a *conceptio Dei*, a concept in the mind of God, who is the author of generic and specific states of nature (*generales vel speciales naturae status*).[48] The cause of the imposition of the universal noun 'man' (for example) or of the universal 'being man (*esse hominem*)' is a *status*.[49] In the last analysis the universal seems to be based on divine ideas. This is close to Platonism, although men who know things by means of their senses do not know the pure nature of things; the conceived forms which words express are not forms as they exist in the divine mind.[50] Furthermore, in studying the relationship between what signifies (*vox* or *vocabulum*) and what is signified (*res*), Abelard arrives at a Platonic idea of *essentia* as *res*. He writes in the *'Ingredientibus'* that the Aristotelian categories (substance and the nine accidents) signify a thing in its essence, for every thing subsists in its essence before being received by its subject.[51] So the word 'essence' is used by Abelard in ways that suggest that universals name essences which underlie

45 *Ibid.* p. 522.28–31.
46 *Logica 'Ingredientibus'* ed. Geyer 1919–27, p. 24.29–30.
47 See on this W. L. Gombocz, 'Abaelards Bedeutungslehre als Schlüssel zum Universalien-problem' in *Petrus Abaelardus*, ed. Thomas 1980, pp. 153–64.
48 *Logica 'Ingredientibus'* ed. Geyer 1919–27, pp. 22.25–24.31.
49 See n. 29.
50 Cf. L. M. de Rijk, 'The Semantical Impact of Abailard's Solution of the Problem of Universals', *Petrus Abaelardus*, ed. Thomas 1980, pp. 139–51, at pp. 144–5.
51 '... rem in essentia significant ... in eo statu essentiae qui naturaliter aliis prior est, eam significant. Omnis enim res in essentia sua prius subsistit, quam a subiecto suscipiatur': *Logica 'Ingredientibus'*, ed. Geyer 1919–27, p. 113.5–8.

and are the forms of things.[52] Hereby Abelard comes close to the view of William of Champeaux as we read it in the *Historia calamitatum*.

To sum up, the universal is not a thing (*res*), but it is not nothing, as it is not relegated to being arbitrary. Individuals share in something, and the resemblances they share exist in the world of things (*in re*). These shared *status* or *naturae* objectively depend on the existence of actual individuals. Genera and species are names of material realities; they subsist in these as their names, although they stand outside them in our understanding.[53]

Language, not things, is the concern of logic

Abelard treats logic as an art of language that is closely linked to grammar, for it deals with words and phrases. Logic itself evaluates arguments that are constructed out of words and propositions. Abelard separates logic from the study of the properties of things and of the relations between them, but he admits that logic is based on these properties and on their relations. He sees the reciprocity, not only the contrast, between logic and physics. Logic is an art of language because proofs (both topical and syllogistic) suppose relationships between terms (topical) and between antecedent and consequent propositions (syllogistic). But terms and propositions are in turn rooted in things and in the relationships between them. Arguments and consequences treat things by means of *voces*. Proofs are true if based on things, yet ideally they are independent of the existence of those things. When they are thus independent, they bring necessary consequences into play.

Abelard begins with reflection on Porphyry, with an idea of the predicate as only a *vox*. He arrives at a theory of the *status naturae* which is expressed not by a noun (*homo*) but by an infinitive (*esse hominem*). The doctrine of the

52 See J. Jolivet, 'Notes de lexicographie abélardienne', in *Pierre Abélard. Pierre le Vénérable* 1975, pp. 531–43, at pp. 538–43. Jolivet brings together a remarkable selection of passages from Abelard's writings. E.g. 'universalia, quae licet confusae significationis sint, quantum ad nominatas *essentias*, ad communem illam conceptionem status dirigunt animum auditoris': *Logica Ingredientibus*', ed. Geyer 1919–27, p. 23.27–9. Also: '(Nomen substantia) habet . . . in rebus duas consuetas significationes, quia modo pro omni essentia sumitur iuxta illud Prisciani: "Significans substantiam cum qualitate", modo pro illis tantum *essentiis* quae per se subsistunt, nulli scilicet subiectae materiae adhaerentes ut formae eorum': *Logica 'Ingredientibus'*, ed. Geyer 1919–27, p. 140.5–9.

53 'Solvens ita: genera et species quaedam, non omnia in sensibilibus sunt posita, hoc est sensibilia habent appellare vel nominare, et ponuntur extra sensibilia, id est res habent significare et non cum aliqua forma quae sensui subiaceat, quia si res omnes formas quae sensui subiacent, amitterent, non ideo minus a genere et specie nominari possent. Sunt igitur genera et species in sensibilibus posita per appellationem, extra vero per significationem.'

                                   Logica 'Nostrorum', ed. Geyer 1973, p. 527.23–9.
      Cf. Gombocz 1980, p. 160; de Rijk 1980, pp. 145–6.

universal and the theory of proof bring into play concepts of signification and of nature. Abelard is concerned both with language from which content has been eliminated and with language as the bearer of meaning. He is concerned with pure formalism and also with real relationships between things. His nominalism in logic is not incompatible with a degree of philosophical realism.[54]

Logic and Christian faith

Abelard attacks the opponents of dialectic (by which he means the opponents of Aristotle) in the Prologue to *Tractatus* IV of his *Dialectica* and in his *Theologia*.[55] He writes that St Augustine himself used dialectic and that dialectic provides faith with a sharp sword with which to counter the sophisms of the heretics. Knowledge even of wrong things can never be wrong (*mala*) in itself, although it can become wrong in its application (*nefarium exercitium*). Misused logic is sophistry. Dialectic is the means of distinguishing between truth and falsehood. In matters of Christian faith logic is subordinate to divine revelation. But logic can construct arguments that show that what faith offers is not absurd. Book I of the *Theologia 'Summi boni'* presents the objection of pseudo-dialecticians, that the doctrine of God as one substance and three persons is a contradiction, and in Book III Abelard replies to this. Book III is full of similarities to Abelard's logical works; here he is applying logic to matters of faith.

In his autobiography, the *Historia calamitatum*, Abelard describes how he came to write the first version of his *Theologia*:

I first applied myself to writing about the foundation of our faith with the aid of analogies provided by human reason, and I wrote a treatise of theology – on the divine unity and trinity – for our scholars, who were asking for human and philosophical reasons and clamouring more for what could be understood than for what could be said. They said in fact that the utterance of words was superfluous unless it were followed by understanding, and that it was ridiculous for anyone to preach to others what neither he nor those taught by him could accept into their understanding.[56]

54 See de Rijk in his introduction to *Dialectica* 1970, pp. xcviif.
55 *Dialectica* 1970, pp. 469–71. *Theologia 'Summi boni'* II, ed. H. Ostlender, BGPTM xxxv.2/3 (1939), pp. 28–36. *Theologia Christiana* III 4–55, ed. E. M. Buytaert, *Opera Theologica II*, CC CM XII (Turnhout 1969), pp. 195–218; *Theologia 'Scholarium'* II 2 (P.L. 178, 1040–6). On the versions of the *Theologia* (*Theologia 'Summi boni'*, *Theologia Christiana*, *Theologia 'Scholarium'*) see Buytaert I, 1969, xiv–xviii; also C. J. Mews, 'Peter Abelard's *Theologia Christiana* and *Theologia 'Scholarium'* re-examined', *RTAM* LII (1985) 109–58. The preparation of these versions extends over a long period.
56 Abelard, *Historia calamitatum*, ed. Monfrin 1962, pp. 82–3, lines 690–700.

In the *Theologia 'Summi boni'*, to which Abelard here refers, he declares his intention to expound the truths of faith with the aid of logic and of human reason, and to say 'something plausible, something close to human reason' in order to answer on their own ground those dialecticians who found the doctrine of the Trinity to be absurd.[57] Neither the authority of the saints nor that of the philosophers can refute importunate arguments; only human reasonings can be used to oppose those who are swayed by human reasonings.[58]

Words and God

Words used of God do not bear their original meaning. For example, God cannot properly be called substance because Aristotle, Porphyry, and Boethius teach that substance is susceptible of accidents or forms. So God eludes the rules of the Aristotelians, who have to be content with the study of creatures.[59]

In the successive versions of his *Theologia* Abelard demonstrates how the words that men use of God — words such as 'lord', 'eternal', 'immense', or 'creator' — have undergone a change from their habitual meaning. God is beyond human understanding and nomination. He is ineffable. When we say that God is anterior to the world, or that the Son is generated by the Father, we do not mean that God may be truly described by our notions of time or of the human person. Rather language, as here used of divine realities, undergoes a necessary alteration, or *translatio*, a translation of meaning.[60] There do exist resemblances between creatures and the Creator, and therefore the words we use for creation may designate God without incongruity (*non incongrue*). But the formulas used to define Christian faith cannot be understood unless account is taken of these transpositions.

---

57 'Those who attack our faith . . . assail us above all with philosophical reasonings. It is those reasonings which we have principally enquired into and I believe that no one can fully understand them without applying himself to philosophical and especially to dialectical studies': *Theologia 'Summi boni'* III 5, ed. Ostlender 1939, pp. 107.32–108.5.
58 Cf. *ibid.* II, Introduction, ed. Ostlender 1939, p. 36.1–3.
59 *Ibid.* II 3, ed. Ostlender 1939, pp. 47–52. On substance and God see too *Theologia Christiana* III 119–24, ed. Buytaert II, 1969, 238–42; *Theologia 'Scholarium'* II 10 (P.L. 178, 1059B–1062A).
60 *Theologia 'Summi boni'* II 3, ed. Ostlender 1939, pp. 52–3; *Theologia Christiana* III 44, III 126–8, ed. Buytaert II, 1969, 212, 242–3; *Theologia 'Scholarium'* II 10 (P.L. 178, 1062A–63A).

Words and the divine Trinity

Dialecticians raise objections to the possibility of there being any known mode of diversity by which persons may be distinguished in an individual substance. Abelard replies that the vocabulary of philosophy is deficient when it comes to speaking of God. Nonetheless in his *Theologia*, in an effort to reply to other dialecticians, he examines identity and difference by constructing propositions in which the names of persons and of the divine essence enter as subject or as predicate. God is *essentially* identical but *numerically* plural in the divine persons. Father, Son, and Spirit have one essence but differ in their definitions or in their *propria*. Abelard's account of identity and difference varies a little from one version of his *Theologia* to another. In his *Theologia 'Summi boni'* he presents six modes:[61] (1) Some things are identical in essence, e.g. 'sword' and 'blade';[62] (2) some things are identical in number;[63] (3) some things are identical by definition, e.g. a sword is a blade;[64] (4) some things are identical by resemblance, e.g. species in their genus;[65] (5) some things are identical by immutableness, e.g. God is always the same;[66] (6) some things are the same by their effect, e.g. when two words express the same conception.[67] Difference (*diversum*) has a corresponding set of six meanings in the *Theologia 'Summi boni'*: (1) difference in essence, e.g. a part is not a whole;[68] (2) difference in number, e.g. 'Socrates' and 'Plato';[69] (3) difference in definition, e.g. 'substance' and

---

61 *Theologia 'Summi boni'* II 4, ed. Ostlender 1939, p. 54.20–6. The six modes are reduced to five in the *Theologia Christiana* III 138–64 ed. Buytaert II, 1969, 247–55. Later Abelard reduces them to three in his *Theologia 'Scholarium'* II 12, P.L. 178, 1065A.

62 *Theologia 'Summi boni'* II 4 ed. Ostlender 1939, pp. 54.27–55.5.

63 *Ibid.* II 4, ed. Ostlender 1939, p. 55.6–25 (and see the references to the *Logica* there cited). But identity of essence is seen as identity of number in *Theologia Christiana* III 139, ed. Buytaert II, 1969, 247, and in *Theologia 'Scholarium'* II 12 (P.L. 178, 1065A).

64 *Theologia 'Summi boni'* II 4, ed. Ostlender 1939, pp. 55.26–56.26. Cf. *Theologia Christiana* III 142–4, ed. Buytaert II, 1969, 248–50; *Theologia 'Scholarium'* II 12: 'proprietate autem seu definitione idem' (P.L. 178, 1065A).

65 *Theologia 'Summi boni'* II 4, ed. Ostlender 1939, p. 56.26–31. Cf. *Theologia Christiana* III 145, ed. Buytaert II, 1969, 250; *Theologia 'Scholarium'* II 12 (P.L. 178, 1065A).

66 *Theologia 'Summi boni'* II 4, ed. Ostlender 1939, p. 56.32–5. Cf. *Theologia Christiana* III 146, ed. Buytaert II, 1969, 250.

67 *Theologia 'Summi boni'* II 4, ed. Ostlender 1939, p. 57.1–4.

68 *Ibid.* II 4, ed. Ostlender 1939, p. 57.10–26. Cf. *Theologia Christiana* III 148, ed. Buytaert II, 1969, 250–1.

69 *Theologia 'Summi boni'* II 4, ed. Ostlender 1939, pp. 57.27–59.5. Cf. *Theologia Christiana* III 149–53, ed. Buytaert II, 1969, 251–2.

'body';[70] (4) difference in resemblance;[71] (5) difference by change, e.g. 'now Socrates is standing' and 'now Socrates is sitting';[72] (6) difference by effect, e.g. things act diversely.[73] Abelard concludes his discussion of identity and difference with a brief examination of the differences between persons in God, who is absolutely one and the same *essentialiter*.[74] The persons in God are different by their definitions, that is by their *propria* or *proprietates*.[75] The *proprium* of the Father is to be by himself; that of the Son, to be eternally engendered by the Father; that of the Spirit, to proceed from the Father and the Son. Identity of essence entails numerical identity but not vice versa. Identity of essence or of number does not entail identity of definition. Difference in definition is not incompatible with identity of essence. Essential difference may be compatible with identity through resemblance, e.g. of individuals in a species.[76] This analysis provides Abelard with a basis for maintaining the essential unity of God and the numerical plurality of definitions or properties or persons in God. It enables him moreover to expound the generation of the Son by the Father in terms of the production of the Wisdom of God by the Power of God (species out of genus).[77]

Similes and analogies

God is ineffable, yet there exist resemblances between God and his creatures. When we apply to God the words we use to name creatures, these words indicate a limited resemblance but are transformed and enigmatic.[78] To

70 *Theologia 'Summi boni'* II 4, ed. Ostlender 1939, pp. 59.6–60.16. Cf. *Theologia Christiana* III 154–8, ed. Buytaert II, 1969, 252–4.
71 *Theologia 'Summi boni'* II 4, ed. Ostlender 1939, p. 60.17–18. Cf. *Theologia Christiana* III 159, ed. Buytaert II, 1969, 254.
72 *Theologia 'Summi boni'* II 4, ed. Ostlender 1939, p. 60.19–21. Cf. *Theologia Christiana* III 160, ed. Buytaert II, 1969, 254.
73 *Theologia 'Summi boni'* II 4, ed. Ostlender 1939, pp. 60.22–61.13. This disappears in *Theologia Christiana* III 147, ed. Buytaert II, 1969, 250.
74 *Theologia 'Summi boni'* II 4, ed. Ostlender 1939, pp. 61.14–62.8. Cf. *Theologia Christiana* III 164, ed. Buytaert II, 1969, 255.
75 'Sunt autem ab invicem diversae personae, id est pater et filius et spiritus sanctus, ad similitudinem eorum quae diversa sunt secundum diffinitiones, eo videlicet quod, cum eadem penitus essentia sit pater, quae est filius, vel spiritus sanctus, aliud tamen proprium est patris, in eo scilicet quod pater est, et aliud filii, et aliud spiritus sancti': *Theologia 'Summi boni'* II 4, ed. Ostlender 1939, p. 61.19–24. Cf. *Theologia Christiana* III 164, ed. Buytaert II, 1969, 255.
76 *Theologia 'Summi boni'* II 4, ed. Ostlender 1939, pp. 56, 58, 61; *Theologia Christiana* III 139, 140, 143, 153, 164, ed. Buytaert II, 1969, 247, 249, 252, 255.
77 *Theologia 'Summi boni'* III 2, ed. Ostlender 1939, pp. 86–93. Cf. *Theologia Christiana* IV 82–115, ed. Buytaert II, 1969, 303–22; *Theologia 'Scholarium'* II 13 (P.L. 178, 1067–71).
78 '... in deo nullum propriam inventionem vocabulum servare videtur, sed omnia quae de eo dicuntur, translationibus et parabolicis aenigmatibus involuta sunt et per similitudinem

account for the relationship between the three divine persons in the Trinity Abelard explores the notions of identity and difference and the notion of person;[79] he also illustrates the generation of the Son by the Father, and the procession of the Spirit, with the aid of analogies. These analogies are taken from things which are composed of matter and form, such as a waxen image which comes from wax but is of identical essence with the wax,[80] and a bronze seal in which the matter is bronze and the form is the figure. A bronze seal – a single thing – has two different properties and is also capable of sealing, this being a third property. As in the Trinity, the seal is in a manner generated by the bronze.[81] But every analogy is imperfect (*ex parte inducitur*); every resemblance is dissimilar in some respect.[82] There is no matter, and there are no forms, in God.[83] Analogies, like words used of God, involve transpositions (*translationes*). Nonetheless, it was by consideration of the world that philosophers found the Trinity. Things bear the traces of God, and in studying analogies such as the bronze seal or the wax statue Abelard tries as a dialectician to establish what predications are possible in God. He argues that a belief in the Trinity is natural to all men.[84]

Reason and faith

St Bernard saw in Abelard a rash man seeking to penetrate to the heart of divine mysteries. Some more recent scholars have on this account seen in Abelard a rationalist. A distinction should be drawn between the application of dialectic to theology and the relationship between reason and faith. Abelard applied to the content of faith procedures of interpretation and explanation which were tested in another domain. His adversaries transferred to the level of faith what was initially only a means of confronting and resolving difficulties found by dialecticians. Abelard was more concerned with the formulations of the faith and with knowledge of them (*intelligentia*);

aliquam vestigantur ex parte aliqua inductam, ut aliquid de illa ineffabili maiestate suspicando potius quam intelligendo degustemus': *Theologia 'Summi boni'* II 3, ed. Ostlender 1939, p. 53.5–10. In Latin rhetorical treatises *translationes* is a normal word for 'metaphors'.
79 On the notion of person see *Theologia 'Summi boni'* II 5, ed. Ostlender 1939, pp. 63–4; *Theologia Christiana* III 176–82, ed. Buytaert II, 1969, 261–3; *Theologia 'Scholarium'* II 12 (P.L. 178, 1067BC).
80 *Theologia 'Summi boni'* III 2, ed. Ostlender 1939, pp. 89.30–90.6. Abelard's discussions of analogies are in part prompted by reflections on the use of analogies by Anselm of Canterbury; cf. D. E. Luscombe, 'St Anselm and Abelard', *Anselm Studies* I (1983) 207–29.
81 *Theologia 'Scholarium'* II 13–15 (P.L. 178, 1068C–1070B, 1073B–5A).
82 *Theologia 'Summi boni'* II 2, III 2, ed. Ostlender 1939, pp. 43.18–19, 94.24–6.
83 *Ibid.* III 2, ed. Ostlender 1939, pp. 96.23f.
84 *Ibid.* III 5, ed. Ostlender 1939, p. 107.

with showing the conformity of revelation to the laws of predication; with the task of commentary with the aid of the disciplines of the Trivium; with understanding the *sacra pagina* through the similitudes of human reason; with human and philosophical reasons. The words used by authority give birth to questions which have to be judged before they can be invoked, even if the judgement is plausible rather than certain.

Logic and the sacred authors

In the Prologue to his *Sic et Non* – a collection of excerpts from sacred writers who appear to disagree on matters of Christian belief – Abelard outlines some principles which may reduce or eliminate the difficulties arising from apparent conflicts of meaning. Sometimes such conflicts can be resolved on the level of logic, by determining the meaning of the terms used by different authors in varying ways. However, examination of the meaning of the teaching of the authorities should also stimulate questioning and methodical doubting which, upon enquiry, leads towards truth. Abelard's suggestions relate to history as well as to logic, insofar as he asks his readers to consider who the authors were, in what circumstances they wrote, and how we can prove or disprove their authorship of particular writings.[85]

Abelard as a philosopher

Logic together with physics and ethics is a branch of philosophy, and philosophy is the science of discernment (*discernendi scientia*). Only those who have outstandingly subtle intelligences possess this science and can know and understand the hidden causes of things.[86]

From Aristotle Abelard could derive little philosophy beyond what he found in the *Categories* and *On Interpretation*. In his *Logica* and *Dialectica* Abelard uses Aristotle, Boethius, and Porphyry largely to explore and resolve technical questions in logic. For a wider philosophy, Abelard, like such contemporaries as William of Conches, Thierry of Chartres, and Gilbert of Poitiers, relied on the writings that derive directly or indirectly from Plato: a part of the *Timaeus* as translated and commented on by Calcidius; Macrobius; Boethius' *Consolation of Philosophy*; Augustine's *City of God*. He used these especially in his *Theologies*.

85 *Sic et Non*, ed. B. B. Boyer and R. McKeon (Chicago–London 1976–7). See also Jolivet 1982, pp. 238–51.
86 *Logica 'Nostrorum'*, ed. Geyer 1973, p. 506; *Logica 'Ingredientibus'*, ed. Geyer 1919–27, p. 1.

In the main it was as a theologian that Abelard turned to the pagan philosophers who found God by using reason and by investigating the world God has made. Abelard liked to cite St Paul: 'What is known of God is manifest in them for God has manifested it unto them. The invisible things of God are clearly seen from the creation of the world, being understood from the things that are made.' Abelard also liked to explain that the pagans, using natural law, which is in human reason, had gained a knowledge of God, even of the Trinity.[87] To Abelard the natural law had also a moral connotation; reason and the natural law guided the philosophers to lead lives of abstinence and continence.[88] In his *Theologies* Abelard illustrated the moral lives led by the pagan philosophers by means of many examples taken from Jerome's *Against Jovinian* and Augustine's *City of God*. Among them are examples of philosophers who promoted the well-being of their fellow-citizens by providing good government; other examples are of philosophers who withdrew from society and held the world in contempt.[89] By their lives as much as by their teaching the philosophers gained a knowledge of God and came also to believe in the Trinity, in the immortality of the soul, and in eternal retribution.[90] In his *Historia calamitatum* Abelard tells how Heloise

87 'Quod notum est Dei manifestum est in illis: Deus enim illis manifestavit. Invisibilia enim ipsius, a creatura mundi per ea quae facta sunt intellecta conspiciuntur': Romans 1: 19–20; see also '. . . gentes, quae legem non habent, naturaliter ea, quae legis sunt, faciunt': Romans 2: 14. Cf. *Theologia 'Summi boni'* I 5, III 5, ed. Ostlender 1939, pp. 11, 107.21. Also *Theologia Christiana* I 54, 58, II 6, 12–13, 19–21, IV 85, 159, ed. Buytaert 1969, pp. 94, 95, 135, 138–9, 141, 305, 345. '. . . ipse perhibet Apostolus Deum sui notitiam reprobis quoque contulisse, iuxta quod ad Romanos scribens, inexcusabilem omnem hominem esse convincit et de contemptu sui conditoris arguendum, cum eius notitiam lex ipsa naturalis, quae in ratione consistit, etiam sine scripto in ipsa operum eius exhibitionem omnibus afferret': *Theologia Christiana* v 4, ed. Buytaert II, 1969, 348. Cf. *Theologia 'Scholarium'* I 15 (P.L. 178, 1004D–6A, 1007B; II 1 (P.L. 178, 1037CD, 1039BC); III 1 (P.L. 178, 1086D, 1087A); III 18 (P.L. 178, 1085AB). See too Abelard's *Commentary on Paul's Epistle to the Romans* I 19–20: the gentiles knew God without the aid of revelation ('sine scripto') but by the use of reason (which is the natural law) and by knowledge of his visible works. Gentile philosophers, as the Christian Fathers have shown, found much evidence of the divine Trinity in the works of God which exhibit the divine power, wisdom, and loving kindness. However, the mystery of the divine Incarnation could not be discovered by human reason from the study of God's works. Ed. Buytaert I, 1969, 67–8.

88 'Quis itaque non attendat quantum in omni gente semper Deo accepta fuerit carnis integritas, et continentia vitae . . . Et quid mirum, cum hoc illis continentia vitae contulerit, si magna apud Deum promeruerit tanta philosophorum abstinentia et continentia, cum haec tanto laudabiliora in eis videantur et maiori reputanda merito, quanto minus ad haec aliorum praedicatione vel exemplis incitati sunt, sed propria ratione et naturali legis instructione commoti.'
Theologia Christiana II 108, ed. Buytaert II, 1969, 180.

89 *Theologia Christiana* II 43–115, ed. Buytaert II, 1969, 149–84. J. Jolivet, 'Doctrines et figures de philosophes chez Abélard', in *Petrus Abaelardus*, ed. Thomas 1980, pp. 103–20.

90 'Quod si post fidem ac moralem doctrinam philosophorum finemque seu intentionem recte vivendi ab eis assignatum, vitam quoque ipsorum inspiciamus, et quam diligenter rei publicae statum instituerint atque ipsorum civium simulque conviventium vitam ord-

sought to dissuade him from marriage by invoking the examples of ancient philosophers who renounced the pleasures of this world.[91] Later, in establishing his school at the Oratory of the Paraclete at Quincey, Abelard compared his pupils to the philosophers of old whom Jerome described in *Against Jovinian*, men who gave up the comforts of life and forsook the distractions which impeded thought about God.[92] As abbot of the monastery of St Gildas, in his *Sermon on St John the Baptist*, Abelard offered to monks the examples of the philosophers as well as of John himself: Socrates and Diogenes lived off little and held the world in contempt.[93] Heloise openly compares monks and gentile philosophers.[94] Abelard's image of the wise man in times past embraces Jews as well as gentiles. Natural law was followed by both the patriarchs and the philosophers. Before the Law was granted to Moses, natural law was followed by Abel, Enoch, Noah and his sons, by the Jewish patriarchs Abraham, Isaac, Jacob, Lot, and Melchisedech.[95] In his *Theologia 'Summi boni'* Abelard writes that the gentile Job

inaverint, reperiemus ipsorum tam vitam quam doctrinam maxime evangelicam seu apostolicam perfectionem exprimere, et a religione Christiana eos nihil aut parum recedere. Qui nobis tam rationibus morum quam nomine ipso iunctissimi reperiuntur: nomine quidem cum nos a vera sophia, hoc est sapientia Dei Patris quae Christus est, Christiani dicamur, vere in hoc dicendi philosophi, si vere Christum diligimus; fide quoque et spe morumque et honestatis rationibus secundum caritatis libertatem qui in gratia vocati sumus, non secundum servitutem Iudaicam ex timore poenarum et ambitione terrenorum, non ex desiderio aeternorum, nobis plurimum philosophos certum est assentire. Quibus, ut diximus, et fides Trinitatis revelata est et ab ipsis praedicata, et spes immortalitatis animae et aeternae retributionis exspectata.'
Theologia Christiana II 43, ed. Buytaert II 1969, 149.
Cf. *ibid.* II 65, p. 158. Also *Theologia 'Summi boni'* I 6, ed. Ostlender 1939, p. 24; and *Theologia 'Summi boni'* II, ed. Ostlender 1939, p. 33: 'Quod nec ipsos latuit philosophos, qui notitiam dei non ratiocinando, sed bene vivendo acquirendam censebant et ad eam moribus potius quam verbis intendendum esse suadebant.'

91 *Historia calamitatum*, ed. Monfrin 1962, lines 425–558. Cf. *Theologia Christiana* II 67, 87, 96–101, ed. Buytaert II, 1969, 159–60, 170, 173–7; and also P. Delhaye, 'Le dossier antimatrimonial de l'*Adversus Jovinianum* et son influence sur quelques écrits latins du XIIe siècle', *Mediaeval Studies* XIII (1951) 65–86.

92 *Historia calamitatum*, ed. Monfrin 1962, lines 1038–119. Cf. *Theologia Christiana* II 61–3, 67, 69, ed. Buytaert II, 1969, pp. 156–7, 160, 161–2.

93 *Sermo XXXIII* (P.L. 178, 582–607, esp. 591C–2B). See D. E. Luscombe, 'Pierre Abélard et le monachisme', in *Pierre Abélard– Pierre le Vénérable* 1975, pp. 271–8; J. Leclercq, '"Ad ipsam sophiam Christum"'. Le témoignage monastique d'Abélard', *Revue d'ascétique et de mystique* XLVI (1970) 161–81.

94 '... apud nos vero monachi ... apud gentiles autem ... philosophi': *Historia calamitatum*, ed. Monfrin 1962, lines 506–9.

95 Peter Abelard, *Dialogus inter Philosophum, Iudaeum et Christianum*, ed. R. Thomas (Stuttgart–Bad Cannstatt 1970), pp. 53–4. Peter Abelard, *A Dialogue of a Philosopher with a Jew and a Christian*, trans. P. J. Payer, Mediaeval Sources in Translation XX (Toronto 1979), pp. 36–7. The *Dialogue* may have been written between 1135 and 1139, but an earlier date has been suggested by Mews 1985, pp. 104f.

attested faith in the immortality of the soul, even in the resurrection of the body, more clearly than all the prophets.[96]

The moral precepts of the Gospels are nothing other than a reform of the natural law which has been followed by the philosophers.[97] The wisdom of gentile philosophy is close to that of Christianity. In his *Soliloquy* Abelard explores the links between Christian faith and philosophy.[98] Abelard argues that the word 'Christian' comes from Christ; Christ is Wisdom or *Sophia*; therefore a Christian is a philosopher or lover of *Sophia*. Moreover, since Christ is the Word and the Word is *Logos*, Christians are logicians and therefore philosophers.[99] These arguments are found also in the *Invectiva in quemdam ignarum dialectices*.[100] Abelard in his own career exemplified the varieties of philosopher, being himself a logician, a teacher, a hermit, a theologian, and a monk.

Interpreting the writings of the pagan philosophers

Abelard made generous use of the writings of philosophers in his theological works, but the perspective in which he did so needs to be understood. Much of his knowledge of pagan philosophy came through the works of the Church Fathers. What Abelard knew of the teaching of the Platonists he found largely in the works of St Augustine.[101] It was not confidence in reason alone which led him to seek in the works of the Platonists the doctrine of the Trinity. The philosophers, like the prophets, had received a divine revelation which was to be complete after the coming of Christ.[102] There is

96 *Theologia 'Summi boni'* 1 6, ed. Ostlender 1939, pp. 24.35–25.3.

97 '... si enim diligenter moralia evangelii praecepta consideremus, nihil ea aliud quam reformationem legis naturalis inveniemus, quam secutos esse philosophos constat': *Theologia Christiana* II 44, ed. Buytaert II, 1969, 149.611–14.

98 P.L. 178, 1876C–1880A; new ed. by C. S. F. Burnett, 'Peter Abelard, Soliloquium', *Studi medievali*, ser. 3a, XXV (1984), 857–94. In the *Soliloquium* Abelard refers to his (now lost) *Exhortatio ad fratres et commonachos nostros*: 'Quam quidem Exhortationem quisque legerit, videbit philosophos non tam nomine quam re ipsa Christianis maxime sociatos': P.L. 178, 1878A and ed. Burnett 1984, pp. 888f.

99 *Soliloquium* P.L. 178, 1878AB and ed. Burnett 1984, p. 889.

100 *Epistola XIII*, ed. E. R. Smits, in *Peter Abelard. Letters IX-XIV. An Edition with an Introduction* (Rijksuniversiteit te Groningen 1983), pp. 271–7, at lines 97–128. Previous ed. P.L. 178, 351–6, at 355. Smits discusses the content of this letter on pp. 172–88 and suggests that it may have been written when Abelard was Abbot of St Gildas or shortly afterwards.

101 *Theologia Christiana* II 12, ed. Buytaert II, 1969, 137–8; *Theologia 'Scholarium'* II 1 (P.L. 178, 1039AB). See T. Gregory, 'Abélard et Platon', in *Peter Abelard. Proceedings of the International Conference Louvain, May 10–12, 1971*, ed. E. M. Buytaert, *Mediaevalia Lovaniensia*, ser. 1/Studia II (Leuven 1974), pp. 38–64.

102 *Theologia 'Summi boni'* I, ed. Ostlender 1939, p. 24: 'Cum itaque dominus et per prophetas Iudaeis et per praestantes philosophos seu vates gentibus catholicae fidei tenorem annuntiaverit ...': *Theologia Christiana* I 136, ed. Buytaert II, 1969, 130; cf. also *Theologia*

harmony between evangelical and philosophical teaching,[103] but the
meaning of the teaching of the philosophers, like that of the prophets, is
presented in fables.[104] The doctrine of the Trinity can be found in the
writings of the Platonists only by means of an exegesis like that used to
understand the allegories in the Bible.[105] In both philosophical and sacred
writings we find symbols hidden in veils or myths (*involucra*); and these have
to be interpreted in a mystical manner (*mystice*) in order to appreciate their
multiple meanings. The surface of the letter (*litterae superficies*) is heavily
charged with *mysteria*.[106] But, when properly interpreted, Plato – *maximus
philosophorum* – and his followers may be seen to have expressed the mystery
of the Trinity (*totius Trinitatis summam post prophetas patenter ediderunt*).[107]
Christian teaching on the Son of God resembles the philosophers' teaching
on *nous*.[108] The Platonic 'world soul (*anima mundi*)' adumbrates Christian
belief in the Holy Spirit.[109]

'*Scholarium*' I 25 (P.L. 178, 1034C); 'hanc Trinitatis distinctionem omnibus annuntiatam . . .
quam quidem divina inspiratio et per prophetas Judaeis, et per philosophos gentibus
dignata est revelare, ut utrumque populum ad cultum unius Dei ipsa summi boni perfectio
agnita invitaret . . . et facilius haec fides Trinitatis tempore gratiae susciperetur ab utroque
populo, cum eam a doctoribus quoque antiquis viderent esse traditam': *Theologia* '*Scholarium*' I 12 (P.L. 178, 998BC). Cf. *Theologia* '*Summi boni*' I 2, ed. Ostlender 1939, p. 4;
Theologia Christiana I 7 ed. Buytaert II, 1969, 75. In the *Theologia Christiana* Abelard writes:
'hanc divinae Trinitatis distinctionem non a Christo inceptam, sed ab ipso apertius ac
diligentius traditam esse . . .'
103 '. . . evangelicae ac philosophicae doctrinae concordia': *Theologia Christiana* II 44, ed.
Buytaert II, 1969, 150.618–19.
104 *Theologia* '*Summi boni*' I 5, ed. Ostlender 1939, p. 14.22f; *Theologia Christiana* I 103f, ed.
Buytaert II, 1969, 114f; *Theologia* '*Scholarium*' I 19–20 (P.L. 178, 1022B f).
105 *Theologia Christiana* II 15–16, ed. Buytaert II, 1969, 139–40.
106 *Theologia* '*Summi boni*' I 5, ed. Ostlender 1939, pp. 13–14:
'Hoc quippe loquendi genus (*sc.* involucri figura) philosophis sicut prophetis familiarissi-
mum est, ut videlicet, cum ad arcana prophetiae pervenerint, nihil vulgaribus verbis
efferant, sed comparationibus similitudinum lectorem magis alliciant. Quae enim quasi
fabulosa antea videbantur et ab omni utilitate remota secundum litterae superficiem,
gratiora sunt, cum magnis plena mysteriis postmodum reperta magnam in se doctrinae
continent aedificationem.'
Cf. *Theologia Christiana* I 98, ed. Buytaert II, 1969, 112; *Theologia* '*Scholarium*' I 19 (P.L.
178, 1021C). On the notion of *involucrum* or *integumentum* in the twelfth century see also
E. Jeauneau, 'L'usage de la notion d'integumentum à travers les gloses de Guillaume de
Conches', *AHDLMA* XXIV (1957) 35–100 (repr. in E. Jeauneau, *Lectio Philosophorum*
(Amsterdam 1973), pp. 125–92); P. Dronke, *Fabula* (Leiden–Cologne 1974), pp. 55–67.
107 *Theologia* '*Summi boni*' I 5, ed. Ostlender 1939, p. 13; *Theologia Christiana* I 68, ed. Buytaert
II 1969, 100; *Theologia* '*Scholarium*' I 17 (P.L. 178, 1012CD).
108 *Theologia* '*Summi boni*' I 5, ed. Ostlender 1939, p. 13; *Theologia Christiana* I 68, ed.
Buytaert II, 1969, 100; *Theologia* '*Scholarium*' I 16 (P.L. 178, 1009C–1012C).
109 *Theologia* '*Summi boni*' I 5–6, ed. Ostlender 1939, pp. 13–20; *Theologia Christiana* I 69–96,
ed. Buytaert II 1969, 100–12; *Theologia* '*Scholarium*' I 17 (P.L. 178, 1013B–1021C).

Abelard and moral philosophy

Abelard discusses the relationship between revealed and philosophical teaching about goodness in a work entitled the *Dialogue of the Philosopher with a Jew and a Christian*. The differences of belief and opinion which the three participants express and debate reflect a division of history into three periods: the period of the natural law, when men used only reason to establish the moral law; the period of the written law which was given by Moses to the Jews; the period of grace inaugurated by Christ. The Philosopher claims that many people were content with the natural Law before the handing down of the Law by Moses; natural law, which he calls ethics, consists in the love of God and neighbour. The Philosopher rejects the Jewish Law as an unnecessary extra burden to the natural law. His debate with the Christian concentrates on the nature of the supreme goodness as it is defined by pagan philosophers in ancient Greece and Rome and by Christian authors. Pagans have called the study of goodness ethics, Christians divinity.[110] The Philosopher alleges that supreme goodness, as it is defined by Christians, is that which, when attained, makes one blessed, and supreme evil is that whose possession makes one wretched. But supreme goodness has also been defined as virtue or as pleasure by non-Christian thinkers. These differences may be differences of terminology, if it is accepted that pleasure consists in an inner peace of the soul achieved through the practice of virtue, and also if blessedness results from being excellent in virtue.[111] The Philosopher raises the question whether the supreme good or supreme evil for man may be attained in this or in a future life, that is, whether man may become better or worse in an afterlife. To this the Christian replies that the time for earning merit is in this life only; the time for receiving a reward is in the future life. Now is the time for planting, then the time for gathering. The Philosopher is persuaded by the Christian that the supreme good for man is the perpetual rest or joy which the meritorious receive in a life after death. What the Epicureans have called pleasure is the enjoyment of the kingdom of heaven according to the teaching of Christ. Supreme evil for man is the supreme misery or punishment received for one's failings.[112] But the Christian is not prepared to accept a definition of the supreme good or the supreme evil for

---

110 Abelard 1970, pp. 88–9; cf. pp. 44 and 53. Abelard 1979, p. 76; cf. pp. 24 and 36. Cf. M. de Gandillac, 'Le *Dialogue*', in *Abélard* (1981), pp. 3–20. On the Philosopher see *Peter Abelard's Ethics*, ed. and trans. D. E. Luscombe, Oxford Medieval Texts (Oxford 1971), p. xxxv n. 6, and the references there cited.

111 Abelard 1970, pp. 98–9; Abelard 1979, pp. 88–90.

112 Abelard 1970, pp. 100–6; Abelard 1979, pp. 91–7.

man that reduces good and evil to rewards or penalties earned by man; rather, the supreme good or the supreme evil for man is the supreme state of inner blessedness or inner wretchedness that man can achieve. The Christian defines this supreme blessedness or wretchedness in terms of what gains for man his eternal reward, namely man's supreme love of God, or those faults committed by him which make him bad.[113] The Philosopher and the Christian next discuss the nature of supreme goodness in itself. To the Christian the supreme good is God, who alone is properly and absolutely called the supreme good and whose supreme love is extended to us. No greater good can be found than God, and unless the supreme good is God, the glory and the blessedness of God cannot be supreme. Beatitude for man is therefore the vision of God.[114] The Philosopher finds this acceptable and observes that this view is not unknown to philosophers.

Goodness in general is defined by the Christian as that which does not obstruct the advantage or benefit of anything; evil in general is that which does so obstruct. For this reason actions are morally neutral, that is, they are neither good nor bad, because an action in itself does not promote or obstruct goodness.[115] Both the tyrant and the prince wield a sword; their act of using the sword is the same and it is morally indifferent, although the tyrant uses the sword evilly and for the sake of spreading violence, whereas the prince uses it well to punish wrongdoing. Doing good and doing wrong therefore mean acting well (that is, with a good intent) or acting evilly (that is, with an evil intent). By virtue of a difference of intention the same act may be done well or evilly. Two men may hang a criminal, the one because he hates him, the other in the exercise of justice. The second acts well because of his right intention; the first acts unjustly, through not acting out of love of justice.[116] What it is good or wrong to do is laid down by the command of God.[117]

In his work called the *Ethics* or *Know Thyself* Abelard explores in greater detail the role of intentions and of consent in determining morality.[118] His teaching on actions is that they only come to be called right or wrong on

113 Abelard 1970, pp. 132–3; Abelard 1979, p. 129.
114 Abelard 1970, p. 138; Abelard 1979, p. 135.
115 Abelard 1970, pp. 160–1; Abelard 1979, pp. 158–9.
116 Abelard 1970, pp. 163–5; Abelard 1979, pp. 161–2.
117 Abelard 1970, pp. 170–1; Abelard 1979, pp. 168–9.
118 *Ethics* 1971, pp. 22–5, 46–9. The *Ethics* was probably written between 1135 and 1139. Of great value to the study of Abelard's moral teaching are R. Blomme, *La doctrine du péché dans les écoles théologiques de la première moitié du XIIe siècle* (Louvain 1958), Pt II, pp. 101–294; O. Lottin, *Psychologie et morale aux XIIe et XIIIe siècles* (6 vols., Louvain–Gembloux 1942–60); and P. Anciaux, *La théologie du sacrement de pénitence au XIIe siècle* (Louvain–Gembloux 1949), pp. 66–7, 286–92.

account of the intention of their human agent. An action cannot increase a man's merit or guilt, because no external, physical happening can profit or blemish a man's soul. Only the intention to conform to the law of God can win merit for man, and only the knowing consent to committing a deliberate contempt of God incurs guilt.[119] Sin lies neither in being tempted to do nor in doing what is wrong; it lies between these two moments, in consenting to the initial temptation.[120] Abelard eliminates a series of definitions of sin: sin is not vice nor an evil will nor an evil desire nor concupiscence. All these are incitements to sin which may be resisted. Sin itself is yielding to what the mind knows to be wrong.[121] Abelard emphasizes therefore the non-substantiality of sin.[122] What matters in morality is not what we do but why we do it, our intentions rather than our acts.[123] It is the modality of actions that counts, whether, that is, they are done well or wrongly, for a good intention or an evil one. As in his discussions of logic (though without direct reference to them), Abelard refers the study of ethics away from the third branch of philosophy, namely, physics or the study of things, towards the realm of understanding. Consent is the pivot of morality, yet it is not a thing. For consent to be sinful a man has to know that it is evil to which he consents; likewise an intention only becomes good, and therefore capable of earning merit for man, if it is in conformity with divine law. Abelard chose the provocative example of the crucifixion of Christ to argue that those who put Christ to death did no wrong, for they believed they acted rightly.[124]

Conclusion

Over a period of about forty years Abelard extended the range of his learning and thought. In his early studies of the arts of the Trivium he explored the role of language in expressing truth and falsehood, and also the double

119 *Ethics* 1971, pp. 52–7.
120 *Ibid.* pp. 4–7.
121 Abelard 1971, pp. 2–17.
122 'Cum itaque peccatum diffinimus abnegative, dicentes scilicet non facere vel non dimittere quod convenit, patenter ostendimus nullam esse substantiam peccati quod in non esse potius quam esse subsistat, veluti si tenebras diffinientes dicamus absentiam lucis ubi lux habuit esse': *Ethics* 1971, pp. 6–7. Abelard's dismissal of the significance in ethics of actions reminds one of his dismissal of the view that verbal utterances and *status* and *dicta* are things: 'A man is hanged on account of a theft he performed which is now nothing and a man dies because he does not eat and is damned because he does not act rightly, yet not eating and not acting rightly are not things (*non sunt essentiae aliquae*)': *Logica 'Ingredientibus'*, ed Geyer 1919–27, p. 369.3–6.
123 'Non enim quae fiunt, sed quo animo fiant pensat Deus, nec in opere sed in intentione meritum operantis vel laus consistit': *Ethics* 1971, p. 28.
124 *Ibid.* pp. 54–7.

relationship of language to things and to concepts. When he came to write on ethics he similarly explored the relationship between things (actions) and mental decisions and judgements about them. He criticized a form of realism which allowed that physical acts may be the carriers of goodness or evil, just as he criticized the view that physical utterances (words) may themselves convey general ideas. In his properly theological writings Abelard was similarly disposed towards non-realism. In respect of the Trinity Abelard raised the question whether the three divine persons exist *in re* or in words only, and whether there are other ways of elucidating the three aspects of God than by speaking of three persons.[125] In his account of the creation of the universe, he offered a partially non-literal account of some of the content of the opening of Genesis, and he interpreted it as a text that conveys spiritual meaning to us as well as scientific lore.[126] Discussing the redemption of mankind by Christ, Abelard questioned the view that the actions of Christ, and especially Christ's physical suffering and death, themselves liberated mankind from the grip of the devil. He apparently favoured an alternative view, that Christ provided, through the example of his preaching and his humble love of man, an incitement to fallen man to desert the ways of sin.[127] In one of his poems, the lament or *Planctus* on the death of Samson, Abelard likewise explored not so much the fact of Samson's tragic death as the motives which led Samson to commit suicide.[128] In his autobiography and in the correspondence which he shared with Heloise, much emphasis is laid on the distinction between the external realm of happenings and the inner realm of intentions and of motives, which alone lead to rewards or to punishments. In his exploration of the writings of the ancient philosophers of Greece and Rome Abelard underlines the virtuous lives led by the philosophers themselves, the purity of their motives, the goodness of their intentions. The inner meaning of their words may often be found to be in close conformity with Christian teaching once the physical layer of their words is removed. Such a penetration beyond an actual text to its underlying purpose required

---

125 *Theologia 'Summi boni'* II 2, III 1, ed. Ostlender 1939, pp. 42, 67; *Theologia christiana* IV 1–6, ed. Buytaert II, 1969, 266–8. To some extent Abelard's question whether the divine substance is present in three divine persons is similar to the question he faced as a logician as to whether a universal may be present in a number of individuals which belong to a species or genus.

126 P.L. 178, 729–84.

127 *Commentary on St. Paul's Epistle to the Romans*, ed. Buytaert I 1969, 113–18. See R. E. Weingart, *The Logic of Divine Love: A Critical Analysis of the Soteriology of Peter Abelard* (Oxford 1970).

128 P.L. 178, 1820–1. Cf. P. Dronke, *Poetic Individuality in the Middle Ages: New Departures in Poetry, 1000–1150* (Oxford 1970), ch. 4.

the use of hermeneutics; intellection was always more important to Abelard than the raw data.

Abelard encountered much criticism from his contemporaries, who complained of his novelty and his departures from tradition. Much criticism of his theology was well-grounded. Yet Abelard always defended the integrity of his motives and of his Christian faith. In a *Confession* of his faith to Heloise he admitted that logic had made him odious to the world, but he added: 'I do not wish to be a philosopher if it means conflicting with Paul, nor to be an Aristotle if it cuts me off from Christ.'[129] Abelard's work clearly represents more than the culmination of the old logic, for he applied logic so widely in philosophy and theology.[130] He exerted a strong influence as a teacher on his immediate pupils and followers, as well as upon his critics. Yet future generations of philosophers were not much aware of Abelard's writings or ideas. The reasons for this still await elucidation.

129 'Nolo sic esse philosophus, ut recalcritem Paulo. Non sic esse Aristoteles, ut secludar a Christo': P.L. 178, 375–8, at 375.
130 On 'the culmination of the old logic' see Kretzmann 1982; also M. M. Tweedale, 'Abelard and the culmination of the old logic', *CHLMP* pp. 143–57.

11

WILLIAM OF CONCHES

DOROTHY ELFORD

In his day William of Conches's work evoked a variety of responses: admiration from John of Salisbury, his best-known pupil; scorn and impatience, it seems, from the 'Cornificians', who favoured a utilitarian approach to education and considered old-fashioned the thorough, painstaking study of literary expression which characterized William's teaching; alarm and anger from some who feared they saw unorthodox, unchristian influences at work in his philosophy.[1] The manuscript tradition suggests that in the years which followed his death (some time after 1154) William's writings attracted many readers, compilers, and excerptors. His two systematic works, the *Philosophia* and the *Dragmaticon*, are each known in around seventy manuscripts,[2] and many of his sets of glosses on texts, particularly those on the *Timaeus* and on Boethius' *Consolation of Philosophy*, were also widely copied and used. After many centuries of neglect William has been drawing considerable scholarly interest for the past hundred years and more.[3] As before, reactions differ; William's ideas and those of people associated with him have been interpreted both as original and as unduly conservative.[4] Aspects of his system, notably his element-theory and his doctrine of the world-soul or *anima mundi*, are once again controversial, although they are not now being studied as theologically dangerous novel-

---

1 John of Salisbury, *Metalogicon*, ed. C. C. J. Webb (Oxford 1929), I 5, I 24, II 10; J. O. Ward, 'The Date of the Commentary on Cicero's *De Inventione* by Thierry of Chartres (*ca.* 1095–1160?) and the Cornifician Attack on the Liberal Arts', *Viator* III (1972), 219–73; William of Saint-Thierry, *De erroribus Gulielmi de Conchis ad sanctum Bernardum*, ed. J. Leclercq, *Revue Bénédictine* LXXIX (1969) 375–91.
2 A. Vernet, 'Un remaniement de la *Philosophia* de Guillaume de Conches', *Scriptorium* I (1946–7) 243–59.
3 T. Gregory, *Anima mundi: La filosofia di Guglielmo di Conches e la Scuola di Chartres* (Florence 1955), is the outstanding modern work and contains an extensive bibliography. Many of the more recent articles and books are mentioned in my 'Developments in the natural philosophy of William of Conches: a study of the *Dragmaticon* and a consideration of its relationship to the *Philosophia*' (unpublished Cambridge Ph.D. thesis, 1983).
4 According to R. W. Southern, *Medieval Humanism and Other Studies* (Oxford 1970), pp. 61–85, at p. 83, 'all their thoughts were old thoughts'. P. Dronke, 'New Approaches to the School of Chartres', *Anuario de Estudios Medievales* VI (1969) 117–40, speaks of 'the radical, challenging qualities of [William's] mind' (p. 132 n. 50).

ties. Much progress has been made, but the majority of William's own works still lack critical editions. This is most to be regretted in the case of his *Dragmaticon*, a greatly enlarged and revised survey of the ground he had covered many years earlier in his *Philosophia*.

William has been seen as a figure in a tradition of 'Christian Platonism'. This is a good starting-point, so long as we remember that Platonism itself is 'an extremely slippery concept',[5] which takes on different forms in different people's hands. We should recognize that his thought is characterized by a determination to go beyond Plato and yet not away from him. As he himself expressed it in the *Dragmaticon* when asked to explain a puzzling statement in the *Timaeus*: 'It is not my intention to expound here the words of Plato, but to set down here the view of natural scientists (*physici*) concerning substances; but even if I have not expounded Plato's words, I have said all that he said about elements, and more'.[6] This attitude, which will have arisen from the breadth of William's reading, was no doubt strengthened by his scholarly contacts.[7]

Analysis of the sources of William's philosophy has made it clear that he drew on Platonist and Neoplatonist texts, on the Bible and the Fathers, and on some of the works (particularly of a medical and astronomical nature) which the process of translation from Arabic had made accessible to men of his generation. It is customary to view him as a great systematizer – indeed he is – but at how profound a level has the integration of ideas taken place, and was his attempt a fruitful one? Some feel that his 'system' is the best possible amalgamation of all the inconsistent information which he knew.[8] Others have found in him an impulse towards a genuinely consistent view of nature.[9] The divergence of opinion is closely related to the question of exactly what difference William's reading of 'new' authors made to his

---

5 R. W. Southern, *Platonism, scholastic method, and the School of Chartres* (Reading 1979), p. 5.
6 *Dragmaticon*, ed. G. Gratarolus (Strasbourg 1567), p. 52. E. Maccagnolo, *Il Divino e il Megacosmo* (Milan 1980), pp. 241–453, gives an Italian translation of the work made from an unpublished 1943 edition; see the Bio-bibliographies, p. 456. Cf. H. Flatten, *Die Philosophie des Wilhelm von Conches* (Koblenz 1929), p. 18.
7 The issue of the relations between William and the cathedral school at Chartres forms part of a much broader complex of questions about the significance of that school and the validity of 'the label of Chartrian Platonism' (Southern 1979, p. 40). Dronke 1969 and N. Häring, 'Chartres and Paris Revisited', in *Essays in honour of A. C. Pegis*, ed. J. R. O'Donnell (Toronto 1974), pp. 268–329, stress the individuality of Chartres. Southern (cf. also his 'The Schools of Paris and the School of Chartres', *Harvard 1982* pp. 113–37) opposes that position. I myself believe that William both studied and taught at Chartres.
8 Southern 1979, pp. 16–25.
9 H. Liebeschütz, 'Kosmologische Motive in der Bildungswelt der Frühscholastik', in *Vorträge der Bibliothek Warburg 1923–24* (Leipzig 1926), pp. 83–148, at p. 128.

thought and to his Platonism. I believe there is both more 'consistency' and more 'inconsistency' in him than has yet been shown.

Because my concern will be to present William as a natural philosopher, rather than as a teacher of literature, I shall base the discussion on his systematic works and his glosses on the *Timaeus*. Since William's method of glossing a text involved him in giving scientific/philosophical explanations as well as literary ones, and since the systematic works were written, so he tells us, 'to facilitate reading the philosophers',[10] there is no sharp division of subject-matter, but the remaining glosses add relatively little to his picture of the physical world. In order to present William's thought in its mature form, I shall pay particular attention to the *Dragmaticon* – a work of great importance both for its content and for the light it sheds on William's techniques of argument.

One of the most interesting aspects of William's thought is the way it changes. Manuscript studies are revealing how complex is the question of the order of his works and the number of redactions of each,[11] but we do know that William modified his views on certain topics.[12] Is this in itself a sign of inconsistency? I do not think we have to take that line. I should like to draw attention to some intriguing developments from the *Philosophia* to the *Dragmaticon* on the question of elements – developments which have not previously been properly studied. Here, I would suggest, we can see William as a member of his generation and catch a glimpse of the influences at work in his milieu in the period from the 1120s to the 1140s. Few things in study are more fascinating than to be able (in however small a degree) so to get inside the minds of a generation of thinkers that we can see the process of stimulation, information, and criticism going on between them and contrast their reactions to new ideas from outside. This kind of endeavour is beginning to be possible for those studying William and his contemporaries, as we have greater access both to what they wrote and to the texts at their disposal.

There are two main discussions of elements in William's works.[13] In the

10 *Dragmaticon*, pp. 5, 235; cf. *Philosophia*, ed. G. Maurach (Pretoria 1980), p. 95.
11 See the Bio-bibliographies, p. 456.
12 Gregory 1955, pp. 223–31 (astronomy); see below (nn. 79, 53, 68 respectively) for works by B. Lawn (meteorology, medical matters), Y. V. O'Neill (the brain), C. Picard-Parra (meteorology). For the world-soul, see the end of this chapter.
13 See R. McKeon, 'Medicine and Philosophy in the Eleventh and Twelfth Centuries: the Problem of Elements', *The Thomist* XXIV (1961) 211–56.

Philosophia[14] and the *Glosae super Platonem*,[15] we find him quoting the authority of Constantinus[16] for confining the term 'elements' to the simple minimal particles which compose all bodies. These particles are simple as to quality and minimal as to quantity. They occur in four varieties – hot and dry (fire), hot and moist (air), cold and moist (water), and cold and dry (earth) – and it is the preponderance of a different kind of particle in each of the four large-scale visible 'elements' which gives it its name. These visible 'elements' should be called *elementata*, 'things made from elements', or *elementa mundi*, 'elements of the world' – for, as William explains, just as the particles are the first principles of individual bodies, so the four visible masses are the constituent parts of the universe. We must not be discouraged by our inability to grasp particle-elements with our senses, for they may be found by the intellectual method of division, which is merely an extension of the physical dissection of a body.[17]

This passage illustrates the complexity of William's use of sources. He dwells on Constantinus' name (it comes six times!), as if he were pleased to be able to include him in his bibliography, but relatively little of the argument is drawn from the *Pantegni*. As Gregory has seen, Constantinus' whole discussion centres on *qualitative* requirements for elements; it is William who explains that the term 'minimal' in the definition is to be understood in a quantitative sense. This is by no means the only difference between the two accounts.[18] Why should William have projected his own, more developed view back onto Constantinus? He may have wished to quote an authority for a theory which involved a perhaps surprising transfer of the term 'element' from the familiar four masses to tiny particles we can never apprehend with our senses.[19]

We may observe a certain flourish when William introduces his distinction between elements and *elementata*. The sentence in which he does so is closely modelled on a famous Boethian distinction between eternity, which belongs

---

14 Pp. 26–30.
15 Ed. E. Jeauneau (Paris 1965), chs. 58–9, pp. 128–30; cf. ch. 164, pp. 272–4.
16 Constantinus died at Monte Cassino in 1087 after translating many medical works from Arabic into Latin. See H. Schipperges, *Die Assimilation der arabischen Medizin durch das lateinische Mittelalter, Sudhoffs Archiv*, III (Wiesbaden 1964) 17–54. For a recent reappraisal and bibliographical information, see M.-Th. d'Alverny, 'Translations and Translators', in *Harvard 1982*, pp. 421–62, especially pp. 422–5.
17 Cf. Constantinus, *Pantechni*, in *Omnia opera Ysaac . . .* (Lyons 1515) II iv b – 2r b (elements), iv a (mental 'dissolution' and 'composition' of the human body). This work is a translation of the *al-Kunnāsh al-Malikī* of Ali ibn al-'Abbas al-Majūsī.
18 Gregory 1955, pp. 204–6.
19 Fuller discussion in Elford 1983, pp. 17–26.

to God alone, and perpetuity.[20] The non-Constantinian word *elementatum* raises interesting questions, for it was only around this time that it began to appear in Latin literature. Did William invent it,[21] or was it coined by a translator seeking to express the meaning of his Arabic original?[22] A third possibility is that the word originated in an early-twelfth-century commentary on a newly translated medical work.[23] In this case the 'flourish' would mark the use of a word that might be new to the general reader. There are also some Greek terms in this passage which are not from Constantinus but, it would seem, from another 'new' author.[24]

William's tone here is supremely confident, his attitude towards opponents scathing. He pours scorn on those who are ignorant of the writings of Constantinus and the medical authors. How intriguing, then, to turn to the *Dragmaticon* and discover that he has rewritten the entire section.[25] The exposition of Constantinus' definition of an element has been replaced by pages of puzzles and arguments in which perhaps the most curious feature is that we see William (under the guise of the Duke of Normandy, the interlocutor in the dialogue) setting himself problems to which he cannot give a fully convincing answer – that is, the questions are better than the solutions. What is going on? One thing is clear: the famous passage in the *Philosophia* had ceased to express what William wanted to say about elements. Let us look more closely at the *Dragmaticon*.

PHILOSOPHER: An element is what is found first in the building-up of a body and last in its breaking-down. That which is first in building-up is what builds up but is not built up; that which is last in breaking-down is what divides off but is not divided up. Now reason requires that just as every body can be divided into two largest parts, so it can be broken down into infinite smallest parts, for every body has a limit and a boundary. There are therefore in every single body certain things which compose it in such a way as not to be composed of parts; these things are first as to building-up and last as to breaking-down.

DUKE: In the same breath you are contradicting both yourself and Boethius. For

20 *Philosophia*, p. 28; cf. Boethius, *De Consolatione Philosophiae* v, pr. 6.
21 See Dronke 1969, pp. 128–32.
22 See T. Silverstein, 'ELEMENTATUM: Its Appearance among the Twelfth-Century Cosmogonists', *Mediaeval Studies* XVI (1954) 156–62. R. Lemay, *Abu Ma'shar and Latin Aristotelianism in the Twelfth Century* (Beirut 1962), is convinced that William took the word from John of Seville's 1133 translation of Abū Ma'shar's *Introductorium Maius*. Lemay's account of William's elements and *elementata* seems confused.
23 *Elementatum* occurs in the anonymous commentary on Johannitius' *Isagoge* in the Oxford Bodleian MS Digby 108, fol. 5v. See below, p. 325.
24 See T. Silverstein, 'Guillaume de Conches and the Elements: *Homiomeria* and *Organica*', *Mediaeval Studies* XXVI (1964) 363–7; 'Guillaume de Conches and Nemesius of Emesa', *Harry Austryn Wolfson Jubilee Volume* (Jerusalem 1965) II 719–34.
25 In the preface to the *Dragmaticon*, pp. 5–6, William undertakes to reproduce those parts of his earlier work which were correct.

you say that every body can be broken down into infinite smallest parts, but then you add that certain things in bodies are last as to breaking-down; and Boethius says 'magnitude decreases to infinity'.

PHILOSOPHER: 'Infinite' can refer to several different realms – number, size, kind …[26]

In this passage we have William's new definition of an element, the explanation of that definition and the first of three puzzles concerning the exact status of the elements. The definition and explanation develop points made in the *Philosophia*, and do so in words which call to mind the *De essentiis* of Hermann of Carinthia.[27] The puzzle may be stated as follows: an element must be indivisible, but how can the process of division in matter come to an end? William's 'corpuscular' elements, which are fixed units of matter, would seem to be ruled out by Boethius' statement that 'magnitude, beginning from a finite quantity, has no limit in division, for it allows the most infinite cuttings of its body'.[28] He defends himself against possible criticism by assuming that Boethius' concern is with *numerical* infinity and by explaining that both in his own exposition and in Boethius' statement 'infinite' means 'too many to know'. There does come a stopping-point in the subdivision of a body, but the number of parts involved (i.e. elements) exceeds our ability to count them.

But this 'solution' violates the plain meaning of Boethius' text. Boethius had been dealing with the subdivision of lengths or bodies, not with number, and had stated that they were susceptible to absolutely infinite division. This would indeed leave no room for the kind of elements proposed by William. That is why he quotes the dictum in the truncated form 'magnitude decreases to infinity' and 'explains' it in such a way that his particles seem to escape the need to be infinitely *divisible* by being infinitely (i.e. merely unknowably) *numerous*. Unwilling either to ignore Boethius' authority or to confront it, he misinterprets him and says that he agrees with him! This kind of verbal quibbling is not uncharacteristic of William.

A few pages later, William faces two further puzzles concerning the nature of the elements. The first is this: elements must be capable of producing a world which is perceptible to our senses, but are elements themselves perceptible? If they are, they cannot be indivisible, but if they are not, how

26 *Dragmaticon*, pp. 23–4.
27 Ed. C. Burnett (Leiden–Cologne 1982), 60v CD. See Burnett's commentary, pp. 22–5, 252–60. Hermann's book appeared in 1143, early enough to have influenced William. An obvious link between them could have been Thierry of Chartres, Hermann's teacher.
28 *De institutione arithmetica* I 1 (P.L. 63 1081C). See A. White, 'Boethius in the Medieval Quadrivium', in *Boethius: His Life, Thought and Influence*, ed. M. Gibson (Oxford 1981), pp. 162–205.

could they ever alter their nature so as to constitute solid reality? This would contradict principles laid down by Lucretius[29] and Macrobius.[30] William responds by defining 'imperceptible' in such a way as to exclude the particles. The distinction he makes is between things which are truly immaterial and could never be perceived by the senses and those which can be perceived *en masse* even if not singly. Souls would be an example of the first category, but element-particles belong in the second.[31]

The final problem, which follows on directly from the second, is this: elements must be capable of producing body, but are they themselves body or not?

DUKE: If these particles are perceptible in their own right, they are bodies; but if they are bodies, they have the three dimensions of length, breadth and thickness, because, as Boethius says, no body can be found without these three dimensions.[32]

PHILOSOPHER: That troublesome group of questions stems from the fact that you are ignorant of the applications and transferred usages of terms. The man who [first] applied this term 'body' applied it to something visible composed of the four elements . . . Later, philosophers considering the first principles of things transferred the terms to the principles and called the first principles of bodies 'bodies', but, to distinguish them from composite ones, 'simple' . . .

Boethius' statement about dimensions was made in accordance with the original meaning of the word 'body'. The particles, on the other hand, 'are bodies according to the scientific usage but do not have three dimensions'.[33]

This, the hardest of the three problems, receives the most paradoxical solution. Elements that were three-dimensional would not be ultimate – a contradiction of William's definition of them. He therefore turns once again to his old friend in adversity, the redefinition of his opponents' terms in order to deflect their force, and claims that while everyday, visible bodies obey a certain set of rules, their first principles (called 'simple bodies' by philosophers[34]) need not.

What can have prompted William's surprising assertion that the first principles of physical bodies are non-dimensional entities? I should like to

---

29 *De rerum natura* II 888 (known to William through Priscian).

30 *Commentarii in somnium Scipionis*, ed. J. Willis (Leipzig 1970) II xv 30.

31 *Dragmaticon*, pp. 28–9 *init.*

32 *De inst. arithmetica* II 4 (P.L. 63, 1120D); cf. Calcidius, *Timaeus a Calcidio translatus commentarioque instructus*, ed. J. H. Waszink (2nd ed., London–Leiden 1975), ch. 319; Nemesius, *Premnon phisicon*, trans. N. Alfanus, ed. C. Burkhard (Leipzig 1917), p. 26.

33 *Dragmaticon*, pp. 29–30.

34 William's authorities generally say that bodies are composite, not simple, e.g. Calcidius 1975, ch. 319. Cf. perhaps Nemesius 1917, p. 63, where, however, 'simple' has a qualitative sense.

draw attention to a passage in Boethius' *De institutione arithmetica* where the geometrical point is defined as follows:

> It is agreed that the point itself, without any bodily magnitude or extension in a dimension, since it lacks length and breadth and depth, is the principle (beginning) of all the dimensions, and by nature uncuttable, which the Greeks call 'atom', that is, so minute and small that no part of it can be found. So it is the principle (beginning) of all the dimensions yet not a dimension . . .[35]

This combination of characteristics has many echoes in the *Dragmaticon* and could go far towards explaining William's readiness to call the elements 'bodies without three dimensions' on the grounds that they are not natural bodies but the first principles of body.[36] We must recognize that in his determination to safeguard their indivisibility and minimum nature, without however making body from non-body,[37] William has overreached himself. He was aware of the problems involved in this kind of approach to elements – I do not feel that he was merely trying to reconcile all the 'authorities' – but could not fully overcome them.

Comparison between the *Philosophia* and the *Dragmaticon* reveals a noteworthy development in William's thinking. In the earlier work he was chiefly concerned to establish that the particles described by Constantinus deserved to be thought of as elements. The contrast was always between the elements and something larger and more complex, with the result that the formula 'simple minimal particle' could pass relatively unchallenged. The emphasis on grasping the elements intellectually also directed attention away from asking what they were in themselves. In the *Dragmaticon*, the focus shifts to the status of individual elements. Questions about their divisibility, perceptibility, and corporeality come to the fore. There is greater precision, allied with a new tone of defensiveness. Was William aware that a rather different conception of elements was gaining acceptance among his contemporaries? Hermann of Carinthia, for one, was very critical of the idea that the tiny parts of bodies were their elements. It is not implausible that he had William's *Philosophia* and *Glosae super Platonem* in mind.[38] Whether or not he was reacting to specific criticisms, William was determined to retain and refine his own theory.

35 *De inst. arithmetica* II 4 (P.L. 63, 1121AB).
36 Cf. pseudo-Bede, *De mundi celestis terrestrisque constitutione*, ed. C. Burnett (London 1985), p. 76, sections 475–80; White 1981, pp. 178–9.
37 Calcidius 1975, ch. 320 and Boethius, *Contra Eutychen et Nestorium* VI, both deny this possibility.
38 See Hermann 1982, 60v E, 62r CD and Burnett's commentary, pp. 252, 260–1. For Hermann, the elements were non-corporeal universals which come together to produce body (61r E – 62r C).

Towards the end of the *Glosae super Platonem* there are two chapters which throw into relief the divergent tendencies in William's element-theory. In chapter 164, William, having reached that point in the *Timaeus* where Plato rejects the right of visible fire, earth, water, and air to these names because of their mutability, and asserts that true fire must be unchanging,[39] attempts to establish his own particle-elements as the unvarying fire, earth, and the others as required by Plato. We learn that the particles are unchangeable, that they are never found by themselves even if they are understood by themselves, and that they are not only substances but corporeal substances.[40]

A little later, William turns back to the same lines of the *Timaeus*. True unchanging fire, he says,

> . . . can be understood by itself but cannot exist by itself, for all true elements are mixed [i.e. exist in combination]. But 'the function of the intellect is to distinguish things which are joined together'[41] . . . So true elements are things which do not exist by themselves but are understood by themselves . . . But there are some bestial people who imagine that nothing is real unless they can touch it, and so they do not believe that the true elements or the ideas or other intelligibles exist.[42]

Are the 'true elements' of this passage the 'particles' of the earlier chapter, or not? It seems hard to reconcile the 'corporeal substances' of chapter 164 with the implication here that the true elements belong, like the ideas, with the intelligibles, the other class of existence. Yet William must intend to refer to the same entities as particles and as true elements, for both, in their contexts, are exemplified by the fire which deserves its name because it is unchanging.[43]

I believe that this same tension would surface in any attempt to make the Platonism of the Latin *Timaeus* the foundation of a worked-out system of nature. The apparent contradiction highlights William's search for a class of things which are corporeal by nature but imperceptible and intelligible in our experience because they are extremely small and always occur within larger bodies. *What I can't touch or see* easily become assimilated to *what is intelligible and not sense-perceptible or corporeal* whenever there is a sharp Platonist distinction between the objects of intellect on the one hand and of sense and opinion on the other. The particle-elements on which William bases his

---

39 *Timaeus* 49DE.
40 *Glosae*, pp. 272–4.
41 William paraphrases Boethius, *In Porphyrium* I (P.L. 64, 84D). See Jeauneau, *Glosae*, p. 129 n. (a).
42 *Glosae* 170, pp. 280–1.
43 This prompts a question: if particles are unchangeable, what is it that undergoes the transformation when one element changes into another? William never really resolves this issue. See Elford 1983, pp. 47–8 n. 103.

scheme of nature fall at a boundary where Platonists[44] traditionally had no fence on which to sit. This is why it is possible for William to treat them as intelligibles *qua* objects of intellection, even though he has previously called them corporeal substances.

In the *Dragmaticon* we find William trying to limit the role of our bodily senses as the arbiters of perceptible and imperceptible, body and non-body. This is the lesson of the second and third puzzles. Faced with the particles, the senses impose a cut-off point which is not inherent in matter; reason must take over where the senses' limited range ends.[45] Adelard of Bath, who gives atoms as an example of something the senses cannot apprehend, also speaks of particles in a way which may have stimulated William to look for elements below the level of sense-perception.[46] In the *Philosophia* William had quoted Boethius to the effect that 'the function of the intellect is to distinguish things which are joined together and join together those which are separate'.[47] In the *Dragmaticon*, it is the meanings of words which are distinguished, and the second task is attempted when William argues that there is continuity all the way from the single particle, with its rather uncertain status, to the whole physical body.[48]

Should William be criticized for imagining that a purely verbal and logical solution would deal with the physical problem of finding the elements in bodies? The limitations of his approach are obvious, but it is interesting as an attempt to go beyond inherited ideas to develop a fitting physical basis for the natural world. There is originality both in William's actual theory and in the way he first presents it almost in the form of a manifesto, then reveals, in interaction with the text of Plato, the tensions inherent in it, and finally subjects it to his own searching criticisms.

Students of William of Conches have frequently drawn attention to his wish to answer the question 'how?' and to the importance he attaches to secondary causes. The concept of the 'autonomy of nature' has been invoked: William and certain of his contemporaries wanted to show that the origin and

44 Cf. Calcidius 1975, chs. 319–20: 'if *silva* [primordial matter] is a body it is sense-perceptible ... but if *silva* is something incorporeal, its nature is intelligible'.
45 Cf. Boethius, *De musica* i 9 (P.L. 63, 1176c).
46 Adelard, *De eodem et diverso*, ed. H. Willner, BGPTM iv.1 (1903), 13. In his *Questiones naturales*, ed. M. Müller, BGPTM xxxi.2 (1934), ch. 1, we read that earth is a mixture such that 'in its individual particles, at least those which are accessible to the senses, it contains all four elements with their qualities'.
47 See n. 41.
48 William now also sees creation itself in terms of particles, whereas previously he had spoken of the *elementa mundi* being created (*Dragmaticon*, pp. 27, 30; *Philosophia*, p. 29) – a further separation of what is joined together.

functioning of the world could be understood in terms of natural processes without this constituting any threat to the Christian belief in an all-powerful Creator.[49] William's best-known statement of this principle can be found in the *Philosophia*, in a passage where he defends his naturalistic exegesis of the Genesis account of the creation of the first man and woman. The expression he uses for what his obscurantist enemies do not want him to investigate is *vires naturae*, 'the forces of nature'.[50]

William's search for explanations led him to focus on a number of basic physical mechanisms. They can be traced back to his sources, notably to the Constantinian corpus – indeed this is the most fundamental aspect of his dependence on that tradition – but we find him applying them with great boldness and originality far beyond their original contexts. His readiness to identify in the macrocosm processes corresponding to those described by Constantinus for the microcosm is notable; as Liebeschütz commented many years ago, 'Here we seem unmistakably to encounter a rational attempt to trace manifold reality back to simple factors'.[51] William's systematic use of corresponding macrocosmic/microcosmic processes is fully as important as his element-theory, for these processes are the means by which he undertook to explain movement, change, and growth.

One of the most central of these physical principles is the idea that there are four forces (*vires*) – attractive, retentive, digestive, and expulsive – each produced by a different combination of the four basic qualities. In the Constantinian corpus, these forces operate within the realm of the 'natural power (*virtus naturalis*)' which presides over such processes as nutrition and growth.[52] William applies them not only to these areas but also to the thinking process[53] and to cosmology and meteorology. Their importance in his understanding of the macrocosm may be gathered from a passage in the

49 Gregory 1955, ch. 4, esp. pp. 178–82.
50 *Philosophia*, p. 39. William often appeals to *physica* – defined in *Glosae* 5, p. 61, as the science of the natures and complexions of bodies – and to *natura rerum*, 'the nature of the world'.
51 Liebeschütz 1926, p. 128.
52 *Pantegni* (printed as *De communibus medico cognitu necessariis locis* in Constantini Africani *Operum reliqua*, (Basle 1539)), IV 1–4; *De stomacho* (in Ysaac 1515, II), fols. 178v–179r.
53 *Philosophia*, pp. 106–7; *Dragmaticon*, pp. 276–8. William describes the combination of qualities in each of the three sections (*cellulae*) of the brain, together with reasons (e.g. the 'memory section' at the back is cold and dry in order to retain well) and the effects of any departure from the norm. Constantinus had localized faculties but not qualities; the brain is cold and moist (*Pantegni* IV 19; *De oculis* (in Ysaac 1515, II), fols. 172v–173r – cf. *Pantegni* IV 2, *De stomacho*, fol. 178v). Adelard 1934, chs. 17–18, also localizes faculties but not qualities, although he says that moisture promotes quick understanding (localized in the front section of the brain) and dryness promotes memory (back section). Could this have encouraged William to link the scheme of the four forces with mental processes? Cf. Y. V. O'Neill, 'William of Conches' Descriptions of the Brain', *Clio Medica* III (1968) 203–23.

Dragmaticon where the four 'elements' as seen in concentric positions in the universe are beginning to be discussed. The Duke is unwilling to concede the presence of cold or moist particles in fire.

PHILOSOPHER: No true philosopher doubts that fire is consuming by nature and consumes itself and other things. Also, it is certain that in winter some fire is very much thickened and is changed into air. Therefore that fire which is consumed either by itself or by something else in one season has to be restored in a different one. So in summer the fire first changes part of the water into air, then attracts it into itself – hence the fact that natural scientists have said that fire feeds on water. But it cannot transform what it attracts unless it retains and digests it. Now all natural scientists agree that coldness and dryness operate a retaining force, heat and moistness a cooking force. For a dry heat consumes and bakes something, a dry cold freezes it, a moist cold dissipates it . . . In fire there is also an expulsive force, which comes from what is cold and moist; there is an attractive force, which comes from what is hot and dry. Therefore there exist in fire the four kinds of particles, but with the hot dry ones predominating.[54]

In this analysis of the balance of the seasons, the effect of fire on the lower world-elements each summer is said to demonstrate the presence in it of all four types of particles. This explicit link between particles and the four forces belongs to William, not to Constantinus. It represents an extension of the realm of both concepts: we are to think of particles as the physical basis of the four forces, and we can no longer confine the operation of those forces within the old bounds.

William's originality shows itself again when he integrates the working of the four Constantinian forces with a traditional scheme[55] according to which each element possesses three qualities, one from each of the pairs fine/corpulent, blunt/sharp, mobile/immobile. In this scheme fire is fine, mobile, and sharp. He argues that if God had put fire and earth into contact in the universe without air and water as intermediaries, the fire would devastate the earth. The form of such an attack would be a direct outworking of the qualities of fire:

. . . the fire by its *fineness* would enter the pores of the earth and by its *movement* and *sharpness* would divide part from part, and it would *bake* the earth by *drying up* whatever was on its surface . . .[56]

In this description the fineness, mobility, and sharpness of fire are shown in

---

54 *Dragmaticon*, pp. 38–9.
55 Cf. Calcidius 1975, chs. 21–2, on *Timaeus* 31B f; Nemesius 1917, pp. 68–9; Isidore, *De natura rerum* 11.
56 *Dragmaticon*, p. 45.

action, in pulverization,[57] along with the 'baking' that we recognize from the passage about the four forces as one of the effects of a dry heat. There is an imaginative quality here, a consciousness of the real world, which brings alive the inherited formulae and is characteristic of a new twelfth-century attitude to nature.[58]

The whole of this section of the *Dragmaticon* is an expression of William's conviction that the world owes its stability as much to balanced changes between its parts as to any static system of proportions. To Plato's argument, that the world is indissoluble because of the balanced proportions between the elements (*Timaeus* 32C–33A), William adds one inspired by *Timaeus* 49C, where we read that the elements turn into one another by processes of thickening and thinning (this is not, for Plato, a proof of stability). In the *Glosae* William had brought out much more clearly than Plato the agency of heat in thinning and of cold in thickening, and had put these changes in the context of the seasonal cycle.[59] In the *Dragmaticon*, he describes this same process to illustrate regular movements between the elements.[60] The result is a far more dynamic picture of the world: 'By this alternation of changes the world remains indissoluble.'[61]

The four forces even enter the realm of astronomy. When detailing theories about the movements of the three upper planets, William includes the suggestion that the sun attracts them; here, as so often, he supplies an explanatory *mechanism* for a suggestion that had been made by others.[62] On this occasion he hesitates (in the *Dragmaticon*) between the new 'Chaldaean' theory of eccentric circles and epicycles and one which would be a more direct outworking of his own system of nature.[63]

---

57 Cf. p. 170: 'When the sun's rays touch this (cloud), they penetrate it by their sharpness and separate part from part . . .'; pp. 162, 173–4.

58 See Gregory 1955, pp. 175–88. In William's proof that the earth cannot be in flux, the traditional heaviness and immobility of earth are shown to be the product of its corpulence, coldness, and dryness (*Dragmaticon*, pp. 58–9). Cf. p. 278: if the front section of someone's brain is cold and dry, he will be slow-witted and 'stolid (*stupidus*)' – the very word used on p. 59 to describe the earth! This demonstrates again William's deep sense that our constitution is parallel with that of the macrocosm.

59 Ch. 162, p. 270.

60 Pp. 55–6.

61 *Dragmaticon*, p. 56. William thus gives a number of different models of seasonal change (see also *Philosophia*, pp. 58–63; *Dragmaticon*, pp. 121–32). They are neither unconnected ('thickening' is mentioned along with the four forces in *Dragmaticon*, p. 38) nor fully integrated. William must have seen something very significant in this process.

62 *Dragmaticon*, p. 103; cf. Macrobius 1970, I xx 4–5; Martianus, *De Nuptiis* VIII 887; Isidore, *Etymologies* III lxvi.

63 *Dragmaticon*, pp. 103–9; *Philosophia*, pp. 53–4, lacks the 'Chaldaean' theory. Burnett (Hermann 1982, p. 24) characterizes William's approach to natural science as 'biological',

Seasonal and physiological ideas come together in two further explanatory mechanisms used by William. His commentary on Juvenal contains an interesting explanation of why a man died when he took a bath after eating a peacock. In such a case the heat of the water opens the man's pores; his natural heat evaporates, the food cannot be properly digested, 'and from it are produced raw humours which are the cause of death or of serious illnesses'.[64] The principle that pores are closed by cold but opened by heat is used in the *Dragmaticon* to account for three apparently unconnected phenomena: our need to eat more in winter than in summer, the fact that the roots of plants stay alive during the winter, and the anomaly of well-water being cold in summer but warm in winter.[65] Clearly William has connected the obvious freezing of the ground in winter and its relaxation in spring with the medical themes of pores and natural heat in the human body, and has retained the doctors' term.

Again, we read that when the air above our temperate zone is inflamed by the sun in midsummer it 'feels itself being emptied *(suam inanitionem sentiens)*' and begins to act on the water beneath it and change it into itself. It is experiencing the same sensation and taking the same action as a plant or tree whose root moisture is drawn up by the sun in spring, or a person's skin dried up by work and a warm atmosphere, or a stomach from which the moisture has been sucked out to supply moisture to the dry skin.[66] The phrase *suam inanitionem sentiens* is from Constantinus, who uses it of the stomach;[67] William's extension of the concept is a striking example of microcosm/macrocosm parallelism.

William's debt to Seneca's *Naturales quaestiones* for the meteorological section of the *Dragmaticon* has been documented.[68] It is Seneca who seems to have furnished him with the principle that warmth cannot be produced except in something dense: this, he says, is why the lower air becomes warmer than the fine upper air when the sun shines.[69] William employs this

whereas Hermann's is 'mathematical'. Certainly for William the functioning of *organic* life serves as a pattern by which to interpret the whole of nature.

64 William of Conches *Glosae in Iuvenalem*, ed. B. Wilson (Paris 1980), pp. 132–3. This edition is faulty: see P. Dronke in *Medium Aevum* LII (1983) 146–9. Cf. *Dragmaticon*, p. 239: making love after eating is harmful because it too diminishes natural heat.

65 *Dragmaticon*, pp. 121–2, 125; p. 121; p. 204.

66 *Dragmaticon*, pp. 55–6, 123, 251–2.

67 *De stomacho*, fol. 178v. For the background to the theme of man as an upside-down tree *(arbor inversa)*, cf. C. Edsman, 'Arbor Inversa', in *Festschrift Walter Baetke* (Weimar 1966); *Dragmaticon*, p. 299.

68 C. Picard-Parra, 'Une utilisation des *Quaestiones naturales* de Sénèque au milieu du XIIe siècle', *RMAL* v (1949) 115–26. Cf. Elford 1983, pp. 142–3, 147–62.

69 *Naturales quaestiones*, ed. A. Gercke (Leipzig 1907) IVB 10f.

principle in a variety of contexts. He generally stresses the need for something to be moist as well as dense if heat is to be generated in it by the heavenly bodies.[70] This is perhaps a sign that he has combined the Senecan theme with the doctrine that the heavenly bodies draw up water to feed on.[71] He also links it with something Plato said about the different qualities of fire. The context is the Duke's refusal to accept that the planet Saturn is cold. The fiery nature of all stars is clear from their mobility and brightness, so how can there be such a thing as a cold star? William replies that the heat and brightness of fire are present together in some bodies but separately in others.[72] Stars may indeed be fiery, but they cannot be hot in the absence of thick moist material, and the aether in which they exist is extremely fine.[73]

But Saturn's 'coldness' is a subject that seems to have caused real problems for William, and this argument leads him into an inconsistency. Earlier in the *Dragmaticon*, when opposing the Fifth Essence theory – according to which the four elements exist below the moon and everything above it is made of a different substance, which is not hot, cold, moist, or dry – he had insisted on Saturn actually being cold and causing cold in the air.[74] Afterwards, however, he finds it no easy task to prove that this is so. He ends up by saying that perhaps Saturn is not himself cold and does not cause cold but merely signifies it[75] – a far cry from his previous confidence! One might have expected him to account for the traditional qualities and effects of Saturn and the other planets by saying that they contain different proportions of element-particles, but this is not attempted. We are left not knowing if all the information William gives is to be interpreted symbolically. It was presumably the manifest difficulty of describing fiery bodies as cold or capable of causing cold that made William agnostic with regard to Saturn. Indeed, quite a number of the weak points which we can discover in his physical system involve details of the relationship between the upper and lower parts of the world.[76] It is here that his four-element and four-quality framework

70 *Philosophia*, pp. 50, 74–6; *Dragmaticon*, pp. 180, 226.
71 Cf. Ambrose, *Hexaemeron* II iii 13 (P.L. 14, 151); Cicero, *De natura deorum* II xxxiii 83; Macrobius 1970, II x 10f etc; *Philosophia*, pp. 36, 54; *Dragmaticon*, pp. 38, 73, 104.
72 Cf. *Timaeus* 45B.
73 *Dragmaticon*, pp. 99–101; cf. *Philosophia*, pp. 49–50.
74 *Dragmaticon*, pp. 80–3; cf. pp. 118–19, 218–19. The fact that the Fifth Essence theory was not mentioned in the *Philosophia* suggests there must have been growing interest in Aristotelian astronomy among William's public in the intervening years. He himself refers to 'some of our people ... who ... falsely claim to be that man's sons' (p. 80).
75 *Dragmaticon*, pp. 101–2. In the *Philosophia*, p. 50, Saturn is hot but causes cold; does William now regard that position as unsatisfactory? Cf. R. Klibansky, E. Panofsky, and F. Saxl, *Saturn and Melancholy* (London 1964), p. 182.
76 For example, when William tries to explain how different planets can cause variations in our climate and seasons, he seems to have a number of mutually exclusive models in his mind

shows itself most inadequate to account for and integrate the phenomena. Elsewhere we can accept that it is for the sake of completeness that he gives the reader a choice of explanations;[77] here there are signs of irresolution.

In the final part of this chapter I should like to focus on a passage in the last book of the *Dragmaticon* which I feel both illustrates William's individuality and raises questions about the extent and above all the *nature* of his debt to the medical literature. To go through *Dragmaticon* VI in detail, attempting to pinpoint the source of each item of information, is a worthwhile exercise, and any future edition of the work will require a full commentary of this kind. It will reveal the great variety of William's medical reading,[78] document the relationship between him and Salernitan question-literature,[79] and demonstrate an important debt to his near-contemporary Adelard of Bath for what he has to say about the mechanism of sight and about the 'airy substance' that operates the senses.[80] But we also need to ask ourselves questions about the spirit in which the sources are being used.

PHILOSOPHER: There is no person who is not hot and moist, but some are more so, some less. For the first man was balanced between the four qualities, but when, after his expulsion from the loveliness of Paradise, he began to live on his own bread produced by the labour of his own hands in the valley of tears and misery, he began to dry up through his toil, hunger and lack of sleep, and his natural heat began to be extinguished, and the imbalance of the air and the quality of his food and drink had the same effect on him. Therefore all descended from him are corrupt, since they come from someone corrupt, and perfect health has never been found in man since that time. For something perfectly healthy is what is well balanced (*eucraticum*) in its 'homoeomeries' and equal in its organic parts – that is, what is well balanced (i.e. of a good complexion) in those members which can be divided into parts identical to one another, which the Greeks call 'homoeomeries', and does not overshoot or fall short

---

(*Dragmaticon*, pp. 130–2: cf. *Philosophia*, p. 62; *Dragmaticon*, pp. 205–7: cf. *Philosophia*, p. 86, and *Glosae* 25, p. 88). There are also problems concerning the relationship between the earth and the moon (*Dragmaticon*, p. 112, contradicts p. 100).

77 William himself upholds multiple explanations: 'As it may happen that plausible explanations of the same thing lead to a contradiction, both yours and mine (*et tua et mea*, MS Cambridge Gonville and Caius 240/225, p. 13; Gratarolus, *et tua in ea*) should be entertained as plausible, but neither of them as necessary' (*Dragmaticon*, p. 41).

78 Cf. O'Neill 1968 and her 'William of Conches and the Cerebral Membranes', *Clio Medica* II (1967) 13–21; Elford 1983, pp. 220–2.

79 B. Lawn, *I quesiti salernitani* (Salerno 1969), pp. 69–75, 236–8; *The Prose Salernitan Questions* (London 1979), Introduction and pp. 2–17. Lawn here edits a set of medical questions which incorporate a version of part of *Dragmaticon* VI.

80 Cf. Elford 1983, pp. 233–7. For sight, compare *Dragmaticon*, pp. 283–7, with Adelard 1934, chs. 24–5, 27, 23.

of the mean either in size or in number in its official members, which the Greeks call 'organic parts'.[81]

The theme of balance and correct proportion is of very great importance in William's system. In the *Philosophia*, he had taken the Genesis description of the making of Eve from Adam's side as a way of saying that she was created from ground close beside that perfectly balanced spot where he originated. This is why the complexion (proportion of qualities) of women is always less balanced than that of men.[82] This exegesis, which had scandalized William of Saint-Thierry,[83] is condemned in the preface to the *Dragmaticon*, and the creation of Eve is described in the most orthodox terms.[84] Yet the interpretation of Genesis 3 cited above makes it clear that the basic naturalism of William's outlook had remained unimpaired: at one and the same time he is showing that he takes the story of Adam being driven out of Eden literally and is turning that story to good account: the conditions of Adam's life after the Fall were such as to make him lose heat and moisture, and this is why his descendants fall short of perfect health.

This passage also provides the key to the otherwise puzzling fact that William can refer to the same things both as hot-and-moist and as temperate (balanced). It is because all men are now deficient in heat and moisture that temperate things are, by comparison with us, hot and moist.[85] These qualities are consistently used by William in his explanations of life, growth, and change;[86] by contrast, death and disease are associated with imbalance.[87] We see here again what I have called William's dynamic picture of the world. The hot-and-moist complexion, which stands for balance and correct

---

81 *Dragmaticon*, pp. 261–2. The passage on health is corrupt in Gratarolus' text; see MSS Cambridge Gonville and Caius 240/225, p. 89; Montpellier École de Médecine 145, fol. 51v; B.L. Add. 18210, fol. 62v; and B.L. Arundel 377, p. 137. The translation of Maccagnolo 1980, p. 419, seems faulty.

82 *Philosophia*, p. 38.

83 William of Saint-Thierry 1969, p. 390.

84 *Dragmaticon*, pp. 7 and 77.

85 Spring is temperate: *Dragmaticon*, pp. 122–4; spring resembles air, blood, and childhood in being hot and moist, *ibid*. pp. 124–5. See Klibansky 1964, pp. 97f.

86 When the world began, the warm, muddy surface of the earth produced living creatures (*Dragmaticon*, p. 76; *Philosophia*, p. 38). Heat and moisture are vital in sexual intercourse (best suited to spring and to people of sanguine complexion); they also characterize infants (*Dragmaticon*, pp. 238–9; 248–9; *Philosophia*, p. 52). The same qualities preside over our digestion and growth (cf. *Dragmaticon*, p. 39, on the 'digestive force', and pp. 261 and 258–9 – where blood is transformed into all parts of the body) and over our sensory and intellectual powers (an adaptable 'airy substance' works the senses, and the central section of the brain, where reasoning occurs, is temperate: *Dragmaticon*, pp. 282, and 277–8). Many meteorological phenomena are caused by the rising of hot moist vapour (*fumus*).

87 For the principle, see *Dragmaticon*, p. 79; cf. p. 288 (the evil eye is caused by a badly balanced visual ray) and p. 112 (the moon's rays might 'unbalance' the earth).

proportion, is the very one that generates processes of change and new life in both macrocosm and microcosm. This conviction, which is William's own integration of many strands of medical and other tradition,[88] leads him to take the Genesis 3 story 'literally'[89] in a very individual way; the hot-and-moist combination is basic to life because in it alone is preserved the balance lost by Adam.

If we look closely at the picture William gives of Adam's life outside Paradise, we find that nearly all the 'non-natural things' (variables relevant to the condition of the human body) from the schemes given by Constantinus and Johannitius[90] are mentioned as having an effect on Adam: emotions, sleep patterns, physical activity, food and drink, the atmosphere. The theme of the corruption of humanity is being treated in such a way that physical factors are emphasized to the exclusion of spiritual ones. This becomes all the more clear when we contrast it with a passage in Hildegard of Bingen's *Causae et curae*[91] in which Adam's humours are said to have undergone a change into something corrupt and bitter *at the moment when he sinned.*

William's definition of perfect health appears at first sight to be a combination of a passage in Constantinus[92] with some Greek terms from Nemesius.[93] However, a strikingly close parallel may be found in an anonymous commentary on Johannitius' *Isagoge* in an Oxford manuscript. This same commentary contains, on the next page, a passage on elements and *elementata* which makes the same distinction as William.[94] If Brian Lawn, who has studied this manuscript, is correct in dating the commentaries in it to the beginning of the twelfth century,[95] we may have here further evidence of

---

88 I believe Constantinus' teaching on the 'digestive force' and on the three kinds of spirit or breath (*spiritus*) which bring about our nutrition/reproduction, respiration, and mental/sensory powers (*Pantegni* IV 19) may have prompted William to make explicit the role of heat and moisture. The ancient assimilations between elements, humours, ages, seasons, and complexions (see n. 85) were available in Bede, *De temporum ratione* 35 (P.L. 90, 457–9); cf. Johannitius, *Isagoge ad Thegni Galeni*, in *Articella* (Lyons 1527), fol. 3v.

89 Cf. Thierry's promise to expound the beginning of Genesis 'according to natural science and literally (*secundum physicam et ad litteram*)': *Tractatus de sex dierum operibus* I, ed. N. M. Häring, *Commentaries on Boethius by Thierry of Chartres and his School* (Toronto 1971), p. 555.

90 *Pantegni* V 1; *Isagoge*, 2v–3r.

91 Text in P. Dronke, *Women Writers of the Middle Ages* (Cambridge 1984), pp. 244–5; discussion *ibid.* pp. 176–7.

92 *Pantegni* IV 20; cf. I 5.

93 Nemesius 1917, pp. 35, 59, 60.

94 Oxford, Bodleian Library, MS Digby 108, fol. 5r (health), fol. 5v (*elementata*). Cf. William of Saint-Thierry, *De natura corporis et animae*, P.L. 180, 696–7 (*eucraticum* and *eucrasia* in a passage on health); Lawn 1979, pp. 2–3 (*eucraticum* and *elementatum*).

95 Lawn 1979, pp. xx, 2–16. He notes close parallels between William and the Digby commentaries in gynaecological matters.

connections between William and the tradition of scholarly commentaries on medical works that was becoming established in his time.[96]

At the very end of the *Dragmaticon*,[97] William explains why infants are irrational. This passage brings together in a remarkable way the Christian, the Platonist, and the Constantinian views of man. First, the theme of our corruption since the Fall is developed in a thoroughly Platonist and dualist direction with the use of material from Macrobius, Vergil, and the Book of Wisdom: the *body* is corrupted, and the soul, weighed down by being joined to it, needs instruction if it is to develop its innate powers.[98] We are then told that infants cannot learn, because a vapour (*fumus*) produced from their frequent meals (they are hot and moist and therefore digest food very quickly) impedes the soul's activity in the brain. Here William has taken a starting-point in the *Timaeus* – Plato had said that a child's soul is linked as if to a swift torrent because of the process of nutrition – and has built on it with help from both Calcidius and Constantinus.[99] It is characteristic of William that he takes up those themes in the *Timaeus* which lend themselves to being filled out with more precise and technical information drawn from 'new' sources.

Scholars have been fascinated by William's changing attitude towards the world-soul described by Plato in the *Timaeus*. His works reveal an early confidence in identifying it with the Holy Spirit, followed by greater caution, until by the time of the *Dragmaticon* the world-soul receives not so much as a mention. The issue was an exciting yet difficult one for any Christian philosopher who took Plato seriously. William of Saint-Thierry, who found in the *Philosophia* views which seemed to him to ignore the Spirit's position within the Trinity, and to confuse the uncreated Spirit with the created order, accused William of developing the ideas of Abelard – ideas which had just received the official condemnation of a Church Council.[100]

96 Cf. E. Jeauneau, 'Note sur l'école de Chartres', *Studi medievali*, ser. 3, v.2 (1964) 821–65, at p. 851; P. O. Kristeller, 'Bartholomaeus, Musandinus and Maurus of Salerno and other early commentators of the *Articella*', *Italia Medioevale e Umanistica* XIX (1976) 57–87; and *La scuola medica di Salerno secondo ricerche e scoperte recenti*, *Quaderni del Centro studi e documentazione della Scuola medica salernitana* V (1980).

97 Pp. 310–12; cf. *Philosophia*, pp. 113–14; *Glosae*, ch. 120, p. 213; chs. 128–32, pp. 226–33.

98 Cf. *Timaeus* 41DE; Macrobius 1970 I ix–x, xiv 14–15 (here Macrobius quotes *Aeneid* VI 731); Wisdom 9: 15.

99 *Timaeus* 43A f; Calcidius 1975, chs. 206–7; *Pantegni* IV 2–4, *De stomacho* fol. 178v (headaches caused by *fumus* from the stomach rising to the brain).

100 The following works provide an introduction to this subject: Gregory 1955, pp. 15–16, 123–74 (esp. pp. 141f); and *Platonismo medievale* (Rome 1958), pp. 122–50; *Glosae*, ch. 71, pp. 144–6 and n. (c), p. 145; P. Dronke, 'L'amor che move il sole e l'altre stelle', *Studi Medievali* ser. 3, VI I (1965) 389–422 (at pp. 410f). See also William of Saint-Thierry 1969.

William's speculations regarding the world-soul, the elements and natural processes were all motivated by a wish to discover what underlies the world and what holds it together. The particular attraction of the world-soul as a cosmological principle was that, stemming as it does directly from God, it could guarantee the relationship not only between different levels of existence but also between the world and its source. But there were also advantages in stressing the role of physically based processes: they could be given specific applications, while the world-soul, despite its greater poetic and imaginative appeal, was liable to remain a rather imprecise concept. Thus the physically based processes might in the end prove more fruitful. William's confidence in the consistency and dynamic order of the natural world – a confidence grounded in the properties he saw God as having built into matter, and nourished by his medical reading and his interpretation of the *Timaeus* – increased to the point where he no longer needed the doctrine of the world-soul; the *natura rerum* itself constituted a sufficient guarantee of the unity of the cosmos.[101]

101 Gregory 1955, pp. 149f, suggests a link between William's final abandoning of the world-soul doctrine and his growing interest in the Constantinian explanation of organic life with reference to different kinds of vapour (see n. 88).

12

GILBERT OF POITIERS[1]

JOHN MARENBON

There is one distinction which Gilbert of Poitiers uses so pervasively in his masterpiece, the commentary on Boethius' *Opuscula sacra*,[2] that it is difficult even to begin an account of his thought without explaining it. According to Gilbert, everything except God is what it is (*quod est*) by virtue of something which makes it so (*quo est*). For instance, a man is what he is (a man) by humanity; a stone is a stone by stone-ness; a white thing is white by whiteness, a rational thing rational by rationality, a body corporeal by corporeality, Plato Plato by Plato-ness. Gilbert calls the men, stones, white things, rational things, bodies, Plato *quod ests*;* the humanity, stone-ness, whiteness, rationality, corporeality and Plato-ness *quo ests*. Whether such a distinction is valuable, trivial, or merely confusing depends on how it is used and developed. What, more precisely, are *quo ests*? And what is made of the fact that, for example, Plato is Plato, a man, a white thing, a rational thing and a body? Gilbert's answers to these questions will be examined in due course.[3] To consider them immediately would lead to a particular view of Gilbert's interests and strengths as a thinker, one which is widely accepted, and which this chapter will dispute.

Only three works can be attributed with confidence to Gilbert: the commentary on Boethius' theological essays, and commentaries on two

---

1 Gilbert, of Poitiers (his birthplace and the seat of his bishopric), is variously surnamed by modern scholars Porretanus, de la Porrée or (probably most correctly) Porreta: see F. Pelster, 'Gilbert de la Porrée, Gilbertus Porretanus oder Gilbertus Porreta', *Scholastik* XIX–XXIV (1949) 401–3.

2 *The Commentaries on Boethius by Gilbert of Poitiers* ed. N. M. Häring (Toronto 1966) [=H]. An uncritical and textually unsatisfactory edition can be found in P.L. 64, 1247ff.

3 The distinction between *quod ests* and *quo ests* is discussed in detail below, pp. 341–3. Gilbert frequently refers to the same distinction using different terms, either because he is referring to a particular sort of *quo est* and *quod est*, or under the influence of the passage he is commenting on. *Quo ests* are variously termed *subsistentiae* (see below, p. 339 and n. 50), *formae* (e.g. H pp. 82.1–4, 98.80, 124.67, 262.39–42, *substantiae* (e.g. H pp. 116.36–8, 120.49–50, 135.95–1), *esse* (e.g. H pp. 81.73–4, 194.90, 195.20, 279.12), *materia* (e.g. H p. 81.73–5); *mathematica* (e.g. H pp. 199.21, 245.80; cf. below, pp. 339–40); *quod ests* are termed *subsistentes* (see below, n. 50) and *substantiae* (e.g. H pp. 111.99–100, 116.36–9). On the origins of the terms *quod est* and *quo est*, see M. A. Schmidt, *Gottheit und Trinität nach dem Kommentar des Gilbert Porreta zu Boethius, De Trinitate* (Basel 1956), pp. 210–15.

* [For convenience, the hybrid plural forms (*quod ests, quo ests*) have been italicized in the same way as the singulars throughout this chapter.]

books of the Bible – the Psalms and the Pauline Letters.[4] The subjects about which Gilbert chose to write suggest that his place in medieval thought will be alongside two of his teachers, Anselm and Ralph of Laon, as an interpreter of Scripture and pioneer of systematic theology. But historians have viewed him otherwise. Gilbert's thought starts, they believe, from the philosophical distinction between *quod est* and *quo est*, which is developed, by purely rational argument, into a theory about concrete wholes and their parts, individuals and universals. Nineteenth- and early twentieth-century scholars usually restricted themselves to setting out what they described as Gilbert's philosophy, with little reference to his treatment of Christian doctrine.[5] Over the last fifty years the treatment of the Trinity and the Incarnation in the commentary on the *Opuscula sacra* has received attention; but it has been presented as following from a philosophical position which Gilbert had developed by rational reflection, independent of revelation. Assessment of Gilbert's thought has rested on the view taken of his philosophy. One account makes him a logician, misguidedly applying conceptual distinctions to reality and consequently falling into theological error.[6] Another, much more popular today, maintains that the orthodoxy and subtlety of Gilbert's theology emerge once its derivation from his philosophical use of grammatical theory, or from his sophisticated metaphysics,[7] is recognized.

4 On works attributed to Gilbert and their authenticity see: H. C. van Elswijk, *Gilbert Porreta. Sa vie, son oeuvre, sa pensée* (Louvain 1966), pp. 40–73; and L. O. Nielsen, *Theology and Philosophy in the Twelfth Century* (Leiden 1982), pp. 40–6. One authentic letter of Gilbert's (to Matthew, Abbot of Saint-Florent at Saumur) survives (ed. P.L. 188, 1255–8). A set of *quaestiones* based to some extent on Gilbert's teaching, and other works sometimes attributed to Gilbert are discussed in the Appendix: see below, pp. 353–4. The present chapter will be concerned almost exclusively with the commentary on the *Opuscula sacra*. Gilbert's two other commentaries (both unedited) are far less original in their thought and more narrowly doctrinal in their concerns. They contain little of importance for a history of twelfth-century *philosophy*. For further information on Gilbert as a biblical exegete see M. Fontana, 'Il commento ai Salmi di Gilberto della Porrée', *Logos* xiii (1930) 282–301; M. Simon, 'La glose de l'épître aux romains de Gilbert de la Porrée', *Revue d'Histoire Ecclésiastique* lii.1 (1957) 51–80; and Nielsen 1982, pp. 115–31. For details of manuscripts, see F. Stegmüller, *Repertorium biblicum medii aevi* ii (Madrid 1950), n. 2511 (Psalms), n. 2528 (Pauline Epistles).
5 For example, B. Hauréau, *Histoire de la philosophie scolastique* i (2nd ed., Paris 1872), pp. 447–78; M. de Wulf, *Histoire de la philosophie médiévale* (2nd ed., Louvain–Paris 1905).
6 A. Hayen, 'Le concile de Reims et l'erreur théologique de Gilbert de la Porrée', *AHDLMA* x (1935/6) 29–102. This account is followed in D. Knowles, *The Evolution of Medieval Thought* (London 1962), pp. 133–5.
7 N. M. Häring was the first to suggest grammatical theory as Gilbert's point of departure: 'The Case of Gilbert de la Porrée Bishop of Poitiers (1142–1154)', *Mediaeval Studies* iii (1951) 1–40; and 'Sprachlogische und philosophische Voraussetzungen zum Verständnis der Christologie Gilberts von Poitiers', *Scholastik* xxxii (1957) 373–97. See also Elswijk 1966, pp. 127–52; and B. Maioli, *Gilberto Porretano. Dalla grammatica speculativa alla metafisica del concreto* (Rome 1979). For the view that Gilbert began his thinking from metaphysics see A. Forest, 'Gilbert de la Porrée et les écoles du xiie siècle', *Revue des Cours et des Conférences* xxxv.2 (1934) 410–20, 640–51; and 'Le réalisme de Gilbert de la Porrée dans le commentaire

But there are two reasons why an account of Gilbert's thought (even one which belongs to a history of *philosophy* and is not concerned with doctrinal discussions for their own sake) should not follow the usual practice and separate his philosophy from his theology. First, the common assumption that Gilbert's theology is based on a set of independent, rationally based distinctions is unfounded: in commenting on Boethius, Gilbert is the respectful exegete of theological monographs by a recognized authority; he unifies his work by developing a theory about the nature of theological arguments; and where he investigates concepts which are not specifically Christian, he is almost always reflecting the topics Boethius chooses to discuss, and these discussions are linked, more closely than in the *Opuscula sacra* themselves, to doctrinal problems. Secondly, even if they make no assumption about Gilbert's own aims, scholars who restrict their interest to his rationally based arguments and omit those concerned with revelation will find themselves faced by material which is incoherent and often explicable neither in its own terms nor by reason and self-evidence. They will be forced to admit themselves baffled, or to baffle their readers.

The following account aims to avoid these alternatives by beginning with a discussion of Gilbert as commentator (of Boethius) and the theory about theological reasoning which unifies his commentary. In connection with this theory, and the doctrinal concerns of the *Opuscula sacra*, the conceptual arguments and analyses gain their direction and coherence; and a motive becomes clear for the positions Gilbert adopts, although not in every case a justification.

Gilbert the commentator

The most immediately striking feature of Gilbert's commentary on the *Opuscula sacra* is its thoroughness as an exposition. The early medieval glosses, which circulated widely between the tenth and twelfth centuries and were known to Gilbert, combined an uneven beginners' explanation of the text with passages of information and metaphysical speculation, for which

du *De hebdomadibus*', in *Hommage à Monsieur le Professeur Maurice de Wulf* (Louvain 1934) = *Revue Néoscolastique de Philosophie* XXXVI (1934) 101–10; E. Gilson, *La philosophie au moyen âge* (Paris 1947), pp. 262–7; M. E. Williams, *The Teaching of Gilbert Porreta on the Trinity as Found in his Commentaries on Boethius* (Rome 1951); G. Leff, *Medieval Thought. St Augustine to Ockham* (Harmondsworth 1958); R. J. Westley, 'A Philosophy of the Concreted and the Concrete', *The Modern Schoolman* XXXVII (1960) 257–86; L. Nielsen, 'On the Doctrine of Logic and Language of Gilbert Porreta and his Followers', *CIMAGL* XVII (1976) 40–69; and Nielsen 1982, pp. 103–4.

Boethius' phrases provided no more than a point of departure.[8] Twelfth-century commentators who were not directly influenced by Gilbert tended to approach the *Opuscula* selectively, ignoring some passages, using others as the basis for long discussions in which they developed their own views.[9] Gilbert himself aims to give an exegesis which is complete in its grasp both of the detail and of the overall argument of his text. Gilbert's commentary consists of passages where he interlaces Boethius' words with his own paraphrases, expansions, qualifications, and explanations (he 'endeavoured', as his editor remarks, 'not to omit a single word' of the four *Opuscula* from his commentary[10]); sections where Gilbert develops, in his own terms, concepts and distinctions which he believes are necessary for understanding an *Opusculum*; and a series of devices designed to help the reader grasp the author's intentions – a prologue to each treatise identifying Boethius' aim and the method of reasoning used, references back to this summary,[11] cross-references,[12] warnings about unstable terminology,[13] identification of logical techniques.[14]

But, in spite of this closeness to the text, many of the ideas which Gilbert's commentary puts forward are very different from those of Boethius. How can Gilbert consistently combine originality of thought with professed fidelity to his author? The answer to this question lies in Gilbert's under-

---

8 These glosses are edited (as the work of Eriugena) in E. K. Rand, *Johannes Scottus* (Munich 1906). On their authorship, see M. Cappuyns, 'Le plus ancien commentaire des "Opuscula sacra" et son origine', *RTAM* III (1931) 237–72; and G. Schrimpf, *Die Axiomenschrift des Boethius (De hebdomadibus) als philosophisches Lehrbuch des Mittelalters* (Leiden 1966), pp. 37–8. Minor borrowings indicate that Gilbert knew these glosses: e.g. H pp. 66.25–67.31 draws on Rand 1906, p. 31.29–35; the interpretation of *ebdomades* as *conceptiones* and the contrast between them and *entimemata* at H p. 185.52–4 is suggested by *ibid.* p. 50.6–15. For a general survey of the use of the *Opuscula sacra*, see M. Gibson, 'The *Opuscula sacra* in the Middle Ages', in *Boethius. His Life, Thought and Influence* (Oxford 1981), ed. M. Gibson, pp. 214–34. The best text of the *Opuscula sacra* is ed. (with trans.) H. F. Stewart, E. K. Rand, and S. J. Tester (London–Cambridge, Mass. 1973); all references here are to this edition [= R].

9 See the various commentaries attributed to Thierry of Chartres in *Commentaries on Boethius by Thierry of Chartres and his School*, ed. N. M. Häring (Toronto 1971). Although most of these works contain some (hostile) allusions to Gilbert's teaching, they are not closely influenced by his commentary. For further discussion of them, see P. Dronke's contribution to this volume: below, pp. 358–85. For the commentary by Clarembald of Arras, see Appendix, below p. 355.

10 H p. 43.

11 E.g. H pp. 109.16–21, 142.10–16, 215.31–6, 326.1–327.10. Gilbert used the same technique in his commentary on the Pauline Epistles: see Simon 1957, pp. 55–9.

12 E.g. H p. 146.22–3, 167.19–20. In commenting on the third *opusculum*, Gilbert points out which of the axioms given by Boethius at the beginning of the work underlie each stage of the subsequent argument: see Schrimpf 1966, p. 66 n. 3, for a list of instances.

13 E.g. H p. 288.19–24.

14 E.g. H pp. 289.52–3 (hypothetical syllogisms), 69.4–6, 271.2–3, 327.16 (division and definition).

standing of an exegete's duties and his view of Boethius' style of writing. The usual meanings of words (their *significationes*) provide a starting-point for the interpreter, but only that. Often, Gilbert says, the words of a text can have many different meanings; the commentator must decide which is intended by judging the author's sense. If he fails, he will not grasp what the author is discussing.[15] The *Opuscula sacra*, Gilbert believes, are deliberately obscure. Boethius himself refers to the obscurities of brevity (*obscuritates brevitatis*) and the unfamiliar vocabulary (*significationes novorum verborum*) with which he protects his secret doctrines from those who are envious or unworthy. Gilbert draws attention to these passages, and he begins the general prologue to his whole commentary by making it clear that in Boethius' 'intricate discussion his reasoning is not explicit, figures of speech guide his choice of words and their senses, his unwonted syntax breaks the rules of grammar': devices designed to mislead the proud and leave his teachings open to the wise, who study his works with careful attention.[16] By Gilbert's own standards, it will be a mark of his wisdom and care as an interpreter that he uncovers a sense different from that yielded by the ordinary meanings of Boethius' words.

The modern reader may be surprised to find Boethius' elegant Latin described as obscure, and he might suspect Gilbert of attributing illusory difficulties to his author's style in order to gain freedom as a commentator. Yet on the level not of style but of argument, the *Opuscula sacra* are obscure: written at different times, for various purposes, using many sources, the four treatises Gilbert commented on do not present a coherent set of thoughts; some sections require a knowledge of Neoplatonic terminology and assumptions (beyond that available to Gilbert) in order to be understood; and some passages remain loose or vague. By arguing that the *Opuscula* are deliberately obscure in their language, Gilbert is able to recognize the apparent instances of incoherence and vagueness in Boethius' reasoning without either disparaging his author or removing precision and connectedness of argument from his aims as a faithful interpreter.

The quaestio-*technique and Gilbert's theory of arguments*

Convinced that, beneath an obscure surface, the *Opuscula sacra* contain complex and compelling arguments, Gilbert attributes to their author the

---

15 H pp. 67.55–68.74, 297.79–298.97; cf. Nielsen 1982, pp. 105–7.
16 H p. 54.24–9. Boethius mentions his deliberate obscurity at R pp. 4.16–20 and 38.11–13; cf. H pp. 66.24–67.54, 188.36–189.49.

techniques and preoccupations of a sophisticated twelfth-century thinker. At the school of Laon, where Gilbert had studied, scholars were beginning to use the *quaestio*, a way of organizing thought which would become dominant in medieval universities.[17] A *quaestio* – as Gilbert explains – consists of an affirmation and a negation that contradicts it, each of which seems to be true. But contradictories cannot both be true: the *quaestio* is to be resolved by showing how the two statements are ambiguous and, in so far as they are true, not contradictory.[18] Gilbert believes that Boethius, like the scholars of his own day, engages in theology by propounding and resolving *quaestiones*. The *Opuscula sacra* are Boethius' 'books of *quaestiones*'.[19] Boethius' remark, at the beginning of his first treatise, the *De trinitate*, that he is about to tackle 'a question which [he] has long considered (*investigatam diutissime quaestionem*)', is taken to mean that the discussion which follows is a *quaestio* in the twelfth-century sense.[20] Gilbert analyses the argument of the third *opusculum*, *De hebdomadibus*, as the presentation and resolution of a seeming contradiction.[21] Although Gilbert does not think that the final piece, *Contra Eutychen et Nestorium*, has like these the overall structure of a *quaestio*, one of the important problems it raises is treated by the *quaestio*-technique.[22] And, throughout his commentary, Gilbert often uses the technical formulae of the *quaestio* to indicate the shape of Boethius' argument.[23]

The ambiguity revealed in the solution of a *quaestio* can be of various types. Gilbert mentions two which were often recognized by his contemporaries: ambiguity produced when the same term has a different range of reference on each side of the contradiction, and that which results from figurative language. But his interest lies in a third type, unknown to others, which arises 'from different arguments of different types (*diversorum* . . .

---

17 A succinct summary of modern discussions is given by A. Kenny in his section, 'The Origins of Disputation', in *CHLMP*, pp. 24–6.
18 H p. 63.17–25. Gilbert's comments on the *quaestio* were first discussed in M. Grabmann, *Geschichte der scholastischen Methode* II (Freiburg im Breisgau 1911) 424–30. See also Elswijk 1966, pp. 271–6; and L. M. de Rijk, *Logica Modernorum* I (Assen 1962) 157–8.
19 H p. 53.1: 'Libros quaestionum Anicii . . .'
20 R p. 2.1; cf. H pp. 63.17–64.57. The short second treatise on the Trinity is also taken as a *quaestio* – one which is not 'simplex, sed ex diversis questionibus iuncta' (H p. 165.61–2).
21 H. p. 206.90–100, 211.26–8, 215.31–41; cf. Grabmann 1911, p. 428.
22 See below, pp. 346f.
23 E.g. H pp. 97.37–40 ('Contra illud vero quod nobis opponunt . . . respondemus . . .'); 139.31–3 ('At opponit quis dicens . . . Respondemus . . .'). Gilbert also uses *quaestiones* in his commentary on the Pauline Epistles: see e.g. his gloss on 1 Corinthians 11:29, 'Quaeritur an cotidie sit sumenda eucharistia . . .' (Cambridge Pembroke Coll. MS 76 (s. xii), fol. 52r), and Simon 1957, pp. 71–3.

generum diversis rationibus)'.[24] The *quaestiones* which, Gilbert thinks, form much of the *Opuscula sacra*, rest for the most part on ambiguities of this sort. In consequence, Gilbert's theory about types of argument underlies his whole treatment of Boethius' text and provides both direction and unity for it.

By the term *ratio* Gilbert means, not any instance of reasoning, but a self-evident argument which can be used in one or many disciplines. Every discipline has such general statements. Rhetoricians call them 'common-places', dialecticians 'maximal propositions', geometers 'theorems', musicians 'axioms', moralists and philosophers 'general statements'.[25] Boethius refers to them, Gilbert believes, at the beginning of the *De hebdomadibus* when he talks of 'a common conception of the mind' which anyone who hears accepts as true; to deny one, Gilbert adds, would be a sign of insanity.[26] Some *rationes* are 'common (*communes*)': they can be used in every subject. But many (the *rationes propriae*) are appropriate only to a particular discipline and its objects.[27] Ambiguity 'from different arguments of different types' depends on this distinction. A pair of *rationes* (or conclusions derived from them) can be apparently contradictory, yet both true, if each is a *ratio propria* of a different discipline. For instance, 'No species can be predicated of its genus' is true, where definitions are concerned (*in diffinitionum genere*); its contrary, 'Every species can be predicated of its genus' is true, where divisions are being made (*in divisionum genere*).[28]

Gilbert does not have a definite list of how many disciplines there are, each

---

24 H pp. 63.26–39, 64.69–65.72; cf. de Rijk 1962, *passim*, on twelfth-century theories of fallacy. Gilbert's discussion does not, according to de Rijk, indicate acquaintance with the *De sophisticis elenchis*.

25 H pp. 189.67–190.74.

26 R p. 40.18–19, H pp. 190.94–191.97.

27 H p. 57.1–2: 'Omnium, que rebus percipiendis suppeditant, rationum alie communes sunt multorum generum, alie proprie aliquorum.' It has been asserted (Nielsen 1982, p. 89) that 'there can be no doubt that Gilbert has found the distinction between proper and common rules in Aristotle's *Analytica Posteriora* II, 10'. Yet there *is* room for great doubt about Gilbert's acquaintance with this work. Although it is not impossible that, already in the 1130s or 1140s, he had access to James of Venice's translation of the *Posterior Analytics*, the theory of arguments in his commentary is, by Nielsen's own admission, not the same as Aristotle's. It is more probable that Gilbert developed his own theory from the logic of topical argument, as expounded in Boethius' widely read *De topicis differentiis*. On this work and its use in the twelfth century, see E. Stump, *Boethius's 'De topicis differentiis' Translated with Notes and Essays on the Text* (Ithaca–London 1978); and 'Boethius's Theory of Topics and its Place in Early Scholastic Logic' in *Congresso internazionale di studi Boeziani: Atti*, ed. L. Obertello (Rome 1981), pp. 249–62; and 'Topics: their Development and Absorption into Consequences', in *CHLMP*, pp. 273–99, especially pp. 275–81.

28 H p. 63.38–41.

with its *rationes propriae*.[29] But he concentrates his attention on the three branches of knowledge described by Boethius in the *De trinitate*: natural science, mathematics, and theology.[30] In particular, the distinction between the *rationes propriae* of natural science and those of theology is seen as fundamental to the *Opuscula sacra*. Ignorance of it leads not merely to intellectual error but to heresy; by trying to apply arguments which are appropriate only to created things (the province of natural science) to the creator (one of the objects of theology), heretics misrepresent God's nature. For example, in the *De trinitate*, Boethius wishes (in Gilbert's view) to show that it is possible, according to a theological *ratio*, to infer from 'the Father is God, the Son is God and the Holy Spirit is God' that 'the Father and the Son and the Holy Spirit are one God, not three Gods'.[31] Those who mistakenly judge this inference by the *rationes propriae* of natural science (where it is not true to say that, for instance, Plato is a man, Cicero is a man, Aristotle is a man: therefore they all are one man)[32] discover a contradiction between reason and faith and, in some cases, seek to overcome it by distorting orthodox doctrine. Had they understood the propriety of *rationes* to particular disciplines they would have seen that the contradiction was only apparent.

Although Gilbert introduces his theory of arguments in the context of solving the *quaestiones* which he believes Boethius has posed himself, he develops it in a way which goes beyond its original object. Boethius is not, his commentator thinks, just concerned to resolve the contradictions which have been the occasion of heresy; he also wishes to give the orthodox a closer understanding of Christian doctrine. For example, having shown, by theological *rationes propriae*, that Father, Son and Holy Spirit are one, he goes on to explain how the persons of the Trinity are nonetheless 'different from one another by diversity of properties'.[33] This is accomplished, not by using the arguments peculiarly appropriate to theology, but by taking the *rationes propriae* of natural science and transferring – or, as Gilbert often calls it, 'transuming' – them 'proportionately'. An argument from transumption (*transsumptio*), Boethius says in his *De topicis differentiis* (a work probably much in Gilbert's mind),[34] is one in which a problem is solved by trans-

---

29 See H pp. 115.3–4, 190.70–4, 216.60, 220.79, 229.28 for references to the special *rationes* of a variety of disciplines.
30 The three subjects are distinguished at R p. 8.5–16; cf. H pp. 79.43–88.69.
31 H p. 72.46–9; cf. R p. 6.7–9.
32 See H p. 72.56–65.
33 H p. 157.58–63; cf. p. 109.17–21.
34 See above, n. 27.

ferring it from its own terms into terms which are better known. Plato's
Republic provides his illustration. Wishing to discover the nature of justice in
the individual, Plato transferred the problem to a larger scale and examined
the nature of justice in the state. By solving this problem, he was also able to
find the solution to his initial one about the individual.[35] Similarly, Gilbert
extends his doctrinal discussions beyond the limited scope which theological
rationes propriae would allow him by transuming arguments from the
accessible field of natural science to the remote and ultimately incomprehensible[36] objects of theology. Such transumption cannot be complete; and
Gilbert must introduce the concept of *proportionate* transumption in order to
avoid the confusion between common and proper arguments for which he
has blamed the heretics.[37]

Gilbert does not develop the theory of *rationes propriae* and proportionate
transumption in isolation from his more celebrated discussions of essence,
concrete wholes, parts, individuals, persons, and matter. On the one hand,
his treatment of these subjects reveals the differences between the three main
disciplines and enables him to illustrate the proportion by which the
arguments of natural science can be transferred to theology. On the other,
the theory about the arguments of natural science and theology provides the
framework for linking analyses of created things with the doctrines of the
Trinity and the Incarnation. Although Gilbert in this way manages to unify
the disparate discussions of his text, the coherence of his arguments varies:
some cogently link clear and penetrating rational analyses of created things
with the theory of *rationes*; others, despite their ingenuity and sophistication,
make assumptions and contain confusions explicable only in the light of the
theological doctrines which Gilbert, using proportionate transumption,
aims to defend.

---

35 Boethius, P.L. 64, 1192A. *Transsumptio* is also a term used by grammarians as an equivalent
   for *metalepsis* (cf. Quintilian *Institutio oratoria*, III 6 46, VIII 6 37); but only Boethius provides
   Gilbert with the notion of transuming not just words, but also arguments.
36 See H p. 247.35–8: 'Sed quoniam nulla eius proprietate, vel quid sit genere vel quantus
   mensura vel qualis forma vel huiusmodi, percipit, ipsum [*sc.* Deum] minime comprehendit.
   Nam intelligibilis quidem est: non vero comprehensibilis.'
37 For 'proportionate transumption', see e.g. pp. 120.68–9, 143.42–7, 170.87–93, 184.43–4.
   Sometimes Gilbert talks of 'proportionate translation (*transfero, translatio*)' in the same sense:
   e.g. pp. 115.2–18, 156.38–40, 163.10–12. He refers to a similar idea ('Non enim omnia
   neque nulla, que in naturalibus aut mathematicis intelliguntur, in theologicis accipienda
   sentimus') at p. 294.88–96. Gilbert's most detailed and explicit discussion of proportion in
   an analogy is found in his commentary to Hebrews 1: 3 (Cambridge Pembroke MS 76, fols.
   117v–118r) – a gloss printed and discussed in Elswijk 1966, pp. 265–6, and Nielsen 1982,
   pp. 134–6; but this notion of proportion is rather different from that which Gilbert uses
   when transuming arguments in the commentary on Boethius.

God, the branches of knowledge and mathematics

Two of Gilbert's most successful analyses are his treatment of divinity and essence, and his description (in the context of his division of knowledge) of what he calls 'mathematics'. Each is a reinterpretation of the *Opuscula sacra* in logical terms which do not involve Boethius' Platonic assumptions.

(1) Divinity, essence and denomination

For many Christian thinkers strongly influenced by Platonism (including Boethius, who makes this assumption, though not explicitly, in *De hebdomadibus*),[38] God is the essence in which all other things participate in order to be. Gilbert, too, believes that without God there could be nothing else; but he cannot accept without reinterpretation either that essence is to be identified with God or that all things participate in it. Gilbert allows that, as a 'way of speaking (*usus loquendi*)', it is not incorrect to say 'God is essence itself (*ipsa essencia*)', just as someone might say of a wise man 'you're entirely wisdom'. But strictly speaking, one can say only 'God is.'[39] It is from this bare statement that Gilbert establishes the relation between God and his creation.

For Gilbert, the existential sense of 'is' can be used properly only in theology. When natural science and other disciplines use the verb literally, it functions as part of a statement about how things are. According to natural science, everything is what it is by something. There is no parallel, therefore, in the description of created things to the bare statement, 'God is': a man is a man by humanity; Socrates is by all the different *quo ests* which make him what he is.[40] But Gilbert is aware that created things are frequently said to be, in the existential sense. He explains such cases by saying that the existential sense of the verb is transferred from the Creator – to whom alone it really belongs – to his creation; transumed from theology to natural science. Gilbert uses a grammatical term to describe such transumptions. When something takes its name from that of something else related to it, grammarians say that it has been named 'denominatively (*denominative*)'.[41] One of

38 Cf. R p. 42.41–2: 'Omne quod est participat eo quod est esse ut sit.'
39 H p. 90.28–36; cf. p. 193.54–5. When Gilbert states (p. 193.54–5) that 'in theology we say that the divine essence . . . is the *esse* of all created things', he need not be taken as suggesting that, in any simple sense, all things participate in the divine essence. 'The divine essence', Gilbert says, 'is what we predicate of God when we say "God is"'; and Gilbert goes on to describe the relationship between God and his creatures by analysing the relations between the statement 'God is' and statements such as 'a body is', 'a man is'.
40 H pp. 88.70–5, 193.51–194.77.
41 See e.g. Priscian, *Institutiones* IV, 'De denominativis'; Isidore, *Etymologiae* X 1; Martianus Capella, *De nuptiis* IV (ed. A. Dick (rev. ed., Stuttgart, 1969)), pp. 171.20, 172.10, 179.7–9. Boethius gives a detailed discussion of denomination in his commentary on the *Categories*

the relations between the bearer of a name and what is denominated from it is that of cause and effect.[42] Gilbert extends this usage and says that in statements like 'a man is', 'a body is', 'is' can be understood existentially only if it is regarded as a denomination from the essence which is predicated of God in the statement 'God is'.[43]

Gilbert uses the idea of 'denominative transumption' to solve the puzzle posed in *De hebdomadibus* and to reach the conception which it hides. Boethius considers that goodness is a transcendental quality: everything which exists has it. His problem is to explain how, if all things are good simply by virtue of existing, it is not therefore the case that they are good in substance and so indistinguishable from God himself.[44] Gilbert envisages the problem rather differently. If the sentence 'Everything which exists is good by virtue of existing' is understood in terms of natural science, then it will indeed follow that everything is good in substance (because were it good merely by accident it would not be good by virtue of existing). In natural science predicates always name a thing's substance (*subsistentia*[45]) or its accidents. But the sentence, Gilbert argues, does not belong to natural science, but to ethics, where it is understood not literally but denominatively. All things, say the *ethici*, are good, because the Creator of all things is good. They are said to be good *not* in the way that a man can be described as a 'human animal', but rather as an artifact can be described as a 'human work' – 'human' because a man has made it.[46] By this 'transumptive denomination' or 'denominative transumption' of God's goodness to his creation, all things are not merely good, but good by virtue of existing[47] – presumably because everything which exists is God's creation: nothing could *be* which fell outside the appropriateness of this denomination from cause to effect.

(2) The branches of knowledge and the function of mathematics

Boethius divides speculative knowledge, following a well-established Neoplatonic pattern, according to the extent to which the forms which are the

(P.L. 64, 167D–8C). Unlike Gilbert, all these writers treat denomination as a way of deriving one word from another similar, but different, word. Boethius makes explicit the requirement that the verbal form should be changed: e.g. a man is 'strong' denominatively from 'strength'; but Boethius would refuse to say that a 'safe' was denominated from being 'safe'.

42 Cf. H p. 99.98–9.
43 H p. 193.55–8: 'Cum enim dicimus "corpus est" vel "homo est" vel huiusmodi, theologici hoc esse dictum intelligunt quadam extrinseca denominatione ab essentia sui principii.'
44 *Quomodo substantiae, in eo quod sint, bonae sint, cum non sint substantialia bona* (R p. 38) – as the title frequently given to the treatise in medieval manuscripts puts it.
45 See below, p. 339.
46 H p. 220.58–82.
47 H p. 221.94–1.

object of each science can be separated from matter. Knowledge can be of concrete wholes in which forms are inseparable from matter (natural science); or forms entirely separate from matter (theology); or of the partly separable forms of mathematics.[48] The mathematician studies numerical and geometrical relations, which are separable from the objects numbered and the individual geometrical figures but are not of the same kind as the transcendental objects of theology. Gilbert approaches Boethius' scheme with a different set of presuppositions. The objects of theology, he agrees, are special: God, matter, and the Ideas.[49] But natural science and mathematics both approach the same objects, concrete wholes, although in distinct ways. A concrete whole is the sort of thing it is by genus, *differentiae* and species; and it also has accidental attributes. Gilbert accordingly distinguishes between the substantial *quo ests*, which he often calls *subsistentiae*, and the *quo ests* by which it has its accidental attributes.[50] *Subsistentiae* make things the sort of things they are: sometimes Gilbert speaks of a thing's *subsistentia* (in the singular), regarding it as complex; sometimes of the many *subsistentiae* (generic, differential, and specific) which make a thing the sort it is. Every concrete whole is both created and concreted. It is created by receiving a *subsistentia*, by becoming a particular sort of thing. It is concreted by the *quo ests* which give it its accidental attributes.[51] The study of creation (*creatio*) does not lie within the natural scientist's or the mathematician's scope, and even the theologian can only study it in general terms (not surprisingly, for what is the 'it' before it is made something by its *subsistentia*?). The natural scientist's task is to analyse, not only this concretion (*concretio*), but also the

---

48 R p. 8.5–16; cf. H. Chadwick, *Boethius. The Consolations of Music, Logic, Theology and Philosophy* (Oxford 1981), pp. 110–11.

49 H p. 85.97–100. Occasionally (e.g. H pp. 219.51, 246.18–247.20) Gilbert uses the term *genuina* to refer to at least two of the three objects of theology, God and matter; and, more frequently, (e.g. H pp. 83.44, 84.70, 85.97, 247.19, 248.74 – and see passage quoted in n. 59 below), the contrasting term *nativa* to refer to concrete wholes which, in different ways, are studied by natural science and by mathematics. For Gilbert's different approaches to matter, see below pp. 348–51.

50 Gilbert takes the term *subsistentia* from *Contra Eutychen* (cf. R pp. 86.23–90.93 and Schmidt 1956, pp. 231–6) and adapts it to his own purposes. The term is very widely used in his commentary and, just as *quo est* is contrasted with *quod est*, so *subsistentia* is contrasted with *subsistens* – the thing which is the sort of thing it is by the *subsistentia* which makes it so: e.g. H pp. 58.44, 93.33–4, 135.99–100, 199.24–5, 261.13–14, 292.21–32, 320.87–93. Gilbert does not always keep to his distinction between *subsistentiae* and *quo ests* in general: for instance, at one point (H p. 262.40–2) he talks of *generales, speciales, differentiales* and also *accidentales subsistentiae*!

51 H p. 84.54–6: 'Creatio . . . subsistenciam inesse facit ut, cui inest, ab ea aliquid sit. Concretio vero eidem subsistencie naturas posterioris rationis accomodat ut, cui cum illa insunt, simplex non sit.'

concretion of generic, differential, and specific *quo ests* which makes a thing's complex *subsistentia*.[52]

Whereas natural science analyses the concretion of *quo ests* in an object, mathematics considers *quo ests* (accidental or substantial) 'other than they are, that is abstractly':[53] it takes a *quo est* apart from the other *quo ests* with which it is naturally concrete. The mathematician's job is to class *quo ests* into one or more of the nine categories other than substance in Aristotle's list. For instance, '*animatio* (ensouledness)' belongs to the category of relation (*habitus*); 'rationality' belongs to the category of quality. A complex *quo est* belongs to the categories of its genus and *differentia*: 'humanity' (which belongs to the genus *animatio* and has rationality as a *differentia*) is both relation and quality.[54] Whereas the natural scientist is concerned with how genera are divided by their *differentiae* into species (evident in the concretion of *quo ests* in the individual), the mathematician places *quo ests* into 'genera of genera' – the nine categories.[55] The natural scientist, then, is concerned to understand the objects of the world by classifying them according to genus, *differentia* and species, and noting their accidents. The mathematician's interest is not in numbers or geometrical figures, but in the logical description of the classifications used by the natural scientist. His subject has much in common with an area singled out for special treatment by later medieval logicians: second intentions.[56] But there is an important difference. The theory of second intentions studies the first-order distinctions made by logicians; the relation of those distinctions to reality is a question open to discussion. Mathematics studies a set of distinctions which – it quickly emerges from Gilbert's treatment of *quo ests* and *quod ests* – belong to reality, not just to logic.

The concept of quo est: Gilbert's difficulties and his theological aims

What exactly does Gilbert mean by a *quo est*? Why does he introduce the concept? These questions (mooted at the beginning of this chapter) lead to some of the most intricate, and most questionable, passages in his commentary, about parts, singularity, individuality, and personality.

52 See below, pp. 341f.
53 H p. 84.70–1.
54 H pp. 117.84–118.91.
55 H p. 86.31–7.
56 Cf. Nielsen 1982, pp. 94–5: 'In mathematics a sort of secondary intention is predicated (though Gilbert does not use this expression), in such a way that by means of a predication of this kind we can show to which superior category a form or collection of mutually similar

(1) Quo ests

Quo ests, according to Gilbert, do not merely explain how *quod ests* are as they are, but why. A man is made a man by humanity; a white thing white by whiteness: *quo ests* make (*efficiunt*) *quod ests* what they are.[57] Completely different in genus and definition,[58] *quod ests* and *quo ests* belong equally to reality, but epistemologically and ontologically they are interdependent. Natural things (*quod ests*) can be conceived only through their cause; the objects of mathematics (*quo ests*) only through their power to make – 'a white thing through whiteness; whiteness through its making white'.[59] *Quo ests* cannot even exist (except in mental abstraction) apart from their corresponding *quod ests*; nor *quod ests* apart from their corresponding *quo ests*. 'Bodiliness', says Gilbert, 'is nothing in actuality unless it is in a body. And what we call a body would not be one unless there were in it the bodiliness by which it is what it is.'[60] *Quo ests*, as well as *quod ests*, are singular – the whiteness by which this white thing is white is a singular, by which this thing alone is white, not the universal, by which all white things are white.[61] Indeed, the singularity of *quo ests* is for Gilbert a necessary consequence of their reality, since he accepts that 'whatever is, is one in number'.[62]

Many *quo ests*, each of them real and singular, are brought together by 'natural concretion'. To the 'whole form of [a man's] substance (*tota forma substancie*)' – the humanity by which he is a man – can be added the genera and *differentiae* from which it is composed (such as bodiliness and ensouledness) and the *quo ests* which give a man his accidental features (such as colour and knowledge).[63] That each thing is made what it is by a multiplicity of

forms belongs.' For second intentions in later medieval logic, see C. Knudsen, 'Intentions and Impositions' in *CHLMP*, pp. 479–95.

57 H pp. 91.51–8, 116.47–9.

58 H p. 293.57–8.

59 H p. 245.77–81: 'Nativa nanque per aliquam sui vel efficientem vel efficiendi proprietatem concipiuntur: ut album per albedinem et albedo per naturam faciendi album. Nichil enim naturalium nisi per causam et nichil mathematicorum nisi per efficiendi potestatem concipi potest.'

60 H pp. 278.8–279.12 (esp. 10–12): 'Actu nanque corporalitas nichil est nisi sit in corpore. Et corpus non est, quod vocatur, nisi in ipso sit corporalitas que est eius esse'. *Esse* here means *quo est*: cf. n. 3 above.

61 H pp. 144.58–60, 145.95–100.

62 H pp. 270.73–4 ('Quicquid enim est, singulare est'), 300.69–301.95 ('. . . Quodcumque enim est, unum est . . .'). Gilbert is basing himself here on Boethius' statement that *unum* and *esse* are convertible; cf. R p. 94.35–40. As these two phrases make clear, for Gilbert the extensions of unity and singularity are the same; nor is there any indication that he wishes to distinguish intensionally between the two concepts. In this chapter, the concepts are treated as identical. For a finely nuanced discussion of the question, see J. J. E. Gracia, *Introduction to the Problem of Individuation in the Early Middle Ages* (Munich–Vienna 1984), pp. 164–5.

63 H pp. 90.43–91.67.

singular *quo ests* does not, for Gilbert, mean that it is not itself one in number. On the contrary, he argues that the singularity of each *quo est* makes its corresponding *quod est* singular.[64] Rationality, for instance, not only makes something rational but also, because it is itself one, makes the rational thing one.

Gilbert's theory of *quod est* and *quo est* is based on the logical distinctions of Porphyry's *Isagoge*, which would have been familiar to any twelfth-century logical student: substance, accident, species, *differentia*, genus. Its originality lies in the assertion it makes of the reality and singularity of *quo ests*. But what are the grounds for this position? Gilbert's theory is not an attempt to explain why *quo ests* are concreted in particular groups; why this whiteness and this book-ness, for instance, make the book on my left white, and that red-ness and that book-ness make the book on my right red. *Quo ests* can be known only from their effects; the concretion of *quo ests* only from the way in which their effects combine in a single object; and Gilbert simply assumes that he knows what objects are single.

If Gilbert is to justify his positing of real *quo ests*, it must be on the basis of the role they play in establishing or explaining universals. Although every *quo est* is singular, *quo ests* which have exactly similar effects (each 'humanity' which makes its *quod est* a man; each 'whiteness' which makes its *quod est* white) are described as 'exactly alike (*conformes*)'. *Quo ests* which are exactly like each other (all 'humanities' or all 'whitenesses') together form what Gilbert calls 'one dividual'[65] (and the same term can be used of the *quod ests* which the conformity of their *quo ests* makes exactly alike).[66] Gilbert thinks that this concept of the dividual is similar to that of a universal. At one point he says that universals are those *quo ests* which, because they have exactly similar effects (are *conformes*), are predicated of many single things;[67] at another, more explicitly, he equates a universal, a dividual, a common genus and a same nature – calling them collections of substantial, not accidental, *quo ests* which, when compared, are similar.[68] The similarity of real, singular *quo ests* therefore provides the basis for universal classifications. But this is not a reason for granting the existence of real, singular *quo ests*, unless no other supposition provides an equally plausible basis. As the variety of theories about universals from Gilbert's own time illustrates,

64 H pp. 144.58–62, 145.95–100, 175.10–176.22.
65 H p. 75.28–31.
66 H pp. 270.75–7, 144.64–5.
67 H p. 269.39–50.
68 H p. 312.100–13.

many other explanations are possible.[69] Gilbert's is distinguished only by its inability to respond to the questions that any collection-theory[70] must face (How can a collection of *quo ests* be one in number? Or if it is not one, how can it be a universal?), and the extravagance of its metaphysical claims.

Although the real existence of *quo ests* cannot be justified simply by the analysis of created things, the need to posit it is evident within the theological plan of Gilbert's commentary. On the one hand, Gilbert wishes to show that created things are *really* complex, and God *really* simple. He can do this by contrasting the necessarily complex *quo est* of any created thing (concreted of species, genera, *differentiae* and accidents) with the simple *quo est* of God[71] – the divinity by which he alone is, and which is only because God is God by it.[72] On the other hand, Gilbert wishes to gain an understanding of the Trinity and the incarnation by proportionate transumption from the arguments of natural science: analysis into *quo est* and *quod est* provides a way of explaining the proportion, but only if these are what really constitute things, not just a way of talking about them. The theory of parts – a ramification of Gilbert's view of *quo ests* and *quod ests* – provides an example of such transumption; and also a separate illustration of how Gilbert's perspectives are determined by his theological aims.

(2) Parts

According to Gilbert, if a whole is made of parts, the parts are not another thing (*aliud unum*) from the whole, although the whole is another thing from its parts.[73] The complex *quo est* of the whole includes the *quo ests* of all its parts and their accidents.[74] What it is true to say of the part, it is also true to say of the whole; and two things stand in the relation of part to whole when the *quo ests* by which the part is what it is are the same (numerically, not just by conformity) as those by which the whole has those characteristics. A man, for instance, is made of the parts body and soul: colour is an accident of his

69 On the debate about universals in the twelfth century, see above, ch. 7.
70 See J. Marenbon, *Early Medieval Philosophy (480–1150): an Introduction* (London 1983), pp. 132–3.
71 H p. 90.38–41.
72 H 98.63–4: 'Non enim est a divinitate aliud quo Deus sit. Nec est unde divinitas ipsa sit nisi quod ea Deus est.' Does Gilbert – as many of his contemporaries thought – compromise divine unity by applying to God the very distinction, between *quod est* and *quo est*, by which he hopes to illustrate and explain that unity? He can be defended from this charge both by his general admission of God's incomprehensibility (see above, p. 336 and n. 36), and by the absolute simplicity of God's *quo est*, which results in the perfect unity of *Deus* and *divinitas* expressed in the passage quoted here. For a detailed discussion of the question, see Nielsen 1982, pp. 158–63.
73 H pp. 203.22–204.27.
74 H p. 90.42–50.

body, knowledge an accident of his soul. It is true to say of the whole man that he is coloured and possesses knowledge; and it is by numerically the same *quo est* that the man is coloured and his body is coloured, and by numerically the same *quo est* that he, and his soul, have knowledge .[75]

Gilbert does allow two exceptions to his general principle. Only positive predicates, not negative ones, which indicate a privation rather than an attribute, are true of the whole if they are true of the part. A man's soul, but not the man himself, is incorporeal.[76] And some descriptions which do not belong to natural science but are at a higher level of abstraction apply to the part but not the whole: the term 'part' is itself an example – a man's soul is part of him, but the whole man is not part of himself.[77] But neither of these exceptions meets the obvious objection that it simply is not the case for most wholes that what is true of their parts is true of them too. A hand is part of a man: it may be reasonable to say that the hand-ness, by which the hand is what it is, belongs to the complex of the whole man; but the man himself, unlike the hand, is not nine inches long and has more than five fingers. Gilbert does not take such points into account, because the only example of parts and a whole he considers are body and soul which make up a man. To this example alone the principles he sets out might, arguably, be applied. Indeed, it is perhaps best to consider these, not as constituting a general theory of wholes and parts, but as an attempt to discuss the relations between soul and body by a writer who, although unfamiliar with Aristotle's view, shares his concern to stress the unity of each human being. Gilbert's strong interest in this problem[78] indicates one of the reasons why he views the theory of parts so narrowly; but there is another. The principles which Gilbert lays down about wholes and their parts are just those which he needs to explain how a *ratio* of natural science can be transumed in order to show the diversity of Father, Son, and Holy Spirit in one God.

In natural science, a group of nouns and/or adjectives can be used either to refer to ('repeat') the same object (*repetitio*), or to refer to ('enumerate') different objects (*numeratio*); and this is so whether the words in the group are the same (for instance, 'man, man, man' used to 'enumerate' three different men) or different (for instance, 'Cicero', 'Tully' used to 'repeat' a single man). Since in everything *quod est* can be distinguished from *quo est*, there will be four main ways in which groups of nouns/adjectives can denote: (1) They can enumerate both *quod ests* and *quo ests* ('man, stone'); (2) they can repeat

75 H p. 94.42–64.
76 H pp. 97.37–46, 272.38–42.
77 H p. 272.35–8; cf. p. 97.45: *naturaliter*.
78 See below, pp. 348f.

both *quod ests* and *quo ests* ('book, volume, tome' – all referring to the same object); (3) they can repeat *quod ests* but enumerate *quo ests* ('rational animal' – with reference to the same man; since he is rational by rationality and an animal by animality); (4) they can repeat *quo ests* but enumerate *quod ests*. (4) depends directly on Gilbert's theory of parts: an example of it is 'rational rational', where these words enumerate two distinct *quod ests* – a man and his soul – but repeat the single *quo est* by which both the man and his soul are rational. These methods of repetition and enumeration can be used in theology, but only in a limited way: neither (1), (2) nor (3) applies to the persons of the Trinity; but (4) does. When the words 'God, God, God' are used, applying in turn to the Father, the Son, and the Holy Spirit, then those which are God are enumerated, that by which they are God is repeated.[79]

(3) Singularity, individuality, personality

The analysis of personality provides an even clearer example of how Gilbert develops his theory of *quod est* and *quo est* in ways which only his theological purposes can explain. But his approach to the problem is also complicated by the difficulty of accommodating Boethius' definition to the terms Gilbert has developed. A person, says Boethius, is 'an individual substance of a rational nature (*naturae rationabilis individua substantia*)'.[80] In explaining the terms of this formula, Boethius makes no apparent distinction between an individual, a singular, and a particular: they are distinguished from universals because they cannot be predicated. Whereas 'man' is predicated of single men and 'stone' of single stones, there can be no predication, for instance, of 'Cicero' or 'this stone'.[81] Gilbert cannot follow Boethius here, because, if he were to accept all singulars as individuals, every *quo est* would be an individual. This would have unacceptable consequences: for instance, the *quo est*, humanity, by which I am a man – being of a rational nature ('rational' is its *differentia*), a substance (in one sense of the word,[82]) and individual – would be a person.

Not surprisingly, then, Gilbert says that, whilst everything which is individual is one in number, not everything which is one in number is individual.[83] To be an individual is not to belong to a *dividuum*. Every *quo est* (including complex ones) is singular; but only those *quo ests* which are exactly alike (*conformes*) to no other are individuals (and so are their corresponding

79 H pp. 109.33–110.54.
80 R pp. 84.4–5, 92.21–2.
81 R p. 84.37–52. For a sophisticated discussion of singularity and individuation in Boethius and Gilbert, see Gracia 1984, pp. 97–107. (Boethius's *De trinitate*), 155–78 (Gilbert).
82 See n. 3 above for *substantia* = *quo est*.
83 H pp. 144.55–7, 270.71–4.

quod ests).[84] But *which* are the *quo ests* that are unlike any other? The lack of obvious criteria for answering this question provides Gilbert with the means, when he turns to the definition of a person, to develop his theory in line with his larger theological purposes.

In his commentary on *De trinitate*, Gilbert says that the only sort of *quo ests* which are individuals are the 'whole properties' of things, the complex *quo ests* collected from all of something's substantial and accidental attributes, such as the 'Plato-ness collected from all those things which have been, are or will be, in act and in nature, Plato's'.[85] He goes on to define a person as a substance which meets what seem to be three requirements:

(1) It is individual (and therefore singular, since every individual is singular);
(2) It is not part of anything;
(3) It is rational.[86]

(1) and (3) correspond to Boethius' definition (in *Contra Eutychen*); and Gilbert explains that (3) is just an arbitrary distinction, a matter of general usage. But (2) does not seem to enter into Boethius' formula. This difference between what Boethius seems to allow and what Gilbert requires is made explicit in the commentary on *Contra Eutychen* and resolved in a discussion which takes the form of a *quaestio*. According to Boethius' definition, Gilbert says, 'the human soul seems to be (*videtur esse*) a person': it is a substance – not, as some say, '*endilichia*, which is form'; and it is of rational nature; and the soul of each man is an individual since its whole property (*plena proprietas*), the complex *quo est* by which it is what it is, seems to be individual.[87] But it is impossible that the human soul should be a person, 'because no person can be part of a person'.[88]

Gilbert's task is to resolve this apparent contradiction which – as befits a *quaestio* – he considers in fact merely verbal (*ut ergo pugnas verborum sensuum convenientia dirimat, dicendum est* ...).[89] He does so by exploring the conditions under which a *quo est* is dividual or individual. He has already said that any *quo est* to which another is exactly alike is a dividual; now he makes it clear that this conformity need not be actual. It is enough to make a *quo est* dividual for it to be exactly like another potentially. And, for Gilbert, whatever is logically possible is potentially the case. For instance, 'man' and 'sun' are both words used by logicians to refer to dividual things. 'Man'

84 H pp. 144.65–8, 274.85–8.
85 H p. 144.75–8; for the expression 'whole property (*plena proprietas*)', see p. 273.73.
86 H pp. 143.52ff: especially, for (1) and (2), p. 146.24–8; for (3), p. 146.19–23.
87 H pp. 271.15–272.26.
88 H p. 272.27–44.
89 H p. 272.45–6.

refers to what is dividual actually and potentially – the *quo est* by which, not just a single man, but all men past, present and future, actual and potential, are men. 'Sun' refers to what is only potentially dividual. There is, has been and will ever be only one sun, Gilbert affirms; but 'potentially there have been and are and will be infinite suns'.[90]

The requirements for individuality are therefore stricter than they had seemed: not merely that in actuality a *quo est* is exactly like no other, but also in potentiality. It must be logically impossible for any other *quo est* to conform to it. Gilbert feels confident in asserting that this condition is met only in the case of something which is not part of something else: by, for instance, Plato's whole property (his Plato-ness), but not by his body or his soul. And so the conflict between Boethius' and Gilbert's definitions of 'person' turns out to be illusory. Since the soul is not even an individual, it cannot be a person by Boethius' own definition.[91]

Gilbert does not explain why he feels able to assert with such confidence the logical impossibility of there being any other complex *quo est* exactly like the whole property of a thing. But there is a good reason for holding this position. The whole property of a thing includes the *quo ests* of all its accidents, past, present, and future. However alike two members of the same species may be, they cannot – if they are corporeal – have identical accidents of place, because two objects cannot occupy the same place at the same time. And so their whole properties cannot be exactly alike. Variety of accidents (or, failing other variety, just of the accident of place) is, for Boethius, the basis of numerical difference; whereas for Gilbert it is merely a sign of the numerical difference which, ontologically, is based on the singularity of *quo ests*.[92] Yet it seems that – implicitly and perhaps without noticing it – Gilbert has used Boethius' principle as the foundation for his concept of the individual.

But why does Gilbert think that it *is* always logically possible for there to be another *quo est* exactly like the whole property of a *part* of something? The argument for the uniqueness of the whole property of a man holds equally well for the whole property of his body. Perhaps here (just as in his treatment of parts), Gilbert's mind is so fixed on a particular example that it displaces the wider problem it is supposed to exemplify. The example, in this case, is the soul; and the argument about the whole property of the man does not

90 H p. 273.50–74.
91 H p. 274.75–92. In his commentary on the *De trinitate*, Gilbert uses, but does not explain or justify, the ideas he develops here. All composite *quo ests*, which are not made from all the properties of a thing, are – he says (p. 144.71–8) – 'vel actu vel natura' exactly like some other *quo est*.
92 H p. 77.86–90; cf. Gracia 1984, pp. 169–73.

apply to it – though not because the soul is a part, but because it is incorporeal. And Gilbert's theological aims make it particularly important for him to show that the soul (rather than any other part of any other whole) is not an individual. If it were an individual, then it would have all that is required to be a person; but if it were possible for two persons to be conjoined in the relationship of soul to the whole man, then Gilbert's argument against the heretical Christology of Nestorius – who envisaged two persons in Christ – would be ruined.[93]

Gilbert's insistence that a person cannot be a part also serves another theological purpose, since it enables him to explain the proportion by which the concept of person can be transumed into theology. According to Gilbert's theory of parts, a part is not another thing from a whole but a whole is another thing from its part, and something is part of a whole when the *quo est*, by which it is what it is, is numerically the same as the *quo est* by which the whole has those attributes.[94] If, then, no part can be a person, nothing can be a person unless 'no other person is what it is by any of those things by which it is itself'.[95] But, in the case of the Trinity, Father, Son, and Holy Spirit are each different (*alius*), but they are all what they are by the same *quo est*. 'That by which one [of the persons of the Trinity] is, is that by which another [of them] is.'[96] 'Person' in theological use does not, therefore, obey all the same conditions as it does in natural science. By showing the rule of natural science which it disobeys, Gilbert has succeeded in elucidating the proportion of its transumption.

Corporeality and matter

Gilbert analyses concrete wholes into their different forms, substantial and accidental, rather than into matter and form. But he cannot, in commenting on Boethius, ignore the concept of matter. In the course of his work he uses two different approaches to the materiality of things. The first is a straight-forward development within the theory of *quod est* and *quo est*, which – in a manner typical of Gilbert – centres upon the example of a man and seems to have been evolved with its requirements in mind. Some things are spiritual; some are bodily; some are both. Whatever is spiritual (such as man's soul) will perpetually remain spiritual; whatever is bodily will perpetually remain bodily. When the relationship between body and spirit is sundered, no

93 H pp. 287.1ff.
94 See above, pp. 343f.
95 H p. 147.53–4.
96 H p. 147.41–55.

longer does the man or the animal exist; but body and spirit remain. Bodiliness and spirituality can therefore be described as the two 'perpetual *subsistentiae*'.[97] By contrast, embodiment (*incorporatio*) and ensouledness (*animatio*) are the *subsistentiae* of 'generation and corruption'. They are substantial *quo ests* of a whole man, but merely accidental with regard to his soul and his body. Gilbert develops this point by making a division of *quo ests* rather different from that between *subsistentiae* and accidental *quo ests*: substantial *quo ests* and those which produce the intrinsic accidents, quantity and quality, give a thing its 'nature (*natura*)'; *quo ests* which produce the other, extrinsic accidents, merely give it its *status*. Although embodiment and ensouledness are *subsistentiae* of the whole man, they do not even contribute to the nature of the body and soul separately, but merely to their *status*.[98]

Using this distinction, Gilbert goes on to tackle a difficult theological problem about body, soul, and the whole man. Philosophers define man as a 'rational, mortal animal': 'misled by this philosophical way of talking', Christian thinkers of Gilbert's own day had been led to doubt whether the conjoined bodies and souls of the blessed after the Resurrection will be truly men, since they will lack 'part of the human *subsistentia*', mortality. But in Gilbert's view neither mortality nor immortality are *subsistentiae* of man, but rather his *status*, variable from time to time according to God's will. To say that man is immortal means that the conjunction of body and soul cannot be dissolved; to say he is mortal means it cannot not be dissolved. Before the Fall, man was neither immortal nor mortal, in Gilbert's terms: it was possible that the conjunction of body and soul might be dissolved and possible that it might not. By sinning, man merited the change of his *status* to mortality; had he not sinned, he would have become immortal, and such will be the *status* of the blessed after the Resurrection.[99]

Gilbert's second approach to the concept of matter is quite different. It introduces ideas much at variance with the rest of the commentary; and Gilbert shows his skill by keeping it apart from the theory of *quod est* and *quo est*.

In the *De trinitate*, Boethius distinguishes between two different kinds of forms: those which are in matter and produce bodies, and those which are outside matter. Only the ones outside matter can properly be called forms; the forms in matter derive from these and should be called 'images'.[100]

97 H pp. 320.89–321.97.
98 H pp. 319.56–320.88.
99 H pp. 321.98–323.63, 358.28–42.
100 R p. 12.51–6.

Boethius – a thinker who asserted the harmony of Plato and Aristotle[101] – thus admits one sort of forms (the forms properly so called) which are like Platonic Ideas, and another (the images) which are like Aristotelian embodied forms. Neither type has an obvious place in the main scheme of Gilbert's thought about concrete wholes. But Gilbert finds a way out of a potential difficulty by remembering another late antique author who also contrasts disembodied Ideas with embodied forms. In his commentary on Plato's *Timaeus*, Calcidius puts forward a theory about the formation of the material world. Matter without form or quality (*silva*) is formed by an 'intelligible species' into the four 'elements' or 'pure substances (*sincerae substantiae*)' – fire, water, earth, and air – from which sensible matter which is fiery, watery, earthy or airy derives. Without acknowledgement, Gilbert borrows not merely Calcidius' argument but his words (one of the few instances of direct quotation in the commentary).[102]

The great advantage of this theory for Gilbert is that it concerns the production of the bodily matter of things, not their nature as members of a species affected by certain accidents. Gilbert places matter (*yle*) and the Idea along with God (*principium/opifex*) as the objects of theology.[103] The study of how the four pure elements are made by God from formless matter and the Idea(s) therefore belongs to the theologian; and the derivation of sensible matter from these elements is seen as a different process from the concretion of substantial and accidental forms which the natural scientist analyses. The materiality of bodies – but not their specific or accidental natures – is to be explained by forms which are images of their exemplars.

Normally these two types of discussion are kept apart.[104] The one passage in which they seem to be brought together does not involve a natural scientist's analysis of the concretion of *quo ests*, but rather considers what Gilbert has earlier called 'creation'[105] and here calls 'generation' – the barely describable reception of the *subsistentia* by which something is. Generation

101 *De interpretatione* II, ed. C. Meiser (Leipzig 1880), pp. 79.10–80.6.
102 Compare Calcidius, *Commentary on 'Timaeus'*, ed. J. H. Waszink (2nd ed., London–Leiden 1975), p. 276.11–15, with H pp. 81.96–82.100; and pp. 275.22–276.3 with H p. 81.69–71. Both parallels are noted by Häring, but they have received little attention from scholars. It is probable that, in the second of these borrowings, Gilbert has either misunderstood or deliberately adapted the tenet of his source: Calcidius refers here to the four, pure elements which exist in *concretione mutua*; but Gilbert (cf. H pp. 81.94–5, 100.15–17) distinguishes the elements which have *concretio mutua in yle* from the pure elements. Gilbert also borrows his names for matter from Calcidius: see E. Gilson, 'Notes sur les noms de la matière chez Gilbert de la Porrée', *RMAL* II (1946) 173–6.
103 H p. 85.97–100.
104 See e.g. H p. 100.13–20.
105 See above, p. 339 and n. 51.

and material formation are necessarily connected in the case of material things: nothing can be without a *subsistentia*, and material things exist by the coming-together of matter and form. Even so, Gilbert is careful to distinguish the two processes, referring first to a thing's generation, and then to its material formation as the image (*ycon*) of an exemplar.[106] Despite Gilbert's care, many modern scholars have confused his discussion of exemplars and his analysis of concrete wholes. According to Gilbert, they say, the *quo ests* which make something what it is are images, derived from immaterial Ideas.[107] The Platonic (or, rather, Calcidian) feature, which Gilbert borrows but compartmentalizes, is thus allowed to dominate and distort the whole interpretation of his commentary.

Conclusion

The historian who approaches Gilbert as a thinker who tackled a set of changeless metaphysical problems – identical to those which faced, for instance, Plato and Aristotle, or Kant and Hegel – must either end by confessing that Gilbert's treatment is inadequate and confused, or must disguise this confusion by his own. But if Gilbert's commentary is seen as a theological work – an attempt to understand, in twelfth-century terms, Boethius' doctrinal analyses – its author emerges as a clear-minded and subtle writer. He unifies Boethius' various discussions by developing a theory about arguments in different disciplines, which is used throughout his commentary. His analysis of concrete wholes takes place within the

---

106 H p. 195.100–7:
  '[1] AT VERO id QUOD EST, ACCEPTA in se FORMA ESSENDI (i.e. ea, quam abstractim intellectus concipit, subsistentia) – que acceptio dicitur "generatio" – EST; [2] ATQUE materie (que Grece "yle" dicitur) formeque huius (que Grece "usyosis" vocatur) concursu – opifice illa forma (que nominatur "usya"), iuxta exemplar illius (que dicitur "ydea") – YCON (hoc est illius exemplaris exemplum et imago) CONSISTIT; [3] ut corpus eo quod ut esse corporalitatem habet est corpus, et homo eo quod humanitatem.'
  The punctuation (designed to bring out the sense) is my own. I follow the suggestion in Nielsen 1982, pp. 70–1, that *id quod est* is the subject of *est*, and *ycon* is the subject of *consistit*. But [3] is not, as Nielsen wishes to take it, an explanation of material formation ([2]), but rather of the process of generation ([1]), with which – in the case of material things – material formation is necessarily combined.
107 E.g. Hauréau 1872, pp. 459–62; E. Gilson, 'Le platonisme de Bernard de Chartres', *Revue Néoscolastique de Philosophie* XXV (1923) 5–19, esp. pp. 15–16; Forest 1934 ('Le réalisme...'), p. 102; Gilson 1947, pp. 264–5; Schmidt 1956, pp. 63–85; Elswijk 1966, pp. 166–71, 199–200 (but some important qualifications are added on pp. 201–2). Behind this view there often lie the unclear and probably misleading remarks of John of Salisbury in his *Metalogicon* II 17 (ed. C. C. J. Webb (Oxford 1929), p. 94). Not all commentators follow this approach: e.g. Williams 1951, p. 16 ('Gilbert's teaching on exemplars does not play an important part in his commentaries, and it seems as if he rejects them altogether, as he nowhere gives a full treatment of them'), and Nielsen 1982, pp. 72–7.

context of this theory. Much in it which is puzzling can be explained, if not justified, by reference to Gilbert's theological aims, and by his tendency to limit his consideration of wholes and parts to the particular example of a man, made of body and soul. As a result of this tendency, the relations between body and soul receive a detailed treatment, which Gilbert would perhaps not have wished the wise interpreter of *his* work to overlook. Although at times a distraction in his general discussion, Gilbert's half-concealed theory is as sustained an examination of the conditions of human wholeness and mortality as any which was made between the time of Augustine and Aquinas.

A NOTE ON THE PORRETANI

JOHN MARENBON

Gilbert of Poitiers had many followers in the later twelfth century. In most cases, they were influenced by his particular theological doctrines rather than by his techniques of argument or conceptual analyses. One group of texts (the products of Gilbert's 'little school', as it has been called) is concerned to support the controversial features of his trinitarian and Christological teaching with Patristic testimony.[1] Another group puts forward ideas and uses language so close to Gilbert's that the works which belong to it have (with varying degrees of probability) been attributed by some to Gilbert himself.[2]

---

1 For a general account see A. Dondaine, *Écrits de la 'petite école' porrétaine* (Montreal 1962). The individual texts are edited and/or discussed as follows: ADHEMAR OF SAINT RUF: *De trinitate*, ed. N. Häring, 'The Tractatus de trinitate of Adhemar of Saint-Ruf (Valence)', *AHDLMA* XXXI (1964) 111–206, at p. 126; Collection of Patristic Texts, lost but partly reconstructable: see N. Häring, 'Die Vätersammlung des Adhemar von Saint-Ruf in Valence', *Scholastik* XXXVIII (1963) 402–20; and 'In Search of Adhemar's Patristic Collection', *Mediaeval Studies* XXVIII (1966) 336–46. ANONYMOUS: *Liber de vera philosophia*, discussed in Dondaine 1963, pp. 20–5. HUGH ETHERIANUS: *Liber de differentia naturae et personae*, ed. N. Häring, 'The "Liber de differentia naturae et personae" by Hugh Etherian and the Letters Addressed to him by Peter of Vienna and Hugh of Honau', *Mediaeval Studies* XXIV (1962) 1–34; cf. N. Häring, 'The Porretans and the Greek Fathers', *ibid.* pp. 181–209. HUGH OF HONAU: *De homoysion et homoeysion*, ed. N. Häring, 'The Liber de homoysion et homoeysion by Hugh of Honau', *AHDLMA* XXXIV (1967) 129–253; XXXV (1968) 211–91; *De diversitate naturae et personae*, ed. N. Häring, 'The Liber de diversitate naturae et personae by Hugh of Honau', *ibid* XXIX (1962) 103–216. Gilbert's defence of himself at the Council of Reims, and the general prologue which he wrote to his commentary on Boethius, probably after his trial, provide the background to these collections of Patristic testimony: for the Council of Reims, see Elswijk 1966, pp. 77–124; and S. Gammersbach, *Gilbert von Poitiers und seine Prozesse im Urteil der Zeitgenossen* (Cologne–Graz 1959); for the general preface, H pp. 53–6.

2 These works are: *Sermo de Natali Domini*, ed. N. Häring, 'A Christmas Sermon by Gilbert of Poitiers', *Mediaeval Studies* XXIII (1961) 126–35; a set of *quaestiones* described in one manuscript as collected from Gilbert's *dicta*, ed. N. Häring, 'Die Sententie Magistri Gisleberti Pictavensis Episcopi', *AHDLMA* XLV (1978) 83–180 (Tortosa MS), and XLVI (1979) 45–105 (Florence MS); a treatise on the Trinity, ed. N. Häring, 'A Treatise on the Trinity by Gilbert of Poitiers', *RTAM* XXXIX (1972) 14–50; and a Commentary on the pseudo-Athanasian Creed, ed. N. M. Häring, 'A Commentary on the pseudo-Athanasian Creed by Gilbert of Poitiers', *Mediaeval Studies* XXVII (1965) 23–53. The attribution of the sermon to Gilbert is probable (but two thirds of it is copied from the commentary on Boethius); that of the commentary on the Creed possible, and those of the other works unlikely; cf. Nielsen 1982, pp. 44–6. (There has been little opportunity for scholars to question Häring's attribution of the *Sentences* to Gilbert. Doubtless they reflect Gilbert's views and perhaps derive in part from his teaching – although

353

And writings by theologians such as Simon of Tournai and Radulphus Ardens show definite borrowings from Gilbert.[3]

Often the theological writers influenced by Gilbert's ideas were those generally most adventurous in their choice of sources. For example, in his commentary on pseudo-Dionysius' *De divinis nominibus* (*ca.* 1169–77), William of Lucca mixes passages derived from Gilbert into a discussion which, for the greater part, reflects the Neoplatonic metaphysics of pseudo-Dionysius himself and his ninth-century Latin follower, John Scotus (Eriugena).[4] And traces of Gilbert's thought appear in another work which also uses Eriugena's *Periphyseon*: the *Liber de causis primis et secundis*, which probably dates from early in the thirteenth century.[5] Before the anonymous author of the *Liber* sets about his ambitious task of bringing together with texts from Eriugena extracts from Avicenna's *Metaphysics* and the *Liber de causis*, he recollects Gilbert's idea of *esse* as a word that is used denominatively.[6]

The two thinkers who made use of Gilbert's theory of arguments were Peter of Poitiers (Peter of Vienna?), who wrote a book of *Sentences* in around 1150 and Alan of Lille. Neither adopts Gilbert's technique completely. Peter takes up the idea of transumption from natural science to

on occasion Gilbert is mentioned as just one authority among others; but they are almost certainly not an independent work written or dictated by Gilbert himself).

3 On Gilbert's wider theological influence, see A. Landgraf, 'Mitteilungen zur Schule Gilberts de la Porrée', *Collectanea Franciscana* III (1933) 182–208; 'Neue Funde zur Porretanerschule', *ibid.* VI (1936) 353–65; J. de Ghellinck, *Le mouvement théologique du XIIe siècle* (Bruges–Brussels–Paris 1948), pp. 175–80; A. Landgraf, *Introduction à l'histoire de la littérature théologique de la scolastique naissante* (French ed., Montreal–Paris 1973), pp. 112–28; and Nielsen 1982, pp. 193ff. For Simon of Tournai's Porretanism, see N. Häring, 'Simon of Tournai and Gilbert of Poitiers', *Mediaeval Studies* XXVII (1965) 325–30; for Radulphus Ardens' Porretanism, see A. Landgraf, 'Der Porretanismus der Homilien des Radulphus Ardens', *Zeitschrift für katholische Theologie* LXIV (1940) 132–48.

4 *Comentum in tertiam ierarchiam Dionisii que est de divinis nominibus*, ed. F. Gastaldelli (Florence 1983): see especially pp. 19, 27 (cf. H pp. 81.94–82.1), 64 (cf. H p. 90.38–41), 76–7, 202 (cf. H p. 190.71–4 – a passage also used by Alan of Lille – see below n. 8) and 203–7. Gastaldelli (pp. lxiii–lxxiv) emphasizes (and probably exaggerates) William's Porretanism. (I should like to thank Peter Dronke for bringing William's commentary to my attention.)

5 The *Liber* is edited in R. de Vaux, *Notes et textes sur l'avicennisme latin aux confins des XIIe–XIIIe siècles* (Paris 1934), pp. 88–140. See M.-T. d'Alverny, 'Une rencontre symbolique de Jean Scot Érigène et d'Avicenne. Notes sur le *De causis primis et secundis et fluxu qui consequitur eas*' in *The Mind of Eriugena*, ed. J. O'Meara and L. Bieler (Dublin 1973), pp. 170–81.

6 See de Vaux 1934, p. 89.7–15: for the passage in Gilbert, above pp. 337f and nn. 39–43. The parallel is pointed out by M. H. Vicaire, 'Les porrétains et l'avicennisme avant 1215', *RSPT* XXVI (1937), 449–82, at p. 460. Vicaire goes on to argue that the whole *Liber de causis primis et secundis* is an exercise in Porretan theology, but succeeds at most in showing some parallels between the *Liber* and arguments advanced by late twelfth-century writers certainly influenced by Gilbert, like Simon of Tournai. On Porretanism and Avicenna, see also P. Dronke, 'New Approaches to the School of Chartres', *Anuario de Estudios Medievales* VI (1969) 117–40, at p. 127 and esp. n. 34.

theology and gives a set of thirty-four rules which apply to created things. From some of these rules, he says, it is also possible to gain some understanding of divine things.[7] But Peter, despite borrowing many of Gilbert's ideas about individuals, persons, and the Trinity, does not use these, like his teacher, in order to establish the proportion by which natural *rationes* may be transumed. Alan begins his *Regulae caelestis iuris* by describing, in almost exactly Gilbert's words, the different sorts of fundamental rules which belong to each discipline.[8] Theology too, says Alan, has its rules; and his treatise sets out one hundred and thirty-four of them. He expounds and attempts to justify each rule, often deriving one from another. Some of the rules themselves and some of Alan's expository remarks are based on Gilbert's ideas; and frequently Alan contrasts what can be said *in naturalibus* with what can be said *in theologicis*. But Alan aims to establish a set of axioms peculiar to theology rather than to discuss proportional transumption as Gilbert had done.[9]

Gilbert's influence on the manner of expounding Boethius' *Opuscula sacra* is seen most clearly in Clarembald of Arras' commentary on the *De trinitate* and *De hebdomadibus*.[10] Clarembald was not, in any straightforward way, a Porretan. He complains of Gilbert's 'complicated words and convoluted style': his fellow-monks' difficulty in understanding them is one of the reasons why Clarembald feels it necessary to produce his own exposition.[11] He rejects many of Gilbert's doctrines, and frequently (if respectfully) his general approach.[12] Yet he owes to Gilbert not merely some passages, but the example of a commentary on the *Opuscula sacra* which explains, sentence by sentence, Boethius' meaning. Clarembald, who shares neither Gilbert's intelligence nor his teachings, inherits his painstakingness.

Among all the texts which bear witness to Porretanism, two are exceptional in that they provide a discussion of Gilbert's conceptual and methodological analyses which is detailed and sympathetic, but not merely derivative.

7 *Die Zwettler Summa*, ed. N. Häring (Münster 1977), pp. 30–3.
8 N. Häring, 'Magister Alanus de Insulis Regulae caelestis iuris', *AHDLMA* xlviii (1981) 97–226, at pp. 121–2; for the passage in Gilbert, see above p. 334 and n. 25; and n. 4 to this appendix.
9 M.-D. Chenu draws attention to the influence of Gilbert's theological method on Alan and others in 'Un essai de méthode théologique au xiie siècle', *RSPT* xxiv (1935) 258–67; but cf. Nielsen 1982, pp. 131–3.
10 The commentary is edited in N. Häring, *Life and Works of Clarembald of Arras. A Twelfth Century Master of the School of Chartres* (Toronto 1965), pp. 61–221. The discussions in W. Jansen, *Der Kommentar des Clarenbaldus von Arras zu Boethius De Trinitate. Ein Werk aus der Schule von Chartres im 12. Jahrhundert* (Breslau 1926), are still valuable.
11 Häring 1965, p. 63.
12 See Häring 1965, pp. 38–45.

One is an anonymous logical textbook, probably written between about 1155 and 1170;[13] the other is a set of interrelated works by Everard of Ypres. Three of the four sections which make up the *Compendium logicae Porretanum* discuss the nature of propositions: their parts, types, and meanings; one long section is devoted to many of the important concepts discussed in Gilbert's commentary, such as parts and wholes, individuals and categories. Many of Gilbert's favoured terms (such as *subsistentia* and *concretio*) are explained and used; and there are explicit references both to the *Opuscula sacra* and to Gilbert's commentary on these. But Gilbert's ideas are removed from their theological context, and are juxtaposed in ways which go beyond their originator. For instance, the *Compendium* explains Gilbert's remarks on creation and concretion in terms of the union of body and soul in man.[14]

Everard of Ypres, a scholar, canon lawyer and, late in life, a Cistercian monk,[15] wrote a letter to Pope Urban III (1185–7) in which he explains and defends Porretan Christological and trinitarian doctrines, without naming Gilbert. Another letter,[16] which purports to be addressed to Everard by a fellow-Cistercian but may well be his own composition, queries some points both in the letter to Pope Urban and in Everard's most ambitious work, a long dialogue written in the 1190s.[17] The chief protagonists of the *Dialogue* are Everard himself and Ratius, a Greek. Ratius is described as a follower of Gilbert's and, in the discussion, he acts as the proponent of Porretanism. His Greek origin reflects both the general association of Greece with learning and intellectual subtlety and the use made of the Greek Fathers by Gilbert and his advocates.[18] Everard – appropriately for a Cistercian – puts into his own mouth the defence of Gilbert's adversary, Bernard. But Ratius is almost always allowed to win in argument; the character Everard is reduced to making excuses for the saintly but theologically incompetent patron of his order; and it becomes clear that the author Everard intends his *Dialogue* as a tactful but firm defence of Gilbert and his teachings.

13 The work is edited by S. Ebbesen, K. M. Fredborg, L. O. Nielsen: 'Compendium logicae Porretanum ex codice Oxoniensi Collegii Corporis Christi 250: a Manual of Porretan doctrine by a Pupil of Gilbert's', *CIMAGL* xlvi (1983) iii–xvii, 1–113; it is discussed by C. J. Martin, 'The Compendium logicae Porretanum: a Survey of Philosophical Logic from the School of Gilbert of Poitiers', *ibid.* pp. xviii–xlvi.
14 Ebbesen, Fredborg and Nielsen 1983, pp. 36.13–37.32; cf. above, p. 339 and n. 51.
15 See N. Häring, 'The Cistercian Everard of Ypres and his Appraisal of the Conflict between St. Bernard and Gilbert of Poitiers', *Mediaeval Studies* xvii (1955) 143–72; cf. Nielsen 1982, pp. 284–6.
16 Both letters are edited as an appendix to Häring 1955.
17 Edited by N. Häring, 'A Latin Dialogue on the Doctrine of Gilbert of Poitiers', *Mediaeval Studies* xv (1953) 243–89.
18 See Häring 1962 ('The Porretans and the Greek Fathers').

Everard handles the dialogue-form with skill and imagination. The discussions stretch over a number of days; there are descriptions, digressions, and interruptions, personal exchanges and witty use of quotations from the Latin poets. Everard uses the latitude this form allows him to connect the controversy over Gilbert's doctrine with more general questions about the relative values of the scholarly and the monastic life, and the differences between the Cistercian ideal and the actual behaviour of many Cistercians. Like Bernard Silvestris and Alan of Lille, he presents abstract discussion in a sophisticated literary form which encourages a reflective assessment of various, conflicting positions. Of the parts of the *Dialogue* directly concerned with Gilbert's teaching, some quote from the commentary on Boethius, summarize its arguments or gloss difficult passages from it.[19] Others show that Everard and his contemporaries have developed Gilbert's thought in their own ways, combining the distinction between natural science and mathematics with late twelfth-century theories about variety in a term's reference.[20] Everard is far less clearly committed than Gilbert to a set of real distinctions in concrete things; rather, the commentary on Boethius has been used to provide techniques of logical and grammatical analysis which can be employed to defend Gilbert's disputed theological doctrines.

Everard's is probably the most intelligent development of Porretanism; and also one of the latest texts so directly and thoroughly concerned with Gilbert's teaching. It was a work by one of Gilbert's opponents at the Council of Reims, the *Sentences* of Peter Lombard, which was chosen as a textbook by university theologians, whilst Gilbert became a shadowy and suspect figure to the masters of the later Middle Ages.[21]

---

19 For example, Gilbert's remarks on the objects of mathematics (H p. 86.31–6) are explained: Haring 1953, p. 257; cf. above p. 340.
20 See e.g. Häring 1953, p. 254.
21 See H p. 6 n. 27; and A. Landgraf, 'Porretanisches Gut beim hl. Thomas von Aquin', *Acta Pontificiae Academiae Romanae S. Thomae Aquinatis* n.s. VI (1939–40) 214–25.

13

THIERRY OF CHARTRES

PETER DRONKE

1.1 The little information that we have about Thierry of Chartres's life and career has become less in recent years: even some of the apparently safer assumptions about him have lately been challenged. It is certain that he was born in Brittany, that he was Chancellor of Chartres in the 1140s, that he retired from this position to a monastery at some point in the 1150s, and died after 1156.[1] It is not certain, though likely, that he was the younger brother of Bernard of Chartres,[2] the renowned teacher – some of whose ideas are recorded by John of Salisbury – who was *magister* at the school of Chartres from before 1117, and later (till 1124) its chancellor. It is also uncertain how far Thierry's teaching activities, in the years before his own chancellorship, can be linked with Chartres itself, rather than with Paris (as is commonly, though on somewhat meagre evidence, affirmed),[3] or with some other centre.

1 Cf. A. Vernet, 'Une épitaphe inédite de Thierry de Chartres', in *Recueil de travaux offert à Cl. Brunel* (2 vols., Paris 1955) II 660–70 (on the date of Thierry's death, p. 667).

2 Doubts were raised by R. W. Southern, 'Humanism and the School of Chartres', *Medieval Humanism* (Oxford 1970), pp. 61–85 (at p. 69); but N. Häring, 'Chartres and Paris Revisited', in *Essays in Honour of Anton Charles Pegis* (Toronto 1974), pp. 268–329, after a careful re-assessment of the evidence (pp. 295–7), concludes that the assumption that Thierry and Bernard were brothers is 'not unreasonable'.

3 As Häring (1974, pp. 284f) notes, 'By calling him "magistrum Teodoricum Carnotensem" Master Balderic [of Trier] indicates the place where he lived at the time, just as "Hugo Parisiensis" means Hugh of St Victor.' I would add that the fact that Thierry was frequently called 'Carnotensis', and never 'Parisiensis', suggests that we should not, in the absence of positive documentation, assume he spent any substantial part of his life in Paris. This assumption is made not only by Southern (*Platonism, Scholastic Method, and the School of Chartres* (Reading 1979), p. 26, and *Harvard 1982*, p. 130), but by Häring himself, who claims, for instance, on the basis of the line 'Ibi doctor cernitur ille Carnotensis' in the poem *Metamorphosis Goliae* (composed 1142/3) that 'the author ... saw Thierry in Paris' (1974, p. 285). In the context of this poem, however, *ibi* plainly refers not to Paris but to a wholly imaginary location, the *locus amenus* described by the author. So, too, it is inadmissible to infer, as Häring does (1974, p. 287), from William of Tyre's references to men who were taught by Thierry of Chartres, that Thierry had taught them in Paris: William's text (ed. R. B. C. Huygens, *Latomus* XXI (1962) 822) gives no indication of place. Similarly, Häring's assertion that Clarembald, who studied with Hugh of Saint-Victor (in Paris) as well as with Thierry, 'seems to have attended Thierry's lectures *at the same time in the same city*' (1974, p. 280; italics mine), is not confirmed by anything in the text of Clarembald's letter where he mentions these two teachers.

Like Bernard of Chartres, Thierry made an unforgettable impact on more than one generation of scholars. Today both men would be known as 'charismatic' teachers. Among Thierry's disciples, Clarembald of Arras calls him 'the foremost philosopher in the whole of Europe',[4] John of Salisbury, 'the most learned of explorers of the liberal arts'.[5] In 1143 Hermann of Carinthia, about to complete his major original work of cosmology, the *De essentiis*, addresses Thierry as his 'fondest teacher (*diligentissime preceptor*)', and dedicates to him, 'the soul of Plato granted once again by heaven to mortals', his translation of Ptolemy's *Planisphere*.[6] In 1147/8, Bernard Silvestris dedicates his epic *Cosmographia* 'to Thierry, by true proclamations of opinion most renowned of teachers'.[7] A long and awestruck epitaph for Thierry also survives, beginning 'Aristotle's worthy successor, Theodoricus, lies here . . .'[8]

Yet Thierry left no finished work comparable in scale or stature to the *De essentiis* or the *Cosmographia*. What survives consists mainly of commentaries, first (probably in the 1130s) on the widely studied pair of works on rhetoric, Cicero's *De inventione* and the pseudo-Ciceronian *Ad Herennium*,[9] then (towards 1150) on Boethius' brief theological treatises;[10] finally, perhaps soon after 1150, there is the incomplete commentary on the opening

The only link between Thierry and Paris that is known to me is made by Anselm of Havelberg in his poetic biography of Adelbert of Mainz, *Vita Adelberti* (ed. P. Jaffé, *Bibliotheca Rerum Germanicarum* III) II 680 ff (pp. 589–92). Anselm states that it was when Adelbert came to Paris ('Parisius, locus eximius bene cultus, initur') that people began to tell him of Thierry's excellence and fame ('cepit ei dici virtus et fama Thedrici'); that he went to visit Thierry *non segniter* (not *non sequitur*, as Häring 1974, p. 283, has it); that he 'deigned to be called and to be Thierry's disciple (*discipulus dici dignatur et esse Thedrici*)' – thus the biographer points the difference of rank between the two men; and finally that, when Adelbert was about to return to Germany, it was in Paris that he bade Thierry a fond farewell ('Hinc facie tristi lugens petit ora magistri . . . largitus et oscula grata, / cum numero turbe prodit pius exul ab urbe'). While these verses allow at least a plausible inference that Thierry was residing in Paris at this time (soon after 1130) – rather than, say, living somewhere relatively near and visiting Paris on occasion – they are hardly a safe basis for constructing an extensive teaching-career in Paris for him. Southern's assertion (1979, p. 26), that 'from about 1115 to 1142 . . . we know him as a Breton master teaching in Paris', has nothing to support it.

4 *Clarembaldi Epistola*, ed. N. Häring, *AHDLMA* XXII (1955) 183.
5 *Metalogicon* I 5 (ed. Webb, p. 16).
6 The dedication has been newly edited in C. Burnett's ed. of Hermann of Carinthia, *De essentiis* (Leiden–Cologne 1982), pp. 347–9.
7 *Cosmographia* (ed. Dronke), p. 96.
8 Vernet 1955, p. 669.
9 Cf. K. M. Fredborg, 'The Commentary of Thierry of Chartres on Cicero's *De inventione*', *CIMAGL* VII (1971) 225–60. A sentence from his commentary on Priscian also survives: cf. K. M. Fredborg, *ibid.* XXI (1977) 40–3. For traces of Thierry's lectures on Martianus Capella, see E. Jeauneau, *Lectio Philosophorum* (Amsterdam 1973), pp. 14–22.
10 See N. Häring, *Commentaries on Boethius by Thierry of Chartres and his School* (Toronto 1971), pp. 24ff. At the same time, it seems to me highly likely that much of the material in these commentaries was first elaborated earlier, in the decade 1135–45.

of Genesis, the 'Treatise on the works of the six days (*Tractatus de sex dierum operibus*)',[11] which has attracted most attention, and brought Thierry most fame, among modern historians of medieval thought.[12] In addition, we have the encyclopaedic collection of his teaching-materials in the *Heptateuchon*, the 'volume of the seven liberal arts', with Thierry's prologue as well as a number of his notes between the texts that were copied. The two large manuscripts, assembling a library of nearly 50 separate works in no fewer than 1170 double-columned pages,[13] remained unfinished at the time of Thierry's death. He left them to the Chartres cathedral library, together with 3 volumes of legal texts and 45 *volumina librorum* on other subjects[14] – a substantial legacy, especially as many of these 'volumes of books' will likewise have contained more than one work.

1.2 The *Heptateuchon* gives striking practical embodiment to a conception that, as will emerge, is crucial to all Thierry's thought – the unity of knowledge. In his prologue[15] he uses the mythopoeic image from Martianus Capella, of the marriage of Mercury and Philology, to evoke this unity in an individual way. The two principal 'instruments of philosophizing', Thierry says, are understanding and interpretation. The one (*intellectus*) is illuminated by the arts of the Quadrivium (arithmetic, geometry, music, and astronomy), that offer matter on which the understanding can work; the other (*interpretatio*) aids understanding by providing it with those powers of language that the Trivium inculcates, so that the expression of intellectual insight may be elegant (with grammar's help), rational (with that of dialectic), and well-composed (with that of rhetoric). The marriage of the arts of Quadrivium and Trivium, 'to beget a noble nation of philosophers', thus means the harmonious union of thought and expression, content and form, reality and language.

The seven arts are not studied primarily for their own sakes but as instruments in the service of Philosophia, the love of that wisdom which

11 While Häring 1971, p. 47, suggests reasons for a date 'before May 1140', I believe the later date argued by E. Maccagnolo, *Rerum universitas: Saggio sulla filosofia di Teodorico di Chartres* (Florence 1976), p. 7, is more plausible. For the *Tractatus*, I here follow Häring's choice of title; the titles it is given in various MSS are noted in Häring 1971, p. 555.

12 A commentary on Boethius' *De institutione arithmetica*, which survives in four MSS and has been claimed for Thierry (cf. G. Beaujouan, *Harvard 1982*, p. 482 n. 84) is – as Charles Burnett kindly informs me – unlikely to be by him.

13 On the *Heptateuchon* (MSS Chartres, Bibl. Mun. 497–8) see most recently C. Burnett, 'The Contents and Affiliation of the Scientific Manuscripts Written at, or Brought to, Chartres...', in *The World of John of Salisbury*, ed. M. Wilks (Oxford 1984), pp. 127–60. Burnett points out (p. 142) that, in MS 498, 104 folios are missing; thus the *Heptateuchon* in Thierry's day will have approached 1400 pages.

14 Häring 1974, p. 291.

15 Ed. Jeauneau 1973, pp. 38f.

(here Thierry adopts a Boethian phrase) 'is the integral comprehension of the truth of the things that are (*integra comprehensio veritatis eorum que sunt*)'. The rich materials in the *Heptateuchon* are gathered and interpreted, that is, in order to lead to *sapientia* – to an understanding of the universe and of God that, for Thierry at least, is 'integral' in being inseparably philosophical and theological. Relying on the arts but going beyond them, Thierry in his commentaries on Boethius and Genesis adumbrates a world-picture for some aspects of which, as he shows, philosophical and scientific arguments are appropriate, whilst for other aspects theological arguments are. Yet underlying both Thierry's ranges of argument – indeed fundamental to both – is his deep awareness that most philosophical and theological language cannot but be 'integumental': it is of its nature to intimate, with the help of mythical and metaphorical statement, what the intellect alone cannot fully grasp. Thierry feels the need to rely on *integumenta* as keenly as Plato did in giving his account of the universe in the *Timaeus*. Whether he is using concepts such as nature or the world-soul, or images such as chaos or the Fates, or using arithmetical 'proofs (*probationes*)' to illuminate the paradoxes of the Trinity, Thierry knows that 'these are only hints and guesses, / hints followed by guesses'.

Not only the prologue but much else about the *Heptateuchon* can indicate Thierry's distinctive cast of mind. While it contains few of the rarest specialist texts, translated from the Greek and Arabic, for which Chartres was celebrated,[16] the section devoted to dialectic, for instance, includes the whole of Aristotle's *Organon*, with the exception of the *Posterior Analytics* (though the oldest manuscript of James of Venice's translation of this work was likewise at Chartres). The longest of the epitaphs written for Thierry indeed commemorates him as the first in France to comprehend Aristotle's *Analytics* and *Sophistical Refutations*.[17] The astronomy section includes not only some older tables ascribed to Ptolemy, that were translated from the Greek in late antiquity, but also the Arabic tables of al-Khwārizmī, newly translated by Adelard of Bath and revised perhaps by Hermann of Carinthia. The section on geometry includes a version by Adelard of Euclid's *Elements*, and a pseudo-Boethian *Altercatio* on points of geometry,[18] in which (as we

16 Cf. P. Dronke, 'New Approaches to the School of Chartres', *Anuario de Estudios Medievales* VI (1969 [but publ. 1971]) 117–40, and Burnett 1984.
17 Vernet 1955, p. 670 ('Primus Analeticos primusque resolvit Helencos, / E Gallis grecas accumulavit opes').
18 Burnett 1984, pp. 142f. The version of Euclid, known as Adelard II, began on the pages missing today (see n. 13). The *Altercatio* has been critically edited by M. Folkerts, 'Die *Altercatio* in der Geometrie I des Pseudo-Boethius', in *Fachprosa-Studien*, ed. G. Keil (Berlin 1982), pp. 84–114.

shall see) Thierry will have perceived the possibility of making geometrical *probationes* point beyond themselves, to adumbrate another kind of *sapientia*.

When studying the *Heptateuchon* manuscripts – or rather, their photocopies (the originals were burnt, save for some fragments, in 1944) – one is struck by the number of columns and parts of columns that have been left blank between the various treatises. These suggest that Thierry, who included prefatory and transitional notes in diverse places, intended to write many more such notes, but that on his retirement, or his death, this task still remained far from complete. This has a bearing on a point that has recently been set in doubt – whether during his years as chancellor Thierry was actually teaching in Chartres. At all events we can say he was still perfecting his teaching-material. So too, if Häring is right in dating the various versions of Thierry's commentary on Boethius' *De trinitate* to *ca.* 1148 and shortly thereafter, then these – which survive in the form of lecture-notes and not of a finished treatise – likewise testify to his teaching in the years of his chancellorship. Finally, the fact that in two separate texts of around 1148 Thierry is designated *magister*[19] seems to me to make further scepticism on this score unreasonable.

1.3 We know that Thierry's predecessor, Gilbert of Poitiers, taught while he was Chancellor of Chartres – but that he was teaching a group of only four students.[20] Were his classes unpopular because of their difficulty, or were they deliberately exclusive? In the vivacious and mordant autobiographical passages that Thierry includes in his commentary on Cicero's *De inventione*, we see that in his case at least exclusiveness was willed:[21]

I have carried out my resolve to shut out, at my whim, the ignorant mob and the mish-mash of the schools. For those who counterfeit genius, hating study, and those who claim to study at home, pretending to be teachers, and the clowns of scholastic disputation, armed with fistfuls of inane words – such in truth are my camp-followers. But let them stay barred from my palace, these men whom only the aura of my name has brought here, so that in their own regions, in their eagerness for fallacious arguments, they may lie about Thierry!

He is wittily – yet not only wittily – aware of being exceptional in the academic world, aware too of being imitated and rivalled and envied. At

19 The texts are cited, one by R. Giacone, 'Masters, Books and Library at Chartres', *Vivarium* XII (1974) 30–51, at pp. 38f, the other by Häring 1974, p. 284. Southern's query of the value of the first testimony (1982, p. 130, n. 52) seems overingenious.

20 Dronke 1969, pp. 119–21.

21 The citations that follow are translated on the basis of the forthcoming critical ed. of the commentary by K. M. Fredborg (PIMS, Toronto), to whom I am grateful for showing me the relevant pages in typescript.

another moment, Thierry pictures the goddess Envy goading the 'mighty goddess Fame' to slander him because he has scorned her:

Much moved, Fama . . . traversed cities and nations with Invidia as her guide, filling them with rumours, accusing Thierry everywhere, calling him ignominious names. When she speaks to uncultivated and scatterbrained men, she calls him 'a Boeotian, born beneath a heavy sky'.[22] When she speaks to religious folk, she calls him a necromancer or a heretic. But among those conscious of the truth she is silent; and if mention is made of him, she changes the subject.

In schools and assemblies of scholars she alters her wares, so as to bring about his shame. She grants him Plato, but in order to take rhetoric away. She allows him rhetoric or grammar, as if for argument's sake, in order to snatch away dialectic – allowing him anything rather than dialectic. She alleges now his immoral life-style, now his negligence in studying, now his long-winded interpretations. Finally, when all else fails, she objects that he lectures to advanced students, so that he holds the younger ones back, or rather, corrupts them in such a way that with him they cannot make any progress.

What emerges from the satire is that, even if he was a controversial figure, Thierry at the time of writing already had a European-wide fame, in an impressive range of subjects – Plato, and all three *artes* of the Trivium, with special emphasis on dialectic. (The passage was doubtless written before he had ventured still further, into theology.) But what Thierry claims is resented most is his exclusiveness, and here, with his final mock-accusation, his implicit self-comparison with Socrates becomes apparent. Like Socrates, Thierry 'corrupts' young men intellectually, he is the gadfly who delights in pricking received truths and in arguing for ideas that seem 'heretical' to the establishment. This passage in my view gives some reason for believing that another Socratic allusion ascribed to Thierry, though recorded in a later source, may also be authentic:

Socrates, as Thierry says, since he was intellectually supreme among philosophers, was so eager in learning that he held it not unworthy of philosophy to learn something of value even from women. That is why he did not blush to call Diotima his teacher.[23]

1.4 Thierry's original contributions to medieval philosophy must be sought in seemingly unpromising places: in the various versions of his commentaries on Boethius' theological essays, and in his *Tractatus* on the opening of

22 Thierry's citation of Horace, *Ep.* II 1 244, has a particular edge, in that the person whom Horace here associates with the proverbial obtuseness of Boeotians is none other than Alexander the Great.

23 Cit. Jeauneau 1973, p. 17, from Walter Burley's *Liber de vita et moribus philosophorum* xxx. On the early Christian conceptions of Socrates, see I. Opelt, 'Das Bild des Sokrates in der christlichen lateinischen Literatur', in *Platonismus und Christentum. Festschrift für Heinrich Dörrie, Jahrbuch für Antike und Christentum*, Suppl. x (1983) pp. 192–207.

Genesis. Only this last suggests stylistically a work that was written 'for publication' (even if it survives incomplete and perhaps was never completed): it is polished, with subtle attention to detail, and has few of the didactic mannerisms and repetitions that pervade the Boethian commentaries. The extent to which these represent Thierry's own lecture-notes, or notes taken by disciples, is hard to gauge. I am inclined to follow Häring in his assessment of the three works *de trinitate* – seeing the *Commentum* as the earliest, followed by the *Lectiones* (which look most like a pupil's notes), and by the *Glosa*, the most mature and advanced version of Thierry's discussion.[24] It is also the work that, in its frequent moments of great succinctness, comparable in manner to the *Tractatus*, is most likely to contain writing that Thierry had substantially finished and made ready for diffusion. Be that as it may, the difficulty of finding the authentic Thierry in these commentaries should not be exaggerated. As with William of Conches, in whose glosses on Plato and Macrobius almost every manuscript (though consisting of reportage rather than authorial fair copy) constitutes a 'version', bringing some new material of value and implying a degree of revision by William himself, so Thierry too will have recast his lectures frequently, and even if no *one* version represents an authorized text, and we must reckon with occasional intrusive matter, where a reporter has added comments from a different source, it is still possible to perceive clearly the thoughts of an exceptional mind. That in the midst of such commentaries, and under such circumstances of transmission, Thierry was able to elaborate a wholly distinctive *imago mundi*, is itself a striking indication of his powers as innovator.

2.1 While the *Tractatus* has been lauded as the 'first systematic attempt to withdraw cosmology from the realm of the miraculous',[25] and seems – at least in its earlier part – daringly to affirm purely physical principles of explanation, the Boethian commentaries appear, by contrast, to present an ultra-Platonic world-view, in which the divine realm and the Ideas are all-important, and physical principles have no place except as a far-off reflection of those Ideas. Are the two tendencies really incompatible? And if not, how does Thierry harmonize them? Central to the discussion of aspects

---

24 Häring 1971, pp. 19–24. All references to the *Commentum*, *Lectiones*, *Glosa* and *Tractatus* in the notes below are to this edition. I signal explicitly the places where I diverge from Häring in readings or (occasionally, where it affects the sense) punctuation. In the citations below, I have also used the abridged version of the *Lectiones* which Häring (pp. 34ff) calls the *Abbreviatio Monacensis*. This includes Thierry's thoughts on Boethius' *De hebdomadibus* and *Contra Eutychen* as well as on *De trinitate*.

25 R. Klibansky, 'The School of Chartres', in *Twelfth-Century Europe and the Foundations of Modern Society*, ed. M. Clagett *et al.* (Madison 1961), pp. 3–14, at p. 8.

of Thierry's thought that follows is the attempt to suggest answers to these questions.

2.2 For Thierry, both the language men use to speak of God and that which they use to speak of the physical universe are inherently metaphorical and approximative. Concerning speech about God, this had been stated notably by pseudo-Dionysius, and up to a point Thierry's stance can be seen as within the Dionysian tradition:[26]

... as 'God' is signified in the mode of substance, this word 'God' being used metaphorically (*translative*), so too with other expressions – such as the power of producing and ordering all things, which is called[27] his creating ... For all words used of God are spoken metaphorically. For otherwise they are not appropriate to God.

Yet Thierry extends these thoughts in more unusual ways. Both philosophical and religious concepts, he suggests, presuppose a human induction, a perception of the possible basis for the metaphors:

... this name 'God', which was first applied to immortal creatures like angels, to signify their essence, was transferred, by way of a likeness, to intimate the ineffable essence of divinity. So too the names 'Father', 'Son', 'Holy Spirit' were first given to created things. But later they were transferred to God by way of a likeness.

Thierry here assumes that human beings have some direct experience or cognition of 'gods' – that is, of the powers that rule the planets and influence mankind – and that such experience provides the ground for the human metaphor of a supreme, unknowable deity. Nonetheless, he also acknowledges that metaphors for God have something intrinsically relative, even arbitrary, about them:

The divine persons are designated in the masculine gender, though they could be designated by these names: mother, daughter, and gift (*donatio*), like the things they intimate – namely omnipotence, wisdom, and benignity (*omnipotentia, sapientia, benignitas* [all three, like *donatio*, of feminine gender]).[28]

At the same time, Thierry envisages the highest human capacity of knowing as, in a sense, coinciding with God. Here it can scarcely be ascertained whether in Thierry's thought this is an ultimate instance of relativism – seeing the summit of cognition as a human construct – or whether a claim to objective truth is implied. In the *Lectiones*, Thierry called

26 *Abbr. Mon. Contra Eutych.* I 51f, III 49f (Häring 1971, pp. 448f, 463).
27 Reading *dicitur* (*dicuntur* Häring).
28 *Glosa* v 22 (p. 297). In the earlier *Commentum* (IV 4, p. 96), however, we read of various reasons why God 'is called father rather than mother, son rather than daughter', including that 'the male sex is the worthier'. It would seem that, by the time he wrote the *Glosa*, Thierry had advanced beyond these more conventional views.

the supreme human capacity both *intelligentia* (like Boethius before him) and *intellectibilitas*. This term, which is his own formation,[29] suggests the capacity of being the object of knowledge rather than the knowing subject. In the *Glosa*, Thierry distinguishes between *intelligentia* and a still higher capacity, for which again he uses a term that seems to have passive force – *intelligibilitas* – a capacity of being known more than knowing, or at least one in which the subject and object of knowledge become indistinguishable. (For his definition of *intelligibilitas*, see below, p. 371.) And here the limitations of human metaphor seem for a moment almost overcome. After saying that 'God is not subject to the motions of reason, and hence is not signified by any name', Thierry continues:

For, if he were signified by any name, that name . . . would signify intelligibility or the simple motions of intelligibility. So its meaning would not be grasped by all mankind, except by so very few, in that this power of intelligibility belongs only to God and very few human beings.[30]

The last phrase echoes a famous passage in the Latin *Timaeus*, though there it is a contrast between the active power *intellectus*, which 'is the property of God and very few chosen human beings', and *opinio*, which is common to all mankind.[31] The special force of Thierry's term *intelligibilitas*, by which he brings together the supreme human construct and the divine object that is constructed, can be seen in other passages, as in a brief aside, on the use of metaphors to intimate the indescribable, in Thierry's commentary on Boethius' *De hebdomadibus*:

. . . as a man does not see his own eye, by which he sees everything, so he cannot see or know the supreme light, by which nonetheless he sees and understands whatever he understands.[32]

The power to speak of the universe is hedged by the limitations of metaphor as much as is the power to speak of God – but this because the physical world itself is merely image. Here Thierry faithfully follows Plato, though adding a somewhat surprising identification of reason with opinion –

29 My remarks here and below concerning Thierry's innovations in philosophical language have been verified in the 'Glossaire du latin philosophique médiéval' at the Sorbonne. I am particularly grateful to Marie-Thérèse d'Alverny for helping me to consult this precious *fichier*. On the epistemological terms discussed here, P. Michaud-Quantin, 'La classification des puissances de l'âme au xiie siècle', *RMAL* v (1949) 15–34, offers valuable background information, though his remarks on Thierry had to be based, in 1949, on the *Commentum* only. On the Boethian distinction between *intelligibile* and *intellectibile*, see esp. M.-D. Chenu, 'Imaginatio', *Miscellanea Giovanni Mercati* II (Vatican City 1946) 593–602.
30 *Glosa* IV 8 (p. 286).
31 Calcidius, *Timaeus*, ed. J. H. Waszink (2nd ed., London–Leiden 1975), 51e (p. 50).
32 *Abbr. Mon. De hebd.* II 37 (p. 411).

two concepts that Plato himself had carefully distinguished.[33] *Ratio*, for Thierry, cannot attain the height of *intelligentia* (let alone – in the *Glosa* – the even greater height of *intelligibilitas*):

Where image, not truth, is perceived, opinion is at work. But in physics only the image – that is, the embodied form – not the truth, is considered. So there one must use reason, that is, opinion (*ratione, id est opinione*). For reason perceives the image of things and not their truth. It is called reason, in the sense of opinion, from *reor, reris* – which means to opine (*opinari*).[34]

2.3 To turn now to the content of what Thierry intimates within these limitations of metaphor and image: first and foremost it concerns, as we might expect from one who was both a Christian and a Platonist, the relationship between a divine creator and a created universe. This relationship is defined with the help of many pairs of concepts – God and *Hylê*, necessity and possibility, the changeless and the changing, unity and plurality, among others. But I should like to pause particularly at certain moments that show Thierry's most distinctive approach. Near the opening of the *Tractatus* we read:

Because the things in the world are mutable and corruptible, it is necessary that they should have an author. Because they have been arranged in a rational way and in a very beautiful order, it is necessary that they should have been created in accordance with wisdom. But because the creator, rationally speaking, is in need of nothing, having perfection and sufficiency in himself, it is necessary that he should create what he does create only through benignity and love.[35]

Thierry does not give an argument for the existence of this creator, in the sense of proceeding by steps from what is known to what is unknown. Rather, he suggests an intuitive perception, that a universe which is subject to change and decay is not self-sufficient or self-explanatory, and that nothing in the realm of the mutable can ultimately account for its existence, or for the traces of order that, despite mutability, are manifest in it. But for Thierry this is more than a quasi-tautological assertion that mutability presupposes immutability, and visible order an invisible ordering principle. Notwithstanding the repeated 'it is necessary', Thierry is offering *probationes* not so much in the sense of 'proofs' as in that of 'examinations': he is examining the relationships between his pairs of terms, in the hope that this will illuminate the underlying intuition, which is never itself analysed discursively. Here, indeed, his language evokes something that goes beyond

33 Thus, in the passage cited above (n. 31), *intellectus* is *semper cum ratione vera*, and *opinio* is *sine ulla ratione*.
34 *Lectio* II 29 (p. 164).
35 *Tractatus* 2 (pp. 555f).

any traditional argument from design, or from contingency, for the existence of God; for what Thierry is intimating is that considering the nature of
the universe leads to conceiving its creator along the lines of the Christian
Trinity: not only as begetter (i.e. Father), but as the manifestation of wisdom
(Son) and of benignity or love (Spirit); he links these three modes of looking
at the creator, moreover, with the – ultimately Aristotelian – concepts of,
respectively, the efficient, the formal, and the final cause.[36]

2.4 In the *Lectiones* and *Glosa*, Thierry examines a different range of concepts
regarding the creator and the universe. Here his originality of approach is
especially apparent. In the earlier work, after distinguishing speculative
philosophy from ethics and logic, and dividing the speculative (like
Boethius) into theology, mathematics, and physics, Thierry introduces three
terms – simplicity, enfolding, and unfolding (*simplicitas, complicatio, explicatio*) – to show how the universe (*rerum universitas*) can be the subject of all
three branches of speculative thought. The expressions *complicatio* and
explicatio rerum universitatis are Thierry's innovations.

In its simplicity, the universe is the subject of theology. For it is 'enfolded
in a certain simplicity (*complicata in quadam simplicitate*)', which is God. God,
however, not only enfolds the universe but unfolds it (*explicat*), and here we
pass from theology to mathematics (*mathematica*), for the unfolding of the
universe shows how 'the divine unity gives rise to plurality':

> Plurality is the unfolding of unity, unity the principle and origin of plurality. For all
> otherness descends from unity . . . The unfolding of that enfolding is all things that
> were, that shall be and that are.

Yet a *mathematicus*, from the ninth century to the twelfth, is an astrologer
even more than a mathematician. And, as the unfolding that he studies is an
ordered, not a random one, he is *ipso facto* studying 'what the ancients called
fate. For fate is the unfolding of divine providence, and divine providence is
God himself.' Finally, 'the same universe is the subject of physics in yet
another mode – namely, as it is in actuality (*ut in actu est*) . . . For physics
considers the four corporeal elements themselves, as they are in actuality.'[37]

Thierry's argument becomes more complex, and wholly unprecedented,
in what follows. The universe is studied speculatively in three modes; but 'it
exists in four modes':

---

36 *Ibid.*: 'Si quis igitur subtiliter consideret mundi fabricam, efficientem ipsius causam deum
    esse cognoscet, formalem vero dei sapientiam, finalem eiusdem benignitatem . . .'.
37 *Lectiones* II 4–6 (pp. 155f). In the last sentence cited, I read *quatuor elementa corporea ipsa*
    (*corpora* Häring). On the terms *mathematicus* and *mathematica* in medieval Latin, see *Novum
    Glossarium Mediae Latinitatis*, s.v. *mathematicus*.

One and the same universe exists in absolute necessity, in necessity of make-up (*complexionis*), in absolute possibility, and in determinate possibility . . .
It exists in absolute necessity in a certain simplicity and union of all things, which is God. It exists in necessity of make-up in a certain order and progression – but immutably. It exists in absolute possibility – that is, in possibility only, without any actuality. And it exists in determinate possibility – both possibly and actually.
Absolute necessity is the enfolding of all things in simplicity. Necessity of make-up is their unfolding in a certain order (which the physicists call fate). Absolute possibility is the enfolding of that same universe in that pure possibility from which all things come to actuality (which the physicists call primordial matter or chaos). Determinate possibility is the unfolding of absolute possibility in actuality, with possibility remaining.[38]

Once more all four expressions – *necessitas absoluta, necessitas complexionis, possibilitas absoluta,* and *possibilitas determinata* – are of Thierry's own devising.[39] His conception of these four modes of existence of the universe is enriched in the *Glosa*. Absolute necessity is now also called unity and eternity and 'form of forms (*forma formarum*)' – since for Thierry, as for Boethius, 'form is the source of being (*ex forma enim esse*)' and 'being exists through participation in unity (*est enim esse ex unitatis participatione*)'.[40] Necessity of make-up is here linked with the unfolding of the universe 'into the truths of forms and images, which we call Ideas', and into the patterns of causality:[41]

Simplicity arranges these Ideas in a certain order, into the series of causes, which of necessity is as it is. For a thing follows[42] that series once it has come to be governed by a particular cause. And this is called determinate necessity, or necessity of make-up, in that, when we consider a particular material expression of it, we cannot avoid the rest of its series of causal connexions.

38 *Lectiones* II 9f (pp. 157f).
39 *Necessitas absoluta* also occurs (under Thierry's influence?) in a theological context in a twelfth-century MS (Vat. Reg. Lat. 135, fol. 99r), where it is contrasted with *necessitas implicita* and *necessitas vehemens* (see A. Landgraf, *Dogmengeschichte der Frühscholastik* I. I (Regensburg 1952), p. 113 n. 69 – where, however, *Alia, dum res manet* should be corrected to *Absoluta, dum res manet*).
   It is difficult to know the precise connotations of *complexio* in Thierry's *necessitas complexionis*. Of the senses given in *Mittellateinisches Wörterbuch*, s.v. 'Verflechtung' (I A 2 b), 'Zusammenhang' (I A 2 d) and 'Gefüge' (I B) among the general meanings, 'Beschaffenheit (des Körpers)' (II C 1) and '(körperliche) Verfassung' (II C 2) among the medical meanings, could all be relevant.
40 *Glosa* II 15f (p. 272). Häring 1971, p. 410, cites Augustine, *Sermon* 117, where God is *forma . . . omnium formatorum*, adding that 'the expression *forma formarum* was apparently coined by Thierry'. But here Thierry was preceded by Gerbert, *De rationali* XI (ed. A. Olleris, Clermont–Ferrand–Paris 1867, p. 305): 'Substantiales quippe differentiae, itemque species et genera, semper sunt. Alia sunt quidem rerum formae, vel, ut ita dixerim, formae formarum; alia sunt actus; alia sunt quaedam potestates.' Gerbert's *ut ita dixerim* strongly suggests he was introducing the expression.
41 *Glosa* II 20ff (p. 273).
42 Reading *sequitur* (*sequuntur* Häring).

With his exceptional gift for synthesis, bringing together concepts from the most disparate ranges of literature and thought, Thierry goes on to say of this necessity of make-up: 'some have called it natural law (*legem naturalem*), others Natura, others the world-soul . . . others Eimarmenê, yet others again have called it fate, others the Fates (*Parcae*), others the divine intelligence'. The last concept here is theological, the rest are mythographic, Platonic, or (in the case of *lex naturalis* and *Eimarmenê*) Stoic and Hermetic.[43] Thierry suggests, however, that underlying all these terms is a particular way of looking at the universe, as subject to, and the product of, immutable principles.

So, too, there are many names that correspond to the notion of absolute possibility:

This, then, is the primordial matter which some have called Hylê, others Silva, others chaos, others the underworld, others aptitude and neediness . . .[44]

Again Thierry suggests that the Platonic and Aristotelian expressions familiar through Calcidius (*chaos*, *Hylê*, *Silva*, *carentia*),[45] the Boethian *aptitudo*, and the *infernus* that is both pagan underworld and Christian hell, are so many approximations to his own philosophical construct.

2.5 Corresponding to the four modes of existence of the universe he envisages the four modes of human knowledge. In the *Glosa* Thierry, like Boethius, sees sense-perception, imagination, reason, and intelligence hierarchically,[46] each attaining a greater degree of abstraction from the corporeal and coming closer to the perception of pure forms. Like Boethius too, Thierry sees each of the higher powers 'as it were reigning over' those below it, relying on and subsuming the information that they provide. Thus imagination gathers up sense-data, as reason does images, and intelligence those forms (still 'with little abstracting of mutability') with which reason furnishes it.

But the concept 'intelligibility (*intelligibilitas*)', the faculty Thierry sees as higher than Boethius' *intelligentia*, is his own contribution:[47]

43 Thierry knew *Eimarmenê* from *Asclepius* 19 (ed. Nock–Festugière, *Corpus Hermeticum* II 319): 'The seven spheres, as they are called, have as their Ousiarchs or chiefs that which men call fortune and *Eimarmenê*, through which all things are transformed by natural law (*lege naturae*) and varied by perpetual movement within an absolutely firm order.' It is noteworthy that already in this passage *Eimarmenê* is related to *lex naturae*. On the Stoic origins of both concepts, see Ch. 3, pp. 99, 103, 112.

44 *Glosa* II 18 (p. 272).

45 Cf. Calcidius 1975, p. 167. 6 ('chaos, quam Graeci hylen, nos silvam vocamus'); on *silva* and *carentia*, in the context of Aristotle's *Physics* 192a, see *ibid.* pp. 289–93.

46 *Glosa* II 3ff (pp. 269f); cf. Boethius, *Cons. Phil.* v pr. 4. Thierry here also uses *disciplina* as a synonym for *intelligentia*.

47 *Ibid.* II 8 (p. 270).

... it is the power of the soul that removes from the forms all those limits that make them distinct, contemplating what remains of them only as existence (*esse*) and essence (*entia*);[48] thereby the soul frightens away all plurality, and beholds the simple union of all unions – just as, if you were to take away the limit of being-a-circle from the circle, and the limit of being-human from humanity, only the essence (*entia*) of these remains – and this, containing all things in itself, is the simple simplicity enfolding all, and the simple whole.

This supreme power of cognition (which, as we noted, only a few human beings share with God) is what we need in order to consider absolute necessity. On the other hand, intelligence considers the necessity of make-up; and reason (or opinion), along with imagination and sense-perception, considers both determinate and absolute possibility. For, in speculative science, both these modes – the universe as it is, and as it came to be – are the domain of the physicist; just as the necessity of make-up is the domain of the mathematician–astrologer, and absolute necessity that of the theologian.

Fundamental to Thierry's epistemology is the congruence between the modes of knowledge of the human soul and the modes of existence of the universe. Again the question arises: is it an objective correspondence, a 'pre-established harmony', or are the modes of existence, in the last resort, only a metaphor projected by the soul in its effort at understanding? One passage at least in the *Lectiones* suggests this. There Thierry alludes to one of the most enigmatic moments in Plato's *Timaeus*: 'the soul, as Plato says, is composed of undivided and divided substance, and of the same and the different nature'.[49] Where Plato meant this of the world-soul, and William of Conches made a brilliant attempt to account for Plato's fourfold distinction in terms of the world-soul,[50] Thierry boldly disregards the question of Plato's literal meaning and makes of the distinctions a statement about human knowledge, about the four powers, by means of which the human

---

48 Thierry uses *entia* as a feminine singular noun: Häring lists fourteen occasions in his Index (p. 604). The term appears to be a coinage of Abelard's, *Theologia Christiana* IV (ed. Cousin II 549). Cousin's speculation – 'forte legendum *essentiam*' – is groundless, both because of the confirmation of the word in Thierry's writings and because of its confirmation in Abelard's own sentence, by the complementary coinage *entialiter*: 'res omnino recte dici non possit, quae in se veram non habet entiam, ut sit in se una res numero a ceteris omnibus, quae ipsa non sunt, rebus entialiter discreta'. Unfortunately E. M. Buytaert in his new edition (CC CM XII 343, 2468f) has substituted the *lectiones faciliores*, *essentia* and *essentialiter*, relegating *entia* and *entialiter* to the apparatus.

On the other hand, Thierry's two terms signifying 'state of being' – *entitas* and *onitas* – were apparently his own inventions. (For their occurrences, see Häring's Index, pp. 604, 613). *Onitas* was formed with Greek ὤν in mind: a relation with *anitas* (the later twelfth-century formation, from Arabic *anniyya*, on which see M.-T. d'Alverny, 'Anniyya-Anitas', *Mélanges Etienne Gilson* (Toronto–Paris 1959), pp. 59–91) seems unlikely.

49 *Timaeus* 35A (Calcidius 1975, p. 27).

50 *Glosae super Platonem*, ed. E. Jeauneau (Paris 1965), pp. 152f.

mind comprehends the four modes – understanding 'undivided substance, namely divinity, that is, the universe in its simplicity; . . . divided substance, namely absolute possibility; . . . the nature of the same – that is, the universe in the necessity of its make-up, which is undivided and immutable; . . . and the nature of the different, in determinate possibility'.[51]

In the *Glosa* it is not so much the powers as the movements of the soul that Thierry stresses, movements which, as the soul comprehends the universe in its different modes, correspond to the divine unfolding (*explicatio*) and enfolding (*complicatio*):

The soul is proportioned to the nature of the universe. For now as it were she unfolds herself, now gathers herself into a certain simplicity, as when she is intelligibility. When she is brought down from that, she dilates herself, evolving what she had enfolded.[52]

This correspondence with the divine activity, according to Thierry, extends also to the human mind's creative aspect. If the divine mind is *forma formarum*, the human is 'the form of artistic forms (*forma artificialium specierum*)':

God is the form of forms, because, when only the possible lay waiting in advance, he, conceiving forms in relation to that possible, generated a certain perfection of actuality (*actus*), whose form exists because he gave it being.

This can be seen similarly in the soul of man. For the human mind conceives a form and the composition of some object of art, forming what is in the mind before linking it to matter, but taking account of matter. For the mind could not beget any exemplary figure if there were absolutely no matter.

Thus the human mind is the form of artistic forms. For between it and matter lies only the artistic form which, subsisting as something possible, through being adjoined to matter turns into an object of art.[53]

2.6 What is true of artistic creation is equally so for Thierry of verbal creation. In particular, he sees the human naming of things as creative, as not merely imitating but reproducing a primordial divine act that consisted inseparably of creating and naming. Here we encounter the most extreme aspect of Thierry's Platonism. Boethius (*De trinitate* II) had said 'All being (*esse*) comes from form. For a statue is called (*dicitur*) the likeness of a living being not on account of its bronze, which is matter, but on account of the form by which the likeness is impressed on it.' Thierry, commenting on this,

---

51 *Lectiones* II 30f (pp. 164f). In the *Lectiones*, as was mentioned above, Thierry still identifies the highest power of the soul with Boethius' *intelligentia* (for which he likewise uses the term *intellectibilitas*).
52 *Glosa* II 12 (p. 271).
53 *Ibid.* II 33f (pp. 275f).

says something much more unusual. For him all being stems inseparably from form and name (*vocabulum*). He praises Boethius' subtlety in using the expression 'is called (*dicitur*)', but only to invest it with a meaning Boethius could never have foreseen:[54]

Form and name accompany each other. The form cannot exist without the name. From the same source as each thing has its form, it also has its name. Otherwise it could not exist.[55] Names indeed give things their being (*Nomina quippe essentiant res* [*essentiare* is yet another of Thierry's new formations]). Something is a man because it is called 'man', an animal because it is called 'animal'. And so with the rest . . . For the names were united in the divine mind from eternity even before the imposing of them by human beings. Later man imposed them on the things with which they were united in the divine mind.

Thus in the end Thierry does not see the necessary human reliance on metaphor and image negatively: he is convinced that the human mind can penetrate the world of forms in the divine mind, that human language, for all its approximateness, is not a random groping for words but can reach the true reality of the names as they are, as they give rise to forms. In the *Glosa* Thierry, in one of his characteristic passages of daring synthesis, summons testimonies to this which range from the grammarian Priscian to Moses (as the reputed author of Genesis), to Cicero and his commentator Victorinus, Boethius and the Church Fathers, and at last to the theological confirmation of the unity of name and form in the Logos: 'Once did God speak'. Priscian, Thierry begins, glosses 'the things that exist' by '[the things] that fall beneath a particular name'; and he continues:

In the same way Moses says: 'he called the light day and the darkness night' . . . as if to say, he united the names to the realities, in such a way that the realities themselves exist on account of the names. For a thing exists in virtue of God's naming. Otherwise God's providence would be in error [i.e. if God had conceived a name to which no reality corresponded].

Boethius too confirms this union, saying: each thing is called that which pleased him who first imposed names on things. So biblical commentators affirm that Adam imposed names on things through the Holy Spirit – for only in this way, not otherwise, could he have discerned the primordial unity of names and forms. It is in accordance with this that Cicero, in his *Tusculan Disputations*, calls him the happiest and most blessed who first imposed names on things.[56]

54 *Lectiones* II 52f (pp. 172f).
55 Reading *res non posset esse* (*esse non posset esse* Häring).
56 *Glosa* II 41f (pp. 277f). Cf. also P. Dronke, 'La creazione degli animali', *Settimane di Studio* XXXI (1985) 809–48, at pp. 811f; J. Jolivet, 'Quelques cas de "platonisme grammatical" du VIIe au XIIe siècle', in *Mélanges René Crozet* (2 vols., Poitiers 1966) I 93–9; M.-D. Chenu, 'Un cas de platonisme grammatical au XIIe siècle', *RSPT* LI (1967) 666–8.

3.1 If the human mind, like the universe in the divine mind, both unfolds itself and gathers itself into *simplicitas*, does this not suggest the intended unity and complementarity of the two seemingly so disparate parts of Thierry's *Tractatus* on the six days of creation? In the so-called empirical or naturalistic part he shows the unfolding, from absolute possibility to determinate possibility. Then, in the incomplete later part, he considers the enfolded *simplicitas*.

Again, if forms and names are conjoined in the way Thierry believes, can we not say that the *Tractatus* is concerned with *explicatio* in two senses – the 'unfolding' of the universe, and the 'explication' of that unfolding in human language? Thierry's verbal explication imitates the cosmogonic unfolding, just as the human artist imitates the divine one. And, as on the divine plane there are two 'poles' of creation – absolute necessity and absolute possibility – so the human explicator, Thierry, will have planned to consider creation from both these poles. Plato began his account in the *Timaeus* from the upper pole, the design of the Demiurgos, and then completed this with an account that took its departure from the lower pole, *Hylê*, the 'nurse and receptacle of becoming'.[57] Thierry, after a brief initial acknowledgment of the upper pole, proceeds with a detailed account that begins from the lower, and concludes the extant part of his work with a theological excursus that considers the creator in himself. The further cosmological account, of the descent from absolute necessity – Thierry's counterpart to the first section of the *Timaeus* – will also have been included in his overall design, even if this part is lost or was never completed.

3.2 Near the beginning of the *Tractatus*, the passage (cited above p. 367) in which Thierry infers from the nature of the universe a creator who orders in accordance with wisdom and love continues: 'Because all ordering is brought to unordered things, it was necessary that something unordered should precede.' What preceded, which in other contexts Thierry calls absolute possibility, primordial matter, chaos, or *Hylê*, is here said to be the four elements, the 'material cause' of the universe. But though the elements preceded the formed universe, Thierry stresses that they are not eternal: 'the creator himself created them in the beginning out of nothing'.

Thereby Thierry was trying, like Boethius before him, to guard against the notion (which for a Christian was fraught with Manichaean implications) that the material world is 'coeternal (*coeterna*)' with God. Yet Thierry did not accept Boethius' resolution of this point near the close of his *Consolation of Philosophy*, where Boethius had argued that, whilst God is eternal, the world

57 *Timaeus* 49A (Calcidius 1975, p. 46).

is perpetual[58] – not self-sufficient in its own eternity, hence not on a par with God, but eternally dependent on God for its existence. Perhaps this Boethian conception – though clearly compatible with belief in a divine creator – was too daring for the orthodoxy of twelfth-century theologians[59] (and indeed in Boethius' day it was rejected by his Christian Neoplatonist colleagues, Zacharias and Philoponus).[60] At the same time, both Platonic and Aristotelian cosmology seemed to presuppose divine and physical principles of creation collaborating from the outset, as did the Hermetic cosmology (preserved in the *Asclepius*) from which Thierry himself cites the key phrase: 'There was God and *Hylê*.'[61] For Thierry's friend and admirer Bernard Silvestris, in the *Cosmographia*, it was possible to develop this phrase, and to see primordial matter (personified as Silva) as itself a theophany and a protagonist in the labour of creation.[62] But there the evidently 'integumental' nature of the account afforded a certain safeguard. The nearest Thierry came to Bernard's Silva or Boethius' perpetual world was in a passage in the *Glosa* (II 32), where he says that, when God conceived the forms of all things, matter lay waiting in advance (*preiacente materia*), and adds, to characterize the relation between mutable matter and immutable creator: 'though mutability was created by immutability, immutability did not precede it in time'.

In the *Tractatus*, by contrast, 'God created matter in the first moment of time' (5). Thierry here preferred to make a clear obeisance to the – still basically Augustinian – orthodoxy of his day. But this gave him far greater freedom of manoeuvre in all that followed. From the instant of the divine creation of matter onwards, Thierry sees nature as autonomous: everything unfolds 'naturally (*naturaliter*)', as 'the natural order demanded (*ordo naturalis exigebat*)'.

Historically perhaps the most astonishing aspect of Thierry's conception of natural unfolding is that of animate from inanimate: Thierry sees the emergence of animal and human life as part of the material process. Where even a thinker as audacious as William of Conches had felt obliged to accept the Augustinian notion that for mankind 'God creates new souls each day'[63]

---

58 *Cons. Phil.* v pr. 6.
59 Cf. Dronke 1969, pp. 137–9.
60 Cf. P. Courcelle, *La Consolation de Philosophie dans la tradition littéraire* (Paris 1967), p. 229.
61 *Asclepius* 14 (ed. Nock–Festugière, *Corpus Hermeticum* II 313), cit. *Tractatus* 26. The *Asclepius*, composed in Greek probably in the third century AD and translated into Latin in the fourth, was thought in the Middle Ages and Renaissance to be by a sage, Hermes, who was more ancient than Plato. See also below, p. 379.
62 Cf. *Cosmographia* (ed. Dronke), pp. 29–31.
63 *Philosophia* IV 51 (ed. G. Maurach (Pretoria 1980), pp. 112, 228 n. 200).

– conceding, that is, that the natural order is not sufficient to account for the emergence of human souls, each of which presupposes a direct divine intervention in nature – Thierry, having secured the divine beginning for *explicatio* as a whole, felt free to develop the idea of *explicatio* with full consistency.

At the opening of the *Tractatus*, in a passage that, I would suggest, is closely modelled on one in Eriugena's *Periphyseon*,[64] Thierry promises to expound the account of creation in Genesis 'in accordance with physics and literally (*secundum phisicam et ad litteram*)', leaving allegorical and moral reading wholly aside, 'for this has clearly been accomplished by the holy Fathers'. What, then, is the physical meaning for Thierry of the 'work of the six days'?

3.3 A day, he says, is literally the space of time of one complete rotation of the highest heaven (the outer sphere known in later Scholastic thought as the Primum Mobile). This rotation began in the first moment of time, because the heaven, consisting of the element fire, is of such lightness that it cannot stay still; again, since it encompasses everything else, it cannot move forward from one place to another, and hence cannot but rotate (5).

In its first rotation this fire lit up the air below it –

But when the air was lit by the power of the highest element, it followed naturally that, through the mediating illumination of the air, fire would warm the third element, water, and, warming it, would suspend it in the form of vapour above the air. For it is the nature of heat to divide water into the minutest drops and to lift these above the air by the power of its motion – as is apparent in the smoke of a steam-bath, just as it is manifest in the clouds of the sky . . .

Thus it happened that the second element, air, was midway between flowing water and water suspended as vapour. And this is what Moses says in the words 'And he placed the firmament in the middle of the waters' . . . And the space of time of that rotation was called 'second day'. (7–8)

64 Compare:

Periphyseon 693B–C:	*Tractatus* 1:
(A). '*De operibus sex primorum dierum*, quoniam multi et grece et latine multa *exposuere*, . . . nunc disputandum est . . .' (N.) 'Ac prius dicendum quod de *allegoricis intellectibus moralium interpretationum nulla nunc nobis intentio* est, sed de sola rerum factarum creatione *secundum historiam pauca disserere* . . .' (A.) '*Satis* enim *a sanctis patribus* de talium *allegoria* est actum.'	'*De septem diebus et sex operum* distinctionibus primam Geneseos partem *secundum phisicam et ad litteram* ego *expositurus*, inprimis de intentione auctoris et de libri utilitate *pauca* premittam. Postea vero *ad sensum littere hystorialem* exponendum veniam, ut et *allegoricam et moralem lectionem, que a sanctis doctoribus aperte* execute sunt, *ex toto pretermittam*.'

The remarkable thing about this passage is less that Thierry supports his physical interpretation of Moses' statement by an empirical analogy (the wording indeed suggests that his 'observation' also owes something to Cicero),[65] than that he tries to show that the notion of waters above the firmament – which William of Conches had argued was a scientific impossibility – is scientifically not merely acceptable but necessary: that it is in conformity with physical laws. William had mocked the fundamentalists of his day, who accepted the existence of such waters as a miraculous divine contravention of the laws of nature; Thierry is insisting, by contrast, that what Moses gives at the opening of Genesis is not an account of creation as miracle but an account of the emergence of the universe which is soundly based on physical laws. Admittedly Moses expressed himself in oracular utterances, that have to be scrutinized carefully for their literal meaning. And it needs a physicist to elucidate that meaning accurately.

Each of the next four rotations of the Primum Mobile entails, naturally and necessarily, certain physical effects that correspond to what Moses evoked in his 'days' of creation. And (even if one might take it to be otherwise from Moses' obscure text!) none of these effects presupposes any specific divine intervention in the natural processes, for these themselves result, step by step, in the emergence of plant life, marine and other animal life, and human life:

When the water was suspended above the air in the form of vapour, the natural order of things demanded that, since the flowing water below had been diminished, earth would appear, not continuously, but as it were in the manner of islands. This can be shown in many ways. For, the more the steam rises from a steam-bath, the more the water in the bath is diminished . . .

In that same rotation [Moses' 'third day'] it happened that – through the warmth of the upper air mingled with the moisture in the earth . . . – the earth conceived the power of producing herbs and trees. This power proceeds naturally from the warmth of heaven into the newly-bared moist earth . . .

But if the firmament by now contained enough warmth to contract the flowing water below, it naturally happened that, from the multitude of waters drawn together to the firmament through the warmth of the third day, the bodies of stars were created. (9–10)

Thierry goes on to prove that stellar bodies are in fact composed of water, and then relates this emergence of stars to the fourth rotation or day. But in the fifth, the warmth generated by the motion of the stars became a

65 *De natura deorum* II x 27 (cf. Dronke 1969, p. 133 n. 51).

'life-giving warmth (*calor vitalis*)' – this Stoic phrase, which Thierry knew through Cicero,[66] probably also having for him the Neoplatonic astrological connotations by which the stars are causes of life on earth:

> ... the warmth coming from their motion, increasing and proceeding to a life-giving warmth, first came to rest on the waters, that is, on the element higher than earth. And thereby the living beings of the water and the birds were created ...
>
> But through the mediation of moisture that life-giving warmth naturally reached earth, and thereby the living beings of the earth were created, in whose number man was made to the image and likeness of God.[67] And the space of time of this sixth rotation was called 'sixth day'. (14)

Thierry then tries to show that there could be no new modes of creation beyond those he has outlined (and that this is what Moses really meant by his declaration, 'The Lord rested on the seventh day'!) Everything that emerges thereafter is produced through some of the modes already described, and 'through the seminal causes [that is, powers of bringing forth new life] which God inserted in the elements'.

These 'seminal causes' are characterized in one of Thierry's most unusual insights (though again a certain Stoic influence is perceptible):[68]

> Fire is wholly active, earth wholly passive. So fire is as it were the artificer and efficient cause, and earth, underlying, is as it were the material cause; the two elements between them are as it were an instrument or binding power by which the activity of the highest is transmitted to those below. (17)

For Thierry, that is, there is a mimesis of divine creation on the elemental level – where fire is the artist working upon his material – just as there is on the human, when the artist's mind conceives forms.

3.4 At this point Thierry proceeds to a more detailed 'literal exposition' of the opening of Genesis. Yet he remains as far as ever from the traditional works of this kind. Explaining the words 'heaven and earth' in verse 1 enables him to propound (to borrow Jeauneau's telling phrase) 'a kinetic theory of bodies'.[69] The elements, he argues, can be transmuted into one another because they consist of particles of the same kind but of greater or lesser compression – they are most closely compacted in earth, most lightly

---

66 *Ibid.* II ix–x 23–7 (esp. 27 *ad fin.*, of *ignis*): 'Iam vero reliqua quarta pars mundi: ea et ipsa tota natura fervida est et ceteris naturis omnibus salutarem inpertit et vitalem calorem.'

67 Häring (*Tractatus*, p. 561) attempts to separate the making of man from that of the *animalia terre* by setting a full stop before the phrase 'in quorum numero homo ad imaginem et similitudinem dei factus est', which he construes as a separate sentence. But syntactically this is not possible: lacking a finite verb, the phrase can only qualify the preceding words, *animalia terre*.

68 Cf. Dronke 1969, p. 135 n 56.

69 Jeauneau 1973, p. 9.

in fire. There is a reciprocity by which the lighter elements and the heavier make one another what they are: the looser assemblage of particles in fire and air is more agile and mobile, and, by imprisoning the denser assemblages of water and earth, makes these more solid and corpulent, while fire and air, if they are not to disperse completely, need something solider to lean upon. The mobility of the lighter elements both causes and presupposes the fixity of the heavier ones.

According to Thierry, Moses, in his enigmatic sayings, showed himself well aware of the nature of the elements; yet his words are at times susceptible of more than one literal construction. What did he mean, for instance, by 'darkness on the face of the abyss'? Thierry first takes it as a description of water alone, in its unformed state, and adds that, 'according to some', the spirit borne over the waters is air, 'which because of its subtlety in some sense approaches the tenuousness of the divine Spirit' (22). But then he gives an alternative reading of his own, which he prefers: the darkness was air, still unformed, looming like tenebrous mist over an abyss that was a chaotic mire of earth and water intermingled. And the spirit borne over the waters was 'the power of the artificer', working upon matter and ordering it.

Here Thierry is no longer thinking of the *artifex* fire, but of 'the operative power of the [divine] creator'. He lets us glimpse another aspect of his cosmology, the universe in the mode of its 'necessity of make-up'. And, still more than in the *Glosa*, he stresses that the shaping, life-giving principle works upon matter not from above but from within. For this immanent principle, to characterize which Thierry in the *Glosa* brings together a range of concepts and images extending from natural law to world-soul, he now considers the particular aptness of the concept 'spirit'. In his most dazzling demonstration that the great thinkers of the past were, however different their approaches, pointing to the same cosmological truths, Thierry finds the moving power inherent in the universe understood as spirit by the pagan philosophers, Hermes (whose testament, *Asclepius*, was deemed to be a work of immense antiquity), Plato, and Vergil (the inspired *vates* who speaks of 'the spirit within'), just as it is by the biblical prophets, Moses, David, and Solomon. And it is this same power, Thierry concludes triumphantly, that Christians call 'the Holy Spirit'.[70]

3.5 Then, before resuming his elaborate literal explanation of the verses in Genesis, from the creation of light onwards, Thierry decides to insert a

---

70 *Tractatus* 26f (pp. 566f). In the case of David, the term *spiritus* comes not in the words (from Psalm 32: 6) cited by Thierry, but in their continuation: 'et spiritu oris eius omnis virtus eorum'.

theological digression (*ex vera et sancta theologia sumptum*: 29) on the Logos and the Holy Spirit. The extant *Tractatus* breaks off near the beginning of this digression, in which Thierry promises four kinds of reasoning 'that lead man to cognition of the creator – *probationes* of arithmetic, music, geometry, and astronomy'. Only the first kind are in fact broached, and themselves remain incomplete. These *probationes*, as Jeauneau observed, proceed *rationabiliter* (30) in a sense somewhat similar to that implied in Anselm's arguments concerning the existence and nature of God.[71] They do not exist autonomously, but in relation to definitions which the author takes as points of departure, and which he tries to make evident by way of the examination (*probatio* in its other sense) of related concepts, the aptness of which to the divine context the reader is intended to perceive. Thierry takes as his basis a dictum of Augustine's about the Trinity: 'In the Father there is unity, in the Son equality, in the Holy Spirit the concord of unity and equality.'[72] From this Thierry develops a series of *integumenta*, treating the concept 'unity' in particular in a wide-ranging metaphorical fashion in order to illuminate both the Christian Trinity and the relations between God and the cosmos.

These *integumenta* move too far into purely theological discourse to consider in detail here. Yet something of their intellectual daring and elegance can be conveyed even by a brief quotation. As Thierry, like Boethius, held that in each thing its existence is inseparable from its unity, he saw *unitas* as an apt name for the divine *forma formarum*. And he was the first, to my knowledge, to use the two ways in which *unitas* can be said to 'generate' numbers as an image of the cosmogonic and the trinitarian process. Unity, multiplied by other numbers, engenders the entire series of whole numbers –

> ... but numbers are infinite, so it is necessary that unity should have no limit to its power. Unity therefore is omnipotent in the creation of numbers. But the creation of numbers is the creation of realities (*rerum*).[73] So unity is omnipotent in the creation of realities ... So unity is necessarily deity.

On the other hand, unity can be multiplied by itself, and then the result is again unity ($1 \times 1 = 1$):

> For unity multiplied by one is nothing other than unity. So the begetting one and the begotten one are one and the same substance, since each of them is true unity. For unity can beget nothing other than the equality of that same unity. (38–9)

71 Jeauneau 1973, pp. 95f.
72 *De doctrina Christiana* 1 5.
73 Thierry probably implies in this – his most often cited phrase – not only the Platonic claim that numbers are real, like forms, but also the (ultimately Pythagorean) one, that each thing is as it is by virtue of its proportioning. Some aspects of the background and the *Nachleben* of

The *Tractatus* breaks off before Thierry's *integumentum* for the Holy Spirit, seen as the 'binding *(connexio)*' of equality and unity,[74] but we can reconstruct it with the help of moments in his Boethian commentaries. The equation $1 \times 1 = 1$, we might say, can be read in two ways: in the first, just cited, the Father, multiplying himself, brings forth the Son, who is equal to himself. But if we read it another way, we can say that the equality here affirmed proceeds (like the Spirit) from both the terms on the lefthand side of the equation, and is equal to both these terms.

3.6 So, too, we can reconstruct at least approximately some of the ways in which Thierry might have gone on to use *probationes* from music, geometry, and astronomy to 'lead man to cognition of the creator'. In the case of geometry, consider a passage such as this in the pseudo-Boethian *Altercatio* on geometry, that was copied in the *Heptateuchon*:

Certainly you can see how great is the power of the point. For the line begins from the point, the figure is completed by it. Indeed we see that no rectilinear figure can come into existence unless the angle is closed by the point. Moreover, wherever a line can be intersected, it is intersected through the point, though the point itself admits absolutely no intersection in itself. No line is joined to any other line except through the point. Finally, since reason shows us that the figure formed by a circle is to be preferred to all other plane figures, because of its equality, what is the principle of that evenness if not the point set at the circle's centre?[75]

Thierry's phrase are discussed by F. Brunner, '*Creatio numerorum, rerum est creatio*', in *Mélanges Crozet* (n. 56) II 719–25.

74 In two of the seven MSS that preserve Thierry's treatise complete as far as here (Häring 1971, pp. 48ff), it is preceded by a letter and followed by a *tractatulus* by his disciple Clarembald. These were printed together with Thierry's work by Häring in *AHDLMA* XXII 183 (letter) and 200–16 *(tractatulus)*, and separately in Häring's *Life and Works of Clarembald of Arras* (Toronto 1965), pp. 225–49. Clarembald repeats a number of Thierry's detailed insights regarding the natural unfolding of the universe, but does not fully grasp Thierry's underlying *principles* of natural explanation. Instead, he mingles sentences drawn from Thierry with sentences drawn from St Augustine, seemingly unaware of the vast difference in orientation between the two writers on Genesis, so that the *tractatulus*, though assembling some valuable materials, uses them for little more than a banal essay in Christian apologetics. That Southern (1979, p. 32) could describe Thierry's *Tractatus* as 'a somewhat confused and repetitive commentary on Genesis, indistinguishable (so far as I can see) in style and method from that part of the work [sic] which was written by Clarembald', is to me incomprehensible.

75 MS Chartres Bibl. mun. 498, fol. 142r a:
'Vides certe etiam quantum valeat punctum. Nam ab ipso incipit linea. Ipso terminatur figura. Utique rectis lineis nullam figuram videmus fieri posse, nisi ab ipso puncto angulus claudatur. Deinde undecumque secari linea potest per ipsum sequatur, cum ipsum omnino nullam in se ammittat sectionem. Nulla (*Nullam* MS) linea linee nisi per ipsum copulatur. Postremo cum ceteris planis figuris eam preponendam ratio demonstraverit que circulo clauditur, propter summam equalitatem, que alia ipsius equitatis moderatio est quam punctum in medio constitutum?'
Cf. Folkerts (n. 18), p. 106. While these lines, as M. Geymonat first recognized (see ibid. p. 92), form part of a section, ultimately Pythagorean in inspiration, excerpted from

Thierry will have read this not only as geometrical doctrine but as *integumen-tum*: he was well aware that the real Boethius had chosen the point (*punctum*) as his image for divine providence, to which the unfolding of fate is related 'as time is to eternity, as the circle to its central point (*uti est . . . ad aeternitatem tempus, ad punctum medium circulus*)' (*Cons.* IV pr. 6).

Similarly, Thierry's *probationes* from music and astronomy can be sur-mised to some extent, for instance from the descriptions of these arts in Alan of Lille's epic, *Anticlaudianus*, which throughout shows the imprint of Chartres. Alan characterizes all the arts of the Quadrivium as culminating in insights into the nature of God. Thus the study of music shows what is the reason (*ratio*)

> why every song and the sweet melodies of sounds
> are brought forth not by one voice but by union of voices,
> sound like and unlike, diverse and the same,
> unique and simple, double, biformed and still another.

Similarly, the study of astronomy bears witness to divine love at work in the heavens, showing

> by what reason the stars move, by what law a planet
> goes on a forward course, by what law it flees,
> retrograde, or lingers at a station of its journey,
> by what reason the Signs move on their oblique path . . .[76]

It is motifs of this kind that Thierry is likely to have developed.

It is harder to conjecture what material the rest of the 'literal exposition' would have contained. The scale of the comments on the first two verses of Genesis (in *Tractatus* 18–28) implies that the continuation might have been substantial. And the deep influence of the *Timaeus* on Thierry's cosmology suggests that in his '*Timaeus*' too an account of the unfolding from the creator's mind was still to come.

4.1 How did Thierry envisage the passage from absolute necessity – in which the universe lies enfolded in the simplicity of the divine mind – to necessity of make-up? We have at least some indications of an answer in a remarkable passage in his Boethian *Commentum*, which has no counterpart in the later *Lectiones* and *Glosa*, possibly because Thierry was still searching to give these ideas a fully satisfying shape. On this one occasion, in the *Commentum*, he availed himself of Boethius' distinction between the eternal and the perpetual. He suggests that from the eternal Trinity of the theo-

---

Augustine's *De quantitate animae* XI–XII, they will have been known to Thierry only through the pseudo-Boethian dialogue on geometry.

76 *Anticlaudianus*, ed. R. Bossuat (Paris 1955), III 426–9, IV 36–9.

logians there 'descends' a perpetual one, in which the foundations of the cosmos can be perceived:[77]

From this holy and supreme Trinity descends, as it were, a trinity of perpetuals. Unity, inasmuch as it is unity, creates matter; inasmuch as it is the equality of unity, it creates form; by being love and binding, it creates spirit.

It is fitting that it is said to create matter by being unity. Indeed otherness (*alteritas*) descends from unity, and thus mutability descends from the immutable . . . But what is mutable is apt to take on diverse conditions – and matter is this aptitude. So matter itself is the mutability that descends from unity.

To show that the equality of unity (theologically the Son or Logos) creates form, Thierry uses 'equality' in a sense close to 'perfect balance of parts':[78]

For form is the integrity and perfection of a thing – as humanity, for instance, to use an unfamiliar mode of expression, is the 'equality' of being human . . . So the forms of all things are rightly said to emanate (*emanare*) from the simple divine form, because each thing has the 'equality' of its being in accordance with that form.

Finally, unity inasmuch as it is 'love and binding' creates spirit:

All that exists is moved, that is, tends naturally, to what it loves. It tends towards being, as far as in it lies, and thus towards unity. So . . . unity is rightly said to create spirit by being that love and binding.

Matter, form, and spirit are thus the perpetual constituents of the universe. Though Thierry repeatedly uses the term 'to create' here, it is possible that he later abandoned the term 'perpetual', lest it suggest that the universe as such is a divine emanation rather than creation. There are indeed sentences in the *Commentum* that give the impression of a mystical monism:

As a face reflecting in diverse mirrors is one in itself, but is thought, because of the diversity of the mirrors, to be now one face, now another, so too, if one may make the comparison, the divine form in a sense sparkles in all things, and is but one in being the form of all.[79]

Yet such perceptions are redressed in the *Tractatus* by the strong insistence that the shaping spirit within the universe – even if it can be identified with the Holy Spirit – works 'in accordance with physics (*secundum physicam*)'. Thus the cosmos is no mere mirror-image of divinity.

77 *Commentum* II 39–42 (pp. 80–2).
78 On Thierry's concept *aequalitas*, and how it applies both to the transcendent God and, by participation, to created things, see M.-D. Chenu, 'Une définition pythagoricienne de la vérité au Moyen Age', *AHDLMA* xxviii (1961) 7–13. Chenu, however, fails to mention Thierry's use of the expression *emanare* in the passage here cited (an expression that suggests a rather less 'orthodox' concept than participation).
79 *Commentum* II 48 (p. 83). As P. Lucentini, *Platonismo medievale* (2nd ed., Florence 1980), p. 51, has well observed, this passage is deeply Eriugenian in inspiration.

4.2 If there is something unfinished about Thierry's thought in these directions, this is bound up with the fecundity of his ideas and the sheer range of what he was trying to combine and newly harmonize. We could say, negatively, that – unlike Boethius in his *Opuscula* – Thierry did not have a clear sense of the difference between philosophical and theological argument, or of the limitations of philosophy in relation to theological questions. Boethius distinguished carefully between the concepts furnished by Christianity and what he could do as philosopher to define and elucidate those concepts, to show that 'person', 'nature', 'substance', 'being' and the rest could be used meaningfully and without logical contradiction even in the paradoxical language involved in speaking of Trinity or Incarnation.

Thierry gives at times the impression of ignoring Boethius' distinction between theological concepts and philosophical analysis, at times of overriding it. Yet the Boethian position, with its admirable intellectual lucidity, admitted only a restricted number of moves and was not of itself capable of generating new ways of looking and ways of enquiry. If he had remained strictly Boethian in this respect, Thierry might also have remained simply a faithful exegete of Boethius, rather than become an innovator.

Thierry's originality lay in combining an extreme Platonism – in which forms and names exist indissolubly in the mind of God, and in which 'names essentiate things' – with a far-reaching naturalism. And this combination was no capricious yoking together of incompatibles, but the direct consequence of his individual way of envisaging *rerum universitas* in four modes. It was this that enabled Thierry to complement an account of the universe from the perspective of the *forma formarum* with one from the perspective of *primordialis materia*.

It is important to see the precise scope of Thierry's naturalism. There had indeed been attempts before him to give physical explanations for phenomena that theologians had held to be miraculous. Such attempts at explanation feature prominently in the waywardly original *De mirabilibus sacrae scripturae* of Augustinus Hibernicus (655).[80] But Thierry was unusual in the *systematic* way that he withdrew cosmology from the miraculous – in the way, that is, that (once having conceded that primordial matter was created) he accepted

---

80 P.L. 35, 2149–2200. While I have found no evidence that Thierry knew this work itself, it is significant that at *Glosa* IV 13 he cites the only slightly later *Liber de ordine creaturarum*, which, under the influence of *De mirabilibus*, likewise shows a tendency to naturalistic explanation of many aspects of creation. Thierry cites the *Liber* as 'Ysidorus de ordine creaturarum': as M. C. Díaz y Díaz has shown in his excellent edition (Santiago de Compostela 1972), this attribution, very frequently found in the MSS, cannot be correct: it is an anonymous work of Irish provenance, of the later seventh century.

empirical principles pervasively, not selectively. It was easy in his time to admit such principles in particular contexts, such as mythography – to interpret stories about Jupiter and Juno, for instance, as statements about physics or astronomy.[81] Thierry, however, went much further: he admitted the validity of empirical interpretation at the heart of his Platonic conception of reality. He is audaciously innovative in uniting the two seemingly conflicting models, the empirical and the Platonic, and in admitting the principles of natural explanation in every aspect of *explicatio*.

Again, perhaps no previous thinker had been as keenly aware of the 'integumental' nature of the language used in connection with both models: for Thierry, the Platonist considering the Ideas in the divine mind and the physicist considering the material processes by which the universe evolves rely equally on image and metaphor; their languages are necessarily no more than approximations to reality, and perhaps no more than constructs of minds aspiring to an *intelligibilitas* that remains beyond them.

Finally, Thierry is outstanding for his breadth of vision, for what I called his sense of the unity of knowledge. This can be seen embodied in the *Heptateuchon* as an educational ideal. It can likewise be seen in Thierry's epistemological ideal, the gradual ascent from sense-perception to *intelligibilitas*, in which each higher stage of cognition integrates the findings of the lower ones. And it can be seen in Thierry's passages of *concordia* – on names and things, on nature and fate and spirit – which, far from being mere encyclopaedic parading of authorities, are integrations of a creative kind, bringing together diverse disciplines and diverse authors – grammarians and metaphysicians, poets and prophets – in the service of more precise insight into *rerum universitas*.

81 Cf. P. Dronke, *Fabula* (Leiden–Cologne 1974), pp. 27–9.

14

HERMANN OF CARINTHIA

CHARLES BURNETT

Hermannus de Carinthia, Hermannus Dalmata, Hermannus Sclavus, or, as he preferred to call himself, Hermannus Secundus[1] occupies a special place in twelfth-century philosophy and science in that he was 'skilled in two languages',[2] and therefore familiar with both Latin and Arabic learning. Details concerning his life are meagre to an extreme.[3] He calls Carinthia his native land, and the rubrics to his works sketch a shadowy existence in the South of France and the North of Spain between the years 1138 and 1143. We do not know what Hermann owed to his upbringing in the Duchy of Carinthia. His mother-tongue may have been a local Slavic dialect and he may have had some acquaintance with Greek there. Though he uses no Greek sources directly, he seems to know how Greek words are formed.[4] His higher education must have taken place in the northern French schools, which attracted bright young men from far and wide, and it is probably with the French and, in particular, the Cluniac, interest in the newly conquered

---

1 Hermann of Carinthia, De essentiis, ed. C. Burnett (Leiden–Cologne 1982): see Appendix I, 'Hermann's Name'. All references to the De essentiis are to this edition, and to the folio number, and division of the folio, of MS Naples, Biblioteca nazionale VIII c 50, which provides the system of reference used in this edition.
2 Rubric to Hermann's translation of Doctrina Mahumet, ed. T. Bibliander (Basel 1543), p. 189: '... ab eodem Hermanno translata, cum esset peritissimus utriusque linguae, Latinae scilicet atque Arabicae'. This rubric was probably added by Peter the Venerable who, in a letter to St Bernard, recommended the translators Robert of Ketton and Hermann of Carinthia as 'viri utriusque linguae periti', and further qualified Hermann as 'acutissimi et literati ingenii scholasticus' (Epistola ... de translatione sua, ibid. p. 1 and P.L. 189, 650).
3 This chapter brings up to date the information in C. H. Haskins, Studies in the History of Mediaeval Science (2nd ed., Cambridge MA 1927), pp. 43–66; C. Burnett, 'Arabic into Latin in Twelfth-Century Spain: the Works of Hermann of Carinthia', Mittellateinisches Jahrbuch XIII (1978), 100–34; and 'Hermann of Carinthia's Attitude towards his Arabic Sources', in L'Homme et son universe au moyen âge, ed. C. Wenin, Philosophes médiévaux XXV (Louvain, 1986), pp. 306–22.
4 He uses the Greek declension of diametros, treating it as a feminine noun with accusative in -on, and ablative -o. He recognizes or creates Greek forms for words he finds in Arabic sources, such as telesmatici for aṣḥāb al-ṭilasmāt ('masters of the talismans'), or Archimedes (where other translators from the Arabic wrote Ersimedes, Arsamithes, Archimenides or other garbled forms). See also T. Silverstein, 'Hermann of Carinthia and Greek', in Medioevo e Rinascimento: Studi in onore di Bruno Nardi (2 vols., Florence 1955) II 683–99.

areas of Spain that Hermann's move south must be associated.[5] He dedicated his translation of Ptolemy's *Planisphere* to Thierry, the well-known Platonist and Chancellor of Chartres Cathedral, addressing him as a 'most loving teacher (*diligentissime preceptor*)', whose character he has used as a model (*tuam ... virtutem ... quasi propositum ... speculum*).[6] He was recruited by Peter the Venerable, Abbot of Cluny and leader of the Cluniac movement, to translate works illustrating the Islamic religion, while he was working on the banks of the Ebro. His colleagues were Anglo-Norman or French-speaking: Robert of Ketton, Archdeacon of Pamplona, his boon-companion and fellow-translator, and Rudolph of Bruges, his only known pupil. However, he was also aware of belonging to an intellectual tradition which was not exclusively French and which stretched back to the time when the first astronomical works were being translated from Arabic into Latin and introduced to Western audiences – the time of Lupitus of Barcelona, Gerbert d'Aurillac, and Hermannus Contractus.[7] As the 'second Hermann' he would have wished people to understand that he was following in the footsteps of that first Hermann, whose works in the field of the Quadrivium were well-known and respected.

Hermann's earliest dated work is a translation of an astrological treatise from Arabic in 1138. In 1141 he was with Robert of Ketton beside the Ebro, and soon afterwards he was translating the *De generatione Mahumet* for Peter the Venerable at León. In 1143 he was completing the translation of Ptolemy's *Planisphere* (as always from an Arabic version) at Toulouse, and later that same year he was in Béziers. In 1144 Rudolph of Bruges referred piously to his teacher Hermann and used Béziers in an astronomical example, but nothing more is heard of Hermann's movements.

The littoral of Provence and Languedoc had close cultural links with northern Spain, and Hermann could have had intimate contact with Arabic scholarship on either side of the Pyrenees. There is evidence of an Arabic community in Montpellier in the mid-twelfth century,[8] and Muslims still formed one fifth of the population of Aragon after the Christian conquest of

5 See J. M. Lacarra, 'A propos de la colonisation "franca" en Navarre et en Aragón', *Annales du Midi* LXV (1953), 331–42.
6 This preface is edited in Hermann 1982, pp. 347–9.
7 To the classic study of J. M. Millàs Vallicrosa, *Assaig d'Història de les idees físiques i matematiques a la Catalunya Medieval* (Barcelona 1931), pp. 164–235, one may add G. Feliu i Montfort, 'Sunfred, Anomenat Llobet, ardiaca de Barcelona (finals del segle X)', in *II Col.loqui d'Història del Monaquisme Català* I (Abadia de Poblet 1972) 51–63.
8 J. Jomier, 'Notes sur les stèles funéraires arabes de Montpellier', in *Islam et chrétiens du Midi (xiie–xive s.)*, *Cahiers de Fanjeaux* XVIII (1983), pp. 60–3. One of the tombstones commemorates the death of a Muslim fakih in 1138–9.

1087. The most northerly outpost of Arabic rule was the kingdom of the Banū Hūd, who did not capitulate to the Christians until 1140. One of the Banū Hūd – Abū ʿAmir Yūsuf al-Muʾtaman – was a well-known mathematician, and his works show that he had access to a remarkably large collection of mathematical works.[9] The translator Hugo of Santalla tells us that Michael, Bishop of Tarazona from 1119 to 1151, sought out an astronomical text in the library of Rūṭa, the capital of the Banū Hūd from 1110 until 1140. He may well have been benefiting from the resources of Abū ʿAmir's collection.[10]

Hermann's literary output consists of two commissioned works concerning Islam – the *De generatione Mahumet* and the *Doctrina Mahumet* – his own original work, the *De essentiis*, and about a dozen translations or compendia of Arabic science. These last could be said to cover the whole of the Quadrivium with the exception of music (Arabic musical theory had very little impact on the West). For arithmetic there are two lost works, concerning the function of numbers and finding a square root, and for geometry there are Euclid's *Elements* and Theodosius' *Spherics*. It would be under the heading of 'astronomy', however, that most of the works would fall. These include astronomical tables (not extant), an important introduction to astrology by Abū Maʿshar, a work on prognosticating affairs of national significance, and compendia on weather-forecasting and finding hidden treasure.

Hermann alludes to the four-part division of science known as the Quadrivium at the beginning of his *De essentiis*, when he presents the figure of Minerva in the presence of counters (for arithmetic), a measuring-rod (for geometry), a pair of scales (for music), and a lamp (for astronomy). This is the Goddess, he says to Robert of Ketton, who has inspired his work.[11] Minerva's accoutrements, however, are the traditional symbols of the Quadrivium and do not evoke the new science of the Arabs. The measuring-rod was more appropriate to the land-measurers (*agrimensores*), whose works preserved the scant remnants of Classical geometry in the Latin West, than to Euclid's *Elements*, and the pair of scales recalled the story of Pythagoras' discovery of the mathematics of music when observing the blacksmiths working in their forge.

9 See J. P. Hogendijk, 'Discovery of an 11th-Century Geometrical Compilation: the *Kitāb al-Istikmāl* of Yūsuf al-Muʾtaman ibn Hūd . . .', *Historia Mathematica* XIII (1986) 43–52.
10 Haskins 1927, p. 73 (Hugo's preface to Ibn al-Muthannā's revision of al-Khwārizmī's astronomical tables, addressed to Michael): 'opus edictum in Rotensi armario et inter secretiora bibliotece penetralia tua insaciabilis filosophandi aviditas meruit repperiri'.
11 *De essentiis* 58r G–H.

Cutting across the traditional Quadrivium was a new division of science which Hermann sought to promote. This was the division of theoretical science into mathematics and physics. Hermann explains the two divisions in the preface to his translation of Ptolemy's *Planisphere*. The study of the movements of the stars – what we might call 'astronomy' – is 'mathematical speculation' and is the subject of Ptolemy's *Planisphere* and al-Battānī's *Science of the Stars*. The study of the effects of the movements – our astrology – belongs to natural speculation or physics, and is the subject of Ptolemy's *Tetrabiblos* and the *Greater Introduction to Astrology* of Abū Ma'shar. Hermann's immediate source for this division, which cuts the quadrivial *astronomia* into two species, is this last work. In the second chapter of his first book, Abū Ma'shar differentiated between a 'science of the whole (*'ilm al-kullī*)', which dealt with the quality and size of the heavenly spheres and the spheres of the planets and their movements, and which required a knowledge of arithmetic and geometry, and a 'science of (astrological) judgements (*'ilm al-aḥkām*)', which dealt with the natures of the planets and their indications, and what happens as a result of their movements. The first science, Abū Ma'shar said, was necessary for the second.[12] In his characteristically free translation of this passage Hermann introduces significant changes of sense.[13] He calls the first science 'mathematical' (*Prima quidem species mathematica*), and the second 'natural' (*Secunda vero naturalis*). The first species, Hermann writes, adapting the biblical phrase,[14] 'introduces a necessary argument based on three reasonings: number, proportion and measure'; the second 'investigates the nature of the heavenly bodies . . . and their influence over the accidents of this world, investigating partly by certain experiences of the senses, partly by a certain natural speculation'.

Hermann has introduced the words *mathematica* and *naturalis* (*speculatio*) from his reading of Boethius' *De trinitate*[15] – a favourite text of his teacher, Thierry of Chartres.[16] According to Boethius, theoretical knowledge

---

12 Leiden, University Library, MS Or. 47, pp. 5–6.
13 *Introductorium ad astronomiam Albumasaris abalachi* (Venice 1506), fol. a2v.
14 Wisdom 11:21: 'omnia in mensura et numero et pondere disposuisti'.
15 Boethius, *The Theological Tractates, The Consolation of Philosophy*, ed. H. F. Stewart, E. K. Rand, and S. J. Tester (Cambridge MA 1973), p. 8.
16 Nikolaus Häring published a *Commentum* and a *Glosa* to the *De trinitate* which he believed had been written by Thierry, and *Lectiones* on the *De trinitate* which he thought were a *reportatio* of Thierry's lectures, in his *Commentaries on Boethius by Thierry of Chartres and his School* (Toronto 1971). Häring's attributions have not been accepted without question, but these works are evidence for at least one outstanding northern French interpretation in the first half of the twelfth century. Boethius' division of speculation is discussed in *Commentum* II 8–16 (ed. Häring, pp. 70–3), *Lectiones* II 17–32 (*ibid.* pp. 160–5), and *Glosa* II 24–8 (*ibid.* pp. 272–4).

(*speculatio*) is of three parts: a natural, a mathematical, and a theological part (*naturalis, mathematica, theologica*). But while recalling Boethius' terminology, Hermann does not adopt Boethius' schematic definition of the three parts of theoretical knowledge. Moreover, Hermann changes the order of the three kinds of speculation. He elevates physics above mathematics:

The end of all mathematical study is the beginning of the physical study.[17]

In the same preface to Ptolemy's *Planisphere* Hermann goes on to describe the subject-matter of physics, in words very different from those of Boethius and Thierry:

The first part [of physics] considers the nature of the upper world; the second part, the nature of the lower world – that is, the material causes of things, just as the nature of the upper world is the formal causes of things – both being the principles of all coming-to-be, after that first cause which is the origin of both [i.e. God].[18]

Hermann's conception of physics is based not on Boethius' definitions or the speculations of the French schools, but rather on his acquaintance with Arabic thought. As we have seen, Hermann takes over Abū Ma'shar's two-part division of the science of the stars, while colouring his translation with the vocabulary of Latin philosophical works. Hermann's translations and adaptations of Arabic works fit more easily into this two-part division than into the traditional Latin Quadrivium. Alongside the works which Hermann mentions as belonging to the mathematical division – Ptolemy's *Almagest* and al-Battānī's *Science of the Stars* – one may place his translation of Euclid's *Elements*, Theodosius' *Spherics*, and, possibly, a translation of the astronomical tables of al-Khwārizmī. To Ptolemy's *Tetrabiblos* and Abū Ma'shar's *Greater Introduction to Astrology* one may add Hermann's translation of Sahl ibn Bishr's astrological works and his compendia on weather-forecasting and finding lost treasure, as representing the physical division.[19] All these works, however, specialize in one aspect of physics: i.e. the influence of the heavenly bodies on changes in the sublunar world, and, with the important exception of substantial portions of Abū Ma'shar's *Greater*

17 Preface to the *Planisphere* (Hermann 1982, p. 348): 'ut finis est disciplinalis studii, naturalis quoque speculationis extitit origo'.
18 (Continuation of text in previous note): '... cuius prior pars superioris mundi, ut sequens inferioris, naturam contemplatur – id autem est materiales rerum causas, quemadmodum illa formales, omnis videlicet geniture principia post primam ipsam causam utrumque moventem'.
19 Hermann refers to his own translations of al-Khwārizmī's astronomical tables, and Sahl's *Introduction to Astrological Judgements* (see Burnett 1978, pp. 106 and 120), and shows a close acquaintance with Theodosius' *Spherics* (*ibid.* pp. 104–6).

Introduction,[20] concentrate on classifying the effects of, rather than discovering the underlying causes of, this influence. Hermann was aware from his Arabic sources of a much broader range covered by the subject of physics. This broader range he promises, addressing Thierry of Chartres, to describe in his master-work, the *De essentiis*:

This [the subject-matter of physics] will be shown more fully in the work concerning the essences, which we have already begun.[21]

The conception of theoretical science amongst the Arabic philosophers of whose works Hermann would have been aware is represented by al-Fārābī's *Classification of the Sciences*[22] and the *On the Rise of the Sciences*, attributed in the anonymous Latin translation to al-Fārābī.[23] These Arabic works, following Aristotle,[24] place physical speculation between mathematical and theological speculation. In *On the Rise of the Sciences*, physics (*ars naturalis*) follows the four mathematical sciences (*ars numeri, ars mensurandi, scientia de stellis* and *ars musicae*) and precedes theology (*scientia divina*). In al-Fārābī, the mathematical or disciplinary science (*'ilm al-ta'ālīm*) precedes the natural science (*al-'ilm al-ṭabī'ī*), which in turn is followed by the divine science (*al-'ilm al-ilāhī*). The definition of physics in *On the Rise of the Sciences* could be the description of the subject-matter of the *De essentiis* itself:

Because a substance now reddens, now pales; now has a longer existence, now a shorter; now becomes larger, now smaller; now comes-to-be, now passes away; now is sick, now is healed; for this reason there had to be a science which pointed out all this, i.e. through which we might arrive at the knowledge of how such a kind of change takes place, and when and why it happens, and how we might, when we wished, both drive away those effects which were harmful and encourage those [which were beneficial]. This was the science of natures, which is the science of action and passion.

After seeking its origin we will find four elements – fire, air, water and earth (this is the material of sublunary substance), and from their four qualities (heat, coldness, moisture and dryness) the accidents to substance take place, and action and passion appear. And from these four roots [i.e. the elements], with those first four which are the mathematical sciences, emerged the science of all sublunary things ... There remained therefore the science of the material of the higher substance (because everything about its disposition and accidents had already been covered [i.e. in the *scientia de stellis*]). I can only understand the higher substance as being the sphere, able

20 The theoretical aspects of Abū Ma'shar's work have been well considered by Richard Lemay in his *Abū Ma'shar and Latin Aristotelianism in the Twelfth Century* (Beirut 1962).
21 Burnett 1982, p. 348: '... ut in eo quod de essentiis instituimus, plenius patebit'.
22 Ed. A. González Palencia, al-Fārābī, *Catálogo de las ciencias* (2nd ed., Madrid 1953).
23 Ed. C. Baeumker, in *BGPTM* XIX (1918). The Arabic original of this work has not been found.
24 *Metaphysics* E 1, 1026A6–19.

to revolve and move by a natural motion, ministering to the constitution of this world [i.e. sublunary substance] in accordance with the power and wisdom and will of God who is blessed and exalted.[25]

Hermann describes his method of speculation in the *De essentiis* just before he attempts to describe the soul:

All speculation resides in the nature of the soul. Reason approaches the composition [of the universe], demonstration its disposition, while intellect approaches the governing cause. Reason relies on plausibility (*probabilitas*), demonstration depends on necessity, whereas intellect trusts in a certain simple and unmixed intuition . . . We both support what we profess with reason, and establish it by demonstration.[26]

The distinction between 'probable arguments' and 'necessary arguments' is also made by Hermann's colleague Robert of Ketton in a letter to Peter the Venerable:

I promise to your celestial highness a celestial gift which embraces within itself the whole of science. This reveals according to number, proportion and measure, all the celestial circles, and their quantities, orders and conditions, and, finally, all the various movements of the stars and their effects and natures and everything else of this kind . . . based now on plausible arguments, sometimes on necessary arguments.[27]

In mathematics, the 'disciplinary' science,[28] the arguments are those from necessity and demonstration. In physics, the arguments are based on reason and plausibility. Throughout the *De essentiis* we can see these two approaches being used (Hermann explicitly disclaims using theological arguments).[29] Reason is applied to working out how the universe is put together (i.e. the *compositio*), while demonstration shows forth the resulting arrangement (i.e. the *dispositio*). The composer or creator of the universe is the supremely rational divine being himself. Since God knows how to, and has the ability to, make a perfect universe, man, as far as lies in his nature, should be capable

25 Ed. Baeumker, pp. 20–1.
26 *De essentiis*, 72v A–B: 'Omnis autem speculatio in natura anime. Accedit igitur ad compositionem ratio, ad dispositionem demonstratio, ad causam moderatricem intellectus – ratio quidem probabilitate contenta, demonstratio necessitate nitens, intellectus simplici quadam et mera conceptione fidens . . . ea quidem que profitemur tum ratione fulcimus, tum demonstratione firmamus.'
27 *P.L.* 189, 660: 'Tibi celesti . . . celeste munus voveo, quod integritatem in se scientie complectitur. Que secundum numerum et proportionem et mensuram celestes circulos omnes et eorum quantitates et ordines et habitudines, demum stellarum motus omnimodos et earumdem effectus atque naturas, et huiusmodi cetera . . . aperit, nunc probabilibus, nonnumquam necessariis argumentis innitens.'
28 The equation of *disciplinalis* or *doctrinalis* with 'mathematics' is based on the literal meaning of the Greek term μαθηματική (= 'of learning').
29 *De essentiis* 72v C: 'In his autem [sc. theology] fidem habere sufficiat auctoritati eorum qui divinitus illustrati puriore mentis visu divina penetrare potuerunt.'

of discovering through reason what this best possible universe should be, and, as a consequence of God's omnipotence, *must* be. The working out of the consequences of reason in forming the universe in the *De essentiis* is closely modelled on the work of 'intellect' in Plato's *Timaeus*.[30]

The starting-point is the essences which give the work its title. These are conceived as ultimate principles from which the whole universe evolves. They have a greater reality than the physical world and are the unchanging principles which underlie all change:

These are the things which, although they are disturbed in some way by the inconstancy of their subjects, nevertheless preserve their own proper and natural constancy intact ... They are properly called 'essences' ... They are cause, movement, place, time, and 'habitude' ... These, perfect in their substance and consummate by nature, lead all coming-to-be into existence.[31]

The five essences not only bring into being the created universe, but also determine the plan of the book, as Hermann states at the end of the first section:

These are the things which complete the wholeness of our project concerning the essences ... It seems completely necessary that ... there must be a well-ordered plan, so that we may ... find the contents organized in the natural order of sequence itself. Since as much has been said as the space demanded about the first and moving cause ['cause'], it seems that we must now start from the movement which is next, and prior to, and more general than, the rest, and preferably from that which is the first of those which are the principles for the rest – i.e. the movement of form and matter ['movement']. Then, after we have looked at the 'habitude' of the other [movements], and also at the receptacle of place and the space of time, so that the facts have been put forward from all sides concerning 'as a result of what' and 'in what', 'where', and 'when', and finally 'by what law' each thing is made – then, at the very end, may the *ratio* of the whole instrument be added and may it be established, having finally returned to the beginning, in the craftsman of the universe himself, just as it started from him.[32]

The work of reason is based on certain presuppositions which would have been more self-evident to Hermann's audience than they are to present-day readers. These include the axiom that circular movement is better than movement in straight lines; symmetry is better than lack of symmetry; even

---

30 *Timaeus*, trans. Calcidius, ed. J. H. Waszink (2nd ed., Leiden–London 1975) 47E: 'Nunc quoniam cuncta exceptis admodum paucis executi sumus, quae *providae mentis intellectus instituit*, oportet de illis etiam, quae necessitas invehit, dicere.'

31 *De essentiis* 58v B–D. Hermann's source for the definition of essences is Boethius, *De institutione arithmetica* I 1, ed. G. Friedlein (Leipzig 1867), pp. 7–8.

32 *Ibid.*, 60r C–E. See also Introduction, pp. 46–8.

numbers are better than odd numbers; higher is better than lower; similarity is better than difference.[33]

Several lines of reasoning can follow from these kinds of axioms:

(1) If the universe is to be immortal it must be bound together by firm bonds. Firm bonds cannot exist between things which are completely the same (for they would coalesce into each other and lose their separateness) or between things which are totally different (for they would never agree). Therefore a mixture of the same and the different is necessary.

(2) The elemental seeds cannot be entirely the same as one another because then they would not produce the variety of things required in the world. Therefore they have to be differentiated into four qualities. These are the hot, the cold, the moist, and the dry. The qualities themselves must be marked in such a way that illegitimate combinations, such as hot with cold, do not arise. One way of doing this is to make the qualities alternately masculine and feminine, so that only pairings between opposite sexes are made.

(3) The elements resulting from these pairings – fire, air, water, and earth – have to have the shape which ensures least disturbance from outside. The most suitable is the spherical shape.

(4) The sublunary universe has to have the best possible relationship with the superlunary universe. This can be ensured through the ratio of the numbers of their respective parts. The most appropriate ratio is eight to four. Thus there are eight celestial spheres (the seven planets and the sphere of the fixed stars, or outer extreme).

(5) For there to be generation there has to be an active and a passive entity. The active entity, being more perfect, must be higher in the universe; the passive must be lower. To be passive requires immobility. Therefore the lower part of the universe must be immobile. To be active requires motion. Therefore the upper part of the universe must be perpetually in movement. Since the universe is perfect, its movement is the one movement which is perfect in that it has no beginning or end – i.e. circular movement. Thus the whole universe is a revolving sphere. The 'lowest' point of a sphere is its centre, and this, as reason demands, is immobile. The earth, therefore, is immobile at the centre of a revolving sphere.

33 Hermann frequently uses phrases such as *ratio habet*, 'reason holds [that]', or *ratio exigebat*, 'reason demanded', or *exigebat* with other subjects ('place required' or 'the earth required' etc), or *id debitum habebat*, 'it had that need'. At other times Hermann appends the word *merito* to a statement of fact. The striving of creation towards perfection is brought out in *De essentiis* 62v H, where Herman writes: 'Ita siquidem habet ratio ut, quoniam omnia quidem valde bona futura essent, que prima, ipsa et optima fierent (id enim in ordine boni primum, quod optimum)' ('for reason holds that, since all creation was certainly destined to be good,

At certain significant points in the *De essentiis* Hermann corroborates these arguments from reason with arguments from mathematical demonstration. Using proofs from geometry, he shows how the earth is at the centre of the universe. Then he uses proofs from Ptolemy's *Almagest* to show that the apparent movement of the heavens must be due to a revolving heaven rather than a rotating earth.[34]

At one point demonstration overrides an apparently rational train of thought. This occurs when Hermann is investigating whether the intervals between the planets can be deduced from the periods of their orbits, on the supposition that the velocity of each planet is the same. Hermann introduces the argument by restating his methodology:

First we take the reasoning (*ratio*) of the most long-standing authority, then the evidence of demonstration.[35]

The authority he refers to is that of the Platonists and the Pythagoreans – who could be more venerable? – who believe that the planets have a uniform rate of motion. For two criteria are involved in the movement of the planets: first, the higher the planet, the lighter it is, and, consequently, the faster it moves; secondly, the closer the planet is to the outermost sphere which is moving in the opposite direction, the more the planet is retarded. These criteria would seem to cancel each other out, and thus the planets would seem to move at the same velocity.

Hermann sets against this 'reasonable argument' the proofs of demonstration:

Their grounds for [claiming] equality of movement are not sufficiently firm ... In contrast, we will measure the distances of some of the intervals, and, from that, demonstrate that the movements themselves are far from being equal.[36]

Once again Hermann turns to the *Almagest* (or possibly al-Battānī's reworking of the *Almagest*), from which he takes the values for the distance of the moon from the earth and for the size of its diameter. Then he sets up a geometrical construction and uses theorems from Euclid's *Elements* to work out the distance of the sun from the earth. He concludes from his mathematical calculations (which he sets forth in such detail that one can detect the

those things which were first were also made best (for, in the order of goodness, the best is first)'.
34 *De essentiis*, 64r G–64v D.
35 *Ibid*. 66v D: 'Quod primum sumimus secundum vetustissime auctoritatis rationem, tunc secundum quod demonstratio constituit.'
36 *Ibid*. 67r B: 'Nec enim satis constans est unde motus equalitatem sumunt ... Nos igitur converso et distantias intervallorum partim metiemur, et inde motus ipsos longe inequales demonstrabimus.'

mistakes he makes), that the sun is 1,210 earth-radiuses from the centre of the earth, whereas the moon is only 64 earth-radiuses away. From these values the lengths of the orbits of the sun and the moon are calculated and their ratio is found to be considerably higher than the ratio of the orbital periods of the moon and the sun (13 : 1). Hence the sun must be travelling faster than the moon, and the reasoning of the followers of Plato and Pythagoras is proved false.

That Hermann makes elementary mistakes in using his mathematical sources is not so important as that he attempts to make his own calculations, to corroborate or disprove what reason might suggest. It must be emphasized that neither his arguments from reason nor his arguments from demonstration are based on observation. Hermann follows the Platonic line in believing that the senses provide the least reliable kind of information. They delude one into thinking that the elements one sees are the true elements.[37] The soul would 'see' all the more clearly if it did not have material eyes which confuse it with the obfuscations of matter.[38] Hermann is merely setting one group of authorities against another. However, in introducing the mathematical authorities of Euclid, Theodosius, and Ptolemy, Hermann is innovating. The arguments of the followers of Plato and Pythagoras concerning planetary movement had long been known in the Latin West through the works of Boethius, Macrobius, and Martianus Capella. The demonstrations of Euclid, Theodosius, and Ptolemy were taken from works which Hermann himself had introduced or planned to introduce to his Latin-reading public. Hermann is aware of the significance of mathematical calculation in a cosmological work. For he places the two most detailed calculations at focal points in the two books that make up the *De essentiis*: in each case just before the final section of the book.

Hermann's arguments from probability and necessity are not taken from thin air but derive from his reading of a wide range of authorities and from direct acquaintance with scholars from within both the Latin and the Arabic tradition. The model for the form of the *De essentiis* is Plato's *Timaeus*; much of the contents can be generally defined as Aristotelian. However, within this overall framework Hermann favours certain lines of reasoning which can be distinguished, and whose sources are different. The most pervasive I would classify as the 'biological', the 'mechanical', and the 'numerological'.

37 *Ibid.* 60v H.
38 *Ibid.* 72r D (describing the soul): 'Igitur videtne etiam sine oculis? Videt plane, et multo purius, cum plerumque et in corpore, sine oculis tamen ipso etiam spiritu visibili quiescente, et multo expeditius videat, nichil materie presentia, nichil extrinseci corporeive luminis auxilio, egens.'

The structures resulting from these lines of reasoning are not always compatible with one another, and one should perhaps consider them as 'likely arguments'[39] rather than as true descriptions concerning the functioning of the universe.

First one may isolate the biological line of reasoning. The universe is imagined as a large animal with a living body and with the potential within itself for perpetual generation and regeneration. Hermann seems to have a concept of God not only as creator, but also as begetter of the universe, and of the universe as his consort.[40] The elemental qualities are called seeds, and are divided into masculine and feminine. It is from the 'marrying' of these masculine and feminine seeds that the elements, earth, water, air, and fire are born.[41] These elements, when mixed together, bring about the birth of minerals, plants, and animals. Minerals are conceived directly from the mating of the elements;[42] plants and animals are born through the mediation of a seed of their own nature. In the case of plants, that seed produces offspring without mating; in the case of animals, the seed must be exchanged in the process of mating.[43]

The heavenly bodies initiate this manifold fruitful generation. First of all, they provide an analogy:

Ptolemy claims that in the conjunction of the luminaries, as if in the very mating of the parents of the world, the moon becomes pregnant with the seeds of things, like someone who conceives. In planetary opposition, the moon finally brings forth the completed births.[44]

This can only be a metaphor, because in fact there can be no mixing of elemental seeds in the superlunary universe, which is not subject to change. However, the movement of the heavenly bodies regulates the reproductive activity. For example, spring makes

39 Cf. *Timaeus*, trans. Calcidius, 29C.
40 While echoing Plato's language in *Timaeus* 29D–E ('Optimus erat, ab optimo porro invidia longe relegata est. Itaque consequenter cuncta sui similia . . . effici voluit'), Hermann adds the idea that the universe is the 'partner' or consort of God (60r F): 'Optimus omnium auctor deus summeque beatus nequaquam invidit quin aliquid sibi gratie sue tanteque glorie consors efficeret.' The matter of the universe is the *semina* laid down by God (*ibid*. 60r G): 'Iecit itaque semina commiscendi potentia virtutisque generative.'
41 *De essentiis* 63r D (God is the subject): 'Deinde siccitati ex proximo frigus, frigori ex contiguo humorem, humori ex vicino calorem, calori a latere siccitatem copulans, singulas commixtiones ex utroque sexu legitimo federe maritavit, ne ulla posset intercidere dissensio singulis equali sorte beatis.'
42 *Ibid*. 75v E: 'Metalli quidem pars in primo elementorum coitu . . . ultra omne occidue geniture evum stabilis, pauca siquidem in hoc genus concedunt usque nunc nascentia.'
43 *Ibid*. 74v F–G.
44 *Ibid*. 76v E–F: 'Sic enim Ptholomeus asserit in coniunctione luminum, tamquam in ipso mundi parentum coitu, lunam more concipientis rerum seminibus gravidari; in oppositione demum plenos absolvere partus.'

. . . the lower substance pregnant by the very mating of the elements excited by the force of the heavens. The approach of the sun arouses and leads out the seed into various forms.[45]

The sun, being masculine, also ensures masculine births, whereas the moon leads to the birth of girls.[46] In that the superlunary sphere (which Hermann calls 'essence' *tout court*, as distinct from the five 'essences' discussed above) is active, formative, and engendering, whereas the sublunary sphere (or 'substance') is open to that activity, provides the materials, and is nurturing, these two parts of the universe too have masculine and feminine roles.[47]

Words such as *semina, maritare, commixtio, conceptio, partus*, abound in the *De essentiis*. Hermann owes this vocabulary partly to medical writers. He follows the authority of Galen rather than that of Aristotle in believing that the progeny is conceived from an equitable mixing of a female seed and a male seed, and not simply from a male seed placed inside a female vessel. However, on the whole, Hermann takes issue with the *medici*. He attributes to Galen the statement that the sex of a child is determined simply by a difference in the heat of the sexual parts of the parents when they engender it; he pours scorn on such a statement, in that it does not credit the higher parts of the universe with any role in determining sex.[48]

It is not so much with medical works as with works belonging to an alchemical or Hermetic tradition that the *De essentiis* must be associated in using these arguments. Hermann refers – rather obscurely – to the artificial production of metals and their assignment to respective planets.[49] He knows the credo of the alchemists – a set of verses attributed to Hermes Trismegistus known as the *Emerald Tablet*. Hermann retells the tale of the discovery of this text in a cave beneath a statue of Hermes, and he quotes from the *Tablet* the statement that the sun and moon are the parents of the universe.[50]

It is difficult to ascribe any Latin alchemical or Hermetic text (other than the *Asclepius*) with certainty to the time before Hermann wrote the *De essentiis*.[51] However, he could have known several works on the subject in

45 *Ibid.* 76v D: 'inferiorem substantiam ipso elementorum coitu superna vi concitato gravidet. Quod semen accessus solis eliciens in varias educit effigies.'
46 *Ibid.* 74r H.
47 *Ibid.* 61r E. The parts of substance are the *causae nutrientes*; the parts of essence are the *causae generantes* (see also 63r B).
48 *Ibid.* 74r G.
49 *Ibid.* 75v H.
50 *Ibid.* 65v C and 72v D–E.
51 One group of Arabic Hermetic texts and their translations into Latin has been discussed in my 'Arabic, Greek and Latin Works on Astrological Magic attributed to Aristotle', in *Pseudo-Aristotle in the Middle Ages*, ed. Jill Kraye, W. F. Ryan, and C. B. Schmitt (London 1986), pp. 84–96.

Arabic.[52] The *Emerald Tablet* was included in the *Secret of Creation* (*Sirr al-khalīqa*), attributed to Apollonius of Tyana, which was already known in Spain in the late eleventh century, for it was copied in Arabic in 1092, and was translated into Latin by Hermann's contemporary, Hugo of Santalla, some time between 1119 and 1152.[53] Although Hermann does not appear to have known Hugo's translation, it was through this work that Hermann knew the *Emerald Tablet*, for he cites the authority of Apollonius for the *Tablet* and the story of its discovery. He may well have been influenced also by other passages in 'Apollonius'.

The *Secret of Creation* purports to be Hermes' account of God's creation of the world and of the origins of minerals, plants, animals, and men. Although it does not describe alchemical processes, it provides the cosmology which is presupposed in works describing the practice of alchemy.[54] Here we find ideas concerning the elements which are very similar to those of Hermann. The elemental qualities are alternately masculine and feminine, and are married together:

Each quality sought out its like, and the dry chose the cold, and the moist the hot. The dry entered into the cold because of its likeness to it, and the moist entered into the hot because of its likeness to it, and when both pairs came together, they were married. And from the marriage of the dry and the cold came the earth, and from the marriage of the moist and the hot came the air. The dry was husband to the cold and the cold was wife to the dry ... Each of them demanded the other and needed the other's help, just as a husband needs the help of his wife and the wife needs the help of her husband.[55]

52 Hermann refers to Hermes' *Aurea virga* and quotes a passage allegedly from 'Aristotle's *Data neiringet*', which has been identified with a passage in the Arabic Hermetic work, the *Kitāb al-Isṭamāṭīs* (see my 'Hermann of Carinthia and the *Kitāb al-Isṭamāṭīs*', *Journal of the Warburg and Courtauld Institutes* XLIV (1981) 167–9). Hermann's distribution of the elements amongst the planets corresponds to that found in the Hermetic *Ghāyat al-ḥakīm* (*Picatrix*) (*De essentiis* 63r F–G = *Picatrix* I 3, ed. H. Ritter, *Pseudo-Maǧrīṭī, Das Ziel des Weisen* (Leipzig 1933), p. 13). Hermann shares with the *Kitāb al-Isṭamāṭīs* his partition of the openings of the head amongst the planets (79v A = Oxford, MS Marsh 556, fol. 41v).
53 Pseudo-Apollonios von Tyana, *Buch über das Geheimnis der Schöpfung und die Darstellung der Natur*, ed. U. Weisser (Aleppo 1979). MS Madrid, Biblioteca nacional Gg 153 gives a text which is dated 485 of the Muslim era (= 1092 AD). This is probably the date of the exemplar, since the manuscript itself is of the fifteenth century (Weisser, p. 10). The recension in this manuscript corresponds to that represented by Hugo of Santalla's translation, *De secretis nature*, an edition of which is being prepared by Mlle M.-T. d'Alverny and Mme F. Hudry. I have used the single surviving medieval manuscript of Hugo's translation, Paris B.N. lat. 13951.
54 A detailed summary of the contents of the work can be found in U. Weisser, *Das 'Buch über das Geheimnis der Schöpfung' von Pseudo-Apollonius von Tyana* (Berlin 1980), pp. 73–153.
55 *Sirr al-khalīqa* II 5 1, pp. 109–11. Hugo's translation reads (fol. 9r–v):
'Eorumque singula propria similitudine reliqua beare nituntur. Siccitas ergo frigus ingrediens, quadam habitudine eidem congruit. Humor etiam calori adherens, id ipsum. Ex huiusmodi alterno ingressu facto coniugio, dum frigus et siccitas coeunt, terra

The elements themselves are alternately masculine and feminine, and from the mating of the masculine elements, fire and air, and the feminine elements, earth and water, are born the smallest and the greatest things in the universe. The elements are 'mothers' of them all.[56]

Throughout the _Secret of Creation_ there is the idea of an underlying unity in nature, and a bond connecting all things. This was evident already in the _Emerald Tablet_:

The higher is from the lower, and the lower from the higher. The performance of marvels is one thing, just as all things derive from one arrangement, whose father is the sun, and whose mother is the moon.[57]

Near the beginning of the _Secret_, pseudo-Apollonius writes that everything is connected to everything else because all things derive from one substance (_jawhar_) and one seed (_nutfa_[58]). God himself created the bond (_ittiṣāl_) connecting all creation.[59]

The words _izdiwāj_ (connecting of two things together) and _ittiṣāl_ (connecting of several things) recur frequently in the _Secret of Creation_, and Hermann, too, constantly emphasizes the _nodus_ or the _nexus_ (also the _retinaculum_ and _vinculum_) – whether between the elemental qualities,[60] between the spheres of the planets,[61] between the superlunary and sublunary world,[62] between essence and substance,[63] or between the body and the soul.[64] However, Hermann weaves his bonds from numbers and musical proportions. In the _Secret of Creation_ dimensions and ratios have little part to play and there are no exact astronomical measurements. Hermann owes his numerical values on the one hand to the works of exact science that he knew, on the other to the numerology of Plato and the Platonists.

generatur, humoris namque et caloris facta adiunctio, aera producit. Que dum ita se habeant siccitatem sponsum frigoris, frigus siccitatis nuptam manifeste liquet . . . Hoc illud exigit, communique adinvicem prout vir femine, mulier etiam vice mutua viri fruitur amminiculo.'

56 _Sirr al-khalīqa_ III 20, ed. Weisser, pp. 306–7; trans. Hugo, fol. 16r.
57 _Sirr al-khalīqa_ VI 33 2, ed. Weisser, p. 524. Hugo translates (fol. 31r): 'Superiora de inferioribus, inferiora de superioribus. Prodigiorum operatio ex uno, quemadmodum omnia ex uno eodemque ducunt originem, una eademque consilii administratione, cuius pater sol, mater vero luna.'
58 _Sirr al-khalīqa_ I 1 3, ed. Weisser, p. 3. Hugo translates (fol. 1r): '[Omnia] ex eadem . . . materia et ex eiusdem seminarii germine procedunt.'
59 _Sirr al-khalīqa_ I 2 3 5, ed. Weisser, p. 35. Cf. Hugo's translation (fol. 3v): 'totius rursum materialis substantie et extra – omnium videlicet que in hac mundi fabrica sensus concipit – idem opifex adinvenit nexus.'
60 _De essentiis_ 60r G.
61 _Ibid._ 63r G.
62 _Ibid._ 63v B.
63 _Ibid._ 63r E.
64 _Ibid._ 79v C.

Hermann's mathematical sources provided a model for a mechanical universe. He uses the term *machina* on two occasions in reference to the structure of the universe.[65] The universe could be regarded as a giant clockwork within which motion was relayed and diversified by mechanical means. The outermost sphere of the universe imparts movement to the whole, but since it is of an utterly simple movement itself, within it is placed, first, a sphere with an equator at an angle to the equator of the outermost sphere, so that when the latter revolves, the equator of the former will appear to rise and to fall. This movement is further diversified by the several movements of the planets. These provide a sufficient variety to excite all the movements necessary in the sublunary world:

The Creator placed the mediators [i.e. the planets] below the highest extreme which impelled them all, in such a disposition that they might have the potential to provide sufficient variation for all the movements of subject nature, by the multiformity of their different motions.[66]

Hermann compares the mechanism of this diversification of movement to the one breath which produces different pitches by being blown through pipes of different lengths.[67] He gives some numerical values for the dimensions of certain parts of this mechanism – such as the distances of the sun and the moon from the earth – and hints that it is possible to work out all the parameters of the system.[68] Like clockwork, the system is self-motivating and does not require, as does Plato's system, a soul to impart movement into the body of the universe.

Hermann does not handle astronomical figures with ease. The kind of numbers he feels more at home with are those familiar from Boethius' *De institutione arithmetica* and the other Neopythagorean sources within the Latin tradition. The last dimension of Hermann's thought that we shall explore in the *De essentiis* may be called the 'numerological'.

In several cases it is the rightness of the number which is thought to corroborate the accuracy of a statement. The fact that there are forty-eight constellations is proved by the fact that forty-eight is the product of the first cubic number (eight) and the first 'perfect' number (six).[69] There are eight parts to essence and four parts to substance, because 8 : 4 forms the most

65 *Ibid.* 74r D and 79v A.
66 *Ibid.* 68r D–E: 'Media namque infra summam extremitatem cuncta cogentem in tantum relegavit auctor, ut gemina libertate sue seorsum legis potentia cunctis subiectorum motibus omnimoda diversitate satisfacerent.'
67 *Ibid.* 63v H.
68 *Ibid.* 67v G–H: 'perpetuum studium per intervalla interpositarum sperarum usque ad octavum celum demum conscendere possit.'
69 *Ibid.* 64r C.

perfect kind of bond.[70] The relation of the parts of the zodiac to those of essence (the superlunary parts of the universe) also provides a sufficiently binding ratio (12 : 8).[71] The order by which the elemental qualities are distributed through the planetary spheres is determined by considerations of symmetry.[72] The soul of man is perfected by having a 'perfect number' of faculties.[73]

Side by side with the biological arguments concerning matter are numerological ones. The elemental seeds seem to be understood as undifferentiated units, for, like numbers, according to Boethius' system, they are the 'same' when considered individually, but are 'different' when massed together.[74] As each 'different' number is conceived as being built up geometrically from units – a triangle of units represents three, a square four etc[75] – so each material object can be imagined as being filled by unitary seminal elements. Hermann follows Plato in saying that bodies are composed of planes.[76] So, just as the aggregate of units provides the internal dimensions of the body, the two-dimensional plane wraps up the body on the outside. Rational numerical values and ratios determine both the arrangement of the units within the individual object (the *compositio* or 'internal habitude') and the shape of the surrounding cover or limit (the *dispositio* or 'external completeness').[77] All these numerical values are relayed by the heavenly bodies.

The words 'same' and 'different' have been put in inverted commas in the previous paragraph because, for Hermann, these have a special meaning. The terms are clearly derived from Plato's *Timaeus*, where they designate ingredients of the world-soul. While not finding the concept of a world-soul

70 *Ibid.* 63r E–F.
71 *Ibid.* 63r H–63v A.
72 *Ibid.* 63r F–G. Cf. 63r G: '[The order of the elements is such] ut per utramque seriem pari ordine eadem cognatio reperiatur a mediis usque in utrumque extremorum, qualis apud Euclidem equa proportionalitas appellatur – artissimus rerum omnium nodus.'
73 *Ibid.* 71v C.
74 *Ibid.* 60r G–H: 'semina . . . que per se quidem eiusdem nature ac substantie individue, collata vero ad invicem, diverse'.
75 See Boethius, *De institutione arithmetica* II 7ff.
76 *Ibid.* 60r H–60v A: 'numerum pariter parem [i.e. 4] . . . non solidum sed planum, unde omnia solida conficienda erant' (cf. Plato, *Timaeus* 53–4, reported in Aristotle, *De generatione et corruptione* 315B31–2).
77 *Ibid.* 62v E–F: 'Constat autem omnis forma geminis quibusdam partibus tamquam integralibus, eo quod totam integritatem absolvunt. Quarum altera intrinseca habitudo, altera extrinseca absolutio. Atque intrinseca quidem habitudo in commixtionis proportione, extrinseca vero absolutio in figure dispositione – secundum utrumque videlicet genus quantitatis rerum omnium exemplar.' The two kinds of quantity are the 'discrete' and the 'continuous' and these are defined in Boethius, *De institutione arithmetica* I 1, while in the second chapter of the same book the 'exemplar in the mind of God' is described as the *ratio numerorum* by which all first things in the universe were composed (*De institutione arithmetica* I 2, ed. G. Friedlein (Leipzig 1867), p. 12).

useful, Hermann brings Plato's Same and Different to the forefront of his own system. The priority for God in creating the universe was to establish the Same and the Different, so that from their mixture all things might be generated.[78] The progression from Same (*idem*) through Different (*diversum*) to Mixed (*mixtum* or *medium*) at the elemental level is mirrored at the celestial level. For the outermost sphere is identified with the Same, the zodiac with the Different, and the sphere of the fixed stars with the Mixed. A similar relationship obtains at another level, for the outer extreme of the universe (which includes the three spheres just mentioned) is also called the Same, the sublunary world, the Different, and the spheres of the planets, the *medium*. Nature, too, is Same, Different, and Mixed.[79]

Finally, number is the constituent of musical harmony, and the last of the overlapping reasonings that Hermann uses to describe the functions of the universe are the reasonings of music.[80] The sublunary and the superlunary parts of the universe conform to each other in the number and proportions of their parts. They can be said to be tuned to the same pitches. Thus, when the superlunary parts of the universe are set in motion, the sublunary parts will vibrate in sympathy. This is an explanation of how causation at a distance works. Both the world of nature and the soul of man are governed by this celestial harmony. As Hermann states in the concluding sentence of the first book of the *De essentiis*:

Hence [Hermes] Trismegistus understood that nothing is a more pleasing gift to the Gods from the service of men than the performance of music, and the experience of almost all ages has proved that music alone is worthy for the veneration of the divine, since those wonderful dancing rounds of celestial virgins chant it in perpetual harmony to preserve the peace of the whole body of the universe.[81]

The celestial virgins would seem to be the Muses, each assigned to one of the nine spheres.

Hermann made a daring attempt to combine various ways of reasoning, taken from different sources. He tried to reconcile the Platonism of his Latin,

---

78 *De essentiis* 60r G: 'Primum ergo necessaria fuit huiusmodi fabrice eiusdem diversique propositio.'

79 *Ibid*. 69r C.

80 The first book of the *De essentiis* ends with a description of the consonances between the two parts of the universe, whereas the second ends with a description of man, which includes an account of the harmony of the soul.

81 *Ibid*. 68r H–68v A: 'Unde et Trimegistus intellexit nichil superis ex hominum officio musice munere gratius, et omnium fere seculorum usus expertus solam musicam divinitatis veneratione dignam, quippe quam admirabiles ille celestium choree virginum in universi mundi fedus perpetuo concentu modulantur.' Hermann is referring to Hermes Trismegistus, *Asclepius* 38 (ed. A. D. Nock and trans. A.-J. Festugière, *Corpus Hermeticum* II (2nd ed., Paris 1960)).

and the Aristotelianism of his Arabic, sources, while also coming under the spell of Hermetic writings. The contortions in some of the arguments in the *De essentiis* indicate that the materials were ultimately incompatible. However, the *De essentiis* remains essentially a philosophical work. For it demonstrates what can be achieved by using reason to work out the principles on which the universe is based.

Hermann's master-work had little influence. Only two full copies and two fragments have survived,[82] and the only known clear citations of his work are in a treatise by a contemporary translator.[83] Hermann was better known to posterity for his translations of astronomical and astrological works. Of all his writings it was the few pages he devoted to summarizing the opinions of the 'Indians' concerning weather-prediction that were copied most frequently. His attempt to advertise the *De essentiis* to Thierry of Chartres as an introduction to natural science was evidently unsuccessful. Perhaps it was premature. Nevertheless Hermann pointed to the new direction which scientific learning in the West was destined to take. He broke out of the old moulds of the Christian cosmologies that took the Bible as their starting-point, or of the late Classical cosmologies and their medieval derivatives, which were rather encyclopaedias of the curiosities of nature or sets of questions concerning natural philosophy. He did this by making meta-physical principles (the 'essences') the beginning of his investigation. He could not have done this had he not glimpsed the outline of Aristotelian physics through his Arabic sources. It is unlikely that Hermann knew any of Aristotle's works on natural philosophy directly, nor does he seem to have been aware of the writings of Avicenna. Nevertheless he was in touch with those currents of Arabic Aristotelianism which were about to burst upon the European schools. It might be precisely the spread of the translations of Avicenna and Aristotle that eclipsed his own work, which had so bravely paved the way for them.

---

82 The manuscripts are described in Hermann 1982, pp. 63–6. The second fragment came to light only recently and is briefly described in *Bookhands of the Middle Ages*, Bernard Quaritch Ltd., Catalogue no. 1036 (1984), item 109.
83 The work is Gundissalinus, *De processione mundi*, ed. G. Bülow, BGPTM xxiv. 3 (1925).

IV

THE ENTRY OF THE 'NEW' ARISTOTLE

15

ARISTOTELIAN THOUGHT IN SALERNO *

DANIELLE JACQUART

For the past sixty years or so, the name of Salerno has been associated with the history of medieval Aristotelianism. Although the role of the famous medical school is often mentioned in connection with the propagation of 'the new Aristotle', and more particularly with the treatises on natural philosophy, before their condemnation in Paris in 1210, the actual contribution of Salerno remains open to question. The chief difficulty lies in the fact that most of the source material is still unpublished, as regards both the Latin translations of Aristotle known in the twelfth century and the vast corpus of Salernitan writings. A major disadvantage ensues: the establishment of an accurate chronology has so far proved impossible; all one can do is to suggest approximations, which are often inadequate to shed light on the influence of one text on another. Researchers who tackle this question take up alternative attitudes: either waiting for the publication of critical editions before pronouncing themselves, or putting forward hypotheses – which become convictions in course of time – on the basis of a few easily accessible manuscripts. What seems most profitable in the present state of research is to blaze a trail by offering examples of explicit quotations or of the recognizable influence of Aristotelian thought. As a preliminary we shall examine the scientific motivation which may have led to the interest in Aristotle. The ground was largely prepared, in fact, by medical translations at the end of the eleventh century.

Background: Alexander Birkenmajer and his successors

Alexander Birkenmajer, in a paper given in 1928,[1] provided a decisive stimulus to research by ascribing a special role to 'physicians and naturalists' in the discovery and dissemination of Aristotle's treatises on natural phil-

---

* Translated by Jean Stewart.
1 A. Birkenmajer, 'Le rôle joué par les médecins et les naturalistes dans la réception d'Aristote au xiie et xiiie siècle', in *La Pologne au VIe Congrès International des Sciences Historiques, Oslo 1928* (Warsaw 1930), pp. 1–15; repr. in A. Birkenmajer, *Etudes d'histoire des sciences et de la philosophie du Moyen Age* (Wrocław–Warsaw–Cracow 1970) [*Studia Copernicana* i], pp. 73–87.

osophy. Whereas the traces of Aristotelian influence previously discovered in William of Conches, Thierry of Chartres, or Gilbert of Poitiers had been ascribed to indirect sources, such as Calcidius, Macrobius, Martianus Capella or, in a different connection, Constantine of Africa, the question now arose of the possible direct use of Latin translations. Birkenmajer, basing his theory on the available published texts and on a few manuscripts, attributed to the Salernitan scholars Maurus and Urso, 'round about 1170', direct recourse to the *libri naturales*, in the Graeco-Latin versions prepared in Italy towards the middle of the twelfth century. This tended to diminish the importance of the Latin translations from the Arabic of Gerard of Cremona († 1187) in making Aristotle's physics known in the West. Birkenmajer credited the Salernitan scholars not merely with using but with diffusing the Aristotelian texts, since he showed that their works were quoted in the earliest years of the thirteenth century in the *De natura rerum* of Alexander Nequam and in Raoul of Longchamps's commentary on the *Anticlaudianus* of Alan of Lille.[2]

Although Birkenmajer's article is still authoritative as regards the use made of Aristotle by Salernitan scholars, several points have become open to discussion. First the quest for manuscripts undertaken in connection with the *Aristoteles Latinus*[3] provided important details as to the development and propagation of the Graeco-Latin versions. The study of a group of twelfth-century manuscripts containing marginal and interlinear glosses led Lorenzo Minio-Paluello to suggest a different way in which the *libri naturales* may have become known.[4] These manuscripts, some of which come from the library of Mont Saint-Michel, were transcribed in northern France. Lorenzo Minio-Paluello established that they must have come into Normandy about 1160 and that the glosses could be ascribed to the circle of Richard Bishop, Archdeacon of Coutances and former teacher of John of Salisbury, whose *Metalogicon* contained moreover the first quotation from the *Posterior Analytics* in the version of James of Venice. The conclusion was inevitable: 'One thing seems to be sure: that there was a centre of interest in the *new* Aristotle

---

2 Alexander Nequam, in the *De natura rerum*, composed between 1197 and 1204, cites the *Aphorisms* of Urso with their commentary: cf. B. Lawn, *The Salernitan Questions* (Oxford 1963), p. 32 (rev. Italian ed. *I Quesiti Salernitani*, trans. A. Spagnuolo (Salerno 1969)).

Raoul of Longchamps cites Maurus' commentary on the *Prognosticon* of Hippocrates, as well as Urso's *Aphorisms*: cf. Radulphus de Longo Campo, *In Anticlaudianum Alani commentum*, ed. J. Sulowski (Wrocław–Warsaw–Cracow–Gdansk 1972), pp. 56, 214, 32, 37, 48.

3 *Aristoteles Latinus: Codices, Pars prior* (Rome 1939), *Pars posterior* (Cambridge 1955), *Supplementa altera* (Bruges–Paris 1961; repr. in 3 vols., Leiden 1979).

4 L. Minio-Paluello, 'Iacobus Veneticus Grecus, Canonist and Translator of Aristotle', *Traditio* VIII (1952) 265–304; repr. in L. Minio-Paluello, *Opuscula: The Latin Aristotle* (Amsterdam 1972), pp. 189–228.

in northern France, which produced the first known attempt at Latin exegesis and at propagation of these works.' Normandy thus appeared as a possible route by which the newly translated treatises of Aristotle were made available to philosophers and theologians. The influence of works produced in Toledo and Salerno was thus restricted to 'scientists'.

Thirty years after Birkenmajer's article, Paul Oskar Kristeller put forward the hypothesis that the *libri naturales* had been studied at Salerno shortly after 1150.[5] He based this theory on an examination of a number of manuscripts containing commentaries attributed to a certain 'Bartholomew'. The fact that this name was linked in certain cases to that of the Salernitan scholar Petrus Musandinus, who was active during the second half of the twelfth century, led Kristeller to identify the commentator with the author of the celebrated *Practica*, Bartholomew of Salerno.[6] As it seems possible that this scholar was teaching in Salerno in the first half of the twelfth century, the date of the commentaries attributed to him could not have been much later than 1150–60. Thus the Aristotelian treatises must have been put to use almost as soon as they were translated from the Greek. It was, in fact, in the middle of the twelfth century, or shortly before, that James of Venice translated into Latin Aristotle's *Physics*, the *De anima*, the *Metaphysics* (Books I–IV 4), known as 'Metaphysica vetustissima', and part of the *Parva naturalia*; the partial version of the *Meteorologica* (Book IV) by Henricus Aristippus is roughly contemporary, and the anonymous translations of the *De generatione et corruptione* and the *Nicomachean Ethics* (Books II–III, 'Ethica vetus'),[7] slightly later.

The favoured position of Salerno at the junction of Eastern and Western

---

5 P. O. Kristeller, 'Nuove fonti per la medicina salernitana del secolo XII', *Rassegna Storica Salernitana* XVIII (1957) 61–75; 'Beitrag der Schule von Salerno zur Entwicklung der scholastischen Wissenschaft im 12. Jahrhundert', in *Artes Liberales von der antiken Bildung zur Wissenschaft des Mittelalters*, ed. J. Koch (Leiden–Cologne 1959) [*Studien und Texte zur Geistesgeschichte des Mittelalters* v], pp. 84–90; 'Bartholomaeus, Musandinus and Maurus of Salerno and Other Early Commentators of the *Articella*, with a Tentative List of Texts and Manuscripts', *Italia Medioevale e Umanistica* XIX (1976) 57–87 (trans. and rev. in his *Studi sulla Scuola medica salernitana* (Naples 1986), pp. 97–151).

6 The *Practica* was edited long ago by Salvatore de Renzi (*Collectio Salernitana* IV (Naples 1856) 321–406). This text contains a reference to a commentary by the same author on the *Ysagoge* of Iohannitius; cf. Kristeller 1976, p. 62.

7 *Parva Naturalia*, trans. James of Venice: *De memoria, De iuventute, De longitudine vitae, De vita, De respiratione*. To this brief recapitulation of twelfth-century translations, which seeks to be clear rather than exhaustive, we must add that other translations were made from the Greek towards the end of the century: an almost complete version of the *Metaphysics*, known as 'Metaphysica media'; Book I and part of Book II of the *Physics*, known as 'Physica Vaticana'; the *De somno et vigilia*, the *De sensu et sensato*, and the *De divinatione per somnum*. For an illuminating analysis and the list of editions, see M.-T. d'Alverny, 'Translations and Translators', in *Harvard 1982*, pp. 435–7.

influences has suggested furthermore that the teachers at this school may have known Greek and Arabic. Paul Oskar Kristeller rates Bartholomew a respectable Hellenist.[8] In this connection, reference is often made to the statement of Stephen of Antioch that many scholars in Sicily and Salerno understood Greek and Arabic.[9] There is no solid proof for this assumption, but relations were still being established in the twelfth century between translators and the school of Salerno. It was for instance at the request of Bartholomew of Salerno that Burgundio of Pisa completed an early version of Galen's *Ars Medica*.[10] Again, we know that a former student of Salerno living in Sicily translated Ptolemy's *Almagest* about 1160, and, shortly before that, the *Elementatio physica* (or *De motu*) of Proclus.[11] Such contacts undoubtedly encouraged exchanges between scholars, by which some fragments of texts as yet untranslated might have changed hands. In this context the question has been raised with respect to the oldest Salernitan anatomical text, the *Anatomia porci* or *Cophonis*,[12] of a possible acquaintance with certain passages of Aristotle's *De animalibus*, which was not translated into Latin until the thirteenth century. An explanation by 'oral tradition', as a last resort, too often only conceals a failure to identify the intermediary author.

The role of indirect sources, particularly Arabic ones, no longer needs demonstrating. In 1962 Richard Lemay questioned the importance of Salerno's 'new' Aristotle,[13] suggesting instead an indirect transmission by way of astrological texts, especially the *Introductorium Maius in Astronomiam* of Abū Ma'shar, the two versions of which are slightly earlier than the mid-twelfth century. The author comments moreover that 'some tentative probing into the naturalistic writings issued from the Salernitan school which were available in print yields disappointing results'.[14] Morris H. Saffron, discussing the commentary on the *Prognostics* of Hippocrates, declares: 'But while Maurus may have been eager to demonstrate to his students an easy familiarity with Aristotelian logic and terminology, these novelties seem to have been poorly understood by him, and aside from their usefulness as teaching aids, bear only a superficial relevance to the subject

---

8 Kristeller 1976, and 'Ancient Philosophy at Salerno in the Twelfth Century', communication to the Society for Ancient Greek Philosophy, 1958 (mimeographed).
9 Cf. d'Alverny 1982, p. 438, n. 71.
10 R. J. Durling, 'Corrigenda and Addenda to Diels' Galenica, 1: Codices Vaticani', *Traditio* XXIII (1967), 463.
11 Ed. H. Boese, *Die Mittelalterliche Übersetzung der Στοιχείωσις φυσική des Proclus; Procli Diadochi Elementatio physica* (Berlin 1958).
12 Cf. Y. V. O'Neill, 'Another look at the Anatomia Porci', *Viator* I (1970) 115–24.
13 R. Lemay, *Abu Ma'shar and Latin Aristotelianism in the Twelfth Century* (Beirut 1962).
14 *Ibid.* p. 137.

matter of our very practical text.'[15] Again, Wolfgang Stürner is unable to identify precisely the three quotations made by Urso of Calabria in his *De commixtione elementorum*.[16] The question can therefore no longer be posed in exactly the same terms as at the time of Alexander Birkenmajer. The use made of Aristotle at Salerno seems limited to specific areas. Before attempting to identify these we must describe the medical context which made possible an opening to natural philosophy.

Two basic medical texts: the Ysagoge ad artem Galeni *and the* Pantegni

The origin of the school of Salerno is surrounded by legends;[17] as early as the tenth century it seems to have enjoyed a certain renown, and historians are apt to quote in this connection the account by Richer of Reims of the rivalry between Derold, future Bishop of Amiens, and a physician from Salerno visiting the court of Charles the Simple (about 907–17). The twelfth century represents the school's apogee, at a period that German historians have named 'Hochsalerno'. The capture and sack of the city by Emperor Henry IV in 1194 mark the end of its greatness.

This century witnessed the production of original anatomical texts,[18] huge pharmacopeial collections[19] which carried weight throughout the Middle Ages, the development of the genre of questions[20] and, above all, with respect to our theme, the constitution of a corpus of writings on which

15 M. H. Saffron, 'Maurus of Salerno: Twelfth-Century *Optimus Physicus* with his Commentary on the Prognostics of Hippocrates', *Transactions of the American Philosophical Society*, N.S. LXII. 1 (1972) 20.

16 Urso of Salerno, *De commixtionibus elementorum libellus*, ed. W. Stürner (Stuttgart 1976), pp. 9–11.

17 The bibliography on the School of Salerno is vast; only some of the most essential items will be signalled here: F. Hartmann, *Die Literatur von Früh- und Hochsalerno und der Inhalt des Breslauer Codex Salernitanus* (Leipzig 1919, Diss.); K. Sudhoff, 'Die Salernitaner Handschrift in Breslau, ein Corpus medicinae Salerni', *Archiv für Geschichte der Medizin* XII (1920) 101–48; 'Salerno, Montpellier und Paris um 1200', *ibid.* XX (1928) 51–62; 'Salerno, eine mittelalterliche Heil- und Lehrstätte am Tyrrhenischen Meere', *ibid.* XXI (1929) 43–62; C. and D. Singer, 'The Origin of the Medical School of Salerno, the First University', in *Essays on the History of Medicine presented to Karl Sudhoff* (Zurich 1924), pp. 121–38; P. O. Kristeller, 'The School of Salerno: Its Development and its Contribution to the History of Learning', *Bulletin of the History of Medicine* XVII (1945) 138–94, repr. in P. O. Kristeller, *Studies in Renaissance Thought and Letters* (Rome 1956), pp. 495–551, trans. in Kristeller 1986, pp. 11–96; A. Pazzini, 'La letteratura medica salernitana e la storia della Scuola di Salerno', *Salerno* I (1967) 5–17; and 'La scuola vescovile di Salerno, origine della scuola medica di Salerno', *ibid.* II (1968) 3–17.

18 Cf. M. H. Saffron's article 'Salernitan Anatomists' in *Dictionary of Scientific Biography* XII (New York 1975) 80–3.

19 The Salernitan contribution is summarized in D. Goltz, *Mittelalterliche Pharmazie und Medizin, Dargestellt an Geschichte und Inhalt des Antidotarium Nicolai* (Stuttgart 1976).

20 Cf. Lawn 1963, 1969, and B. Lawn, *The Prose Salernitan Questions* (London 1979) [*Auctores Britannici Medii Aevi* V].

teachers commented in the course of their lectures. They were renewing a tradition established in Ravenna in the fifth and sixth centuries[21] but expanding it considerably. This corpus, known later as *Articella*, took shape gradually during the early twelfth century and eventually became fixed in the following form:[22] *Ysagoge ad artem Galeni* by Johannitius, the *Aphorisms* and *Prognostics* of Hippocrates, *De urinis* by Theophilus, *De pulsibus* by Philaretus, and Galen's *Tegni* or *Ars parva*. Before entering the university curriculum in the thirteenth century, this corpus was adopted at Chartres at an early date, as seems confirmed by the fragments of commentary that have come down to us.[23]

The first of these texts deserves attention. Many questions are still unanswered as regards the *Ysagoge* and its translation.[24] Salernitan commentators considered it a product of the Alexandrian school and attributed it to the son, or a disciple, of John of Alexandria. Whereas no Greek original is known to this day, there is an Arabic text that corresponds to it, the *Masā'il fi ṭ–ṭibb* of Ḥunayn ibn Isḥāq.[25] Since Ḥunayn was one of the greatest

21 These commentaries on some works of Hippocrates and Galen are listed and described in A. Beccaria, 'Sulle tracce di un antico canone latino di Ippocrate e di Galeno', *Italia Medioevale e Umanistica* II (1959) 1–56; IV (1961) 1–75; XIV (1971) 1–23. The commentary on Galen's *De medendi methodo ad Glauconem* has been edited by N. Palmieri, 'Un antico commento a Galeno della Scuola medica di Ravenna', *Physis* XXIII (1981) 197–296.

22 Cf. Kristeller 1976.

23 C. Burnett, 'The Contents and Affiliation of the Scientific Manuscripts Written at, or Brought to, Chartres in the Time of John of Salisbury', in *The World of John of Salisbury*, ed. M. Wilks (Oxford 1984), pp. 127–60. We must add that, apart from the commentaries considered as Chartrian and the Salernitan commentaries, another group, which Paul Oskar Kristeller calls the 'Digby commentary', seems to provide one of the earliest pieces of evidence; this group cannot at present be connected with any certainty to a precise intellectual centre: see S. P. Hall, 'Commentaries on the Aphorisms of Hippocrates', in *Manuscripts at Oxford: R. W. Hunt Memorial Exhibition*, ed. A. C. de la Mare and B. C. Barker-Benfield (Oxford 1980), p. 49. The prologue to the commentary on the *De urinis* by Theophilus (MS Oxford, Bodl. Libr. Digby 108, fol. 76r) is published in the article by Burnett quoted above (pp. 149–50).

24 Johannicius, '*Isagoge ad Techne Galieni*', ed. G. Maurach, *Sudhoffs Archiv* LXII (1978) 148–74. The editor is unfamiliar with the two earliest manuscripts and continues to attribute this translation, mistakenly, to Mark of Toledo, whereas it is undoubtedly the product of the circle around Constantine of Africa, if not actually Constantine's own work. See D. Jacquart, 'L'*Isagoge Johannitii* et son traducteur', *Bibliothèque de l'Ecole des Chartes* CXLIV (1986) 209–40.

25 Maurus of Salerno specifies: 'Ioannitius vero Iohannis Alexandrini filius seu discipulus ut quidam asserunt' (Commentary on the *Ysagoge*, Paris MS Bibl. nat. lat. 18499, fol. 1r).
    Contrary to what has often been asserted, there seems to be only one edition in Arabic: cf. *Dictionary of Scientific Biography* XV, suppl. 1 (New York 1978) 230–49 (article on Ḥunayn by G. C. Anawati and A. L. Iskandar). English translation of the *Masā'il*: P. Ghalioungui, *Questions on Medicine for Scholars by Ḥunayn Ibn Isḥāq* (Cairo 1980). There is also a Syriac version of this text, part of which has been transcribed in J. B. Chabot, 'Version syriaque de traités médicaux dont l'original n'a pas été retrouvé', in *Notices et extraits des manuscrits de la*

translators from Greek into Arabic, the question arises whether the *Masā'il* is an original work or one derived from a Greek text. In spite of the reservations of some scholars, it is probable that the *Ysagoge*, which was being read in Salerno as early as 1100, was based on an Arabic original. It opens by stating the division of medicine into two parts, theory and practice, and then proceeds to a dry classification of the fields of medicine. In the oldest manuscripts there are two peculiarities of terminology, the first of which was to prove of capital importance.[26] The translator uses the term *commixtio* to describe the combination of primary qualities (heat, cold, moistness, and dryness) characteristic of the temperament of each part or the whole of the body, but the term *compositio* for the four humours (blood, phlegm, bile, and melancholy). Later scribes replaced *commixtio* and *compositio* by the terms that had become current in their days: *complexio* and *humor*. The vocabulary of the *Ysagoge* is markedly tinged with philosophy. For instance, symptoms of illnesses are classified according to accident or substance: 'There are two kinds of signs of homogeneous members; one kind are substantial, the other kind accidental; substantial, such as hot, cold, dry or moist; the accidental are made manifest either by touch, as hard or soft, or by sight, as what is coloured, or by perfection, as with fully accomplished operations.' The implication of this text is that the physician must have knowledge of the categories proposed by philosophy. Comparing the Latin with the Arabic text of the *Ysagoge*, we notice that many sentences are truncated and hard to understand. The Salernitan scholars tried to interpret it with the help of the *Pantegni*, which offered the same kind of information in a more fully developed form.

The *Pantegni* is a translation by Constantine of Africa[27] – a monk from Monte Cassino who, it should be remembered, had had some connection with Salerno in the second half of the eleventh century – of a vast Arabic medical encyclopaedia: the *al-Kunnāsh al-Malikī* of Ali ibn al-'Abbas al-

Bibliothèque Nationale xlii (Paris 1965) 77–143. The Latin version with commentaries by Salernitan authors only includes fragments of the Arabic.

26 D. Jacquart and G. Troupeau, 'Traduction de l'arabe et vocabulaire médical latin: quelques exemples', in *La lexicographie du latin médiéval et ses rapports avec les recherches actuelles sur la civilisation du Moyen Age*, ed. Y. Lefèvre (Paris 1981) [*Colloques internationaux du CNRS* ccclxxvi], pp. 367–76; D. Jacquart, 'De *crasis* à *complexio*: note sur le vocabulaire du tempérament en latin médiéval', in *Mémoires V. Textes médicaux latins antiques* (St Etienne, Centre Jean Palerne 1984), pp. 71–5.

27 The biography of Constantine of Africa (†1087) is still an unsolved enigma; it seems established that he was born in Carthage and studied under Arab teachers, but there is nothing to show that he was a Muslim convert, as has often been said: cf. d'Alverny in *Harvard 1982*, pp. 422–3.

The best edition of the *Pantegni* is the 1515 Lyon edition (*Omnia Opera Ysaac*); the text of the Basle edition, 1535–9 (*Opera Constantini*) has been subject to considerable alteration.

Majūsī (tenth century).[28] This work influenced both the formal structure and the content of Salernitan commentaries during the second half of the twelfth century. It recalled the plan followed in the Alexandrian school for introducing a work: certain things had to be precisely set out – the intention of the book, its usefulness, its title, the field of doctrine it dealt with, the author's name, and the subdivisions of the work.[29] The prologue to the *Pantegni* indicates the originality of the book. Although it follows the tradition of Byzantine medical *summae*, such as those of Oribasius and Paul of Aegina, it is innovatory in that it offers a long development about 'natural things', which are the physical constituents and motive forces of the human body: the elements, temperaments, humours, members, virtues (or forces), operations, spirits (or *pneumata*). With certain variations, it repeats Galen's three ways of approaching medicine: by analysis (*dissolutio, resolutio*), by synthesis (*compositio*), and by definition (*descriptio, notatio*).

The *Pantegni* is in two parts, one theoretical, the other practical. This division of subjects gave rise to a definition which was repeated and discussed by the scholars of Salerno: 'The theoretical part is the perfect knowledge of things that can be apprehended by the intellect alone, subject to the memory of things to be performed. Practice consists in demonstrating theory, subject to the sensory field and to manual operation, according to a previous understanding of theory.' This twofold definition, somewhat ambiguous, led to long discussions in an attempt to decide which came first, theory or practice. It also provided the opportunity to enquire into the faculties necessary to a physician: reasoning power, memory, sense perception, manual skill. In its theoretical aspect, medicine was connected with philosophy and other sciences: 'he who would attain the first rank in this art must have a knowledge of dialectics and of the whole Quadrivium'. The *Pantegni* thus provided a direct incitement to the medical man to go beyond the narrow limits of his art and accept other influences.

The *Ysagoge* begins, like the theoretical part of the *Pantegni*, by setting forth the seven natural things; in the first place, the elements, which it

28 There is a German translation of the preface of the Arabic text in M. Ullmann, *Die Medizin im Islam* (Leiden–Cologne 1970).
29 To recall some types of *accessus ad auctores* used by medical commentators: in the Ravenna version of a commentary, of Alexandrian origin, on the *De sectis* of Galen: *intentio, utilitas, si verus est liber Galieni, causa suprascriptionis, ordo legendi, habitus doctrine*; cf. Beccaria 1971, pp. 14–15. Bartholomew's commentary on the *Ysagoge*, after asking about authorship, decides to treat: *intentio auctoris, causa operis, utilitas libri, ad quam partem philosophie spectet, quo genere doctrine utatur, que divisio operis vel quis ordo, quis titulus* (MS Winchester 24, fol. 22v; cf. Kristeller 1976, p. 85). As for Maurus: *materia et intentio, intentionis causa, utilitas, suppositio operis, modus et ordo tractandi, libri titulus* (Commentary on the *Ysagoge*, MS Paris, Bibl. nat. lat. 18499, fol. 1r); these headings come similarly after discussion of the authorship.

enumerates without defining them. 'There are four elements, fire, air, water, and earth. Fire is hot and dry, air is hot and moist, water is cold and moist, earth is cold and dry.' The *Pantegni* develops the subject further: 'An element is the smallest simple particle of a composite body.' The idea of oneness being rejected, the four elements are said to be simple according to the senses, composite according to the intellect. It is specified that to philosophers these four elements are heat, cold, moistness, and dryness, and that they are not to be understood as qualities but as substances: perfect, active heat is fire, perfect, active cold is earth etc. Each element acquires a complementary quality through proximity: fire owes its dryness to its proximity to the circle of the moon, air its heat to proximity to fire etc. The paragraph devoted to the elements concludes with a statement of other elemental qualities: heaviness, lightness, thinness, and thickness.

On the problem of temperament – Galen's *crasis* – there is a difference in vocabulary between the *Ysagoge*, which uses *commixtio*, and the *Pantegni*, which offers, possibly for the first time in medical terminology, the word *complexio*. In the latter text the term *commixtio* refers to a different concept, which is set forth before the paragraph on temperaments: the mixture of elements. The word is related to Aristotle's *mixis*: the product of wine and water mixed together cannot be described as *commixtio*, since each retains its individual quality; there is no transformation. Complexion results from the mixture of elements.[30] Since any body destined to 'construction and destruction' is born of this mixture, the dominant elements assign their own specific qualities to the final product. Faced with this terminological ambiguity, the Salernitan commentators sought greater precision: they established that *complexio* is the effect of *commixtio*, the combination of primary qualities resulting from the mixture of elements.[31] The notion of temperament is a central one in Galen's science, since it underlies both the physiological explanation and the therapeutic system: the physician has in fact to find the means to establish agreement or opposition, depending on his purpose, between the qualities of the body or of some organ and those of a

30 'Illud autem complexionem esse dicimus quod ex elementorum commixtione conficitur' (*Pantegni, Theorica* I 6). Constantine here translates the Arabic faithfully; *complexio* corresponds to *mizāj*, which translates Galen's *crasis*, the mixture of qualities that characterize the temperament, *commixtio* to *imtizāj*, the mixture properly so called: 'these qualities are called "temperament" (*mizāj*), for it derives from the mixing (*imtizāj*) of the elements' (MS Paris, Bibl. nat. ar. 2871, fol. 8r). In the *Ysagoge, commixtio* was used indifferently for *mizāj* and *imtizāj*.

31 For example, Maurus: 'Queritur autem hic utrum complexio sit de rebus naturalibus vel non. Dicemus eam non esse de naturalibus quoniam ad minus naturalia essent octo, sed eam dicemus contineri sub commixtione tamquam effectus a causa' (Commentary on the *Ysagoge*, MS Paris, Bibl. nat. lat. 18499, fol. 9r).

medicament, either simple or compound. It can thus be understood how, at a time when the essential writings of Galen were not well known,[32] the Aristotelian theory of mixture found its way into medical discussions.

The citations from Aristotle's Physics and De generatione et corruptione

As several scholars have pointed out (Alexander Birkenmajer in the first place), the Salernitan commentaries on the *Ysagoge* are the works which make the most obvious use of Aristotle. We must therefore analyse a few passages from these, beginning with the one ascribed by Paul Oskar Kristeller to Bartholomew of Salerno. As certain titles or colophons of manuscripts also mention the name of Petrus Musandinus, it is probable that the state of this text is the result of a *reportatio* or subsequent writing-up of notes taken during a lecture.[33] In the absence of an edition or even of a comparison of the different versions, we shall take as our basis the Winchester manuscript.[34]

The definition of the theoretical part of medicine as 'the science that contemplates nature or the principle of nature' leads the author to examine the meaning of the word 'nature'. Here he quotes Aristotle's *Physics*: 'Nature is the principle of the movement and rest of a thing that moves by itself.'[35] This quotation recurs in the same form in Maurus.[36] Although not completely literal, it is closer to the Graeco-Latin version that has been preserved than that adduced in an anonymous treatise on the elements: 'Nature is the natural movement of an element by itself.'[37] After referring to the *Categories*[38] to enumerate the six species of movement (generation, corruption,

---

32 It should be noted, however, that Galen's *Peri Craseôn* was translated in the mid twelfth century by Burgundio of Pisa, who, it seems, had some links with Salerno (cf. above, p. 410): see *Burgundio of Pisa's Translation of Galen's 'Peri Craseôn', 'De complexionibus'*, ed. R. J. Durling (Berlin–New York 1976) [*Ars Medica* II, *Galenus Latinus* I].

33 The commonest incipit is *Rectus ordo doctrine*. The Winchester MS, dating from the end of the twelfth and the beginning of the thirteenth century, attributes the commentary on the *Ysagoge* to Petrus Musandinus alone, whereas the incipit of the commentary on Galen's *Tegni* states precisely: 'Incipiunt Glosule Tengni quas ad locutionem Bartholomei theorici in artem Practiche magister Petrus Musandinus composuit.' Most of the other MSS attribute the commentary on the *Ysagoge* to Bartholomew. Cf. Kristeller 1976, pp. 60–1, 77–9.

34 MS Winchester (Winchester College, The Warden and Fellows' Library) 24, fols. 22v–52.

35 'Natura est principium motus et quietis rei per se mobilis': fol. 22v. In the Graeco-Latin version in the MS Avranches 221, we read: 'est natura principium alicuius et causa movendi et quiescendi in quo est primum per se et non per accidens'. Cf. Aristotle, *Physics* II 1, 192B.

36 Commentary on the *Ysagoge*, MS Paris, Bibl. nat. lat. 18499, fol. 3v.

37 'Phisis est naturalis motus alicuius elementi ex se'; cf. R. C. Dales, '*Anonymi De elementis*: from a Twelfth-Century Collection of Scientific Works in British Museum MS Cotton Galba E.IV', *Isis* LVI (1965) 181.

38 It should be recalled that the *Categories* had been translated by Boethius.

augmentation, diminution, alteration, change of place), the commentator dwells on the causes of movement. He sets out the twofold principle of movement, its efficient cause and its material cause, the necessary existence of a mover and of that which is moved. He refers to the subdivision of the efficient cause into two kinds, the intrinsic and the extrinsic principles, the latter being either with or without movement. The extrinsic principle without movement is unique: it is the prime mover, itself unmoving, as defined by Aristotle, the first cause, God, 'principle and cause of all movements'. The extrinsic principle with movement refers to the heavenly bodies, whose action is exerted over the sublunary world. These notions are fairly elementary and their formulation cannot be identified with any precise source; it seems, however, that the author was directly acquainted with the eighth book of the *Physics*, not only when he speaks of the unmoving prime mover, but when he declares that every mover, if it is not self-moved, needs an intermediary that moves of itself. The second explicit reference to the *Physics* – after that which provides the definition of nature – again concerns the principle of movement: 'Aristotle says it is twofold, form and matter, but chiefly form.' The author here seems to be referring to the discussion contained in the second book of the *Physics* on the problem of whether nature is matter or form.

More extensive use is made of the *De generatione et corruptione*, which is more directly devoted to the sublunary world. The treatise is first quoted in connection with the action of superior bodies: 'the sun as it draws nearer engenders, as it moves further away corrupts'.[39] But it is obviously on the problem of the elements and their combination that the *De generatione et corruptione* is introduced at greater length. The impossibility for one element to be the principle of another is reaffirmed; Aristotle is referred to, in a truncated version which somewhat alters the meaning of the sentence:

(Winchester commentary:) Aristotle concludes briefly by saying that those who have admitted only two elements posit that the other two are created by rarefication and condensation. For instance, air, when rarefied becomes fire, when condensed becomes water. Aristotle refutes these assertions in the *De generatione et corruptione*. Indeed he declares and proves that no element can be the principle of another.[40]

(Aristotle, 330B:) Among those who admit simple bodies as elements some admit one element, others two, others three, others again four elements. Those who admit a

---

39 'Sol adveniendo generat, recedendo corrumpit' (MS Winchester 24, fol. 23r); almost the same citation is found in Urso: 'A sole vero fit mutatio, corporaque adveniendo generat, recedendo corrumpit' (*Glos. Aph.* 32, ed. Creutz, p. 64).

The Graeco-Latin version: 'Videmus enim quoniam adveniente quidem sole generatio est, recedente autem diminutio' (MS Avranches 232, fol. 58r).

40 Fol. 25v.

single element, unless they assume that the others arise from the condensation and rarefication of this element, admit basically two principles, which are the agents, whereas the single element is merely acted upon by them insofar as it is matter . . . (332A) There is no one [element] from which the others might be derived.[41]

The Salernitan commentator, by confusing elements and principles, has presumably not fully grasped what is at stake in the problem. He may simply have misunderstood the complex sentence offered by the Latin translator, and retained only the end of it: *qui igitur unum dicunt solum, deinde densitate et raritate alia generant, his contingit duo facere principia* . . .[42]

The common opinion is that there are four elements, but the author points out that for Aristotle there is a fifth, situated above the moon's sphere. He thus mentions the *quinta essentia*, which had already been referred to by the Chartrian writers.[43] The account of the transformation of elements by the play of qualities entails a direct, even if apparently superficial, reference to the *De generatione et corruptione*. The author retains such notions as the need for contact in order for bodies to act or be acted upon reciprocally, and the limits and place proper to each: 'Aristotle asserts that a true form of elements can only remain, and a species can only be found, within such limits.'[44] This phrase is in fact drawn from the *De generatione et corruptione*: 'Now each element is naturally borne to its own place and the shape and form of all of them reside in their limits'.[45] The same idea is more briefly phrased by Maurus and Urso: 'the true species of elements are found within their limits alone'.[46] The commentary differs according to authors. Bartholomew connects this phrase with another taken from the *De generatione et corruptione*: 'The extreme and purest bodies are fire and earth; the intermediate bodies, which are more mixed, are water and air.'[47] He then glosses: 'in fact the intermediate elements like air and water are infected by the extreme ones'.

41 *De generatione et corruptione* II 3 and II 5.
42 MS Avranches 232, fol. 42r.
43 MS Winchester 24, fol. 25v: 'Communis autem sentientia est et fere ab omnibus probata quatuor esse tantum elementa; Aristoteles tamen preter hoc quintam essentiam esse constituit cuius secundum locum est a lunari globo superius.' Compare William of Conches in the *Dragmaticon*: 'Aristoteles praeter quatuor elementa unam quintam voluit esse essentiam; quatuor vere elementa a Luna esse deorsum, quintam essentiam ab eadem sursum. Omnia quae sunt infra Lunam vel esse elementa vel eis constare: omnia quae supra Lunam sunt esse quintam essentiam vel ex ea constare'; cf. T. Gregory, *Anima mundi, La filosofia di Guglielmo di Conches e la Scuola di Chartres* (Florence 1955), p. 233.
44 MS Winchester 24, fol. 25v.
45 *De generatione et corruptione* II 8, 335A.
46 Maurus, Commentary on the *Ysagoge*, MS Paris Bibl. nat. lat. 18499, fol. 6r; Urso, *De commixtionibus elementorum*, ed. Stürner, p. 47 (for this citation, the editor refers to the *De caelo*, whereas there is no doubt that the *De generatione et corruptione* is in question).
47 *De generatione et corruptione* II 3, 330B.

Maurus lays greater stress on the notion of the localization in space of simple bodies: 'we call limits the poles of the world in which the elements are contained and where each is what it is of itself, without undergoing contagion from any other'.

One peculiarity of vocabulary has its importance in the history of medicine. To indicate the change undergone by one element in contact with another, Bartholomew uses the verb *inficere*, the primary meaning of which is 'to impregnate'. We have translated this as 'infect' because Maurus, repeating the same idea, chooses the word *contagio*. We see that the notion of contagion, not recognized scientifically when it refers to a disease being passed from one person to another, is applied only to bodies, such as the elements, capable of exchanging qualities by contact. Urso, for his part, adds this quotation to the theory of the 'elemented body (*elementatum*)': 'Indeed, as a body is enclosed within a double limit, namely the end and the beginning, the same elements are found at the end in the corruption of an *elementatum* and at the beginning in the composition of another engendered *elementatum*.'

The paragraph that the *Ysagoge* devotes to temperaments, which it calls *commixtiones*, in the Latin version, leads Bartholomew to define mixture, following Aristotle: '*Commixtio* is the union of miscibles, joined by the smallest parts (*minima*).'[48] The miscibles must first touch, then be united as a whole. This quotation, which is also found in Maurus,[49] is not literal and conveys the meaning inadequately. The commentator does not seem to have quite understood the difference between a compound and a mixture; it looks as if in this case, here again, he is paraphrasing an awkwardly chosen fragment of a sentence. To recall Aristotle's words (328A):

We shall say, on the contrary, that in order for there to be a mixture, it is necessary for the parts of that body obtained by mixing to have the same properties as the whole, and that just as any part of water is water, any part of the mixture must be that mixture. But if the so-called mixture is actually a compound through juxtaposition of small particles, none of these phenomena will occur.[50]

The *minima* are not determinant in Aristotle's definition of mixture; they appear however a few lines further on, when it is said that bodies which are delimited and divisible into small particles are more easily miscible. The author of the commentary is more interested in the respective roles played by

48 MS Winchester 24, fol. 26r: 'Commixtio miscibilium per minima sibi iunctorum unio'. The Graeco-Latin translation: 'Mixtio autem miscibilium alteratorum unio' (MS Avranches 232, fol. 37v).
49 'Conmixtio est miscibilium per minima coniunctorum unio' (MS Paris, Bibl. nat. lat. 18499, fol. 8v).
50 *De generatione et corruptione* I 10.

the primary qualities. He states that for philosophers the most important qualities are those 'according to which elements operate in the constitution of the world, such as lightness and heaviness'. Physicians, on the other hand, are more concerned with qualities 'according to which elements operate in composite bodies', namely heat, cold, moistness, and dryness. The author then gives the definition of those qualities in a quotation, this time almost wholly accurate, from the *De generatione et corruptione*: 'Heat is that which unites homogeneous bodies . . . Cold that which unites dissimilar bodies . . . Moistness is indeterminate, having no proper limit, but being easily delimitable . . . Dryness is determined by its own limit, but not easily delimitable . . .' His quotation corresponds to the Graeco-Latin version, as it is preserved for instance in a manuscript at Avranches.[51]

Bartholomew, then, must undoubtedly have himself consulted a version of the *De generatione et corruptione*, which he quotes on several occasions. He furthermore retains from this reading the importance of the sense of touch in the determination of qualities, and also the distinction between a circular or reciprocal generation, affecting the elements, and a linear or non-reciprocal generation, which is that of 'animals, plants, and trees'.[52] With regard to the humours, he repeats this distinction and notes, 'The generation of humours is in a straight line and not recriprocal, whereas that of the elements is reciprocal; that is why Aristotle calls it circular.'[53] This reading of the *De generatione et corruptione* seems to correspond to a first stage in which only the most fundamental definitions are retained, without the link with the whole of the system being always apparent, or at any rate perceptible through the commentary at our disposal.

As we have pointed out incidentally, Maurus' commentary on the *Ysagoge* includes certain quotations already found in the Winchester manuscript. We cannot recognize any new textual borrowings. It is possible, however, that Maurus himself may have been directly acquainted with the *De generatione et corruptione*, certain formulae from which seem to emerge, mingled with the commentary itself. He repeats the assertion from the *Pantegni* that the four

51 MS Winchester 24: 'Calidum est quod congregat omogenea . . . Frigidum enim quod congregat dissimilia . . . Humidum est indeterminatum proprio termino, bene terminabile . . . Siccum est determinatum proprio termino male terminabile ens' (fol. 25v). The Graeco-Latin translation: 'Calidum enim est quod congregat homogenea . . . Frigidum autem quod coniungens et congregans similiter et singenea et non homofyla. Humidum autem indeterminatum proprio termino, bene terminabile ens. Siccum autem bene terminabile proprio termino, male autem terminabile' (MS Avranches 232, fol. 40r). Cf. Aristotle, *De gen. et corr.* II 2, 329B.
52 Fol. 27r.
53 Fol. 29r.

elements are simple according to the senses and composite according to the intellect, and he analyses the process of alteration by contact: earth and air invariably contain some particles of water, air invariably contains a particle of fire. This leads him to assert that each element intrinsically contains a single quality: fire – heat, air – cold, water – moistness, earth – dryness.[54] This formulation seems closer to the *De generatione et corruptione* than to the *Pantegni*, although this cannot be definitely asserted. Maurus does not devote much time to the question of *commixtio*; he takes this notion for granted. After giving the same definition as the Winchester manuscript, he specifies that mixture occurs not through any casual conjunction of elements, but when the bodies commingled undergo alteration in form and in substance.[55]

With the last of the great Salernitan authors, Urso of Calabria, a wholly different tonality appears. Whereas for Maurus philosophical considerations are most frequently only digressions, Urso constructs a coherent system: the study of matter, of the alteration and mixture of primary qualities, enables him to give a detailed explanation of biological phenomena and of the processes of action of substances ingested.[56] Since the Middle Ages, Urso has been nicknamed 'the philosopher'.[57] It is true that his philosophical knowledge was greater than that of other Salernitan scholars, but his point of view was always that of the medical man; in his *De effectibus qualitatum* and *De commixtionibus* as well as in his *Glosule super Aphorismis* the functioning of the human body is at the centre of his arguments. The medical doctrine set forth in the *Ysagoge*, which devotes a considerable space to the pores,[58] to the relaxation and contraction of the channels of penetration, associated with the pneumatic theory amply dealt with in the *Pantegni*, enables Urso to

---

54 Commentary on the *Ysagoge*, Paris Bibl. nat. lat. 18499, fol. 7v; cf. Aristotle, *De gen. et corr.* II 4, 331A.

55 *Ibid.* fol. 8v.

56 Four of Urso's works are directly concerned with the problem of the mixing of elements or the interaction of qualities: *De commixtionibus elementorum* (ed. Stürner 1976); *De effectibus qualitatum* and *De effectibus medicinarum* (ed. C. Matthaes, *Der Salernitaner Arzt Urso* (Leipzig 1918, Diss.), pp. 16–17); *De qualitatum effectibus accidentalibus* (ed. Sudhoff 1920, pp. 139–43). The problem is again treated extensively in the *Aphorismi cum Glosulis* (ed. R. Creutz, 'Die medizinisch- naturphilosophischen Aphorismen und Kommentare des Magister Urso Salernitanus', *Quellen und Studien zur Geschichte der Naturwissenschaften und der Medizin* v.1 (1936).)

57 R. Creutz, 'Urso, der Letzte des Hochsalerno, Arzt, Philosoph, Theologe', *Abhandlungen zur Geschichte der Medizin und der Naturwissenschaften* v (1934) 3–15.

58 It should be remembered that for Galen, for instance, *poroi* are both the pores of the skin and other channels through which the spirits or *pneumata* can pass. In stressing the importance of the 'pores' the *Ysagoge* was reviving one factor in the teaching of the 'methodist' school. Maurus, in the *Regulae urinarum*, distinguishes between the *pori manifesti* through which superfluous matter is evacuated and the *pori occulti* which give vent to sweat, hairs, and the 'different respirations of the body'; cf. Saffron 1972, p. 95, n. 55.

introduce certain elementary principles of Aristotelian physics at every level of the vital processes. The actual name of Aristotle is, however, seldom quoted by this last of the Salernitan authors. He was doubtless familiar with the contents of the *De generatione et corruptione* when setting forth the processes of the transformation of qualities by the play of opposites, and the principles of circular or linear generation. When he quotes Aristotle specifically it is usually, as with his predecessors, a case of truncated sentences or marginal problems. Thus in one of his glosses on the *Aphorisms* we find a curious reference to Aristotle: 'So Aristotle says that one handful of water gives nine of air (*Unde Aristoteles ex uno pugillo aquae fiunt novem aeris*)'.[59] This quotation may be compared with a proposition from the *De generatione et corruptione*: 'Now if it is quantitatively that the elements are equal, there must be something common to all the elements being compared with one another by which they can be measured. If for example one *cotyle* of water could produce ten *cotyles* of air, these two elements would be, in some sort, the same thing, since they are measured by the same measure.'[60] This sentence appears in Aristotle's criticism of Empedocles' system, in which it is shown that if one admits a plurality of elements, while denying their power of mutual transformation, it is hard to maintain that they can be compared to one another. In Urso's argument, the few words extracted from this context serve to demonstrate that 'a thing engendered by dissolution becomes more subtle than its matter; being rarer, it is more subtle and changeable, hence more apt to undergo the action of the agent, except where the violence of the quality makes up for the lack of substance'. This explanation is probably inspired by a passage from the fourth book of the *Physics*, in which, regarding the non-existence of the vacuum, Aristotle repeats the example of air produced from water:

... in fact, when air is engendered from water, the matter which undergoes generation is the same, without any extrinsic addition, but merely becoming actually what it was potentially. And similarly when, inversely, water is engendered from air; in the one case generation goes from the smaller to the greater, in the other from the greater to the smaller.[61]

Urso retains from the *De generatione et corruptione* only what is useful for his argument. The criticism of Empedocles' system and the question of the vacuum are not mentioned: the aim is solely to demonstrate that relaxing

59 *Glosula* 8, ed. Creutz, p. 31.
60 Aristotle, *De generatione et corruptione* II 6, 333A. The Graeco-Latin version in the MS Avranches 232 (fol. 39r) includes the proposition corresponding to that cited by Urso: 'Si ex aque pugillo erunt pugilli aeris decem'. The numerical error is clearly not significant.
61 Aristotle, *Physics* IV, 9, 217A.

agents weaken the substance by increasing its quantity, whereas contracting agents, applied in moderation, do the contrary. From the same passage, devoted to the vacuum and to the statement of the unity of matter, Urso derives another quotation which he places in the *De commixtionibus elemento- rum: Unde Aristoteles: yle potestate est omne id, quod ex ea est,*[62] which corresponds to "it is matter which, being potentially this or that, becomes this or that".

The significance of Aristotle in Salernitan works

Apart from the *Physics* and the *De generatione et corruptione*, the only texts explicitly cited in the Salernitan works which we have examined for the present study deal with logic: the *Categories*, the *Topics*, the *Ysagoge* of Porphyry, and the *De interpretatione*. Extensive use was made of the older versions of Boethius, for instance by Maurus.[63] Again, the tradition of the pseudo-Aristotelian *Problemata* played a key role, as Brian Lawn has shown.[64] Other newly translated works have been traced: the influence of the fourth book of the *Meteorologica* on Urso has been noted.[65] In the commentaries on the *Ysagoge* and on Galen's *Tegni* by Bartholomew and Petrus Musandinus, we find some echoes of the *Metaphysics*[66] and, in particular, actual quotations from the *Nicomachean Ethics*, ascribed to Aris- totle without specific mention of the work's title. They are introduced in a discussion of the role of habit in the acquirement of virtues:[67] actions beget virtue as well as vice. Just as by playing the cithern one can become either a good or a bad performer on the cithern, and by building either a good or a

---

62 Ed. Stürner, p. 42; cf. Aristotle, *ibid.*
63 Commentary on the *Ysagoge*, Paris Bibl. nat. lat. 18499, and Saffron 1972, p. 92, n. 9.
64 The form of the so-called Salernitan Questions is in part derived from the tradition of these *Problemata*. An early version of this pseudo-Aristotelian work, known as 'vetustissima translatio' (ed. V. Rose, *Aristoteles Pseudepigraphus* (Leipzig 1863), pp. 666–76) was in fact in circulation before its complete translation by Bartholomew of Messina. The Salernitan authors appear to have known a more complete version of the 'vetustissima translatio' than that edited by V. Rose. Cf. Lawn 1963, p. 25, and 1979, p. xxiii.
65 Cf. Matthaes 1918.
66 Paul Oskar Kristeller sees an influence of Aristotle's *Metaphysics* (XI, 7, 1064B) in Bar- tholomew's subdivisions of natural science: metaphysics or theology, mathematics, physics (Commentary on the *Ysagoge*, MS Winchester 24, fol. 22v, and Kristeller 1958, p. 3). An echo of the opening of *Metaphysics* I (1, 981A) may perhaps also be found in this commentary: 'Nam sicut Aristoteles ait ex multis experimentis una regula et ex multis regulis ars una perficiatur' (MS Winchester 24, fol. 25v). Cf. 'Metaphysica vetustissima': 'Fit autem ars, cum ex multis experimento intellectis universaliter una fit de similibus opinio' (ed. G. Vuillemin-Diem *Aristoteles Latinus* XXV. 1–1A (Brussels 1970) 5).
67 Commentary on the *Tegni*, MS Winchester 24, fols. 108v–144v. Cf. *Eth. Nic.* II 1, 1103A–1103B.

bad builder, so 'the habitual conditions of a character are the result of activities that are of the same nature'. The comparison with health and sickness also comes from the *Nicomachean Ethics*: the corruption of health is due to excessive or inadequate nourishment, just as the corruption of courage is due to an excess of fear, which makes one timorous, or to a lack of it, which makes one audacious. Moderation saves both the body and the soul. If we set the text of Bartholomew–Petrus Musandinus beside the Graeco-Latin version, known as 'Ethica vetus', the results are conclusive enough:[68] there can be no doubt that this translation was known to the authors of this commentary on Galen's *Tegni*.

Hitherto the writings of Aristotle that we have mentioned are all known to have been translated, at least partially, from Greek into Latin. It remains to be asked whether the Scholars of Salerno may have made use of others not included in this category. Certain similarities in formulation suggest that Urso may have known the second book of the *Meterologica*, which was translated only from the Arabic by Gerard of Cremona.[69] As we have said, the action of the breath of life is an essential feature in Urso's medical theory. His commentary on the 6th Aphorism[70] seeks to show that 'an animal's life

---

68 (MS Winchester 24):

> 'Anime quidem virtus ex eisdem secundum Aristotelem servatur et corrumpitur, ex operationis enim mediocritate non solum fit virtus sed etiam servatur et augetur, ex earum autem indigentia et superfluitate corrumpitur. Verbi gratia: quicumque audet terribilia quelibet et nihil timet et timenda et non timenda in audendo superhabundat, in timendo deficit. Similiter qui omnia timet et timenda et non timenda in timendo superhabundat, in audendo deficit ... Secundum Aristotelem ex similibus operationibus similes habitus fiunt, scilicet virtutes et vitia. Operationes enim domine et magistre sunt habituum, sicut enim in artibus apparet, quoniam fabricantes bene vel male boni vel mali fabri fiunt, cittarrantes cithariste, sic in virtutibus apparet et vitiis ... Sic eadem ratione que circa animam attenditur virtus corporis et eius sanitas ex superfluitate eorumdem et indigentia corrumpitur ex quorum mediocritate salvatur.'
>
> ('Ethica vetus') 'Quemadmodum et in artibus aliis. Que enim oportet discentes facere, hec facientes discimus. Verbi gracia. Fabricantes, fabri fiunt; et citharizantes, cithariste ... Adhuc ex eisdem ipsis et per eadem ipsa, et fit omnis virtus et corrumpitur. Similiter et ars. Ex citharizare autem, boni et mali fiunt cithariste; proportionaliter autem, et fabri; et reliqui omnes. Ex bene enim fabricare, boni fabri fiunt; ex male autem, mali ... Et uno utique sermone, ex similibus actibus, habitus fiunt ... Necesse est scrutari que circa operationes, quomodo faciendum eas; hee enim dominent quales fiant habitudines, quemadmodum diximus ... Quemadmodum in virtute et sanitate videmus. Superflua enim ginnasia et indigencia, corrumpunt virtutem. Similiter utique potus et cibus amplius vel minus fiens, corrumpit sanitatem. Commensuratus autem, et facit et auget et salvat ... Qui enim omnia fugit et timet et nichil sustinet, timidus fit; qui autem nichil omnino timet, set ad omnia vadit, audax.'
>
> (Ed. R. A. Gauthier, *Aristoteles Latinus* XXVI.2 6–7)

69 Gerard of Cremona translated the first three books of the *Meterologica* and stopped at the beginning of the fourth, when he realized that for this book Henricus Aristippus' version was already in existence: cf. d'Alverny in *Harvard 1982*, p. 454.

70 Ed. Creutz, pp. 27–9.

comes from the aerial substance enclosed within it', and that 'when this is compressed within the pores, without free exhalation, it overheats'. This question leads to a comparison with earthquakes, tremors that arise when 'the substance enclosed in the earth's cavities is violently shaken by the wind which has made its way into them'. Aristotle's explanation of earthquakes was repeated by many writers, including Seneca in the *Quaestiones naturales*,[71] which may have been Urso's source; however, the formulation, the adjacent reference to the formation of thunder and the insistence with which Urso develops the notion of some impediment to free exhalation through the pores, gives plausibility to the hypothesis of a direct acquaintance with Aristotle's treatise, which also includes the comparison with the internal motions of the human body.[72]

The question of a possible familiarity with the *De caelo* has been put by the editor of Urso's *De commixtionibus elementorum*.[73] As we have pointed out, one of the passages mentioned in fact relates to the *De generatione et corruptione*. Two other cases may be more plausibly connected with the *De caelo*. One is concerned with the definition of movement in space, rectilinear or circular, and the distinction between simple and composite, centrifugal and centripetal movements.[74] Urso does not claim to be quoting here, and the idea is not sufficiently developed to be directly connected with Aristotle's authentic treatise. We should note, moreover, that the same definitions are to be found in the Arabic–Latin paraphrase *De caelo et mundo*, which was in circulation in the twelfth century under the name of Avicenna.[75] Another coincidence, in a passage of the *De commixtionibus elementorum* devoted to the movements of elemental bodies, cannot be associated with this Arabic–Latin paraphrase. Urso's formula, 'It is manifest from this that each element has by nature a force of attraction either from the centre or towards the centre', is very close to Aristotle's phrase, 'Hence it is clear that among these elements

71 Seneca, *Quaest. nat.* VI 3 1.
72 *Meteorologica* II 8M, 366A–367B.
73 Stürner 1976, pp. 31–2.
74 *Ibid.* p. 126: 'Motus localis communis a virtute locativa innatus duplex est. Alius enim est circularis, alius rectus. Circularis vel rectus alius perficitur in contento, alius in continente. Circularis perfectus in contento alius est simplex, alius compositus. Simplex alius de centro, alius ad centrum, compositus de centro et ad centrum.' Cf. *De caelo* I 2, 268B.
75 *De caelo et mundo* I 2: 'Sequitur ergo ex hoc necessario, ut omne quod est corpus habeat motum naturalem. Sed motuum alii sunt simplices, alii compositi; motus autem simplices sunt duo, circularis et rectus et motus compositus est ex duobus motibus ... Invenimus etenim ex quibus naturalem sibi quemdam motum consequitur motum omnis corporis quod est in mundo, aut ad suum medium aut circa suum medium' (ed. Venice 1508, fol. 37r). The *De caelo et mundo* which circulated with Avicenna's *Physics* is in reality a compilation of extracts from a commentary by Themistius: cf. M.-T. d'Alverny, 'La tradition manuscrite de l'Avicenne latin', in *Mélanges en l'honneur de Taha Husein* (Cairo 1962), p. 68.

there is one which naturally moves away from the centre and another which moves towards it'.[76] The presence in Salernitan writings of certain key ideas of the *De caelo*, and the similarity between occasional formulae, do not constitute sufficient proof that this work was in fact consulted; we must note however that there is no chronological incompatibility.

In fact, the versions of the *De caelo* and the *Meteorologica* by Gerard of Cremona were the first to circulate and the most widely read of the translations of Aristotle produced in Toledo. We find them transcribed in the same manuscripts as the Graeco-Latin versions of the *Physics*, the *De generatione et corruptione*, the *De anima* and the *Parva naturalia*. This collection, generally known as the 'corpus vetustius', is often accompanied by the Arabic–Latin translation of Costa ben Luca's *De differentia spiritus et anime*.[77] Now the commentary on the *Ysagoge* in the Winchester manuscript refers explicitly to this text: 'Certain philosophers, such as Democritus, consider that the *pneuma* is the soul, but others, displaying greater subtlety of mind, have said that it is not the soul, but the instrument through which the soul acts on the body; the difference between *pneuma* and soul is perfectly demonstrated in the book *Stabili vita constabilicione*.'[78]

The commentaries attributed to Bartholomew and to Petrus Musandinus provide indubitable evidence that Latin versions of an Aristotelian corpus were consulted. The *De generatione et corruptione* and the *Nicomachean Ethics*, in Latin versions that have been attributed to the same translator,[79] are the works we find quoted with the greatest literal accuracy. Maurus and Urso are less faithful in their rendering of Aristotle's texts; we find in their works sometimes the same quotations as in the Winchester Manuscript, sometimes mere echoes rather than actual borrowings. Must we therefore question the priority of the commentaries attributed to Bartholomew and Petrus Musandinus? This does not seem necessary; these commentaries, on the contrary, may be seen as bearing witness to the arrival in Salerno of an Aristotelian

76 Urso, *De commixtionibus elementorum*: 'Ex his manifestum est, quod quodlibet elementum habet vim attractionis naturaliter seu de centro vel ad centrum' (ed. Stürner, p. 54). Aristotle, *De caelo* I 8, 276A, in Gerard of Cremona's translation: 'Tunc manifestum est et patens quod eorum alia sunt que vadunt ad medium et alia que vadunt ex medio' (MS Paris, Bibl. nat. lat. 16082, fol. 247r). The possibility that a Graeco-Latin version of the *De caelo* existed in the twelfth century was raised by C. Haskins, *Studies in the History of Mediaeval Science* (2nd ed., Cambridge, Mass. 1927), p. 149; this hypothesis was discarded by S. D. Wingate, *The Mediaeval Latin Versions of the Aristotelian Scientific Corpus, with Special Reference to the Biological Works* (London 1931), p. 39.

77 The *De differentia spiritus et anime* seems to have been translated twice – by John of Seville and by an anonymous translator: cf. *Aristoteles Latinus: Pars Prior*, pp. 15–16.

78 MS Winchester 24, fol. 33v. It should be noted that the name of the medical writer Costa ben Luca was frequently distorted in the twelfth century.

79 Cf. L. Minio-Paluello 1952, p. 279, n. 28.

corpus, whereas later commentaries depend on notes or recollections. The current state of research does not allow us to go beyond such suppositions.

Borrowings from Aristotle by Maurus and Urso are confined to specific sectors, and they appear mixed up with discussions often very remote from the thought of Aristotle. The long digression on primordial matter with which Maurus opens his commentary on the *Ysagoge* is based essentially on Plato's *Timaeus* as commented on by Calcidius.[80] On the other hand, the development of the theme of the *elementatum* (the element in the world, as opposed to the pure element), which is chiefly found in the writings of Urso, must be compared with writings of the school of Chartres.[81] The theory of the elements[82] amply elaborated by the scholars of Salerno has still to be studied in detail; unquestionably, it cannot be seen as Aristotelian, even if the works of the Philosopher are referred to on specific points, sometimes in commonplace or quite insignificant observations. There remains a certain ambiguity in the Salernitan teaching: according to different authors, or depending on the context, the elements are envisaged either as immaterial principles or as actual physical constituents of the universe.

The few somewhat disparate examples we have offered doubtless provide sufficient evidence of the appearance in Salerno of hitherto unfamiliar works of Aristotle. In contrast to the case of David of Dinant,[83] there is no immediate proof of recourse to the Greek, and an acquaintance with Latin versions seems more probable. If this incursion of Aristotle plays its part in the history of Aristotelian thought in the Middle Ages, how important is it in the framework of Salernitan thought? True, the teachers in the famous school directed medicine decisively towards philosophy, but their recourse to Aristotle appears more as a consequence of this trend than as a determinant impulse. The assimilation of the corpus of Constantine's translations forms the real basis of Salernitan thought, as expressed in the works of Bartholomew, Petrus Musandinus, Maurus, and even Urso. The *Ysagoge* and the *Pantegni* provide the intellectual framework to these writings, which also

---

80 MS Paris Bibl. nat. lat. 18499, fols. 4r–6r.
81 Ed. Stürner, p. 28. The problems concerning *elementatum* falls outside this chapter; they are outlined in P. Dronke, 'New Approaches to the School of Chartres', *Anuario de Estudios Medievales* VI (1969) 128–31.
82 We have left aside the *Liber Marii de elementis*, since it seems it can no longer be ascribed to the school of Salerno (Marius, *On the Elements*, ed. and trans. R. C. Dales (Berkeley–Los Angeles–London 1976)): Petrus Alfonsi's name has been put forward (J. H. L. Reuter-Beaumont, *Petrus Alfonsi: an Examination of his Works, their Scientific Content and their Background* (Oxford 1975), D. Phil. Diss).
83 The *Quaternuli* refer notably to the *De animalibus*, translated directly from the Greek: cf. M. Kurdziałek, *Davidis de Dinanto quaternulorum fragmenta*, Studia Mediewistyczne III (Warsaw 1963), p. lx.

show a close acquaintance with other translations, such as the *Viaticum*, the *De gradibus*, and the treatises of Isaac Israeli. Karl Sudhoff was right to stress the omnipresence of Constantine of Africa,[84] and there are no grounds for questioning his verdict. The reticence of the Salernitan scholars with regard to their use of Arabic texts has more to do with legend (or their vanity) than with actual fact.[85] Yet we can distinguish no break in continuity between the utilization of works already in circulation in the early Middle Ages and these new translations. The Salernitan scholars exploited the content of both conjointly. Similarly, references to the 'new Aristotle' may serve to explain Platonic or Neoplatonic texts. This is what makes it so hard and so risky to seek for sources in these works, which were produced in an environment open to numerous and multiform influences. The pioneer article of Alexander Birkenmajer emphasized the contribution of Graeco-Latin translations, about which there can be no question. Perhaps future research should look again at a hypothesis which the Polish scholar had discarded, and attempt to trace in greater depth the importance of the infiltration of translations from the Arabic, other than those by Constantine of Africa.

84 K. Sudhoff, 'Konstantin der Afrikaner und die Medizinschule von Salerno', *Sudhoffs Archiv* XXIII (1930) 293–8; and 'Constantin, der erste Vermittler muslimischer Wissenschaft ins Abendland und die beiden Salernitaner Frühscholastiker Maurus und Urso, als Exponenten dieser Vermittlung' *Archeion* XIV (1932) 359–69.
85 This reticence has been emphasized by H. Schipperges, *Die Assimilation der arabischen Medizin durch das lateinische Mittelalter* (Wiesbaden 1965) [Sudhoffs Archiv, Beiheft III].

16

DAVID OF DINANT AND THE BEGINNINGS OF ARISTOTELIANISM IN PARIS*[1]

†ENZO MACCAGNOLO

The Parisian Synod of 1210, presided over by Peter of Corbeil, the Archbishop of Sens, and by Peter of Nemours, the Bishop of Paris, with the participation of the bishops of the ecclesiastical province, was concerned with three different problems: the Amalrician heresy, the appearance in Paris of Aristotelian texts translated by David of Dinant, and, finally, the order that the 'theological books' written in the vernacular (in Romano) should be handed in to the bishops of the individual dioceses.[2] Of these three matters, the most serious was that of the persistence and wider expansion of the Amalrician movement after the death of Amalric of Bène in 1206. The Synod ordered that Amalric's body should be removed from the graveyard and cast on unhallowed ground.[3] As for the presence in Paris of Aristotelian texts, the Synod decreed thus:

David of Dinant's notebooks (Quaternuli) are to be handed in before Christmas to the Bishop of Paris and burnt; and no lectures are to be held in Paris either publicly or privately using Aristotle's books on natural philosophy or the commentaries,[4] and

---

* Translated by Jonathan Hunt.
1 [All citations of David's writings below are fom M. Kurdziałek's edition, Davidis de Dinanto Quaternulorum Fragmenta, Studia Mediewistyczne III (Warsaw 1963). The editor gives an extensive bibliography of the older literature on pp. lvii–lix. Since then, Kurdziałek has made further important contributions to the study of David's thought, especially 'David von Dinant als Ausleger der Aristotelischen Naturphilosophie', Miscellanea Mediaevalia x (1976) 181–92, and 'L'idée de l'homme chez David de Dinant', in Images of Man in Ancient and Medieval Thought: Studia Gerardo Verbeke ... dicata (Louvain 1976), pp. 311–22. For the historical context of David's speculations, see M.-T. d'Alverny, 'Les nouveaux apports dans les domaines de la science et de la pensée au temps de Philippe Auguste: La philosophie', in La France de Philippe Auguste: Le temps des mutations, Colloques internationaux du CNRS, DCII (Paris 1982), pp. 863–80.]
2 [Romanus was used substantivally to refer to Romance vernaculars: see A. Blaise, Lexicon Latinitatis Medii Aevi, s.v.]
3 Cf. Chartularium Universitatis Parisiensis I, ed. H. Denifle and A. Chatelain (Paris 1889) 70, no. 11.
4 I.e., the commentaries of Averroes. [Thus Maccagnolo, following Chartularium I, ad loc. But there are chronological difficulties about this hypothesis: see R. de Vaux, 'La première entrée d'Averroës chez les Latins', RSPT XXII (1933) 193–243. According to de Vaux (p. 237), the first sure traces of Averroes in Paris are found in William of Auvergne's De universo and De anima (1231–6) and in Philip the Chancellor's Summa de bono (today thought to be 1225–8). The commenta condemned in the decree are works of other Arabic philosophers who were considered as commentators on Aristotle – al-Kindī, al-Fārābī, Avicenna and Algazel – some

we forbid all this under pain of excommunication. If, from the birthday of our Lord onwards, anyone is found to be in possession of Master David's *Quaternuli*, he shall thereafter be considered a heretic.[5]

The text of the synodal decree does not express any judgement about David's person; in fact it does not talk about David, but rather about his *Quaternuli*, the Aristotelian books of 'natural philosophy', and the commentaries. It may be, however, that since David did not belong to the Parisian ecclesiastical province he could not be judged by a Parisian tribunal; the synodal Fathers, if I am not mistaken, were chiefly concerned that Aristotle's naturalistic writings should not be further disseminated, even though they were already circulating in Paris and the province.[6] The anonymous chronicler from Laon, after briefly discussing Amalric, writes:

> Master David, another heretic of Dinaunt (*sic*) and the inventor of this novelty, was often in the company of Pope Innocent, because the Pope dedicated himself passionately to subtle questions. For David himself was more subtle than was fitting; from his *quaterni*, as it is believed, Master Amalric and the other heretics of that time absorbed David's error.[7]

This passage suggests that David, whom we know to have studied in Greece, had before 1210 returned to the West and been welcomed by Innocent III (1198–1216). The author's scant knowledge leads him to conclusions which are chronologically inaccurate and in some respects unwarranted. He seems not to have a very high regard for Pope Innocent, since he states that Innocent kept among his entourage a man who was a 'heretic'; but, though the chronicler knows of the existence of the *quaterni*, he seems unable to give any details about them. Yet what is most astonishing is the chronological and historical distortion: the notion that from David's *quaterni* Amalric and his contemporaries absorbed David's error.

of whose writings, translated in Toledo in the second half of the twelfth century, had made their way to France, Italy, England, and even Austria before the coming of the Latin Averroes (cf. d'Alverny 1982, p. 867). It is noteworthy that the Englishman John Blund, whose *De anima*, inspired by his Aristotelian studies in Paris, was composed at the beginning of the thirteenth century, refers to Algazel as *commentator* (cf. d'Alverny 1982, p. 879).]

5 *Chartularium* I, *ibid.* 'Quaternuli magistri David de Dinant infra natale episcopo Parisiensi afferantur et comburantur, nec libri Aristotelis de naturali philosophia nec commenta legantur Parisiis publice vel secreto, et hoc sub pena excommunicationis inhibemus. Apud quem invenientur quaternuli magistri David a natali Domini in antea pro heretico habebitur.'

6 Alan of Lille had already in the later twelfth century reproved those who abandon theology to dedicate themselves 'ad inanes et transitorias scientias . . . contempnimus celestem scientiam et currimus ad inanem philosophiam . . . florem iuventutis offerunt naturali scientie, fecem vero senectutis theologie': Alain de Lille, *Textes inédits*, ed. M.-T. d'Alverny (Paris 1965), pp. 274–5.

7 Anonymi Laudunensis Canonici, *Cronica, Recueil des historiens des Gaules et de la France* XVIII (Paris 1822) 714–15.

Thus a confusion arose out of the account of the anonymous author of Laon, who, though writing only two years after the Parisian Synod, attributes to David the responsibility for the theses maintained by Amalric.[8] Yet at this time David was not in Paris but probably with the Pope, as is indicated by a letter from Innocent III himself addressed to the Abbot and Chapter of the church of Dinant in the diocese of Liège, and dated 6 June 1206.[9] In 1206 Amalric died; how could he have known the texts translated by David, if they appeared at a date close to that of the Parisian Synod? More accurate and better informed is William the Breton, who, in the *Gesta Philippi Augusti*, after discussing the problem of the Amalricians, concludes with these words:

During those days certain short writings (*libelli*), said to be by Aristotle and teaching metaphysics, were being read in Paris, having been recently brought from Constantinople and translated from Greek into Latin. These writings provided an opportunity not only for the subtle doctrines of the Amalrician heresy but also for other doctrines which had not yet been invented, and it was therefore decreed that they should all be burnt. Moreover, it was laid down in the same Council that no one should henceforth dare to transcribe or read those books, however they might have come into their possession.[10]

During these years, shortly before 1210, Alexander of Hales had come to Paris, where, after leaving the Faculty of Arts, he moved to the Faculty of Theology; there he wrote a commentary, the first ever, on Peter Lombard's *Sententiae*. In the first book of his *Glossa*, at the thirty-sixth *Distinctio*, we find him referring, after the citation of a passage of the *Monologion* by St Anselm,[11] to Anselm's having been interpreted as meaning that

. . . the things created in God (*in ipso*) are the very essence of God; and this is very close to that heresy according to which 'all things are God', just as it is said that 'Jove is everything that you see'.[12]

8 Amalric of Bène, after teaching in the Faculty of Arts, moved to the Faculty of Theology without obtaining his doctorate. In 1204 the Faculty of Theology condemned Amalric's theses. Not convinced by the replies of the theologians, he appealed to the Pope, who found against Amalric.

9 Innocent III recalls the merits of David's life, and assigns him the title 'cappellanus noster' [P.L. 215, 901–2].

10 William the Breton, *Gesta Philippi Augusti* 155:
    'In diebus illis legebantur Parisius libelli quidam ab Aristotele, ut dicebatur, compositi qui docebant metaphysicam, delati de novo a Constantinopoli, et a greco in latinum translati, qui, quoniam non solum predicte heresi sententiis subtilibus occasionem prebebant, imo et aliis nondum inventis prebere poterant, jussi sunt omnes comburi, et, sub pena excommunicationis, cautum est in eodem concilio, ne quis eos de cetero scribere, legere presumeret vel quocumque modo habere.'
    (*Gesta Philippi Augusti*, ed. F. Delaborde, *Société de l'Histoire de France* I (Paris 1882) 231)

11 *Monologion* 34; S, I 53f.

12 Alexander of Hales, *Glossa in quatuor Libros Sententiarum Petri Lombardi, in Librum Primum* (Quaracchi–Florence 1951), p. 356. The citation 'Iupiter est quodcumque vides' is from Lucan, *Pharsalia* IX 593.

Here Alexander underlines the difference between saying that 'all things are divine essence (*omnia sunt divina essentia*)', and saying that 'all things in God are divine essence (*omnia sunt in ipso divina essentia*)':

For when we say, 'all things are divine essence', created things are understood, inasmuch as they are in their being; but when we say that 'all things in God are divine essence', the eternal reasons (*rationes aeternae*) stand in the place of the transient things; and these *rationes* are God's essence inasmuch as they are God's wisdom.[13]

This passage refers to Amalric of Bène's theory, and a few pages further on we read:

But wisdom and knowledge designate that which is proper to the knowing God; for created things do not have wisdom or knowledge. Potency (*potentia*), on the other hand, is the disposition proper to the agent; therefore we do not say that in the agent all things are in potency, unless we are speaking in a privative sense (*ablative*), and we take *potentia* to mean possibility, as against material potency, so as not to fall into that heresy which states, 'God is the matter of all things.'[14]

It is significant that Alexander, though present at the University of Paris in 1210, makes no reference to Master David. In the discussions of the Parisian Synod David's person was not subjected to examination: the intention was to prevent the dissemination of the Aristotelian texts he had translated.

To the *Quaternuli* we may add another work of David's which was picked out by Brian Lawn among the spurious writings of Galen.[15] Its title is *De iuvamento anhelitus* (or *De utilitate respirationis*). Part of this work was printed at the end of William of Conches's *Dragmaticon* in Gratarolus' edition (1567). There the treatise is followed by two others, the *De mari et aquis* and the *De fluminum origine*, which correspond to a section of David's *Liber de effectibus colere nigre* (*Quaternuli*, pp. 55–64).[16]

Since Innocent III, writing to the church of St Mary of Dinant, referred to David as 'our chaplain', we may infer that David at that time held an appointment relating to some office or duty in the Apostolic See; and this is confirmed by the *Chronica* of the anonymous author of Laon. David's

---

13 Alexander, *loc. cit.*
14 *Ibid.* pp. 359–60: 'Sapientia autem et cognitio nominant illud quod proprium est Dei cognoscentis: non enim creatura sapit aut cognoscit. Potentia autem est propria dispositio agentis; ideo non dicuntur omnia in eo esse potentia, nisi ablative dicatur. Et sumitur potentia pro potestate, ad differentiam potentiae materialis, ne incidamus in illam haeresim quae dixit Deum esse omnium materiam.'
15 B. Lawn, *I Quesiti salernitani*, trans. A. Spagnuolo (Salerno 1969), pp. 101–15.
16 [See most recently d'Alverny 1982, pp. 868f.]

absence from France allowed scope for the fanciful notion that he had been put to flight, as we read in the *Compilatio de novo spiritu*;[17] but a more likely explanation is that David was in Rome at the papal court, while his *Quaternuli* had appeared in Paris, either in complete or partial form. Certainly the doctrinal positions of the Amalricians, which precede the reference to David in the decree, generated a confusion that resulted in a fantastic marriage in which Amalric and David were put on the same level, by those to whom David's translations from Greek into Latin were unknown; thus the Amalrician theses were given equivalent status with the writings of David. Anyone who has read the proceedings of 1210 will have noticed the diversity of treatment with regard to the Amalricians, who were punished severely, whereas, when the presence of the natural-istic works of Aristotle is dealt with, there is no reference to the personalities concerned; it is simply decreed that the *Quaternuli* must be handed in to the Bishop of Paris and burnt. From this it may be under-stood that the ecclesiastical worries concerning Aristotle were limited to the writings on natural philosophy and David's *Quaternuli*, because these works dealt with physical and naturalistic themes. As for the 'metaphysical' *libelli* to which William the Breton alludes, there already existed in the twelfth century a translation from Greek into Latin of Aristotle's *Metaphysics* – though only as far as the fourth chapter of Book IV – known as the 'Metaphysica vetustissima'. At the beginning of the thirteenth century, shortly before 1210, there was in circulation a fuller version of the *Metaphysics* – though it still lacked Book XI – called the 'Metaphysica media': Ezio Franceschini considered it to be 'without doubt the version mentioned by William the Breton'.[18]

In August 1213 Robert of Courson was present in Paris in his capacity as legate for the Apostolic See, on the occasion of the provincial Council in connection with the university. Courson decreed that

> ... no one who is responsible for a parish may learn the secular sciences, through which he can in no way benefit the salvation of the parishioners. And if anyone obtains from his superior the permission to attend the schools, let him not learn anything that is not the true letter of the law or holy writ, for the education of his parishioners. For if from his schools he brings everyone merely the dregs of secular sciences, and not a single flower from the fields of heavenly philosophy, according to

---

17 [Cited by Kurdziałek, *Quaternuli*, p. l, n. 219, from two manuscripts: 'temporibus nostris pro hac heresi de Francia fugatus est'.]

18 E. Franceschini, 'Aristotele nel medioevo latino', in *Atti del IX Congresso Nazionale di Filosofia* (Padua 1936), p. 9.

the Gospel he shall be rejected like one besotted and trampled underfoot by all people.[19]

Then Courson addresses the 'regulars':

For certain regulars, to use the words of the Third Lateran Council,[20] under the pretext of caring for the body of their ailing brothers and devoting greater care to ecclesiastical activities, do not fear to leave their cloisters to study secular law and medical preparations ... These men must return to their cloisters within two months, or face excommunication.

After the decrees of 1213 Robert of Courson, now a cardinal legate, prescribed the forms of teaching both in the Faculty of Arts and the Faculty of Theology. In addition he indicated which books the 'masters of arts' were not to use in the schools, and lastly issued directives concerning the discipline of the students; thus he reorganized and reformed the University of Paris. What is interesting is that he in his turn prohibited the use in lectures of Aristotle's writings on metaphysics and natural philosophy and the compendia of these works. Robert also again banned the teachings of David of Dinant, those of the heretic Amalric of Bène, and those of Maurice Hispanus.[21] In the Fourth Lateran Council (1215), however, there is no longer any mention of David and Maurice Hispanus, but only of Amalric of Bène. The silence concerning David caused Father Théry some perplexity, for he saw the Pope on the one hand calling David 'our chaplain', and on the other branding him with the name of heretic.[22] In my opinion the Council's silence about David and Maurice Hispanus suggests that David, for his part, only explored the naturalistic treatises of Aristotle, and that in the case of Maurice, who was a fervent disciple of Dionysius and at the same time a 'cultivator of Muslim theology', his interest in the knowledge of Islamic culture, and the possibility of understanding it, may have been seen as an obstacle in the Christian Latin world. Of the three authors condemned by

19 'Ordinationes Concilii Provincialis Parisiensis sub legato apostolicae sedis magistro Roberto de Courçon celebrati circa studia, Parisiis 1213'; see *Chartularium Universitatis Parisiensis* I 77, no. 19.
20 The words originate from the Council of Tours. Cf. *Chartularium, ibid.*: 'Verba relata non inveniuntur in actis Concilii Lateranensis *iii*, sed in illis Concilii Turonensis.'
21 Various authors have attempted to identify Mauritius Hispanus. M. Grabmann discussed the question, but without coming to any definite conclusion; see *I divieti ecclesiastici sotto Innocenzo III e Gregorio IX* (Rome 1941), pp. 49–52. A few years later in a learned essay M.-T. d'Alverny gathered together various pieces of information which probably identify Mauritius: see 'Deux traductions latines du Coran au Moyen Age', *AHDLMA* xvi (1948) 69–131, at pp. 128–9. Maurice Hispanus had a keen interest in Islamic theology, and some may have misunderstood the attention he devoted to Islam.
22 [G. Théry, *Autour du Décret de 1210: I David de Dinant* (Kain 1925), p. 10. The citations of Théry below are on the same page.]

Courson, only Amalric and his teachings continued to be considered as certainly heretical.[23]

Théry insisted at length on his view that David of Dinant was a heretic and condemned as such, and that on the other hand

... it seems extremely likely that Master David, the heretic, sojourned for some time at the papal court. Furthermore, behind the official phraseology of Innocent III's letter to the Chapter of Dinant it is possible to perceive the signs of a certain liking for David on the part of the Pope.

And Théry continued:

This liking can explain to us why in 1215 the Fourth Lateran Council solemnly condemned Amalric's heresy, whereas no mention is made of David's name.

Again, Théry was astonished at David's presence at the court of Innocent III, 'whose goodwill he seems to have won', and adds, 'this favourable silence of the Council can probably be explained by an intervention on the Pope's part'. As far as the date of David's death is concerned we know nothing. Théry examines the authors of the time: William of Auvergne, whose combative temperament would have found material on which to exercise itself, never mentions the name of David of Dinant in his *De universo*, and does not seem to have any knowledge of his doctrines. Roland of Cremona, who is not averse to involving himself in theological debates, does not mention this 'heretic'. The reconstruction of the texts from David present in the works of Albert the Great made it possible for Théry to organize and structure the material he had gathered, while steadfastly preserving his conviction as to David's unorthodoxy. Théry added, 'there is a silence on the part of the great representatives of medieval theology which the historian must explain'.[24] In discussing the Parisian Synod, Théry gratuitously assumed the presence at it of David of Dinant; but, as we have seen, the text of the proceedings of 1210 makes this wholly improbable.

The meagre information regarding David, together with those of his writings which have come down to us, can, however, correct certain assertions which we find in later authors. Thomas Aquinas touches on the subject of David several times.[25] In the *De veritate* we read: 'For some, guided by frivolous motivations, affirmed that God is identical with primal matter:

23 *Contra Amaurianos*, ed. C. Baeumker, BGPTM xxiv. 5/6 (1926).
24 [Théry 1925, p. 15.]
25 [The citations of David by Albert the Great and Thomas Aquinas are valuably listed in Théry 1925, pp. 151–5.]

such as David of Dinant'.[26] The *Contra gentiles* presents a similar picture: 'In this the folly of David of Dinant is refuted, daring to say that God is identical with primal matter'.[27] A reading of the other relevant Thomas passages does not contribute any new facts, but we observe that he takes over what Albert the Great had written.

Later, Nicolas of Cusa shows knowledge of some passages of David. In Nicolas' dialogue *De non-aliud*, also known as *Directio speculantis*, his interlocutor Ferdinand Matim says:

David of Dinant, then, and those philosophers whom he followed, were by no means mistaken when they called God *hylê* and *noys* and *physis*, and said that the visible world is the visible God.

Nicolas replies:

David calls *hylê* the principle of bodies, *noys*, or the mind, the principle of souls, and *physis*, or nature, the principle of all movements, and he saw that those things are not different from one another as it were in their origin, and that is why he said this.

A little further on Ferdinand, replying to Nicolas, concludes with the words of Dionysius:

If someone, seeing God, understood what he saw, he did not see God, but something else. Therefore if David of Dinant saw that God is *hylê* or *noys* or *physis*, he certainly saw something, but he cannot have seen God.[28]

These dicta of David's were already in circulation around the middle of the thirteenth century: they appear in the writings of Albert the Great and Thomas Aquinas and, as we have just seen, were still remembered in the fifteenth century. In his commentary on the *Sententiae* Thomas Aquinas writes concerning David's key terms *hylê*, *mens*, *deus*: 'And these three are [for him] one and the same; from which it follows in turn that all things are one through essence'.[29] We should, however, observe that David's *Tractatus naturalis* begins:

There are three things in the soul: sense, imagination, and desire; and we shall now discuss these. Sense is the perception by the soul of those passions which are formed in the body. For the sense of anything suffers the thing subjected to sense, either

26 *De veritate* XXI 4: 'Quidam enim, frivolis rationibus ducti, posuerunt Deum esse de substantia cuiuslibet rei. Quorum quidam posuerunt Deum esse idem quod materia prima, ut David de Dinando.'

27 *Contra gentiles* I 17: 'In hoc autem insania David de Dinant confunditur, qui ausus est dicere Deum esse idem quod prima materia.'

28 [*De non-aliud* XVII: Nikolaus von Kues, *Philosophisch-Theologische Schriften* (3 vols., Vienna 1966) II 522–4.]

29 Thomas Aquinas, *In IIum Sententiarum* XVII I I: 'Et haec tria esse unum et idem: ex quo iterum consequitur esse omnia per essentiam unum.'

without intermediary or through an intermediary. The intermediary both acts and suffers: it suffers the thing sensed, and acts on the instrument of sense.[30]

In my view David proposes a parallel between the triad 'sense, imagination, desire' and the other triad, *hylê, mens, deus*. In this perspective it seems to me that David intends to establish a progression, in which the first triad presents a 'natural' itinerary, as an approach to the triad which concludes with the term 'God'.

The first three sections of the *Tractatus naturalis* are the *De visu*, the *De imaginatione* and the *De affectu*. In the *De visu* David, following Aristotle, expounds his doctrine and rejects that of Plato, according to which vision forms through the action of fire and the eye emits light from itself towards the thing seen, light being conceived as a body:

Aristotle opposes this theory and demonstrates that vision derives from the liquid which is in the eye, and that the eye receives light from the thing seen, and that light is not a body but a passive colour. Some will ask whether, if the eye sees colours, it is affected by contrary colours. I say that from those contrary colours a single colour is formed by mixing, and this colour is in the eye and in the air that is near the eye.[31]

A little further on David writes:

The colour seems, however, to be in that place from which it took its first origin, that is, in the thing subjected to vision. And this is why the eye suffers through the contrary colours, which mingle in the eye, and yet the sight perceives the colours unmixed and far from the eye. Something similar happens in the hearing. For even if the sound – which is simply a movement of air, or beating on the eardrum by the moved air – is produced in the air, it is perceived as being as far from the ear as that which produces the sound in the air is far from it. I say that when we see a thing in the mirror, the light is emitted from the thing seen to the mirror and then again from the mirror to the eye. Something similar happens when we hear an echo, which is simply the reflection of the movement of air. But it happens naturally that we see and hear correctly. Therefore the thing seen appears in the mirror to be as large as the distance between the thing seen and the mirror. The ray of light which is emitted from the thing seen towards the mirror is rightly understood as being prolonged within the mirror. And the echo which is heard in a cave, and which causes a repercussion of the air, is heard as if it were as far inside as the thing which makes the sound is distant from the cave.[32]

30 *Quaternuli* 1963, p. 65.
31 *Ibid.* p. 66.
32 *Ibid.*:
  'Videtur tamen in eo loco, a quo cepit primam sui originem, hoc est in re visui subiecta. Et inde est, quod oculus patiatur per colores contrarios, qui miscentur in oculo, visus tamen percipit eos inpermixtos longe ab oculo. Cuius simile apparet in auditu; nam etsi sonus fiat in aere, qui nichil aliud est quam motus aeris aut percussio timpani auditus ab aere moto, percipitur tamen tam longe ab aure, quantum distat illud quod sonum facit in aure. Dico, quod cum videmus rem in speculo, lux emittitur a re visa ad speculum et iterum a speculo

The first step in the progression mentioned above is limited to presenting two senses: sight and hearing, which are the senses that permit us to know and to communicate. To these senses is added the *imagination*. David affirms that any act of imagination is formed from a pre-existent sense perception, and adds that

... sense and imagination are formed in the same parts of the body, but differ in this way: sense perceives the passion which is formed on the instrument of sense by the thing sensed; imagination, on the other hand, perceives the passion which remains on the instrument of sense even after the removal of the thing sensed. For there remains, if not the whole passion, at least a certain part of it, which Aristotle calls the 'sign' or 'trace' of the pre-existent passion, and this thing he calls the 'phantasm', when he says, 'without a phantasm it is impossible to understand'.[33]

Moreover, after rejecting the Platonic theory of ideas, David, referring back to Aristotle, says that

... memory is identical with imagination. For memory is created by the persistence of the phantasms in the place of the imagination. Recollection (*rememoracio*), on the other hand, is an investigation of the phantasms in the place of the imagination. And a dream is simply an imagining, which is frequently either brought about through a passion that has formed on the instruments of the senses before sleep, or brought about during sleep itself, whether from within or from without. For when a small sound is produced in the ear, either from within or from without, to the sleeper it seems a clap of thunder.[33]

In the *De affectu* David deals with affective status (such as joy, sadness, hope, fear, anger, or hate). He begins by saying that every affective state forms as a result of a disturbance of the heart; and without the 'fellow-suffering (*compassio*)' of the heart the affective state cannot be formed in the soul. David asks himself 'if an affect forms because of the suffering of the heart or vice versa', and answers:

That the things which befall externally are not joint causes of the affects which are formed in the soul, as some have thought, is clear from the fact that some people can experience joy and sadness without any external cause. Or again, two men hear something equally grave for both of them, and one is moved to sadness, but not the other. And it happens that a person may be timid if he has a large, cold heart or if there is a cold humour or exhalation in his heart. Sickness or death may occur as the result of excessive fear or love, or indeed through any affect whatsoever. It is manifest

ad oculum. Simile autem contingit, cum audimus ecco, que nichil aliud est, quam reflectio motus aeris. Sed naturaliter accidit recte videre et audire. Ideo quidem res visa apparet tanta intra speculum, quanta est distancia rei vise a speculo. Radius, qui a re visa ad speculum mittitur, intelligitur recte intra speculum protendi; ecco, que auditur intra antrum, a quo fit repercussio aeris, auditur autem tantum intrinsecus, quanta est distancia eius, quod facit sonum, ab antro.'

33 *Ibid.* p. 67.

therefore that although the suffering of the heart and the affect of the soul are formed simultaneously, nevertheless the suffering of the heart is the cause of the affect which forms in the soul.

A littler further on David says that

. . . the change in the movement of the heart produces a greater or lesser warming or cooling of the blood or spirit in the heart, which Aristotle said was the cause of the affects that are formed in the soul. I say that the heart warms the body by its motion alone, because the heart, according to its complexion, is not warm, but is a more earthly part of the body. Similarly Aristotle believed that the sun warms the world by its movement alone, since in itself the sun is not warm, nor cold, but ethereal. For Aristotle posits three elements: the hot, the cold, the ethereal; and correspondingly he posits three natural movements, one upwards, one downwards, and one in a circle. Since, therefore, man is the image of the universe, the sun corresponds to the heart; the spirit, which is in the heart and the arteries, to fire and air; water to the blood, and earth to the solid limbs. And the spirit in the first place takes its heat from the heart, as does the air from the sun, and the spirit, spreading throughout the body by way of the arteries, heats the blood and the limbs as the air warms the earth and the water.[34]

The progression developed in the *Tractatus naturalis* culminates in the chapter *Mens, hylê, deus*. The operation concludes with the term 'God', as a sign that even nature can be a guide to the religious man. David writes:

I say that in the soul there are three things: knowledge and intellect and will (*scientia, intellectus, voluntas*); and each one of these is passible. I say that passible knowledge is the sense, passible intellect is the imagination, and passible will is the desire or affective state. For what the sense perceives is simply the suffering which is formed on the instrument of sense by the thing sensed. But because it is impossible for an imagining to be formed except from a pre-existent sense perception, it is clear that what the imagination perceives is simply the sign or vestige of the suffering that is sensed. Neither can the affect be formed in the soul except through the mutation of the systole and diastole, according to the warming and the cooling of the blood, or of the spirit which is in the heart . . .

None, therefore, of the aforementioned three things can be formed except from the body, because none of these is formed except together with the suffering of the body.

34 *Ibid.* p. 68:
'Dico autem quod mutatio motus cordis facit maiorem aut minorem calefactionem aut frigefactionem sanguinis sive spiritus in corde, quam dixit Aristoteles esse causam affectuum, qui fiunt in anima. Dico autem, quod cor solo motu calefacit corpus, cum ipsum secundum complexionem non sit calidum, sed sit terrestrior pars corporis. Similiter quoque visum est Aristoteli, quod sol solo motu calefacit mundum, cum ipse non sit calidus nec frigidus, sed ethereus. Ponit enim tria elementa: calidum, frigidum, ethereum. Et ponit propter hoc tres naturales motus, qui fiunt sursum et deorsum et in circuitu. Cum ergo homo ymago sit mundi, sol quidem proportionalis cordi, et spiritus, qui in corde est et in arteriis, et igni et aeri, aqua vero – sanguini, terra – solidis membris. Spiritus autem primo loco calefit a corde, sicut et aer a sole, qui per arterias in totum corpus diffusum calefacit sanguinem et membra, sicut aer terram et aquam.'

A further problem is whether nothing is separable from the soul or whether something is separable. But something in the soul is separable from the body in its being, and we call this 'mind' (*mens*); therefore it is evident that the mind is something impassible, and that knowledge, intellect, and will are contained in it, inasmuch as they are impassible. And I say that as the body is to matter (*hylê*), so the soul is to the mind. But if the body and matter are passive, the soul and the mind must also be passive.

I say, moreover, that there is only one mind, but many souls; and there is only one matter, but many bodies. For since only received attributes, that is, accidents or properties, differentiate things from one another, it follows that that being which is not subject to any received attribute must be only one; and such are mind and matter. And it follows that passive things must be many, and because the properties which are in them establish a difference with respect to other things (such are the bodies and the souls), it is clear that there is only one mind and only one matter.

We must enquire, moreover, if mind and matter are one single entity, or if they are different. Since, then, only passive things differ from one another, it appears that mind and matter do not differ in any way, because neither of them is subject to any received attribute. Again, just as the passive intellect, which is in the soul, only understands the body, so the impassible intellect, which is in the mind, only understands matter. It is manifest, furthermore, that the passive intellect (that is, the imagination) does not understand being (*esse*) unless it assimilates itself to the thing sensed, for that exceeds its nature. Similarly we observe that the passible intellect cannot understand matter unless it has some similarity to it or is identical with it. But it cannot be similar to it, because similarity only occurs in those realities which are passive and subject to the same received attribute, such as two white things or two black things.

From all this, then, we may conclude that mind and matter are identical. Plato seems to agree with this, when he says that the world is the perceptible God. For the mind of which we are speaking, and which we say is one and impassible, is none other than God. If, therefore, the world is God himself outgoing himself and perceptible to sense, as Plato, Zeno, Socrates, and many others have said, the matter of the world is God himself, and the form that comes to matter is nothing other than God's making himself into what is perceptible. For quantity, as Aristotle says, is the first thing that comes upon matter, and the corporeal is produced; natural motion comes to the corporeal, and an element is produced. For although matter is, by the force of its nature, as it were imperceptible and immobile, nevertheless the sense recognizes size and motion in it.

It is clear, therefore, that there is only one substance, not only of all bodies but also of all souls, and this substance is nothing other than God himself. And the substance from which all bodies come is called 'matter' (*hylê*), while the substance from which all souls come is called 'reason' or 'mind' (*racio sive mens*). It is therefore manifest that God is the reason of all souls, and the matter of all bodies.[35]

The *Tractatus naturalis* presents both philosophical and religious aspects, as if David wished to demonstrate that it is possible to reach the religious level

35 *Ibid.* pp. 69–71.

by moving from what is natural. The procedure which he adopts seems to be a sort of marriage: both nature and sacrality are involved in being human; man can dissociate nature and the sacred, or else unite them. In other words, one observes the liberty of man, who has to choose his path and assume his responsibilities. Kurdziałek gives the following analysis of the *Tractatus naturalis*:

David expounds the problem of nature, the mind and the soul in the light of Aristotle's doctrine, and poses precisely the same problem as Aristotle had posed: 'whether some part of the soul is separable from the body or not'. Furthermore, and above all, he examines the three manifestations of the psychic life: sense, imagination, and affection. Sensible knowledge (*sensus*) is none other, in his opinion, than 'the perception by the soul of those passions which are formed in the body'.[36]

The forms which remain in the organ (i.e. the signs or vestiges of a pre-existent passion) constitute the material of imaginative knowledge. For the latter is based on the *phantasma*, just as sensible knowledge is based on 'passion'. Both kinds of knowledge have their place in the same parts of the soul and in the same corporeal instruments.

In the chapter *Mens, hylê, deus* we observe a new approach, which moves away from the naturalistic aspect and closer to the anthropological theme of the mind. David, asking like Aristotle before him whether or not something is separable from the soul, replies in the affirmative: something in the soul is separable from the body in its being, and we call that 'mind'. The term 'mind', however, takes on a wider force: we read that the body is to matter as the soul is to mind. When David affirms that 'there is only one mind', to be consistent with the language appropriate to a *Tractatus naturalis* he does not use theological terms, but nevertheless gives an indication which modestly approaches religious themes.

At this point the question arises as to why David inserted the chapter *Mens, hylê, deus* into his *Tractatus naturalis*. It is certainly true that in the *De affectu* we read that man is the 'image of the world'; but it is also true that man is part of that world. It is this double aspect of the human being that underlies David's conception of a continuity that extends from simple sense-impressions to the perception of the universe as 'God outgoing himself'. To cite Kurdziałek once more:

Particular human souls, like bodies, are only individualized manifestations of the divine substance, produced 'out of the passions, that is, the accidents or properties (*ex passionibus, hoc est accidentibus sive proprietatibus*)'. Man as 'manifestation' does not

36 M. Kurdziałek, 'David von Dinant und die Anfänge der Aristotelischen Naturphilosophie', in *La filosofia della natura nel medio evo. Atti del III Congresso Internazionale di filosofia Medievale* (Passo della Mendola 1964), pp. 413–14.

differ essentially from all the other individualized manifestations. Like the others, he is only a participating detail on the *peplum Palladis* – that is, on that garment of God which is the world. Nonetheless, in the case of the human being the manifestation is in a sense exceptional, since it reflects better than the rest 'the visible God' – in other words, the world. David's conception of man as 'image of the world' seems to be the most radical, and at the same time the most consistent, among those formulated in the twelfth century.[37]

37 'L'idée de l'homme', 1976, pp. 321–2.

BIO-BIBLIOGRAPHIES

The list that follows includes only in exceptional cases figures who are important primarily for neighbouring disciplines, such as the history of spirituality (see the Introduction, pp. 5–6). A number of the attributions, datings and localizations suggested below are, inevitably, debatable; where possible, further documentation is given in the course of the book. In principle references in this list are to primary sources; a few exceptions have had to be made for authors whose writings are unpublished or known chiefly through indirect testimonies.

ABELARD: see 'Peter Abelard'

ADAM PARVIPONTANUS (Adam of Balsham, Adam du Petit Pont) † 1181
Born at Balsham, near Cambridge, Adam studied with Peter Lombard in Paris and then (from *ca.* 1132) taught there, John of Salisbury being one of his disciples.[1] He was the author of a treatise on Aristotelian logic (*Ars disserendi*),[2] as well as of one on rare words (*De utensilibus*, or *Fale tolum*).[3]

[1] John of Salisbury, *Metalogicon*, ed. C. C. J. Webb (Oxford 1929), II 10, III Prol., III 3.
[2] Ed. L. Minio-Paluello, *Twelfth Century Logic: Texts and Studies* I (Rome 1956).
[3] Ed. A. H. Hoffmann von Fallersleben, *Epistola Adami Balsamiensis ad Anselmum* (Neuwied–Cologne–Hanover 1853).

ADELARD OF BATH   *fl. s.* XII[1]
Of English origin, Adelard studied at Tours and taught at Laon. It is difficult to assign an exact date to his travels in southern Italy and Sicily, and thereafter in various regions in the Near East; the possibility that he was also in Spain cannot be excluded. He is attested at Bath in 1130. Adelard's numerous philosophical and scientific works and translations from the Arabic include, among the early writings, *Regulae abaci*[1] and *De eodem et diverso*[2] (before 1116, perhaps in the first years of the century), followed (before 1137 and probably much earlier) by the *Quaestiones naturales*.[3] Adelard's translations of mathematics and astronomy include Euclid's *Elements*[4] and works by al-Khwārizmī.[5] A treatise on the astrolabe, dedicated to the young Henry II (between 1142 and 1146), remains unpublished.

[1] Ed. B. Boncompagni, *Bollettino di bibliografia e di storia delle scienze matematiche e fisiche* XIV (1881) 1–134.
[2] Ed. H. Willner, BGPTM IV.1 (1903).
[3] Ed. M. Müller, BGPTM XXXI.2 (1934).
[4] Ed. H. L. L. Busard (Toronto 1983).
[5] (?) *Liber ysagogarum Alchorismi* I–III, ed. M. Curtze, *Abhandlungen zur Geschichte der Mathematik* VIII (1898) 1–27; *Die astronomischen Tafeln*, ed. H. Suter, *Det Kongelige Danske Videnskabernes Selskabs Skrifter*, 7th ser., Hist. og filos. afdeling III (Copenhagen 1914); A. Allard, *Les plus anciennes versions latines du XIIe siècle issues de l'arithmétique d'al-Khwārizmī* (Louvain 1975).

ALAN OF LILLE (Alain de Lille, Alanus ab Insulis)   *ca.* 1120–1203
Born in Lille, Alan studied with Gilbert Porreta in Chartres or Paris, and probably
with Bernard Silvestris in Tours. After *ca.* 1150 he taught in Paris and Montpellier,
and in old age entered the Cistercian order at Cîteaux, where he was buried. His
prodigiously varied writings,[1] which earned him the title *doctor universalis,* include
two cosmological epics, that show the influence of Bernard Silvestris' *Cosmographia*
(1147): the first, *De planctu Naturae*[2] (*ca.* 1160–70), a *prosimetrum* like that of Bernard,
the second, *Anticlaudianus*[3] (1182–3), in hexameters. Likewise rich in philosophical
elements are Alan's *Summa 'Quoniam homines',*[4] his *Regulae caelestis iuris*[5] (where he
uses a demonstrative method akin to that of the *Liber de causis*) and *Contra haereticos,*[6]
his *De virtutibus et vitiis,*[7] and his *Sermo de sphaera intelligibili*[8] (a brief work of his
youth, discovered only recently).

[1] The majority of these are collected in P.L. 210; for a full account of Alan's writings and an ed.
   of some of the previously unpublished ones, see M.-Th. d'Alverny, *Alain de Lille: Textes
   inédits* (Paris 1965).
[2] Ed. N. M. Häring, *Studi Medievali* ser. 3, XIX (1978) 797–879; English trans. by J. J. Sheridan
   (Toronto 1980).
[3] Ed. R. Bossuat (Paris 1955); English trans. by J. J. Sheridan (Toronto 1973).
[4] Ed. P. Glorieux, *AHDLMA* XX (1953) 113–364.
[5] Ed. N. M. Häring, *AHDLMA* XLVIII (1981) 97–226.
[6] P.L. 210, 305–430.
[7] Ed. O. Lottin, *Psychologie et morale aux XIIe et XIIIe siècles* VI (Gembloux 1960) 27–92.
[8] Ed. M.-Th. d'Alverny (n. 1), pp. 295–306.

ALEXANDER NEQUAM (Alexander Neckam)   1157–1217
Born and schooled at St Albans and later a student in Paris, Alexander taught at Dun-
stable, St Albans, Paris, and Oxford. Before 1202 he became an Augustinian canon at
Cirencester, and was elected abbot there in 1213. His prolific writings include a commentary on Martianus Capella[1] (*ca.* 1177) and two encyclopaedic works: the prose *De
naturis rerum*[2] (before 1205), and the verse *De laudibus divinae sapientiae*[3] (*ca.* 1213), with
a sequel, *Suppletio defectuum*[4] (1216–17). Alexander is among the earliest northern
writers to cite Aristotle's *De caelo* and *Ethics* and the *Metaphysics* of Algazel.

[1] Unpublished: see R. W. Hunt, *The Schools and the Cloister: The Life and Times of Alexander
   Nequam* (Oxford 1984), p. 128.
[2] Ed. T. Wright, *Alexandri Neckam De naturis rerum libri duo,* Rolls Series (London 1863),
   pp. 1–354 (Books I–II only; Books III–IV are unprinted).
[3] *Ibid.* pp. 357–503.
[4] Unpublished: see R. W. Hunt (n. 1), pp. 78–83, 139f.

ALFRED OF SARESHEL (Alfredus Anglicus)   fl. s. XII/XIII
An Englishman who studied and worked in Spain in the second half of the twelfth
century, Alfred translated from the Arabic the pseudo-Aristotelian *De plantis* and
some chapters *De mineralibus* by Avicenna. He wrote a commentary on Aristotle's
Meteorologica, as well as on the *De plantis.* A larger group of Aristotelian commentaries
by Alfred, lost today but still extant in Beauvais in the seventeenth century – 'de
mundo et celo, de generatione et corruptione, de somno et vigilantia, de morte et vita,
de colore celi' – suggests he was the earliest major commentator in northern Europe
on the 'new Aristotle'. Alfred's own treatise *De motu cordis,* [1] which he dedicated to
Alexander Nequam (q.v.), shows his knowledge of Aristotle's physical writings as
well as of the *De anima, Metaphysics* and *Ethics.*

[1] Ed. C. Baeumker, BGPTM XXIII. 1–2 (1923)

AMALRIC OF BENE (Amaury de Bène) † 1206
Born at Bène, near Chartres, Amalric studied and taught in Paris, where his teachings were condemned by a synod in 1210. His thought, usually termed pantheistic, is known only through hostile citations and paraphrases,[1] and appears to be related to the thought of John Scotus Eriugena.[2]

[1] Collected in G. C. Capelle, *Amaury de Bène: Etude sur son panthéisme formel* (Paris 1932); see also M.-Th. d'Alverny, 'Un fragment du procès des Amauriciens', *AHDLMA* XVIII (1950–1) 325–36.
[2] See P. Lucentini, 'Giovanni Scoto e l'eresia di Amalrico', in *Colloquium zur Wirkungsgeschichte Eriugenas*, ed. W. Beierwaltes (forthcoming).

ANSELM OF CANTERBURY (St Anselm) 1033–1109
Born in Aosta, Anselm left Italy in 1056, and settled at the monastery of Bec in Normandy in 1059, where he studied with Lanfranc. He became Abbot of Bec in 1078, and succeeded Lanfranc as Archbishop of Canterbury in 1093. Among Anselm's *Opera Omnia*,[1] the following are of particular importance for the history of philosophy: *Monologion*[2] (1076); *Proslogion*[3] (1077–8); *De grammatico*[4], *De veritate*[5], *De libertate arbitrii* (1080–5); *De concordia* (1108); and among the *Memorials of St Anselm*,[6] *De humanis moribus* (assembled posthumously, before 1130). Anselm's two treatises on the Incarnation, however – *De incarnatione verbi* (1092–4), and *Cur deus homo*[7] (1094–8) – likewise contain elements crucial to the perception of his philosophical premises.

[1] *S. Anselmi Opera Omnia*, ed. F. S. Schmitt (6 vols., Seckau–Rome–Edinburgh 1938–61; repr. Stuttgart–Bad Cannstatt 1968); *Obras Completas*, with Spanish trans. by J. Alameda (2 vols., Madrid 1952–3); English trans. by J. Hopkins and H. Richardson (4 vols., London–Toronto– New York 1974–6).
[2] Ed. with German trans. by F. S. Schmitt (Stuttgart–Bad Cannstatt 1964).
[3] Ed. with German trans. by F. S. Schmitt (Stuttgart–Bad Cannstatt 1962); ed. with French trans. by A. Koyré (3rd ed., Paris 1964); ed. with English trans. by M. J. Charlesworth (Oxford 1965).
[4] Ed. with English trans. by D. P. Henry (Notre Dame 1964).
[5] Ed. with German trans. by F. S. Schmitt (Stuttgart–Bad Cannstatt 1966).
[6] Ed. R. W. Southern and F. S. Schmitt, Auctores Britannici Medii Aevi I (London 1969).
[7] Ed. with German trans. by F. S. Schmitt (Darmstadt 1965); ed. with French trans. by R. Roques (Paris 1963).

ARCHIMATTHEUS: see 'Bartholomew of Salerno'

BARTHOLOMEW OF SALERNO (Bartholomaeus Salernitanus) *fl.* s. XII med.
For a long time Bartholomew's name was associated only with the famous *Practica Bartholomaei*.[1] Today he is also regarded as the author of a series of commentaries on the collection of texts called *Articella*,[2] which he helped introduce into the curriculum. The first of these texts to receive a commentary in Salerno was the *Isagoge Iohannitii*, which was glossed by a master prior to Bartholomew, Archimattheus (MS Trier, Bibl. des Priesterseminars 76, s. XIII med., fol. 1r–53v). The name of Petrus Musandinus, Bartholomew's pupil, is linked with or substituted for that of Bartholomew in certain MSS; diverse redactions of the *Articella* commentaries can be discerned, suggesting the form of *reportata*. Bartholomew can doubtless be identified with the author of the medical advice addressed in epistolary form to Peter the Venerable, Abbot of Cluny († 1156)[3], and to King Louis VII of France († 1180).[4]

[1] Ed. S. de Renzi, *Collectio Salernitana* IV (Naples 1856) 321–406.
[2] See P. O. Kristeller, *Studi sulla Scuola medica salernitana* (Naples 1986), pp. 124f, 140–2.
[3] Ed. H. Quentin, in *Scritti di storia e paleografia: Miscellanea Francesco Ehrle* I (Rome 1924) 85f.
[4] Ed. C. H. Talbot, *Bulletin of the History of Medicine* XXX (1956) 326–8.

BERNARD OF CHARTRES (Bernardus Carnotensis) † *ca.* 1130
Breton in origin, probably the elder brother of Thierry of Chartres, Bernard is
attested as a master at the cathedral school of Chartres from before 1117, and later, till
1124, as its chancellor. His writings have not survived; a commentary on the
Timaeus, however, has recently been ascribed to him.[1] Apart from this, the principal
testimonies to Bernard's thought and teaching are to be found in John of Salisbury's
Metalogicon[2] and *Policraticus*;[3] there are traces also in William of Conches's *Glosae super
Priscianum*.[4]

[1] See P. E. Dutton, 'The Uncovering of the *Glosae super Platonem* of Bernard of Chartres',
   Mediaeval Studies XLVI (1984) 192–221, and the Introduction above, pp. 14–17.
[2] Ed. C. C. J. Webb (Oxford 1929), I 5, 11, 24; II 17; III 2, 4; IV 35.
[3] Ed. C. C. J. Webb (2 vols., Oxford 1909), VII 13.
[4] See E. Jeauneau, *Lectio Philosophorum* (Amsterdam 1973), p. 358; also *ibid.* pp. 51–73.

BERNARD SILVESTRIS (Bernardus Silvestris) *ca.* 1100 – *ca.* 1160
Bernard taught at the cathedral school of Tours, the city where he probably spent the
greater part of his life. Some scholars still question the attribution to Bernard of his
two early commentaries – on Vergil's *Aeneid*[1] (*ca.* 1125–30) and on Martianus
Capella's *De nuptiis*[2] (*ca.* 1130–5). Bernard's masterpiece is his cosmological *prosimetrum*, *Cosmographia*[3] (completed 1147); he also has a long poem, *Mathematicus*[4]
(*ca.* 1150), based on one of the *Declamations* ascribed to Quintilian, in which, as in the
Cosmographia, he considers the problem of fate. This problem is likewise central to
Bernard's introduction to the *Experimentarius*,[5] a manual of divination apparently
translated by him from the Arabic, of which, on account of the very heterogeneous
MSS that preserve it, the exact composition and extent remain uncertain.[6] Bernard's
treatise on *Dictamen*,[7] often alluded to by his disciples, has not been convincingly
identified, and his commentary on Plato's *Timaeus* is either lost or still awaiting
identification.

[1] Ed. J. W. Jones and E. F. Jones (Lincoln–London 1977); English trans. by E. G. Schreiber and
   T. E. Maresca (Lincoln–London 1979).
[2] Ed. H. J. Westra (Toronto 1986).
[3] Ed. P. Dronke (Leiden 1978); English trans. by W. Wetherbee (New York–London 1973);
   Italian trans. by E. Maccagnolo, *Il divino e il megacosmo* (Milan 1980), pp. 457–552.
[4] Ed. B. Hauréau (Paris 1895).
[5] Ed. M. Brini Savorelli, *Rivista critica di storia della filosofia* XIV (1959) 283–342.
[6] See C. Burnett, 'What is the *Experimentarius* of B. Silvestris?', *AHDLMA* XLIV (1978) 79–125.
[7] The text printed by M. Brini Savorelli, *ibid.* (n. 5) XX (1965) 182–230, is unlikely to be
   Bernard's.

BURGUNDIO OF PISA *ca.* 1110–93
Born in Pisa, Burgundio had a varied career as jurist and physician, and as
ambassador to Constantinople, where in 1136 he was present with James of Venice
and Moses of Bergamo at the theological disputation between Anselm of Havelberg
and Patriarch Nicetas. Burgundio's achievements lie in his translations from the
Greek, including theological writings of St John Damascene[1] and St John Chryso-
stom, a new translation of Nemesius of Emesa's *De natura hominis*[2] (1155–9), which
he dedicated to Frederick Barbarossa, and a number of medical treatises, especially by
Galen,[3] not all of them yet determined with certainty.

[1] *De fide orthodoxa: Versions of Burgundio and Cerbanus*, ed. E. M. Buytaert (New York–
   Paderborn 1955).
[2] Ed. G. Verbeke and J. R. Moncho (Leiden 1975).

[3] *Burgundio of Pisa's Translation of Galen's* Περὶ κράσεων, *'De complexionibus'*, ed. R. J. Durling (Berlin 1976).

CLAREMBALD OF ARRAS (Clarembaldus) † *ca.*1187
Clarembald studied with Hugh of Saint-Victor and Thierry of Chartres, and later taught both at Arras and Laon. He is the author of a major commentary on Boethius' *De trinitate*[1] and a brief one on *De hebdomadibus*[2] (both *ca.*1157–8). He helped to preserve Thierry's treatise *De sex dierum operibus*, to which he wrote a sequel, *Tractatulus*[3] (*ca.*1160–70).

[1] Ed. N. M. Häring, *Life and Works of Clarembald of Arras* (Toronto 1965), pp. 61–186.
[2] *Ibid.* pp. 187–221.
[3] *Ibid.* pp. 223–49.

DANIEL OF MORLEY *ca.*1140 – *ca.*1210
Born in Norfolk, Daniel, disappointed with the narrow scope of studies in Paris, went to Toledo and became a disciple of Gerard of Cremona, who introduced him to Arabic philosophy and science. On his return to England (1187), bringing MSS of the new learning back with him, Daniel composed his cosmological treatise, *De naturis inferiorum et superiorum*.[1].

[1] Ed. K. Sudhoff, *Archiv für Geschichte der Naturwissenschaften und Technik* VIII (1917) 6–40; corrections by A. Birkenmajer, *ibid.* IX (1918) 45–51.

DAVID OF DINANT † *ca.*1214
Born in Dinant (Belgium), David became a physician and cosmologist as well as a key figure in the interpreting and translating of the 'new' Aristotle. During travels in Greece David found texts of Aristotle's scientific writings, including *De generatione animalium*, *De partibus animalium*, *De somno et vigilia* and the *Meteorologica*, as well as the *Problemata* ascribed to Aristotle. He excerpted, translated, and expounded these in his *Quaternuli*,[1] which survive in fragmentary form as a record of his lectures in Paris. A medical treatise by David, *De iuvamento anhelitus*,[2] has been discovered among the spurious writings of Galen. David became chaplain (*ca.*1205–6) to Pope Innocent III (1198–1216). His *Quaternuli* were condemned by a Parisian synod in 1210.

[1] Ed. M. Kurdziałek, Studia Mediewistyczne III (Warsaw 1963).
[2] See B. Lawn, *I Quesiti salernitani* (Salerno 1969), pp. 101–5.

DOMINICUS GUNDISSALINUS (Dominicus Gundisalvi) † after 1181
Gundissalinus was Archdeacon of Segovia and then Toledo (to whose diocese Segovia belonged). His life spans perhaps almost the entire twelfth century, but his scholarly activity does not seem to have begun before the decade 1140–50; while it is abundantly attested during the episcopate of John of Toledo (1152–6), Gundissalinus is still recorded in Toledo as late as 1178–81. One of his translations of Avicenna[1] (*De anima*) is addressed to John of Toledo; he collaborated with a 'magister Iohannes' in translating Algazel[2] and Avencebrol.[3] Using his translations as a basis, Gundissalinus also composed a number of independent works: *De unitate*,[4] *De divisione philosophie*,[5] *De processione mundi*,[6] and *De anima*.[7]

[1] *Avicenna Latinus. Liber de anima*, ed. S. van Riet (2 vols., Louvain–Leiden 1968–72); *Liber de philosophia prima*, ed. S. van Riet (3 vols., Louvain–Leiden 1977–83).
[2] *Algazel's Metaphysics*, ed. J. T. Muckle (Toronto 1933).
[3] *Avencebrolis Fons vitae*, ed. C. Baeumker, BGPTM I.2–4 (1892–5).
[4] Ed. P. Correns, BGPTM I.1 (1891).
[5] Ed. L. Baur, BGPTM IV.2–3 (1903).

[6] Ed. G. Bülow, BGPTM xxiv.3 (1925).
[7] Ed. J. T. Muckle, *Mediaeval Studies* ii (1940) 31–103.

EVERARD OF YPRES *ca.* 1115 – after 1191
Born in Ypres (Flanders), Everard became a close disciple of Gilbert of Poitiers, whom he followed from Chartres (in the 1130s) to Paris (*ca.* 1137) to Poitiers (1142). Later (1162–5) Everard was in the entourage of Cardinal Hyacinthus, who became Pope Celestine III (1191–8). During Celestine's pontificate Everard, having become a Cistercian at Clairvaux (after 1185), wrote his *Dialogus Ratii et Everardi*,[1] a vivacious defence of the teachings of his master, Gilbert, against St Bernard of Clairvaux († 1153), who had attacked them. Everard is also the author of a *Summula decretalium quaestionum* (unpublished),[2] and of two letters on trinitarian speculation, the second in the fictive persona of a 'Frater B'.[3]

[1] Ed. N. M. Häring, *Mediaeval Studies* xv (1953) 243–89.
[2] See N. M. Häring, *Mediaeval Studies* xvii (1955) 143ff.
[3] Ed. N. M. Häring, *ibid.* pp. 162–72.

GARLANDUS COMPOTISTA (Garland the Computist) *ca.* 1015–1084/1102
Born in Lorraine and educated at Liège, Garland went to England in the reign of Harald I (1036–40) and stayed there till 1066. Later he was a *magister* at Besançon, where he died after 1084. His prolific writings, for the most part still unpublished, extended to chronology (*Compotus*), astronomy (*Tabulae astronomicae*), arithmetic (*De abaco*), and music (*De fistulis, De nolis*), to a comprehensive treatise on logic, *Dialectica*[1] (probably towards 1040) and perhaps one on grammar, to an encyclopaedic work on theology, *Candela*, and commentaries on the Psalms and Gospels combining excerpts from older sources.

[1] Ed. L. M. de Rijk (Assen 1959), on whose introduction the note above is based.

GERARD OF CREMONA (Gerardus Cremonensis) 1114–87
Gerard was the leading twelfth-century translator of scientific and philosophical works from Arabic into Latin. Daniel of Morley heard Gerard lecturing in Toledo *ca.* 1170, and a 'Gerardus dictus magister' is a witness to a document in the cartulary of Toledo cathedral dated 1176. The date of Gerard's death, and his age at the time, are given in the *Eulogium* written by his students.[1] According to this, Gerard came to Toledo because of his longing to read Ptolemy's *Almagest*, which he could not find among the Latins, and when he discovered there such an abundance of books in Arabic on every scientific discipline, for which nothing corresponding existed in Latin, he learnt Arabic in order to translate them. The *Eulogium* mentions some seventy translations made by Gerard, classifying them under logic, astronomy/astrology, philosophy, and medicine. Gerard appears to have attempted to translate complete syllabuses in astronomy and medicine. In the field of philosophy he translated several of the works of Aristotle (including the *Posterior Analytics*,[2] *Physics*, *De caelo, De generatione et corruptione*, and *Meteorologica*), some short treatises by al-Kindī,[3] al-Fārābī's *Catalogue of the Sciences*,[4] and the *Liber de causis*.[5] Gerard's translations are literal and accurate, and particularly suitable for scientific works.

[1] Ed. K. Sudhoff, *Archiv für Geschichte der Medizin* viii (1914) 73–82.
[2] Ed. L. Minio-Paluello, *Aristoteles Latinus* iv.3 (Leiden 1954).
[3] Ed. A. Nagy, BGPTM ii.5 (1897).
[4] Ed. A. González Paléncia, *Al-Fārābī, Catálogo de las ciencias* (2nd edn., Madrid–Granada 1953), pp. 119–76.
[5] Ed. A. Pattin, *Tijdschrift voor Filosofie* xxviii (1966) 90–203.
On Gerard's translations see most recently M.-Th. d'Alverny, *Harvard 1982*, pp. 452–4.

GILBERT OF POITIERS (Gilbert de la Porrée, Gilbertus Porreta) 1085/90–1154
Gilbert, born in Poitiers, studied first in his native town under Hilary, a schoolmaster
there, then at Chartres with the celebrated Bernard, and then at Laon with Anselm
and Ralph of Laon. Under Anselm's tutelage he composed a commentary on the
Psalms (unedited). By *ca.*1116 Gilbert had left Laon, and spent some time in Poitiers
before becoming, by 1124, a canon of Chartres. From 1126 till *ca.*1137 he was
chancellor at Chartres. Gilbert taught both at Chartres and in Paris before being made
Bishop of Poitiers in 1142. In the mid-1130s he composed a commentary on the
Pauline epistles (unedited) and, probably after this, his most ambitious and important
work, a commentary on four of Boethius' *Opuscula sacra*.[1] Gilbert's teachings on the
Trinity and Incarnation laid him open to charges of heresy. He was forced to defend
his views before Pope Eugene III, first in Paris (April 1147) and then at a consistory
after the Council of Reims (March 1148). There Bernard of Clairvaux was joined by a
number of eminent theologians (among them Peter Lombard and Robert of Melun)
in attacking Gilbert. But, despite Bernard's devious attempts to ensure a condemnation, the consistory allowed Gilbert to return to his diocese with his reputation
unharmed. The correction of his commentary on Boethius in accord with an agreed
profession of faith was left to the author himself; it seems unlikely that Gilbert saw
any need to alter it.

[1] *The Commentaries on Boethius by Gilbert of Poitiers*, ed. N. M. Häring (Toronto 1966). For
details of works sometimes attributed to Gilbert, and works by Gilbert's followers, the
Porretani, see above pp. 353–7.

GUNDISSALINUS: see 'Dominicus Gundissalinus'

HENRY ARISTIPPUS (Henricus Aristippus) *fl.* 1154–62
Archdeacon of Catania, Henry began his translation of Plato's *Phaedo*[1] in 1156, in the
camp of William I during the king's siege of Beneventum. Between 1158 and 1160 he
was William's ambassador to Constantinople, from where he brought back Greek
manuscripts, including Ptolemy's *Almagest*. In 1160 Henry became Admiral at
William's court in Palermo; he died in prison, captured during William's expedition
against Salerno. Henry also made translations of Plato's *Meno*[2] (1154–60) and of Book
IV of Aristotle's *Meteorologica* (still unpublished). His translations of Gregory Nazian-
zen and Diogenes Laertius, to which he alludes in his preface to the *Meno*, no longer
survive.

[1] Ed. L. Minio-Paluello, *Plato Latinus* II (London 1940).
[2] Ed. V. Kordeuter and C. Labowsky, *Plato Latinus* I (London 1940).

HERMANN OF CARINTHIA *fl.* 1138–43
Hermann – scientist, cosmologist, and translator of works from Arabic – was
probably a Slav by birth. He was a disciple of Thierry of Chartres, whom he
addresses as his teacher, and probably learnt Arabic in Spain. By 1138 Hermann was
sufficiently well versed in Arabic to translate an astrological work by Sahl ibn Bishr.
He is attested on the banks of the Ebro in 1141, at León soon afterwards, and in 1143
in the South of France, successively at Toulouse and Béziers. Hermann's translations
include the *Planisphere* of Ptolemy (dedicated to Thierry),[1] the *Greater Introduction to
Astrology* of Abū Ma'shar,[2] and, in all likelihood, Euclid's *Elements*,[3] alongside several
other works of astrology and astro-meteorology and two texts concerning the Muslim
faith. Some of his own scientific writings are free adaptations of, or compilations
from, Arabic works. However, the work in which he shows most originality is his

De essentiis,[4] a treatise on the coming-to-be of the world, on the underlying causes of the cosmos, and on man, which Hermann completed at Béziers in the second half of 1143. Hermann's only known pupil is Rudolph of Bruges, who wrote a work on the astrolabe.

[1] Ed. J. L. Heiberg, *Cl. Ptolemaei opera astronomica minora* (Leipzig 1907), pp. 225–59.
[2] Augsburg 1489; Venice 1506.
[3] Ed. H. L. L. Busard, *Janus* LIV (1967) 1–140: Books I–VI; and *Mathematical Centre Tracts* LXXXIV (1977): Books VII–XII.
[4] Ed. with English trans. by C. Burnett (Leiden–Cologne 1982).

HONORIUS AUGUSTODUNENSIS   *ca.* 1080 – *ca.* 1140

Probably of German birth, Honorius spent some time in England (perhaps as a disciple of Anselm at Canterbury), but the greater part of his life and work thereafter was linked with Regensburg. His vast output[1] includes didactic and historical, liturgical, exegetical, homiletic and ascetic works, and topical writings on the quarrel over investitures,[2] as well as the widely diffused and often translated encyclopaedic treatises *Elucidarium*[3] and *Imago mundi*.[4] Of greatest importance for the history of philosophy is Honorius' adaptation of Scotus Eriugena's *Periphyseon*, the *Clavis Physicae*.[5]

[1] P.L. 172 (with the exception of William of Conches's *Philosophia [mundi]*, 39–102, *De solis effectibus*, 101–16, and Salonius of Geneva's *Quaestiones*, 311–48).
[2] Ed. J. Dietrich, *Libelli de lite* III (MGH, 1897) 38–80.
[3] Ed. Y. Lefèvre, *L'Elucidarium et les Lucidaires* (Paris 1954), pp. 361–477.
[4] Ed. V. I. J. Flint, *AHDLMA* XLIX (1982) 7–153.
[5] Ed. P. Lucentini (Rome 1974).

HUGH OF SAINT-VICTOR (Hugo de Sancto Victore)   *ca.* 1096–1141

Born in Saxony, Hugh became a pupil of William of Champeaux at Saint-Victor in Paris, and later taught at Saint-Victor and became prior there (1133). Among his prolific writings on theology, Scripture, and contemplation,[1] those that treat especially of the arts and philosophy include the *Didascalicon*,[2] the *Opera propaedeutica (Practica geometriae, De grammatica, Epitome Dindimi in philosophiam)*[3] and *De contemplatione*.[4]

[1] P.L. 175–7.
[2] Ed. C. H. Buttimer (Washington 1939); English trans. by J. Taylor (New York 1961).
[3] Ed. R. Baron (Notre Dame 1966).
[4] Ed. R. Baron (Paris 1958).

HUGO OF SANTALLA (Hugo Santallensis)   *fl. s.* XII[1]

Hugo was born in Spain, and dedicated his works – translations of scientific texts from the Arabic – to Michael, Bishop of Tarazona (1119–51). He is presumably the 'magister Hugo' who witnessed two charters at Tarazona on 11 November 1145. Hugo translated works on scapulimancy, geomancy, astro-meteorology and astrology. One of these last, surviving in two Oxford MSS, is entitled 'Aristotle's book based on 255 Indian volumes of universal questions'[1] and contains genuine Indian material. Hugo's translation of Ibn al-Muthannā's commentary on al-Khwārizmī's astronomical tables is one of the means by which we know their contents, and his translation of pseudo-Apollonius' *Sirr al-khalīqa*, under the title *De secretis naturae*,[2] introduced into Latin Europe the *Tabula Smaragdina* ascribed to Hermes Trismegistus – a canonical text for alchemists. The Arabic texts which Hugo used for his translations may have come from the library of the Banū Hūd in the stronghold of Rueda de Jalón. A collection of his translations[3] appears in a MS that belonged to John Dee (now Oxford Bodl. Savile 15).

[1] Bodl. Digby 159 and Savile 15 (an ed. by C. Burnett and D. Pingree is in preparation).
[2] MS Paris B.N. lat. 13951 (an ed. by M.-Th. d'Alverny is in preparation).
[3] On Hugo's translations see C. H. Haskins, *Studies in the History of Mediaeval Science* (2nd ed., Cambridge, Mass. 1927), pp. 67–81; T. Charmasson, *Recherches sur une technique divinatoire: la géomancie dans l'occident médiéval* (Geneva–Paris 1980), pp. 95–109; C. Burnett, *Cambridge Medieval Celtic Studies* VI (1983) 31–42, and *Miscellanea Mediaevalia* XVII (1985) 161–71.

JAMES OF VENICE (Iacobus Veneticus Graecus) *fl.* 1125–50
Either a Greek born in Venice or a Venetian by birth or extraction who studied in Constantinople, James's achievements as a translator of Aristotle have been brought to light through the researches of L. Minio-Paluello.[1] James's translations include the *Posterior Analytics*,[2] *Sophistici elenchi*,[3] *Physics, De anima*, some of the *Parva naturalia*, and *Metaphysics*[4] I–IV 4, and an introduction to the *Physics* (*De intelligentiis*).

[1] *Opuscula: The Latin Aristotle* (Amsterdam 1972), esp. ch. 12.
[2] Ed. L. Minio-Paluello and B. G. Dod, *Aristoteles Latinus* IV (2nd ed., Leiden 1968).
[3] Fragments ed. B. G. Dod, *Aristoteles Latinus* VI (Leiden 1973).
[4] Ed. G. Vuillemin-Diem, *Aristoteles Latinus* XXV (Leiden 1976).
(Further Aristotelian translations by James will appear in the corpus, Aristoteles Latinus).

JOHN BLUND (Iohannes Blund) *ca.* 1175–1248
A student and teacher both in Oxford and Paris, John wrote his *Tractatus de anima*[1] probably in Paris *ca.* 1200. It is remarkable for its independent use of Avicenna's *De anima*, of much of the 'new' Aristotle, and of the *Metaphysics* of Algazel. John's later career was that of theologian and Chancellor of York Cathedral; he was elected Archbishop of Canterbury in 1232 but never consecrated.

[1] Ed. D. A. Callus and R. W. Hunt, Auctores Britannici Medii Aevi II (London 1970).

JOHN OF SALISBURY *ca.* 1115–80
Born near Salisbury, John studied especially in Paris and Chartres. In philosophy his most outstanding teachers were Abelard, William of Conches, Gilbert of Poitiers, and Thierry of Chartres. After his years of study, John served as a papal official, and later at the court of the Archbishop of Canterbury, first under Theobald then under Becket, whom he championed both before and after Becket's murder (1170). Among his numerous writings,[1] there are philosophical elements notably in the *Metalogicon*,[2] the *Policraticus*[3] (1159), and the verse *Entheticus de dogmate philosophorum*.[4]

[1] *Opera omnia*, ed. J. A. Giles (5 vols., Oxford 1848), and P.L. 199, 1–1040.
[2] Ed. C. C. J. Webb (Oxford 1929); English trans. by D. D. McGarry (Berkeley 1955).
[3] Ed. C. C. J. Webb (2 vols., Oxford 1909); the partial English trans. of J. Dickinson (New York 1927) is completed by that of J. B. Pike (Minneapolis 1938); Spanish trans. by M. A. Ladero and M. Alcalá (Madrid 1984).
[4] Ed. R. E. Pepin, *Traditio* XXXI (1975) 127–93.

JOHN OF SEVILLE *fl.* s. XII 2/4
John, an astrologer–astronomer and translator of scientific works from Arabic into Latin, has been confused in the past with a mysterious 'Avendauth' (s. XII[2]) and with another John who, together with Dominicus Gundissalinus, was involved in translating works of Avicenna and Algazel. John of Seville translated Abū Maʿshar's *Greater Introduction to Astrology*[1] (1133), the *Rudiments of Astronomy* of al-Farghānī

(1135), Thābit ibn Qurra's *De imaginibus* (about making talismans), and a few astrological works by Māshā'allāh and Sahl ibn Bishr, and wrote his own *Epitome of Astrology* (1135).[2] He appears to have ventured into the field of medicine, if he can be identified as the translator of an extract from the *Secret of Secrets* (dedicated to a queen of Spain), and of Costa ben Luca's *De differentia spiritus et animae*,[3] dedicated to Raymond, Archbishop of Toledo (1125–52). John's translations are exceedingly literal, and his name and style of writing suggest that he was a Mozarab.

[1] See R. Lemay, *Abū Ma'shar and Latin Aristotelianism in the Twelfth Century* (Beirut 1962).
[2] See especially M.-Th. d'Alverny, *Harvard 1982*, pp. 444–7.
[3] Ed. C. S. Barach (Innsbruck 1878).

MANEGOLD OF LAUTENBACH   *ca.*1045 – after 1103
Manegold, who was born at Lautenbach (Alsace) and travelled to study both in France and Germany, entered the order of the Augustinian canons regular; he died in his native region, probably at Marbach. Manegold's *Liber contra Wolfelmum*[1] (1085) is notable for its attack on certain Platonic and Macrobian motifs and on the abuses of dialectic, as well as for Manegold's vehemently pro-papal political philosophy. This is central to his other polemical treatise, *Ad Gebehardum liber*,[2] where in defining the nature of sovereignty he to some extent anticipates more recent conceptions of social contract.

[1] Ed. W. Hartmann (MGH, Weimar 1972).
[2] Ed. K. Francke, *Libelli de lite* I 308–430 (MGH, Berlin 1891).

MAURUS OF SALERNO (Maurus Salernitanus)   *ca.*1130–1214
Born of an aristocratic family in southern Italy, Maurus studied medicine in Salerno (*ca.*1150–60) as a pupil of Platearius, the author of the celebrated *Circa instans*, and of Petrus Musandinus. He had a long career as a teacher in the school of Salerno. At his death in 1214 Maurus left behind two sons, Matthew and John, themselves *magistri in phisica*, and his wife Theodora († 1239). Without neglecting the philosophical foundations of medicine and the use of logical argumentation, Maurus' work shows a constant preoccupation with medical praxis. The following among his works have received modern editions: *Anatomia*;[1] *De flebotomia*;[2] *Regulae urinarum*;[3] *Super Pronostica Hippocratis*;[4] and *Super Aphorismos Hippocratis*.[5] Maurus' commentaries on texts of the *Articella* (Iohannitius, Theophilus, Philaretus and Galen) also survive.[6]

[1] Ed. W. L. H. Ploss (Diss., Leipzig 1921).
[2] Ed. R. Buerschapper (Diss., Borna–Leipzig 1919).
[3] Ed. S. de Renzi, *Collectio Salernitana* III (Naples 1854) 2–51.
[4] Ed. with English trans. by M. H. Saffron, *Transactions of the American Philosophical Society*, N.S. LXII.1 (1972).
[5] Ed. S. de Renzi, *Collectio Salernitana* V (Naples 1856) 513–57.
[6] See P. O. Kristeller, *Studi sulla Scuola medica salernitana* (Naples 1986), pp. 126f, 147, 149f.

PETER ABELARD (Petrus Abaelardus)   1079–1142/4
Born in 1079 at Le Pallet in Brittany, from *ca.*1095 Abelard studied under Roscelin of Compiègne at Loches or Tours and then under William of Champeaux in Paris (before 1106 and again in 1108). He taught in various schools (Corbeil, 1102; Melun, *ca.*1104; the Mont Sainte-Geneviève outside Paris), and perhaps at this time wrote his short glosses on logical texts;[1] he briefly studied divinity under Anselm of Laon (after 1113) before returning to Paris to teach at Notre Dame from *ca.*1116. About this time he probably wrote his *Logica 'Ingredientibus'*.[2] *Ca.*1117–18 he married Heloise, but they were forced to separate shortly afterwards, Abelard becoming a monk at Saint-Denis,

Heloise a nun. In 1121 Abelard's *Theologia 'Summi boni'*[3] was condemned as heretical by a council at Soissons. In 1122 he taught again, at a rural retreat in Champagne that he called the oratory of the Paraclete. There he wrote his *Logica 'Nostrorum petitioni sociorum'*,[4] *Theologia Christiana*,[5] and further versions of a work begun previously, *Sic et Non*.[6] *Ca*.1127 Abelard became Abbot of Saint-Gildas-de-Rhuys in Brittany; the Paraclete was occupied in 1129 by a group of nuns led by Heloise. Before 1135 Abelard wrote an account of his life (*Historia calamitatum*).[7] In 1136 and 1140 he was again teaching in Paris, and during this period he wrote or revised his *Dialectica*,[8] and wrote his *Theologia 'Scholarium'*,[9] *Ethics*,[10] and *Dialogus*.[11] In 1140 he was again condemned for heresy, by a council at Sens. He retired to the abbey of Cluny and died at the priory of Saint-Marcel near Chalon-sur-Saône. Abelard's writings also include *Letters*,[12] and a short *Soliloquy*.[13] Some works are lost, among them a book on fallacies.[14] Other works attributed to him by some scholars include a treatise on *intellectus*[15] and further glosses on Porphyry *'secundum vocales'*.[16]

[1] Ed. M. Dal Pra, *Pietro Abelardo. Scritti di logica* (2nd ed., Florence 1969).
[2] Ed. B. Geyer, BGPTM xxi.1–3 (1919–27).
[3] Ed. H. Ostlender, BGPTM xxxv.2–3 (1939).
[4] Ed. B. Geyer, BGPTM xxi.4 (2nd ed., 1973).
[5] Ed. E. M. Buytaert, *Petri Abaelardi opera theologica* ii, CC CM XX (1969).
[6] Ed. B. B. Boyer and R. McKeon (Chicago–London 1976–7).
[7] Ed. J. Monfrin (3rd ed., Paris 1967).
[8] Ed. L. M. de Rijk (2nd ed., Assen 1969).
[9] (= *Introductio ad theologiam*), P.L. 178, 979–1114.
[10] Ed. with English trans. by D. E. Luscombe (Oxford 1971).
[11] Ed. R. Thomas (Stuttgart–Bad Cannstatt 1970); English trans. by P. J. Payer (Toronto 1979).
[12] *Letters I-VIII* (i = *Historia calamitatum*): ed. J. T. Muckle, *Mediaeval Studies* xii (1950) 163–213; xv (1953) 47–94; xvii (1955) 240–81; English trans. by B. Radice (Harmondsworth 1974). *Letters IX-XIV*: ed. E. R. Smits (Groningen 1983).
[13] Ed. C. Burnett, *Studi Medievali* ser. 3, xxv (1984) 857–94.
[14] *Sentences* which may have formed part of a lost work on fallacies have been ed. by L. Minio-Paluello, *Twelfth-Century Logic. Texts and Studies II: Abaelardiana Inedita* (Rome 1958).
[15] Ed. L. U. Ulivi (Rome 1976).
[16] Ed. C. Ottaviano, Fontes Ambrosiani iii (Florence 1933): extracts in BGPTM xxi.4, 581–8.

PETER ALFONSI (Petrus Alfonsi) *ca*.1060 – *ca*.1140

Peter, a Spanish Jew born at Huesca, who became Rabbi Moises Sephardi, changed his name at his conversion to Christianity in 1106. Well versed in Judaism, Islam, and Arabic literature and thought, Peter was court physician to both Alfonso I of Aragon and Henry I 'Beauclerc' of England. He wrote works on astronomy (*De dracone*)[1] and translated the *Astronomical Tables* of al-Khwārizmī;[2] his polemical work, the *Dialogus*,[3] aimed at converting the Jews, contains much of cosmological interest. Peter is probably also the author of the work known as *Liber Marii de elementis*.[4] He is most renowned, however, for his lively collection of Oriental tales and *exampla*, *Disciplina clericalis*.[5]

[1] Ed. J. M. MillásVallicrosa, *Sefarad* iii (1943) 65–105, at pp. 97–105.
[2] Ed. O. Neugebauer, *Historisk-filosofiske Skrifter udgivet af Det Kongelige Danske Videnskabernes Selskab* iv.2 (Copenhagen 1962).
[3] P.L. 157, 535–706.
[4] Ed. with English trans. by R. C. Dales (Berkeley–Los Angeles–London 1976); on the attribution to Peter, see M.-Th. d'Alverny, 'Pseudo-Aristotle, *De elementis*', in *Pseudo-Aristotle in the Middle Ages*, ed. J. Kraye *et al.* (London 1986), pp. 72f.

[5] Ed. A. Hilka and W. Söderhjelm (Helsingfors 1911; Editio minor, Heidelberg 1911); ed. with Spanish trans. by M. J. Lacarra and E. Ducay (Zaragoza 1980); English trans. by E. Hermes and P. R. Quarrie (Berkeley–Los Angeles–London 1977).

PETER HELIAS (Petrus Helias)   *fl.* 1130–66
Peter, a student of Thierry of Chartres, was an influential teacher of grammar and rhetoric in Paris from the 1130s to the 1150s, and an official of the cathedral of Poitiers from 1147 to 1166. His *Summa super Priscianum,*[1] partly based on the Priscian commentary of William of Conches,[2] contains important elements of speculative grammar. He is also the author of a commentary on Cicero's *De inventione*[3] (1130–9).

[1] Ed. J. E. Tolson (with an introd. by M. Gibson), *CIMAGL* XXVII–XXVIII (1978) 1–210.
[2] See K. M. Fredborg, *CIMAGL* XI (1973) 1–57.
[3] See K. M. Fredborg, *CIMAGL* XIII (1974) 31–41.

PETER MUSANDINUS (Petrus Musandinus)   s. XII
Peter Musandinus will have died before 1194, the probable date of Gilles de Corbeil's poem *De laudibus et virtutibus compositorum medicaminum,* ed. L. Choulant (Leipzig 1826), in which Peter is praised. He was the pupil of Bartholomew of Salerno, and the teacher of Maurus. Apart from his contributions to the commentaries that bear Bartholomew's name (see above), he composed works on dietetics and therapeutics.[1]

[1] See TK, cols. 217, 228, 344, 367, 999.

PHILIP THE CHANCELLOR   *ca.*1165–1236
Born in Paris, Philip, attested as Archdeacon of Noyon in 1211, became Chancellor of Notre Dame in Paris in 1217, a position he held, amid stormy disputes with the papacy, the University and the bishops, till his death. Famed as a lyrical poet and as a homilist, Philip in his *Summa de bono*[1] (*ca.*1225–8) makes extensive and original use of works of the 'new' Aristotle, including the *Physics, De anima,* and above all the *Ethics.* Philip is also one of the very first to cite Averroes, though his debt to Avicenna is more substantial.

[1] Ed. N. Wicki, Corpus Philosophorum Medii Aevi II–III (2 vols., Berne 1985).

PLATO OF TIVOLI   *fl.* 1134–45
Plato, a translator of scientific works from Arabic, was active in Barcelona. He contributed to the introduction of trigonometry into Europe through his translation of Abraham ibn Ezra's *Liber embadorum* ('*Book of* [*measuring*] *areas*'), and appears to be the author of the earliest translation into Latin of Archimedes' theorem for measuring the area of a circle.[1] Most of his translations, however, are of works of astronomy and astrology. The most important of these are al-Battānī's *Science of the Stars* (a revision of Ptolemy's *Almagest*) and Ptolemy's *Tetrabiblos.*[2] His commentary on the alchemical *Tabula Smaragdina* has been printed in modern times.[3]

[1] See M. Clagett, *Archimedes in the Middle Ages* I (Madison 1964) 16f.
[2] See L. Minio-Paluello, *Dictionary of Scientific Biography* XI (1975) 31–3.
[3] Ed. R. Steele and D. W. Singer, *Proceedings of the Royal Society of Medicine* XXI. 1 (1928) 485–501.

RADULPHUS DE LONGO CAMPO   1153/60 – after 1213
Roman by origin, Radulphus became a master of arts, physician, scientist, and Cistercian monk in France. He lived much of his life in Provence, teaching at Montpellier, where he wrote a *Summula de elocutione* (lost today). He lived in the abbey of Cîteaux during Alan of Lille's sojourn there, but himself died in Provence.

He is the author of *Cornicula, seu Summula de philosophia*, a youthful work dependent on William of Conches's *Philosophia*,[1] and of a *Computus*, both unpublished; of an encyclopaedic *Distinctiones*,[2] and of a remarkable commentary on his friend Alan of Lille's *Anticlaudianus*[3] (as far as IV 78). This, composed 1212/13, is dedicated to Arnald Amalric, Archbishop of Narbonne and persecutor of Cathars, who had been Abbot of Cîteaux in 1201–2. It shows knowledge of many medical writings, including those translated by Constantine and Gerard of Cremona's translation of Avicenna's *Canon*. Among Radulphus' lost works, mentioned by himself, were a medical treatise, *Regimentum sanitatis*, and one on optics, *De speculis*.

[1] See M. Grabmann, *Handschriftliche Forschungen zum Schrifttum des Wilhelm von Conches . . .*, *Sitzungsberichte der Bayerischen Akademie* (1935) X 33ff.
[2] Ed. J. Sulowski, Mediaevalia Philosophica Polonorum XXII (Académie polonaise des sciences, 1976).
[3] Ed. J. Sulowski (Wrocław 1972).

THIERRY OF CHARTRES (Theodoricus Carnotensis) † after 1156
A Breton by birth, probably the younger brother of Bernard of Chartres, Thierry was the most influential teacher of his generation. John of Salisbury, Peter Helias, Hermann of Carinthia, and Clarembald of Arras were among his disciples. Thierry taught at Chartres and quite possibly for a time elsewhere, perhaps (soon after 1130) in Paris. In the 1140s he was Chancellor at Chartres, and it is with the cathedral school there that, with the possible exception of his early commentaries on Cicero's *De inventione*[1] and on the *Ad Herennium*,[2] we can link Thierry's chief surviving works. These consist of a series of commentaries, often rich in philosophical insight, on Boethius' theological treatises,[3] an original treatise on cosmology (*De sex dierum operibus*),[4] and an encyclopaedic assemblage of texts on the seven Liberal Arts, *Heptateuchon*, to which Thierry contributed a prologue as well as various notes (left incomplete).[5] At some date in the 1150s Thierry resigned from Chartres to end his days in a monastery, perhaps the Cistercian abbey of Vaux-de-Cernay.

[1] Ed. K. M. Fredborg (Toronto 1987).
[2] Unpublished: see K. M. Fredborg, *CIMAGL* VII (1971) 225–60.
[3] Ed. N. M. Häring, *Commentaries on Boethius by Thierry of Chartres and his School* (Toronto 1971); Italian trans. of the *Glosa* (Häring, pp. 259–310) in E. Maccagnolo, *Il divino e il megacosmo* (Milan 1980), pp. 103–78.
[4] Ed. N. M. Häring, *ibid.* pp. 553–75; trans. E. Maccagnolo, *ibid.* pp. 179–206.
[5] The prologue and one of the notes are ed. in E. Jeauneau, *Lectio philosophorum* (Amsterdam 1973), pp. 37–9.

URSO OF SALERNO (Urso of Calabria, Urso Salernitanus) *fl. s.* XII[2]
Urso, born in Calabria, was the last of the masters of the School of Salerno's greatest period. He was a contemporary of Maurus; the date of his death, generally given as 1225 (on the basis of the necrology in the *Liber Confratrum* of San Matteo di Salerno), is somewhat problematic, in that some of Urso's works were already copied *ca.* 1160–80 in the celebrated Codex Salernitanus (formerly MS Breslau 1302), which today is lost. It is not easy to characterize Urso's scientific achievement, because of the complexity of his work, which to a large extent goes beyond medicine in the strict sense towards problems of philosophy and physics, even towards mysticism. Urso is the author of *Aphorismi cum Glossulis*,[1] *De commixtionibus elementorum*[2] (where he mentions two other works, *De pulsibus* and *De diebus creticis*, that have not survived), *De effectibus qualitatum*,[3] *De effectibus medicinarum*,[4] *De effectibus qualitatum*

accidentalibus,[5] *De gradibus,*[6] *De saporibus et odoribus,*[7] *De coloribus,*[8] and perhaps of the brief *De urinis*[9] and *Anatomia.*[10]

[1] Ed. R. Creutz, *Quellen und Studien zur Geschichte der Naturwissenschaften und der Medizin* v.1 (1936).
[2] Ed. W. Stürner (Stuttgart 1976).
[3] Ed. C. Matthaes (Diss., Borna–Leipzig 1918).
[4] Ed. C. Matthaes, *ibid.*
[5] Ed. K. Sudhoff, *Archiv für Geschichte der Medizin* xii (1920) 139–43.
[6] Ed. K. Sudhoff, *ibid.* pp. 135–8.
[7] Ed. G. F. Hartmann (Diss., Borna–Leipzig 1919).
[8] Ed. L. Thorndike, *Ambix* vii (1959) 7–16.
[9] Ed. P. Giacosa, *Magistri Salernitani nondum editi* (Turin 1901), pp. 283–9. G. Keil, *Der 'Kurze Harntraktat' des Breslauer 'Codex Salernitanus' und seine Sippe* (Diss., Bonn 1959), casts doubt on the attribution.
[10] Ed. K. Sudhoff, *Archiv für Geschichte der Medizin* xx (1928) 40–50.

WILLIAM OF CHAMPEAUX *ca.*1070–1122

Born at Champeaux (near Melun), William taught in Paris at the Cathedral school of Notre Dame, where Abelard was his pupil and soon became his opponent, and from 1110 at Saint-Victor, the Parisian abbey-school of the Augustinian canons regular that William helped to found. In 1113 he was elected Bishop of Châlons-sur-Marne. Together with his teacher, Anselm of Laon, William was one of the founders of early scholasticism, teaching rhetoric, logic, and theology. His theological works[1] are transmitted chiefly in collective texts; his rhetorical commentaries[2] are still unpublished; his logic[3] is known only indirectly, particularly through Abelard.

[1] See O. Lottin, *Psychologie et morale aux XIIe et XIIIe siècles* v (Gembloux 1959) 189–227.
[2] See K. M. Fredborg, *CIMAGL* xvii (1976) 1–39.
[3] See N. J. Green-Pedersen, *CIMAGL* xiii (1974) 13–30.

WILLIAM OF CONCHES (Guillaume de Conches) *ca.*1085 – after 1154

Born at Conches in Normandy, William was a pupil of Bernard of Chartres and then most probably went on to teach at Chartres himself. To the early period of his activity belong commentaries on Boethius' *Consolation of Philosophy,*[1] on Macrobius,[2] Priscian (a later redaction is also extant),[3] and Juvenal,[4] and lost commentaries on Martianus Capella[5] and Vergil's *Aeneid,*[6] as well as his comprehensive and innovative *Philosophia*[7] (*ca.*1125). Later, as tutor to Geoffrey Plantagenet, Duke of Normandy, William wrote the dialogue *Dragmaticon*[8] (1144–9), which, like the *Philosophia,* deals with every aspect of the cosmos and man. To this period likewise belongs William's commentary on Plato's *Timaeus,*[9] though, as in his earlier commentaries, there are traces of more than one recension. William's approach to cosmological problems owes something to medical writings translated from the Arabic (Constantine, Johannitius) and Greek (Theophilus), to Seneca's *Quaestiones naturales* and to Nemesius' *De natura hominis* (in Alfanus of Salerno's translation). It is possible though not certain that William was also responsible for the influential ethical compilation, *Moralium dogma philosophorum,*[10] which was translated into several medieval vernaculars.

[1] Extracts ed. C. Jourdain, *Notices et extraits des manuscrits de la Bibliothèque Nationale* xx.2 (Paris 1862) 40–82, and J. M. Parent, *La doctrine de la création dans l'école de Chartres* (Paris–Ottawa 1938), pp. 122–36.
[2] Extracts ed. P. Dronke, *Fabula* (Leiden–Cologne 1974), pp. 68–78.
[3] Extracts ed. E. Jeauneau, *Lectio philosophorum* (Amsterdam 1973), pp. 335–70.
[4] Ed. B. Wilson (Paris 1980 – often giving a garbled text).

5 See P. Dronke, *Fabula* (n. 4), pp. 167–83.
6 See P. Dronke, 'Bernardo Silvestre', *Enciclopedia Virgiliana* I (Rome 1985) 497–500.
7 Ed. with German trans. by G. Maurach (Pretoria 1980).
8 Ed. G. Gratarolus (Strasbourg 1567; repr. Frankfurt a. M. 1967); Italian trans. by E. Maccagnolo, *Il divino e il megacosmo* (Milan 1980), pp. 241–453.
9 *Glosae super Platonem*, ed. E. Jeauneau (Paris 1965).
10 Ed. J. Holmberg (Uppsala 1929), with the Old French and Middle Frankish translations.

WILLIAM OF LUCCA (Wilhelmus Lucensis) † 1178
Born in Lucca, William, who underwent the influence of the *Porretani* in northern France, returned to teach both in Lucca and in Bologna, where he is buried. Of his work, only the first part of a vast commentary on pseudo-Dionysius' *On the Divine Names*[1] survives (written 1169–77). The unique manuscript (Troyes 1003), from Clairvaux, has glosses that may be by Everard of Ypres. The work is notable for its assimilation of the thought of John Scotus Eriugena as well as of Gilbert of Poitiers.

1 *Comentum in tertiam ierarchiam Dionisii que est de divinis nominibus*, ed. F. Gastaldelli (Florence 1983).

GENERAL BIBLIOGRAPHY

Abelard, Peter, *see* Peter Abelard.

Abeloos, E. B. (1972). 'Un cinquième manuscrit du "Tractatus de anima" de Dominique Gundissalinus', *Bulletin de Philosophie Médiévale* XIV: 72–85.

Abū Ma'shar, *Introductorium maius, see* Hermann of Carinthia.

Abū Rīda (1950). *Rasā'il al-Kindī al-falsafiyya* I, Cairo.

Actas del V Congreso Internacional de Filosofia Medieval (1979). (2 vols.), Madrid.

Actes du Colloque de Neuchâtel, 16–17 nov. 1979 (1981). *Abélard*, Cahiers de la Revue de Théologie et de Philosophie VI, Geneva.

Actes du IVe Congrès International de Philosophie Médiévale, Montréal, 27 août–2 sept. 1967 (1969). *Arts libéraux et philosophie au moyen âge*, Montreal–Paris.

Adam Parvipontanus (1853). *Epistola Adami Balsamiensis ad Anselmum*, ed. A. H. Hoffmann von Fallersleben, Neuwied–Cologne–Hanover.

(1956). *Adam Balsamiensis Parvipontani Ars disserendi (Dialectica Alexandri)*, ed. L. Minio-Paluello, *Twelfth Century Logic: Texts and Studies I*, Rome.

Adams, M. (1972). 'Was Anselm a Realist? The *Monologium*', *Franciscan Studies* XXII: 5–14.

Adelard of Bath (1881). *Regulae abaci*, ed. B. Boncompagni, *Bollettino di Bibliografia e di Storia delle Scienze Matematiche e Fisiche* XIV: 1–134.

(1898). *Liber ysagogarum Alchorismi I–III*, ed. M. Curtze, *Abhandlungen zur Geschichte der Mathematik* VIII: 1–27.

(1903). *De eodem et diverso*, ed. Hans Willner, BGPTM IV.1.

(1914). *Die astronomischen Tafeln*, ed. H. Suter, *Det Kongelige Danske Videnskabernes Selskabs Skrifter*, 7th ser., Hist. og Filos. Afdeling III, Copenhagen.

(1934). *Quaestiones naturales*, ed. M. Müller, BGPTM XXXI.2.

(1983). *The First Latin Translation of Euclid's Elements, commonly ascribed to Adelard of Bath*, ed. H. L. L. Busard, Toronto.

Adhémar of Saint-Ruf, see N. M. Häring.

d'Agostino, V. (1962). *Studi sul Neostoicismo* (2nd ed.), Turin.

Alan of Lille (P.L. 210). *Contra haereticos* (= *De fide catholica*): 305–430.

(P.L. 210). *Distinctiones*: 685–1012.

(1953). *Summa 'Quoniam homines'*, ed. P. Glorieux, *AHDLMA* XX: 113–364.

(1955). *Anticlaudianus*, ed. Robert Bossuat, Paris.

(1960). *De virtutibus et vitiis*, ed. O. Lottin, *Psychologie et morale aux XIIe et XIIIe siècles* VI, Gembloux.

(1965a). *Alain de Lille: Textes inédits*, ed. M.-T. d'Alverny, Paris.

(1965b). *Sermo*, 'De clericis ad theologiam non accedentibus', in M.-T. d'Alverny (ed.), *Alain de Lille: Textes inédits*, Paris.

(1965c). *Sermo de sphaera intelligibili*, in Alan of Lille (1965a).

(1978). *De planctu Naturae*, ed. N. M. Häring, *Studi Medievali*, ser. 3, XIX: 797–879.

(1981). 'Magister Alanus de Insulis. *Regulae caelestis iuris*' (= *Theologicae regulae*), ed. N. M. Häring, *AHDLMA* XLVIII: 97–226.

Albert, K. (1976). 'Amalrich von Bena und der mittelalterliche Pantheismus', *Miscellanea Mediaevalia* X: 193–212.

Alessio, Franco (1965). 'La filosofia e le "artes mechanicae" nel secolo XII', *Studi Medievali*, ser. 3, VI: 110–29.

Alexander, J. J. G., and Gibson, M. T. (eds.) (1976). *Medieval Learning and Literature: Essays presented to Richard William Hunt*, Oxford.

Alexander of Hales (1951). *Glossa in quatuor libros Sententiarum Petri Lombardi, in librum primum*, Quaracchi–Florence.

Alexander Nequam (1863). *Alexandri Neckam De naturis rerum libri duo*, ed. T. Wright (Books I–II only; Books III–IV are unprinted), Rolls Series, London, pp. 1–354. *De laudibus divinae sapientiae*, ibid., pp. 357–503.

Alexander de Villa-Dei (1974). *Doctrinale*, ed. D. Reichling, New York.

Alfanus of Salerno (1917). *Nemesii episcopi Premnon physicon . . . in Latinum translatus*, ed. C. Burkhard, Leipzig.

Alfonsi, Peter, see Peter Alfonsi.

Alfred of Sareshel (1923). *De motu cordis*, ed. C. Baeumker, BGPTM XXIII.1–2.

Algazel (1933). *Algazel's Metaphysics*, ed. J. T. Muckle, Toronto.

Allard, A. (1975). *Les plus anciennes versions latines du XIIe siècle issues de l'arithmétique d'Al-Khwārizmī*, Louvain.

Allard, B. C. (1976). 'Note sur le "De immortalitate animae" de Guillaume d'Auvergne', *Bulletin de Philosophie Médiévale*, XVIII: 68–72.

Allard, G. H., and Lusignan, S. (eds.) (1982). *Les arts mécaniques au Moyen Age*, Cahiers d'Etudes Médiévales VII, Montreal–Paris.

d'Alverny, M.-T. (1948). 'Deux traductions latines du Coran au Moyen Age', *AHDLMA* XVI: 69–131.

(1950–1). 'Un fragment du procès des Amauriciens', *AHDLMA* XVIII: 325–36.

(1952). 'Notes sur les traductions médiévales des oeuvres arabes d'Avicenne', *AHDLMA* XIX: 337–58.

(1953). 'Le cosmos symbolique du XIIe siècle', *AHDLMA* XX: 31–81.

(1959). 'Anniyya–Anitas', in *Mélanges Etienne Gilson*, Toronto–Paris.

(1960). 'Liber XXIV philosophorum', in *Catalogus translationum et commentariorum* I, Washington, D.C.

(1962). 'La tradition manuscrite de l'Avicenne latin', in *Mélanges en l'honneur de Taha Husein*, Cairo.

(1964). 'Alain de Lille et la *Theologia*', in *L'homme devant Dieu. Mélanges Henri de Lubac* II, Paris.

(1973). 'Une rencontre symbolique de Jean Scot Erigène et d'Avicenne. Notes sur le *De causis primis et secundis et fluxu qui consequitur eas*', in J. J. O'Meara and L. Bieler (eds.), *The Mind of Eriugena*, Dublin.

(1982a). 'Les nouveaux apports dans les domaines de la science et de la pensée au temps de Philippe Auguste: La philosophie', in *La France de Philippe Auguste: Le temps des mutations*, Colloques Internationaux du CNRS, DCII, Paris.

(1982b). 'Translations and Translators', in *Harvard 1982*.

(1986). 'Pseudo-Aristotle, *De elementis*', in J. Kraye, W. F. Ryan and C. B. Schmitt (eds.), *Pseudo-Aristotle in the Middle Ages*, London.

d'Alverny, M.-T., and Vajda, G. (1951). 'Marc de Tolède, traducteur d'Ibn Tumart', *al-Andalus* XVI: 99–110.

Amalric of Bène, see Albert, K.; d'Alverny, M.-T.; Capelle, G. C.; *Contra Amaurianos*; Lucentini, Paolo

Anawati, G. C. A., and Iskandar, A. L. (1978). Article on Ḥunayn, *Dictionary of Scientific Biography* XV, suppl. I, New York.

Anciaux, P. (1949). *La théologie du sacrement de pénitence au XIIe siècle*, Louvain–Gembloux.
Anonymous (1927). *Liber XXIV philosophorum*, ed. C. Baeumker, BGPTM xxv. 1–2: 194–214.
Anonymous (1942). *Liber Hermetis de XV stellis*, ed. L. Delatte, *Textes latins et vieux français relatifs aux Cyranides*, Paris.
Anonymous (1955). *Liber Hermetis Mercurii Triplicis de VI rerum principiis*, ed. T. Silverstein, *AHDLMA* xxii: 217–302.
Anonymous (1972). *Liber de ordine creaturarum*, ed. M. C. Díaz y Díaz, Santiago de Compostela.
Anonymous (1979). *The Prose Salernitan Questions*, ed. B. Lawn, Auctores Britannici Medii Aevi v, London.
Anonymous (1984). *Liber Alcidi de immortalitate animae: Studio e edizione critica*, ed. Paolo Lucentini, Naples.
Anselm of Canterbury (1936). 'Ein neues unvollendetes Werk des hl. Anselm von Canterbury' ('Lambeth Fragments' or 'Philosophical Fragments'), ed. F. S. Schmitt, BGPTM xxxiii.3: 23–45.
 (1938–61). *S. Anselmi Opera omnia*, ed. F. S. Schmitt (6 vols.), Seckau–Rome–Edinburgh; reprinted Stuttgart–Bad Cannstatt, 1968.
 (1952–3). *Obras completas*, with Spanish trans. by J. Alameda (2 vols.), Madrid.
 (1962). *Proslogion*, ed. with German trans. by F. S. Schmitt, Stuttgart–Bad Cannstatt.
 (1963). *Anselme de Cantorbéry, Pourquoi Dieu s'est fait homme*, ed. and trans. R. Roques, Paris.
 (1964a). *The De grammatico of St. Anselm*, ed. with English trans. by D. P. Henry, University of Notre Dame Publications in Medieval Studies xviii, Notre Dame.
 (1964b). *Monologion*, ed. with German trans. by F. S. Schmitt, Stuttgart–Bad Cannstatt.
 (1964c). *Proslogion*, ed. with French trans. by A. Koyré (3rd ed.), Paris.
 (1965a). *Cur deus homo*, ed. with German trans. by F. S. Schmitt, Darmstadt.
 (1965b). *Proslogion*, ed. with English trans. by M. J. Charlesworth, Oxford.
 (1966). *De veritate*, ed. with German trans. by F. S. Schmitt, Stuttgart–Bad Cannstatt.
 (1969). *Memorials of St Anselm*, ed. R. W. Southern and F. S. Schmitt, Auctores Britannici Medii Aevi i, London.
 (1974–6). *Anselm of Canterbury, [Works]*, English trans. by J. Hopkins and H. Richardson (4 vols.), London–Toronto–New York.
Aristippus, Henry, *see* Henry Aristippus.
Asclepius (1961). *Corpus Hermeticum* ii, ed. A. D. Nock and A.-J. Festugière (2nd ed.), Paris, pp. 257–401.
Atti del Convegno Internazionale di Storia della Logica, San Gimignano, 4–8 Dec. 1982 (1983). Bologna.
Atti del iii Congresso Internazionale di Filosofia Medioevale, Passo della Mendola – Trento, 31 Aug.–5 Sept. 1964 (1966). *La filosofia della natura nel Medioevo*, Milan.
Audet, T. A. (1949). 'Une source augustinienne de l'argument de saint Anselme', in J. Maritain *et al.*, *Etienne Gilson, philosophe de la Chrétienté*, Paris.
Augustinus Hibernicus (P.L. 35). *De mirabilibus sacrae scripturae*: 2149–2200.
Avencebrol (1891–5). *Fons vitae*, ex Arabico in Latinum translatus ab Johanne Hispano et Dominico Gundissalino, ed. C. Baeumker, BGPTM i.2–4.
[Avicenna Latinus] (1968). *Liber de anima IV–V*, ed. S. van Riet, Louvain–Leiden.
 (1972). *Liber de anima seu sextus de naturalibus I–III*, ed. S. van Riet, Louvain–Leiden.
 (1977, 1980, 1983). *Liber de philosophia prima sive scientia divina*, ed. S. van Riet (3 vols.), Louvain–Leiden.
Baader, G., and Keil, G. (eds.) (1982). *Medizin im mittelalterlichen Abendland*, Wege der Forschung ccclxiii, Darmstadt.

Baeumker, C. (1890). *Das Problem der Materie in der griechischen Philosophie*, Münster.

Barnes, J. (1981). 'Boethius and the Study of Logic', in M. Gibson (ed.), *Boethius, His Life, Thought and Influence*, Oxford.

Baron, Roger (1957). *Science et sagesse chez Hugues de St. Victor*, Paris.

Bartholomew of Salerno (1856). *Practica Bartholomaei*, ed. S. de Renzi, Collectio Salernitana IV, Naples.

(1924). [Letter to Peter the Venerable], ed. H. Quentin, in *Scritti di storia e paleografia: Miscellanea Francesco Ehrle* I, Rome, 85f.

(1956). [Letter to Louis VII], ed. C. H. Talbot, *Bulletin of the History of Medicine* XXX: 326–8.

Beaujouan, Guy (1975). 'Réflexions sur les rapports entre théories et pratique au moyen âge', in J. E. Murdoch and E. D. Sylla (eds.), *The Cultural Context of Medieval Learning*, Dordrecht–Boston.

(1982). 'The Transformation of the Quadrivium', in *Harvard 1982*.

Beaumont, J. (1981). 'The Latin Tradition of the *De consolatione Philosophiae*', in M. Gibson (ed.), *Boethius: His Life, Thought and Influence*, Oxford.(*See also* Reuter-Beaumont, J.)

Beccaria, A. (1959, 1961, 1971). 'Sulle tracce di un antico canone latino di Ippocrate e di Galeno', *Italia Medioevale e Umanistica* II: 1–56; IV: 1–75; XIV: 1–23.

Beckmann, J. P., *et al.* (eds.) (1981). *Sprache und Erkenntnis im Mittelalter*. Proceedings of the 6th International Congress ... of the S.I.E.P.M., Bonn 29.8–3.9, 1977 (*Miscellanea Mediaevalia* XIII.1), Berlin–New York.

Bede, pseudo- (1985). *De mundi celestis terrestrisque constitutione*, ed. Charles Burnett, Warburg Institute Surveys and Texts X, London.

Benson, R. L., and Constable, G. (eds.) (1982). *Renaissance and Renewal in the Twelfth Century*, Cambridge, Mass. (= *Harvard 1982*).

Benton, John F. (1975). 'Philology's Search for Abelard in the *Metamorphosis Goliae*', *Speculum* L: 199–217.

Benz, E. (1929). *Das Todesproblem in der stoischen Philosophie*, Stuttgart.

Beonio-Brocchieri Fumagalli, M. T. (1969). *The Logic of Peter Abelard*, Dordrecht.

Beonio-Brocchieri Fumagalli, M. T., *et al.* (1985). *Momenti e modelli nella storia dell'enciclopedia* (= *Rivista Critica di Storia della Filosofia* XL. 1).

Bernard Silvestris (1895). *Mathematicus*, ed. B. Hauréau, *Le Mathematicus de Bernard Sylvestris et la Passio S. Agnetis de Pierre Riga*, Paris.

(1959). *Experimentarius*, ed. M. Brini Savorelli ('Un manuale di geomanzia presentato da Bernardo Silvestre da Tours, XII secolo: l'Experimentarius'), *Rivista Critica di Storia della Filosofia* XIV: 283–342).

(1973). *The Cosmographia of Bernardus Silvestris*, English trans. by W. Wetherbee, New York.

(1977). *The Commentary on the First Six Books of the Aeneid of Vergil*, ed. J. W. Jones and E. F. Jones, Lincoln–London.

(1978). *Cosmographia*, ed. Peter Dronke, Leiden.

(1979). *The Commentary on the First Six Books of the Aeneid of Vergil*, English trans. by E. G. Schreiber and T. E. Maresca, Lincoln–London.

(1980). *Cosmographia*, Italian trans. by E. Maccagnolo, in his *Il divino e il megacosmo*, Milan.

(1986). *The Commentary on Martianus Capella's De nuptiis Philologiae et Mercurii*, ed. H. H. Westra, Toronto.

Berschin, W. (1980). *Griechisch-lateinisches Mittelalter*, Bern–Munich.

Bird, O. (1959). 'The Logical Interest of the Topics as seen in Abelard', *Modern Schoolman* XXXVII: 53–7.

(1960). 'The Formalizing of the Topics in Mediaeval Logic', *Notre Dame Journal of Formal Logic* I: 138–49.

(1962). 'The Tradition of the Logical Topics: Aristotle to Ockham', *Journal of the History of Ideas* XXIII: 307–23.

Birkenmajer, Alexander (1930). 'Le rôle joué par les médecins et les naturalistes dans la réception d'Aristote aux XIIe et XIIIe siècles', in *La Pologne au VIe Congrès International des Sciences Historiques, Oslo 1928*, Warsaw; reprinted in his *Etudes* (1970).

(1933). 'Découverte de fragments manuscrits de David de Dinant', *Revue Néoscolastique de Philosophie* XXXV: 220–9; reprinted in his *Etudes* (1970).

(1970). *Etudes d'histoire des sciences et de la philosophie du Moyen Age*, Studia Copernicana I, Wrocław–Warsaw–Cracow.

Bloch, Ernst (1963). *Avicenna und die Aristotelische Linke* (2nd ed.), Frankfurt.

Blomme, R. (1958). *La doctrine du péché dans les écoles théologiques de la première moitié du XIIe siècle*, Louvain.

Bloos, L. *Probleme der stoischen Physik*, Hamburger Studien zur Philosophie IV, Hamburg.

Blund, John, *see* John Blund.

Bodson, A. (1967). *La morale sociale des derniers stoïciens, Sénèque, Epictète et Marc-Aurèle*, Paris.

Boeft, J. den (1970). *Calcidius on Fate. His Doctrine and Sources*, Leiden.

Boese, H. (ed.) (1958). *Die Mittelalterliche Übersetzung der Στοιχείωσις φυσική des Proclus; Procli Diadochi Elementatio physica*, Berlin.

Boh, I. (1982). 'Consequences', in *CHLMP*.

Bos, E. P. (forthcoming). 'Quelques remarques sur les vues sémantiques des *Introductiones Montanae Maiores et Minores*', in A. de Libera's forthcoming ed. of the 7th Symposium on Medieval Logic and Semantics, Poitiers 1985.

Bottin, F. (forthcoming). 'Quelques discussions sur la transitivité de la prédication dans l'école d'Albéric du Mont', in A. de Libera's forthcoming ed. of the proceedings of the 7th Symposium on Medieval Logic and Semantics, Poitiers 1985.

Braakhuis, H. A. G. (1980). *De 13de Eeuwse Tractaten over Syncategorematische Termen* (2 vols.), Nijmegen.

Braakhuis, H. A. G., Kneepkens, C. H., de Rijk, L. M. (eds.) (1981). *English Logic and Semantics. From the End of the Twelfth Century to the Time of Ockham and Burleigh*, Acts of the 4th European Symposium on Medieval Logic and Semantics (*Artistarium*, suppl. I), Nijmegen.

Bréhier, E. (1943). *Histoire de la philosophie* I, Paris.

Bresson, L. (1974). *Le même et l'autre dans la structure ontologique du Timée de Platon. Un commentaire systématique du Timée de Platon*, Paris.

Briard, Joel (forthcoming). 'La signification des termes dans l'*Ars Meliduna*', in A. de Libera's forthcoming ed. of the proceedings of the 7th Symposium on Medieval Logic and Semantics, Poitiers 1985.

Brooke, C. (1984). 'John of Salisbury and his World', in M. Wilks (ed.), *The World of John of Salisbury*, Oxford.

Brunner, F. (1966). '*Creatio numerorum, rerum est creatio*', in *Mélanges René Crozet* II, Poitiers.

Bruyne, Edgar de (1946). *Etudes d'esthétique médiévale* (3 vols.), Ghent.

Bulmer-Thomas, I. (1971). 'Euclid', in C. C. Gillispie (ed.), *Dictionary of Scientific Biography* IV, New York.

Burgundio of Pisa (1955). [Trans. of St John Damascene] in E. M. Buytaert (ed.), *De fide orthodoxa: Versions of Burgundio and Cerbanus*, New York–Paderborn.

(1975). *Némésius d'Emèse, De natura hominis: Traduction de Burgundio de Pise*, ed. G. Verbeke and J. R. Moncho, Leiden.

(1976). *Burgundio of Pisa's Translation of Galen's Περὶ κράσεων, 'De complexionibus'*, ed. R. J. Durling, Ars Medica II, Galenus Latinus I, Berlin–New York.

Burnett, C. S. F. (1977). 'A Group of Arabic-Latin Translators working in Northern Spain in the mid-12th Century', *Journal of the Royal Asiatic Society*, 62–108.

(1978a). 'What is the *Experimentarius* of Bernardus Silvestris? A Preliminary Survey of the Material', *AHDLMA* XLIV: 79–125.

(1978b). 'Arabic into Latin in Twelfth-Century Spain: the Works of Hermann of Carinthia', *Mittellateinisches Jahrbuch* XIII: 100–34.

(1981). 'Hermann of Carinthia and the kitāb al-Isṭamāṭīs', *Journal of the Warburg and Courtauld Institutes* XLIV: 167–9.

(1983). 'Arabic Divinatory Texts and Celtic Folklore', in *Cambridge Medieval Celtic Studies* VI: 31–42.

(1984). 'The Contents and Affiliation of the Scientific Manuscripts written at, or brought to, Chartres in the Time of John of Salisbury', in M. Wilks (ed.), *The World of John of Salisbury*, Oxford.

(1985). 'Some Comments on the Translating of works from Arabic into Latin', *Miscellanea Mediaevalia* XVII: 161–71.

(1986a). 'Arabic, Greek and Latin Works on Astrological Magic attributed to Aristotle', in J. Kraye, W. F. Ryan and C. B. Schmitt (eds.), *Pseudo-Aristotle in the Middle Ages*, London.

(1986b). 'Hermann of Carinthia's Attitude towards his Arabic Sources', in C. Wenin (ed.), *L'homme et son univers au moyen âge*, Louvain.

Buytaert, E. M. (ed.) (1974). *Peter Abelard*, Proceedings of the International Conference, Louvain, May 10–12, 1971, Louvain–The Hague.

Callus, D. A. (1941). 'Philip the Chancellor and the *De anima* ascribed to Robert Grosseteste', *MARS* I.1: 105–27.

Capelle, G. C. (1932). *Autour du décret de 1210: III. – Amaury de Bène. Etude sur son panthéisme formel*, Paris.

Cappuyns, M. (1931). 'Le plus ancien commentaire des "Opuscula sacra" et son origine', *RTAM* III: 237–72.

Cenacchi, G. (1974). *Il pensiero filosofico di Anselmo d'Aosta*, Padua.

Chabot, J. B. (1965). 'Version syriaque de traités médicaux dont l'original n'a pas été retrouvé', *Notices et Extraits des Manuscrits de la Bibliothèque Nationale* XLII: 77–143.

Chadwick, H. (1981). *Boethius. The Consolations of Music, Logic and Philosophy*, Oxford.

Charmasson, T. (1980). *Recherches sur une technique divinatoire: la géomancie dans l'occident médiéval*, Geneva–Paris.

Chenu, M.-D. (1935). 'Un essai de méthode théologique au XIIe siècle', *RSPT* XXIV: 258–67.

(1946). 'Imaginatio. Note de lexicographie philosophique médiévale', in *Miscellanea Giovanni Mercati* II, Vatican City.

(1954). 'Platon à Cîteaux', *AHDLMA* XXI: 99–106.

(1957). *La théologie au XIIe siècle*, Paris (Translated by Jerome Taylor and L. K. Little as *Nature, Man and Society in the Twelfth Century*, Chicago 1968).

(1961). 'Une définition pythagoricienne de la vérité au Moyen Age', *AHDLMA* XXVIII: 7–13.

(1967). 'Un cas de platonisme grammatical au XIIe siècle', *RSPT* LI: 666–8.

Christensen, J. (1962). *An Essay on the Unity of Stoic Philosophy*, Copenhagen.

Chroust, A. H. (1963). 'Some Historical Observations on Natural Law and "According to Nature"', *Emerita* XXXI: 285–98.

Cicchetti, A. (1951). *L'Agostinismo nel pensiero di Anselmo d'Aosta*, Rome.

Ciotti, Andrea (1960). 'Alano e Dante', *Convivium* XXVIII: 257–88.

Clagett, M. (1964). *Archimedes in the Middle Ages*, Madison, Wisc.

(1970). 'Adelard of Bath', in *Dictionary of Scientific Biography* I, New York.

(ed.) (1954). 'King Alfred and the *Elements* of Euclid', *Isis* XLV: 269–77.

Clagett, M., Post, G., and Reynolds, R. (eds.) (1961). *Twelfth Century Europe and the Foundations of Modern Society*, Madison, Wisc.

Clarembald of Arras (1955). *Clarembaldi Epistola*, ed. N. M. Häring, *AHDLMA* XXII: 183.

(1965). *Life and Works of Clarembald of Arras*, ed. N. M. Häring, Toronto.

see also Jansen.

Colish, M. (1969). 'Eleventh-Century Grammar in the Thought of St. Anselm', in *Arts libéraux et philosophie au Moyen Age*, Actes du IVe Congrès International de Philosophie Médiévale, Montréal 27 août–2 sept. 1967, Montreal–Paris.

(1983a). *The Mirror of Language. A Study in the Medieval Theory of Knowledge* (2nd ed.), Lincoln, Nebraska.

(1983b). 'St. Anselm's Philosophy of Language Reconsidered', *Anselm Studies* I: 113–23.

(1985). *The Stoic Tradition from Antiquity to the Early Middle Ages* (2 vols.), Leiden.

Constantinus Africanus (1515). *Pantechni*, in *Omnia opera Ysaac...*, Lyons.

(1536, 1539). *Operum reliqua*, Basle.

Contenson, P. M. de (1959). 'Avicennisme latin et vision de Dieu au début du 13e siècle', *AHDLMA* XXVII: 29–97.

Contra Amaurianos (1926). Ed. C. Baeumker and M. Grabmann, BGPTM XXIV.5–6.

Copleston, F. (1950). *A History of Philosophy II: Augustine to Scotus*, London.

Corbin, H. (1960). *Avicenna and the Visionary Recital*, trans. W. Trask, London.

Costa ben Luca (1878). *De differentia spiritus et animae*, [trans. John of Seville], ed. C. S. Barach, Innsbruck.

Courcelle, P. (1948). *Les lettres grecques en Occident. De Macrobe à Cassiodore*, Paris.

(1967). *La Consolation de philosophie dans la tradition littéraire*, Paris.

Cremaschi, G. (1945). *Mosè del Bergamo e la cultura a Bergamo nei secoli XI e XII*, Padua.

Creutz, R. (1934). 'Urso, der Letzte des Hochsalerno, Arzt, Philosoph, Theologe', *Abhandlungen zur Geschichte der Medizin und der Naturwissenschaften* V: 3–15.

Cruz Hernández, M. (1950–1). 'El "Fontes quaestionum" ('Uyūn al-Masā'il') de Abū Naṣr al-Fārābī', *AHDLMA* XVIII: 303–23.

Curtius, E. R. (1943). 'Zur Geschichte des Wortes Philosophie im Mittelalter', *Romanische Forschungen* LVII: 290–309.

Dahan, G. (1982). 'Une introduction à la philosophie au XIIe siècle. Le *Tractatus quidam de philosophia et partibus ejus*', *AHDLMA* XLIX: 155–93.

Dales, R. C. (1965). 'Anonymi *De elementis*: from a Twelfth-Century Collection of Scientific Works in British Museum MS Cotton Galba E. IV', *Isis* LVI: 174–89.

Dambska, I. (1977). 'La sémiotique des "Dictiones Indefinitae" dans la Dialectique d'Abélard', *CIMAGL* XXI: 10–20.

Daniel of Morley (1917). *De naturis inferiorum et superiorum*, ed. K. Sudhoff, *Archiv für Geschichte der Naturwissenschaften und Technik* VIII: 6–40 (Corrections by A. Birkenmajer, *ibid.* IX (1918): 45–51).

David of Dinant (1963). *Davidis de Dinanto Quaternulorum fragmenta*, ed. M. Kurdziałek, Studia Mediewistyczne III, Warsaw.

Déchanet, J. M. (1940). 'Le "naturam sequi" chez Guillaume de Saint-Thierry', *Collectanea Ordinis Cisterciensium reformatorum* VII: 141–8.

(1951). '*Seneca noster*: des Lettres à Lucilius à la Lettre aux frères du Mont-Dieu', in *Mélanges J. de Ghellinck* II, Gembloux.

Delhaye, Philippe (1947): 'L'organisation scolaire au XIIe siècle', *Traditio* V: 211–68.

(1949). 'L'enseignement de la philosophie morale au XIIe siècle', *Mediaeval Studies* XI: 77–99.

(1949, 1950). 'Une adaptation du *De officiis* au XIIe siècle: le *Moralium dogma philosophorum*', *RTAM* XVI: 227–58; XVII: 5–28.

(1951). 'Le dossier antimatrimonial de l'*Adversus Jovinianum* et son influence sur quelques écrits latins du XIIe siècle', *Mediaeval Studies* XIII: 65–86.

Delhaye, P., and Talbot, C. H. (eds.) (1956–61). *Florilegium Morale Oxoniense MS. Bodl. 633* (2 vols.), Analecta Medievalia Naumurcensia V–VI, Lille–Louvain.

Denifle, H., and Chatelain, A. (eds.) (1889). *Chartularium Universitatis Parisiensis* I, Paris.
Dod, Bernard G. (1982). 'Aristoteles Latinus', in *CHLMP*
Dominicus Gundissalinus (1891). *De unitate*, ed. P. Correns, BGPTM I.I.
    (1903). *De divisione philosophie*, ed. L. Baur, BGPTM IV.2–3.
    (1925). *De processione mundi*, ed. G. Bülow, BGPTM XXIV.3.
    (1940). *De anima*, ed. J. T. Muckle, *Mediaeval Studies* II: 31–103.
    see also Algazel; Avencebrol; [Avicenna Latinus].
Dondaine, A. (1963). *Ecrits de la 'petite école' porrétaine*, Montreal.
Draak, M. (1956). 'Construe Marks in Hiberno-Latin Manuscripts', *Mededelingen der Koninklijke Nederlandse Akademie van Wetenschappen, Nieuwe Reeks deel 20.10, Afdeling Letterkunde*: 261–82.
Dronke, Peter (1965). 'L'amor che move il sole e l'altre stelle', *Studi Medievali*, ser. 3, VI, 1: 389–422; reprinted in Dronke (1984a).
    (1969). 'New Approaches to the School of Chartres', *Anuario de Estudios Medievales* VI: 117–40.
    (1974). *Fabula: Explorations into the Uses of Myth in Medieval Platonism*, Leiden–Cologne.
    (1983). [Review of] *Guillaume de Conches, Glosae in Iuvenalem*, ed. B. Wilson, Paris 1980, *Medium Aevum* LII: 146–9.
    (1984a). *The Medieval Poet and his World*, Rome.
    (1984b). *Women Writers of the Middle Ages*, Cambridge.
    (1985a). 'Bernardo Silvestre', in *Enciclopedia Virgiliana* I, Rome.
    (1985b). 'La creazione degli animali', *Settimane di Studio* XXXI: 809–48.
    (1985c). 'Integumenta Virgilii', in *Lectures médiévales de Virgile*, Collection de l'Ecole Française de Rome LXXX, Rome.
    (1986). *Dante and Medieval Latin Traditions*, Cambridge.
Dutton, P. E. (1983). *'Illustre ciuitatis et populi exemplum*: Plato's *Timaeus* and the Transmission from Calcidius to the End of the Twelfth Century of a Tripartite Scheme of Society', *Mediaeval Studies* XLV: 79–119.
    (1984). 'The Uncovering of the *Glosae super Platonem* of Bernard of Chartres', *Mediaeval Studies* XLVI: 192–221.
Eadmer (1962). *The Life of St. Anselm, Archbishop of Canterbury, by Eadmer*, ed. and trans. by R. W. Southern, London.
Ebbesen, S. (1972). 'Anonymi Bodleiani in Sophisticos Elenchos Aristotelis Commentarii fragmentum', *CIMAGL* VIII: 3–32.
    (1973a). 'Manlius Boethius on Aristotle's *Analytica Posteriora*', *CIMAGL* IX: 68–73.
    (1973b). 'Paris 4720A. A 12th-Century Compendium of Aristotle's *Sophistici Elenchi*', *CIMAGL* X: 1–20.
    (1976). 'Anonymus Aurelianensis II, Aristotle, Alexander, Porphyry and Boethius', *CIMAGL* XVI: 1–128.
    (1977). 'Jacobus Veneticus on the Posterior Analytics', *CIMAGL* XXI: 1–9.
    (1979). 'Anonyma Aurelianensis I, Commentarium in Sophisticos Elenchos', *CIMAGL* XXXIV.
    (1981a). *Commentators and Commentaries on Aristotle's Sophistici Elenchi. A Study of Post-Aristotelian Ancient and Medieval Writings on Fallacies* (3 vols.), Corpus Latinum Commentariorum in Aristotelem Graecorum VII, Leiden.
    (1981b). 'Early Supposition Theory (12th–13th Cent.)', *Histoire, Epistémologie, Langage* III.I.
    (1981c). 'The Present King of France Wears Hypothetical Shoes with Categorical Laces. Twelfth Century Writers on Well-formedness', *Medioevo* VII: 91–113.
    (1982). 'Ancient Scholastic Logic as the Source of Medieval Scholastic Logic', in *CHLMP*.
Ebbesen, S., Fredborg, K. M., and Nielsen, L. O. (eds.) (1983). 'Compendium logicae

Porretanum ex codice Oxoniensi Collegii Corporis Christi 250: a Manual of Porretan Doctrine by a Pupil of Gilbert's', *CIMAGL* XLVI.

Ebbesen, S., and Iwakuma, Y. (1983). 'Instantiae and 12th Century "Schools"', *CIMAGL* XLIV: 81–5.

Economou, George D. (1972). *The Goddess Natura in Medieval Literature*, Cambridge, Mass.

Edelstein, L., and Kidd, I. G. (eds.) (1972). *Posidonius I: The Fragments*, Cambridge.

Edsman, C. (1966). 'Arbor inversa', in *Festschrift Walter Baetke*, Weimar.

Elford, Dorothy (1983). 'Developments in the Natural Philosophy of William of Conches: a Study of the *Dragmaticon* and a Consideration of its Relationship to the *Philosophia*'. Unpublished Ph.D. thesis, University of Cambridge.

Elswijk, H. C. van (1966). *Gilbert Porreta. Sa vie, son oeuvre, sa pensée*, Louvain.

Evans, G. R. (1975). 'The "Secure Technician". Varieties of Paradox in the Writings of St. Anselm', *Vivarium* XIII: 1–21.

(1976a). 'St. Anselm's Analogies', *Vivarium* XIV: 81–93.

(1976b). 'St. Anselm's Images of Trinity', *Journal of Theological Studies* XXVII: 46–57.

(1977). 'St. Anselm's Technical Terms of Rhetoric', *Latomus* XXXVI: 171–9.

(1978). *Anselm and Talking about God*, Oxford.

(1979). 'St. Anselm's Technical Terms of Grammar', *Latomus* XXXVIII: 413–21.

(1980a). *Anselm and a New Generation*, Oxford.

(1980b). *Old Arts and New Theology*, Oxford.

(1982). 'A Work of "Terminist Theology"? Peter the Chanter's *De tropis loquendi* and some *Fallacie*', *Vivarium* XX.2: 40–58.

(1983a). *Alan of Lille: The Frontiers of Theology in the Late Twelfth Century*, Cambridge.

(1983b). 'The Uncompleted "Heptateuch" of Thierry of Chartres', *History of Universities* III: 1–13.

Evdokimov, P. (1959). 'L'aspect apophatique de l'argument de saint Anselme', *Spicilegium Beccense* I: 233–58.

Everard of Ypres (1953). *Dialogus Ratii et Everardi*, ed. N. M. Häring, *Mediaeval Studies* XV: 243–89.

(1955). [Letters on the Trinity], ed. N. M. Häring, *Mediaeval Studies* XVII: 162–72.

Eynde, D. van den (1962). 'Les écrits perdus d'Abélard'. *Antonianum* XXXVII: 467–80.

Faggiotto, P. (1954). 'La fonte platonica dell'argumento ontologico di Anselmo d'Aosta', *Rivista di filosofia neoscolastica* XLVI: 493–5.

al-Fārābī (1918). *De ortu scientiarum*, ed. C. Baeumker, BGPTM XIX.

(1929–30). *De intellectu et intellecto*, ed. E. Gilson, in 'Les sources gréco-arabes de l'augustinisme avicennisant', *AHDLMA* IV: 115–26.

(1953). *Catálogo de las ciencias*, ed. A. González-Palencia (2nd ed.), Madrid–Granada. *see also* Gerard of Cremona.

Feliu i Montfort, G. (1972). 'Sunfred, Anomenat Llobet ardiaca de Barcelona (finals del segle X)', in *II Colloqui d' Història del Monaquisme Català* I, Abadia de Poblet

Fernández, I. P. (1979). 'Influjo del árabe en el nacimiento del término latino medieval "Metaphysica"', in *Actas del V Congreso internacional de filosofia medieval* II, Madrid.

Festugière, A.-J. (1949–54). *La révélation d'Hermès Trismégiste* (4 vols.), Paris.

Flasch, K. (1970). 'Der philosophische Ansatz des Anselm von Canterbury im Monologion und sein Verhältnis zum augustinischen Neuplatonismus', *Analecta Anselmiana* II: 1–43.

Flatten, H. (1929). *Die Philosophie des Wilhelm von Conches*, Koblenz.

Flint, V. (1981). 'The "Liber Hermetis Mercurii Triplicis de VI Rerum Principiis" and the "Imago Mundi" of Honorius Augustodunensis', *Scriptorium* XXXV: 284–7.

Folkerts, M. (ed.) (1970). '*Boethius' Geometrie II*, Wiesbaden.

(ed.) (1982). 'Die *Altercatio* in der Geometrie I des Pseudo-Boethius', in G. Keil (ed.), *Fachprosa-Studien*, Berlin.

Fontaine, J. (1959). *Isidore de Séville et la culture classique dans l'Espagne wisigothique* (2 vols.), Paris.

Fontana, M. (1930). 'Il commento ai Salmi di Gilberto della Porrée', *Logos* XIII: 282–301.

Forest, A. (1934a). 'Gilbert de la Porrée et les écoles du XIIe siècle', *Revue des Cours et des Conférences* XXXV.2: 410–20, 640–51.

(1934b). 'Le réalisme de Gilbert de la Porrée dans le commentaire du *De hebdomadibus*', in *Hommage à Monsieur le Professeur Maurice de Wulf (Revue Néoscolastique de Philosophie* XXVI: 101–10), Louvain.

Fredborg, K. M. (1971). 'The Commentary of Thierry of Chartres on Cicero's *De inventione*', *CIMAGL* VII: 225–60.

(1973). 'The Dependence of Petrus Helias' *Summa super Priscianum* on William of Conches' *Glose super Priscianum*', *CIMAGL* XI: 1–57.

(1974). 'Petrus Helias on Rhetoric', *CIMAGL* XIII: 31–41.

(1976). 'The Commentaries on Cicero's *De inventione* and *Rhetorica ad Herennium* by William of Champeaux', *CIMAGL* XVII: 1–39.

(1977). '*Tractatus Glosarum Prisciani* in Ms. Vat. Lat. 1486', *CIMAGL* XXI: 21–44.

(1980). 'Universal Grammar according to some 12th c. Grammarians', *Historiographia Linguistica* VII: 69–83.

(1981). 'Some Notes on the Grammar of William of Conches', *CIMAGL* XXXVII: 21–41.

Frickel, M. (1956). *Deus totus ubique simul. Untersuchungen zur allgemeinen Gottgegenwart im Rahmen der Gotteslehre Gregors des Grossen*, Freiburg i. Br.

Gagnér, S. (1960). *Studien zur Ideengeschichte der Gesetzgebung*, Uppsala.

Gammersbach, S. (1959). *Gilbert von Poitiers und seine Prozesse im Urteil der Zeitgenossen*, Cologne–Graz.

Gandillac, Maurice de (1954). 'Le platonisme au XIIe et au XIIIe siècles', *Association Guillaume Budé. Congrès de Tours et de Poitiers, 1953*, Paris.

(1981). 'Le Dialogue', in *Abélard. Actes du colloque de Neuchâtel, 16–17 nov. 1979*, Geneva.

Gardet, L. (1979). 'De la terminologie à la problématique (quelques exemples à propos de l'Avicenne latin', in *Actas del V Congreso Internacional de Filosofia Medieval* I, Madrid.

Garin, E. (1958). *Studi sul platonismo medievale*, Florence.

Garlandus Compotista (1959). *Dialectica*, ed. L. M. de Rijk, Assen.

Gastaldelli, F. (1979a). 'Il manoscritto Troyes 1003 e il commento di Guglielmo da Lucca al De Divinis Nominibus', *Salesianum* XLI: 37–72.

(1979b). 'Linguaggio e stile in Guglielmo da Lucca', *ibid.* 441–88.

Gauthier, R.-A. (1951). 'Pour l'attribution à Gauthier de Châtillon du *Moralium dogma philosophorum*', *Revue du Moyen Âge Latin* VII: 19–64.

Gerard of Cremona (1953). [Trans. of al-Fārābī, *De scientiis*], ed. A. González-Palencia, *Al-Fārābī, Catálogo de las ciencias* (2nd ed.), Madrid–Granada 1953, pp. 119–76.

(1954). [Trans. of Aristotle, *Analytica Posteriora*], ed. L. Minio-Paluello, *Aristoteles Latinus* IV.3, Leiden.

(1966). [Trans. of *Liber de causis*], ed. A. Pattin, *Tijdschrift voor filosofie* XXVIII: 90–203.

(1980). *The Latin Translation of the Arabic Version of Euclid's Elements Commonly Ascribed to Gerard of Cremona*, ed. H. L. L. Busard, Leiden.

see also al-Kindī; al-Nairīzī.

Gerbert of Aurillac (1867). *De rationali et ratione uti*, ed. A. Olleris, *Oeuvres de Gerbert*, Clermont-Ferrand–Paris.

Gersh, Stephen (1982). 'Platonism – Neoplatonism – Aristotelianism: A Twelfth-Century Metaphysical System and its Sources', in *Harvard 1982*.

(1986). *Middle Platonism and Neoplatonism: The Latin Tradition* (2 vols.), Notre Dame, Indiana.

Geyer, B. (1913). 'Die Stellung Abaelards in der Universalienfrage nach neuen handschriftlichen Texten', BGPTM Supplementband I: 101–27.

al-Ghazālī, *see* Algazel.

Ghellinck, Joseph de (1948). *Le mouvement théologique du XIIe siècle* (2nd ed.), Bruges–Brussels–Paris.

Giacone, R. (1974). 'Masters, Books and Library at Chartres', *Vivarium* XII: 30–51.

Gibson, Margaret (1969). 'The Study of the *Timaeus* in the Eleventh and Twelfth Centuries', *Pensiamento* XXV: 183–94.

(1971). 'Lanfranc's Notes on Patristic Texts', *Journal of Theological Studies* XXII: 435–50.

(1977). 'The Collected Works of Priscian: the Printed Editions 1470–1859', *Studi Medievali*, 3rd series, XVIII. 1: 249–60.

(1978). *Lanfranc of Bec*, Oxford.

(1979). 'The Early Scholastic *Glosule* to Priscian, *Institutiones grammaticae*: the Text and its Influences', *Studi Medievali*, 3rd series, XX. 1:235–54.

(1981). 'The *Opuscula sacra* in the Middle Ages', in M. Gibson (ed.), *Boethius: His Life, Thought and Influence*, Oxford.

(ed.) (1981). *Boethius: His Life, Thought and Influence*, Oxford.

Gilbert of Poitiers (1961). *Sermo de Natali Domini* ('A Christmas Sermon by Gilbert of Poitiers'), ed. N. M. Häring, *Mediaeval Studies* XXIII: 126–35.

(1965). 'A Commentary on the Pseudo-Athanasian Creed by Gilbert of Poitiers', ed. N. M. Häring, *Mediaeval Studies* XXVII: 23–53.

(1966). *The Commentaries on Boethius by Gilbert of Poitiers*, ed. N. M. Häring, Toronto.

(1972). 'A Treatise on the Trinity by Gilbert of Poitiers', ed. N. M. Häring, *RTAM* XXXIX: 14–50.

(1978, 1979). 'Die Sententie Magistri Gisleberti Pictavensis Episcopi', ed. N. M. Häring, *AHDLMA* XLV: 83–180 (Tortosa MS) and XLVI: 45–105 (Florence MS).

Gilbertus Porreta, *see* Gilbert of Poitiers.

Gilson, Etienne (1923). 'Le platonisme de Bernard de Chartres', *Revue Néoscolastique de philosophie* XXV: 5–19.

(1929). 'Les sources gréco-arabes de l'augustinisme avicennisant', *AHDLMA* IV: 5–149.

(1946). 'Notes sur les noms de la matière chez Gilbert de la Porrée', *RMAL* II: 173–6.

(1947). *La philosophie au Moyen Âge* (3rd ed.), Paris [English trans.: *History of Christian Philosophy in the Middle Ages*, London 1955].

(1969). 'Avicenne en Occident au Moyen Age', *AHDLMA* XXXVI: 99–110.

Giusberti, F. (1982). *Materials for a Study on Twelfth Century Scholasticism*, History of Logic II, Naples.

Glorieux, P. (1948). 'Le *Moralium dogma philosophorum* et son auteur', *RTAM* XV: 360–6.

(1952). 'Le "Contra quatuor labyrinthos Franciae" de Gauthier de Saint-Victor', *AHDLMA* XIX: 187–335.

(1954). 'Mauvaise action et mauvais travail: le "Contra quatuor labyrinthos Franciae"', *RTAM* XXI: 179–93.

Godefroy de Saint-Victor (1951). *Microcosmus*, ed. Philippe Delhaye, Namur.

(1956). *Fons philosophiae*, ed. Pierre Michaud-Quantin, Namur.

(1966). *Ordo artium*, ed. Ludwig Gompf, *Mittellateinisches Jahrbuch* III: 107–10.

Goltz, D. (1976). *Mittelalterliche Pharmazie und Medizin, dargestellt an Geschichte und Inhalt des Antidotarium Nicolai*, Stuttgart.

Gombocz, W. L. (1975). 'Zu neueren Beiträgen zur Interpretation von Anselms Proslogion', *Salzburger Jahrbuch für Philosophie* XX: 131–5.

(1980). 'Abaelards Bedeutungslehre als Schlüssel zum Universalienproblem', in R. Thomas *et al.* (eds.), *Petrus Abaelardus (1079–1142): Person, Werk und Wirkung*, Trier.

Grabmann, M. (1911). *Geschichte der scholastischen Methode* (2 vols.), Freiburg im Breisgau.

(1935). *Handschriftliche Forschungen zum Schrifttum des Wilhelm von Conches, Sitzungsberichte der Bayerischen Akademie* x.

(1941). *I divieti ecclesiastici sotto Innocenzo III e Gregorio IX*, Rome.

Grabowski, S. (1954). *The All-Present God. A Study in St. Augustine*, St Louis, Missouri.

Gracia, J. J. E. (1984). *Introduction to the Problem of Individuation in the Early Middle Ages*, Munich–Vienna.

Green-Pedersen, N. J. (1974). 'William of Champeaux on Boethius' *Topics* according to Orléans Bibl. Mun. 266', *CIMAGL* xiii: 13–30.

(1977). 'The Doctrine of "maxima propositio" and "locus differentia" in Commentaries from the 12th Century on Boethius' "Topics"', *Studia Mediewistyczne* xviii: 125–63.

(1984). *The Tradition of the Topics in the Middle Ages. The Commentaries on Aristotle's and Boethius' Topics*, Munich–Vienna.

Gregory, Tullio (1955). *Anima mundi. La filosofia di Guglielmo di Conches e la Scuola di Chartres*, Florence.

(1958). *Platonismo medievale: studi e ricerche*, Rome.

(1966). 'L'idea di natura nella filosofia medievale prima dell'ingresso della fisica di Aristotele – il secolo xii', in *La filosofia della natura nel Medioevo*, Atti del iii Congresso Internazionale de Filosofia Medioevale, Passo della Mendola–Trento, 31 Aug.–5 Sept. 1964, Milan.

(1974). 'Abélard et Platon', in E. M. Buytaert (ed.), *Peter Abelard*, Louvain.

(1975a). 'La nouvelle idée de la nature et de savoir scientifique au xiie siècle', in J. E. Murdoch and E. D. Sylla (eds.), *The Cultural Context of Medieval Learning*, Dordrecht–Boston.

(1975b). 'Ratio et Natura chez Abélard', in *Pierre Abélard-Pierre le Vénérable*, Colloques Internationaux du CNRS dxlvi, Paris.

Grunwald, G. (1907). *Geschichte der Gottesbeweise im Mittelalter*, BGPTM vi.3.

Guglielmo da Lucca, *see* William of Lucca.

Guillaume de Conches, *see* William of Conches.

Gundissalinus, *see* Dominicus Gundissalinus.

Györy, Jean (1963). 'Le cosmos, un songe', *Annales Universitatis Scientiarum Budapestensis: Sectio Philologica* iv: 87–110.

Hadot, I. (1984). *Arts libéraux et philosophie dans la pensée antique*, Paris.

Hall, S. P. (1980). 'Commentaries on the Aphorisms of Hippocrates', in A. C. de la Mare and B. L. C. Barker-Benfield (eds.), *Manuscripts at Oxford: R. W. Hunt Memorial Exhibition*, Oxford.

Happ, H. (1971). *Hyle. Studien zum aristotelischen Materie-Begriff*, Berlin.

Häring, N. M. (1951). 'The Case of Gilbert de la Porrée Bishop of Poitiers (1142–1154)', *Mediaeval Studies* xiii: 1–40.

(1955a). 'The Cistercian Everard of Ypres and his Appraisal of the Conflict between St. Bernard and Gilbert of Poitiers', *Mediaeval Studies* xvii: 143–72.

(1955b). 'The Creation and Creator of the World according to Thierry of Chartres and Clarembald of Arras', *AHDLMA* xxii: 137–216.

(1957). 'Sprachlogische und philosophische Voraussetzungen zum Verständnis der Christologie Gilberts von Poitiers', *Scholastik* xxxii: 373–97.

(1962). 'The Porretans and the Greek Fathers', *Mediaeval Studies* xxiv: 181–209.

(1963). 'Die Vätersammlung des Adhémar von Saint-Ruf in Valence', *Scholastik* xxxviii: 402–20.

(1965a). *Life and Works of Clarembald of Arras. A Twelfth Century Master of the School of Chartres*, Toronto.

(1965b). 'Simon of Tournai and Gilbert of Poitiers', *Mediaeval Studies* xxvii: 325–30.

(1966). 'In Search of Adhémar's Patristic Collection', *Mediaeval Studies* xxviii: 336–46.

(1974). 'Chartres and Paris Revisited', in J. R. O'Donnell (ed.), *Essays in Honor of Anton Charles Pegis*, Toronto.

(ed.) (1962a). 'The "Liber de differentia naturae et personae" by Hugh Etherian and the Letters addressed to him by Peter of Vienna and Hugh of Honau', *Mediaeval Studies* XXIV: 1–34.

(ed.) (1962b). 'The Liber de diversitate naturae et personae, by Hugh of Honau', *AHDLMA* XXIX: 103–210.

(ed.) (1964). 'The Tractatus de trinitate of Adhémar of Saint-Ruf (Valence)', *AHDLMA* XXXI: 111–206.

(ed.) (1967–8). 'The Liber de homoysion et homoeysion by Hugh of Honau', *AHDLMA* XXXIV: 129–253; XXXV: 211–91.

see also Everard of Ypres; Gilbert of Poitiers; Thierry of Chartres.

Hartmann, F. (1919). *Die Literatur von Früh- und Hochsalerno und der Inhalt des Breslauer Codex Salernitanus*. Dissertation, Leipzig.

Haskins, C. H. (1927). *Studies in the History of Mediaeval Science* (2nd ed.), Cambridge, Mass.; reprinted New York 1960.

Hauréau, B. (1872). *Histoire de la philosophie scolastique* I (2nd ed.), Paris.

Hayen, A. (1935–6). 'Le concile de Reims et l'erreur théologique de Gilbert de la Porrée', *AHDLMA* X: 29–102.

Henry Aristippus (1940). *Meno*, ed. V. Kordeuter and C. Labowsky, *Plato Latinus* I, London.

(1950). *Phaedo*, ed. L. Minio-Paluello, *Plato Latinus* II, London.

Henry, D. P. (1967). *The Logic of St. Anselm*, Oxford.

(1974). *Commentary on De grammatico: the Historical-Logical Dimensions of a Dialogue of St. Anselm's*, Dordrecht–Boston.

Hermann of Carinthia (1489). [Trans. of Abū Ma'shar]: *Introductorium ad astronomiam Albumasaris abalachi*, Augsburg; reprinted Venice 1506.

(1543). [Trans. of *De generatione Mahumet* and *Doctrina Mahumet*], ed. T. Bibliander, Basel.

(1907). [Trans. of Ptolemy's *Planisphere*], in *Cl. Ptolomaei opera astronomica minora*, ed. J. L. Heiberg, Leipzig, pp. 225–59.

(1967, 1977). [Trans. of Euclid's *Elements*], ed. H. L. L. Busard, *Janus* LIV: 1–140 (Books I–VI) and *Mathematical Centre Tracts* LXXXIV (Books VII–XII).

(1982). *De essentiis, A Critical Edition with Translation and Commentary* by Charles Burnett, Leiden–Cologne.

Hogendijk, J. P. (1986). 'Discovery of an 11th-century Geometrical Compilation: the *kitāb al-Istikmāl* of al-Mu'taman ibn Hūd', *Historia Mathematica* XIII: 43–52.

Honorius Augustodunensis (P.L. 172). *Opera*.

(1954). *L'Elucidarium et les Lucidaires*, ed. Y. Lefèvre, Paris.

(1974). *Clavis Physicae*, ed. P. Lucentini, Rome.

(1982). *Imago mundi*, ed. V. I. J. Flint, *AHDLMA* XLIX: 7–153.

Hopkins, Jasper (1972). *A Companion to the Study of St. Anselm*, Minneapolis.

(1976). 'The Anselmian Theory of Universals', in J. Hopkins and H. Richardson, *Anselm of Canterbury* IV, Toronto–New York.

Horsley, R. A. (1978). 'The Law of Nature in Philo and Cicero', *Harvard Theological Review* LXXI: 35–59.

Hugh Etherian, see N. M. Häring.

Hugh of Honau, see N. M. Häring.

Hugh of Saint-Victor (P.L. 175–7). *Opera*.

(1939). *Hugonis de Sancto Victore Didascalicon, De Studio Legendi: A Critical Text*, ed. C. H. Buttimer, Washington D.C.

(1958). *De contemplatione*, ed. R. Baron, Paris.

(1961). *The Didascalicon of Hugh of St. Victor*, trans. J. Taylor, New York.

(1966). *Opera propaedeutica (Practica geometriae, De grammatica, Epitome Dindimi in philosophiam)*, ed. R. Baron, Notre Dame.

Hugo of Santalla (forthcoming). 'Aristotle's Book based on 255 Indian Volumes of Universal Questions', ed. C. Burnett and D. Pingree.

Hugo Santallensis, *see* Hugo of Santalla.

Hugonnard-Roche, H. (1984). 'La classification des sciences de Gundissalinus et l'influence d'Avicenne', in J. Jolivet and R. Rashed (eds.), *Etudes sur Avicenne*, Paris.

Humbertus de Balesma (1984). *Sermo*, ed. M.-T. d'Alverny ('Humbertus de Balesma'), *AHDLMA* LI: 127–91.

Ḥunayn Ibn Isḥāq (1980). [Masāʾil.] *Questions on Medicine for Scholars*, English trans. by P. Ghalioungui, Cairo.

Hunt, R. W. (1941–3). 'Studies on Priscian in the Eleventh and Twelfth Centuries I', *MARS* I.2: 194–231.

(1948). 'The Introductions to the "Artes" in the Twelfth Century', in *Studia medievalia in honorem . . . R. J. Martin*, Bruges.

(1950). 'Studies on Priscian in the Eleventh and Twelfth Centuries II', *MARS* II: 1–56.

(1975). '*Absoluta*. The Summa of Petrus Hispanus on Priscianus Minor', *Historiographia Linguistica* II.1: 1–23.

(1980). *Collected Papers on the History of Grammar in the Middle Ages*, ed. G. L. Bursill-Hall, Amsterdam.

(1984). *The Schools and the Cloister: The Life and Writings of Alexander Nequam (1157–1217)*, ed. M. Gibson, Oxford.

Hunt, R. W., Pantin, W. A., and Southern, R. W. (eds.) (1948). *Studies in Medieval History presented to F. M. Powicke*, Oxford.

Hunt, Tony (1978). 'Redating Chrestien de Troyes', *Bulletin Bibliographique de la Société Internationale Arthurienne* XXX: 209–37.

(1981–2). 'Chrestien and Macrobius', *Classica et Mediaevalia* XXXIII: 211–27.

Iacobus Veneticus Graecus, *see* James of Venice.

Ibn Gabirol, *see* Avencebrol.

Ibn Sina, *see* Avicenna Latinus.

Inwood, B. (1985). *Ethics and Human Action in Early Stoicism*, Oxford.

Iohannes Blund, *see* John Blund.

Iwakuma, Y. (1981). 'Instantiae. A Study of Twelfth Century Technique of Argumentation with an Edition of MS Paris BN Lat. 6674 f. 1–5', *CIMAGL* XXXVIII: 1–91.

(1983). 'Instantiae Revisited', *CIMAGL* XLIV: 61–80.

Jacobi, Klaus (1980a). 'Diskussionen über Prädikationstheorie in den logischen Schriften des Petrus Abaelardus, Versuch einer Übersicht', in R. Thomas *et al.* (eds.), *Petrus Abaelardus (1079–1142): Person, Werk und Wirkung*, Trier.

(1980b). *Die Modalbegriiffe in den logischen Schriften des Wilhelm von Shyreswood und in anderen Kompendien des 12. und 13. Jahrhunderts. Funktionsbestimmung und Gebrauch in der logischen Analyse*, Studien und Texte zur Geistesgeschichte des Mittelalters XIII, Leiden–Cologne.

(1981a). 'Drei Theorien über die Funktion aussagenverknüpfender Zeichen. Die Diskussion des Junktors "si" bei Wilhelm von Shyreswood', in J. P. Beckmann *et al.* (eds.), *Sprache und Erkenntnis im Mittelalter*, Proceedings of the 6th International Congress . . . of the S.I.E.P.M., Bonn 29.8–3.9, 1977 (*Miscellanea Mediaevalia* XIII.1), Berlin–New York.

(1981b). 'Die Semantik sprachlicher Ausdrücke, Ausdrucksfolgen und Aussagen in Abaelards Kommentar zu *Peri Hermenias*', *Medioevo* VII: 41–89.

(1981c). 'Wilhelm von Shyreswood und die Dialectica Monacensis', in H. A. G.

Braakhuis, C. H. Kneepkens and L. M. de Rijk (eds.), *English Logic and Semantics. From the End of the Twelfth Century to the Time of Ockham and Burleigh*, Nijmegen.

(1983). 'Abelard and Frege: the Semantics of Words and Propositions', in *Atti del Convegno Internazionale di Storia della Logica, San Gimignano, 4–8 Dec. 1982*, Bologna.

(1985a). 'Diskussionen über unpersönliche Aussage in Peter Abaelards Kommentar zu *Peri Hermenias*', in *Medieval Semantics and Metaphysics. Studies dedicated to L. M. de Rijk, Ph.D. on the Occasion of his 60th Birthday*, Artistarium Supplementa II, Nijmegen.

(1985b). 'Peter Abelard's Investigations into the Meaning and Functions of the Speech Sign "Est"', in Simo Knuuttila and Jaakko Hintikka (eds.), *The Logic of Being*, Dordrecht.

Jacquart, D. (1984). 'De *crasis* à *complexio*: note sur le vocabulaire du tempérament en latin médiéval', *Mémoires V. Textes médicaux latins antiques*, Centre Jean Palerne, St Etienne.

Jacquart, D., and Thomasset, C. (1985). *Sexualité et savoir médical au Moyen Age*, Paris.

Jacquart, D., and Troupeau, G. (1981). 'Traduction de l'arabe et vocabulaire médical latin: quelques exemples', in Y. Lefèvre (ed.), *La lexicographie du latin médiéval et ses rapports avec les recherches actuelles sur la civilisation du Moyen Age*, Colloques Internationaux du CNRS CCCLXXVI, Paris.

Jaeger, W. W. (1914). *Nemesios von Emesa*, Berlin.

James of Venice (1968). [Trans. of *Analytica Posteriora*], ed. L. Minio-Paluello and B. G. Dod (*Aristoteles Latinus* IV (2nd ed.)), Leiden.

(1970). [Trans. of *Metaphysica* (I–IV.4)], ed. G. Vuillemin-Diem (*Aristoteles Latinus* XXV.I–Ia), Leiden.

(1973). [Trans. of *De Sophisticis Elenchis* (fragment)], ed. B. G. Dod (*Aristoteles Latinus* VI), Leiden.

Jansen, W. (1926). *Der Kommentar des Clarenbaldus von Arras zu Boethius De trinitate. Ein Werk aus der Schule von Chartres im 12. Jahrhundert*, Breslau.

Jeauneau, Edouard (1957). 'L'usage de la notion d'*integumentum* à travers les gloses de Guillaume de Conches', *AHDLMA* XXIV: 35–100; reprinted in Jeauneau (1973).

(1960a). 'Deux rédactions des gloses de Guillaume de Conches sur Priscien', *RTAM* XXVII: 212–47; reprinted in Jeauneau (1973).

(1960b). 'Macrobe, source du platonisme chartrain', *Studi Medievali*, ser. 3, I: 3–24; reprinted in Jeauneau (1973).

(1963). 'Mathématiques et Trinité chez Thierry de Chartres', *Miscellanea Mediaevalia* II: 289–95; reprinted in Jeauneau (1973).

(1964). 'Note sur l'Ecole de Chartres', *Studi Medievali* ser. 3, V: 821–65; reprinted in Jeauneau (1973).

(1967). 'Nani gigantum humeris insidentes', *Vivarium* V: 79–99; reprinted in Jeauneau (1973).

(1973). *Lectio philosophorum*, Amsterdam.

(1980). 'Jean de Salisbury, évêque de Chartres', *Notre-Dame de Chartres* XI (September): 4–9.

Johann, H. T. (1981). *Gerechtigkeit und Nutzen. Studien zur ciceronischen und hellenistischen Naturrechts- und Staatslehre*, Heidelberg.

Johannitius (1978). '*Isagoge ad Techne Galieni*', ed. G. Maurach, *Sudhoffs Archiv* LXII: 148–74.

John Blund (1970). *Iohannes Blund, Tractatus de anima*, ed. D. A. Callus and R. W. Hunt, Auctores Britannici Medii Aevi II, London.

John of Salisbury (1848). *Opera omnia*, ed. J. A. Giles (5 vols.), Oxford.

(1909). *Ioannis Saresberiensis Episcopi Carnotensis Policratici sive de nugis curialium et vestigiis philosophorum libri VIII*, ed. C. C. J. Webb (2 vols.), Oxford.

(1927). [*Policraticus*] *The Statesman's Book*, (partial) English trans. by J. Dickinson, New York.

(1929). *Ioannis Saresberiensis Episcopi Carnotensis Metalogicon*, ed. C. C. J. Webb, Oxford.

(1938). [*Policraticus*] *Frivolities of Courtiers and Footprints of Philosophers*, (partial) English trans. by J. B. Pike, Minneapolis.

(1955). *The Metalogicon of John of Salisbury*, English trans. by D. D. McGarry, Berkeley, Calif.–Los Angeles.

(1975). *Entheticus de dogmate philosophorum*, ed. R. E. Pepin, *Traditio* xxxi: 127–93.

(1984). *Policraticus*, Spanish trans. by M. A. Ladero and M. Alcalá, Madrid.

Jolivet, Jean (1966a). 'Eléments du concept de nature chez Abélard', in *La filosofia della natura nel Medioevo*, Atti del III Congresso Internazionale di Filosofia Medioevale, Passo della Mendola – Trento, 31 Aug.–5 Sept. 1964, Milan.

(1966b). 'Quelques cas de "platonisme grammatical" du viie au xiie siècle', in *Mélanges offerts à René Crozet* i, Poitiers.

(1971). *L'intellect selon Kindī*, Leiden.

(1974). 'Les *Quaestiones naturales* d'Adélard de Bath, ou la nature sans le Livre', in *Mélanges E. R. Labande*, Poitiers.

(1975). 'Notes de lexicographie abélardienne', in *Pierre Abélard. Pierre le Vénérable*, Colloques Internationaux du CNRS dxlvi, Paris.

(1977). 'Intellect et intelligence. Note sur la tradition arabo-latine des 12e et 13e siècles', in *Mélanges Henry Corbin*, Tehran.

(1980). 'Remarques sur les *Regulae theologicae* d'Alain de Lille', in H. Roussel and F. Luard (eds.), *Alain de Lille, Gautier de Châtillon, Jakemart Giélée et leur temps*, Lille.

(1982). *Arts du langage et théologie chez Abélard* (2nd ed.), Paris.

(1983). 'Les rochers de Cumes et l'antre de Cerbère. L'ordre de savoir selon le Commentaire de Bernard Silvestre sur l'Enéide', in *Pascua medievalia. Studies voor Prof. Dr. J. M. de Smet*, Louvain.

(1987). 'L'Islam et la raison, d'après quelques auteurs latins des xie et xiie siècles', in *L'art des confins (Mélanges Maurice de Gandillac)*, Paris.

Jolivet, Jean, and Rashed, R. (eds.) (1984). *Etudes sur Avicenne*, Paris.

Keil, G. (1959). *Der 'Kurze Harntraktat' des Breslauer 'Codex Salernitanus' und seine Sippe*. Dissertation, Bonn.

Kenny, A. (1982). 'The Origins of Disputation', in *CHLMP*.

Kerner, Max (1979). 'Natur und Gesellschaft bei Johannes von Salisbury', *Miscellanea Mediaevalia* xii: 188–96.

Kienzler, K. (1981). *Glauben und Denken bei Anselm von Canterbury*, Freiburg–Basle–Vienna.

al-Kindī (1897). *Die philosophischen Abhandlungen (Liber de intellectu, Liber de somno et visione, Liber de quinque essentiis, Liber introductorius in artem logicae demonstrationis)* [trans. Gerard of Cremona], ed. A. Nagy, BGPTM ii.5.

see also Abū Rīda.

King, Peter O. (1982). 'Peter Abailard and the Problem of Universals'. Unpublished doctoral thesis, Princeton University.

Klibansky, Raymond (1961). 'The School of Chartres', in M. Clagett, G. Post and R. Reynolds (eds.), *Twelfth Century Europe and the Foundations of Modern Society*, Madison, Wisc.

(1981). *The Continuity of the Platonic Tradition during the Middle Ages*, with a new preface and four supplementary chapters, Munich.

Klibansky, R., Panofsky, E. and Saxl, F. (1964). *Saturn and Melancholy*, London.

Kluge, E.-H. W. (1976). 'Roscelin and the Medieval Problem of Universals', *Journal of the History of Philosophy* xiv.4: 405–14.

Kneale, W. and M. (1962). *The Development of Logic*, Oxford.

Kneepkens, C. H. (1978). 'Master Guido and his View on Government: On Twelfth-Century Linguistic Thought', *Vivarium* xvi.2: 108–41.

(1980). '"Legere est agere": the First *Quaestio* of the First *Quaestiones*-collection in MS Oxford C.C.C. 250', *Historiographia Linguistica* vii: 109–30.

(1981). 'Robert Blund and the Theory of Evocation', in H. A. G. Braakhuis, C. H.

Kneepkens and L. M. de Rijk (eds.), *English Logic and Semantics. From the End of the Twelfth Century to the Time of Ockham and Burleigh*, Nijmegen.

(1983). 'The Quaestiones grammaticales of MS Oxford, Corpus Christi College 250: an Edition of the First Collection', *Vivarium* XXI.1: 1–34.

(1987). *Het Iudicium Constructionis. Het Leerstuk van de Constructio in de 2de Helft van de 12de Eeuw*, 4 vols., Nijmegen.

Knowles, D. (1962). *The Evolution of Medieval Thought*, London.

Knudsen, C. (1982). 'Intentions and Impositions', in *CHLMP*.

Knuuttila, Simo, and Hintikka, Jaakko (eds.) (1985). *The Logic of Being*, Dordrecht.

Koch, Joseph (1953). 'Die Grundlagen der Geschichtsphilosophie Ottos von Freising', *Münchener Theologische Zeitschrift* IV: 79–94; reprinted in W. Lammers (ed.), *Geschichtsdenken und Geschichtsbild im Mittelalter*, Darmstadt 1961.

(ed.) (1959). *Artes Liberales von der antiken Bildung zur Wissenschaft des Mittelalters*, Studien und Texte zur Geistesgeschichte des Mittelalters V, Leiden–Cologne.

Kohlenberger, H. (1972). *Similitudo und Ratio. Überlegungen zur Methode bei Anselm von Canterbury*, Bonn.

(1973). 'Konsequenzen und Inkonsequenzen der Trinitätslehre in Anselms Monologion', *Analecta Anselmiana* V: 149–78.

(ed.) (1970). *Sola ratione. Anselm-Studien für F. S. Schmitt zum 75. Geburtstag*, Stuttgart.

Koyré, A. (1923). *L'idée de Dieu dans la philosophie de saint Anselme*, Paris.

Kraye, J., Ryan, W. F., and Schmitt, C. B. (eds.) (1986). *Pseudo-Aristotle in the Middle Ages*, London.

Kren, C. (1972). 'Gundissalinus, Dominicus', in *Dictionary of Scientific Biography* V, New York.

Kretzmann, N. (1967). 'Semantics, History of', in P. Edwards (ed.), *The Encyclopedia of Philosophy* VII–VIII, New York–London.

(1982). 'The Culmination of the Old Logic in Peter Abelard', in *Harvard 1982*.

Kretzmann, N., Kenny, A., and Pinborg, J. (eds.) (1982). *The Cambridge History of Later Medieval Philosophy*, Cambridge (= *CHLMP*).

Kristeller, P. O. (1945). 'The School of Salerno: its Development and its Contribution to the History of Learning', *Bulletin of the History of Medicine* XVII: 138–94; reprinted in his *Studies in Renaissance Thought and Letters*, Rome 1956.

(1957). 'Nuove fonti per la medicina salernitana del secolo XII', *Rassegna Storia Salernitana* XVIII: 61–75.

(1959). 'Beitrag der Schule von Salerno zur Entwicklung der scholastischen Wissenschaft im 12. Jahrhundert', in J. Koch (ed.), *Artes Liberales von der antiken Bildung zur Wissenschaft des Mittelalters*, Leiden–Cologne.

(1976). 'Bartolomaeus, Musandinus and Maurus of Salerno and other early Commentators of the *Articella*, with a tentative List of Texts and Manuscripts', *Italia Medioevale e Umanistica* XIX: 57–87.

(1980). *La scuola medica di Salerno secondo ricerche e scoperte recenti*, Quaderni del Centro Studi e Documentazione della Scuola Medica Salernitana V, Salerno.

(1986). *Studi sulla scuola medica salernitana*, Naples.

Kritzeck, J. (1964). *Peter the Venerable and Islam*, Princeton, N.J.

Kurdziałek, M. (1966). 'David von Dinant und die Anfänge der aristotelischen Naturphilosophie', in *La filosofia della natura nel medioevo*, Atti del Terzo Congresso Internazionale di Filosofia Medioevale, Passo della Mendola–Trento, Milan.

(1971). 'Der Mensch als Abbild des Kosmos', *Miscellanea Mediaevalia* VIII: 35–75.

(1976a). 'David von Dinant als Ausleger der Aristotelischen Naturphilosophie', *Miscellanea Mediaevalia* X: 181–92.

(1976b). 'L'idée de l'homme chez David de Dinant', in *Images of Man in Ancient and Medieval Thought: Studia Gerardo Verbeke . . . Dicata*, Louvain.

Ladner, Gerhart B. (1982). 'Terms and Ideas of Renewal', in *Harvard 1982*.

Landgraf, A. (1933). 'Mitteilungen zur Schule Gilberts de la Porrée', *Collectanea Franciscana* III: 182–208.

 (1936). 'Neue Funde zur Porretanerschule', *Collectanea Franciscana* VI: 353–65.

 (1939–40). 'Porretanisches Gut beim hl. Thomas von Aquin', *Acta Pontificalis Academiae Romanae S. Thomae Aquinatis* n.s. VI: 214–25.

 (1940). 'Der Porretanismus der Homilien des Radulphus Ardens', *Zeitschrift für katholische Theologie* LXIV: 132–48.

 (1952–6). *Dogmengeschichte der Frühscholastik* (4 vols.), Regensburg.

 (1973). *Introduction à l'histoire de la littérature théologique de la scolastique naissante*, Montreal–Paris.

Lapidge, M. (1973). 'ἀρχαί and στοιχεῖα: A Problem in Stoic Cosmology', *Phronesis* XVIII: 240–78.

 (1980). 'A Stoic Metaphor in Late Latin Poetry: The Binding of the Cosmos', *Latomus* XXXIX: 817–37.

Lawn, Brian (1963). *The Salernitan Questions. An Introduction to the History of Medieval and Renaissance Problem Literature*, Oxford.

 (1969). *I quesiti salernitani*, rev. Italian ed. of Lawn (1963), trans. A. Spagnuolo, Salerno.

Le Goff, Jacques (1957). *Les intellectuels au Moyen Age*, Paris.

Leclercq, J. (ed.) (1943–5). 'Le "De grammatica" de Hugues de St. Victor', *AHDLMA* XIV: 263–322.

 (1970). '"Ad ipsam sophiam Christum". Le témoignage monastique d'Abélard', *Revue d'Ascétique et de Mystique* XLVI: 161–81.

Lefèvre, G. (1898). *Les variations de Guillaume de Champeaux et la question des universaux*, Lille.

Lefèvre, Y. (ed.) (1981). *La lexicographie du latin médiéval et ses rapports avec les recherches actuelles sur la civilisation du Moyen Age*, Colloques Internationaux du CNRS CCCLXXVI, Paris.

Leff, G. (1958). *Medieval Thought. St Augustine to Ockham*, Harmondsworth.

Lemay, Richard (1962). *Abu Ma'shar and Latin Aristotelianism in the Twelfth Century*, Beirut.

Levy, F. (1928). 'Der Weltuntergang in Senecas *Naturales quaestiones*', *Philologus* LXXXIII: 459–66.

Lewry, O. (1981). 'Boethian Logic in the Medieval West', in M. Gibson (ed.), *Boethius. His Life, Thought and Influence*, Oxford.

Lewry, O. (ed.) (1985). *The Rise of British Logic*, Acts of the 6th European Symposium on Medieval Logic and Semantics (1983), Toronto.

Ley, Hermann (1957). *Studie zur Geschichte des Materialismus im Mittelalter*, Berlin.

Libera, A. de (1981). 'Abélard et le dictisme', in *Abélard*, Actes du Colloque de Neuchâtel, 16–17 novembre 1979, *Cahiers de la Revue de Théologie et de Philosophie* VI: 59–97.

 (1985). 'La littérature des *abstractiones* et la tradition logique d'Oxford', in O. Lewry (ed.), *The Rise of British Logic*, Acts of the 6th European Symposium on Medieval Logic and Semantics, Toronto.

 (forthcoming). 'Logique et théologie dans la Summa "Quoniam homines" d'Alain de Lille', in his edition of the proceedings of the 7th Symposium on Medieval Logic and Semantics, Poitiers 1985.

Liccaro, V. (1979). 'Ugo di San Vittore di fronte alla novità delle traduzioni scientifiche greche e arabe', in *Actas del V Congreso Internacional de Filosofia Medieval* II, Madrid.

Liebeschütz, Hans (1926). 'Kosmologische Motive in der Bildungswelt der Frühscholastik', *Vorträge der Bibliothek Warburg 1923–4*, Leipzig.

 (1951). *Medieval Humanism in the Life and Writings of John of Salisbury*, London.

Lindberg, D. C. (ed.) (1978). *Science in the Middle Ages*, Chicago.

Lohr, C. H. (1982). 'The Mediaeval Interpretation of Aristotle', in *CHLMP*.

(1986). 'The Pseudo-Aristotelian *Liber de causis* and Latin Theories of Science in the Twelfth and Thirteenth Centuries', in J. Kraye, W. F. Ryan and C. B. Schmitt (eds.), *Pseudo-Aristotle in the Middle Ages*, London.

Lottin, O. (1942–60). *Psychologie et morale aux XIIe et XIIIe siècles* (6 vols.), Louvain–Gembloux.

Lubac, H. de (1959). 'Sur le chapitre xiv du Proslogion', *Spicilegium Beccense* i: 295–312.

(1959–64). *Exégèse médiévale* (2 vols. in 4), Paris.

(1976). '"Seigneur, je cherche ton visage". Sur le chapitre xive du Proslogion de saint Anselme', *Archives de Philosophie* xxxix: 201–25, 407–25.

Lucentini, Paolo (1980). *Platonismo medievale: Contributi per la storia dell'eriugenismo* (2nd ed.), Florence.

(forthcoming). 'Giovanni Scoto e l'eresia di Amalrico', in W. Beierwaltes (ed.), *Colloquium zur Wirkungsgeschichte Eriugenas*.

Łukasiewicz, J. (1957). *Aristotle's Syllogistic* (2nd ed.), Oxford.

Luscombe, D. E. (1966). 'Nature in the Thought of Peter Abelard', in *La filosofia della natura nel medioevo*, Atti del Terzo Congresso Internazionale di Filosofia Medioevale, Passo della Mendola – Trento, Milan.

(1970). *The School of Peter Abelard*, Cambridge.

(1975). 'Pierre Abélard et le monachisme', in *Pierre Abélard. Pierre le Vénérable*, Colloques Internationaux du CNRS dxlvi, Paris.

(1983). 'St Anselm and Abelard', *Anselm Studies* i: 207–29.

(1984). 'John of Salisbury in Recent Scholarship', in M. Wilks (ed.), *The World of John of Salisbury*, Oxford.

Maccagnolo, Enzo (1976). *Rerum universitas: Saggi sulla filosofia di Teodorico di Chartres*, Florence.

(1980). *Il divino e il megacosmo: Testi filosofici e scientifici della scuola di Chartres*, Milan.

McGill, A. C. (1967). 'Recent Discussions of Anselm's Argument', in J. Hick and A. C. McGill (eds.), *The Many-Faced Argument*, New York.

McIntyre, J. (1959). 'Premises and Conclusions in the System of St. Anselm's Theology', *Spicilegium Beccense* i: 95–101.

McKeon, Richard (1961). 'Medicine and Philosophy in the Eleventh and Twelfth Centuries: the Problem of Elements', *The Thomist* xxiv: 211–56.

(1975). 'The Organization of Sciences and the Relations of Cultures in the Twelfth and Thirteenth Century', in J. E. Murdoch and E. D. Sylla (eds.), *The Cultural Context of Medieval Learning*, Dordrecht–Boston.

Magister Siguinus (1979). *Ars lectoria*, ed. J. Engels, Leiden.

Mahoney, M. S. (1978). 'Mathematics', in D. C. Lindberg (ed.), *Science in the Middle Ages*, Chicago.

Maierù, A. (1972). *Terminologia logica della tarda scolastica*, Lessico Intellettuale Europeo vii, Rome.

Maioli, Bruno (1979). *Gilberto Porretano. Dalla grammatica speculativa alla metafisica del concreto*, Rome.

Manegold of Lautenbach (1891). *Ad Gebehardum*, in K. Francke (ed.), *Libelli de lite* i: 308–430 (MGH), Berlin.

(1972). *Liber contra Wolfelmum*, ed. W. Hartmann (MGH), Weimar.

Marenbon, John (1983). *Early Medieval Philosophy (480–1150): an Introduction*, London.

Maritain, J. et al. (eds.) (1949). *Etienne Gilson, philosophe de la Chrétienté*, Paris.

Marius (1976). *On the Elements*, ed. and trans. by R. C. Dales, Berkeley–Los Angeles–London [probably by Peter Alfonsi].

Marshall, Linda E. (1979). 'The Identity of the "New Man" in the *Anticlaudianus* of Alan of Lille', *Viator* x: 77–94.

Martin, C. J. (1983). 'The Compendium Logicae Porretanum: a Survey of Philosophical Logic from the School of Gilbert of Poitiers', *CIMAGL* XLVI: xviii–xlvi.

(forthcoming). 'Embarrassing Arguments and Surprising Conclusions in the Development of Theories of the Conditional in the Twelfth Century', in *Proceedings of the VIIth European Symposium on Medieval Logic and Semantics, Poitiers 17–21 June 1985*.

Maurus of Salerno (1854). *Regulae urinarum*, in S. de Renzi (ed.), *Collectio Salernitana* III, Naples.

(1856). *Super Aphorismos Hippocratis*, in S. de Renzi (ed.), *Collectio Salernitana* V, Naples.

(1919). *De flebotomia*, ed. R. Buerschapper. Dissertation, Borna–Leipzig.

(1921). *Anatomia*, ed. W. L. H. Ploss. Dissertation, Leipzig.

(1972). [*Super Pronostica Hippocratis*] 'Maurus of Salerno: Twelfth-century *Optimus Physicus* with his Commentary on the Prognostics of Hippocrates', ed. with English trans. by M. H. Saffron, *Transactions of the American Philosophical Society*, n.s. LXII.1.

Mazzarella, P. (1962). *Il pensiero speculativo di S. Anselmo d'Aosta*, Padua.

(1969). 'L'esemplarismo in Anselmo d'Aosta e in Bonaventura da Bagnoreggio', *Analecta Anselmiana* I: 145–64.

Meier, Christel (1977). 'Zum Problem der allegorischen Interpretation mittelalterlicher Dichtung', *Beiträge zur Geschichte der deutschen Sprache und Literatur* (Tübingen) XCIX: 250–96.

(1985). 'Eriugena im Nonnenkloster?', *Frühmittelalterliche Studien* XIX: 466–97.

Metamorphosis Golye episcopi (1962). Ed. R. B. C. Huygens, 'Mitteilungen aus Handschriften', *Studi Medievali*, ser. 3, III: 764–72.

Mews, C. J. (1984). 'A Neglected Gloss on the "Isagoge" by Peter Abelard', *Freiburger Zeitschrift für Philosophie und Theologie* XXXI: 35–55.

(1985a). 'On Dating the Works of Peter Abelard', *AHDLMA* LII: 73–134.

(1985b). 'Peter Abelard's *Theologia Christiana* and *Theologia "Scholarium"* Re-examined', *RTAM* LII: 105–58.

Meyer, H. (1914). *Geschichte der Lehre von den Keimkräften von der Stoa bis zum Ausgang der Patristik*, Bonn.

Michaud-Quantin, P. (1949). 'La classification des puissances de l'âme au XIIe siècle', *RMAL* V: 15–34.

Millàs Vallicrosa, J. M. (1931). *Assaig d'Història de les idees físiques i matematiques a la Catalunya Medieval*, Barcelona.

Minio-Paluello, L. (1952). 'Iacobus Veneticus Grecus, Canonist and Translator of Aristotle', *Traditio* VIII: 265–304; reprinted in his *Opuscula* (1972).

(1954). 'The "Ars disserendi" of Adam of Balsham "Parvipontanus"', *MARS* III: 116–69.

(1965). 'Aristotele dal mundo arabo a quello latino', in *L'Occidente e l'Islam nell'alto medioevo* (= *Settimane di Studio* XII: 603–37); reprinted in his *Opuscula* (1972).

(1972). *Opuscula: The Latin Aristotle*, Amsterdam.

(1975). 'Plato of Tivoli', in *Dictionary of Scientific Biography* XI, 31–3.

Monnot, G. (1986). 'Les citations coraniques dans le "Dialogue" de Pierre Alfonse', in his *Islam et religions*, (Paris).

Morrison, Karl (1980). 'Otto of Freising's Quest for the Hermeneutic Circle', *Speculum* LV: 207–36.

Mueller, I. (1969). 'Stoic and Peripatetic Logic', *Archiv für Geschichte der Philosophie* LI: 173–87.

Munk Olsen, B. (1979, 1980). 'Les classiques latins dans les florilèges médiévaux antérieurs au XIIIe siècle', *Revue d'Histoire des Textes* IX: 47–121; X: 123–72.

(1982). *L'étude des auteurs classiques latins aux XIe et XIIe siècles* I, Paris.

Murdoch, J. E. (1968). 'The Medieval Euclid', *Revue de Synthèse* LXXXIX: 67–94.

(1971). 'Euclid: Transmission of the *Elements*', in *Dictionary of Scientific Biography* IV, New York.

Murdoch, J. E., and Sylla, E. D. (eds.) (1975). *The Cultural Context of Medieval Learning*, Dordrecht–Boston.

Murray, Alexander (1978). *Reason and Society in the Middle Ages*, Oxford.

al-Nairīzī (1899). *Euclides supplementum. Anaritii commentarii* (trans. Gerard of Cremona), ed. M. Curtze, Leipzig.

Nelson, N. E. (1933). 'Cicero's de *officiis* in Christian Thought: 300–1300', *University of Michigan Publications: Language and Literature* x: 59–160.

Nemesius of Emesa, *see* Alfanus of Salerno; Burgundio of Pisa.

Nequam, Alexander, *see* Alexander Nequam.

Nicolas of Amiens (P.L. 210). *De arte catholicae fidei*: 593–618.

Nielsen, L. (1976). 'On the Doctrine of Logic and Language of Gilbert Porreta and his Followers', *CIMAGL* XVII: 40–69.

(1982). *Theology and Philosophy in the Twelfth Century*, Leiden.

Nothdurft, K. D. (1963). *Studien zum Einfluss Senecas auf die Philosophie und Theologie des zwölften Jahrhunderts*, Leiden–Cologne.

Nuchelmans, G. (1973). *Theories of the Proposition. Ancient and Medieval Conceptions of the Bearers of Truth and Falsity*, Amsterdam–London.

(1982). 'The Semantics of Propositions', in *CHLMP*.

O'Donnell, J. R. (ed.) (1974). *Essays in Honor of Anton Charles Pegis*, Toronto.

O'Meara, J. J., and Bieler, L., (eds.) (1973). *The Mind of Eriugena*, Dublin.

O'Neill, Y. V. (1967). 'William of Conches and the Cerebral Membranes', *Clio Medica* II: 13–21.

(1968). 'William of Conches' Descriptions of the Brain', *Clio Medica* III: 203–23.

(1970). 'Another Look at the *Anatomia Porci*', *Viator* I: 115–24.

Orlandi, G. (1979). 'Per una nuova edizione del "Dialogus" di Abelardo', *Rivista Critica di Storia della Filosofia* XXXIV: 474–94.

Palmieri, N. (ed.) (1981). 'Un antico commento a Galeno della Scuola medica di Ravenna', *Physis* XXIII: 197–296.

Parent, J. M. (1938). *La doctrine de la création dans l'Ecole de Chartres*, Paris–Ottawa.

Pazzini, A. (1967). 'La letteratura medica salernitana e la storia della Scuola di Salerno', *Salerno* I: 5–17.

(1968). 'La scuola vescovile di Salerno, origine della scuola medica di Salerno', *Salerno* II: 3–17.

Pelster, F. (1949). 'Gilbert de la Porrée, Gilbertus Porretanus oder Gilbertus Porreta', *Scholastik* XIX–XXIV: 401–3.

Perino, R. (1952). *La dottrina trinitaria di S. Anselmo nel quadro del suo metodo teologico e del suo concetto di Dio*, Rome.

Peter Abelard (1836). *Ouvrages inédits d'Abélard*, ed. V. Cousin, Paris.

(P.L. 178). *Theologia 'Scholarium'* [here *Introductio ad theologiam*]: 979–1114.

(1859). *Petri Abaelardi Opera* (2 vols.), ed. V. Cousin, Paris.

(1919–27). *Logica 'Ingredientibus'*, ed. B. Geyer in *Peter Abaelards philosophische Schriften*, BGPTM XXI.1–3.

(1933a). *Logica 'Nostrorum petitioni sociorum'*, ed. B. Geyer in *Peter Abaelards philosophische Schriften*, BGPTM XXI.4.

(1933b). *Glossae super librum Porphyrii secundum vocales*, ed. C. Ottaviano [*Un opuscolo di Abelardo*], Testi Medioevali Inediti, Fontes Ambrosiani III, Florence.

(1939). *Theologia 'Summi boni'*, ed. H. Ostlender, BGPTM XXXV.2–3.

(1950, 1953, 1955). [Letters], ed. J. T. Muckle, *Mediaeval Studies* XII: 163–213; XV: 47–94; XVII: 240–81.

(1954). *Pietro Abelardo Scritti filosofici: Editio super Porphyrium, Glossae in Categorias, Editio* super *Aristotelem De interpretatione, De divisionibus, Super topica glossae*, ed. M. dal Pra, Rome–Milan.

(1958). *Abelardiana inedita: 1. Super Periermenias XII–XIV 2. Sententie secundum M. Petrum*, ed. L. Minio-Paluello, *Twelfth Century Logic. Texts and Studies* II, Rome.

(1967). *Historia calamitatum*, ed. J. Monfrin (3rd ed.), Paris.

(1969a). *Pietro Abelardo. Scritti di logica*, ed. M. dal Pra (2nd ed.), Florence.

(1969b). *Theologia Christiana*, ed. E. M. Buytaert in CC CM XII, Turnhout.

(1970a). *Petrus Abaelardus: Dialectica*, ed. L. M. de Rijk (2nd ed.), Assen.

(1970b). *Petrus Abaelardus: Dialogus inter Philosophum, Iudaeum et Christianum*, ed. R. Thomas, Stuttgart–Bad Cannstatt; *see also* Orlandi.

(1971). *Peter Abelard's Ethics*, ed. with English trans. by D. E. Luscombe, Oxford.

(1973). *Logica 'Nostrorum petitioni sociorum'*, ed. B. Geyer, BGPTM XXI.4 (2nd ed.).

(1974). *The Letters of Abelard and Heloise*, English trans. by B. Radice, Harmondsworth.

(1976). *La psicologia di Abelardo e il 'Tractatus de Intellectibus'*, ed. L. U. Ulivi, Rome.

(1976–7). *Sic et Non*, ed. B. B. Boyer and R. McKeon, Chicago–London.

(1979). *A Dialogue of a Philosopher with a Jew and a Christian*, trans. P. J. Payer, Medieval Sources in Translation XX, Toronto.

(1983a). *Letters IX–XIV. An Edition with an Introduction*, ed. E. R. Smits, Groningen.

(1983b). *Sententie Magistri Petri Abelardi (Sententie Hermanni)*, ed. S. Buzzetti, Florence.

(1984). 'Peter Abelard, Soliloquium', ed. C. S. F. Burnett, *Studi Medievali*, 3a serie, XXV: 857–94.

Peter Alfonsi (P.L. 157). *Dialogus*: 535–706.

(1911). *Die Disciplina clericalis des Petrus Alfonsi*, ed. A. Hilka and W. Söderhjelm, Helsinki [Editio minor: Heidelberg 1911].

(1943). *De dracone* [Letter to the Peripatetics of France], ed. J. M. Millás Vallicrosa, in 'La aportación astronómica de Pedro Alfonso', *Sefarad* III: 65–105.

(1962). [Trans. of al-Khwārizmī], ed. O. Neugebauer, *Historisk-filosofiske Skrifter udgivet af det Kongelige Danske Videnskabernes Selskab* IV.2, Copenhagen.

(1977). *Disciplina clericalis*, English trans. by E. Hermes and P. R. Quarrie, London.

(1980). *Disciplina clericalis*, ed. with Spanish trans. by M. J. Lacarra and E. Ducay, Saragossa.

see also Marius.

Peter Helias (1975). 'Petrus Helias' *Summa super Priscianum* I–III: an Edition and Study', ed. L. Reilly. Unpublished D.Phil. dissertation, University of Michigan, Ann Arbor.

(1978). *Summa super Priscianum, Books XVII–XVIII*, in J. H. Tolson (ed.), 'The Summa of Petrus Helias on Priscianus Minor', with an introduction by M. Gibson, *CIMAGL* XXVII: 1–158, XXVIII: 159–210.

Peter of Poitiers (1961). *Sententie*, ed. P. S. Moore and M. Dulong (2nd ed.), Notre Dame.

(1977). *Die Zwettler Summa*, ed. N. M. Häring, Münster.

Pfister, R. (1976). 'Zur Geschichte der Begriffe von Subjekt und Praedikat', *Münchener Studien zur Sprachwissenschaft* XXV: 105–21.

Philip the Chancellor (1985). *Summa de bono*, ed. N. Wicki, Corpus Philosophorum Medii Aevi II–III (2 vols.), Berne.

Picard-Parra, C. (1949). 'Une utilisation des *Quaestiones naturales* de Sénèque au milieu du XIIe siècle', *RMAL* V: 115–26.

Picatrix (1933). [Arabic version] Pseudo-Maǧrītī, *Das Ziel des Weisen*, ed. H. Ritter, Leipzig.

(1962). [German trans.] *'Picatrix': Das Ziel des Weisen von Pseudo-Maǧrītī*, trans. H. Ritter and M. Plessner, London.

(1986). *Picatrix: The Latin Version*, ed. D. Pingree, London.

Piehler, Paul H. (1971). *The Visionary Landscape*, London.

Pinborg, J. (1967). *Die Entwicklung der Sprachtheorie im Mittelalter*, Münster–Copenhagen.

(1972). *Logik und Semantik im Mittelalter – Ein Überblick*, Stuttgart–Bad Cannstatt.

[Plato Latinus] (1975). IV: *Timaeus a Calcidio translatus commentarioque instructus*, ed. J. H. Waszink, Corpus Platonicum Medii Aevi (2nd ed.), London–Leiden.

Plato of Tivoli (1928). [Commentary on the *Tabula smaragdina*], ed. R. Steele and D. W. Singer, *Proceedings of the Royal Society of Medicine* XXI.1: 485–501.

Pohlenz, M. (1970). *Die Stoa. Geschichte einer geistigen Bewegung* (2 vols.) (4th ed.), Göttingen.

Poirion, Daniel (1980). 'Alain de Lille et Jean de Meun', in H. Roussel and F. Suard (eds.), *Alain de Lille, Gautier de Châtillon, Jakemart Giélée et leur temps*, Lille.

Porcelloni, E. M. (1970). 'Le problème de la dérivation du monde à partir de Dieu chez Scot Erigène et chez saint Anselme', *Analecta Anselmiana* II: 195–208.

Post, Gaines (1964). *Studies in Medieval Legal Thought*, Princeton, N.J.

pseudo-Apollonius of Tyana (1979). *Buch über das Geheimnis der Schöpfung und die Darstellung der Natur*, ed. U. Weisser, Aleppo.

pseudo-Maǧrīṭī, *see Picatrix*.

Quṣṭa b. Lūqā, *see* Costa ben Luca.

Radulphus de Longo Campo (1972). *In Anticlaudianum Alani commentum*, ed. Jan Sulowski, Wrocław.

(1976). *Distinctiones*, ed. J. Sulowski, Mediaevalia Philosophica Polonorum XXII, Académie Polonaise des Sciences, Warsaw.

Ralph of Beauvais (1982). *Glose super Donatum*, ed. C. H. Kneepkens, Nijmegen.

Raoul of Longchamps, *see* Radulphus de Longo Campo.

Reuter-Beaumont, J. (*See also* Beaumont, J.) (1975). 'Petrus Alfonsi: an Examination of his Works, their Scientific Content and their Background'. Unpublished D.Phil. thesis, Oxford.

Reynolds, L. D. (1965). *The Medieval Tradition of Seneca's Letters*, Oxford.

(1968). 'The Medieval Tradition of Seneca's Dialogues', *Classical Quarterly* XVIII: 355–72.

(ed.) (1983). *Texts and Transmission: A Survey of the Latin Classics*, Oxford.

Riché, P. (1984). 'Jean de Salisbury et le monde scolaire du XIIIe siècle', in M. Wilks (ed.), *The World of John of Salisbury*, Oxford.

Rico, F. (1986). *El pequeño mundo del hombre* (2nd ed.), Madrid.

Riet, S. van (1979). 'Influence de l'arabe sur la terminologie philosophique latine médiévale', in *Actas del V Congreso Internacional de Filosofía Medieval* I, Madrid.

Rijk, L. M. de (1962–7). *Logica modernorum: A Contribution to the History of Early Terminist Logic*. I. 'On the Twelfth Century Theories of Fallacy' (1962); II.1: 'The Origin and Early Development of the Theory of Supposition'; II.2: 'Texts and Indices' (1967), Assen.

(1966a). 'Some New Evidence on Twelfth Century Logic: Alberic and the School of Mont Ste. Geneviève (Montani)', *Vivarium* IV: 1–57.

(1966b). 'Some Notes on the Medieval Tract *De insolubilibus*, with an Edition of a Tract Dating from the End of the Twelfth Century', *Vivarium* IV: 83–115.

(1975). 'La signification de la proposition (*Dictum Propositionis*) chez Abélard', in *Pierre Abélard. Pierre le Vénérable*, Colloques Internationaux du CNRS DXLVI, Paris.

(1980a). 'Peter Abälard (1079–1142): Meister und Opfer des Scharfsinns', in R. Thomas *et al.* (eds.), *Petrus Abaelardus (1079–1142): Person, Werk und Wirkung*, Trier, pp. 125–38.

(1980b). 'The Semantical Impact of Abailard's Solution of the Problem of Universals', in Thomas *et al., ibid.* pp. 139–51.

(1982). 'The Origins of the Theory of the Properties of Terms', in *CHLMP*.

(1985). *La philosophie au Moyen Age*, Leiden.

Rist, J. M. (1969). *Stoic Philosophy*, Cambridge.

(ed.) (1978). *The Stoics*, Berkeley–Los Angeles–London.

Robins, R. H. (1967). *A Short History of Linguistics*, London.
Ross, G. M. (1974). 'Seneca's Philosophical Influence', in C. D. N. Costa (ed.), *Seneca*, London.
Rouse, R. H. (1979). 'Florilegia and Latin Classical Authors in Twelfth- and Thirteenth-Century Orléans', *Viator* x: 131–60.
Rouse, R. H. and M. A. (1976). 'The *Florilegium Angelicum*: its Origin, Content and Influence', in J. J. G. Alexander and M. T. Gibson (eds.), *Medieval Learning and Literature: Essays presented to Richard William Hunt*, Oxford.
    (1978). 'The Medieval Circulation of Cicero's "Posterior Academics" and the *De finibus bonorum et malorum*', in M. B. Parkes and A. G. Watson (eds.), *Medieval Scribes, Manuscripts and Libraries: Essays presented to N. R. Ker*, London.
Roussel, H., and Suard, F. (eds.) (1980). *Alain de Lille, Gautier de Châtillon, Jakemart Giélée et leur temps*, Lille.
Saffron, M. H. (1975). 'Salernitan Anatomists', in *Dictionary of Scientific Biography* xii, New York.
Sánchez-Albornoz, C. (1965). 'El Islam de España y el Occidente', in *L'Occidente e l'Islam nell'alto medioevo*, Settimane di Studio xii, Spoleto.
Sandbach, F. H. (1975). *The Stoics*, London.
Sanford, E. M. (1943). 'The *Verbum abbreviatum* of Petrus Cantor', *Transactions of the American Philological Association* lxxiv: 33–48.
Schipperges, Heinrich (1956). 'Die Schulen von Chartres unter dem Einfluss des Arabismus', *Sudhoffs Archiv für Geschichte der Medizin und der Naturwissenschaften* xl: 193–210.
    (1962). 'Einflüsse arabischer Medizin auf die Mikrokosmosliteratur des 12. Jahrhunderts', *Miscellanea Mediaevalia* i: 129–53.
    (1965). *Die Assimilation der arabischen Medizin durch das lateinische Mittelalter*, Sudhoffs Archiv iii, Wiesbaden.
Schlanger, J. (1968). *La philosophie de Salomon Ibn Gabirol. Etude d'un néoplatonisme*, Leiden.
Schmaus, M. (1970). 'Die metaphysisch-psychologische Lehre über den Heiligen Geist im Monologion Anselms von Canterbury', in H. Kohlenberger (ed.), *Sola ratione. Anselm-Studien für F. S. Schmitt zum 75. Geburtstag*, Stuttgart.
    (1975). 'Die theologiegeschichtliche Tragweite der Trinitätslehre des Anselm von Canterbury', *Analecta Anselmiana* iv.1: 29–45.
Schmidt, M. A. (1956). *Gottheit und Trinität nach dem Kommentar des Gilbert Porreta zu Boethius, De Trinitate*, Basel.
Schmidt, P. L. (1974). *Die Überlieferung von Ciceros Schrift "De legibus" im Mittelalter und Renaissance*, Munich.
Schmidt, T. (1897). *Ambrosius. Sein Werk De officiis libri tres und die Stoa*, Erlangen.
Schmitt, F. S. (1932). 'Zur Chronologie der Werke des hl. Anselm von Canterbury', *Revue Bénédictine* xliv: 322–50.
    (1969). 'Anselm und der (Neu-)Platonismus', *Analecta Anselmiana* i: 39–71.
Schrimpf, G. (1966). *Die Axiomenschrift des Boethius (De hebdomadibus) als philosophisches Lehrbuch des Mittelalters*, Leiden.
Silverstein, T. (1952). 'Adelard, Aristotle and the *De natura deorum*', *Classical Philology* xlvii: 82–6.
    (1954). 'ELEMENTATUM: Its Appearance among the Twelfth-Century Cosmogonists', *Mediaeval Studies* xvi: 156–62.
    (1955). 'Hermann of Carinthia and Greek', in *Medioevo e Rinascimento: Studi in onore di Bruno Nardi* ii, Florence.
    (1964). 'Guillaume de Conches and the Elements: *Homiomeria* and *Organica*', *Mediaeval Studies* xxvi: 363–7.

(1965). 'Guillaume de Conches and Nemesius of Emesa: On the Sources of the "New Science" of the Twelfth Century', in *Harry Austryn Wolfson Jubilee Volume* II, Jerusalem.

Simon, H. and M. (1956). *Die ältere Stoa und ihr Naturbegriff*, Berlin.

Simon, M. (1957). 'La glose de l'épître aux romains de Gilbert de la Porrée', *Revue d'Histoire Ecclésiastique* LII.1: 51–80.

Singer, C. and D. (1924). 'The Origin of the Medical School of Salerno, the First University', in *Essays on the History of Medicine presented to Karl Sudhoff*, Zurich.

Sirat, C. (1985). *A History of Jewish Philosophy in the Middle Ages*, Cambridge–Paris.

Smalley, Beryl (1952). *The Study of the Bible in the Middle Ages* (2nd ed.), Oxford.

(1973). *The Beckett Conflict and the Schools*, Oxford.

Solmsen, F. (1957). 'The Vital Heat, the Inborn Pneuma and the Aether', *Journal of Hellenic Studies* LXXVII: 119–23.

Sorabji, R. (1980). *Necessity, Cause and Blame*, London.

(1983). *Time, Creation and the Continuum*, London.

Southern, R. W. (1948). 'Lanfranc and Bec and Berengar of Tours', in R. W. Hunt, W. A. Pantin and R. W. Southern (eds.), *Studies in Medieval History presented to F. M. Powicke*, Oxford.

(1963). *St. Anselm and his Biographer. A Study of Monastic Life and Thought 1059–c.1130*, Cambridge.

(1970). *Medieval Humanism and other Studies*, Oxford.

(1979). *Platonism, Scholastic Method and the School of Chartres*, Reading.

(1982). 'The Schools of Paris and the School of Chartres', in *Harvard 1982*.

Spanneut, M. (1969). *Le Stoïcisme des pères de l'église de Clément de Rome à Clément d'Alexandrie* (2nd ed.), Paris.

(1973). *Permanence du Stoïcisme de Zénon à Malraux*, Gembloux.

Stahl, G. (1964). 'Die *Naturales quaestiones* Senecas. Ein Beitrag zum Spiritualisierungsprozess der römischen Stoa', *Hermes* XCII: 425–54.

Steiger, L. (1969). 'Contexte syllogismos. Über die Kunst und Bedeutung der Topik bei Anselm', *Analecta Anselmiana* I: 107–43.

Steinen, W. von den (1954). 'Natur und Geist im 12. Jahrhundert', *Die Welt als Geschichte* II: 71–90.

Stewart, H. F., Rand, E. K., and Tester, S. J. (eds.) (1973). *Boethius, The Theological Tractates, The Consolation of Philosophy*, London–Cambridge, Mass.

Stock, Brian (1972). *Myth and Science in the Twelfth Century: A Study of Bernard Silvester*, Princeton, N.J.

(1983). *The Implications of Literacy*, Princeton, N.J.

Stolz, A. (1935). 'Das Proslogion des hl. Anselm', *Revue Bénédictine* XLVII: 331–47.

Struve, Tilman (1978). *Die Entwicklung der organologischen Staatsauffassung im Mittelalter*, Stuttgart.

(1984). 'The Importance of the Organism in the Political Theory of John of Salisbury', in M. Wilks (ed.), *The World of John of Salisbury*, Oxford.

Stump, E. (1980). 'Dialectic in the Eleventh and Twelfth Centuries: Garlandus Compotista', *History and Philosophy of Logic* I: 1–18.

(1981). 'Boethius's Theory of Topics and its Place in Early Scholastic Logic', in L. Obertello (ed.), *Congresso Internazionale di Studi Boeziani: Atti*, Rome.

(1982). 'Topics: their Development and Absorption into Consequences', in *CHLMP*.

(ed.) (1978). *Boethius's De topicis differentiis. Translated with Notes and Essays on the Text*, Ithaca, N.Y.–London.

Sudhoff, Karl (1920). 'Die Salernitaner Handschrift in Breslau, ein Corpus medicinae Salerni', *Archiv für Geschichte der Medizin* XII: 101–48.

(1928). 'Salerno, Montpellier und Paris um 1200', *Archiv für Geschichte der Medizin* XX: 51–62.

(1929). 'Salerno, eine mittelalterliche Heil- und Lehrstätte am Tyrrhenischen Meere', *Archiv für Geschichte der Medizin* XXI: 43–62.

(1930). 'Konstantin der Afrikaner und die Medizinschule von Salerno', *Archiv für Geschichte der Medizin* (= *Sudhoffs Archiv*) XXII: 293–8.

(1932). 'Constantin, der erste Vermittler muslimischer Wissenschaft ins Abendland und die beiden Salernitaner Frühscholastiker Maurus und Urso, als Exponenten dieser Vermittlung', *Archeion* XIV: 359–69.

(ed.) (1914). 'Die Kurze "Vita" und das Verzeichnis der Arbeiten Gerhards von Cremona', *Archiv für Geschichte der Medizin* VIII: 73–82.

Sullivan, M. W. (1967). *Apuleian Logic: The Nature, Sources and Influence of Apuleius's Peri Hermeneias*, Amsterdam.

Tarabocchia Canavero, A. (1981). *Esegesi biblica e cosmologia. Note sull'interpretazione patristica e medioevale di Genesi 1,2*, Milan.

Theodoricus Carnotensis, *see* Thierry of Chartres.

Théry, G. (1925). *Autour du décret de 1210: I, David de Dinant. Etude sur son panthéisme matérialiste*, Kain.

(1926). *Autour du décret de 1210: II, Alexandre d'Aphrodise. Aperçu sur l'influence de sa noétique*, Kain.

Thierry of Chartres (1964). *Prologus in Eptatheuchon*, ed. E. Jeauneau, in his 'Note sur l'Ecole de Chartres', *Studi Medievali*, ser. 3, V: 821–65; reprinted in Jeauneau's *Lectio philosophorum*, Amsterdam 1973.

(1971a). *Commentaries on Boethius by Thierry of Chartres and his School*, ed. N. M. Häring, Toronto.

(1971b). *De sex dierum operibus*, in N. M. Häring (ed.), *Commentaries on Boethius by Thierry of Chartres and his School*, Toronto.

(1980). *Glosa super Boethii librum de Trinitate* and *De sex dierum operibus*, Italian trans. by E. Maccagnolo in his *Il divino e il megacosmo*, Milan.

(1987). *Commentary on Cicero's De inventione*, ed. K. M. Fredborg, Toronto.

Thomas, R., *et al.* (eds.) (1980). *Petrus Abaelardus 1079–1142: Person, Werk und Wirkung*, Trier.

Thonnard, F. J. (1959). 'Caractères augustiniens de la méthode philosophique de saint Anselme', *Spicilegium Beccense* I: 171–83.

Thorndike, L., and Kibre, P. (eds.) (1963). *A Catalogue of Incipits of Mediaeval Scientific Writings in Latin*, rev. and augmented, London.

Thurot, C. (1869). *Extraits de divers manuscrits latins pour servir à l'histoire des doctrines grammaticales au Moyen-Age*, Paris; reprinted Frankfurt a. Main, 1964.

Troncarelli, F. (1981). *Tradizioni perdute. La 'Consolatio Philosophiae' nell'alto medioevo*, Medioevo e Umanesimo XLII, Padua.

Tweedale, M. M. (1976). *Abailard on Universals*, Amsterdam.

(1982). 'Abelard and the Culmination of the Old Logic', in *CHLMP*.

Ueberweg, F. (1927). *Grundriss der Geschichte der Philosophie II: Die Patristische und Scholastische Philosophie*, ed. B. Geyer (11th ed.), Basel–Stuttgart.

Ullmann, M. (1970). *Die Medizin im Islam*, Leiden–Cologne.

Ulrich, F. (1975). 'Cur non video praesentem? Zur Implikation der "griechischen" und "lateinischen" Denkform bei Anselm und Scotus Eriugena', *Freiburger Zeitschrift für Philosophie und Theologie* XXII: 70–170.

Urso of Salerno (1901). *De urinis*, ed. P. Giacosa, in *Magistri Salernitani nondum editi*, Turin.

(1918). *De effectibus qualitatum* and *De effectibus medicinarum*, ed. C. Matthaes, in his *Der Salernitaner Arzt Urso*. Dissertation, Borna–Leipzig.

(1919). *De saporibus et odoribus*, ed. G. F. Hartmann. Dissertation, Borna–Leipzig.

(1920a). *De gradibus*, ed. K. Sudhoff, *Archiv für Geschichte der Medizin* XII: 135–8.

(1920b). *De effectibus qualitatum*, ed. K. Sudhoff, *Archiv für Geschichte der Medizin* XII: 139–43.

(1928). *Anatomia*, ed. K. Sudhoff, *Archiv für Geschichte der Medizin* XX: 40–50.

(1936). [*Aphorismi cum Glossulis*] 'Die medizinisch-naturphilosophischen Aphorismen und Kommentare des Magister Urso Salernitanus', ed. R. Creutz, *Quellen und Studien zur Geschichte der Naturwissenschaften und der Medizin* V.1.

(1959). *De coloribus*, ed. L. Thorndike, *Ambix* VII: 7–16.

(1976). *De commixtionibus elementorum libellus*, ed. W. Stürner, Stuttgart.

Van de Vyver, A. (1929), 'Les étapes du développement philosophique du haut moyen âge', *Revue Belge de Philologie* VIII: 425–52.

(1936). 'Les plus anciennes traductions latines médiévales (x–xi siècles) de traités d'astronomie et d'astrologie', *Osiris* I: 658–91.

Vaux, R. de (1933). 'La première entrée d'Averroës chez les Latins', *RSPT* XXII: 193–243.

(1934). *Notes et textes sur l'avicennisme latin aux confins des XIIe–XIIIe siècles*, Paris.

Verbeke, Gerard (1945). *L'évolution de la doctrine du pneuma du stoïcisme à S. Augustin*, Paris–Louvain.

(1979). 'L'influence du Stoïcisme sur la pensée médiévale en occident', in *Actas del V Congreso Internacional de Filosofia Medieval* I, Madrid.

(1983). *The Presence of Stoicism in Medieval Thought*, Washington, D.C.

Vergnes, J. (1924). 'Les sources de l'argument de Saint Anselme', *Revue des Sciences Religieuses* IV: 576–9.

Vernet, A. (1946–7). 'Un remaniement de la *Philosophia* de Guillaume de Conches', *Scriptorium* I: 243–59.

(1955). 'Une épitaphe inédite de Thierry de Chartres', in *Recueil de travaux offert à Cl. Brunel* II, Paris.

(1981). *Etudes médiévales*, Paris.

Vicaire, M. H. (1937). 'Les porrétains et l'avicennisme avant 1215', *RSPT* XXVI: 449–82.

Vignaux, P. (1947a). 'Note sur le chapitre LXX du Monologion', *RMAL*, iii: 321–34.

(1947b). 'Structure et sens du Monologion', *RSPT* XXXI: 192–212.

Vuillemin, J. (1971). *Le Dieu d'Anselme et les apparences de la raison*, Paris.

Walter of Mortagne (1892). *Tractatus 'Quoniam de generali'*, ed. B. Hauréau in his *Notices et extraits de quelques manuscrits latins de la Bibliothèque Nationale* V, Paris.

Ward, J. O. (1972). 'The Date of the Commentary on Cicero's *De inventione* by Thierry of Chartres (*ca.* 1095–1160?) and the Cornifician Attack on the Liberal Arts', *Viator* III: 219–73.

Weijers, O. (1984). 'The Chronology of John of Salisbury's Studies in France (*Metalogicon* II 10)', in M. Wilks (ed.), *The World of John of Salisbury*, Oxford.

Weingart, R. E. (1970). *The Logic of Divine Love: A Critical Analysis of the Soteriology of Peter Abelard*, Oxford.

Wenin, C. (1982). 'La signification des universaux chez Abélard', *Revue Philosophique de Louvain* LXXX: 414–48.

(ed.) (1986). *L'homme et son univers au moyen âge*, Philosophes Médiévaux XXVI–XXVII, Louvain.

Westley, R. J. (1960). 'A Philosophy of the Concreted and the Concrete', *The Modern Schoolman* XXXVII: 257–86.

Wetherbee, W. (1972). *Platonism and Poetry in the Twelfth Century: The Literary Influence of the School of Chartres*, Princeton, N.J.

White, A. (1981). 'Boethius in the Medieval Quadrivium', in M. Gibson (ed.), *Boethius: His Life, Thought and Influence*, Oxford.

Wilhelmus Lucensis, *see* William of Lucca.

Wilks, Michael (1977). 'Alan of Lille and the New Man', in D. Baker (ed.), *Renaissance and Renewal in Christian History*, Oxford.

   (ed.) (1984). *The World of John of Salisbury*, Studies in Church History III, Oxford.

William of Conches (1567). *Dragmaticon – Dialogus de substantiis physicis . . . a Vuilhelmo Aneponymo philosopho*, ed. G. Gratarolus, Strasbourg; reprinted Frankfurt/Main, 1967.

   (1862). 'Des commentaires inédits de Guillaume de Conches et de Nicolas Triveth sur la Consolation de Philosophie de Boèce', [Extracts] ed. C. Jourdain, *Notices et extraits des manuscrits de la Bibliothèque Nationale* XX.2, Paris, pp. 40–82.

   (1929). *Moralium dogma philosophorum*, ed. J. Holmberg (with the Old French and Middle Frankish translations), Uppsala [attribution to William not certain].

   (1935). *Compendium philosophiae*, ed. C. Ottaviano (*Un brano inedito della 'philosophia' di Guglielmo di Conches*), Naples [a compilation based on William and other sources].

   (1938). [Extracts from the commentary on Boethius], in J. M. Parent, *La doctrine de la création dans l'Ecole de Chartres*, Paris–Ottawa, pp. 122–36.

   (1965). *Glosae super Platonem*, ed. E. Jeauneau, Paris.

   (1973). [Extracts from the commentary on Priscian], in E. Jeauneau, *Lectio philosophorum*, Amsterdam, pp. 335–70.

   (1974). [Extracts from the commentary on Macrobius], in P. Dronke, *Fabula*, Leiden–Cologne, pp. 68–78.

   (1980a). *Dragmaticon*, Italian trans. in E. Maccagnolo, *Il divino e il megacosmo*, Milan.

   (1980b). *Glosae in Iuvenalem*, ed. B. Wilson, Paris.

   (1980c). *Philosophia*, ed. G. Maurach, Pretoria.

William of Lucca (1983). *Comentum in tertiam ierarchiam Dionisii que est de divinis nominibus*, ed. F. Gastaldelli, Florence.

William of Saint-Thierry (P.L. 180). *De natura corporis et animae*, 695–726.

   (1956). *Lettre d'or aux frères du Mont-Dieu*, ed. J. M. Déchanet, Paris.

   (1969). *De erroribus Gulielmi de Conchis ad sanctum Bernardum*, ed. J. Leclercq, *Revue Bénédictine* LXXIX: 375–91.

   (1983). *Guillaume de Saint-Thierry, La lettera d'oro*, ed. Claudio Leonardi, trans. C. Piacentini and R. Scarcia, Florence.

Williams, J. R. (1931). 'The Authorship of the *Moralium dogma philosophorum*', *Speculum* VI: 392–411.

Williams, M. E. (1951). *The Teaching of Gilbert Porreta on the Trinity as found in his Commentaries on Boethius*, Rome.

Winden, J. M. C. van (1962). *Calcidius on Matter. His Doctrine and his Sources*, Leiden.

Wingate, S. D. (1931). *The Mediaeval Latin Versions of the Aristotelian Scientific Corpus, with Special Reference to the Biological Works*, London.

Woolsey, R. B. (1948). 'Bernard Silvester and the Hermetic *Asclepius*', *Traditio* VI: 340–4.

Wulf, M. de (1905). *Histoire de la philosophie médiévale* (2nd ed.), Louvain–Paris.

Ziolkowski, Jan (1985). *Alan of Lille's Grammar of Sex. The Meaning of Grammar to a Twelfth-Century Intellectual*, Cambridge, Mass.

INDEX OF MANUSCRIPTS

GENERAL INDEX

In the transliteration of Arabic words and names, it has not been practicable to standardize to a single system, both because certain forms (e.g. Abū Ma'shar, al-Khwārizmī) have become too familiar in the English-speaking world to ignore, and because the titles of works cited in the course of the volume themselves vary in their usage. In the rare cases where confusion might arise, cross-references are given below.

DATE DUE

5 1999